CRIMINOLOGY AND THE CRI

CRIMINOLOGY AND THE CRIMINAL JUSTICE SYSTEM

A Historical and Transatlantic Introduction

Cyrille FIJNAUT

intersentia

Cambridge – Antwerp – Portland

Intersentia Ltd
Sheraton House | Castle Park
Cambridge | CB3 0AX | United Kingdom
Tel.: +44 1223 370 170 | Fax: +44 1223 370 169
Email: mail@intersentia.co.uk
www.intersentia.com | www.intersentia.co.uk

Distribution for the UK and Ireland:
NBN International
Airport Business Centre, 10 Thornbury Road
Plymouth, PL6 7 PP
United Kingdom
Tel.: +44 1752 202 301 | Fax: +44 1752 202 331
Email: orders@nbninternational.com

Distribution for Europe and all other countries:
Intersentia Publishing nv
Groenstraat 31
2640 Mortsel
Belgium
Tel.: +32 3 680 15 50 | Fax: +32 3 658 71 21
Email: mail@intersentia.be

Distribution for the USA and Canada:
International Specialized Book Services
920 NE 58th Ave. Suite 300
Portland, OR 97213
USA
Tel.: +1 800 944 6190 (toll free) | Fax: +1 503 280 8832
Email: info@isbs.com

Criminology and the Criminal Justice System. A Historical and Transatlantic
Introduction
© Cyrille Fijnaut 2017

ISBN 978-1-78068-506-9
D/2017/7849/90
NUR 821/824

British Library Cataloguing in Publication Data. A catalogue record for this book is available from
the British Library.

PREFACE

In the 1989–90 academic year, it was my pleasure to take over the course on *General Criminology* from the late Prof. Steven de Batselier, a course that had been taught for decades as part of the special programme in criminology at KU Leuven's Faculty of Law. It was my intention from the very start to write an introduction to general criminology for the many students taking the course – both criminology undergraduates and faculty of law graduates – that would facilitate both absorbing the course material and studying it independently. At the same time, I wished to take the opportunity afforded by writing such an introduction not only to make the course suitable for the many law students but also to align it with the ideas that I had about how such an introduction should be structured.

For me, that meant two things. On the one hand, it seemed desirable for various reasons to devote considerable attention to the long history of criminology, in the West in general and in Belgium and the Netherlands in particular. The main reason was and is, however, that without thorough knowledge of that history it is difficult to understand the contemporary developments in theory, research, and practice. On the other hand, I considered it necessary to write not merely a kind of "history of ideas" in criminology but also to show how closely that history has been associated – right up to the present day – with the evolution of criminal law and the administration of criminal justice, and more generally with the combatting of crime in all its forms and varieties.

But actually writing such an introduction proved to be no simple matter. At that time, for instance, because of the absence of systematic and thorough research it was virtually impossible to write a historical introduction to criminology and criminal justice that would, at the very least, properly represent the history of criminology in Belgium and the Netherlands, and its influence on the organisation and operation of the criminal justice systems in those countries. Carrying out that plan was not easy, however, because I did not have access – either directly or indirectly – to the countless foreign publications that I needed in order to analyse, in sufficient depth, the interaction between European and American criminology since the end of the nineteenth century, even though a proper knowledge of that interaction is also necessary for a good understanding of the development of criminology in Belgium and the Netherlands since the 1960s.

These observations led, inter alia, to my starting, in the early 1990s, to collect publications, in both Europe and the United States, that could shed light on the history of criminology in the West and its entanglement with the international history of criminal law and criminal justice. By the mid-1990s, I had reached the stage that I could begin drafting an initial version of the introductory work that I had in mind. But then the time factor proved to be a major problem. All kinds of large-scale research projects – in particular my time-consuming duties on five official committees of inquiry in Belgium and the Netherlands – meant that it was simply impossible from a practical perspective to write this book.

I did, however, find time for two activities. First, I continued through all those years to collect antiquarian and new books on criminology and criminal justice in Europe and America that I thought I would need for the introduction that I envisaged. Second, in the light of the literature that I had collected, I wrote a number of contributions to collections and periodicals that were well suited to inclusion in the present book. The pleasing result was that by 2010 I had gradually progressed to Chapter 5. However, in all that time, I had still not been able to write about the important episodes in the history of criminology since the beginning of the twentieth century. But in 2012 and 2013, I was finally able to carry out my intention and to finish off the book.

The original Dutch edition of this work – *Criminologie en strafrechtsbedeling; een historische en transatlantische inleiding* (Antwerp, Intersentia, 2014) – comes to 924 pages, including the table of contents, bibliography, index of persons, and the numerous illustrations. This English edition has 644 pages and is therefore a significantly abridged version of the original book. A number of chapters have been shortened considerably, namely Chapters 2 (on the medieval origins of the criminal justice system), 3 (on the restructuring of that system during the Enlightenment and the French Period), and 7 (about the early development of criminology in Belgium and the Netherlands). Chapter 8 (on the role of associations and conferences in the internationalisation of criminology) has been completely omitted from this English edition. Chapters 10 (on the reception of European criminology in the United States) and 11 (on the transatlantic integration of criminology) have been retained virtually without excisions. In Chapter 11, those sections have been deleted that relate to the current development of criminology in Belgium and the Netherlands.

The reason for all the various excisions was that the deleted passages are of less relevance for an international readership. The number of illustrations was naturally also reduced, and their selection was tailored to this abridged version of the book. The bibliography has not been adapted to this English edition, however, for the simple reason that in its unabbreviated form it retains its value as a research resource. The index of persons has of course been brought into line with the English edition.

A historical and transatlantic introduction to criminology and the criminal justice system is a work that one writes alone, but not without the help of others. I would therefore like to thank, in the first place, the many booksellers in Belgium, the Netherlands, and elsewhere who have assisted me in the past 25 years in building up my private library, and have thus obviated the need for me to do a great deal of searching in libraries when writing the book. Second, I naturally wish to thank the various librarians who have helped me so effectively during this period, in particular those at KU Leuven's Faculty of Law, the New York University School of Law, the Max Planck Institute for Foreign and International Criminal Law, and the Law Faculty at Tilburg University.

Finally, I consider myself fortunate in the publisher who has guided this abridged edition of the book, Kris Moeremans of Intersentia (Antwerp) and the editors of Intersentia (Cambridge), Rebecca Moffat and Rebecca Bryan, who have been very helpful with the correction of the manuscript. Finally, I also wish to thank the translators at Balance Texts & Translations for producing the translation within a relatively short time.

Tilburg, Spring 2017

CONTENTS

CHAPTER 1

GENERAL INTRODUCTION

1.1. BASIC PRINCIPLES OF THIS WORK

Criminology today definitely cannot be seen as a coherent set of theories, methods, and research topics – quite the opposite. Like many other disciplines, it is nowadays highly differentiated and specialised from the theoretical, methodological, and thematic perspectives. Moreover, it goes without saying that its historical and contemporary complexity increases by leaps and bounds the more it is considered not only as an historically formed assemblage of ideas but also in the light of the development that the criminal justice institutions have undergone, partly because of it, in centuries gone by.

This means that if one wishes to present a true picture of this manifold criminology – or "pluralistic" criminology, as it is sometimes termed – one cannot restrict oneself to writing the kind of introduction that is usually published nowadays. Rather, the present introduction is a deliberate attempt to write a genuinely different kind of treatise. In my view, most of the introductions used nowadays in Western Europe and the United States have major shortcomings. Let me name but a few:

- they generally have a one-sided focus on the development and status of criminology in the country where they are produced, in the countries of the author's own language, or in the English language area;
- they usually view the history of criminology as merely a lead-in to discussion of its contemporary evolution;
- they divide up the history of criminology into relatively sterile portraits of a few individual forerunners or into a fairly insignificant series of quotations from their works;
- they devote either no attention or completely inadequate attention to important episodes in the history of criminology, such as its role in the totalitarian police states of the twentieth century;

- they treat criminology mainly as a loose collection of old and new ideas from Europe and America regarding crime and the response to crime;
- they all too easily disregard the social context within which new ideas about crime and its containment have emerged and have found more or less resonance in the outside world;
- they generally fail to use quotations, disagreements, and references to encourage independent perusal by the reader of important general works or specific studies; and
- they tend to ignore the influence of criminology on the organisation and functioning of the criminal justice system and on the combatting of crime in general.

In writing an introduction to criminology that attempts to avoid such deficiencies, I have in the first place opted explicitly for an introduction that is from start to finish historical. It is therefore an intrinsically *historical introduction* to criminology that is basically limited neither to a theoretical perspective, nor to a method, nor to a particular object. Rather, it aims specifically – in fact entirely in the spirit of the first introduction to criminology ever written, *Criminologia: studio sul delitto, sulle sue cause e sui mezzi di repressione* [*Criminology: A Study of Crime, its Causes and Measures to Repress It*] by Raffaelo Garofalo in 1885 – to outline the developments that criminology has undergone as regards these three aspects. My explicit decision to provide a historical introduction to general criminology is based mainly on the consideration that an effective, i.e. critical, understanding of the present state of criminology, in all its diversity, assumes close familiarity with its past. That is not only because its contemporary developments are obviously rooted in its early evolution, but also because its past – in terms of ideas and practices – is still a living past. In criminology today, history is often used to define one's own points of view. In many discussions, someone who is not familiar with this past cannot adopt a position of their own or properly assess the position adopted by others. One must also not lose sight of the fact that in many current debates on crime and how to combat it, arguments are exchanged that "have always been". Specifically, a historical introduction to general criminology can teach us how to weigh and assess these arguments.

Second, in this book the development of criminology is explicitly and systematically linked to the history of the criminal justice system. This connection is obviously not one I have made in order to appeal to students of law and the social sciences who are interested in the field of criminology. My first major reason for making this connection is that the development of the criminal justice system was to some extent a strategic condition for the development of criminology as a separate scientific discipline towards the end of the nineteenth century. The fact, for example, that in the course of that century imprisonment became the main criminal law penalty meant that a systematic knowledge of crime and criminals needed to be developed with a view to assessing and dealing with inmates. The second major reason is closely related to this, namely that criminology right up to the present has mainly been utilised in the sphere of criminal justice and social assistance. If, therefore, one decides to deal with the history of criminology as not merely an history of ideas, it is an obvious step to link its history to that of the criminal justice system and to systematically elucidate the interaction between that discipline and that institution. The present book does so mainly on the basis of the history of policing and prison systems. These two key executive components of the criminal justice system have, after all, been the focus of criminological interest from the very beginning.

Third, the present introduction deliberately chooses a specific geographical structure in its discussion of the history of criminology and the criminal justice system. In other words, it is constructed in such a way that the discussion operates on three geo-political levels that might best be viewed as concentric circles: their history in the Netherlands and Belgium forms the innermost circle, as it were, of a narrative that takes place simultaneously in the next-largest circle of the neighbouring countries in Western Europe – Italy, France, Germany, and the United Kingdom – and in the largest, transatlantic circle of Western Europe and the United States. This avoids, in particular, the ridiculous situation of Dutch and Belgian students knowing a lot about the history of criminology in the United States but virtually nothing about its history in their own countries. This approach also makes it possible not only to elucidate more clearly the sometimes significant differences between developments in the countries concerned, but also to devote greater attention to the dynamic interactions that have operated over the years between these developments across borders. Of course, this geographical pattern cannot be applied to developments that have been, almost by definition, of a cross-border nature. We need to remember, on the one hand, the history of the international organisations that have functioned, as it were, as the gear wheels driving the increasing internationalisation of criminology. On the other hand, we are dealing here with the history of criminology in the two totalitarian police states that were dominant in Europe in the twentieth century, namely the Third Reich and the Soviet Union.

1.2. ARCHITECTURE OF THIS BOOK

The main thread of this book can be summarised briefly as follows. The institutional structure of today's criminal justice system that was built up in Western Europe during the Middle Ages and the early modern period continued to be developed in the eighteenth century, in terms both of legal protection and of combatting crime, by such thinkers as Cesare Beccaria, subsequently being shaped more towards what it is today at the hands of Napoleon Bonaparte during the French Period. In the course of the nineteenth century, however, it was not only criminals and their crimes that increasingly became the object of focused study, but also society's response to crime problems, in particular the criminal law response. At the end of the nineteenth century, that development crystallised in the work of Cesare Lombroso, spreading from there, in all kinds of varieties and forms, across Western Europe – particularly to France, Germany, Belgium, the Netherlands, and also the United Kingdom – and in the early twentieth century to the United States as well.

While from the 1920s onwards criminology in Western Europe gradually went astray in the two totalitarian police states which increasingly tightened their destructive grip on the continent, in the United States in the same period, due to the work of thinkers including Edwin Sutherland, it in fact developed in many ways gained new vitality – theoretically, methodologically, and thematically. Because criminology in Western Europe after the Second World War had lost its legitimacy or remained stuck in pre-war traditions, it is therefore unsurprising that the version of criminology that had meanwhile developed in the United States was imitated in various ways in Western Europe and brought about renewal on a modest scale. This post-war transatlantic transfer of American criminology then, in turn, formed an important strategic condition for the influence that the critical criminologies which flourished in the 1960s and 1970s in the United States exercised, almost in "real time", on the development of criminology in a number of Western European countries. The unintended effect of these transatlantic interactions has been an increasing fusion of criminologies on both sides of the Atlantic.

The book develops this main thread in ten parts. Unlike most (English-language) introductions to criminology, the discussion begins (in Chapter 2) with an outline of the developments in the criminal justice system and crime prevention in the Middle Ages and the early modern period. This chapter provides the prior knowledge of these developments that is necessary not only to comprehend the shift that thinking about crime and its containment underwent during the Enlightenment, but also to understand the impact that that intellectual renewal had on the organisation of the criminal justice system and the combatting of crime in the eighteenth century and at the time of the French Revolution.

The changes themselves are discussed in detail in Chapter 3. That chapter deals, on the one hand, with the "enlightened" ideas that were propagated at that time about the nature of criminal law, the design of the criminal justice system, and crime prevention. On the other, it discusses the views that existed regarding the reorganisation of the prison and policing systems and also how those ideas were put into practice.

Following on from this, Chapter 4 first discusses how the prison and policing systems evolved further in the first half of the nineteenth century, not only in Western Europe but also in the United States. Benchmarks in the first case are of course the renowned report by Alexis de Tocqueville and Gustave de Beaumont on the prison system in the United States and the formidable role played by Édouard Ducpétiaux in establishing a comprehensive penitentiary system in Belgium modelled on the American system. Where the restructuring of the policing system is concerned, one obviously cannot ignore the creation of the Metropolitan Police in London in 1829–30. Complementary to this description of the institutional changes, the chapter then discusses the emerging scientific approaches to the criminal – biological, psychiatric, and sociological – elucidated on the basis of the work of Franz Gall, Jean Esquirol and, above all, Adolphe Quetelet. It concludes with an exposition of the ideas of revolutionary and evolutionary thinkers in the mid-nineteenth century regarding the background, nature, and development of crime problems and the ways those problems should be addressed. In that context, it deals, on the one hand, with Bénedict Morel and Charles Darwin, and on the other with Karl Marx and Friedrich Engels.

Chapter 5 concerns the establishment of criminology in Italy and France. The first part of the chapter is devoted to the paradigm of the atavistic criminal developed by Cesare Lombroso in his little book *L'uomo delinquente* [*Criminal Man*] (1876), which he subsequently applied to various categories of criminals and all sorts of crime problems. Indeed, the publication of that book marked a radical turning point in the history of thinking about crime and punishment in Europe, and it had a profound influence on the design of the criminal justice system and the "hard" institutions flanking it, namely the policing and prison systems. In that sense, the importance of his book can easily be compared with that of another little book, namely that published by Cesare Beccaria at the end of the eighteenth century, *Dei delitti e delle pene* [*On Crime and Punishment*]. Following on from this exposition of the ideas of the founder of modern criminology, in the narrow sense of the word, Chapter 5 continues by discussing the ideas of his associates in the so-called "Italian School", Enrico Ferri and Raffaele Garofalo. The second part of the chapter considers the strongly sociological response directed from France by Alexandre Lacassagne, Gabriel Tarde, and Émile Durkheim against the bio-anthropological approach – i.e. the Italian approach – to crime and the criminal. The chapter concludes with a discussion of how the burgeoning academic criminology came to be applied in the two countries in criminal policy and criminal justice practice.

Chapter 6 deals with the development of criminology in German-speaking Europe and the United Kingdom. The main focus is on the further development of Italian bio-anthropology in German-speaking Europe up to the time of the Weimar Republic, on the one hand in the direction of *Kriminalbiologie* and on the other of *Kriminalpsychologie*. In this context, a discussion follows of the failure of German universities to appreciate both criminology and its broad application in criminal policy as it was particularly influenced by the works of the Austrian Hans Gross. The underdevelopment of criminology in the United Kingdom up to the Second World War was in stark contrast to the way it flourished in German-speaking Europe prior to the seizure of power by the Nazis in 1933. It is important to emphasise that contrast in this chapter because it makes it possible to demonstrate how unequally or differently criminology developed in the major Western European countries during that period.

Chapter 7 discusses the way criminology became established in the two small countries between France, Germany and the United Kingdom, namely the Netherlands and Belgium. The establishment of criminology in universities and its embedding within criminal policy are treated as similarly as possible for both countries, including with a view to comparing the way it developed in each of them. This means that an indication is first given of who the main pioneers were in the rise of criminology: Gerard van Hamel, Arnold Aletrino, and Willem Bonger in the Netherlands, and Adolphe Prins, Paul Heger, and Jules Dallemagne in Belgium. Second, an explanation is given, based on the most important examples, of how their ideas made themselves felt in the criminal policy pursued in the two countries from the 1890s until the 1930s. Third, the chapter deals with the establishment of criminological research institutes at a number of Dutch universities (Leiden, Utrecht, and Groningen) and of schools of criminology at a number in Belgium (Leuven, Brussels, Ghent, and Liège).

Chapter 8 considers the ideologising of criminology in the totalitarian police states of Europe in the twentieth century. It first deals with the Nazification of criminology, in particular *Kriminalbiologie*, in the Third Reich and the legitimising role that leading researchers played in that process. The Bolshevisation of criminology in the Soviet Union is then discussed, namely how that development initially seemed to bring about a blossoming of criminology, but how it was later – when the terror erupted to its full extent in the 1930s – done away with. Its so-called revival in the 1950s is not, incidentally, ignored.

The reception of European criminology in the United States is the subject of the lengthy Chapter 9. The first part of the chapter discusses not only how the transfer of European criminology to the United States took place but also how that development culminated in the initiative by John Wigmore in 1909 to organise a national conference in Chicago the decisions of which would lead to the institutionalisation of criminology in that country. Following on from a discussion of that critical initiative, an explanation is given of the two divergent paths taken by criminology in the United States: the bio-anthropological route taken at Harvard University, and the more sociological approach taken at the University of Chicago, including in Frederic Thrasher's research on juvenile gangs and the studies by Henry McKay on the influence of social disorganisation. The main theories that were developed in the 1930s by Robert Merton, Thorsten Sellin, and especially Edwin Sutherland are then discussed. Where Sutherland in particular is concerned, both his differential association theory and his ideas on white collar crime are dealt with. Complementary to this, there is a discussion not only of the emerging sociology of organised crime, but also of the studies that Congress ordered of this type of crime. The final section of this chapter examines the impact that criminology has had on the development of the prison system and the policing system in the United States.

Chapter 10 discusses the transatlantic connections between the United States and Western Europe that have developed in the field of criminology since the 1960s. This chapter is specifically intended to form a bridge between the history of criminology, in relation to the criminal justice system, as described in this book, and criminology in the Western world today, whether or not in relation to that system. In order to clarify those connections as much as possible, the first part of the chapter discusses the turmoil that resulted during the 1960s and 1970s from the rise of Marxist, interactionist, and neo-classical trends in American criminology. Complementary to this, the second part of the chapter outlines what developments have manifested themselves in Western European criminology partly through the agency of its evolution in the United States since the 1960s. The evolution of criminology in the United Kingdom, Germany, France, Belgium, and the Netherlands are successively dealt with.

Chapter 11 concludes this historical and transatlantic introduction to criminology in relation to the criminal justice system. It looks first at the past, then outlines the current situation, and finally ventures a look into the future. A full bibliography is included.

CHAPTER 2

ORIGIN OF THE PRESENT-DAY CRIMINAL JUSTICE SYSTEM

2.1.   INTRODUCTION

In the course of the eighteenth century, the criminal justice system – as the main form of combatting crime – became one of the objects of critical discussion regarding the organisation and operation of the nation state. Needless to say, that discussion assumed that the audience addressed would have the necessary prior knowledge of the European political situation regarding these points, or at least the situation in certain European countries. That assumption was probably justified at the time, but it certainly does not apply to readers today.

To ensure a proper understanding of that discussion, this chapter therefore explains some of the main developments that occurred in Europe during the Middle Ages and the early modern period. In particular, an outline is given of how criminal proceedings at the time came to be on an inquisitorial basis and how – in line with that important procedural transformation – a criminal justice system was constructed of which the police force, the judiciary, and the prison system still form the institutional backbone today. Based on one of the best-known Dutch pamphlets from around the year 1600 on tackling the problems of crime – Dirk Volckertszoon Coornhert's *Boeventucht* [*Discipline of Villains*] – an explanation is given of the discussion associated with the emergence of the modern criminal justice system.

Discussing this large-scale institutionalisation of inquisitorial criminal procedure also provides an opportunity to give a taste of the debate taking place in historical criminology and in research on the history of criminal law about important issues such as the establishment of today's prison system and the modernisation of the police.

2.2. TRANSITION FROM ACCUSATORY TO INQUISITORIAL CRIMINAL PROCEEDINGS

Entirely in line with Carolingian criminal law, the "new" medieval state and city criminal law was initially of a predominantly accusatory nature. In the thirteenth, fourteenth, and fifteenth centuries, however, it acquired throughout Europe – in some places under the influence of canon law – an increasingly inquisitorial character, at least as regards more serious forms of crime.[1] For less serious offences, accusatory methods for keeping the peace within the community remained current in many places, right up to the French Revolution. This major shift in criminal law and consequently in the criminal justice system took place not only under the influence of the power struggle within the new princedoms. It was also a result both of the limitations of the accusatory system in combatting serious crime effectively and of a loss of faith in the operation of the traditional, sacrally tinged means of furnishing evidence.[2]

Raoul van Caenegem and other criminal law historians have in any case demonstrated convincingly that the accusatory system – as an autonomous form of organised criminal law – was the result of a gradual process of restructuring the law of retaliation (*lex talionis*). In that system, the authorities still recognised that wrongs between citizens were basically a matter that only concerned them and their families, but that – with a view to the public interest – combatting such wrongs should be effectuated by peaceful means, in accordance with objective standards. The classic accusatory legal system according to which disputes were to be settled was the truce. This amounted to a "cease-fire" between the conflicting parties with a view to mutual reconciliation. In certain circumstances, such a truce could be imposed by the authorities, if necessary by taking one or more of those involved into custody until an agreement had been reached. The truce was therefore merely a temporary measure – although an important one – for maintaining legal order.

That function is apparent from the penalties for those who committed a breach of the peace, namely long-term banishment, destruction of one's home, and capital punishment. In addition, a system of recompense was developed. This involved a solemn agreement between the conflicting parties which put a final end to the feud and guaranteed long-term peace. Essential for this legal concept was that – still entirely in the spirit of Germanic law – the perpetrator paid compensation for the loss or harm sustained. Recompense was mainly applied in cases involving violence: wounding, rape, or manslaughter. As with the

---

[1]   Drenth 1939, pp. 50–101, 124–163, 186–209.
[2]   Coppens 1991.

truce arrangement, the authorities did not simply look on passively, but, over the course of time, furnished themselves with the powers to impose recompense and determine the conditions under which it was to be effectuated.[3]

Whereas in an accusatory system offences are essentially regarded as mainly private matters whose solution is only brought about through mediation by the authorities, in an inquisitorial system they are regarded as violations of the princely or local commandment to keep the peace, and are therefore suppressed by the authorities.

The first major consequence of the rise of the inquisitorial system was that the authorities no longer needed to wait for a complaint to be submitted before taking action. They could initiate criminal investigations on their own initiative and, depending on the outcome, bring the accused before a court.

The second major consequence was a shift in the law of evidence. In criminal proceedings, the authorities were no longer content with the formal truth regarding what had or had not happened, i.e. the truth as presented by the parties to the conflict in the form of confessions, witness statements, ordeals (by water or fire), or armed combat. Quite the contrary: the authorities now actively sought the truth about what had really taken place (i.e. the material truth) by means of objective and rational procedures in which the course of events was reconstructed as closely as possible. This quest for the truth also naturally involved the use of traditional – so-called "ordinary" – evidence such as the examination of witnesses. Gradually, however, "extra-ordinary" means of furnishing evidence were also deployed in that quest – for example secret interrogation and the rack – and the rights of the defence were restricted.[4]

The transition from a predominantly accusatory criminal justice system to a predominantly inquisitorial one was completed in the course of the sixteenth century. That is apparent not only from historical research but also from one of the most important European handbooks of (city) criminal law at the time: *Practycke criminele* [*The Practice of Criminal Law*]. This was written in about 1516 by Filips Wielant but not published until 1555 by Joost de Damhouder (under his own name) as *Practycke ende handbouck in criminele zaeken* [*Practice and Theory in Criminal Matters*], after he had already published a Latin translation in 1554 (*Enchyridion rerum criminalium*). This "first systematic handbook on criminal law north of the Alps" in fact devoted most attention to the application of the inquisitorial procedure, including the use of torture.[5]

---

[3]   Van Caenegem 1954, pp. 230–320; De Vries 1955, pp. 7–81.

[4]   Van Caenegem 1956, pp. 115–245; Frederiks 1918, pp. 263–342.

[5]   De Damhouder 1555.

In the view of Wielant/De Damhouder, the prosecution of criminal offences served not only the interests of the individual aggrieved party but also the general interest. Penalties were therefore intended not only to rectify the loss or harm caused or as retribution for the injury, but also to deter others and

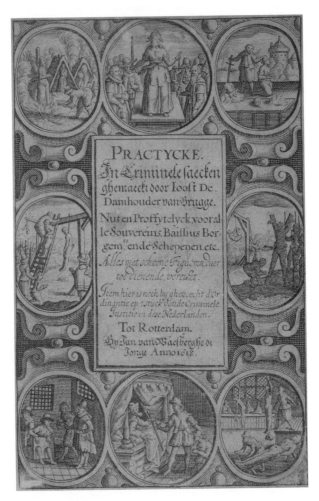

Joost DE DAMHOUDER, *Practycke in criminele saecken*, Rotterdam, Jan van Waesberghe de Jonge, 1618.

thus prevent the commission of new crimes. That did not mean, in their eyes, that the accused was to be punished inhumanely or in an excessive manner; the criminal law should be applied with moderation, with account being taken of mitigating circumstances, the sentence should essentially affect only the guilty party himself and not innocent third parties as well, etc.[6]

---

6   De Monté Verloren 1942, pp. 108–122; Van Heijnsbergen 1925.

2.3.   *BOEVENTUCHT* BY DIRK VOLCKERTSZOON COORNHERT

Given the crime problems arising from poverty and other calamities, it was obvious not only to magistrates but also to scholars that they should consider how those problems should be tackled. The best known of those scholars is Thomas More. In his *Utopia* (1516), More has the figure "Raphael Hythlodaeus" explain at length that the policy pursued in dealing with crime is completely wrong. By failing to intervene in the way the land is used, by accepting grain market monopolies, by allowing the textile industry to decline, etc., the authorities are actually, according to Raphael, raising many young people to be the thieves who they will later punish. And since capital punishment has led to even more murders because robbers are naturally afraid of being identified by their victims – "So in our efforts to terrorise thieves we're actually encouraging them to murder innocent people" – he thinks that alternatives need to be found.

Those alternatives should be sought, on the one hand, in the form of compensation to victims for the loss or harm sustained and, on the other, in the form of forced labour for the perpetrators. Raphael proposes the systematic deployment of convicted offenders to carry out public works as the main method:

> It comes heavily on crime, but it saves the lives of criminals, treating them in such a way that they're forced to become good citizens, and spend the rest of their lives making up for the harm they've done in the past.[7]

This view of the most suitable treatment of criminals can also be found in the only contemporary treatise written in the Netherlands in the late sixteenth century on the causes of crime problems and the means of combatting them. It was published by Dirk Volckertszoon Coornhert as *Boeventucht ofte middelen tot mindering der schadelyke ledighghanghers* [*Discipline of Villains or Means to Reduce the Number of Harmful Idlers*]. Coornhert – still known today as one of the greatest and most versatile intellectuals of his time – wrote the draft of this first Dutch criminological treatise *avant la lettre* in October 1567 when incarcerated in the prison gate in The Hague because of his opposition to Spanish rule. He published the final version in Amsterdam in 1587.[8]

Coornhert begins the work, which was intended for the States of Holland, with the observation that he has seen the tremendous disruption caused by the many *boeven* ("scoundrels", i.e. criminals) who can act as they wish with impunity because of the war. He then states that preventing crime is more praiseworthy than punishing it: a good ruler should make greater efforts to ensure "that few

---

7   More 1965, pp. 49–53.
8   Bonger (H.) 1978, pp. 310–311.

qualify for punishment rather than that many must be punished". Punishment, he argues, is necessary to prevent good citizens from going astray. And because the usual forms of punishment – branding, garrotting, banishment, etc. – do not help, other measures are needed to combat evil. To determine what those measures should be, he first investigates the causes of crime. In his view, there

Dirk Volckertszoon COORNHERT, *Boeventucht*, Utrecht, Instituut De Vooys, 1981 (introduced by M. BOOGAARD et al.).

are three causes: a lack of supervision of young people, the deficient application of the criminal law, and the preference of scoundrels for a quick death.

Complementary to this analysis of the causes, Coornhert adopts two approaches in seeking means of combatting them. To prevent the "proliferation in the number of harmful idlers", it is necessary to have the indigenous population perform useful work, to drastically increase the supervision of women, girls and young men, to intensify control of beggars from outside the city, and to subject the activities of the *schouten* (bailiffs) to strict inspection. As regards the punishment of offenders, he proposes four methods.

The first is to have all healthy beggars, thieves, violent offenders, extortionists, molesters of women, gamblers, profligates, and similar offenders row *beurtships* while chained to the thwarts.

The second method is to have "these bad people" turn the infertile sand dunes and lakes into good land while "linked to one another in pairs with chains or iron fetters".

Coornhert's third proposal is for "a big, solid prison" to be built in each region, with a large number of cells and a spacious courtyard, where every inmate who is already a master of a trade must work, while those who do not yet have a trade will learn "after some time to produce work as described above, or otherwise to fast", i.e. starve.

His fourth proposal is for a prison to be built in every city, and for the inmates either to practise certain trades within its walls or be utilised "riveted together in pairs" to fortify cities, build walls and dykes, dredge bodies of water, and drive piles. To prevent those guilty of capital crimes from attempting to escape, they should be branded in the face or have their nose split. The other criminals should be told that attempting to escape would lead to their term of forced labour being doubled.

Coornhert's treatise concludes with a number of considerations. First, he argues that the Netherlands needs to make money from criminals, in the same way as happens in Italy and Spain, where one pays between 20 and 100 ducats for an uneducated slave. Criminals are "too good to be executed, in other words reduced to nothing, as is the custom here". The convenience and benefit "that one can acquire from healthy scoundrels will certainly not be small but extremely great, if one learns how to utilise them in the right manner". But – his second consideration – that profit will amount to nothing "compared to the enormous benefit to the whole country simply from the reduction in the number of criminals". After all, registering criminals and imprisoning them makes it clear that there is no longer any room for impunity. And their imprisonment will show everyone that crime will henceforth be penalised by painful, miserable, and hopeless slavery. There will no longer be any place for a speedy death, capital punishment, or "foolish charity".

The first comment that one can make about this treatise by Coornhert – widely regarded as one of the great champions of tolerance within society – is that he is absolutely not tolerant of "scoundrels", certainly not "incorrigible criminals". Like More, he too believes that, in the first instance, everything possible should be done through good governance to prevent crime, but that – given that crime does exist – it should be dealt with severely. Without referring to More – we do not know whether Coornhert read More's work; he does not refer to it, in any case – he, like More, advocates unrelenting forced labour as a means of bringing incorrigible criminals to heel. Unlike More, however,

Coornhert does not restrict himself merely to general thoughts on the matter but works out quite specific plans.

It is especially noteworthy that Coornhert justifies this proposal not only with arguments such as the deterrence of others and protection of the innocent, but also with the argument of utility. That argument, in particular, shows in fact that Coornhert was a representative of the utilitarian trend within humanism. What is new to some extent, however, is that he believed that even the most serious criminals should not be executed but punished with forced labour.[9]

But it should be noted that Coornhert's utilitarianism was not only pragmatic but also moralistic. It was, as Florike Egmond writes, one of the manifestations of the "moral offensive" that the upper class and the authorities conducted in the sixteenth century against the poor in general and against all kinds of marginalised groups in particular. The fact that in some passages Coornhert places disobedient children, drunkards, and criminals on a par with one another is the best evidence of this. The idea that they all needed to be disciplined by being put to work went hand in hand with the belief that family life also needed to be kept in order, including by stricter standards of sexual behaviour.[10]

It may be true that Coornhert's proposals for ways of implementing imprisonment were perhaps less original – from the European perspective – than they may seem, given that in Spain offenders were already put to work as galley slaves and miners. The fact remains that the proposal that imprisonment should be the main form of punishment was certainly a ground-breaking one. Indeed, until late in the fifteenth century, this kind of punishment was hardly to be found in the official criminal law, and was only practised on a very small scale. This proposal by Coornhert therefore clearly anticipated a belief that would slowly but surely become commonplace, namely that imprisonment was the preferable form of punishment.

2.4. RENEWAL OF THE PRISON SYSTEM

Even in the Middle Ages, Europe had a great variety of ways of punishing someone by depriving them of their liberty. They might be put to work as galley slaves, used for forced labour on public works, or "simply" locked up in towers and dungeons. There were also a large number of other types of incarceration: political opponents in monasteries, the homeless and the sick in hospices, the feebleminded in special asylums, suspects on remand, etc.[11] Nevertheless, the houses of correction that were established throughout Europe from the second

---

[9]   Huussen 1989, pp. 149–153; Spierenburg 1990.
[10]   Egmond 1990.
[11]   Spierenburg 1991, pp. 12–40.

half of the sixteenth century were in fact an innovation – some would say a radical one. That was not only because of the purposes and organisation of these institutions but also because of the large scale on which they were established. Because the nature of these houses of correction gradually became more and more that of penal institutions, they formed, as it were, the basis for the prison system that we have today.

In the course of the sixteenth century, there were experiments in countless places in Europe involving the establishment of houses of correction as institutions where the needy poor could be imprisoned and – through work, discipline, and prayer – transformed into decent citizens. The first such experiment that was a long-term success, however, was the "bridewell", which takes its name from a castle that the English King Henry VIII made available to the authorities in London in 1553–55 for the detention of, specifically, idlers, beggars, vagrants, and prostitutes. This house of correction was therefore a government institution, as is also evident from the fact that the staff were paid by the city authorities and received an income that did not depend on the work performed by the inmates. Some would say, however, that this initiative was not entirely a success, especially since the original bridewell soon came to be used – contrary to its initial purpose – for the detention of thieves and other criminals. That development did not prevent other bridewells from quickly being established across England – quite the contrary: bridewells were set up in 1562 in Oxford, in 1565 in Norwich, and in 1569 in Ipswich. In 1576, the government even ordered that such institutions be set up throughout the country – with significant results. Eventually there were some 200 bridewells.[12]

Given the frequent contact between England and Holland in the second half of the sixteenth century, and certainly between London and Amsterdam, it is obvious that the creation of the *rasphuis* (rasping house) in Amsterdam in 1596 was partly motivated by the success of the bridewells. But the *rasphuis* was also in fact multifunctional from the very beginning. In accordance with the divergent views of the founders, it was used, on the one hand, as a prison (a penitentiary) for convicted criminals and, on the other, as an institution to house beggars, vagrants, prostitutes, and lunatics. In 1603, moreover, a separate department was established where wealthy families – in return for payment, and in secret – were able to confine their "black sheep" for a time. That department was also used to detain political opponents and sodomites, sometimes for life, because executing them in public presented too much of a risk to public order.[13]

As with the bridewells, the *rasphuis* was managed by the authorities. It held an average of about 100 inmates.[14] It was financed to a large extent by the

---

[12]   Depreeuw 1988, pp. 108–112; Spierenburg 1991, pp. 25–31; Sellin (J.) 1976, pp. 70–76.
[13]   Faber 1990.
[14]   Sellin (J.) 1944, pp. 31–75; Sellin (J.) 1976, pp. 76–79; Spierenburg 1991, pp. 41–50.

income from a special tax on the city's taverns and from the work performed by the inmates. This consisted, on the one hand, of weaving, and on the other of rasping hardwood to create dyestuffs. Despite the monopoly on rasping – which in fact gave rise to much opposition from businessmen – the *rasphuis* was almost always in financial difficulty.

The city authorities did not consider that to be a real problem, however: rasping hardwood in the extremely exhausting but uneconomical traditional manner was seen as a salutary means of punishing both body and spirit. The "ordinary" inmates carried out this forced labour in the cells where they also

THE AMSTERDAM RASPHUIS IN 1663

The Amsterdam Rasphuis in 1663, in: Thorsten SELLIN, *Pioneering in Penology: The Amsterdam Houses of Correction in the Sixteenth and Seventeenth Centuries*, Philadelphia, University of Pennsylvania Press, 1944.

slept. The cells were constructed so as to provide cramped accommodation for between four and 12 people, and looked out onto a common courtyard. The regime was not only extremely tough on paper; in practice too, relatively minor offences were punished by submitting the offenders to a still harsher cellular regime or by the offenders being thrown into chains. There were compulsory prayers at various times of the day. Juveniles received some degree of education.

As soon as the *rasphuis* was opened, discussion began of the need for a house of correction for women too. That discussion did not last long: in 1597, Amsterdam's *spinhuis* (spinning house) was opened, in a former nunnery. Originally, it was intended as a shelter for women who, for whatever reason, found themselves in distress, and not as a penal institution. Within a few years, however, it came to be very similar to the *rasphuis*. In addition to women confined at the request of their family, it was especially disorderly girls and prostitutes who were confined there.[15]

Where the original bridewell served as the model for the other houses of correction in England, the *rasphuis* provided an example for similar institutions which were established in many places in Europe in the first few decades of the seventeenth century. The first were in the Northern Netherlands themselves: in Leiden (1598), Haarlem (1603), Groningen (1609), Utrecht (1616), Delft (1620), and Middelburg (1642). German cities followed: Lübeck (1601), Bremen (1609), Hamburg (1618), and Danzig (1629); a *tukthus* was also set up in Stockholm. To the south, the Amsterdam model was applied in cities including Antwerp (1613), Brussels (1625), Ghent (1626), and Bruges (1675). There was even talk in Paris, in about 1617, of setting up a house of correction on the Amsterdam model. Whether the *maison de discipline* established in Geneva in 1631 was also based on the example of Amsterdam is unknown, but its inmates were certainly similar to those in Amsterdam.[16] It should be noted in this connection that by no means all the new houses of correction were copies of the *rasphuis* in every respect. In more than one city, the system was adapted to local circumstances, for example where financing was concerned. On the latter point: the lack of financial resources was also one of the reasons why some houses of correction were in fact closed down in the course of the seventeenth century. For a long time, the expansion of these institutions in Europe therefore retained something of the experimental character of the original initiative.[17]

To what extent the example of the *spinhuis* was followed in the Netherlands or elsewhere in Europe has never been systematically studied, but it is clear that such an institution was established in Delft in 1628 and another in Bruges in 1675. Interestingly enough, a *spinhuis* of the Amsterdam type was set up in the Dutch East Indies (in 1641), but not a *rasphuis*. Until into the nineteenth century, men were deprived of their liberty there by being deployed on public works, and indeed in chains.[18]

Needless to say, historians, criminologists, and other researchers have not only wondered how this first wave of houses of correction operated in northern Europe, but have also sought an explanation for this phenomenon.

Amongst sociologists and criminologists, this has taken two forms: on the one hand, a broadly functionalist explanation and, on the other, a Marxist-inspired view.

---

[15]   Spierenburg 1991, pp. 50–53; Sellin (J.) 1944, pp. 87–101.
[16]   Roth 1981, pp. 13–23.
[17]   Depreeuw 1988, pp. 116–117; Spierenburg 1991, pp. 55–86; Sellin (J.) 1944, pp. 102–111.
[18]   Hallema 1936, pp. 170–173.

According to the former explanation, as developed by Thorsten Sellin and Wim Depreeuw, the establishment of houses of correction should be seen as one of the remarkable responses by farsighted city governments to the major problems of vagrancy and begging – caused by economic reforms and political

Pieter SPIERENBURG, *The Spectacle of Suffering: Executions and the Evolution of Repression: From a Preindustrial Metropolis to the European Experience*, Cambridge, Cambridge University Press, 1984.

upheavals, i.e. wars – which could not be kept in check by the existing control mechanisms, namely a totally fragmented criminal justice system and church-based charity.

The latter explanation was initially proposed by Georg Rusche and Otto Kirchheimer in their study *Punishment and Social Structure* (1939) and developed further by Dario Melossi and Massimo Pavarini in *Carcere e fabbricca* [*Prison and Factory*] (1977). What it boils down to is basically that the houses of correction were one of the important methods, motivated by Calvinist morality, for making the working class suitable – and disciplining it – for the factory production of goods. The early capitalist development of the Netherlands and the surrounding area was said to be the reason why this development manifested itself earlier here than in other parts of Europe.[19]

Meticulous research by the historian Pieter Spierenburg, in particular, has shown that the Marxist thesis is largely untenable.[20] That is not only because the founders of houses of correction such as the *rasphuis* and the bridewell cannot be suspected of Calvinism – to say nothing of the founders in the Spanish Netherlands – but also because the organisational model of these institutions was based not on that of the emerging factories but on the traditional family model: the inmates were not seen as a reservoir of cheap labour but were viewed – rather paternalistically – as needy fellow human beings who had sinned against the prevailing morality. It was precisely because of this that, for almost two centuries, numerous houses of correction retained the practice of the manual rasping of dyewood even though this was a totally counterproductive method of production from a capitalist perspective.

Spierenburg does consider it possible, however, that in those parts of Europe to which the Reformation had brought the Protestant work ethic, forced labour in prisons was considered more acceptable than in areas that had remained Catholic. He also shares the view of Sellin and Depreeuw that the role of the entrepreneurial elites in cities such as Amsterdam cannot be underestimated: they were simply seeking a pragmatic solution to what they saw as an acute social problem. And since many large cities in northern Europe were confronted by this problem, it is unsurprising – still according to Spierenburg – that the solution developed in Amsterdam was gladly adopted, especially since many of those cities maintained close links with one another in all sorts of fields.

2.5. MODERNISATION OF THE POLICE SYSTEM

While the origins of the modern prison system can be found in England and Holland, those of the modern police system undoubtedly lie in France. The year 1667 saw the police in Paris reorganised in a way that served as a model not only for police forces in other French cities but also, in time, for those in other European cities. In addition, in 1720, the *maréchaussée* was then modernised

---

[19]   Rusche and Kirchheimer 1974; Melossi and Pavarini 1981.
[20]   Spierenburg 1984, p. IX; Spierenburg 1991, pp. 223–227.

according to a model that spread throughout Europe, particularly due to the French Revolution. Modernisation of the police therefore commenced much later than did renewal of the prison system. For all sorts of reasons, it did not take place before the start of the French Period on such a large scale in Europe as the latter renewal. But that does not make it any less important for subsequent developments in the criminal justice system and in the combatting of crime.

It was not the problems in criminal investigation that caused Louis XIV to decide in 1667 to thoroughly reorganise the police force in Paris. The Sun King's main reason was that he wanted to have a force in the capital that would not only be constantly informed of important social developments and thus be able to prevent disturbances of public order in good time, but that would also be in a position to immediately supress any emerging disturbances.

To achieve this, Louis XIV first appointed a lieutenant of police, on whom he conferred not only a wide range of powers but also authority over the many public officials who performed all kinds of policing tasks.[21] By doing this, he was essentially making an institutional separation between two functions that until then, as in the Netherlands, had been combined in a single official, namely the policing and judicial functions. His reason for this separation was that, because of their actual substance, the two functions could not be reconciled and could not therefore be performed by one and the same official. Second, the city watch was transformed into a well-organised uniformed service that in an emergency could call on a special mounted company to maintain or restore order. And third, the already long-established police commissioners were allocated a set of regulations, so that they were not only assured of a regular income but could also be required to obey the lieutenant of police. Each commissioner was responsible for policing in a given part of Paris.[22]

The fact that this modernised police system primarily had a preventive task was expressed clearly in 1671 by the first lieutenant of police, Gabriel Nicolas de la Reynie, in a letter to Minister Jean-Baptiste Colbert: it is much easier to maintain public order than to restore it once it has been disrupted. To that end, La Reynie not only had extensive administrative powers, a watch that constantly monitored the entire city, and commissioners of police, but also made wide use of informants who updated him, directly or indirectly, via the commissioners, on what was happening in the political and the criminal worlds. The prevention principle therefore went hand in hand with the information principle: police officers were required to provide him with written reports of their observations and insights.

It was in fact only La Reynie's successor who in 1708 appointed 40 inspectors of police to gather information on all possible areas: political life in the city, the

---

[21]　Napoli 2003, pp. 34–57; Saint-Germain 1962; Le Nabour 1991.
[22]　Sälter 2004, pp. 97–200; Anglade 1852, pp. 37–48; Clément 1866, pp. 62–71, 130–145.

mood among the populace, the night life of the bourgeoisie, and naturally also the situation in the criminal world. To perform their task, the inspectors could call on an army of informants and observers from all walks of life and sectors of society, some on the payroll and others paid according to the work they actually carried out. In subsequent reorganisations, in particular that in 1750, some of these inspectors were put in charge of a *bureau de sûreté* (security office), the undisputed precursor of today's European criminal investigation services.[23]

Louis XIV had already decreed in 1667 that the other towns in France should follow the example of Paris and reorganise their police apparatus according to this new centralised and integrated model. That decree was not complied with, however. Not a single French town was prepared – particularly for financial reasons – to implement the model voluntarily. The King therefore decreed in 1699 that the larger cities should appoint both a lieutenant of police and commissioners of police. That decree did not have much success either. It was only actually obeyed in a few towns and cities.

Outside France, however, the modernised Paris police force was highly regarded, at least by the great foreign powers of the time. This can be seen from the fact that a police directorate on the Paris model was established in Berlin in 1693, and – after it had disappeared in institutional power struggle – re-established in 1742 by Frederick the Great. In 1718, Tsar Peter the Great followed the example of Paris and also organised a police directorate in St Petersburg. Like Berlin, other German cities also appointed a director of police in the 1750s and 1760s.[24]

The reorganisation of the *maréchaussée* in 1720 was not immediately imitated abroad but that does not make it any less interesting than the reorganisation of the Paris police in 1667. Even before 1720, plans had already been drawn up for reforming the existing provincial *maréchaussées*. Those plans were above all motivated by the concern of central government to maintain public order in the country. That was an understandable concern in a country where wars, domestic political conflicts, agricultural crises, and fiscal measures had led in the early eighteenth century to a loss of a certain amount of stability. Why those plans were repeatedly not implemented is unclear.

But in 1720 a radical reorganisation did finally take place. First, most of the provincial *maréchaussées* were replaced by companies stationed in each *département*, which were in turn divided into a total of 560 brigades. Second, the entire financing of this *maréchaussée générale* was taken over by the state, which immediately used its new position of power to standardise the system of ranks and other organisational matters. Just how radical this reorganisation in fact was is clearly shown by the following example: in the later *départements* of Languedoc,

---

[23]   Fijnaut 1979, 1, pp. 518–527; Williams (A.) 1979, pp. 17–61.
[24]   Fijnaut 1979, 1, pp. 533–540, 542–547.

Touraine and Poitou, the number of officers' posts, spread out over some 80-odd *maréchaussées*, was reduced from 487 to 52, divided across three companies.[25]

That this modernisation of the *maréchaussée* on a national scale enabled it to suppress public order disturbances more effectively – specifically larger ones – is probably obvious. It is also undeniable, however, that it led to the development of a far more powerful investigative agency in the provinces. A number of historical studies have in fact shown that the "new" *maréchaussée* was better able to combat not only vagrancy and begging on a larger scale but also all the various types of violent crime and property offences. In this sense, the modernisation of the *maréchaussée* reflected that of the police in Paris, although it did not include the establishment of special investigative services within the various companies.[26]

It is precisely the functional similarity between these two reorganisations that allows us to conclude that the modernisation of the policing system essentially consisted of creating professional police forces, i.e. hierarchised and disciplined organisations under a single commander, which could be used to actively and continuously carry out monitoring throughout the entire territory of their political masters, with the special task of gathering information on everything affecting public order, and if necessary able to be mobilised rapidly to quell disturbances. It is therefore not surprising that the term "police" underwent a significant change in the course of the eighteenth century. Whereas it had until then been merely a synonym for a well-governed state – i.e. an *état policé* – it subsequently came to mean the police force: the *corps de police*, the strong arm of the government.[27]

2.6. CONCLUSION

The above allows us to conclude that the public and inquisitorial criminal proceedings that were established during the Middle Ages became embedded in the centuries that followed in a criminal justice system which, seen from an institutional viewpoint, consisted of a judiciary that was flanked, on the one hand, by a modernised police system, and, on the other, by a renewed prison system. At the beginning of the eighteenth century, that evolution of the criminal justice system had by no means progressed equally far everywhere, but here and there it was already possible see what would become the basic structure of

---

[25] Fijnaut 1979, 1, pp. 528–533, 540–542; Alary 2000, pp. 17–42; Larrieu 2002, pp. 79–312.
[26] Cameron 1981, pp. 56–132; Ruff 1984, pp. 24–43.
[27] Fijnaut 1979, 1, pp. 604–615; Rijpperda Wierdsma 1937, pp. 119–193; Von Justi 1759, pp. 3–16, 334–348; Von Pfeiffer 1779, pp. 39–50, Höck 1809, pp. 18–19, 209–221; Lüdtke 1982, pp. 67–82, 143–158, 323–338.

the criminal justice system in Europe today: a system for the administration of justice flanked on the one hand by a police system and on the other by a prison system. The introduction of banishment to the colonies ("transportation") was in a sense diametrically opposed to that evolution, and in fact turned out to be of secondary importance. It was only fully implemented by a single state – Britain – and it died out over the course of the nineteenth century.

CHAPTER 3

RESTRUCTURING OF THE CRIMINAL JUSTICE SYSTEM DURING THE ENLIGHTENMENT AND THE FRENCH PERIOD

3.1.   INTRODUCTION

Most introductions to criminology begin with a discussion of ideas about the foundations of the criminal law and the structure of the criminal justice system that were published anonymously by Cesare Beccaria in his *Dei delitti e delle pene* in Milan in 1764. The previous chapter sufficiently demonstrated that such an approach should be viewed as a false start. The ideas expressed in this masterly treatise did not arrive out of the blue.

The present chapter therefore begins with a brief discussion of the work of two philosophers who greatly influenced Beccaria, namely Charles-Louis de Secondat, Baron de la Brède et de Montesquieu – better known simply as Montesquieu – and Jean-Jacques Rousseau. A discussion then follows of both Beccaria's celebrated treatise and the enormous response that it generated within Europe.

But it is not sufficient merely to describe the battle of ideas that took place in the final decades of the eighteenth century. It is just as important – in line with the previous chapter – to examine how the Enlightenment affected the discussion of the organisation of the criminal justice system at the time, especially in the Austrian Netherlands, because it was there that major reforms of both the prison system and the policing system were implemented, or at least proposed.

The chapter concludes by considering developments during the French Revolution and under the Napoleonic regime. To what extent was the new legislation in line with the ideas previously expressed about the necessary reform of criminal law? And to what extent did the restructuring of the criminal justice system dovetail with what had previously been proposed or tested?

3.2.   THE SPIRIT OF THE AGE: CHARLES-LOUIS DE SECONDAT, BARON DE LA BRÈDE ET DE MONTESQUIEU AND JEAN-JACQUES ROUSSEAU

3.2.1.   MONTESQUIEU: *DE L'ESPRIT DES LOIS*

Montesquieu became world-famous with a work that he published in 1748: *De l'esprit de lois ou du rapport que les lois doivent avoir avec la constitution de chaque gouvernement, les mœurs, le climat, la religion, le commerce, etc.*[1]

---

[1]   De Secondat 1964, pp. 557–564, 598–600. See also Montesquieu 2006, pp. 121–147.

[*On the Spirit of the Laws or on the Relationship that the Laws should have with the Constitution of each Government, the Morals, the Climate, the Religion, the Commerce, etc.*]. He put forward a number of ideas, especially in Chapters VI and VIII, that recur in the work of Beccaria. One of his key principles was that political freedom is not possible if the power to make laws, the power to execute them, and the power to judge crimes and disputes are held by a single person. In line with this principle, he asserted that political freedom essentially consists of the certainty that that freedom is no longer jeopardised by public and private accusations. In other words, the freedom of the citizen is ultimately dependent on good criminal legislation. This naturally raises the question of what behaviour should or should not be made a criminal offence. Montesquieu answers that age-old question by defining four categories of offences: against religion, against morality, against public order, and against the physical and material safety of the citizen.

For how these offences should be punished, Montesquieu worked out a number of rules of thumb. The first rule is that the legislature should not resort to extreme punishments because, on the one hand, people will adapt their behaviour to such punishments and will therefore more easily commit ruthless crimes. On the other, it is because such punishments lead to impunity, for the simple reason that they are either not imposed or not carried out. Following on from this, Montesquieu's second rule is that it is not mild penalties that are the cause of lawlessness but rather the fact that punishment is not imposed, i.e. that there is impunity. In other words, crimes must always be punished. The third rule is that the range of punishments available should be differentiated in a proportionate manner so that serious offences can be punished harshly and minor offences leniently. This rule of thumb provides the fourth rule, namely that the nature and severity of the punishments should correspond as far as possible with the nature and seriousness of the crimes involved.

Offences against religion, for example, should be punished by exclusion from the church, expulsion from the community of believers, etc. Offences against morality should be punished by means of fines, public infamy, or banishment. Offences against public order should result in imprisonment or other correctional penalties that will teach restless spirits what constitutes the established order. And where offences against the security of the citizen are concerned, murder and manslaughter should be punishable by death, property offences by the forfeiture of goods or, if the perpetrator has no assets, by corporal punishment.

Montesquieu considers that the way prosecution is organised should remain as it is. The ruler should appoint an official charged with prosecuting all crimes in the ruler's name. The citizen, for his part, should have all possible means at his disposal to defend his freedom and his life. As regards the gathering of evidence, Montesquieu took the side of those who opposed torture, which he considered a feature of despotic regimes. In his view, the example of England, where it was apparently not used, proved that torture was not necessary to uncover the truth.

3.2.2. ROUSSEAU: *DU CONTRAT SOCIAL*

In his *Du contrat social ou principes du droit politique* [*On the Social Contract or Principles of Political Law*], published in Amsterdam in 1762, Rousseau was far less emphatic about the principles of the criminal law (both material and formal) than Montesquieu.[2] Nevertheless – if only for a proper understanding of *Dei delitti e delle pene* – it is important to be familiar with some of the principles and observations that he set out in his treatise.

Rousseau states that there is a huge difference between the subjection of the masses and the governance of a society that functions as an association, a political body. Such a society is formed at the point when individuals are no longer able to overcome on their own the problems that threaten their survival in their natural state. What changes is that they join forces and jointly deploy those forces. But how does one find a form of association that protects the individual and their goods with all its might but still leaves the individual as free as possible?

The answer is that individuals should unite as sovereign citizens into a single political body and submit to the laws of the state that they thus create. Rousseau goes on to say that although the social contract concluded in this way assigns absolute power over all involved to that political body, this does not mean that the individual citizens no longer have any rights and freedoms. They still have these, he says, because they only relinquish them to the community in so far as that is necessary in the public interest. And that is exactly what happens with laws: they record the reciprocal rights and freedoms of the sovereign and the citizens, without discrimination. The great goal of legislation can therefore only be the greatest wellbeing of all. Criminal legislation ultimately serves the same goal. This explains why Rousseau is certainly not standing up for criminals. In his view, every criminal is an enemy of the state because he has broken the social contract. He must therefore be banished or executed. It should be noted that Rousseau believed that the death penalty and corporal punishment should not be utilised too unrestrainedly because doing so is a sign of authorities that are weak or lazy.

Rousseau's ideas show that the Enlightenment did not therefore mean an absolute break with the past. His views on the use of the death penalty and corporal punishment demonstrate the same utilitarian mind-set as that of More. Similarly, Montesquieu's ideas about the cruelty of punishments and the impact of impunity can easily be found in Coornhert's *Boeventucht*. The range of punishments that Montesquieu considered necessary to respond appropriately to the various types of crime is very similar to what had already existed in most European states since the sixteenth century.

---

[2]   Rousseau (J.-J.) 1962, pp. 243–245, 256–257.

3.3. CESARE BECCARIA'S MANIFESTO *DEI DELITTI E DELLE PENE*

Nobody has been more successful than Lieven Dupont in analysing what principles were considered in the second half of the eighteenth century – particularly by French (criminal justice) philosophers – as those that should

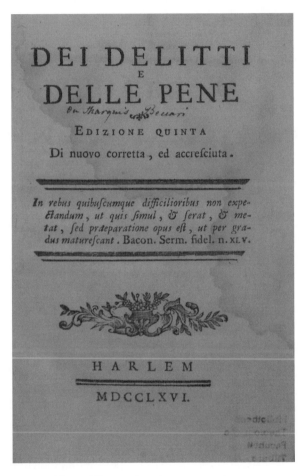

Cesare Beccaria, *Dei delitti e delle pene*, Haarlem, *s.n.*, 1766.

form the basis for a possible reform of the criminal justice system.[3] There were six such principles: legality, equality, proportionality, personality, publicity, and subsidiarity.

We have already looked at some of these when discussing the work of Montesquieu and Rousseau. That there must be a certain relationship between

---

3   Dupont 1979, pp. 48–77.

the seriousness of a crime and the severity of its punishment (proportionality) is an idea that was expressed clearly for the first time by Montesquieu. And the principle of equality – in the sense that the criminal law should apply equally to everyone, i.e. without discrimination – was, of course, implicit in Rousseau's concept of the social contract.

But it was definitely also via *Dei delitti e delle pene* that these principles came to play such a prominent role, later in the period concerned, in public debate on the reform of the criminal justice system.

3.3.1. BASIC PRINCIPLES OF THE MANIFESTO AND THEIR GENERAL CONSEQUENCES

Beccaria (1738–94) began work on his famous manifesto of more than 100 pages in 1763, at the age of 25. He published it anonymously in 1764 because he wanted to avoid being prosecuted in the Milan of that time because of the ideas that he was proclaiming. Beccaria was therefore not a revolutionary and he absolutely did not want to be one. What did he in fact want? That is still the subject of dispute even today, partly because of the rather pamphlet-like style of the work: *Dei delitti e delle pene* contains quite a few passages that could have been clearer, or that are difficult to reconcile with one another.[4]

In his introduction, Beccaria states that his principles are the following.[5] First, he takes issue with the dichotomy in society between a mass of paupers on the one hand and a rich and powerful minority on the other. He advocates legislation that allows everyone to share in the benefits brought by living together in a society. He repeats, word for word, Rousseau's utilitarian maxim: legislation must seek to ensure the greatest happiness for the greatest number. The fact that Beccaria – himself the scion of a noble family – does not seize on this principle to call for far-reaching social and economic reforms is sometimes seen as proof of his conservative attitude.

His second principle is more humanitarian in nature. *Dei delitti e delle pene* was an appeal for opposition to inquisitorial criminal proceedings, and in particular to torture, to the cruelty of many penalties, and to the inhuman conditions in the prisons. Beccaria here refers to Montesquieu as his shining example. The fundamental question that he then raises is that of the origin, i.e. the foundation, of the right to punish (*ius puniendi*). To answer that question, he again invokes Rousseau. In order to preserve the greatest possible freedom, Beccaria asserts, people have decided to sacrifice part of their freedom, because that is the only way they can enjoy, undisturbed, the freedom that remains.

---

4   Jenkins 1984a; Newman and Marongiu 1990.
5   Beccaria 1982; Beccaria 1870.

And the sum total of all the little bits of freedom that they have relinquished constitutes the sovereignty of a nation and is the basis for the right to punish.

Why that right is necessary – why in his view punishment should be imposed in a tangible manner – Beccaria presumably based on the ideas that the British philosopher John Locke had already set out in 1689 in *An Essay Concerning Human Understanding*. In particular, the idea that "pleasure and pain and that which causes them, good and evil, are the hinges on which our passions turn" must have appealed to him.[6] According to Beccaria, punishment – or at least the threat of punishment – is in fact necessary as a counterweight to the strong anti-social impulses of the individual. It is only punishments ("pain") that have the power to eventually subdue the passions that are stirred up by the tempting prospect of real and immediate enjoyment ("pleasure"). Beccaria attaches some important general conclusions to this answer.

In accordance with the legality and equality principles, he first asserts that the penalties for crimes must be established in clearly defined laws that apply to everyone. Such legislation provides a sense of freedom and independence, because everyone knows exactly where he stands; in such a situation, one can even quantify beforehand someone's happiness or unhappiness (if he breaks a law). Beccaria also believes that laws that are formulated in an understandable manner have a preventive effect. After all, laws that are incomprehensible because they are unclear create confusion as to whether certain deeds are liable to be punished, and therefore also regarding the certainty that they will in fact be punished if necessary; this thus increases the temptation to perpetrate those crimes.

Second, it cannot be the case that the sovereign determines whether someone has committed a breach of the social contract, because that would divide the nation into two parties. Instead, it is necessary – and here we can again hear the voice of Montesquieu – for a third power to intervene in order to decide the truth of the matter, namely the judiciary. According to Beccaria, however, judges should not have any freedom of interpretation whatsoever, because then citizens could once more become the victim of all kinds of false reasoning, ill temper or quibbles, or even bribery. Judges must therefore stick to the letter of the law.

And third, the punishments imposed must not be cruel. That would not only be contrary to the civilised character of a society but would also make the objective of punishment unattainable, both because fear of such punishments would lead to ever-crueller crimes being committed, and because such penalties will often not in fact be imposed and carried out, therefore creating a feeling of impunity. Punishment must therefore be moderate. Beccaria does note that in a more civilised, gentler society, penalties can be more moderate than in a less

---

[6] Locke 1973, pp. 108–109; Beirne 1993, pp. 24–29.

civilised society, because in the former proportionately milder penalties already have a preventive effect.

3.3.2. PURPOSES OF PUNISHMENT AND THEIR IMPLEMENTATION

This observation brings us to the question of what purposes Beccaria ascribed to the imposition of punishment. At the beginning of this section, we already saw that he considered that punishments were necessary in order to restrain human passions. We have also just seen that he attached particular importance to the preventive effect of punishment. It is indeed the main effect that he has in mind. Beccaria does not speak of retribution, and he also pays no attention to purposes like the improvement of prisoners. Punishment is for him entirely a matter of specific and general prevention: special prevention in the sense that criminals must be prevented from causing any further harm to their fellow citizens; general prevention in the sense of deterrence, i.e. dissuading others from committing crimes.

With a view to achieving these objectives, Beccaria suggests four general principles that must be taken into account when determining penalties.

The first two principles are an elaboration of the proportionality principle. On the one hand, Beccaria argues that the severity of the punishment earned must be proportionate to the seriousness of the offence. He emphasises that the severity of the crime can only be determined by reference to the harm done to society, and must not be derived, for example, from the intention, i.e. the malice, of the perpetrator. On the other hand, the nature of the punishment imposed must correspond as closely as possible to the nature of the offence.

The third principle expresses the personality principle to a certain extent, but it also demonstrates how Beccaria views the criminal in this connection: this is someone who deliberately – i.e. of his own free will – weighs up the benefits of the intended crime against the disadvantages of the potential punishment. Beccaria consequently states that the punishment must always cause more distress, more disadvantage, to the criminal than the enjoyment, i.e. the benefit, that he gains from his crime. He must always be deprived of that benefit when the penalty is imposed.

Fourth, Beccaria believes that the penalty – especially with a view to its preventive effect – must also be tailored to the spirit, the mentality, of the population. In particular, it is essential that the population immediately associate the commission of a crime with suffering punishment. To achieve this conditioning, it is of great importance, first, for the time that elapses between the point when the crime is committed and the point when the punishment is imposed to be as short as possible. Second, it must be impossible to evade a just punishment. The certainty that one will be punished outweighs the risk of a more severe penalty that one hopes to evade.

3.3.3. CATEGORIES OF CRIMES AND TYPES OF PUNISHMENTS

But what penalties did Beccaria have in mind for what crimes? In the wake of Montesquieu, but also along the lines of the then ideal of science – science should be pursued *more geometrico* – he posits that if geometry could be applied "to the countless, obscure motives that determine human behaviour", it should be possible to draw up "a mathematical scale" of crimes with corresponding penalties. For the "wise legislator", it would be sufficient, however, if the main principles were indicated with which the desired balance can be achieved between crimes and punishments. One must above all ensure that the most serious crimes are not made subject to the mildest penalties.

Crimes, he believes, can be divided into three categories. First, there are those with a direct, undermining impact on society or on those who represent it; these are also the most serious crimes. Second, there are crimes that disadvantage the citizen as a private individual by attacking his life and his goods, or assailing his honour and reputation. The third category includes actions that are contrary to what everyone is obliged to do, or refrain from doing, with a view to the common good.

Beccaria then discusses a number of crimes, or variants of them, in order to clarify what he means. He does not in fact undertake a systematic treatment of the three categories of crimes in terms of the penalties that can or should be applied proportionately. However, when discussing the various specific crimes, he does refer indirectly to previous passages in his manifesto that deal with certain penalties by themselves, i.e. separately from his tripartite categorisation of crimes. It would therefore be in vain to seek in Beccaria's work a systematic discussion of the range of penalties on which a "wise legislator" can draw. The penalties that Beccaria discusses separately are the death penalty, deprivation of liberty, banishment, and forfeiture. Corporal punishment and fines, however, are dealt with when he discusses certain specific crimes.

There is no doubt that Beccaria was against the death penalty as a matter of principle,[7] considering it both unjust and not useful. It was unjust because it cannot possibly be based on a right: "Who has ever wanted to give others the right to murder him if they see fit to do so?" It is not useful because it sets a bad example of bloodthirsty cruelty, because it has never prevented people from committing crimes, and because the ceremony associated with its implementation only strengthens people in their belief that it is a pretext for using force to make an offering "to the insatiable idol of despotism". But he still does not absolutely reject the death penalty. He specifically does not exclude "the deaths of a few civilians" being necessary "at those difficult moments when a nation is on the verge of losing or recovering its freedom, or in times of anarchy, when it is unrest and rioting that make the law".

---

[7]   Badinter 1989.

His preference is plainly for "the penalty of perpetual slavery", which is sufficient to dissuade the most hardened offender from his criminal intent. After all, someone who is aware of the risk of long years of slavery and misery will weigh up that risk against the uncertain fruits of his misdeeds. Beccaria considers that deprivation of liberty in this way is perhaps crueller than execution. Partly for that reason, he believes, it has the advantage of being an even stronger deterrent for those who witness it than those who undergo it.

These views on the death penalty or deprivation of liberty – in many ways reminiscent of those already expressed by Coornhert two centuries previously – are also an excellent illustration of the paradoxical, not to say sometimes contradictory, nature of *Dei delitti e delle pene*. On the one hand, the effectiveness and legitimacy of the existing criminal justice system are strongly criticised because of the inhumane nature of its methods and penalties, while on the other the effectiveness and legitimacy of the upcoming system are based on practices whose inhumane character is beyond dispute. The crimes for which Beccaria envisages deprivation of liberty include those that constitute an attack on people's freedom, security, and property.

Besides deprivation of liberty, Beccaria also considered banishment to be a very acceptable punishment, especially for those who are prosecuted for committing serious crimes but whose guilt cannot be proved. The crucial question here is whether someone who is banished must also have all his goods confiscated. Beccaria does not exclude complete confiscation if the sentence of banishment disrupts all relations between the exile and society. After all, someone who is punished in that way has in fact undergone civil death.

Did Beccaria also see a place for corporal punishment? He does indicate at various points that such punishments certainly deserve a place in the range of punishments that the legislature must have at its disposal. Offences against the person, he asserts, must "definitely be punished by corporal punishment". And in the case of robbery (i.e. with violence being used), the penalty must also "have a physical aspect and an element of slave-like deprivation of liberty". He does not, however, say anything about how corporal punishment should in future be carried out, nor does he raise the question of whether or not it is humane. For him, such punishment can clearly just be continued as before.

There is then the matter of fines. Beccaria upholds the principle that these are ideally suited for punishing thefts perpetrated without the use of violence. But he immediately considers that theft is usually committed out of desperation and poverty – one of the few times when he views perpetrating a crime not only as the result of an individual calculation of benefit and loss by the offender but also directly associates this behaviour with the social conditions in which people find themselves. As a result, fines may in fact increase the number of unfortunates, to an even greater degree than the number of crimes themselves. In this case as well, it is therefore slavery – from which "society benefits fully from the work and person of the penalised party" – that is the most appropriate punishment.

3.3.4. A STAUNCH DEFENDER OF FREEDOM AND A MILITANT OPPONENT OF CRIMINALS

Beccaria was therefore anything but mild when it came to punishing crime. The idea that the preventive effect of criminal justice is increased if an offence is punished swiftly and certainly and also severely – in proportion to the seriousness of the offence – was one that he very much favoured. According to the conclusion of *Dei delitti e delle pene*, this required, however, penalties to be prescribed by law and imposed during proceedings that can meet the fairness test.

It is precisely his criticism of the contemporary approach to criminal proceedings that has led to Beccaria being known as an acute critic and a humane reformer. He did indeed fiercely attack the unnecessary and improper use of pre-trial remand and the dreadful conditions in which that "punishment" had to be served. His championing of the formulation of legal criteria under which suspects could be held in custody is therefore not at all strange. He despised the use of secret accusations and thus the phenomenon of secret criminal trials, and he therefore fiercely advocated for trials to be held in public, with the accusations being brought forward by specially appointed commissioners. And he was totally opposed to torture, which he viewed as a modern variant of divine judgment. Torture was not suitable for uncovering the true circumstances of crimes but rather, in Beccaria's view, the surest way to ensure that physically tough criminals were acquitted and weak innocents condemned.

All in all, Beccaria therefore reveals himself to be both a staunch defender of the freedom of the citizen and a militant opponent of those who do not respect that freedom – governments and criminals alike. In this sense, one can also say that his views on the criminal justice system, and how to reform it, are more coherent and consistent than some of his critics suggest. Is it so strange that when freedom is seen as the supreme good, custodial sentences are regarded as the most effective punishment?[8]

3.3.5. VARIOUS RANDOM THOUGHTS ON CRIME PREVENTION

Finally, one needs to note that Beccaria also pays lip service to the idea that it is better "to prevent crime than to punish it" because, like many of his predecessors, he saw repression, above all, as an appropriate means of prevention. Nevertheless, in *Dei delitti e delle pene* he also made a number of remarks on other ways to prevent crime.

---

[8]   Naucke 1989.

His ideas in that respect concern not only, again, the preventive effect of clearly worded criminal legislation, but also the importance of the intellectual development of the citizen. He considers a "select group" of competent, honest judges to be a blessing for the nation.

But what Beccaria considers most important of all is education. It is the surest way to prevent crime, but also the most difficult because it touches on politics, has to do with methods, concerns good and evil, relies on reason, but also takes account of feelings. That is why he does not expound on it in detail. By enumerating all these factors, he is implicitly indicating that in his eyes the commission of a crime cannot be regarded solely as an entirely individual act, perpetrated in the pursuit of profit, but must also be viewed as the manifestation of a certain social order.

3.4. RECEPTION OF BECCARIA'S MANIFESTO WITHIN EUROPE

Within just a short time, *Dei delitti e delle pene* became a European bestseller. It was quickly translated into a large number of languages, and reprints were sooner or later necessary everywhere. Many naturally wondered why it could become such a resounding success. Was it because Beccaria proclaimed views in a nutshell that had already been adopted here and there but never summarised so succinctly and readably? Was it because his views were in a certain sense not as revolutionary as they might seem at first sight, and were therefore acceptable to many of his contemporaries? Was it because in some countries the existing criminal justice system was proving increasingly unable to cope with crime problems of all kinds, and urgently needed to be restructured? Whatever the precise answer to these questions may be, Beccaria's book was indeed a resounding success.

3.4.1. A MIXED RECEPTION IN ITALY, GERMANY, RUSSIA, SCANDINAVIA, AND FRANCE

In Italy itself, Beccaria's little book was widely distributed and read, despite being almost immediately banned by the secular and ecclesiastical authorities. While it made a deep impression on some leading jurists, it was ignored by others. But the influence that Beccaria's ideas (and, in the background, those of Montesquieu, of course) exerted on the drafting of the new Tuscan criminal code of 1786 – the first in Europe that was infused with "enlightened" ideas – was in all kinds of ways so great that his fame became enduring.[9]

---

9   Pasta 1997; Cartuyvels 1996.

The book also immediately enjoyed a great response in the various German states, being quickly published in three different places. Ardent supporters such as Karl Hommel, professor of criminal law in Leipzig, made it hugely popular.[10] It was specifically Paul Feuerbach, however, who integrated Beccaria's views into German criminal law dogmatics in his *Revision der Grundsätze und Grundbegriffe des positiven peinlichen Rechts* [*Revision of the Principles and Concepts of the Positive Criminal Law*] (1799).[11] Catherine the Great of Russia first became aware of Beccaria's book in the French translation by André Morellet in 1766. She not only immediately invited Beccaria (unsuccessfully) to come to work at her court but also had his ideas and those of Montesquieu incorporated into a new body of criminal legislation.[12] In the 1770s, Beccaria's book also became well known in Scandinavia. There too, it played an important role in the reforms of the criminal justice system that were implemented in that period.[13]

It also goes without saying – given Beccaria's major sources of inspiration – that his manifesto was greeted with great enthusiasm by the *philosophes* in France. Morellet immediately worked hard to produce his translation, which was completed in December 1765 and published in 1766.[14] In his introduction, Morellet stated that he had translated the book because of the deep insights that it articulated. Moreover, he thought that Beccaria deserved great credit for managing to reconcile reason and emotion.[15] Worldwide familiarity with Beccaria's manifesto, particularly in Morellet's translation, was also greatly helped by Voltaire, who used it the same year (1766) to publish, anonymously, a blazing indictment of the criminal justice system in France and, more broadly, in Europe.[16]

That this tremendous reception of *Dei delitti e delle pene* in France would meet resistance among established jurists is not very surprising. It was in particular Pierre-François Muyart de Vouglans – "*avocat au Parlement*" – who attacked it in 1767 in his *Réfutation des principes hasardés dans le traité des délits et des peines* [*Refutation of the Hazardous Principles in the Treatise on Crime and Punishment*]. Not only did he accuse Beccaria of standing up for that part of humanity that is a bane to society but he also suggested that many of Beccaria's criticisms were totally unjustified because many of the principles which he felt needed support had already applied in French criminal law for a long time. Moreover, many of the proposals in the manifesto were quite simply unacceptable. For example, Beccaria's proposal that the death penalty be replaced by deprivation of liberty ("*l'esclavage perpetuel*" [perpetual slavery]) needed to

---

10   Reuter 1989; Kreutziger 1989.
11   Mulder (G.) 1971.
12   Cartuyvels 1996; Steinberg 1989.
13   Tamm 1997.
14   Morellet 1988, pp. 149–155.
15   Beccaria 1766, p. VII.
16   Alff 1989.

be rejected because such a punishment, especially in the case of murder, failed to meet the needs of the survivors sufficiently; they could only draw consolation from the death of the murderer. Nor could a custodial sentence put an end to the harm suffered by society as a result of crime, for one thing because it would become responsible for sustaining so many criminals.

3.4.2. AN UNQUALIFIED SUCCESS IN BRITAIN: JEREMY BENTHAM

In Britain, *Dei delitti e delle pene* was an almost unqualified success, both in Morellet's French translation and in the anonymous English translation published in 1767. What is particularly remarkable is that it was not only leading conservative jurists such as William Blackstone who greatly appreciated Beccaria's ideas but also progressive legal philosophers such as Jeremy Bentham.[17] It is true, however, that most of those who were enthusiastic came from progressive circles. Bentham in fact emerged as the pre-eminent heir to Beccaria.

In numerous places in his enormous oeuvre, Bentham acknowledged that he had been inspired by Beccaria in many ways. It was from him that he learned that thinking about law and legal systems should be guided by reason and not by custom or precedent. It was only when he read *De delitti e delle pene* that he became a convinced utilitarian. What also greatly appealed to him was that Beccaria wished the application of criminal law, or at least of sentencing, to be scientifically based and to be divorced as far as possible from feelings, sympathies and antipathies. It is therefore no surprise that Bentham agreed with Beccaria in numerous respects: determination of the severity of punishment, aversion to the "spectacle of cruelty", the need for swift and certain punishment, the prohibition of judge-made law, opposition to torture, etc. He did have great difficulty, however, with the fact that Beccaria had not always expressed his ideas very clearly, and had certainly not worked them out systematically.[18]

That criticism is easy to understand for anyone who has looked at Bentham's early works on criminal law, his *Theory of Punishment* (1777) and in particular *An Introduction to the Principles of Morals and Legislation*. That treatise – intended as an introduction to the draft of a penal code – was completed in 1780 but not published until 1789. In these studies, Bentham in fact tried to do exactly what he considered Beccaria had failed to do, namely to apply the geometric method with the necessary rigour to the field of morals and thus develop a "moral arithmetic". His premise was perfectly clear:

> The general object which all laws have, or ought to have, in common, is to augment the total happiness of the community; and therefore, in the first place, to exclude, as

---

17   Blackstone 1963; Blamires 1997.
18   Hart 1982, pp. 40–52.

far as may be, everything that tends to subtract from that happiness: in other words, to exclude mischief. But all punishment is mischief: all punishment in itself is evil. Upon the principle of utility, if it ought at all to be admitted, it ought only to be admitted in as far it promises to exclude some greater evil. It is plain, therefore, that in the following cases punishment ought not to be inflicted.[19]

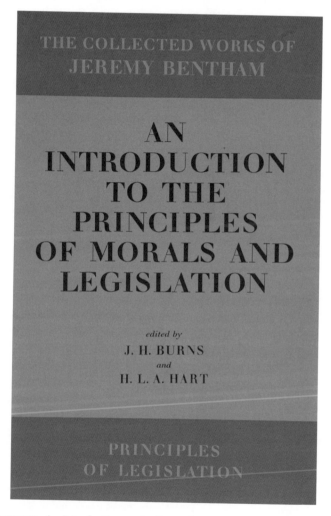

Jeremy BENTHAM, *An Introduction to the Principles of Morals and Legislation*, London, University of London, 1970 (edited by J. BURNS and H. HART).

Bentham then lists four criteria – negative criteria, we would say – for criminalisation, i.e. for determining when behaviour should not be criminalised, namely when doing so is "groundless", "inefficacious", "unprofitable", or "needless". When behaviour should in fact be made punishable, he says, depends

---

[19]   Bentham 1970, pp. 158–159.

largely on the objectives envisioned by the legislature: preventing any crimes whatsoever, ensuring that people commit fewer serious crimes or as few crimes as possible, or attempting to prevent offences as cheaply as possible.

In line with these objectives, he believes that rules should be drawn up with respect to the relationship between crime and punishment. These will include the following: the severity of the penalty must outweigh the benefit resulting from the crime, a more serious crime should be punished more harshly than a less serious one, the penalty must be no more severe than is necessary to enforce compliance with the set standards, etc.[20]

The application of these rules presupposes that penalties have certain characteristics. They must, for example, be variable, comparable with other similar penalties, be characteristic of certain offences, and impress people. According to Bentham, deprivation of liberty meets these requirements to a large extent. It prevents the offender from doing any further harm, it generates the necessary profit, it is impressive, it is very simple in nature, it is the same for everyone, and it can also be subdivided effectively.[21] Bentham was therefore clearly in favour of building prisons.

3.4.3.   A LUKEWARM RESPONSE IN THE AUSTRIAN NETHERLANDS: GOSWIN DE FIERLANT

How was Beccaria's manifesto received in the Austrian Netherlands?[22] It would seem, in any case at first glance, that it completely escaped the attention of jurists, philosophers and administrators; at least, not a single publication was devoted to it, and there was also no public discussion of Beccaria's views. Behind the scenes, however, the manifesto did exert some influence. That was particularly the case in the work of Goswin de Fierlant, for many years president of the *Grote Raad* (Great Council of Mechelen), i.e. the country's highest court.

De Fierlant was certainly not a radical reformer. He was in fact an establishment figure, but one who was open to new ideas such as those proclaimed by Beccaria.[23] That is apparent, inter alia, from the memorandum *Observations sur la torture* [*Observations on Torture*] which he wrote for the *Geheime Raad* (Privy Council) in 1771, and in which he expressed serious doubts about the need for the use of torture in cases when that was still common. If the suspect remained silent, would it not be better to compel him to speak by putting him on bread and water? And why still use torture if there is already sufficient evidence available?

---

20   Bentham 1970, pp. 158–174.
21   Tulkens 1987.
22   Fijnaut 1998.
23   Van den Auweele and Nefors 1993.

The second part of De Fierlant's memorandum is also important because in it he calls for the far-reaching abolition of the death penalty and corporal punishment, and their replacement by imprisonment in provincial houses of correction, where vagrants, beggars, and criminals would be corrected through labour and discipline.[24] In that work, De Fierlant did not yet distinguish between beggars/vagrants and (convicted) criminals, but he did make such a distinction in *Premières idées sur la réformation des loix criminelles* [*First Ideas on the Revision of the Criminal Laws*], a preliminary study for a code of criminal law and criminal procedure on which he began work in 1773. In it, he referred on the one hand to houses of correction and on the other to prisons.[25]

3.4.4. DIVIDED OPINIONS IN THE NORTHERN NETHERLANDS: HENRICUS CALKOEN

Unlike in the Austrian Netherlands, a whole Beccaria literature soon developed in the Northern Netherlands. That was firstly in the sense that Dutch publishers were closely involved in the distribution of Beccaria's manifesto within Europe and also of the pamphlets that were written attacking it. Not only were the fifth and sixth editions of the Italian version published in Haarlem (1766) but Morellet's translation was also published in Amsterdam (1766), followed in 1768 by a reprint in Utrecht of Muyart de Vouglans' criticism. Second, there were also publications in Dutch. The first Dutch translation – *Verhandeling over de misdaaden en straffen* [*Treatise on Crimes and Punishments*] – appeared, anonymously, in Amsterdam in 1768, followed in Utrecht in 1769 by a translation of the commentary by Charles-Auguste de Hautefort. A German pamphlet attacking *Dei delitti e delle pene* was published in Dutch, also in Utrecht, in 1772.

Even just that list shows that Beccaria's ideas were controversial in the Northern Netherlands. If one focuses on the criminal law literature, then a tripartite distinction can be made between the various authors in relation to *Dei delitti e delle pene*.[26] First, there were those who ignored Beccaria's manifesto entirely. An example is Franciscus Kersteman, who in 1789 published *Rechtsgeleerd kweekschool* [*Juridical Training College*], which did adopt critical positions on certain points, for example on the use of torture, but which is not in any way reminiscent of Beccaria. Second, there were authors who were to a certain extent critical of him, for example Bavius Voorda in his study *De crimineele ordonnantien van Koning Philips van Spanje* [*The Criminal Ordinances of King Philip of Spain*] (1792), but also the Groningen professor

---

[24] Depreeuw 1988, pp. 186–189.
[25] Van den Auweele and Nefors 1993.
[26] Fijnaut 1998.

Dionysius van der Keessel.[27] Third, there were authors who truly adored Beccaria. The best known of these is Jan Amalry, who published his *Beschouwinge der crimineele zaaken* [*Observations on Criminal Matters*] in Amsterdam in 1777. This was largely copied, in grandiose wording, from *Dei delitti e delle pene*.[28]

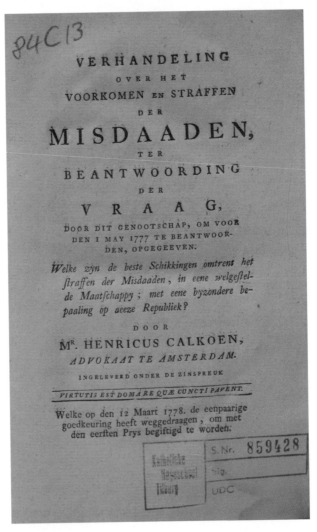

Henricus CALKOEN, *Verhandeling over het voorkomen en straffen der misdaaden*, Amsterdam, Gerrit Warnars, 1780.

The most balanced response was that of Henricus Calkoen, an Amsterdam lawyer whose *Verhandeling over het voorkomen en straffen der misdaaden* [*Treatise on*

---

27   Van Warmelo 1967.
28   Pols 1889.

the Prevention and Punishment of Crimes] won the first prize awarded by the *Floreant Liberales Artes* society in 1778. In 1777, the society had organised a competition to answer the question of how the prosperous Dutch Republic could best punish crime.[29] In answering that question, Calkoen goes much deeper into the prevention of crime (other than through the criminal justice system) than Beccaria, who, as we have seen, only deals with that issue as a rather noncommittal addendum. What is important is that for Calkoen, more than for Beccaria, prevention and repression do not constitute separate and independent means of combatting crime. Calkoen is firmly convinced that prevention and repression influence one another: the more one can prevent crime, the less one needs to rely on repression to curb it (including preventively).

As regards combating crime by means of the criminal law, Calkoen clearly distances himself from the views of Beccaria in several respects. He does so not only because he expressly wishes to maintain a middle course, but also because he wants to focus more systematically on specific improvements in existing practice. There are good reasons why he complains that Beccaria lacks practical experience and apparently knows the criminal justice system only from books. That does not detract from his admiration for Beccaria, however, and he refers to him as *"dat edel vernuft"* (that noble genius). Calkoen assessment of Beccaria's views is therefore a mixed one. On the one hand, he endorses his ideas about the relationship between crime and punishment, the holding of trials in public, the accessibility of criminal legislation, and the role of custodial sentencing. On the other hand, as we have seen, he identifies a number of errors. For example, he considers the argument that courts should be deprived of any freedom of interpretation to be rather foolish; amongst other things, it would lead to a flood of legislation intended to cover every excuse that someone might come up with. He also disagrees that the death penalty should be abolished; it must still be available in cases of rebellion. And he believes that in certain circumstances torture can still be used.

With a view to the adoption of preventive measures against crime, Calkoen first works out a classification of criminal offences.[30] He divides them into five types, with the argument that there is a connection between the different types of crime and the causes that underlie them. He therefore genuinely attempts to proceed in a modern scientific manner, thinking in terms of causal relationships. He asserts, for example, that the first category of crimes – which are also the most frequent: theft, forgery, corruption, bankruptcy – result from "poverty, want, greed, idleness, and laziness".

To prevent this type of crime, Calkoen proposes the following measures. First – as Coornhert had proposed two centuries previously – alms should no

---

[29]   Calkoen 1778. See further, inter alia, De Monté Verloren 1942, pp. 196–205.
[30]   Nagel 1968.

longer be given to "*gevaarlijk tuig*" (dangerous scum), and anyone who could work should be set to work. There was certainly plenty of work to be done: draining lakes, reclaiming peatland, serving in the fleet, and – it is remarkable that Calkoen mentions this – working in the colonies. Second, far more needs to be invested in the education of juveniles, especially the children of indigent parents. If necessary, the support such people receive should be withheld to force them to send their children to school. Such measures, Calkoen argues, would substantially reduce the amount of crime, and as a result the number of penalties carried out in public would also be reduced – and the more infrequent those penalties, the greater would be their deterrent effect on others. He adds, incidentally, that Amsterdam was already very safe compared to other major European cities.

Finally, it should be noted that discussion of the merits of Beccaria's work in the Northern Netherlands was not limited to intellectual debate but that his ideas and those of his philosophical forefathers also had an effect on the revision of the criminal law. The principles underlying the drafts of the criminal code that were drawn up in 1801 and 1804 are in any case fairly "enlightened".[31] Without much effort, one can recognise in them the principles of legality, personality, humanity, and proportionality. At the level of regulation, it is also apparent that – in the spirit of Calkoen – compromises were made between the criminal law which actually existed and that which was advocated in "enlightened" circles. As regards penalties, for example, although the death penalty was retained, deprivation of liberty was clearly the preferred option.

3.5. INITIAL STEPS TOWARDS A DIFFERENT VIEW OF *HOMO CRIMINALIS*

In the literature so far examined, the view of the criminal, *homo criminalis*, is not unambiguous but, as it were, three-dimensional. In one sense, he is presented as a *homo economicus* who first weighs up the advantages and disadvantages, the costs and the benefits, the certainties and the risks, of his criminal behaviour before making his move, either alone or in a group. In another sense, he manifests himself as a *homo sociologicus* who finds it difficult to position himself within the existing social order due to a lack of lack of wealth and education, and can only be deterred from committing crimes through supervision and intimidation. And in addition to these two views, there is also the *homo iuridicialis*, i.e. the citizen who, like the criminal, is entitled to fair and humane treatment by the organs of the state.[32]

---

31   Fijnaut 1998.
32   Fijnaut 1996.

It is also the case that these images are largely abstractions, normatively tinged abstractions – at best, scientifically speaking at least, established *more geometrico*. This means that they are in any case not the result of a systematic empirical investigation of the actual person of the offender and the actual functioning of the criminal justice system. An author such as Calkoen apparently felt it attractive to apply scientific investigative methods to a social problem such as that of crime, but he did not advance any further in that respect than his renowned predecessor Beccaria. He did not know, for example, what to do with "monsters", whether real or supposed.

A change came about at the end of the eighteenth century, particularly at the hands of physicians who, in order to explain human behaviour, began to seek relationships between biological structure and psychological disposition. That reversal was not an isolated phenomenon but took place in the context of a philosophical debate about the relationship between biological phenomena and social developments.[33] One of the first modern French physicians, Julien de La Mettrie (1709–51), assumed, for instance, that a person's mental functions are localised in his brain, and that disorders of the brain can have a whole range of effects on his psyche. Where criminals were concerned, he pursued his rather deterministic view of things so far as to advocate for replacing judges in the courts with physicians. Only they would be able to distinguish the innocent from the guilty.[34]

Another well-known driver of the debate within Europe was undoubtedly Johann Lavater (1741–1801). Between 1775 and 1779, this Swiss scholar published a four-volume work entitled *Physiognomischen Fragmente: zur Beförderung der Menschenkenntnis und Menschenliebe* [*Physiognomic Fragments: to Advance the Knowledge of Human Nature and Philanthropy*]. This work, which caused a great sensation, was in fact an enormous collection of portraits of all sorts of people, with Lavater's comments on the properties of their character, their typical behaviour, their social and intellectual skills, and so forth.[35] These analyses did not involve much, however, in the way of system or method. With the greatest good will, the most one can say is that they formed the as yet unrefined result of inductive but non-methodical research. However, the idea on which these "portraits" were based – namely that there is a correlation between the external form of someone's body, especially his face, and his personality and character – still received great acclaim at the time.[36] Lavater himself hardly applied his "theory" to criminals, if at all. He did not attempt to answer the question whether it was possible to determine whether or not someone would

---

[33] Mucchielli 1994b.
[34] Bonger (W.) 1932, pp. 52–53.
[35] Lavater 1949. See also Bruno s.d. and Rafter 2009, pp. 10–17.
[36] Lavater 1949, p. 15.

be inclined to commit crime by analysing their skull. In a certain sense, his prediction that torture would soon be replaced by *Kriminalphysiognomie* [*Criminal Physiognomy*] is therefore more interesting. Lavater believed that applying this "science" would enable judges to determine more effectively whether a suspect was telling the truth than by using torture.[37]

Especially compared to Lavater, the French physician Philippe Pinel – who became head physician of the Bicêtre Hospital in Paris in 1793 and of the Salpetrière Hospital in 1795 – did in fact proceed methodically in studying mental disorders. Pinel rejected the existing physiological practices, such as bloodletting, for combatting these conditions and applied scientific methodology, i.e. systematic observation and classification of the disturbed, in seeking new ways to cure them. His patient research led him to the conviction that in a limited number of cases mental disorders may possibly be the result of an injury to the central nervous system, but that their substance and development should always be understood in the light of the personality and life experience of the patient him/herself.[38]

In his *Traité medico-philosophique sur l'aliénation mentale ou la manie* [*Medical-philosophical Treatise on Mental Alienation or Mania*] (year IX), Pinel divided mental disorders into five categories: melancholia, mania with delirium, mania without delirium, dementia, and idiocy. Where the manias were concerned, he took the view that these were in the first place generated by moral feelings which – because of their rather extreme violent nature – evoked pathological reactions: religious fanaticism, unrequited love, profound irritation, excessive ambition, etc., and could thus lead to committing crimes. However, he added in the second place that there are no direct relationships between these moral causes and the ways in which manias express themselves. In his view, the factor that determines the type of mania is the sufferer's physical constitution, i.e. his physique. Pinel was also convinced that the mentally ill could be cured, and he developed a method to make that possible. That therapy was based on nurturing self-discipline by means of supervision, work, and submission. Because of this approach, Pinel is sometimes said to have freed the mentally ill from their chains and turned madhouses into clinics.[39]

As regards the development of the *homo criminalis*, one needs to add that Pinel, and also Lavater, with De La Mettrie in the background, developed a fourth type, *homo bio-psychologicus*. That type would gradually play an increasing role in the thinking about crime and criminal justice. The contention that the mentally ill do not belong in prison, for example, was a reason to devote prisons specifically to housing convicted criminals.

---

[37]   Schmid 1984.
[38]   Alexander and Selesnick 1968, pp. 151–156.
[39]   Debuyst 1995.

3.6. FURTHER RENEWAL OF THE PRISON SYSTEM

In the late eighteenth century, Britain was "transporting" (i.e. banishing) many convicts to Australia, on an even larger scale than it had previously done to America. The fleet of 11 ships that set sail for the new colony in January 1788 had 1,030 passengers on board, including 548 male and 188 female prisoners who had in general been convicted of relatively minor offences. In the following decades, an annual total of some 400 were transported. After 1810, however, their number increased to more than 1,000 a year (1810–19), to more than 2,000 a year (1820–29), and to more than 4,000 a year (1830–39). In 1852, the annual total fell to 2,700 and in 1867 to 565. There were numerous reasons why transportation to the colonies was carried out on such a large scale.[40]

In the first place, it was thought that it would not only put an end to the public punishment of offenders but would also relieve the country of what were perceived as the extremely dangerous criminal classes in the major cities. Second, the existing prison system was not large enough to imprison all offenders, and prisons were also not places from which people emerged "better" than they went in. Third, transportation was viewed both as a just penalty for the crimes committed by the convict and as a punishment that would exert a beneficial deterrent effect on those who remained behind. And fourth, this form of banishment was also thought to give those transported a better chance of a new life than confinement in prison.[41]

That the manner in which the successive transports took place was atrocious, and that the fate of most of the deportees in the supposed "promised land" was no less so, was seen by the authorities as no reason to stop this remarkable exodus. Of the 1,000 convicts on the second transport, a quarter died before the end of the voyage; in the case of the third transport, "only" 200 out of 1,864 died. And of those who did reach Australia, the majority were in absolutely no condition to survive in the colony by their own efforts.[42]

This bit of British history should not make us forget that in the course of the eighteenth century there were also repeated proposals in the Northern Netherlands for criminals, including those already confined in a house of correction, to be deported to the colonies on the English model, to the Dutch East Indies and/or Suriname. In the eyes of the proponents of this penalty, the roaming riff-raff were a disgrace to the nation, and the houses of correction were not in any case much use. In the colonies, one could at least make use of the riff-raff and mix them in "among the slaves". The more skilled convicts could possibly make a contribution, through their work, to the development of these

---

[40]   See for similar practices by Prussia to Siberia: Evans 1998, pp. 11–92.
[41]   Radzinowicz and Hood 1990, pp. 465–474.
[42]   Hughes 1988, pp. 129–157, 441–459; Cadogan 1937, pp. 153–201.

countries and reinforce the "white element" vis-à-vis the indigenous population. Unlike in Britain, however, such proposals did not get much of a hearing in the Northern Netherlands, and it was only on odd occasions that convicts were sentenced to be deported. The main reason why transportation to the colonies was not introduced in the Republic was that the costs, which were considerable, had to be paid by the local court that pronounced the sentence.[43]

In all this, it needs to be borne in mind that in the eighteenth century the house of correction, the (penal) prison, was in general viewed more and more as the more appropriate internal solution to crime problems. That was the case not just in the Netherlands but also in other European countries.

This is apparent from the fact that such institutions were established in Italy and the Scandinavian countries: in Rome a house of detention for young delinquents was set up at the *Ospizio di S. Michele* in 1703 followed in 1735 by a kind of *spinhuis*; in Milan a house of correction for women was established in 1766; and in Stockholm a similar institution was set up in 1724. It is also demonstrated by the fact that in the mid-eighteenth century the entire French prison system was adapted to a new model. The abolition of condemnation to the galleys in 1748 led from the 1750s to more and more convicts being put to work in *bagnes* at military establishments in port cities such as Toulon and Brest. The *bagnes* had essentially the same function as the houses of correction in northern Europe.

Ten years later, in 1760, it was decided in France that in order to combat vagrancy and begging *dépôts de mendicité* (colonies for beggars) should be set up throughout the country, in addition to and sometimes in place of the *hôpitaux généraux* (general hospitals).[44] It goes without saying that this reversal in policy gave rise to further differentiation within the prison system, with work camps for the homeless and prisons for convicts. In countries other than France, for example Britain and the Northern Netherlands, such differentiation was reinforced in the same period by the establishment of workhouses and the setting up of training projects for needy fellow citizens. Such initiatives were in fact an expression of the idea that poor people, idlers included, could no longer simply be equated with criminals. That many of these experiments failed is a different matter: the founders were usually "enlightened" persons with a philanthropic attitude who had to get on as well they could without support from the authorities.[45]

---

[43] Van den Eerenbeemt 1968, pp. 111–114.
[44] Spierenburg 1991.
[45] Ignatieff 1978, pp. 13–14; Van den Eerenbeemt 1977, pp. 70–136.

3.6.1. REORGANISATION OF THE HOUSE OF CORRECTION IN GHENT: JEAN VILAIN XIIII

The fact that the higher authorities in the Austrian Netherlands were generally enthusiastic about the establishment of houses of correction after 1750 cannot be viewed separately from the fact that a number of such institutions had already

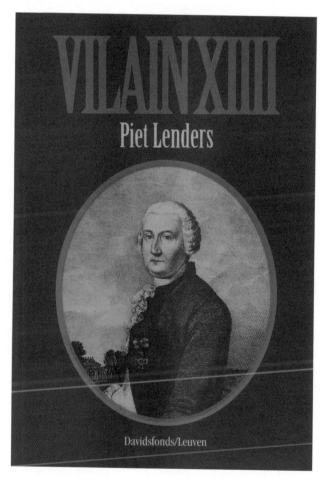

Piet LENDERS, *Vilain XIIII*, Leuven, Davidsfonds, 1995.

been set up in several places in the seventeenth century. This is obviously also connected with the fact that more such institutions were founded in a number of places in the first half of the eighteenth century (Mons in 1717), re-established (Bruges in 1737), or converted, as was done in Ghent, where a prison was established in 1718 in the basement of the existing house of correction.[46]

---

[46]   Bonenfant 1934, pp. 249–345; Stroobant 1898, pp. 206–220.

On the other hand, one should not forget that in 1749 Jean Vilain XIIII, at that time mayor of Aalst and president of the powerful Land of Aalst, had published a pamphlet about his experience in dealing with begging and vagrancy in the area, and in particular his experience as a member of the court that had sentenced a notorious band of robbers. This famous pamphlet – written by a young man who, entirely familiar with the new "enlightened" ideas, would become one of the most versatile, influential, and progressive administrators of his country – called not only for the setting up of a permanent police force, a *maréchaussée*, to confront the problems, but also for the establishment of a reformatory, a house of correction, intended primarily for the employable poor.

Although, for various reasons, that proposal was not welcomed with equal enthusiasm everywhere, the local authorities agreed in 1751 on construction of the house of correction. Machinations within the Privy Council ensured, however, that the project did not proceed, despite the plans already being complete and the stone already ordered. The deeply disappointed Vilain XIIII then resigned as mayor of Aalst and moved to Ghent. He did not remain idle there for long, for in June 1754 he was appointed third *schepen* (alderman) of the city and in March 1755 *burgemeester-voorschepen* (mayor-senior alderman).[47]

The social misery that in the late 1760s no longer manifested itself only in the problems of vagrancy and begging but also in food riots in several cities led Vilain XIIII to produce another work. In 1771 he published an anonymous, untitled pamphlet again setting out his ideas on how the various problems should be tackled. He began with the proposition that man has been condemned by God to eat his bread "in the sweat of his face", and that all countries had recognised the correctness of that judgment. The primary source of evil, according to Vilain XIIII, was that too many people wrongly relied on charity rather than working for their living, because that was how misery and idleness were transmitted from one generation to the next. And how did these people usually end up? Beggars ultimately all became scoundrels. Referring to his experience in dealing with bands of robbers, he then questioned whether one should wait to take action until able vagrants had already become thieves and had perhaps even been condemned to death. He thought not, also given the great extent of the problem in Flanders.

What did he think needed to be done? One of the biggest difficulties was that no sanctions were available between fines on the one hand and the death penalty and corporal punishment on the other, and that beggars and rascals were not impressed by imprisonment, the pillory, or banishment. To deal with this problem, he reverted to an idea that must have sounded familiar to those who had read Coornhert and Beccaria, namely that beggars should be turned into workers for the public good before they became criminals. If that were to

---

47   Lenders 1995, pp. 29–58.

be done, they would forever be deterred by the fear of being incarcerated in a house of correction. This approach would also reduce the cost of the criminal justice system. For Vilain XIIII too, the deterrence of (potential) criminals and the prevention of crime went hand in hand.[48]

Vilain XIIII did not confine himself to merely formulating general ideas; he also explained what an ideal house of correction would look like. Vagabonds, thieves, petty criminals, beggars, and also people who were admitted voluntarily or for payment needed to be kept separate. Church attendance would be mandatory, as would labour (processing textiles, rasping dyewood, knotting fishing nets). There would be a regime of strict discipline and hygiene. Resistance to those in charge would be severely punished, right up to troublemakers being put on starvation rations.[49]

This proposal naturally generated a great deal of discussion, including about the location, the costs (and how they should be distributed), the composition of the prison population, the labour to be performed, and the regime to be enforced. In February 1772, however, the authorities gave the go-ahead. Actual construction commenced towards the end of 1772 and the complex gradually came into use in 1773–74.[50] But that did not mean that discussion was silenced.

For example, the alderman of Ath, François-Joseph Taintenier, published a pamphlet, *Traité sur la mendicité* [*Treatise on Begging*], that generated a great deal of discussion. In it he argued fiercely against the proposal that not only criminals should be confined to the house of correction but also the unemployed. In his view, to tackle unemployment it would be better if all the charitable institutions were to entrust their financial resources to a single fund. The unemployed would then receive allowances from the fund that must not discourage them from seeking work and that would therefore need to be set at the subsistence minimum. The employers, for their part, would then need to provide a greater volume of work, something that was also in their own interest because it would decrease the price of labour.[51]

Despite this debate, the Duchy of Brabant received permission in 1773 to build a house of correction at the site of the former Vilvoorde Castle. The actual establishment of the institution was no easy task. Discussion of the financing and controversy about the quality of the building meant that in was not until 1779 that the first detainees were confined there.[52]

In 1775, Vilain XIIII published his renowned *Mémoire sur les moyens de corriger les malfaiteurs et fainéans à leur propre avantage et de les rendre utiles à l'état* [*Memorandum on the Means to Correct the Wrongdoers and Sluggards, to*

---

[48]   Vilain XIIII 1841.
[49]   Depreeuw 1988, pp. 193–197.
[50]   Stroobant 1898, pp. 226–239.
[51]   Depreeuw 1988, pp. 153–156; Stevens 1993.
[52]   Depreeuw 1988, pp. 207–217.

their Own Advantage and to Make them Useful for the State].[53] Besides a detailed description of the structure of the house of correction, this lengthy study includes an explanation of its administration and management, its industrial activities, and poor relief in general. In the introduction, Vilain XIIII reiterates that idleness is the source of a great deal of evil, and that – given the enormous number of beggars and vagrants – it was high time to implement effective measures. The traditional penalties no longer had any effect whatsoever.

The description of the octagonal building shows that Vilain XIIII still favoured three separate sections, one for the real criminals, one for healthy beggars and petty criminals, and one for girls and women. He also hoped that in the part that was yet to be built, a school could be established for the children of needy parents; these children would not be confined. All the detainees would work during the day in common areas. At night, the men would be locked up in separate cells. Surveillance would be tight, as would be the rules of hygiene to be observed. The men would be obliged to attend not only mass on Sundays and feast days but also prayer services held on weekdays. After all, one of the main purposes of the house of correction was their moral and religious improvement. The strict discipline was necessary to make the offenders understand that they had been living an immoral life. The house of correction was to turn them into new fellow citizens. In the view of Vilain XIIII, their own interests and those of the state and society were therefore aligned.

In the sixth and final chapter – on poor relief in general – Vilain XIIII showed considerable agreement with Taintenier. Setting up a common poor relief fund together with the house of correction and the yet to be established school would certainly constitute an appropriate set of measures to put an end to begging and vagrancy. To ensure the effectiveness of these measures, he added that a total ban was needed on begging and vagrancy in the surrounding countryside, and that it should be stringently enforced by a *maréchaussée*. In other words, in his view reform of the system of houses of correction had to be accompanied by a reorganisation of the policing system. That is also apparent from his proposal for the captains of the Ghent civil guard to be replaced by commissioners and inspectors of police, whose task would be to keep a close eye on what was going on in their district: the makeup of households, people's occupations, births and deaths, relocations, distribution of gifts, etc. In several respects, an organisation of that kind is reminiscent of how the Paris police was organised at the time. What was lacking, in particular, was a proposal to appoint a chief constable of police.

Vilain XIIII died in 1777 and his death is seen as one of the reasons why things subsequently went downhill at the house of correction. The other reason was that the Austrian Emperor Joseph II, visiting the life work of Vilain XIIII in 1781, not only found it to be furnished too "luxuriously" but also thought – this

---

53   Vilain XIIII 1841.

in response to petitions from a number of entrepreneurs – that it was engaged in unfair competition with local industries and therefore had to be dismantled as a "factory". Production must henceforth be restricted to goods that were needed within the institution itself.[54]

3.6.2. ANALYSIS OF EUROPE'S PRISON SYSTEMS: JOHN HOWARD

The house of correction founded in Ghent through the efforts of Vilain XIIII in 1771–75 became just as famous as the *rasphuis* in Amsterdam on which it had been modelled, at least in terms of the regime inside. Its renown was mainly due to the praise expressed by the Englishman John Howard, High Sheriff of Bedfordshire, of the new Ghent house of correction in 1777 (and in subsequent editions) in his highly critical analysis of the prison system in Britain, *The State of the Prisons in England and Wales*.[55] Contrary to what the title of this famous and influential study suggests, it also comprises numerous descriptions, both brief and lengthy, of the prison system, or at least of certain prisons, in other European countries, based on the working visits that Howard paid to them over the years.

Howard's experience as High Sheriff and his personal experience when imprisoned in France were not the only reasons for his great interest in prisons. Equally important was that he frequently rubbed shoulders with believers who had left the Church of England, namely Baptists, Methodists, and Quakers. Among these "Dissenters", for whom philanthropy and asceticism were important, prison reform was a priority of the first order.

That was partly because pioneers among them viewed prisons – in addition to hospitals, factories, schools, etc. – as institutions that were extremely suitable for the institutional reform that they generally had in mind. Such reform – involving tight control and strict discipline – would benefit both the moral health as well as the physical health of their poor and/or "fallen" fellow citizens.

Dissenters also pursued reform because the wretched condition of prisons at that time offered them an excellent opportunity to challenge the political and religious establishment. It is therefore surprising neither that Howard received a lot of support, on the quiet, from co-religionists when writing *The State of the Prisons* nor that the appearance of his book immediately created a sensation in Britain. Howard was quickly admired as one of the greatest reformers of his time.[56] Nor is it surprising that he was also inspired by Beccaria. There are not many explicit references to *Dei delitti e delle pene* in his work, but they do

---

[54] Depreeuw 1988, pp. 203–207.
[55] Howard 1788; Cadogan 1937, pp. 203–226.
[56] Ignatieff 1978, pp. 47–79; England 1993.

concern a number of crucial issues such as the abolition of torture and the death penalty, and the need for swift and certain punishment.[57]

Howard's book – references here are to the widely used French translation, *État des prisons, des hôpitaux et des maisons de force*, published in Paris

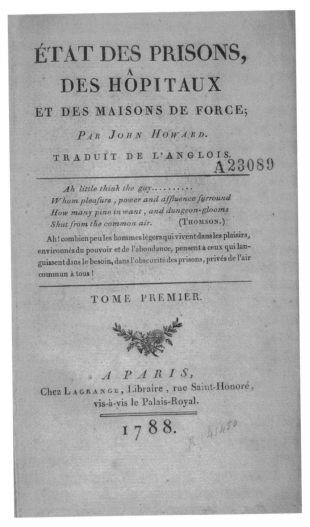

John HOWARD, *État des prisons, des hôpitaux et des maisons de force*, Paris, Lagrange, 1788, 2 vol.

in 1788 – can easily be read as one great indictment of, specifically, the bridewell system that had been developed in the sixteenth century. Howard's experience was that that system turned people into powerless skeletons. His compassion for

---

57   Winkelhorst 1989.

them was his driving force for writing the book, but it was not the only reason. He also wanted to convince Parliament of the need to put an end to this misery by means of a thorough reform of the prison system. His foreign travels were therefore primarily intended to gain ideas for such a reform.

It speaks in Howard's favour that he was not only critical of the existing prison system in his own country but also took the liberty of criticising that in other countries. It is therefore all the more remarkable that he was relatively positive about the houses of correction in Holland, writing that they were so calm and clean that one could scarcely believe they were in fact prisons. It has been noted that the picture sketched by Howard in this regard is much more favourable than the reality according to other sources.[58] Perhaps what appealed to him was that, according to him, the Dutch houses of correction made such efforts to improve the detainees, and that those who did reform were released early. Whatever the case may be, Howard devotes page after page to the *rasphuizen* and/or *spinhuizen* and other prisons in some 15 Dutch cities, usually in positive terms.

Given this positive view, it almost goes without saying that he is also generally favourable when referring to the house of correction in Ghent, at least as he found it on his first visit in 1778. He not only admired the regularity, cleanliness, and order of that institution but also the way in which the detainees were taught moral principles and turned into useful members of society. Not that Howard expressed no criticism at all. For example, he thought that the workplaces for the men were on the small side. Such comments, however, are insignificant if we compare them with his description of the new Ghent house of correction as a *"grand et noble établissement"* (a great and noble establishment). When he visited it in 1778, he wrote that he found a well-regulated factory, but when he returned in 1783 decline had set in. The factory had been closed down by order of the Emperor. Locking up the detainees no longer served any real purpose and a quarter of them were now lodged in the infirmary. Howard's opinion on the houses of correction and prisons in other cities in the country was variable. While he praised the management and staff of the prison in Bruges for their solicitude toward sick prisoners, he described the prison in Aalst as an overcrowded hole where benevolence was hard to find.

The publication of Howard's book in 1777 was greeted with a great deal of enthusiasm. The concept of the model prison that he had expressed throughout his comments and that was closely in line with the organisation of the Amsterdam *rasphuis* and the Ghent house of correction was very well received amidst all the discussion of the need for far-reaching reforms of the criminal justice system. The time was apparently ripe in Britain for criminals to be housed in prisons where cleanliness, discipline, faith and labour prevailed; where the inmates worked communally during the day but were locked up in separate cells at night;

---

[58]   Franke 1990, pp. 19–50.

where the detainees were not all tarred with the same brush but divided into different categories – women and men, young and old; and where the permanent staff no longer depended for their income on the detainees, and the management were not out to make a profit but acted in the spirit of the common good.[59]

Together with William Eden and William Blackstone, Howard was charged in 1778 with drafting what ultimately became the Penitentiary Act 1779. They originally proposed the establishment of a network of "hard labour houses" throughout Britain, but Parliament decided after much debate to initially set up only two such new institutions, in London, one for men and one for women. At the proposal of the three gentlemen, these were referred to as "penitentiary houses" in order to express the idea that they were not only places where labour was carried out but also where the inmates could express remorse and do penance for their erroneous ways. As Blackstone wrote:

> In framing the plan of these penitentiary houses, the principal objects were sobriety, cleanliness and medical assistance, by a regular series of labour, by solitary confinement during the intervals of work and by some religious instruction to preserve and amend the health of the unhappy offenders, to inure them to the habits of industry, to guard them from pernicious company, to accustom them to serious reflection and to teach them both the principles and practice of every Christian and moral duty.[60]

Despite Parliament's decision to have such institutions built, nothing in fact came of them. One reason was the endless discussion of how they should be financed. Another was that local authorities denied that central government had a right to interfere in this matter. Yet another reason that the government was not very enthusiastic about abandoning transportation in favour of a domestic prison system because that would irrevocably mean "the eventual return of convicts to the community".

This failure did not mean, however, that nothing changed. The Penitentiary Act 1779, with *The State of the Prisons* in the background, had already created such a stir, and the problem of overcrowded prisons (because transportation of detainees to America had ceased and transportation to Australia had not yet been organised) was a source of such pressure, that a start was simply made in many places on transforming and reorganising existing prisons and establishing new ones on the model described in the Act and in Howard's book.

In particular, the initiative taken by the local authorities in Gloucestershire, led by George Paul, achieved national renown. In 1792, five new houses of correction and a new county gaol were built there all at once. The organisation of the gaol in Gloucester itself was the object of particular interest. In terms of hygiene and discipline – according to Paul, outward cleanliness was a

---

59   Semple 1993, pp. 62–94.
60   Blackstone 1795, p. 370.

sign of inner order – it in fact surpassed the not inconsiderable requirements that Howard had suggested on these points. The detainees were not only cut off even more completely from the outside world than in Ghent – the entire prison was surrounded by a wall, and visits were only permitted every six months – but they were also separated from one another by means of continuous confinement to their cells, day and night, in the hope of breaking down the criminal subculture, gaining absolute control over their behaviour, and inciting them to examine their conscience.

In practice, and especially after the end of the French Period, it was found that this system could not be maintained. Not only did the detainees repeatedly resist the "inhuman" regime that had supposedly been developed for their own good, but the gaolers had a great deal of difficulty in keeping it operating. Paul was constantly looking for people, preferably ex-soldiers, who could themselves muster the discipline needed to teach the inmates enough self-discipline. After he departed in 1818, "his" regime at the gaol collapsed completely. It is not inappropriate to draw a parallel here with the fate of the Ghent house of correction after the death of Vilain XIIII in 1777.[61]

3.6.3. THE PRISON AS A PANOPTICON: JEREMY BENTHAM ONCE MORE

When Bentham published his *Introduction to the Principles of Morals and Legislation* (1780), it was not yet his masterpiece on the criminal law. In 1776, he had already published *A Fragment of Government*, in which he addressed certain aspects of that legislation, and in 1777 he completed *The Rationale of Punishment*; this did not, however, appear until 1811 (in a French translation). But it was primarily in the latter that Bentham came to the conclusion that incarceration in prison with an obligation to work hard ("laborious punishment") was the most appropriate form of punishment. It was therefore unsurprising that Bentham also provided numerous comments on the draft of the Penitentiary Act 1779. He was broadly in agreement with its contents and praised its "foresight and humanity". On a number of issues, however, he suggested all kinds of improvements, ranging from how the hours of work should be calculated and the central heating maintained, right up to the salary of the director (which in his view needed to be proportionate to the profit made by the prison). Various amendments proposed by Bentham were taken over by Howard et al., either wholly or partly.

In the course of the 1780s, when discussion of the implementation of the Penitentiary Act 1779 was still in full swing, Bentham developed his own ideas about the ideal prison, namely the "panopticon". As that term already indicates,

---

[61]   Ignatieff 1978, pp. 93–109.

Bentham was seeking a type of prison in which everything would be perfectly visible, transparent, and therefore subject to control (a "total institution"). To achieve that objective, he proposed that a prison be built in the shape of a beehive, with the cells in the ascending walls, and with an enclosed tower in the

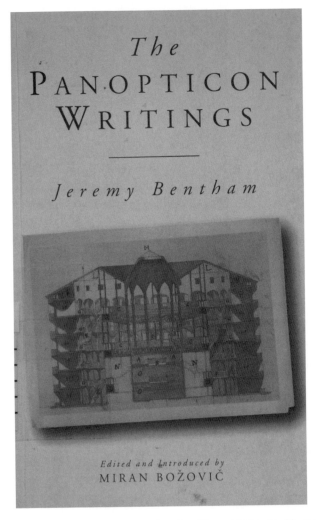

Jeremy BENTHAM, *The Panopticon Writings*, London, Verso, 1995 (edited by M. Božovič).

centre from which the gaolers could observe the inmates without themselves being seen. The inmates would be required to work 16 hours a day, with the profit going to the director-entrepreneur. The latter would therefore have every interest in keeping the detainees in good condition. Similarly, it would not be in his interest to undermine the deterrent effect of punishment by taking care of them too well.[62] It will be clear that this model was far from what had been envisaged by Howard. For Bentham, imprisonment was a matter of "pain and pleasure", not of penance. For Howard, the inmate's cell was a place to pray, for Bentham a place to work. For Howard, the cell was also a place where the detainee was thrown back on himself in order to repent; for Bentham, however, it was just a part of the panopticon prison's wall in which the prisoner could be constantly monitored.[63]

Understandably, not everyone was immediately won over by the idea of the panopticon. For years, Bentham had to strive in all sorts of ways to convince people of the value of what was increasingly becoming his life's work. In 1791, he even sent a French translation of his project to the National Assembly in Paris, but that body merely thanked him kindly for his book as being *plein de vues utiles sur les prisons*" (full of useful views on prisons). Eventually it was major problems with the transportation of convicts to Australia that led some Members of Parliament to conclude in 1793 that the panopticon was perhaps not such a bad solution for implementing custodial sentences. Together with his brother Samuel, a leading engineer, Bentham was then commissioned to work out the plan in greater detail. This led to the design of an exceptionally ingenious building, one that was extremely well thought out in terms of both its principles and its effects.

In this detailed version of the panopticon, Bentham adhered to the main purposes of imprisonment, namely deterrence and reformation. To achieve this, he assumed three basic principles: humanity (the detainee was only to be deprived of his liberty, not of his health or his life, and therefore had to be well looked after), severity (the living conditions of the detainees were to be no better than those of free and innocent poor people), and economy (including to make the panopticon profitable). The building that the Bentham brothers envisioned – a beehive of steel and glass – looked splendid; they did not see why a prison should necessarily be unsightly. A system of pipes not only supplied food and removed waste but also provided heating, and for internal communication there were speaking tubes. To enable the gaolers to see without being seen, the inspection tower, the nerve centre of the panopticon, had peepholes on each floor. The brothers described in minute detail how hygiene should be maintained, what discipline should prevail inside and outside the cells, and what the cells should look like. Bentham even envisaged each cell having a kind of treadmill for physical exercise.

Contrary to what was – and still is – generally thought, when designing the panopticon Bentham was no longer an advocate of absolute solitary confinement ("torture in effect") but in favour of incarceration in groups of three or four. He considered this not only more humane but also more economical. Solitary confinement could, however, be used for punishment. To prevent the prison regime degenerating into tyranny, Bentham proposed not only that the

---

62   Ignatieff 1978, pp. 77–78, 109–113.
63   Semple 1993, pp. 62–94.

various groups within the prison should monitor one another – prisoners and gaolers, gaolers and the director, and also the prisoners one another – he also thought that the public should have access to the institution day and night ("the most effectual and indestructible of all securities against abuse").

This does not alter the fact that Bentham also saw the panopticon as "a mill for grinding rogues honest". He could reconcile this with his utilitarian and democratic views by assuming that criminals – even though they usually came from the poorest strata of the population and their criminal behaviour should be judged in the light of the circumstances in which they had grown up – should still be held accountable for what they had done. They needed to be seen as patients – unruly patients, it is true – who had grown crooked in body and spirit and who could be straightened out through labour and discipline.

An enormous ordeal then began for Bentham. Initially, the prospects for his project looked fairly promising. In 1794, a special Panopticon Bill was even drafted, but discussion in Parliament did not go well. The bill was criticised in all kinds of ways, and it was then shelved. Bentham and his associates nevertheless managed to get it back on the political agenda, but they were ultimately unable to save it. While a parliamentary finance committee in 1796 was still inclined to follow Bentham, a special parliamentary committee decisively rejected his panopticon, instead opting for the ideas of Howard as they had been implemented by Paul in Gloucester.[64]

The prison on the continent that was organised to a certain extent in accordance with Bentham's views – largely due to Étienne Dumont, Bentham's French translator – was that opened in 1825 in Geneva (but soon demolished in 1862 as part of an urban renewal scheme). The building itself was not entirely as prescribed by Bentham, however; it was a semicircle with two wings projecting from the centre. It was only the spy holes in the doors – equipped with a slide – that were strongly reminiscent of Bentham's views on the exercise of control in a prison.[65]

3.7. FURTHER MODERNISATION OF THE POLICE SYSTEM

As we saw when discussing the writings of Vilain XIIII, for "enlightened" reformers of public administration such as he, reorganisation of the prison system was complementary to that of the police system, both in rural and urban areas. Typically, the organisation of the judiciary was left aside in writings on this subject, perhaps because reforming it touched too closely on the core of the

---

[64]   Semple 1993 pp. 166–191.
[65]   Roth 1981 pp. 133–180.

existing political system. Prisons and police were naturally more easily seen as a body of executive services.

3.7.1. REORGANISATION OF THE POLICE IN VIENNA AND LONDON

Reorganisation of public administration was an important matter for progressive authorities in the nation states of the second half of the eighteenth

Johann VON JUSTI, *Grundsätze der Policey-Wissenschaft in einem vernünfigen, auf den Endzweck der Policey gegründeten, Zusammenhange und zum Gebrauch academischer Vorlesungen abgefasset*, Göttingen, im Verlag der Wittwe Vandenhoeck, 1759.

century. So important was it that in German-speaking Europe it became the subject of a new science, *Polizeiwissenschaft*. In this context, the word *Polizei* still had its traditional significance, namely public administration. But in that same context, sight was certainly not lost of the police, in the sense of the police force.[66] Renowned policing experts such as Johann von Justi in fact realised full well that without proper police forces the government was powerless in certain vital respects. In his famous *Grundsätze der Policey-Wissenschaft* [*Principles of Police Science*] (1759), Von Justi wrote, inter alia, that enforcement of the police legislation was entirely dependent on the quality of the police officers charged with carrying out that task.[67] It was partly because of this that there was an enormous increase in interest in the policing system in such an already turbulent period as the eighteenth century. That has usually been lost sight of in the field of criminology because attention tends to focus entirely on the reorganisation of the prison system in that century.

Against this background it is unsurprising that not only in the German states but also in Austria the Paris police organisation was viewed as a model to be imitated. Imitation had already begun in Vienna in 1751 with the introduction of the Paris system, involving the appointment of eight district commissioners. In the 1760s, Maria Theresa clearly wished to go further but was opposed by senior officials, who feared a loss of power. The sovereign was not deterred, however, and through her ambassador in Paris asked the French government for detailed information about the police organisation there. A response to her request was provided in 1771 in a lengthy *Mémoire sur l'administration de la police en France* [*Memorandum on Police Administration in France*], drawn up by commissioner Le Maire.[68] It was some time before this was followed up, but 1776 saw the foundation in Vienna of a *Polizeiamt* (police office) modelled on that of Paris. Under Joseph II, particularly in the years 1785–87, that organisation – after much debate, of course – was extended throughout Austria. In 1787, all the provincial capitals had a police department, directed centrally from Vienna.[69]

In England, matters were more difficult than in Austria in the mid-eighteenth century because – despite the existence of a sizeable urban underworld, familiar from the life and deeds of Jonathan Wild – people wanted absolutely nothing to do with a "French" policing system. That system was considered synonymous with oppression and informing. During this period, only a few marginal changes were made in the existing medieval policing system, for example the appointment of the Bow Street Runners by the famous London magistrate and literary figure Henry Fielding. Even the bloody Gordon Riots (June 1780) brought about no change in the situation. They did lead, however, to a great deal of discussion of the need for a modern, professional police force, but all that happened was that the city watch was reinforced.

In the 1790s, it was above all Patrick Colquhoun who strove to bring about reform of the police in London. In his first and best-known study, *A Treatise*

---

[66]   Fijnaut 1983a.
[67]   Von Justi 1759, p. 344.
[68]   Le Maire 1879.
[69]   Oberhummer 1937, 1, pp. 23–29; Bibl 1927, pp. 216–224; Bernard 1991, pp. 115–139.

on the Police of the Metropolis, he spoke, entirely in the continental spirit, of policing as a "new science", consisting not of "the judicial powers which lead to punishments, and which belong to magistrates alone", but in "the prevention and detection of crimes; and in those other functions which relate to internal regulations for the well ordering and comfort or civil society".[70]

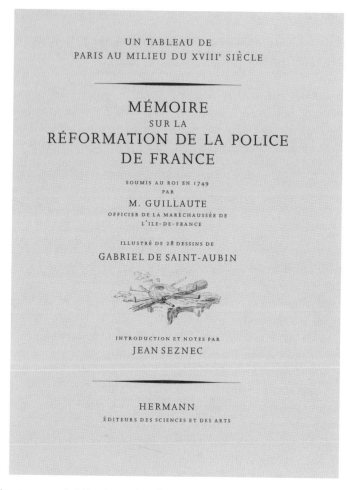

UN TABLEAU DE
PARIS AU MILIEU DU XVIIIᵉ SIÈCLE

MÉMOIRE
SUR LA
RÉFORMATION DE LA POLICE DE FRANCE

SOUMIS AU ROI EN 1749
PAR
M. GUILLAUTE
OFFICIER DE LA MARÉCHAUSSÉE DE
L'ILE-DE-FRANCE

ILLUSTRÉ DE 28 DESSINS DE
GABRIEL DE SAINT-AUBIN

INTRODUCTION ET NOTES PAR
JEAN SEZNEC

HERMANN
ÉDITEURS DES SCIENCES ET DES ARTS

Alexandre GUILLAUTÉ, *Mémoire sur la réformation de la police de France*, Paris, Hermann, 1974 (introduction and notes by J. SEZNEC).

Many English authorities found this rather "French" plea problematic, and for the City of London it was completely unacceptable, especially because Colquhoun had not a good word to say about the existing police organisation.

---

[70]   Colquhoun 1796, pp. 5–9, 23–36, 314–346; Colquhoun 1800, preface, pp. 502–601.

However, London's merchants were indeed open to such reform and in 1798, at their own expense, founded the "marine police establishment" specifically to combat thieving within the port. The first properly organised police force in London was therefore a case of private enterprise. In 1800, however, it was taken over by the central and local authorities, meaning that Colquhoun did have a certain degree of success.[71]

3.7.2. REORGANISATION OF THE POLICE IN THE AUSTRIAN NETHERLANDS

The proposal by Vilain XIIII in the context of poverty reduction for the appointment of police commissioners in Ghent fitted in closely with the development of the metropolitan police forces outlined above. But the city where the battle to modernise the police was really fought was Brussels. The man who called the existing police organisation into question was the *amman* (mayor) appointed in 1775, Ferdinand Rapédius de Berg, like Vilain XIIII a lawyer who had studied at the university in Leuven. Initially, Rapédius de Berg was someone who wanted not to modernise but to restore. In particular, he wanted the office of *amman* to be upgraded into that of a royal commissioner who would supervise the way Brussels was governed, in other words supervise the "policing" of Brussels in the traditional sense of the word, i.e. "police" as internal administration.

The local authorities, however, did not like the idea of such upgrading, for fear of sacrificing power and prestige. To achieve his objective, Rapédius de Berg carried out extensive, detailed studies of the history and current state of governance in Brussels. These writings not only give us a good idea of how "policing" operated in Brussels, but also show how fragmented the policing system was as utilised by the local authorities. One might say that for every administrative task that was carried out, one or more police officers were involved who were charged, subject to the competent authority, with enforcing the associated legislation. In his treatises, Rapédius de Berg restricted himself mainly to descriptions of the existing situation, but if one reads between the lines he was nevertheless expressing considerable criticism. As far as we know, however, he never drew up a plan for a new, perhaps "French", restructuring of the policing system in Brussels. It is quite possible that he in fact realised that that would really be a step too far for Brussels' local authorities.[72]

---

[71]   Fijnaut 1979, 1, pp. 542–563. See further, inter alia, Radzinowicz 1948–56, 1, pp. 400–401; 3, pp. 245–261, 417–426; Emsley 1983, pp. 20–31; Emsley 1996, pp. 8–23; Reynolds 1998, pp. 45–102; Rawlings 2002, pp. 61–105.

[72]   Gérard 1842, 1, pp. 69–91, 133–192.

Another and better-known champion of police reform in the second half of the eighteenth century was Count Jean-Baptiste van der Stegen, the *drossard* (sheriff) of Brabant. Van der Stegen worked exhaustively, particularly in the 1760s and 1770s, on plans for reorganising his *maréchaussée*. Although none of those plans was adopted, they are still interesting for various reasons. Not only do they in some respects provide a splendid reflection of "enlightened" administrative thinking, they are also a precursor to the police restructuring that would take place during the French Period.

Van der Stegen's ideas can best be illustrated by the pamphlet which he published in 1778, *Moyen de rendre les patrouilles utiles et moins onéreuses au plat-pays, surtout en Brabant* [*Means to make Patrols Useful and Less Burdensome in the Country, in particular in Brabant*].[73] In it, he first set out the history, duties, and organisation of his *compagnie*. What his account came down to was that the *maréchaussée*, which operated from a single central point, had for a long time had the task of ensuring that the province remained free from all possible unrest. He then delivered some blunt criticism of the neighbourhood watch system, finishing with what he thought was a highly constructive and ingenious proposal.

He divided up the territory of the Duchy of Brabant into 500 areas of equal size. In each of these, a member of his *compagnie* (unmounted) would be stationed and charged not only with constantly monitoring that area but also of remaining in regular contact with his colleagues in the eight adjacent areas. For every eight *voetgangers* (patrolmen) there would be a junior officer to whom they would submit a daily report. Fifty mounted men would then convey these reports, via fixed routes, to the *drossard*, who would be the head of the *compagnie*. Van der Stegen was therefore clearly attempting not merely to increase the size of his *compagnie* but also to distribute it across the territory according to a system of brigades, like the French *maréchaussée*, so that the advantages of the whole and of the parts would be most effective. This definition of what his *maréchaussée* was intended to be – but failed to become – is entirely in line with the definition given above of a modern police force.

In the wake of the Brabant Revolution (1789–90), plans were nevertheless even drawn up for the formation of a *maréchaussée générale* in the Austrian Netherlands. Before those plans could be implemented, however, the country was occupied by the French. In October 1795 General Louis Wirion was charged with setting up three new divisions of the *gendarmerie nationale* in the former Austrian Netherlands.

---

73   Van der Stegen 1778.

3.8. DEVELOPMENTS IN THE FRENCH PERIOD

Developments in the French Period – including those in the area of criminal justice – cannot be dissociated from the changes that had taken place in preceding centuries or that had already been advocated for a long time. The discontinuity of history should not be overestimated – these developments form the best evidence for that. In discussing them, it is necessary to distinguish between what happened during the period of the French Revolution (1789–99) and what happened during the Napoleonic era (1800–13).

3.8.1. THE FRENCH REVOLUTION AND THE CRIMINAL JUSTICE SYSTEM

The *Déclaration des droits de l'homme et du citoyen* – adopted by the Assemblée nationale on 26 August 1789, after passionate debate – was entirely in the spirit of the Enlightenment. That is certainly true of the articles concerning the criminal justice system. Article 7, for example, states that no one can be accused, arrested, or detained other than in the cases determined by the law, and according to the procedures thereby prescribed. But Article 12 should also not be overlooked in this connection, because it shows that those who drafted the *Déclaration* were not only concerned with the rights of man and the citizen, but also – again in the wake of the "enlightened" thinkers – attached great importance to an effective organisation for maintaining those rights in actual practice. According to that article, a "*force publique*" was necessary to guarantee those rights for the benefit of all. Legal protection and crime prevention went hand in hand.[74] In accordance with this dual principle, a code of criminal procedure and a criminal code were established in September 1791.

The procedures laid down in the former code corresponded largely with the views expressed by Montesquieu and Beccaria regarding the requirements for proper criminal proceedings: there was no longer any question of torture, the accused was entitled to legal assistance, court hearings were entirely public, and the most serious crimes would be tried before a jury.

The criminal code in fact reflects even better the basic values that were to be respected.[75] It embodied, on the one hand, the most important principles, such as those of humanity, legality, equality, proportionality, and transparency. A significant feature was also that offences were carefully divided into three categories – crimes, misdemeanours, and contraventions – and were given fixed

---

74   Rials 1988; Robbers 1987, pp. 64–80.
75   Dupont 1979, pp. 123–126.

penalties so as to eliminate arbitrariness on the part of judges. The death penalty and corporal punishment were in principle abolished.

On the other hand, however, all doubts were dispelled regarding the other goal of this reform, namely combatting crime in a useful and effective manner. Imprisonment, for example – even in the absence of effective alternatives such as transportation and fines – was labelled as the optimum form of punishment. It was also expressly provided that imprisonment would never be for life, so as not to deprive prisoners of all hope of regaining their freedom. The measures involved in implementing that penalty, however, were by no means lenient. Not only were convicted persons required to be exhibited in the marketplace for a number of days prior to their confinement – in order to make an impression on the public – those convicted of more serious crimes were sentenced to hard labour in one of the *bagnes* or in a *maison de force*.

Those who drew up the code had actually wanted to go further and replace the death penalty with confinement in a *cachot* (dungeon) in order to increase the deterrent effect of the criminal law. As the word suggests, this form of punishment meant that the detainee would be locked up alone and in chains in a completely dark cell and fed a diet of bread and water. He would not be permitted to work, thus emphasising that this punishment was actually even crueller than the death penalty. However, the majority of delegates rejected this form of punishment, which is reminiscent in every way of what Coornhert had proposed two centuries previously.[76]

The revolutionary class, the third estate, understood of course that it was not sufficient – with a view to a new order – to adopt legal codes but that an administrative apparatus was also needed. It had already been decided in the course of 1790–91 not only to retain the *maréchaussée* under a new name – *gendarmerie nationale* – but also to develop it into a truly national military-style police force, spread out across the country in 28 divisions (one for every three *départements*). In 1791, the civilian policing system was also reorganised for the entire country, with commissioners of police in the towns and constables in all municipalities that so desired.[77] This laid the foundation for a policing system that would become commonplace in large parts of (Western) Europe, including through the imperialist policy pursued by France in later years. The same can be said about the judicial organisation that was established in the early years of the Revolution, with a justice of the peace in each *canton* and a court of law in each *département*. One typical feature of the early period of the French Revolution was that it was decided that judges and prosecutors would henceforth be elected. This was intended to break the power that the judicial authorities had always had.[78]

---

[76]   Wright 1983, pp. 24–47.
[77]   Luc 2002, pp. 32–38.
[78]   Fijnaut 1979, 2, pp. 643–676; Berlière and Lévy 2011, pp. 45–50; Larrieu 2002, pp. 319–382.

As we know, the Revolution gradually descended into a reign of terror in which little or nothing remained of the ideals enshrined in the *Déclaration*. The latter became merely a symbol that contrasted sharply with the reality of the guillotine, which was used for the first time in April 1792 and which, until the fall of Robespierre in July 1794, gave physical and indeed mechanical shape to the prevailing terror. The regime that subsequently came into being, the *Directoire*, was extremely shaky and could only deal with the effects of *La Terreur* with the greatest difficulty. Moreover, it constantly had to contend with violent political resistance in some parts of the country.

The situation worsened in 1798–99, making room once more for a strongman, this time Napoleon Bonaparte, who seized power on 9 November 1799 by means of a coup.

3.8.2. STRENGTHENING OF THE CRIMINAL JUSTICE SYSTEM IN THE NAPOLEONIC ERA

Napoleon reorganised the criminal justice system so as to bring order to the country. At first, he did this – with the assistance of his Minister of Police Joseph Fouché[79] – by centralising the police even more. The two men had already decided how this should be done, for they had definite ideas about what the position and role of the police should be within the machinery of government. It was to become an active and largely secret tool of the government. Its primary task was to keep an eye on everything, everywhere: "*Le regard de la police est partout et presque toujours son action se borne à voir*" (The eye of the police is everywhere and nearly always its action is limited to looking).[80]

Napoleon and Fouché put this strategy into practice by, for one thing, strengthening the *gendarmerie nationale* – which Fouché referred to as the "*armée de la police*" (police army) – in particular in the more turbulent and problematic regions. They also proceeded to centralise the civilian police under the wing of the Police Ministry. On 17 February 1800, a commissioner-general of police was appointed in all municipalities with more than 10,000 inhabitants. He was given command of the other police commissioners, but was in his turn subordinate to the head of the *département*, the *préfet*. In 1804, this organisation was further expanded, both by the appointment of state councillors who each exercised supervision of the police force in a particular part of the empire, and by the appointment of commissioners-general, including in Antwerp, and of *délegués* of these "chief constables" in specific municipalities such as port cities.

This reorganisation took effect under Fouché's successor, Anne Savary, who issued a decree on 25 March 1811 "*contenant règlement sur l'organisation de la*

---

79 Fouché 1992; Madelin 1945; Madelin 1978.
80 Fijnaut 1979, 2, pp. 753–790.

police de l'empire" (containing regulations for the organisation of the police of the empire). What this meant was that – especially for the *haute police* (political police) – directors-general of police were now appointed in a number of places, including in Holland, and that the *délegués* were replaced by *commissaires spéciaux*, for example in Ostend.[81]

Given the above, it was an obvious step for Napoleon to also attempt to create order within the prison system. One of his main plans in this area was the creation of *maisons centrales* where convicts serving long sentences from several *départements* would be confined, but resources were lacking to implement this plan in its entirety; in addition to the Bicêtre prison, the prisons in Ghent and Vilvoorde were also designated as *maisons centrales*. In a decree promulgated on 20 October 1810, the Minister of the Interior attempted to refine the system somewhat, with *maisons d'arrêt* and *maisons de justice* for detainees and remand prisoners on the one hand, and *maisons de correction* and *maisons de détention* for those serving long sentences (less or more than one year, respectively) on the other. In practice, however, the lack of resources meant that little actually changed.[82] Moreover, it was also decided in 1808 that a colony for beggars – a *dépôt de mendicité* – should be established in each *département*. In Belgium, such institutions were founded between 1809 and 1813 in Mons, Namur, Mechelen, and La Cambre.[83]

Finally, it should be noted that the 1791 Criminal Code did not entirely rule out the possibility of banishment to the colonies. During the Revolution, this option was only considered for political prisoners, but later it was also found suitable for beggars and vagrants. However, both the cost of this form of banishment and the risk of the transports being intercepted by the British meant that hardly anyone was deported to Guyana, Madagascar, or Mauritius. However, under the *Directoire* the system was in fact put into practice, and between 1795 and 1798 almost 400 political dissidents and ordinary criminals were transported to Guyana. Napoleon continued this practice on a small scale, even deporting detainees to the Seychelles in the Indian Ocean.[84]

3.9. CONCLUSION

The evolution of the criminal justice system referred to in the concluding section of the previous chapter – namely that at the beginning of the eighteenth century the basic structure of that system was tending towards a

---

[81] *Motifs* n.d., p. 16; Fijnaut 1995, 1, p. 5; Fijnaut 2007, pp. 48–52.
[82] Wright 1983, pp. 43–44; Eggink 1958, pp. 30–33.
[83] Depreeuw 1988, pp. 265–285.
[84] Wright 1983, pp. 44–47.

concatenation of three separate institutions: the police system, the judiciary, and the prison system – did indeed take effect in the course of that century, in particular during the French Period. General criminology is usually only interested in the history of the prison system. That focus, however, is very much associated with the emergence of criminology in the nineteenth century. As we will see in the next chapter, that was indeed closely linked to the problems in establishing the prison system.

However, the eighteenth-century reformers, and especially those during the French Period, did clearly view the three institutions as interconnected. In their view, effective enforcement of the (criminal) law required more than a properly functioning, "enlightened" judiciary. It also assumed vigorous criminal investigation by a professional police force and an effective system of imprisonment for (convicted) criminals. What had only been tried out here and there within Europe in the early eighteenth century had by the end of that century become systematic, both in theory and increasingly in practice.[85]

A modern writer who understood that connection well was the philosopher Michel Foucault, particularly in his *Surveiller et punir: naissance de la prison* [*Observe and Punish: Birth of the Prison*].[86] Although that book has rightly been subjected to a great deal of criticism by historians and criminologists, it still gives a very good idea of how the rise of the modern police system and of today's prison system have a lot in common.[87] With reference to the title of this book, it is worth repeating that the modern police system is a tool with which it is possible to continuously monitor, from a single point, what is taking place within society.[88] And Foucault's description of the modern penitentiary links up seamlessly with that of Bentham's panopticon.[89] What happens behind prison walls reflects what happens outside those walls: everyone is systematically framed. That was in fact exactly what was envisaged by Van der Stegen, the *drossaard* of Brabant.

But *surveiller* and *punir* are also linked in other ways. Someone who is punished first needs to be tried, and must therefore be tracked down. The punishment of offenders therefore depends entirely on their being detected. Foucault's characterisation of the modern criminal justice system is therefore highly appropriate: "*une quadrillage pénal plus serré du corps social*" (a closer criminal segmentation of the social body). Foucault goes further however – like the eighteenth-century reformers – and describes how this reform of the criminal justice system was merely one component of the overall transformation

---

85   See also Emsley 2005.
86   Foucault 1975.
87   Garland 1992; Lacombe 1993.
88   Foucault 1975, p. 215.
89   Foucault 1975, pp. 233–260.

of society into a *"société disciplinaire"* (disciplinary society). Hospitals, schools, factories, barracks, etc. were in his view also organised according to a similar model of *"quadrillage"*.

By way of transition to the next chapter, it may be noted in closing that the disappearance of public punishment and the appearance of the penitentiary – the

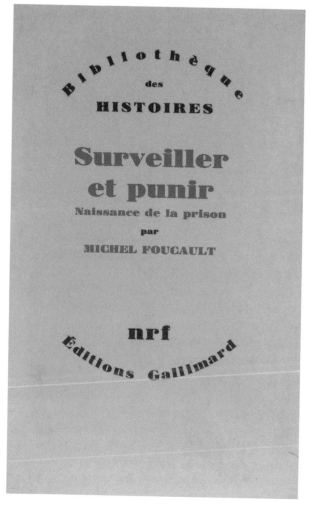

Michel FOUCAULT, *Surveiller et punir: naissance de la prison,* Paris, Editions Gallimard, 1975.

one was associated with the other – not only had the effect, as Foucault wrote, that physical suffering no longer played a central role in the regular criminal justice system; that transition also meant that one could no longer argue solely about the individual offender and his personality in the form of normative abstractions and categories. The aim of putting him back on the right track by means of imprisonment – i.e. by means of special prevention – and making a new man of him presumed an understanding of who he in fact was. That aim could only be achieved if methods and techniques were available to acquire that understanding. Mere observation by gaolers was no longer sufficient.

In other words, the advent of the penitentiary offered scope for further development and eventually also for the application of the medical and psychological insights into the offender that were first written down, although still in a very primitive manner, at the end of the eighteenth century. In this way, the *homo bio-psychologicus* could gradually be given a face.

CHAPTER 4

EMERGENCE OF THE SCIENTIFIC STUDY OF CRIME, CRIMINALS, AND THE COMBATTING OF CRIME

4.1. INTRODUCTION

It goes almost without saying that after the collapse of the Napoleonic empire, discussion arose throughout Western and Central Europe about its institutional legacy in the field of the criminal justice system and the combatting of crime. And given the history of that legacy, it is equally obvious that that discussion was permeated by all kinds of philosophical ideas, religious beliefs, and political theories. Ideas regarding crime and criminals naturally played an important role in this.

This chapter begins by considering the discussion of the prison system. In many countries, the comprehensive reorganisation of that system that gradually took place was more noticeable than the reform of the policing system. In some countries, that restructuring was certainly not unimportant but it was not the subject of public discussion and scholarly polemics to the same extent as reorganisation of the prison system. But that is no reason to ignore the reorganisation of the policing system; it was important from a social perspective and, in particular, it paved the way for an increasing role of the police in how criminals were perceived and in the fight against crime. Reform of the judicial system and of the codified criminal law were generally of less interest than the reorganisation of policing. Relatively speaking, they were to a considerable extent bones of contention within a small political, academic, and professional elite made up of jurists. In this abridged version of the book, they will be left aside.

The focus of the second part of this chapter is on the nascent scientific study of crime and criminals. The decision to deal with the various topics in this order is deliberate. The institutions that were gradually established made it possible to pursue this new science, for example by compiling statistics, but they also required scientific research in order to function in an acceptable manner.

Following on from these considerations, an account will be given of how a number of academic researchers in the mid-nineteenth century attempted to develop a clear picture of crime and its perpetrators. On the one hand, there was someone like Franz Gall who – in the wake of thinkers such as Lavater – adopted a more biological perspective on these issues, while on the other there were statisticians such as Adolphe Quetelet who introduced the sociological study of them. There were also psychiatrists like Jean-Étienne Esquirol – widely viewed as the successor to Pinel – who was particularly interested in the psychopathological aspects of criminal behaviour.

To facilitate a better understanding of the ideas of Cesare Lombroso that will be discussed at the beginning of the next chapter, Chapter 4 concludes with an analysis of the views on crime, criminals, and the combatting of crime held by evolutionary thinkers such as Bénédict Morel and Charles Darwin in the mid-nineteenth century. The ideas of more revolutionary thinkers such as Karl Marx and Friedrich Engels on these topics will naturally not be ignored in this context.

4.2. BATTLE ABOUT THE FUTURE OF THE PRISON SYSTEM

4.2.1. GAP BETWEEN IDEA AND REALITY

Aversion to the Napoleonic regime after the Battle of Waterloo did not by any means entail abandoning the idea that imprisonment was perhaps the optimum form of punishment. That idea had taken root too deeply in the minds of politicians, administrators, and writers of all kinds. The disparity between idea and reality remained significant, however, until late in the nineteenth century. It was only in the final quarter of the century that imprisonment became the dominant criminal penalty almost everywhere, both de jure and de facto. In many countries, people continued to be sentenced to capital and corporal punishment, with these penalties being carried out in public. Nor were these penalties abolished without a struggle. Particularly in the conservative sectors of society, the view persisted that they were indispensable to preserving social order and security.

Just how gradually abolition of the death and corporal punishment came about – precisely because it was so controversial – is clear from the example of the Netherlands. The Lower House of the Dutch Parliament "already" decided in 1839 to put an end to the public branding and flogging of offenders. Opposition to that decision by the Upper House meant, however, that it was not until 1854 that it could be ratified by legislation. In this context, one needs to remember just how normal branding was – for example, between 1827 and 1839, in nine of the 11 provinces, a total of 670 judgments involving branding were imposed, i.e. an average of 55 a year.[1] And although the last (public) execution took place as "early" as 1860 (in Maastricht), it was not until 1870 that capital punishment was formally deleted from the Criminal Code, and then only by small majorities in Parliament – in the Upper House by only 20 votes to 18.[2] One interesting point is that in the majority of cases the death penalty was not actually carried out because the condemned individual was pardoned by the King: of the total of 442 requests for clemency in the period 1814–70, only 75 were refused. This shows how the threat of execution, and its intended deterrent effect, was in practice often mitigated by a form of clemency that was considered equally beneficial. This system therefore gave the authorities considerable policy leeway. When tough criminal law suppression was deemed necessary, it could still in fact be utilised.[3]

When considering the advance of imprisonment towards becoming the dominant form of punishment, one must not forget that Britain long continued to transport convicts to Australia and that France began to apply that penalty on a large scale as late as the mid-nineteenth century. Britain continued the system of transportation until 1867, with the final consignment of convicts arriving in Australia on 10 January 1868. In the preceding decades, between 1,000 and 4,000 convicts had been transported annually to different parts of the colony: to New South Wales, Van Diemen's Land (later renamed Tasmania), and Western Australia. But all that time there had been ongoing debate about the matter, not only in the colony itself but also in Britain. It was becoming more and more evident in all sorts of ways – through eyewitness accounts, reports by commissions of inquiry, newspaper articles – at both "Ends of the Earth" that the objectives of transportation were not being achieved. The motherland was not in fact being increasingly relieved of its "criminal classes". The crime problem was apparently not just ingrained in certain individuals but was also clearly related to poverty and inequality – and these were not being shipped off to the colonies along with the convicts.

Given that development, it is all the more remarkable that France reintroduced the deportation of offenders in 1852. There was in fact a special reason for that decision, namely the revolution in June 1848 and the coup d'état by Napoleon III in December 1851. Both those events were accompanied by the arrest of tens of thousands of rebels and opponents, whom the existing prison system could not possibly accommodate. After a great deal of parliamentary debate, it was finally decided that some of them should be deported to Algeria and others to Guyana. In the wake of this measure, a decision was then taken in 1852 that was in a sense

---

1   Ten Cate 1975; Lensen and Heitling 1986.
2   Van Ruller 1989.
3   Van Ruller 1987, pp. 47–68. See also Franke 1985.

the opposite of what had been decided in Britain a few years previously: closure of the *bagnes* – prisons for those sentenced to long terms of forced labour in the military industry – in large port cities such as Brest and Le Havre, with the labourers involved being banished to Guyana in particular. By 1867, virtually all the *bagnes* had in fact been closed down and the French government had shipped some 17,000 people – almost all of them men – to that colony. Living conditions there were so atrocious, however, that more than half of them died within just a few years. Of the 8,000 people shipped to Guyana between 1852 and 1856, half died within five years due to hardships and illnesses of all kinds. That high mortality rate led to Guyana being nicknamed the *colonie mortuaire* (the colony of death).[4]

4.2.2. DEVELOPMENT OF A PENITENTIARY SYSTEM IN THE UNITED STATES

The fact that after the French Period imprisonment became the preferred form of punishment almost everywhere does not mean that there was consensus as to how it should be implemented. On the contrary, at times there were major differences in many countries between all kinds of publicists and policymakers. That is not surprising of course. In Britain, the ideas of both Howard and Bentham had resulted in a fiasco, and in France Napoleon III had left behind a well-structured prison system on paper but one viewed by many as a disaster in actual practice. Partly due to that hopeless situation, it is no wonder that in many discussions a solution was sought outside Europe, in the New World: the United States. Could the prison system that had evolved there serve as an example? We must therefore first consider that development before returning to the Old World.

The relevant developments in America began in Philadelphia, where, through the work of the Quakers, a "bettering house" – modelled on Amsterdam's *rasphuis* – was set up in Walnut Street in 1767.[5] In the course of the 1780s, however, the Quakers rebuilt that prison under the influence of Howard's analysis of the prison system in Europe. It is therefore unsurprising that although the appearance and internal structure of the building were still not much like a modern prison, the regime – with its emphasis on discipline, work, calm, and moral edification – was strongly reminiscent of the institution set up in Ghent a few years previously by Vilain XIIII. From the very beginning, the Walnut Street prison attracted a great deal of interest from reformers both at home and abroad, as if it was what they had all been waiting for. One of the most famous visitors, in 1785, was a nobleman who would play a major role in the reform of

---

[4] Wright 1983, pp. 91–99, 138–152.
[5] Sellin (J.) 1944, pp. 108–110.

the French prison system after the fall of the Napoleonic Empire, namely the François La Rochefoucauld. Reporting on his visit, he noted that he had been told that the aim of the regime was for the detainee to be "converted, as it were, into a new being". The spirit of Bentham was clearly abroad in Walnut Street.[6]

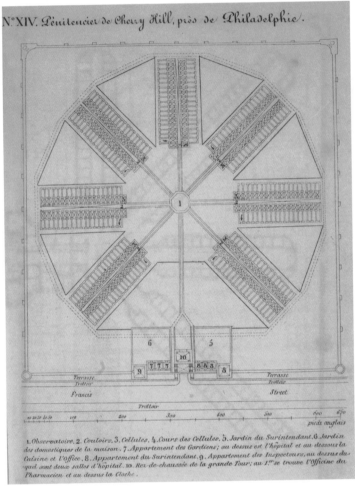

N.°XIV. *Pénitencier de Cherry Hill, près de Philadelphie*.

1.*Observatoire.* 2. *Couloirs.* 3.*Cellules.* 4.*Cours des Cellules.* 5.*Jardin du Surintendant.*6.*Jardin des domestiques de la maison.* 7.*Appartement des Gardiens; au dessus est l'hôpital et au dessous la Cuisine et l'Office.* 8.*Appartement du Surintendant.*9.*Appartement des Inspecteurs, au dessus du-quel sont deux salles d'hôpital.* 10.*Rez-de-chaussée de la grande Tour; au 1.er se trouve l'Officine du Pharmacien et au dessus la Cloche.*

Design of the prisons of Cherry Hill and of Auburn in the *Atlas* that is found in Édouard DUCPÉTIAUX, *Des progrès et de l'état actuel de la réforme pénitentiaire et des institutions préventives, aux Etats-Unis, en France, en Suisse, en Angleterre et en Belgique*, Brussels, Société Belge de Librairie, 1837–1838, 3 vol + *Atlas*.

After the Walnut Street prison came under the partial control of the state of Pennsylvania in 1790, it was modernised once more. A cell block was built in the garden to confine the most serious offenders in complete isolation. Soon,

---

6   Ignatieff 1978, pp. 58–67.

however, this was no longer sufficient either to house the growing number of long-term prisoners or to put them back on the right path in a suitable environment. There were therefore calls from all sides for one or more new state penitentiaries to be built, and that was in fact done. In 1818, construction began near Pittsburgh of the Western Penitentiary and in 1821 of a prison for the eastern part of the state, the Eastern Penitentiary, also known as Cherry Hill.[7]

The latter, in particular, soon gained great fame among prison reformers. This was thanks, on the one hand, to its architecture: a square complex, rather gothic in style, completely surrounded by a wall, with watchtowers at the four corners, and in the centre a kind of tower that served as the focal point of seven self-contained wings, one or two storeys high and each with some 40 cells. On the other hand, Cherry Hill's strict regime also earned it considerable publicity. That regime aimed – entirely in the spirit of the Quakers – to prevent any contact between the inmates, both night and day. The intention was to prevent the "wrong kind" of friendships, to ensure that the inmates were not diverted from their good resolutions, and to give them ample opportunity to reflect on their misdeeds and make their peace again with God. What this in fact amounted to was permanent solitary confinement. Everyone involved agreed that this isolation would have a beneficial effect on inmates and that it would deter potential offenders. Initially, discussion concerned solely whether the inmates should be permitted to work or rather in fact compelled to do so. It was only when the Eastern Penitentiary was about to be opened that it was decided that they should be obliged to carry out work in their cells. Not long after, the same architect – John Haviland – rebuilt the Western Penitentiary along the lines of Cherry Hill, thus completing a model of prison construction that became known as the "Pennsylvania system" or "Philadelphia system".[8]

At the same time, however, a rival model emerged, the "Auburn system" or "New York system". A few years later, for the same reason as in Pennsylvania, construction began in 1819 of a large state prison in Auburn, in central New York State. This was followed by the construction of the Sing Sing in 1825. The difference between this model and the Pennsylvania model was not really very great, with both being based on the principle of isolation. In the Pennsylvania system, however, that principle was converted into permanent confinement to cells and in the Auburn system into a regime in which prisoners were only isolated in their cells at night. During the day, they could work together in communal areas, but with the not inconsiderable restriction that they were prohibited from speaking to one another under any circumstances. They were not even permitted to look at one another; to ensure they could not, they were, inter alia, required to wear a cap with just two small holes for the eyes. In terms of discipline, the

---

[7]   For the regime in this prison, see Livingston 1827.
[8]   Johnston 1960; Petersen 1978, pp. 37–41.

two systems were therefore equivalent. A huge debate nevertheless ensued in the United States in the 1820s and 1830s on the advantages and disadvantages of the two systems, in both theory and practice. As we have already noted, that discussion then extended to Europe.[9]

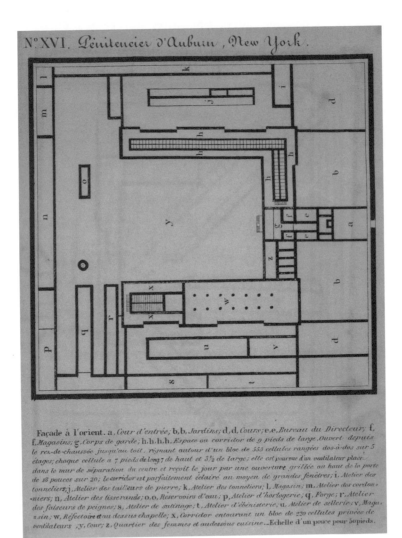

N° XVI. Pénitencier d'Auburn, New York.

Façade à l'orient. a, Cour d'entrée; b,b, Jardins; d,d, Cours; e,e, Bureau du Directeur; f, f, Magasins; g, Corps de garde; h,h,h,h, Espace ou corridor de 9 pieds de large, Ouvert depuis le rez-de-chaussée jusqu'au toit, régnant autour d'un bloc de 555 cellules rangées dos-à-dos sur 5 étages; chaque cellule a 7 pieds de long, 7 de haut et 3½ de large; elle est pourvue d'un ventilateur placé dans le mur de séparation du centre et reçoit le jour par une ouverture grillée au haut de la porte de 18 pouces sur 20; le corridor est parfaitement éclairé au moyen de grandes fenêtres; i, Atelier des tonneliers; j, Atelier des tailleurs de pierre; k, Atelier des tonneliers; l, Magasin; m, Atelier des cordonniers; n, Atelier des tisserands; o,o, Réservoirs d'eau; p, Atelier d'horlogerie; q, Forge; r, Atelier des faiseurs de peignes; s, Atelier de matinage; t, Atelier d'ébénisterie; u, Atelier de sellerie; v, Magasin; w, Réfectoire et au dessus chapelle; x, Corridor entourant un bloc de 220 cellules privées de ventilateurs; y, Cour; z, Quartier des femmes et au dessous cuisine. Echelle d'un pouce pour 50 pieds.

Idem.

In the United States – let it be said right away – the debate was largely won by the proponents of the Auburn system. Arguments that played an important role in

---

9 Rothman 1971, pp. 64–69, 82–88, 95–99; Petersen 1978, pp. 41–45; Melossi and Pavarini 1981, pp. 99–142.

this were the fact – according to proponents of the Auburn model in any case – on the one hand that the Pennsylvania model imposed an unnatural regime on inmates and would lead to their becoming insane, while on the other hand that construction and maintenance were far more expensive than in the Auburn system. The latter system was imitated in Massachusetts, Connecticut, and Illinois, among other places. In Pennsylvania – in any case in the Eastern Penitentiary – the system of solitary confinement of inmates continued until late in the nineteenth century.[10]

4.2.3. REFORM OF THE PRISON SYSTEM IN BRITAIN AND FRANCE

4.2.3.1. From Elizabeth Fry to Mary Carpenter

In Britain, the Prison Act 1877 nationalised the entire prison system, i.e. placed it under the control of the central government. That decision was the culmination of a process that began with the Penitentiary Act 1779. We already saw in Chapter 3 that the prisons built pursuant to that piece of legislation – for example in Gloucestershire under the aegis of Paul – were not as successful as had been hoped because the system of continuous solitary confinement proved to be untenable. The fiasco of the colossal Millbank prison in London – built between 1812 and 1816 on the site where the Tate Britain now stands – merely confirmed this. The inmates – 1,200 of them, confined to cells in seven pentagonal buildings surrounding a chapel – repeatedly rebelled against what they considered an inhuman regime. In 1828, order was permanently restored by the addition of flogging to the disciplinary resources available to the prison management.

For a time, religious and philanthropic groups continued to hope that a workable alternative was still possible. That hope was primarily based on the thoughts and actions of Elizabeth Fry, an ardent Quaker, who since 1816 had made strenuous attempts – through the introduction of work, education, and religious instruction – to transform the Newgate women's prison from a cesspool of depravity into a halfway house on the way to a better life.[11] As the history of the Millbank prison shows, Fry's ideas were in the long run unsuccessful. The Prison Act 1835 left no room for misunderstanding as to which direction the government wished to take. With that legislation, it opted very clearly for a uniform prison regime throughout the country along the lines of the Pennsylvania and Auburn systems. The former system was the basis for the new Pentonville prison built in London in 1842, with capacity for 520 inmates.

---

10   Barnes 1927, pp. 288–309; Barnes 1926, pp. 90–118.
11   Ignatieff 1978, pp. 485–487.

The man who devised the Pentonville prison, William Crawford, had visited America in 1834 to observe the two systems in person, selecting the Pennsylvania system because in his view it was based not on "physical discipline" but on "moral discipline": "The whip inflicts immediate pain, but solitude inspires permanent terror." Not only Fry but also Charles Dickens was highly critical of the regime at Pentonville: "very few men are capable of estimating the immense amount of torture and agony which this dreadful punishment, prolonged for years, inflicts upon its sufferers". But although it was repeatedly proved that prisoners were indeed completely destroyed by it, successive governments nevertheless considered Pentonville a success and therefore an effective alternative to the transportation of convicts to the colonies. In the years that followed, ten new prisons for long-term prisoners were built in Britain on the Pentonville model.[12]

For the rest, we should not forget that in the meantime a whole system of "reformatories" had been established for juvenile delinquents, although not without a struggle. After some philanthropically and religiously inspired experiments with the reception of such young people – including the foundation of the Chelsea School of Reform by the tireless Fry around 1820 – the government took the initiative to some extent. In 1825, it leased the frigate *Euryalus*, on which an average of some 125 boys of about 14 years of age were accommodated between decks, where they were required – under harsh conditions and half-dead from hunger – to manufacture clothing and footwear. There was no question of any education or training, at least not in practice, even though in theory this floating prison was intended precisely for that purpose. The scandals surrounding this "hotbed of vice" led to its closure in 1843.

In the 1850s, the initiative – which should have belonged to the government – was instead taken over for a time by Mary Carpenter, a highly religious philanthropist whose compassion for the "scum" in Bristol led her to set up the "Ragged School" there according to the foreign examples, especially designed to receive young offenders. Her book *Reformatory Schools for the Children of the Perishing and Dangerous Classes and for Juvenile Offenders* (1851) instantly made her the leading national authority in this field. The campaign that she pursued in the years that followed for the establishment of a network of reformatories throughout the United Kingdom was so successful that Parliament already had the Home Office set up such a system in 1854 by means of the Youthful Offenders (Reformatory Schools) Act. By 1860, some 50 institutions had been opened, housing about 4,000 delinquents.[13] The success of this approach also led to it gaining ground in Western Europe, leading in Austria, for example, to great interest in such reformatories.[14]

---

12   Cameron 1983, pp. 92–123. See also Rapport 1848.
13   Radzinowicz and Hood 1990, pp. 148–155, 161–171; Cadogan 1937, pp. 227–257.
14   See Lenz 1894.

4.2.3.2. From François La Rochefoucauld to Alexis de Tocqueville

One of the foreign examples which Carpenter referred to was a famous institution, the agricultural "colony" for juvenile offenders that had been established in Mettray in 1840 by the philanthropist Frédéric-Auguste Demetz.[15] Demetz, and many others, did not really believe in pure punishment, certainly not in the form of solitary confinement, as a means of getting people back on the right track. Their rather romantic premise was that in a caring social environment and in close contact with the soil, juvenile delinquents should, on the one hand, be properly educated and develop a virtuous lifestyle. On the other hand, they should be imbued with the right working discipline *manu militari*. Belief in this approach was so widespread that the Act of 5 August 1850 also made penitentiary agricultural colonies an official component of the prison system, alongside the existing provisions: separate juvenile wings in the central prisons and special reformatories for the youngest long-term prisoners. By about 1885, there were no fewer than 70 such colonies in France, a large number of them in Catholic hands.

This rise of the penitentiary agricultural colonies is in itself surprising because it had gradually become increasingly clear that here too there was a major difference between dream and reality, especially since the basic principles were hard to reconcile. In actual practice, nothing much usually came of the intended education or discipline through work, let alone affection. All too often, the well-intentioned philanthropic discourse had to give way to economic reality, namely the proceeds generated by the colonies, and that was a reality to which their work organisation was unsuited. Moreover, after 1870 the anti-clerical policies of the Third Republic made things very difficult for the colonies. The Mettray movement consequently ended in total failure, and by 1889 only about ten colonies remained.[16]

In France, however, it was not so much the approach to dealing with juvenile offenders that was the main subject of dispute but rather the system of prisons for those serving long sentences. Not long after the defeat of Napoleon at the Battle of Leipzig (October 1813), that discussion immediately received a powerful boost because within just a few weeks the new regime requested La Rochefoucauld to set up an experiment on the lines of the Walnut Street prison, involving a prison in Paris for some 100 long-term prisoners. That initiative came to nothing, but the philanthropists did not allow that to throw them off balance. Using the spoken and written word, they continued to insist that conditions within the prison system were inhumane and that the whole needed to be done away with because it was totally out of date. In 1819, Louis XVIII

---

[15]   Chauvaud 1990; Forlivesi, Pottier and Chassat 2005.
[16]   Jablonka 2000; Lebrun 1980.

allowed himself to be convinced and agreed to the establishment of a *Société royale des prisons* (Royal Society of Prisons) and a *Conseil général des prisons* (General Council of Prisons). That council, in which La Rochefoucauld played an important role, did not waste any time. Before the end of 1819, it came up with a proposal for reorganising the prison system which – what else? – was strongly influenced by the American and British examples, but in particular by the Pennsylvania model. But when all was said and done, things went no further than a proposal.[17]

The result of this was that discussion did not cease. It was kept going in particular by the freethinking *Société de morale chrétienne* (Society of Christian Morality) that was founded in 1821 by celebrities including – of course – La Rochefoucauld and De Tocqueville but also Adolphe Thiers and Alphonse Lamartine. The society gave an enormous impetus to the debate by awarding a prize to Charles Lucas in 1826 for his essay *Du système pénal et de la peine de mort* [*On the Criminal Justice System and the Death Penalty*]. It also encouraged him to continue along his chosen path. This he did, publishing his two-volume *Du système pénitentiaire en Europe et aux Etats-Unis* [*On the Penitentiary System in Europe and the United States*] in 1830. In that work, he vigorously defended the position that it was completely wrong that the French prison system was dominated entirely by punishment and was consequently sustaining the problem of crime because imprisonment amounted to no more than "*un vaste enseignement mutuel au crime*" (an enormous shared education in crime). In Lucas' view, the system needed to be organised completely differently if it was to have a positive effect on that problem. The reorganisation that he advocated was not that of permanent solitary confinement but was based to a large extent on the Auburn model. As might be expected, his views provoked a considerable response.[18]

That response came particularly from De Tocqueville, who succeeded in 1831 in getting the government to allow him, accompanied by his friend Gustave de Beaumont, to travel to the United States to study the penitentiary developments there. They returned in 1833 with a report on the *Système pénitentiaire aux Etats-Unis et de son application en France: suivi d'un appendice sur les colonies pénales et de notes statistiques* [*The Penitentiary System in the United States and its Application in France: followed by an Appendix on the Penal Colonies and Statistical Notes*]. Their report not only dominated penitentiary debate in France for decades but also quickly became a showpiece of international penitentiary literature.[19] It contains, first of all, a still very readable and shrewd comparative analysis of the historical background to the two systems that had developed

---

[17]   Duprat 1980.
[18]   Digneffe 1995.
[19]   De Beaumont and De Toqueville 1833. See further De Beaumont and De Toqueville 1970; De Beaumont and De Toqueville 1977. For an extensive discussion, see also Barnes 1927, pp. 72–180.

in the United States, of the regimes in force in both systems, and of all kinds of management issues involved in maintaining them. Second, it analyses, also comparatively, to what extent the conditions were in place in France for the establishment of one of the two American models. And third, as its subtitle indicates, the report contains a highly critical discussion of the various different types of penal colony. Given the impossibility of dealing exhaustively with the report here, I consider it in general terms.

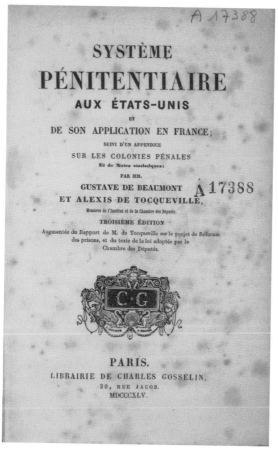

Gustave DE BEAUMONT and Alexis DE TOCQUEVILLE, *Système pénitentiaire aux États-Unis et de son application en France*, Paris, Librairie de Charles Gosselin, 1845.

According to the report's authors, in the summary (pp. 151–152) of the first part of their book, the advantages of the American penitentiary system are in general these: "*impossibilité de corruption pour les détenus*", "*grande probabilité pour eux d'y prendre des habitudes d'obéissance et de travail qui en fassent des citoyens utiles*", and "*possibilité d'une réforme radicale*" (impossibility of the inmates being corrupted, great probability of their learning habits of obedience and work that will make them useful citizens, and the possibility of radical reform). When discussing the differences between the two prevailing models, they clearly express a preference for the Pennsylvania system: first because it makes it impossible for inmates to communicate with one another, and second because they thought it obvious that this system would make a greater impression on the mind of the offender than the Auburn system. Regarding the applicability of the American systems in France, De Tocqueville and De Beaumont do not shy away from any of the counter-arguments: the failures that there had already been elsewhere in Europe when constructing new prisons, the different religious climate in France, aversion to the use of flogging to maintain discipline, the financial burden that building new prisons would involve, etc., but in conclusion they asserted that – linking up with the reform that Napoleon had already wished to carry out – the French government would nevertheless do well to set up a *pénitencier-modèle* (a model penitentiary) in line with the American example. They added, moreover, that such a reform of the prison system was urgently required because of the increasing number of repeat offenders.

Despite the latter argument, the result was not what De Beaumont and De Tocqueville had hoped. To a certain extent, that was their own fault. By opting for a pilot project according to the Pennsylvania system, they positioned themselves in diametric opposition to Lucas, who had earlier advocated the Auburn system. In other words, the conflict that they had encountered in the United States now also divided thinking in France. And even though there was generally already a majority – both within and outside the French parliament – in favour of the Cherry Hill system, the debate swung back and forth for years, whipped up repeatedly by the reports produced by yet more commissions of inquiry. Ultimately, in 1847, the legislature was ready to take a final decision on what should be done, namely introduce the principle of indefinite solitary confinement, replace the *bagnes* with cellular prisons, and retain enforced labour for the former *bagnards* in their cells. However, when the matter was about to be put to the vote early in 1848, the February Revolution broke out and the entire plan collapsed. Under pressure of events, the new regime resorted to banishment to the colonies and abolition of the *bagnes*.[20]

4.2.4. REFORM OF THE PRISON SYSTEM IN THE NETHERLANDS AND BELGIUM

4.2.4.1. Policy in the United Kingdom of the Netherlands

French troops had hardly withdrawn from the Low Countries in November 1813 when the "Sovereign Prince of the United Netherlands", William of

---

[20] Zysberg 1980.

Orange-Nassau (from 1815 King William I of the Netherlands) issued a decree abolishing various penalties contained in the *Code pénal* that were considered typically French. These included the general forfeiture of goods, surveillance by the high state police, the guillotine, and indefinite forced labour. The decree did not put an end, however, to all forms of capital punishment and public corporal punishment, and certainly not to imprisonment.[21]

As in many fields, William I also adopted a systematic approach to the problem of executing penalties. In 1818, he appointed a state commission to advise on the prison system. Its reports led to the establishment of another commission in 1820 that was specifically charged with investigating the state of the country's "*tucht- en gevangenhuizen*" (houses of correction and prisons). In 1821, the work of these two commissions resulted in a Royal Decree ordering the reorganisation of the entire prison system. A further Royal Decree was promulgated in 1825 regulating how that system was to be financed, including payment of the costs involved in adapting the existing buildings and the construction of new institutions. The new organisation that William I had in mind was based on a distinction between prisons for long-term inmates and prisons for those serving short sentences or on remand. In the years that followed, modification of a number of institutions to meet the minimum design requirements turned out to be a major task, one that was further aggravated in 1830 – on both sides of the border – by the division of the United Netherlands into today's Belgium and the Netherlands.[22]

In restructuring the prison system, however, the government had to some extent taken heed of all kinds of philanthropically tinted publications that had appeared in recent years regarding the dire condition of many prisons. But the government considered the aims of the *Nederlandsch Genootschap tot Zedelijke Verbetering der Gevangenen* (Dutch Association for the Moral Improvement of Prisoners) to be more problematical. Inspired by the work by Howard and Fry, that organisation had been founded in 1823, with the consent of William I, by the merchants Willem Suringar, Johannes Nierstrasz, and Willem Warnsinck. In fact, these individuals not only wanted the government to ensure a properly organised and not too costly prison system; as the name of their Association made clear, they, together with like-minded citizens, were also striving to improve the morals of prisoners.

In practice, that actually meant that prison administrators, as it were, "outsourced" everything to do with religious formation, education, and training to the Association's local committees, which – we should not forget – soon numbered 5,000 supporters throughout the country, mainly from the upper classes (civil servants, the nobility, and the merchant class). These committees arranged for lessons in writing and arithmetic, organised prison

---

21   Van Ruller 1987, pp. 27–32.
22   Eggink 1958, pp. 34–117, 163–190; Petersen 1978, pp. 81–86.

visits, distributed morally improving literature, appointed instructors to teach prisoners a trade, etc. Far less was done in the way of providing assistance to former prisoners, including because of a lack of funds. Such assistance was often limited to committee members arranging some kind of job via their own contacts. Nevertheless, this reality could not dampen the enthusiasm of the organisation's founders. In 1825, the Association persuaded the King to arrange for a special "children's prison" to be established in Rotterdam.[23]

But it was not only in the north of the country that a wide range of leading figures were prepared – certainly in name – to strive for the moral improvement of prisoners and for their future after they had been released. The same readiness was also apparent in the south of the country, with the best known organisation being the *Confrérie de la consolation* (Fraternity of Consolation) founded in Namur in 1820, with Christian philanthropic motives, by the canon and former lawyer Lambert-François-Joseph de Hauregard. The rules of this fraternity – which during the 1820s had some 350 members from the upper classes throughout the Southern Netherlands – clearly stated that its members were above all committed to the moral edification of prisoners.[24]

We should also not forget that the authorities in the United Kingdom of the Netherlands not only attempted to harmonise the prison system and improve its organisation, they also attempted to improve matters as regards tackling the problems of begging and vagrancy. The pressure of the economic crisis and the resulting widespread poverty caused the government, first of all, to deal with this by expanding the various institutions to house beggars that had been inherited from the French, and by closely regulating how they were organised and funded. The *Reorganisatiebesluit* (Restructuring Decree) of 12 October 1825, for example, stipulated in detail how many beggars might be accommodated, what support services were to be established (a bakery, an infirmary, etc.), how financing should be arranged, and under what conditions beggars could be released. In the second instance, the government concerned itself mainly with expanding the system of agricultural colonies, both voluntary and involuntary.

On this occasion too, the initiative for such colonies came from a private individual. In 1818, the former military officer and colonial administrator Johannes van den Bosch published a document arguing that poverty was a result of the structure of society and that this social malady should therefore be combatted by making changes to social conditions. Specifically, he came up with a plan to train the able-bodied as farmers and to teach women and children how they could earn additional income by working at home. In order to implement the plan, a number of associates of Van den Bosch, with the support of William I,

---

23   Van Bemmelen 1923, pp. 5–80; Heinrich 1995, pp. 29–62; Rogier 1966, pp. 27–37.
24   Dupont-Bouchat 1993.

founded the *Maatschappij voor Weldadigheid* (Benevolent Society) in 1818. With funds provided by the members, the society bought up large tracts of land in uncultivated areas in order to establish agricultural colonies there: Frederiksoord (1818), Ommerschans (1819), Willemsoord (1820), Wilhelminaoord (1820), Veenhuizen (1823), and Wateren (1823). In 1823 an affiliated organisation in the south of the country purchased the necessary land in Wortel and Merksplas.[25]

It quickly became apparent that these agricultural colonies would not be a financial success, and by 1827 the northern organisation was running at a loss. For one thing, this was because there were no funds to cope with all kinds of natural setbacks, such as cattle dying or the harvest failing. For another, it was because the kind of people and families who were sent to the colonies were often unable to work productively as farmers on the uncultivated land of the north-eastern Netherlands.[26]

4.2.4.2. Continuation of the Policy in the Netherlands: From Louis Bauricius to Anthony Modderman

In the Netherlands, it was Louis Bauricius whose treatise *Over de gevangenissen in Nederland* [*On the Prisons in the Netherlands*] (1838) once more drew attention to the problems of the country's prison system.[27] The main theme of his powerful argument was that although the 1821 reform had been a success from a financial perspective, it was a failure from a moral point of view. This was because making the whole system dependent on the benefits of labour had sacrificed the moral and physical condition of the prisoners.

So what was needed to combat or prevent this? To answer that question, Bauricius discussed the advantages and disadvantages of the two American systems, i.e. the Philadelphia system and the Auburn system. And although he was prepared to accept that in North America the first system had produced better outcomes than the second, he nevertheless came to the conclusion that the Pennsylvania system should certainly not be introduced right across the board. That would not only be extremely expensive because all existing prisons would need to be drastically altered or new cellular prisons would need to be built. It would also not fit in with the Dutch national character, which is by nature "*tot godsdienstigheid geneigd*" (inclined to religiousness) and that inclination would already be aroused and would increase if inmates were locked up only at night. Bauricius considered that permanent solitary confinement was only desirable

---

[25] Bientjes and Offerhaus 1904, pp. 10–37; De Vries (G.) 1995, pp. 19–42.
[26] Depreeuw 1988, pp. 286–300; Dorgelo 1964, pp. 1–21; Berends, Huussen Jr, Mens and De Windt 1984, pp. 9–36; Ros 1986, pp. 9–26.
[27] Bauricius 1838.

for incorrigibles, and because he did not believe that there were many of these, it would suffice to have ten to 20 "Philadelphian cells" in the largest prisons.

Bauricius' treatise played an important role in the parliamentary debate that dragged on in the 1840s – in the context of revision of the Criminal Code – regarding the range of penalties in general and the use of imprisonment in particular. In the draft of Book I that was adopted in 1840 (but which never came into force), the Auburn system was clearly selected for implementing lengthy prison sentences, although the courts were given power to rule that someone who received a heavy sentence should be incarcerated in a separate cell, in solitude, for part of his sentence. In subsequent years, however, attitudes changed. As early as 1842, most Members of Parliament stated that they favoured the Pennsylvania system of imprisonment.[28]

In the years that followed, however, nothing came of the general revision of the Criminal Code. However, with a view to calming down the debate on how imprisonment should be implemented, the Minister of Justice introduced a separate bill in February 1851. This provided that – for a combination of reasons, including a major shortage of appropriate cells and negative reports from abroad about its effects – prolonged solitary confinement would be limited to a maximum of six months. Not long after, that proposal was adopted without any difficulty and in June of the same year the relevant act of parliament was published in the *Staatsblad* (Bulletin of Acts, Orders and Decrees). In 1854, however, the maximum was extended again to a year, with the government letting it be known that the first steps had thus been taken towards general implementation of cellular confinement. But in fact those steps had already been taken. The new gaols that had been built from 1840 on sometimes had more cells than communal areas. The first Dutch cellular prison to leave the drawing board had already been built between 1846 and 1850 at Weteringschans in Amsterdam on the model of Pentonville.[29] By 1871, the country had some 1,100 cells of the Pennsylvania type.

Is that number evidence of a further hardening of the political climate regarding the prison system? The matter is not that simple. The intermediate draft of a new Book I of the Criminal Code of 1859 even stated that in the case of lengthy imprisonment, the inmate should spend the first five years in a separate cell, both day and night. There was, however, the caveat that such solitary confinement could be discontinued in the event of an imminent threat to the health of the prisoner.[30]

---

[28]   Van den Honert 1848.

[29]   Franke 1990, pp. 150–208; Petersen 1978, pp. 316–324; Quintus 1887, pp. 36–99; Van Deinse 1860.

[30]   *Verslag* 1873; Alstorphius Grevelink 1874.

4.2.4.3. Continuation of the Policy in Belgium: From Édouard Ducpétiaux to Édouard Ducpétiaux

Unlike in the Netherlands, in Belgium the establishment of the modern prison system – whose extent and depth were unequalled in Europe – was to a large

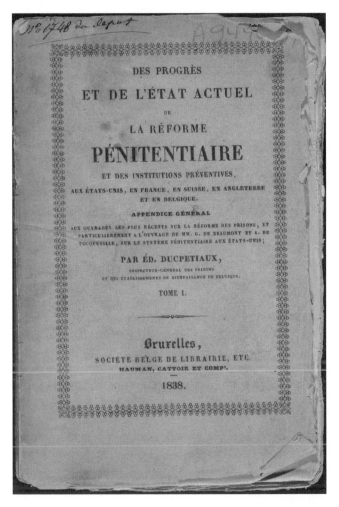

Édouard Ducpétiaux, *Des progrès et de l'état actuel de la réforme pénitentiaire et des institutions préventives, aux Etats-Unis, en France, en Suisse, en Angleterre et en Belgique*, Brussels, Société Belge de Librairie, 1837–1838, 3 vol + Atlas.

extent due to a single man, Édouard Ducpétiaux. In the late 1820s, this liberal Catholic politician and social reformer was one of the leaders in the struggle in the United Kingdom of the Netherlands against the dominance of William I, for which he was himself twice imprisoned. Partly because of that background, he was appointed inspector-general of prisons in 1830, remaining in that post until 1861. The history of the prison system in this period is therefore so intertwined with the course of his life that it can still be best explained on that basis.[31]

Ducpétiaux's law studies at the universities of Liège, Ghent, and Leuven had left him very interested in the combatting of crime and the criminal justice system. In completing his studies, he had gone deeply into international discussions of the impact of poverty and illiteracy on the extent and nature of crime as well as the international literature on criminal law in the strict sense, i.e. what is the basis for the right to punish, and what penalties are justifiable and moreover effective? He was closely familiar with the work of Beccaria and Montesquieu, with the books by La Rochefoucauld and Lucas, and with the activities of the *Société de morale chrétienne*. He disclosed his opinions for the first time in 1827 in two pamphlets concerning the death penalty.[32]

Almost immediately after the Belgian Revolution in 1830, Ducpétiaux began writing about the deplorable state of affairs in the prisons and about the American penitentiary system that he believed was the solution, namely that in Pennsylvania. He brought together the fruits of his reading in 1837–38 in a three-part study entitled *Des progrès et de l'état actuel de la réforme pénitentiaire et des institutions préventives aux Etats-Unis, en France, en Suisse, en Angleterre et en Belgique* [*On the Progress and the Actual State of the Penitentiary Reform and the Preventive Institutions in the United States, in France, in Switzerland, in England and in Belgium*].[33] In today's terminology, this might be called a policy plan in which foreign examples were used to show in detail what needed to be done in Belgium, i.e. fully implement the system of solitary confinement for adult prisoners. According to Ducpétiaux, comparison of the Pennsylvania and Auburn systems showed that the former had more advantages than the latter. He asserted that the clear advantages of the Pennsylvania system were that it:

- guaranteed that the prisons were secure;
- prevented corruption among the prisoners;
- was more effective at preventing recidivism;
- improved the morals of the inmates;
- prevented prisoners interacting with one another after their release;
- made operation of the prisons less dependent on the warders and the other subordinate personnel.

In addition, one should not forget that Ducpétiaux also immediately advocated the complete separation of men and women in prisons and of adults and juveniles.

---

[31] Rubbens 1922–34; Peters 1993; Dupont-Bouchat 1988.
[32] Ducpétiaux 1927.
[33] Ducpétiaux 1837–38.

His study had a direct impact in the Belgian parliament. During the discussion of the 1837 budget for the Ministry of Justice, proposals were immediately made for appropriations to implement Ducpétiaux's plans. The politicians were apparently unaware that he had already begun implementing them. In 1835, 32 cells on the Pennsylvania model had in fact already been prepared in the prison at Ghent, followed shortly afterwards by another 63 in a prison at Aalst.[34] But where the main thrust of Ducpétiaux's study was concerned – legislation for the creation of a Pennsylvanian penitentiary system for adult males – nothing was immediately done. The legal basis for such a system was actually only introduced two years after his death, namely with the Act of 4 March 1870, the single section of which provided that custodial sentences would be enforced in accordance with the principle of solitary confinement, assuming that the condition of the prisons allowed it. The same section then provided that – by way of compensation for this mode of implementation – the length of the prisoner's custodial sentence would be reduced according to the number of years spent in solitary confinement. However, the legislation largely served to formalise the de facto situation that Ducpétiaux had already created, i.e. a network of some 20 cellular prisons throughout the country, with the showpiece being the central prison in Leuven which was completed in 1860 and gained worldwide fame. How could Ducpétiaux and his successors – after his death, another ten cellular prisons were added, including the auxiliary prison in Leuven (1868) and the prison at St Gilles (1885) – create such a unique system of penitentiaries?[35]

Under pressure from debate in the Belgian Parliament, the Minister of Justice Jules d'Anethan submitted a bill in December 1844 which sought to organise a penitentiary system based on solitary confinement. Nevertheless, this proposal for a radical overhaul of the prison system had a number of important consequences for alleviating, to some extent, the plight of those who were subjected to solitary confinement. In the case of inmates sentenced for minor offences, for example, their term of imprisonment would be reduced by a third.[36] Even so, a number of Members of Parliament posed a series of probing questions on the bill that had been drawn up entirely in the spirit of Ducpétiaux's ideals and aims. The minister therefore asked Ducpétiaux to prepare the answers to these questions. This obviously suited Ducpétiaux and a few months later, he published a *Mémoire à l'appui du projet de loi sur les prisons [...] avec un appendice et trois plans de prisons cellulaires* [*Memorandum in Support of the Bill on Prisons [...] with an Appendix and Three Plans for Cellular Prisons*].[37] That report – which came too late in the day, given that the first new cellular prison

---

[34]   Digneffe and Dupont-Bouchat 1982; Dupont-Bouchat 1981, pp. 161–182.
[35]   Rubbens 1922–34; Dupont-Bouchat 1988.
[36]   Van Hoorebeke 1843.
[37]   Ducpétiaux 1845.

(in Tongeren) had already become operational in 1843 – began with a minutely detailed account of the existing prison system. The state of the building, the material conditions, the population, the regime, and so forth were all discussed, almost building by building. Ducpétiaux was not entirely dissatisfied with what had been achieved hitherto and boldly concluded that the prison system could easily stand comparison with other countries in physical and economic terms.

He went on to argue, with equal fervour, that the solution to the prisons issue should not be sought in the Auburn system. For him, the ineffectiveness of that system was indisputable: it failed to intimidate, it did not improve but in fact corrupted, it made any attempt at education futile from the start, it was contrary to human nature, it created dangerous relationships, it formed an obstacle to patronage, and enforcing it required one to resort to barbaric punishments. The only solution was the system of individual confinement, with all its associated advantages. This time, Ducpétiaux backed up his arguments with a detailed discussion of the familiar foreign examples: Cherry Hill, La Roquette, and Pentonville.

Third, Ducpétiaux went into great detail regarding all sorts of issues that had arisen in connection with the construction, financing, work organisation, religious practice, education, and recidivism rates of cellular prisons. He gave a detailed response to all the questions posed, concluding his treatise with a number of reflections that reveal clearly what motivated him, namely the moral edification of prisoners and the improvement of society. He added emphatically that the work accomplished in prisons would remain ineffectual in very many cases if it were not complemented outside the prison by some form of patronage. In his view, Belgium had already made a start, but there was still a great deal of work to be done.[38] And what did the Belgian Parliament do with these answers to the questions that it had itself raised? Nothing! The bill concerned was not put back on the agenda.

The issue was eventually regulated by a separate piece of legislation in 1870, according to the principle of solitary confinement with compensation for the onerousness thereof. That act was therefore the parliamentary enshrinement of the idea to which Ducpétiaux had devoted his life. Many people, both in Belgium and elsewhere, had a high opinion of him and expressed great praise for this immense achievement. It needs to be borne in mind that the international penitentiary conferences held in 1846 and in 1847 declared "the cellular system to be the best form of prison system".[39] That declaration not only expressed support for Ducpétiaux's plans but also meant that the Belgian model immediately became a model worldwide for the most favoured prison system. In 1858, three years before retiring, Ducpétiaux published another lengthy treatise on

---

38   Peters 1993.
39   Ver Loren van Themaat 1910–11, 2, pp. 320, 324.

Des conditions d'application du système de l'emprisonnement séparé ou cellulaire [*On the Conditions for Applying the System of Separate or Cellular Imprisonment*].[40] He apparently wished to provide his successors with a blueprint for how they should continue his life's work.

Against the background of the above, it goes almost without saying that Ducpétiaux also investigated issues related to the prison system, in particular that of institutions to house beggars, agricultural colonies, and *verbeteringsscholen* (reform schools). Unlike in the Netherlands, this issue was indeed placed on the political agenda in Belgium, in 1846. This rethink was mainly at the request of the municipalities, which found themselves confronted due to the economic crisis by ever-increasing expenditure for alleviating extreme hardship. The average occupancy of the five institutions to house beggars remaining from the Napoleonic period, for example, rose from 2,739 individuals in 1840 to 10,033 in 1847. After considerable discussion in Parliament, a law was passed in April 1848 which broadly concerned, on the one hand, the preservation of the institutions for convicted vagrants and beggars, and on the other the establishment of two reform schools (in the form of agricultural colonies) for boys and girls who had been convicted or who were admitted at the request of the municipalities.[41]

Ducpétiaux would certainly have been involved behind the scenes in this legislation being drawn up. Once it had been passed, he at any rate wrote a detailed *Mémoire sur l'organisation des colonies de réforme* [*Memorandum on the Organisation of Reform Colonies*] at the request of the Minister of Justice.[42] Based, inter alia, on the colonies at Mettray and Parkhurst, Ducpétiaux discussed – in his familiar thorough manner – how these schools should be designed in terms of organisation, population, management, staffing, regime and education, funding, equipment, etc. He thus became the founder of the colony for boys which was opened in Ruysselede in 1850 and that for girls which followed shortly after in Beernem.[43] He had a marked preference for these locations because they were in a genuinely agricultural region and therefore in surroundings where the residents could see the value of their work every day. In 1850, besides producing his policy plan for Ruysselede and Beernem, Ducpétiaux quickly visited all the possible versions of agricultural colonies for adults and juveniles in Western Europe with a view to a complete redesign of the system that existed in Belgium. In 1851, he also wrote a comprehensive report on that journey, *Colonies agricoles, écoles rurales et écoles de réforme* [*Agricultural Colonies, Rural Schools and Reform Schools*],[44] in which he described the various institutions in each

---

40   Ducpétiaux 1858.
41   Depreeuw 1988, pp. 332–339.
42   Ducpétiaux 1848.
43   Christiaens 1999, pp. 151–194.
44   Ducpétiaux 1851.

country, starting with Switzerland, followed by Germany, France and Britain, and finally the Netherlands and Belgium.

Given his views on the domestic colonial system, it is not surprising that in 1853 Ducpétiaux was appointed secretary to the state commission whose task was to reconsider the whole issue of the institutions to house beggars. The commission presented its final report a few months later; the findings were not very favourable. Among the conclusions were that the institutions had remained hybrid organisations where all kinds of people were locked up, that most of the workplaces had been dispensed with for fear of competing with private industry – meaning that the inmates were left doing mostly meaningless work – and that their location and premises were unsuited to any improvement. The committee did not of course restrict itself to announcing these findings and it also made a large number of proposals for resolving the problems. After a lengthy parliamentary debate, those proposals were only partly adopted in 1866 in a new act on begging, vagrancy, and institutions to house beggars.[45]

Following on from the above, we will consider an example which shows that, for Ducpétiaux as a social reformer, the prison system was definitely not the panacea to the major problems of overpopulation, poverty, and crime that Belgium was facing in the 1840s in the wake of appalling agricultural crises. That example is his *Mémoire sur le pauperisme dans les Flandres* [*Memorandum on Pauperism in Flanders*] (1850).[46] In the first part of that treatise, Ducpétiaux works out how much crime had increased in both Flemish provinces. He calculates, for example, that between 1830 and 1848 the number of prisoners in the gaols in West Flanders had increased from 2,911 to 6,579 and in those of East Flanders from 3,690 to 13,600. He found it indisputable that the increase in crime was a consequence of the growth in poverty. His great fear was that these trends would lead to an entire generation of criminals growing up in Flanders.

In the second part of his work, Ducpétiaux examines the cause of all the distress, making a distinction between structural and incidental causes. The former, he said, included increasing overpopulation, a lack of employment, the fragmentation of agricultural land, the decline of the textile industry, and the lack of education of the working class. The incidental causes included, in particular, the potato diseases that had appeared, poor harvests, the lack of organisation of assistance, the deficiencies in the legislation on begging and vagrancy, and the failure of the institutions to house beggars. All those causes were then thoroughly discussed one by one.

And Ducpétiaux would not have been himself if he had not indicated in detail in the third part of the treatise how an end could be put to the misery. Even though he had been one of the leaders of the movement for Belgian independence

---

45   Depreeuw 1988, pp. 346–359.
46   Ducpétiaux 1850.

in 1830, he did not now preach revolution. Rather, he proposed drastic measures such as the reconstruction of the textile industry, the restructuring of farmland, encouragement of emigration to the Americas, improvement of general education and vocational training, and of course his familiar pet subjects such as amendment of the legislation on begging and vagrancy and reorganisation of the institutions to house beggars.

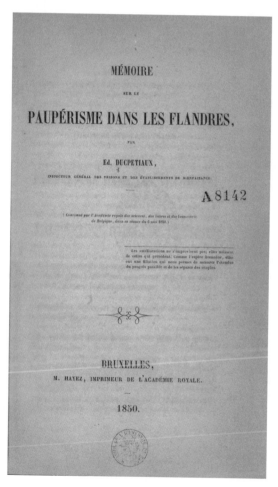

Édouard Ducpétiaux, *Mémoire sur le paupérisme dans les Flandres*, Brussels, M. Hayez, 1850.

4.3. DEVELOPMENT OF THE MODERN POLICING SYSTEM

Unlike the prison system, the policing system played a significant role in implementing the decisions of the Congress of Vienna in 1815. It was an important means of guaranteeing the stability of the geo-political relations within Europe that were redefined at the Congress. In that context, it meant the collection of information on nationalist, liberalist, or Bonapartist groups and individuals that could endanger that stability in one way or another. However, a well-organised police force that could be deployed flexibly anywhere to maintain public order, either preventively and/or repressively, was certainly just as important. In this regard, the new rulers were in fact well aware that the spread of the ideals of the French Revolution meant that the violent suppression of disturbances both large and small had become a very risky strategy; such an approach could easily turn back on them. Deployment of the police in the event of order or security problems needed to be more subtle. In order to implement a more peaceful strategy, citizens were themselves asked to be compliant, namely to behave in an orderly manner: *Ruhe ist die erste Bürgerpflicht* (orderly behaviour is the first duty of the citizen).[47]

4.3.1. FURTHER DEVELOPMENT OF THE POLICING SYSTEM IN FRANCE AND GERMANY

4.3.1.1. Developments in France

In France itself – the home, after all, of modern policing in Europe – part of the system constructed by Fouché was dismantled after 1815, with the positions of Commissioner-General and Special Commissioner being abolished, for example. However, the Police Ministry was not immediately done away with. Quite the contrary: it quickly expanded once more into an *agence secrète de renseignements* (secret intelligence agency) with the task of keeping an eye on those who might oppose the restored regime. Its abolition in 1818 was in itself highly significant because it marked the end of the centralised structure of the police state that had been created at the time of the *Directoire*. This did not mean, however, that its important task ceased to be carried out. It was in fact transferred to the *direction générale de police* (general directorate of police) that was set up at the same time within the Ministry of the Interior.

Just how important political intelligence work remained is most clearly demonstrated by the fact that the criminal investigation service – the *Sûreté* – set up by the Paris prefect of police in 1809 and placed under the leadership of the illustrious former *bagnard* Eugène Vidocq – was used more and more after 1815 for political policing and in 1827 was even incorporated into the political department of the Paris police. Despite this politicisation of the Paris police, the July Revolution of 1830 which put Louis-Philippe I on the throne did not have

---

[47]   Fijnaut 1979.

any major consequences for its overall organisation. A *corps des sergents de ville* (force of city sergeants) was set up, however, in order to maintain public order more effectively.[48]

How the police fared in other cities during this period has never been investigated. As far as the *gendarmerie* is concerned – the strong arm of the police system under Fouché – we know that it was thoroughly purged but certainly not abolished. In September 1815, it was again divided into 24 legions, 1,550 mounted brigades and 620 infantry brigades, with its total strength being fixed at 18,016 men. In 1820, a decree was promulgated which not only again defined as effectively as possible how the force would relate to the various civil, judicial, and military authorities, but which also determined that its strength should be reduced by several thousand men. During the July Revolution of 1830, the *gendarmerie* remained largely out of harm's way. Only in a few places did it act in defence of the autocratic reign of Charles X. Then also, there was also no question of the *gendarmerie* being abolished.[49]

During the February Revolution in 1848, things took a different turn, at least in Paris. The revolutionaries abolished virtually all the existing services, replacing them with new units, including a *force de haute police* and the *garde républicaine*. After the revolution had been crushed in June 1848 and the reactionary Napoleon III elected president, the police clock in Paris was turned back a bit, although there were no real changes to the structure of French policing. What was important, however, was that the *gendarmerie* – which until then had always been organised entirely on a territorial basis – had two battalions of *gendarmerie mobile* added so as to maintain order in a more flexible manner and with greater weight throughout the entire country.

The more general reorganisation took place after Napoleon III's coup d'état in December 1851. In the first place, this not only involved a certain centralisation of the municipal police by making the *préfets* responsible for appointing police commissioners and constables. This police force was restructured extensively in 1854, especially in Paris, by dividing up the city, according to the example of the police in London, into 12 *arrondissements*, which were then subdivided into 850 neighbourhoods so that permanent police surveillance of the population could be organised in a far more sophisticated manner by means of *sergents de ville*. Second, at the central level the *gendarmerie* was strengthened, but parallel to this a separate intelligence service was established in 1855 in the form of the *police spéciale*, which consisted of about 100 commissioners and inspectors of police

---

[48]   Fijnaut 1979, 2, pp. 829–833; Vidocq 1935; Frégier 1850, pp. 359–366; Macé 1891, pp. 139–143; Berlière and Lévy 2011, pp. 95–102. See also Savant 1956; Savant 1957; Froment 1967; Eugène 1968; Edwards 1977; Tudesq 1979; Morton 2004.

[49]   Emsley 1999, pp. 81–119.

stationed at the main nodes of the rail network. This allowed them to keep a close eye on all significant passenger travel.[50]

4.3.1.2. Developments in Germany

Developments in Germany largely ran parallel with those in France. This is strikingly reflected by the fact that the Prussian Ministry of Police was also abolished in 1818, with its tasks being taken over, as in France, by the Ministry of the Interior. Moreover, under pressure from the landed nobility, the influence of the *gendarmerie* was significantly limited in various states after 1815 – in Prussia, Bavaria, and Saxony – by simply reducing its strength. The nobility were very wary of the central authorities using these forces to strengthen their influence on the course of events in rural areas.

There was no real revolution anywhere in Germany in 1830, and thus no regime change, but the 1830s did see considerable unrest, with almost incessant larger and smaller disturbances both in the cities and elsewhere. Needless to say, this did not fail to have its effect on the policing system.[51] A *Sicherheitmannschaft* (security force) was set up in virtually all the major cities and larger towns. In states such as Bavaria and Prussia, the *gendarmerie* was reinforced and *gendarmerie* units were installed in the large towns so as to maintain order more effectively. It is also noteworthy that in 1832 the member states of the *Deutscher Bund* (German Confederation) committed themselves to assisting one another – in particular through the collection and exchange of information – in monitoring groups or individuals who were a threat to state security or who endangered political stability in some other way. This was one of the first official forms of inter-state police cooperation in Europe.

The unsuccessful revolution of 1848 also had consequences for policing. In Berlin, a *Schutzmannschaft* (constabulary) was immediately set up along the lines of the police in London. In terms of equipment and dress, this body had a very civilian appearance – police officers in civilian clothing with a top hat – but internally it was entirely on military lines. Towards the end of 1848, the constabulary immediately demonstrated its value, with new disturbances being nipped in the bud. One important component of this new police force was the *Kriminalpolizei*, led by the notorious Wilhelm Stieber – notorious because of the highly aggressive way in which he carried out his other task, namely political intelligence work.[52]

The other major German cities did not immediately follow the example of Berlin, generally confining themselves to appointing a director of police to ensure

---

50   Fijnaut 1979, 1, pp. 109–116; Larrieu 2002, pp. 567–571; Rey and Féron 1896, pp. 126–167.
51   Fijnaut 1979, 2, pp. 999–1006.
52   Auerbach 1884, pp. 22–108; Funk 1986, pp. 40–93; Fijnaut 1979, 2, pp. 1007–1012; Eibich 2004, pp. 63–80.

better coordination of police work and to coordinate it with the policies of the central government. The army remained the main instrument for maintaining order, if necessary by force. Plans to extend inter-state police co-operation within the German Confederation by setting up a *Zentral-Bundespolizeibehörde* (central police office) fell through due to the argument of some member states that the activities of that office should be carried out in every state in accordance with the legislation that applied there. Ultimately, all that was in fact feasible was to establish a *Verein von Sicherheitsbeamten zur Aufrechterhaltung der öffentlichen Ruhe und Ordnung* (Association of Security Officials for the Maintenance of Public Peace and Order). That association was nevertheless an important channel for the exchange of political information. Moreover, Prussia – in the deepest secrecy – posted a police attaché to its embassy in London, the city to which Karl Marx had fled.[53]

4.3.2. MODERNISATION OF THE POLICE IN THE UNITED KINGDOM

As we saw in the previous chapter, there was great resistance to the French police model in the United Kingdom of the late eighteenth century. We also noted that after 1848 the London police force was the model for reorganisation of the police in both Paris and Berlin. What happened in the United Kingdom, and particularly in London, in the meantime?

The second decade of the nineteenth century was a troubled period for the United Kingdom, with repeated, serious social and political unrest, especially in industrial areas. The forces available to suppress this unrest consisted of the army and the militia. As on the continent, however, these forces proved not to be very effective. Their deployment generally only fanned the flames, certainly after the Peterloo Massacre in 1819, when the army and militia left 11 people dead and 400 wounded. It gradually came to be realised that the police needed to be reorganised, starting in London. To accomplish this, the Home Office minister Robert Peel proposed in 1829 that the patchwork of services that carried out policing in the capital should be entirely replaced by a 3,000-strong police force – divided into divisions, subdivisions, sections, and neighbourhoods – which could maintain order throughout the city at all times and ensure security. Many groups within London were very much opposed to this proposal, seeing in it the outlines of a repressive system on the continental – i.e. French, Parisian – model. Nevertheless, Peel and the Tories persevered and in 1830 work began on organising the force. To emphasise that they were not intended to be a body

---

[53] Fijnaut 1979, 2, pp. 1007–1012.

hostile to the public, the constables were dressed in civilian clothes, including a top hat.[54]

In the ensuing decades, the example of this new police force was followed throughout the country, particularly in the cities and industrial areas, although that was not usually plain sailing. In some places there were insufficient funds and people to establish a modern police force, while in others all kinds of movements – both conservative and socialist – opposed its creation because it was thought to pose a threat to the country's traditional liberties, the risk of oppression was too great, etc. By the early 1850s, however, the new type of police force had become widespread in the United Kingdom. That development was formalised in the County and Borough Police Act of 1856, which authorised the central government – deploying its own inspectors – to monitor the efficiency and effectiveness of the police forces and if necessary provide additional funding to improve them. Partly as a result of this, the army and militia eventually came to play hardly any role in maintaining order. The few times that the army was later deployed on a large scale, for example in London in 1867, subsequently led to the police force being strengthened in order to prevent this recurring.[55]

Where criminal investigation is concerned, it is important to note that a central investigative bureau was set up in London, on the quiet, in 1842. This was expanded in 1868, in the light of a number of attacks in the city, into "a detective establishment covering the whole district", but it was not much of a success, quickly having to deal with problems of corruption. In response, the service was replaced in 1878, on the model of the *Sûreté* in Paris, by a Criminal Investigation Department with 200 officers, led by the lawyer Howard Vincent, who had previously called for such a reorganisation. Like its foreign counterparts, this department also became involved in combatting political opposition. In the 1880s, that mainly meant Irish bombers, whose activities led to the establishment of the Special Irish Branch or Dynamite Branch within the Criminal Investigation Department.[56]

One interesting point – especially in relation to the history of the prison system – is that in the mid-nineteenth century the London police model was imitated to a greater or lesser extent by the creation of police forces in the United States, particularly in the large East Coast cities, and including Boston, New York, Chicago and Buffalo. Here too, labour unrest and the risk of civil unrest played the primary role in the spread of modern urban policing.[57]

---

54   Emsley 1996, pp. 24–31; Reynolds 1998, pp. 103–147.
55   Philips and Storch 1999; Emsley 1996, pp. 32–42; Taylor (D.) 1997, pp. 12–43.
56   Allason 1983, pp. 1–29; Porter 1987, pp. 35–67; Fijnaut 1979, 2, pp. 1014–1016.
57   See, for example, Fosdick 1920, pp. 62–80; Monkkonen 1981, pp. 31–48; Richardson 1970, pp. 23–50; Richardson 1974, pp. 3–34; Bopp and Schultz 1972, pp. 33–47; Carte and Carte 1975, pp. 8–12; Lane 1967, pp. 118–131.

4.3.3. FURTHER DEVELOPMENT OF THE POLICING SYSTEM IN THE NETHERLANDS AND BELGIUM

In the United Kingdom of the Netherlands, the structure of the French police system was retained, with various alterations: on the one hand a civilian local police force that would also carry out certain duties for the central government, and on the other a centrally organised military police. The main difference between the northern and southern parts of the country was that in the former the *gendarmerie* was not retained, whereas it was in the latter, albeit under a traditional name, *marechaussee*. The reason for this body being retained in the south was because the threats to the new Kingdom were much greater here than in the north. For one thing, there were significant power groupings that refused to accept that political creation, and there was also the cross-border interaction with France, with all the risks that entailed. It is therefore unsurprising that the police force in the south was emphatically deployed in the 1820s to curb the swelling opposition to William I. That did not lead, however, to any significant changes to the structure of the policing system. When the Belgian Revolution took place in 1830, the system was broadly the same as in 1815.

4.3.3.1. Developments in the Netherlands

The further history of the Dutch policing system in the course of the nineteenth century was to a large extent determined by discussions of its structure at national level.[58] The food riots that broke out in several regions in 1846 and 1847 led to a proposal for the *marechaussee* – which after the secession of Belgium had been retained only in the three southern Dutch provinces – to operate throughout the country. The plans were presented in 1848. There was to be a national force of 1,800 men divided into five companies. However, disagreement between the Minister of Justice and the Minister of War on the financing for such a force led to the proposal being rejected. It is possible that this failure was also related to the emergency measure adopted in September 1848 to deal with new disturbances, namely the establishment of an auxiliary *marechaussee* formed from the ranks of the cavalry.

Measures had already been taken at local level to better ensure public order and safety. For the most part, this involved establishing a true police force on the London model, as was done in Amsterdam in 1844 and in Rotterdam in 1846. The "bread and potato riot" in Groningen in 1847 led to an 80-man police force being established there in 1849.

For the government, this was all insufficient; it wished to create greater cohesion within the policing system. To achieve that goal, the acclaimed *Gemeentewet* (Municipalities Act) of 1851 provided, on the one hand, that the *burgemeester*

---

58   Fijnaut 2007, pp. 86–177.

(mayor) would have sole responsibility for the maintenance of public order within his municipality and be primarily charged with managing the municipal police force. On the other hand, the Act assumed that the municipal police would be subservient to the *rijkspolitie* (national police); it could in other words be deployed to perform duties subject to the responsibility of the central government. To ensure coordination between these two tasks, the government intended appointing five regional directors of police. The latter proposal met with opposition from the Lower House of Parliament, however, resulting in 1853 in the impasse being resolved by appointing the *procureurs-generaal* as acting directors of police.

This course of events brought about deadlock in solving what had come to be known as the *politievraagstuk* (police question). To break the deadlock, a commission was appointed in 1852 to draw up an entirely new proposal. What that proposal came down to was that the Minister of Justice would be the head of the police, with directors, cantonal police commissioners and inspectors and constables (whether or not mounted) subject to him. The government did not endorse the proposal, however, not only because it considered it too expensive but also – given what had happened in France – because it feared that such a police force could easily be misused for political purposes.

Even so, the proposal was not rejected in its entirety. Between 1854 and 1856, gamekeepers, court officials, and other hitherto unpaid state constables were appointed as salaried state constables and organised into brigades. The Lower House did not agree with this course of events, being clearly opposed to the creation of a *rijksveldwacht* (state constabulary), as the force-to-be quickly came to be known. During the debate on the 1857 budget for the Ministry of Justice, the Lower House cancelled the funding that had been earmarked for the force. The following year, however, the budget item in question was adopted by 30 votes to 29 and the *rijksveldwacht* came into being.

4.3.3.2. Developments in Belgium

After the Revolution of 1830, the young Belgian state wished to distinguish itself from the United Kingdom of the Netherlands, including as regards policing.[59] A good example is the formal abolition of the *haute police*, while the appointment of an *administrateur van de openbare veiligheid* (administrator for public security) showed that the tasks involved would continue to be performed. The same applied to the *marechaussee*. This was abolished in 1830 but simultaneously replaced by the *gendarmerie nationale belge*. However, section 120 of the Constitution provided that the structure and powers of that body should be regulated by law.

Most discussion, however, initially concerned the structure of the municipal police. The local authorities in any case rejected any further explicit involvement

---

59   Fijnaut 1995, pp. 25–26.

of the central government in this regard. The position of director of police was therefore abolished and the appointment of the *hoofdcommissaris* (chief constable) was limited to one year. Even so, the 1836 *Gemeentewet* (Municipalities Act) provided that the chief of police would be appointed by the Crown. That provision made clear that this central figure was also responsible to a certain extent for the performance of the state police duties.

When the Municipalities Act was amended in 1842, it was provided, furthermore, that authority over the municipal police would be exercised entirely by the mayor. This was primarily so as to better ensure the effectiveness of this force as regarded maintaining law and order. After 1848, the structure of a number of municipal police forces was also amended in line with similar reorganisations abroad – in 1848 in Brussels, 1852 in Liège, and 1861 in Antwerp. These police forces were numerically strengthened, their internal hierarchy was tightened up, and the men were divided into smaller units across the area of the municipality.

The *gendarmerie* also became the object of political conflict in the course of the 1830s. As in the Netherlands, the problem was that the Ministers of Justice and War could not agree on the financing for the force in relation to the division of control over it. Under the influence of the public order problems that were encountered in the mid-1840s, a commission was finally appointed in 1847 to prepare a draft act of parliament on the *gendarmerie*. When it was submitted in 1850, however, it became stranded because of the usual differences between the two ministers.

Finally, it is worth noting that – as part of their proposals for an overhaul of the system of criminal investigation on the English model – Adolphe Prins and Hermann Pergameni called for the establishment of a separate judicial police, distributed across the various provinces. However, the commission – chaired by Jean-Joseph Thonissen – that submitted its proposal for a revision of the Code of Criminal Procedure in 1878 rejected this plan. On the one hand, it expressed the fear that such a police force could be misused for political purposes; on the other, it considered that the existing security situation did not justify such radical intervention in the policing system. Parliament agreed with this assessment and the plan was abandoned.[60]

4.4. THREE CONTRASTING SCIENTIFIC APPROACHES TO CRIME AND THE CRIMINAL

As already indicated in the introduction, there were three different scientific approaches during this period to the development of criminology. To put it simply, these were the biological, the psychiatric, and the sociological. These

---

[60] Fijnaut 1995, pp. 26–30.

three approaches will therefore be discussed separately on the basis of the works of the authors who played a leading role, in particular Franz Gall, Jean Esquirol, and Adolphe Quetelet. There is good reason, however, why this section is entitled "contrasting scientific approaches": it indicates that there are no absolute dividing lines between these approaches and that one needs to bear in mind how they impinge on one another and overlap.

4.4.1. BIOLOGICAL APPROACH: THE PHRENOLOGY OF FRANZ GALL

When he settled in Paris in 1807, Franz Gall (1758–1828) was already famous in the states of Germany, and the invitation he received in 1808 to teach in Paris at the *Société de médecine* did not therefore arrive by chance. He was viewed by contemporaries, and later, as a brilliant anatomist with a tremendous surgical record. In his research, Gall was fascinated by the general anatomy and physiology of the brain and in particular by the anatomical and physiological basis of people's mental and emotional life. The guiding scientific idea behind his research was that all one's properties and tendencies are located in a particular place in one's brain, i.e. that is where they have their biological basis. Gall's phrenology or doctrine of the brain therefore consisted of two subdisciplines. On the one hand, there was psychology – intended to determine the basic characteristics and tendencies of a person by means of social observation – and on the other organology – intended to determine the "seat" of those characteristics and inclinations in the brain by means of physical observation.

In line with these ideas, Gall then developed craniology, or the doctrine of the skull. That doctrine was based on the principle that the skull formed, as it were, a mirror of the brain and that cranioscopy – examination of the skull – made it possible, without opening the skull, to determine the state of someone's brain and thus his or her characteristics and tendencies. Unlike Lavater, Gall did not therefore restrict himself to purely associative comparisons between a person's appearance and their character but claimed that this was a positive and scientific means of gaining insights. For that reason, he was for many years held in high regard not only in Europe but also in the United States. Gall's fame declined when he – and also his followers – began to make assertions that had absolutely no empirical support.[61]

But what does all this have to do with the subject of this book? Criminals were excellent research subjects for phrenologists. Sociologically, they were an infamous group of people who naturally attracted a great deal of attention. Unlike most other groups, quite a few of them were to be found in a location

---

[61]   Blondel 1914, pp. 42–43, 50–57, 78–83, 90–92, 128–155; Overholser 1960; Rafter 2005.

where they could be studied without any major problem, namely in prison. And with the rise of ideas regarding moral edification and re-education, a more and better scientific understanding of their abilities and peculiarities became very important. How could those objectives be achieved otherwise? For Gall and other phrenologists, it was therefore quite normal – indeed almost a necessity – to visit prisons and subject inmates to all kinds of observations.

In that way, prisons acquired the status of scientific laboratories within which ground-breaking research was being done. In 1845, for example, the secretary to the *Société phrénologique de Paris* subjected virtually all the inmates of La Petite Roquette to investigation. And what he established was really quite remarkable, namely that in general the growth of their brain was stunted and that in that sense they had ended up outside the species of *Homo sapiens*. From the point of view of evolutionary theory, he could even fairly easily bridge the gap to asserting that criminals formed a category of people who had fallen behind in the development of mankind. As early as 1808, a friend of Gall made a comparison between criminals and prehistoric man.[62]

Propositions such as these also fostered the idea that crime was in fact a disease of the brain and that criminals were therefore actually criminal patients. These not only needed to be punished from the perspective of their crime but also to be treated from that of their capabilities and shortcomings, and if possible cured. In other words, prisons should be converted into hospitals where individually tailored punishment/treatment would seek to improve the inmates' behaviour and adapt them to the values and standards of the society around them. The researchers who – with some hesitation – pointed out these consequences were convinced that the medical approach to criminals would not quickly bear fruit, precisely because of the biological basis of their misconduct. In this way, Gall and his supporters traced the behaviour of murderers back to the innate tendency of people and animals to eat meat, while they saw theft as stemming from the innate tendency to gather food. So how could one reverse behaviour that was rooted in these characteristics?

It should be noted that the phrenologists did not believe that someone was a murderer or a thief from birth. Rather, they asserted that social conditions should be held responsible for a person's criminal career. In disadvantageous conditions, someone's innate characteristics would quite simply develop more readily in the wrong direction than in positive conditions. From the phrenological perspective, thieves were not all that far removed from rich people and the nobility because they displayed "*ce penchant développé à un degré considérable*" (this tendency developed to a considerable degree).[63] The criticisms of society that the phrenologists attached to such principles were naturally not appreciated

---

[62]   Labadie 1995.
[63]   Précis 1829.

by a whole range of power groupings in France, and certainly contributed to their loss of scientific reputation. They did, however, have many supporters in philanthropic circles. Quite a few members of the *Société de morale chrétienne*, for example, were also members of the *Société phrénologique*. It is therefore unsurprising that there was interest in phrenological research among prison reformers.[64]

The demise of phrenology and craniology in the 1840s did not mean, however, the demise of study of the brains and skulls of criminals as such – quite the contrary. A large number of members of the *Société d'anthropologie* – founded in Paris in 1859 by the surgery professor Paul Broca – pursued this kind of research right up to the end of the nineteenth century. In the twentieth century it was resumed, but in different contexts.[65]

4.4.2. PSYCHIATRIC APPROACH: THE MONOMANIA DOCTRINE OF JEAN-ÉTIENNE ESQUIROL

The French psychiatrist Jean-Étienne Esquirol (1772–1840) is generally viewed as the most brilliant and influential pupil of Pinel. Based on the latter's beliefs about manias, he developed in particular his doctrine of monomania, a constant state of delirious fixation on a particular object, which is an extension of what in normal people is referred to as a passion. In his famous book *Des maladies mentales considérées sous les rapports médical, hygiénique et médico-légal* [*On Mental Diseases considered from the Medical, Hygienic, and Medico-Legal Perspectives*] (1838), he categorised monomanias, on the one hand, according to their nature, referring to intellectual, emotional, and instinctive monomanias. On the other hand, he classified them according to their subject. It was in fact mainly elements of the latter classification – namely pyromania, kleptomania, etc. – that for a long time formed part of the standard repertoire of later criminology, including via disciples of Esquirol. A concept that still plays some role is that of the "*monomanie homicide*", both in its affective variant – the murder results from an unreasonable and exalted view of the future victim – and in its instinctive variant – the murder results from an indefinable urge to kill someone.[66]

Esquirol naturally delved deeply into the causes of these and other mental illnesses. In individual cases he took account both of the geographical and socio-economic circumstances in which certain diseases manifested themselves and of the inherited predisposition of the patient him/herself, as well as of the events that had apparently unleashed the manifestation of the disease. As with Pinel, Esquirol's interest was more in the actual treatment of patients. His

---

[64]   Renneville 1994a.
[65]   Blanckaert 1994.
[66]   Esquirol 1838.

central idea in that regard was *traitement moral* (moral treatment), with the principle being that someone could not be cured by compulsion but only by persuasion. He therefore rejected the use of coercion as far as possible, and even of medication. Just how an individual case should be treated was a major point of discussion. There was agreement, however, that treatment could best be given in large enclosed institutions in rural areas. There, the patients would not be unnecessarily distracted or stimulated by their familiar surroundings (i.e. by the negative elements therein) and the medical staff could keep them under their control as much as possible.[67]

These views naturally struck at the core of traditional ideas regarding the criminal responsibility of perpetrators. After all, those ideas basically assumed that people had free will and were able to weigh up the benefits and disadvantages of committing crime in a balanced manner. But according Esquirol and his followers, that assumption was in no way consistent with the facts; it was no more than a legal fiction. Many people apparently committed offences beyond their control, as it were, and could not therefore be held criminally responsible for them. This therefore led to important discussions about the (diminished) responsibility of offenders and about the role of psychiatrists in criminal proceedings, particularly vis-à-vis the court that must ultimately determine guilt or innocence. In French but also Dutch and German criminal law textbooks of the period, it was therefore quite normal for forensic medicine to be classed as an important auxiliary science of criminal law.[68]

As a result of these discussions, a large number of questions naturally arose regarding the organisation of the prison system. Where psychiatrists and prison reformers could perhaps easily agree on the ideal structure of a psychiatric institution or a prison respectively, their views on the ideal prison regime for mentally disturbed criminals could just as easily be miles apart. After all, if criminals, and therefore prisoners, needed to be considered mentally ill, then prisons could definitely not be organised on a cellular footing. According to Esquirol and others, application of prolonged solitary confinement – the means of coercion par excellence – would cure nobody. To actually achieve a cure, prisons needed to be set up as psychiatric hospitals, if necessary as a special category of such. These proposals for "psychiatrisation" of the prison system, which was closely connected with thinking in phrenological circles, naturally met with a great deal of resistance, not only among prison reformers but also in political circles. Nevertheless, the latter could not entirely ignore the criticism from the psychiatrists. Partly because of this, new legislation on the prison system and sentencing generally set maximum limits for solitary confinement and/or options for discontinuing solitary confinement ahead of schedule for psychological reasons.

---

[67]   Debuyst 1995; Binnenveld 1985.
[68]   Van Deinse 1860.

For a better understanding of the further early history of criminology, it should be noted that it was not only in France that Pinel had important followers. A number of British prison doctors definitely gained as much international fame as Esquirol. The first of these was the Scot James Thompson and the second the Englishman James Prichard. For them, it was clear after years of observation and research that criminals – as they knew them, i.e. shut up in dire prisons – were morally, mentally, and physically inferior people, if not indeed an inferior species of people burdened very adversely by heredity for all kinds of reasons. In their eyes, in other words, they formed a separate category of people who had fallen behind in the course of evolution.[69] These ideas became familiar worldwide particularly through Prichard's *Treatise on Moral Insanity* (1837).[70]

4.4.3. SOCIOLOGICAL APPROACH: THE SOCIAL PHYSICS OF ADOLPHE QUETELET

There is a strong case for considering Adolphe Quetelet the most important precursor of modern criminology. More than anyone else in the first half of the nineteenth century, he in any case tried – based on the finding that recorded crime, no matter how one views it, remains virtually unchanged over the years – to make thinking about crime, criminals, and the combatting of crime more scientific, as regards both theory and methods. His ideas therefore merit our attention.

In dealing with the work of this great Belgian scholar, we should not lose sight, however, of that fact that he was not the only person who strove to discover the laws governing the organisation and functioning of society. Besides Quetelet, there was, in particular, André-Michel Guerry, head of the statistical office at the Ministry of Justice in Paris, who attempted to identify those laws. Guerry's *Essai sur la statistique morale en France* [*Essay on Moral Statistics in France*] (1833) is generally seen as a pioneering work in the development of the statistical study of crime and other forms of deviant or undesirable behaviour. That reputation is particularly due to the fact that Guerry came to the conclusion that in all kinds of ways (geography, age, gender) French crime figures exhibited a high degree of regularity over time, and that he attempted, on the basis of that discovery, to identify the factors that could explain such regularity, namely poverty, education, economic activity, etc. His quest took a rather cartographic approach, displaying far less sociological imagination than Quetelet, and he is therefore less highly regarded scientifically than his Belgian counterpart.[71]

---

[69]   Davie 2004, pp. 59–61.
[70]   Prichard 1837.
[71]   Mechler 1970, pp. 6–34; Van Kerckvoorde 1994; Beirne 1993, pp. 65–142.

Moreover, one must not forget that Ducpétiaux always put a lot of effort into statistical study of both crime and its background as well as the settlement of criminal cases and the operation of the prison system. Influenced by Quetelet's work, he also published one of the first criminal statistics studies in Europe in 1835, *Statistique comparée de la criminalité en France, en Belgique, en Angleterre et en Allemagne* [*Comparative Crime Statistics in France, in Belgium, in England, and in Germany*]. There was good reason why he, like Quetelet, was a member of Belgium's *Commission Centrale de Statistique* [*Central Statistical Commission*]. Ducpétiaux is therefore rightly often mentioned together with Quetelet and Guerry as the founder of the Belgian–French "moral-statistical school".

The works of these three individuals, moreover, had a major impact on the discussion of the value and techniques of crime statistics throughout the entire Western world. In Germany, they were closely followed in 1829 by the renowned statistician Carl Mittermaier,[72] while in 1850 the British statistician Joseph Fletcher described their writings as "the greatest work of the kind for its time". Matters also went beyond mere discussion. In more and more countries, separate criminal statistics were eventually drawn up in order to more effectively support policy on crime and the criminal justice system. That development, in its turn, increased the possibilities for comparative criminal-statistical studies that were more thorough than those of Ducpétiaux. In 1864, for example, Guerry published his renowned *Statistique morale de l'Angleterre comparée avec la statistique morale de la France* [*Moral Statistics of England Compared with the Moral Statistics of France*]. But studies such as *Die Gesetzmäßigkeit im Gesellschaftsleben* [*Regularity in Social Life*] (1877) by the German criminal statistician Georg von Mayr would have been unthinkable without the work of the moral statisticians from Belgium and France. Quetelet and Von Mayr in fact corresponded for decades about the best scientific approach to studying crime and the criminal justice system.

4.4.3.1. Quetelet's Life and Ideas

To understand why Quetelet, specifically, could become such an important forerunner of contemporary (criminal) sociology, one should at least know that he received his doctorate in mathematics at the University of Ghent in 1819 and that he spent a long period in Paris, from 1823 to 1824, amidst mathematicians, astronomers and statisticians, preparing for the establishment of an astronomical observatory in Brussels. In those surroundings, he also learned how mathematics and statistics could be applied to demographic data. This explains why he wrote

---

[72] Melchers 1992, pp. 13–17, 135–140.

a treatise for the Royal Academy in 1827 on the development of the population of the United Kingdom of the Netherlands.

However, it was also that treatise that put him on track towards the study of crime and the criminal justice system, namely by analysing the evolution of the populations of prisons and institutions housing beggars. His appointment in 1828 as director of the observatory did not mean that he abandoned the study of social issues. Quite the contrary, because in 1829 he was again involved in the publication of *Recherches statistiques sur le Royaume des Pays-Bas* [*Statistical Inquiries on the Kingdom of the Netherlands*] – the first of which had been published in 1827, also with his involvement – which paid a great deal of attention to the handling of criminal cases by the various courts. In 1831, he published for the first time his ground-breaking ideas on the causes of crime, *Recherches sur le penchant au crime* [*Inquiries on the Tendency to Crime*].[73]

Quetelet explained in a coherent manner how social physics, sociology, should be practised in his book *Du système social et des lois qui le régissent* [*On the Social System and the Laws that Rule It*] (1848).[74] This book makes it clear that he did not think that the methods of Lavater and Gall should be pursued. He greatly valued the work of the latter ("*un monument scientifique du mérite le plus incontestable*" – a scientific monument of the most indisputable value) but he considered its empirical basis to be weak. He also respected Lavater, finding a great deal of truth in his observations; they were not, however, scientifically based. What then did Quetelet consider to be the proper scientific method? That, he believed, was to study people on the basis of their deeds and to trace the effects back to their causes. The field in which he wished to prioritise the application of this method was that of *statistique morale* and consequently also of criminal statistics, because the latter formed an important component of the former. In other words, what Quetelet wanted to do was trace the laws that govern people's morals.

Did that mean denying that one had free will? That was certainly not the view of Quetelet. However, he immediately added that he considered that free will plays only a limited role in social phenomena, merely that of a "*cause accidentelle*" (accidental cause) alongside other random causes (such as natural disasters and famines), and that the consequences of such causes always neutralised one another in the case of large numbers of observations (the law of large numbers). What then are the causes that do have a decisive influence on social phenomena? On one hand, there are constant causes – by which Quetelet means the climate, the course of the rivers, the arrangement of the mountains, and the location of the sea – and on the other there are variable causes – which include public opinion, which extols at morn what it denigrates at eve.

---

73   Quetelet 1831; Dupréel 1942; Dupréel 1977.
74   Quetelet 1848.

Quetelet also assumed that every social system is subject, like physical bodies, to two kinds of forces, those of attraction and repulsion, and that it is therefore very difficult to keep a social system in equilibrium. In that connection, he referred to the role of political revolutions, such as the French Revolution, which always lead to a certain loss of live resources and that are in that sense always calamitous if we fail to impart a useful twist. He made clear – we should remember that it was 1848, with revolutions imminent throughout Europe! – that he was by no means enamoured of such revolutions. They were only rarely absolutely necessary, for example the French Revolution, which was meant to throw off the burden of centuries of oppression of the people. But how many people had it not plunged into the abyss? Despite being a liberal, albeit one who owed much to William I, Quetelet even disagreed with the Belgian Revolution and was sorely afraid of the consequences that the division of the United Kingdom of the Netherlands would have for the population of Belgium.[75] Similarly, he was very averse to philanthropy for the many poor persons who left their firesides and devoted themselves to vagrancy and begging. To counter this, one ought to organise mutual assistance between people, set up insurance companies, and develop savings banks. On that point, Quetelet therefore held positions close to those of Ducpétiaux.

How did Quetelet then wish to study morals? He wished to do so through the theory of averages, and in particular the fiction of the "*homme moyen*" (average man), an abstract being who finds himself "*dans un état d'équilibre entre tous les individus du même âge*" (in a state of balance between all the individuals of the same age). Take, for example, the tendency towards crime. The extent admittedly fluctuates somewhat but never becomes extreme. That is for the simple reason that the majority of people comply with the law and are not inclined to commit crime. In the light of this reasoning, it is less strange than it seems that Quetelet emphasises, a bit further on, that most of a country's crime is perpetrated by only a few families. He did not even rule out hereditary defects being involved, for in some families wickedness was passed on from generation to generation. One might think that at the individual level, Quetelet's views were therefore not far removed from those of Gall and Esquirol. That was not the level, however, at which he wished to study the problems of crime and the criminal. His level was the social level or the level of society.

4.4.3.2. Quetelet's Principles for Studying Crime and the Criminal

We have already seen how Quetelet made clear statements in various publications in the late 1820s and early 1830s regarding the problems of crime and the criminal justice system. He integrated those statements in the standard work that he published in 1835, *Sur l'homme et le développement de ses facultés ou*

---

[75]   Bartier 1977.

essai de physique sociale [*On Man and the Development of his Capacities, or Essay on Social Physics*], an expanded version of which he brought out in 1869 with the title *Physique sociale ou essai sur le développement des facultés de l'homme* [*Social Physics, or Essay on the Development of Man's Capacities*].[76] Right at

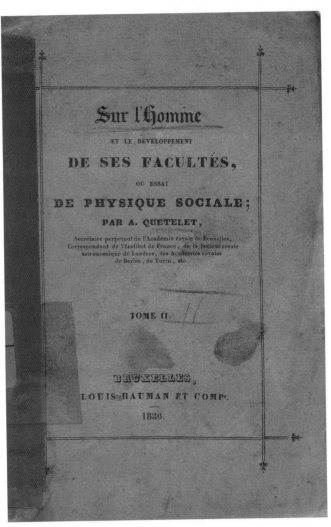

Adolphe QUETELET, *Sur l'homme et le développement de ses facultés ou essai de physique sociale*, Brussels, Hauman, 1836.

the beginning of that book he made it clear that he considered crime and the criminal justice system to be important social issues. Referring to French and Belgian criminal statistics, he noted that the number of crimes remained more

---

76   Quetelet 1835; Quetelet 1869.

or less the same year on year, both in general and according to category (for example the number of murders). He attached the important policy-related conclusion to that finding that money was paid out each year, with appalling regularity, for prisons and scaffolds.

Quetelet therefore concluded that this phenomenon should not be attributed so much to the individual perpetrators but to the way society was organised. That not only contained the seeds of all the crimes committed but also the conditions under which those seeds could flourish. It was therefore actually society that prepared those crimes, with the perpetrator being nothing more than the instrument that carried them out. In Quetelet's view, this was not a discouraging conclusion because it served to demonstrate that it was possible to improve people and their institutions. To do so in a targeted manner, it was necessary, however, to acquire a greater understanding of the organisation of society and thus of the laws that govern it. In his view, that meant above all studying the effects of both natural and human causes on a person's development. That, he believed, would allow one to discover the foundations of what might be termed "*physique sociale*", i.e. the study of the complex of laws that determine the organisation of life within society.

Whether this mechanistic view of the causation and combatting of crime should be read as a veiled criticism of French and Dutch rule, as some claim, is open to question. Nowhere does Quetelet himself in fact suggest such criticism.[77] What is clear, however, is that such a view as his is difficult to reconcile with the notion of individual responsibility as applied in criminal law, even if one does not deny the existence of free will at the individual level. Because what does free will amount to if people are actually no more than mere instruments of the social order? Quetelet's mechanistic view of social phenomena and how they should be studied is unavoidably associated with a deterministic view of human behaviour. This raised the prospect of a full-scale conflict between traditional thinking regarding the criminal law and modern criminology. Quetelet himself did not point out such a conflict, however.

Quetelet set out his main ideas about crime and criminal justice in the second part of this book, in the context of his thoughts on the moral and intellectual qualities of man, Chapter III, entitled *Développement du penchant au crime* [*Development of the Tendency to Crime*]. In this extremely important chapter, he first deals with crime and its suppression in general. The subsequent sections are devoted to the influence of all kinds of factors on the "*penchant au crime*", the tendency towards crime, i.e. upbringing, education and occupation, climate, seasons, gender, and age.

At the beginning of this chapter, Quetelet first defines what he means by "*penchant au crime*" (tendency to crime). For him – assuming that all people

---

[77]   Tixhon 1997.

find themselves in the same circumstances – it means the greater or lesser likelihood of someone committing a crime. He immediately adds that by the same circumstances he means the same in two respects, namely the presence of objects that stimulate temptation and the opportunity to commit the crime. In other words, it is not enough for someone to want to commit a crime: he must also have the opportunity and the means for doing so. In the later version of his book he introduces a distinction between "*penchant apparent*" (apparent tendency) and "*penchant réel*" (real tendency). By the first, he means the likelihood that can be deduced from the volume of crime of which the authorities are aware, and by the second the likelihood that a great deal more crime has been committed but just how much more is unknown. Without using the term, Quetelet here touches on the problem of the "dark number", i.e. the amount of crime that remains unknown. He is well aware that this constitutes a major problem, so much so that criminal statistics would be of no value whatsoever if one did not tacitly accept that there is a somewhat fixed relationship between the number of offences that are known and for which the offender has been convicted and the unknown total number of offences actually committed.

According to Quetelet, the extent of the difference between known and actual crime will vary according to the nature and gravity of the various offences, people's readiness to report them, and the action taken by the police and judicial authorities. That difference will be small in the case of murder and manslaughter but large in that of theft and other less serious offences. Quetelet was therefore well aware of the effect of the interaction between offenders, victims, and police on crime statistics. However, he had not yet developed any methods for clarifying the total amount of crime committed, for example victim or perpetrator surveys.

4.4.3.3. Quetelet's Explanations of the Nature, Extent, and Development of Crime

To understand how Quetelet worked, we need to look at his analysis of the crime figures for both the French *départements* and the Dutch provinces, adjusted for an incorrect count of the population and an uneven level of suppression. He finds that the greatest number of offences against the person and against property are committed in the *départements* around the Rhone, the Rhine and the Seine, with the least number being in the *départements* in central France, along the Atlantic coast, and in northern France. He also notes that in the southern *départements* there are more offences against the person, and in the northern provinces – such as the industrial and commercial provinces of the Netherlands – more offences against property.

How can these differences be explained? Quetelet avoids giving a general answer to that question because for many different offences there are numerous different factors that may play a role. It seems to him that climate itself does not play any major role, given the fact, for example, that the crime figures vary widely between *départements* with a similar climate. As regards education, he hesitates to assign it a particular role because, he now says, what is relevant is perhaps not education as much as moral development.

Poverty is also not necessarily a decisive factor because in some poor areas the level of crime is actually very low. Poverty cannot therefore be the underlying problem in absolute terms but perhaps in relative terms, i.e. poverty as people feel or experience it. In provinces such as the rural Luxembourg, most people can provide for themselves in a secure manner, so that inequality in wealth is felt less sharply and there is thus less temptation to commit crime. It is in busy industrial areas such as Flanders, Holland, and Paris – where large fortunes are built up but where thousands of people may find themselves on the street from one day to the next due to all kinds of market trends – that one finds the major differences and inequalities that cause crime. The decisive reason why the number of property crimes is increasing in the north of France, Flanders, and Holland, he believes, is therefore the unequal distribution of wealth and basic necessities.

Quetelet also attaches a great deal of importance to the factor of race, because no matter how important civilisation is, it can hardly change the character of a people, if at all. Members of the "Pelagic" race, who live mainly in the south of France and in Corsica, commit offences primarily – he says – against the person, while Frisians and the Dutch, who belong to the Germanic race, mainly commit offences against property.

Quetelet also considers gender a very important factor, given that far fewer women are hauled up before the criminal courts than men, with only 23 women for every 100 men. His explanation for this is to be found in his theory (already referred to) that three conditions need to be met for a crime to be committed: *"le vouloir, qui dépend de la moralité, l'occasion et la facilité d'agir"* (the will, which depends on morality, opportunity, and the ability to act). But what is it that makes women far less prone to committing crime than men? In Quetelet's view, it is because they are prevented from doing so by their sense of shame, by social dependence, and by the limited opportunity that they consequently have to commit crime, as well as by their lack of physical strength. Where their role in violent crime, in particular, is concerned, Quetelet believes that the differences to that of men are above all due to the fact that a woman's life largely takes place within the circle of her family and she is therefore less exposed to alcohol abuse and quarrels than a man. He therefore links the role of women in crime in plain terms to their place in society. In that sense, incidentally, lower-class women resemble lower-class men more in their habits than men and women in the higher classes resemble one another. For that reason too, lower-class women find themselves in court more frequently.

What is of the utmost importance – Quetelet believes – is the factor of age, more specifically because someone's physical powers and passions increase with age, and likewise because reason increases with age and also continues to increase as physical powers and passions decline again. He concludes from this that the tendency towards crime in very young and very old people should be practically zero and is at its maximum at the age when physical powers and passions are also at their peak and reason has not yet been able to gain sufficient control over them. On the basis of the available statistics, he concludes that in men the tendency towards committing crime is greatest at about the age of 25 and in women at about 30. His explanation for this difference is that women embark on a criminal career later and also abandon it sooner.

In his final major work, *Anthropométrie ou mesure des différentes facultés de l'homme* [*Anthropometry or Measurement of the Different Capacities of Man*] (1871), Quetelet added nothing new to what he had written about crime and the criminal justice system since the 1830s.[78] He confines himself to repeating moves on his scientific chessboard. In concluding, he merely emphasises strongly once more that the criminal statistics show that people in general instinctively comply with the laws of society and do not question them.

4.5. EVOLUTIONARY AND REVOLUTIONARY THINKERS ON CRIME, CRIMINALS, AND THE COMBATTING OF CRIME

When discussing the phrenological and psychiatric approaches, we saw that many authors freely and easily used terms such as degeneration and heredity in defining and explaining the phenomena that they observed. In most cases, however, they ignored what such terms mean precisely, how the associated processes actually take place, and what underlying causes they are based on. In the mid-nineteenth century, however, there was a shift in thinking that had a major influence on later criminology.

This shift is most clearly embodied by Charles Darwin and his theory of the origin of species. But Darwin was not the only important contemporary researcher in the field of evolutionary theory who wrote about the issues that are central to the present book. Especially in connection with the theories of Gall, Esquirol and Prichard, we must not ignore the work of the French psychiatrist Bénédict Morel.

The writings of these evolutionary thinkers were succeeded, almost as a matter of course, by those of revolutionary thinkers. But why as a matter of course? It was because their criticism of contemporary social circumstances was often similar to that of people like Morel. They did not differ much on that point. Where they did differ was mainly on the matter of the reforms that would need to be implemented to put an end to the abuses.

That is clearest from the work of Karl Marx and Friedrich Engels, to mention just two of the leading contemporary advocates – certainly viewed in

---

[78] Quetelet 1871.

retrospect – of radical social reforms. Whereas Morel clearly favoured gradual adjustments within the existing power structures, the Marxists were striving for revolutionary upheavals in the political system. That difference explains why a close watch was kept on them – but not on Morel – by the political police throughout Western Europe.

4.5.1. TWO EVOLUTIONARY THINKERS: BÉNÉDICT MOREL AND CHARLES DARWIN

4.5.1.1. Morel's Degeneration Thesis

Morel's most influential book was his *Traité des dégénérescenses physiques, intellectuelles et morales de l'espèce humaine et des causes qui produuent ces variétés maladives* [*Treatise on the Physical, Intellectual and Moral Degenerations of the Human Species and on the Causes that Produce these Morbid Varieties*] (1857).[79] As the title already indicates, Morel was thinking not so much in terms of individuals as of whole groups. It is also clear that he placed his views in an evolutionary context. The psychiatrist can be recognised, however, in his use of the adjective "*maladives*" (morbid); Morel therefore considered manifestations of degeneration to be pathological problems.

The fact that Morel nevertheless broke away from the individual patient and concerned himself with the social conditions in which large groups of people had to live was the result of a very pessimistic view of the world around him: crime continued to rise, criminals were getting ever younger, and the number of suicides was also increasing. It should be noted immediately, however, that later in the book Morel hardly talks about crime and criminals as such. Repeatedly, he in fact makes no distinction between criminals and the mentally disturbed, as if there were no difference between the two categories. This is unsurprising given that in medical circles criminals had often been equated in preceding decades with sick people.

The starting point for Morel's actual argument is his definition of the term degeneration, by which he means a pathological deviation from the normal type of person. He leaves aside, however, just what constitutes the latter, suggesting only that everyone has an idea of what that means. He also emphasises that cases of degeneration can admittedly be very different to one another but that they all display a certain mutual cohesion in one way or another: physical degeneration is usually accompanied by moral degeneration and the latter in turn by degeneration of an intellectual nature, as the title of the book in fact implies. In Morel's view, the link between degeneration phenomena and human evolution is

---

[79]   Morel 1857.

generally the result of hereditary transmission but in entirely different and much more difficult circumstances than those in which the normal laws of heredity operate. In certain circles of the population, this genetic transmission leads, from generation to generation, to a special organic condition that provides an increasingly favourable breeding ground for ever more far-reaching degeneration phenomena through the effects of all kinds of external causes.

The greater part of Morel's book is subsequently devoted to an exhaustive description of those causes and of the degeneration phenomena which he believes result from them. Among the primary physical causes discussed are all sorts of poisons – in particular alcohol (i.e. its abuse), but also hashish, opium, and tobacco – toxic substances, food shortages, and infectious diseases. Morel ascribes the primary social causes in particular to the harsh conditions prevailing in the industrial centres, especially mining districts. Based on reports of all kinds, he depicts the physical exploitation of the workers and their children, the deterioration of their bodies, the total lack of proper housing, appalling undernourishment, lack of education and training, etc. The alarming rise in serious crime committed by children under the age of 15 is, in Morel's view, one of the most effective indicators of the degeneration process taking place at that time in the cities and regions of the kingdom. This was because he saw these children as so many manifestations of the degeneration that was fatally undermining the intellectual, physical, and moral health of the population.

To reverse this trend, the lower working classes could not be left to their own devices. After all, on their own they would never be able to participate in the progress of the higher classes. The latter needed to concern themselves with the lot of the lower classes by tackling the manifold causes of degeneration. How should they do so? By instilling morality in the lower classes and by improving them intellectually and physically. With this multi-faceted approach, Morel was explicitly turning against unilaterally economic solutions such as increasing the material welfare of the masses, believing that such a unilateral approach to regenerating the masses had far too many risks for future generations. He does not specify just what those risks actually are. He does clearly resist the idea, however, that society will have done enough by merely punishing the perpetrators of offences and by preventing the mentally ill from disturbing the social order.

That view is entirely in line with the *traitement moral* advocated by Esquirol and applied in prisons by Ducpétiaux. Morel does not offer any opinion on what general preventive measures should be imposed. Apparently, he did not really know because, after all, the moralisation of the masses was "*une science encore toute nouvelle*" (a completely new science).

4.5.1.2. *Darwin's Theory of Natural Selection*

The book that immediately made Darwin (1809–82) world-famous appeared in 1859 (two years after the treatise by Morel): *On the Origin of Species by Means of*

Natural Selection, or the Preservation of Favoured Races in the Struggle for Life.[80] Where Morel concerned himself in particular with those population groups that had lost, or were threatened with losing, in the struggle for existence, Darwin focused especially on those groups that had survived or seemed to be surviving. It should be noted immediately, however, that Darwin – unlike Morel – initially only projected his ideas onto the world of plants and animals. The influence of evolutionary theory in the *Philosophie zoologique* [*Zoological Philosophy*] (1809) of Jean-Baptiste Lamarck – i.e. that new needs of an organism are translated into the development of new organs which are then transmitted to the organism's offspring by heredity – was for good reason one of the main sources of his theory.

Nor is it surprising that in *The Descent of Man, and Selection in Relation to Sex* (1871), Darwin also applied this theory in full to humans. One of his other primary intellectual sources was, after all, the *Essay on the Principle of Population* (1798) by Thomas Malthus, in which the author states that the food supply will always lag behind population growth and thus will lead to major conflicts between nations and people unless growth is curbed by war, famine, disease, or voluntary birth control. Moreover, as everyone knows, Darwin's voyage to South America aboard the *Beagle* (1831–36) also played a major role in the formulation of his theory of evolution.

The essence of his theory was that plant and animal species come in countless varieties with slight differences to one another. The features of one variety therefore make it more suited than another to adapting to the "economy of nature"; thus that variety becomes the dominant one and not only displaces less suitable varieties but again produces new dominant varieties. Because the world does not offer a place for all dominant varieties simultaneously, "the most dominant will beat the less dominant". In other words, in "the struggle for life", the basic rule is therefore "the survival of the fittest".

In *The Descent of Man*, Darwin extended this line of thought to mankind, defending in that work the position that certain races are superior to others. He clearly meant by this that the civilised peoples of the Western world were superior to the barbaric or savage peoples elsewhere. He was also in no doubt that those civilised peoples were in the process of supplanting the others and that that process – as with plants and animals – constituted an entirely natural process (of selection). This was because they were in general better equipped to adapt to their environment and quite naturally prevailed in the struggle for life. Darwin also did not doubt that man was descended "from a hairy, tailed quadruped, probably arboreal in its habits, and an inhabitant of the old world".[81] He considered that the inferior nature of the uncivilised peoples was, inter alia,

---

80   Darwin 1968, pp. 114–172.
81   Darwin 1871.

due to their "low morality" in the social context, although he did note that the morality and thus strength of civilised peoples was also under increasing pressure because "the reckless, degraded, and often vicious members of society, tend to increase at a quicker rate than the provident and generally virtuous members". This was counterbalanced – fortunately, according to Darwin himself and others – by "the constant elimination of imperfect types":

> Malefactors are executed, or imprisoned for long periods, so that they cannot freely transmit their bad qualities. Melancholic and insane persons are confined, or commit suicide. Violent and quarrelsome men often come to a bloody end. The restless who will not follow any steady occupation – and this relic of barbarism is a great check to civilisation – emigrate to newly-settled countries, where they prove useful pioneers.[82]

In Darwin's view, in other words, the criminal justice system played a major positive role in the struggle of civilised peoples for their survival on earth because it brought about the elimination of those who threatened their dominant position.

4.5.2. TWO REVOLUTIONARY THINKERS: KARL MARX AND FRIEDRICH ENGELS

Marx and Engels did not deal directly with issues of crime and the criminal justice system. They used those issues mainly to illustrate or demonstrate their general views on social developments and the need for a complete restructuring of the political system in order to lead it in a better direction.[83] It is nevertheless relevant to mention their comments here, on the one hand so as to demonstrate the contrast between their ideas and those of reformers such as Ducpétiaux and Morel. On the other, it is because they also influenced the practice of criminology in the later communist states of Europe and, moreover, played a role in the "neo-Marxist criminology" which caught on in the 1960s and 1970s in certain university circles in North America and Western Europe.[84]

In *Das Kapital*, Marx describes vividly how – on the one hand through the decline of the feudal structures and the expulsion of masses of people from the land that was once common property, and on the other through the inability of the emerging modern industries to absorb the masses – countless people in the seventeenth and eighteenth centuries were forced to provide for themselves through begging, theft, and vagrancy "partly from inclination, in most cases from stress of circumstances".[85] Moreover, the criminal legislation against

---

[82] Darwin 1871, p. 172.
[83] Greenberg 1993, pp. 11–13.
[84] Digneffe 1995.
[85] Greenberg 1993, pp. 45–48.

vagrancy and begging treated them as common criminals and it was assumed that it was a matter of their own will whether or not they undertook work under conditions that in fact no longer existed.

In other words, Marx is here asserting not only the thesis that crime is a consequence of the changing ownership and production relationships but also suggesting that the perpetrators are criminalised via the criminal law in order to preserve those relationships. In other works, Marx elaborates on the latter suggestion, for example in contributions to the renowned *Rheinische Zeitung* in 1842, in which he refers to the new criminal legislation on the gathering of firewood as a form of usurpation of power by landowners to protect their own interests.[86]

Engels took Marx's arguments further in his equally renowned book *The Condition of the Working Class in England*, where he attributes the deplorable conditions in which the English working class found itself in the nineteenth century to the flourishing of the capitalist system and the class struggle associated with it.[87] It was these abuses that had led to a situation in which the workers had no option other than to become criminals: "If the demoralisation of the worker passes beyond a certain point then it is just as natural that he will turn into a criminal – as inevitably as water turns into steam at boiling point." In England, Engels argued, that point had just about been reached: "Consequently the incidence of crime has increased with the growth of the working-class population and there is more crime in Britain than in any other country in the world." For Engels, this was proof that social warfare was proceeding full tilt and was slowly but surely developing into "combat between two great opposing camps – the middle classes and the proletariat". For him, acts of violence by the workers against the bourgeoisie were therefore purely "frank and undisguised retaliation for the thefts and treacheries perpetrated by the middle classes against the workers". Such offences were for Engels, in other words, expressions of individual protest and individual animosity against those classes. But they were unsuccessful and unintelligent expressions because:

> the mighty forces of society were hurled against the individual law-breaker and crushed him with their overwhelming power. In addition theft was the blindest and most stupid form of protest and consequently this never became the universal expression of the workers' reaction to industrialisation, although many workers doubtless sympathised privately with those who broke the law.[88]

The only proper answer was in fact collective struggle, the organisation of parties and trade unions, etc. Engels therefore considered not only the criminal law as

---

[86] Linebaugh 1993, pp. 100–121.
[87] Greenberg 1993, pp. 48–50.
[88] Greenberg 1993, p. 50.

such but also the criminal justice system, with all its institutions, as a weapon wielded by the propertied classes in the class struggle.

In the light of these ideas, it goes without saying that Marx and Engels – quite unlike Ducpétiaux and Morel, for example – did not pin their hopes for improvement of the lot of the proletariat on the upper classes, with which the proletariat was engaged in a struggle of life and death. In the *Manifest der Kommunistischen Partei* (1848), Marx therefore scorns the "bourgeois socialism" of philanthropists and other benefactors. In his view, that kind of socialism is intended merely to redress social abuses and thus ensure the survival of bourgeois society. That aim, he asserts, is best expressed in the rhetoric of his followers:

> Free trade: for the benefit of the working class. Protective duties: for the benefit of the working class. Prison Reform: for the benefit of the working class. This is the last word and the only seriously meant word of bourgeois socialism. It is summed up in the phrase: the bourgeois is a bourgeois – for the benefit of the working class.[89]

True socialists choose the path of revolution: the proletariat can only elevate itself by blasting official society apart.[90] In the communist society that could thus be established and in which, according to Engels, social peace would replace social warfare, crime would decrease all by itself:

> Crimes against property cease of their own accord where everyone receives what he needs to satisfy his natural and his spiritual urges, where social gradations and distinctions cease to exist.[91]

Moreover, in a society "in which community of interests has become the basic principle, and in which the public interest is no longer distinct from that of each individual" the police and judicial authorities would be well-nigh superfluous. Anyone who is aware of the police states founded in the name of communism in the twentieth century realises, of course, that this idyll cannot be taken seriously. The communist idyll that Engels sketches can to some extent be seen as the counterpart to Marx's satirical story about the productive power of the criminal in a capitalist society.

The criminal, Marx wrote, produces not only crime but also the criminal law, the professor who teaches criminal law, and the textbooks on criminal law that earn significant profits for that professor. And that is not all: the criminal also

---

[89]   Marx and Engels 1966, 3, p. 83.
[90]   Marx and Engels 1966, 3, pp. 59–86.
[91]   Greenberg 1993, p. 51.

produces the entire policing and judicial system and all those novels and plays that revolve around crime:

> The criminal interrupts the monotony and security of bourgeois life. Thus he protects it from stagnation and brings forth that restless tension, that mobility of spirit without which the stimulus of competition would itself become blunted. He therefore gives a new impulse to the productive forces. Crime takes off the labour market a portion of the excess population, diminishes competition among workers, and to a certain extent stops wages from falling below the minimum, while the war against crime absorbs another part of the same population. The criminal therefore appears as one of those natural "equilibrating forces" which establish a just balance and open up a whole perspective of "useful" occupations.[92]

This can in fact be demonstrated in detail. Without thieves, the locksmith trade would never have attained its present perfection! Without forgers the microscope would never have entered into ordinary commercial life!

> Crime, by its ceaseless development of new means of attacking property calls into existence new measures of defence, and its productive effects are as great as those of strikers in stimulating the invention of machines.[93]

4.6. CONCLUSION

The developments that took place in the course of the nineteenth century in the criminal justice system on the one hand and in the study of crime, the criminal, and the combatting of crime on the other can hardly be described as anything other than complicated. Even so, some broad themes can be identified. These will be investigated below against the background of the developments that had occurred in the eighteenth century and in the French Period. That is the best way of making clear their continuity and discontinuity.

From an institutional perspective, what is of course immediately apparent is that in the course of the nineteenth century the death penalty, corporal punishment, and corporal punishment in public were in fact largely abolished, after much dispute, and generally replaced by imprisonment. But even with that victory, the struggle was still far from over, and moved on to the question of what form the prison system should take. And that struggle was also not easily fought and won. There was great aversion to communal undifferentiated confinement, but there was also major disagreement regarding the alternative, namely the

---

[92] See Elster 1999, pp. 320–321.
[93] See Elster 1999, pp. 320–321.

cellular prison. In many countries, debate on the various confinement systems dragged on for decades. There was in fact only a single country – Belgium – where a penitentiary system developed fully.

The development of policing was the subject of intellectual and political debate to a far lesser extent than the development of the prison system. It was also not linked to the adoption of new codes of criminal procedure, although such a link had been supported by some. The further development of the police system along the lines already laid out before the French Revolution was tied far more – and far more directly – to changes in power (or the threat of such) on the occasion of coups d'état and revolutions than was the development of the prison system. This naturally had a lot to do with the fact that the police system, given its duties, powers and resources, was always involuntarily in the firing line of political power struggles, while the prison system was less closely involved. The best evidence for this is the formation of tightly organised urban police forces, the reinforcement of national police forces (whether or not military), the establishment of special riot squads, and the creation of special intelligence services.

But it is not going too far to suggest that the prison system too was expanded in order to cope with the threat from the masses of paupers in the cities and in rural areas, and especially the hard core among them: the subculture of professional criminals. One must bear in mind, however, that whereas the prison system throughout Europe had since the eighteenth century been tailored entirely to controlling that hard core, it was only in the mid-nineteenth century that the policing system in most countries began to professionalise its investigative function on the French model.

There is also no doubt that the strong institutionalisation that the criminal justice system underwent by the modernisation of the police system and the renewal of the prison system significantly promoted the study of crime, the criminal, and the combatting of crime. The prison system as well as the police system not only had a greater need for knowledge of the problems and people that they had to deal with but also created the opportunity to acquire that knowledge in a simple manner. The emergence and flourishing of crime statistics is virtually a model for this double movement: they provided both better insight for policymakers and an important research resource for scientists.

The irony is that the emergence of the scientific study of crime, criminals, and the combatting of crime was to some extent a threat to the criminal law and the criminal justice system as they had developed. The *homo bio-psychologicus* of the phrenologists and psychiatrists was clearly at odds with the *homo economicus* whom the enlightened thinkers had in mind, and certainly also at odds with the penitent of the penal reformers. But Quetelet's *homo sociologicus* was also difficult to reconcile with these ideological abstractions. It is not therefore surprising that the confrontation between these images of the criminal greatly burdened the discussion about the revision of the criminal law and often led to compromises in the application of the penalty of imprisonment. For Darwin, incidentally, this would all have been unnecessary. He viewed a severe criminal justice system precisely as a significant means of maintaining the dominance of the white race in the world.

It is also important to note that even the staunchest defenders of the criminal justice system were in fact aware of its merely relative character when it came to addressing the major social problems –as crime undoubtedly was in their eyes – that manifested themselves at the time. Hence it was not only prison reformers but also crime experts of all kinds who called for radical social reforms in order to bring those problems under control in a preventive manner. Indeed, they not only advocated such reforms but also – as in the case of Ducpétiaux – made enormous efforts to implement them. A not insignificant point is, however, that they wanted to do so within the existing political power structures and explicitly counted on the support of the upper classes. That was because they were diametrically opposed to the revolutionary thinkers who had absolutely no faith in the upper classes, viewed the criminal justice system as a weapon in the class struggle, and called for radical reform of the political system. Where the evolutionary reformers were often undecided as to what extent certain interventions in the political and socio-economic system would lead to a decrease in crime, the revolutionary reformers offered their followers the prospect of a world without crime. That utopia was naturally enticing.

Finally, it should be borne in mind that the developments described in this chapter were to some extent transatlantic developments. As regards the prison system, it has already become clear that its evolution in Europe was very much influenced by the prison models in vogue in the United States. Conversely, the development of the urban police was to a significant extent influenced by the example of the police reorganisation in London in 1830, an example that was very much imitated in continental Europe. And with a view to the reception of the subsequent criminology in the United States, we must also not overlook the fact that a certain amount of transatlantic interaction got underway not only at institutional level but also in the scientific arena. The theories of Gall, in particular, were well received on the other side of the Atlantic.

CHAPTER 5
ESTABLISHMENT OF CRIMINOLOGY
IN ITALY AND FRANCE

5.1. INTRODUCTION

The previous chapter explained how in the course of the nineteenth century –
in part influenced by the further development of the criminal justice

system – authors increasingly wrote about the problems of crime and the combatting of crime, from very different perspectives. In the final two decades of the century, the European literature on these topics increased well-nigh explosively. That enormous growth in the number of publications is not the only difference, however, in the way this field of study had developed in the preceding decades. Another important difference is that, around the turn of the nineteenth century, this domain increasingly took on the form of a separate scientific discipline, namely criminology. The academic institutionalisation of this field manifested itself, inter alia, in the establishment of specialised journals, the founding of new associations, the organisation of dedicated national and international conferences, the publication of specific primers, and the establishment of special university chairs. The man who provided the decisive impulse for the "scientisation" of criminology was undoubtedly Cesare Lombroso. He is quite rightly considered the founder of the discipline.

It is therefore an obvious step for us to begin by devoting ample attention to the views that Lombroso expressed from 1876 on – when the first edition appeared of his renowned *Trattato antropologico sperimentale dell'Uomo Delinquente studiato in rapporto all'antropologia, alla medicina legale e alla discipline carcerarie* [*Anthropological and Experimental Treatise on the Criminal Man Studied in Relation to Anthropology, Legal Medicine and Prison Science*] (usually abbreviated to *Uomo delinquente*) – about the criminal individual and the struggle that Lombroso waged in order to have these views taken seriously in both the scientific and political worlds.[1] But in his homeland of Italy, Lombroso was not alone, and references were already made at the time to the "Italian", "Positive", and also "Anthropological" School of criminology. Lombroso's main associates within that school were the lawyers Enrico Ferri and Raffaele Garofalo. Their work cannot therefore be ignored here, if only to show that the term "school" should not be taken too literally: the opinions of Lombroso, Ferri, and Garofalo in fact differed considerably on a number of points.

It is therefore unsurprising that reactions to Lombroso's ideas were also quite varied outside Italy, with most of the criticism being in France. However, that criticism was half-hearted and ambiguous because it was to some extent dictated as much by intense nationalist feelings as by significant systematic differences. Nevertheless, reference has been made to an alternative to the Italian School, namely the "French School", "Sociological School", or "Environmental School". This French School was even less of a school than was the Italian School. Its leader was the physician Alexandre Lacassagne, who enjoyed the indirect support of the lawyer Gabriel Tarde and also, at a much greater remove, of the sociologist Émile Durkheim. Their views on the personality of the offender and on the nature and development of crime problems will be dealt with below to the same extent as those of the main figures of the Italian School.

---

1   Lombroso-Ferrero 1915.

Following on from this introduction, we will consider how in both cases criminology was incorporated into the university systems in the two countries. In the case of France, we will also go more deeply into the development by Alphonse Bertillon of anthropometry and, more broadly, "scientific police". Although due attention was paid to these subjects in criminology education in Italy, there was no innovator in the field of criminal investigation in that country who could measure up to any real extent to Bertillon.

5.2. ITALIAN SCHOOL: CESARE LOMBROSO, ENRICO FERRI, AND RAFFAELE GAROFALO

Why the school of criminology founded by Lombroso is referred to as the Italian School is obvious. Less obvious, though, is why it is also sometimes called the Positive School. That name derives from the fact that its leaders assumed that it was only through empirical research – i.e. research based on meticulous study of the facts – that one could understand the phenomenon of crime.[2] The adjective "anthropological" reflects the perspective from which that school pursued such research: the required understanding could only be acquired through meticulous study of the personality of the offender, meaning not just his physique but also his psyche. The criminal too was, as an individual, one and indivisible.[3]

These more detailed descriptions of the Italian School of criminology already make clear that the basic principles of its leaders were at odds with those of that other great Italian thinker, Beccaria. In a series of lectures that Ferri gave at the University of Naples in 1901, he praised Beccaria as a revolutionary thinker but at the same time accused the Classical School of criminal law of having lost its way in abstractions and illusions about the extent to which people were free to determine their behaviour (whether or not criminal), about the assumptions and purposes of punishment, and about the applicability of the basic rules for sentencing.[4] In support of these views, Ferri argued that crime in Italy had assumed unprecedented proportions, concluding that the Classical School had been unable to fulfil its promises.

The credo of the new Italian School was that a proper understanding of the personality of the offender was necessary in order to fully understand his crime.[5] That credo was propagated especially in the journal founded in 1880 by Lombroso, together with Ferri and Garofalo, the *Archivio di Psichiatria e Antropologia Criminale*. That title shows clearly how in the Italian School psychiatry and criminology were intertwined from the very outset.

---

[2]   Vervaele 1990, pp. 271–301.
[3]   Horn 2003, pp. 6–16.
[4]   Ferri 1885; Grupp 1968, p. 45.
[5]   Grupp 1968, pp. 70–94.

Given Lombroso's background – he had trained as a physician and psychiatrist – that is unsurprising.

5.2.1. LOMBROSO'S NEW PARADIGM: THE ATAVISTIC CRIMINAL

Lombroso was born in Verona in 1835. He studied medicine not only at Italian universities but also at the University of Vienna. After completing his university studies in 1858–59, he served for several years as a physician in the Italian army. It was clear from the start that he was studious. During the 1860s, he investigated not only the physical features of Italian soldiers but also published his findings on the mentally disturbed. His research made him increasingly interested in both the characteristics of criminals and the differences and similarities between them, the mentally disturbed, and normal people. That interest led him to publish a number of articles in the early 1870s on the personality of the criminal. In 1876, he summarised his ideas on this matter in the aforementioned *Uomo delinquente*. He was also appointed professor of forensic psychiatry at the Faculty of Law of the University of Turin. At the same university, he was appointed to the chair of general psychiatry in 1896 and in 1900 to a full professorship in criminal anthropology.[6] In 1908–09, the first chairman of the American Institute of Criminal Law and Criminology, John Wigmore, offered Lombroso the post of visiting professor for the year 1909–10 at Northwestern University. He would have liked to have accepted but he in fact turned down the offer because his advanced age made him unwilling to risk the journey. Lombroso died on 19 October 1909.[7]

The first edition of his *magnum opus* did not attract much attention, either in Italy or abroad. However, the second edition, published in 1878 and much more extensive (740 pages instead of 252), unleashed a great wave of interest. Ferri asserted that this was because two other publications came out the same year. One was an article by Garofalo arguing that in future the danger posed by the offender should be the criterion for determining his punishment rather than the seriousness of the offence and/or his responsibility for his crime. The other was a book by Ferri himself asserting something similar, namely that free will does not exist and therefore that personal responsibility for crime does not exist either, and that – with a view to protecting society against crime – the science of crime and punishment should concern itself with the true nature of human and social life.[8] Nevertheless, Lombroso's book was a runaway success: the third Italian edition appeared in 1889 (two volumes, of 660 and 581 pages respectively) and

---

6   Kurella 1910, pp. 1–20; Wolfgang 1972.

7   Bondio 1995, pp. 18–51.

8   Sellin (T.) 1968; Martin, Mutchnick and Austin 1990, pp. 21–28.

the fifth and final Italian edition in 1896–97 (ultimately in three volumes with a total of 1,903 pages). The first translations of the book, into French (*L'Homme criminel*) and German (*Der Verbrecher*), both in 1887, led to the worldwide dissemination of Lombroso's ideas. An English translation of excerpts from the various editions was recently published.[9]

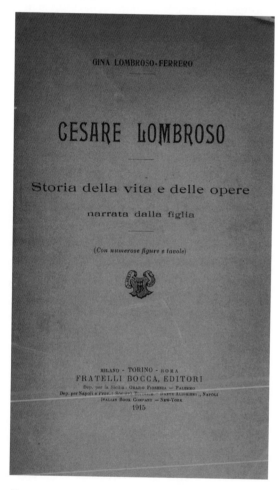

Gina Lombroso-Ferrero, *Cesare Lombroso: storia della vita e delle opere narrata dalla figlia*, Torino, Fratelli Bocca Editori, 1915.

Essentially, Lombroso's views mean that criminals are people whose personal development has not proceeded in the same way as the general evolution of the human species and who therefore exhibit all kinds of features (atavisms) of the human race as it was in the initial stages of its development.[10] How can these

---

[9]   Lombroso 2006, pp. 1–7.
[10]   Becker (P.) 1996.

present-day representatives of the earlier human race be recognised? How do they differ from normal people? It is noteworthy that with a view to answering these questions Lombroso succeeded to some extent in bringing together the main scientific theories and methods that had developed during the nineteenth century in order to better understand the problems of crime and the criminal. He looked back to Gall, i.e. to phrenology, for measurement of the skulls of criminals. He was inspired by Quetelet to carry out statistical research. And the theories of Darwin and other evolutionary biologists provided the basis for the role played in his ideas by atavism.

This integration of such varied theoretical and methodological perspectives caused confusion, particularly because Lombroso did not turn out to be particularly systematic in his writings. Nevertheless, their integration – as the sociologist of science Thomas Kuhn puts it[11] – led to the formulation of a new paradigm that has still not entirely disappeared in criminological research even today, namely that of the atavistic or born criminal. It is precisely for this reason that from the perspective of the history of science Lombroso can be described as a scientific revolutionary. The fact that his actual paradigm has now been largely abandoned does not of course alter the crucial role that he played in the establishment of criminology.[12]

In the first part of the (second) French translation of *Uomo delinquente* (the fifth edition) Lombroso explains in detail his views – in the meantime somewhat modified – on the atavistic criminal. The explanation comprises three parts: first the embryology of the criminal, second the pathological anatomy and anthropology, and third the biology and psychology.[13] Summarising briefly, this produces the following picture of the atavistic criminal.

When dealing with the embryology of the criminal, Lombroso goes deeply into crime and punishment among primitive peoples (*"les sauvages"* – savages). Based on various examples, he describes, inter alia, how they engaged in murder, manslaughter and cannibalism, concluding that as peoples become more civilised, the most hideous forms of these crimes decrease and, conversely, the more primitive the people, the more savage the crime. Parallel to this development in the realm of crime he believes that there has been a development in the field of punishment whereby brutal revenge has been replaced by more civilised forms of repression. The conclusion that Lombroso draws from these observations is no longer expressed in the form of a question. In his opinion, one can state as a fact that if crime persists among the most civilised peoples, then its true cause must be atavism.

That conclusion brings us to the second theme of his study, the anatomy and anthropology of the criminal. It is noteworthy that Lombroso commences

---

[11]   Kuhn 1970.
[12]   Becker (P.) 2002.
[13]   Lombroso 1895a and 1895b.

his description of these with a summary – one that is admittedly extremely muddled – of the findings derived from a study of the skulls of 383 criminals. He is rather disappointed by the fact that the average diameter, etc. of their skulls is in general no different to the skulls of normal people. However, the skulls of criminals – and of males rather than females – exhibit all sorts of anomalies,

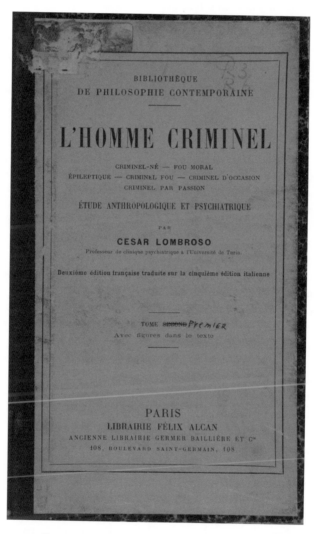

Cesare LOMBROSO, *L'homme criminel; étude anthropologique et psychiatrique*, Paris, Félix Alcan, 1895, 2 vol.

including a low, receding forehead, a small cranial capacity, very heavy eyebrow ridges, and curious wisdom teeth. In an appendix, Lombroso adds an "atlas" of the born criminal to enable the reader to investigate the truth of these assertions for himself. The atlas – which is truly astounding – includes all kinds of photos showing adult and juvenile offenders, as well as drawings of criminals and depictions of their tattoos.

What were Lombroso's findings in this second part of his study? From an anthropometric perspective, criminals, he asserts, are generally smaller in stature than ordinary people, have proportionally longer arms, exhibit on average more abnormalities of the hands and feet, generally have a smaller head but a longer face, have far more skull defects than average, and a smaller brain volume. There are exceptions, however. The brains of gang leaders, for example, are large and look very similar to those of distinguished persons. From a physiognomic perspective, Lombroso believes that criminals, and in particular born criminals, exhibit more than the average of all sorts of defects, for example of the ears, teeth, and nose. For him, it is clear that all these data show similarities between mentally ill persons, savages, and criminals. They also make it clear who the atavistic criminal is:

> *un homme anormal avant sa naissance, par l'arrêt du développement ou par maladie acquise de différents organes, surtout des centres nerveux, comme chez les aliénés; et en font un vrai malade chronique* (an abnormal man before his birth, as a consequence of the stagnation of development or as a consequence of a disease of the different organs, in particular the nerve centres, as in the case of the madmen; and make him a real chronic patient).[14]

In the third part of the study, Lombroso considers a number of topics that he considers highly significant for the biology and psychology of the kind of person who has been born a criminal: tattoos, the feelings and passions of criminals, their morality and intelligence, and the language, literature, and art of criminals. The fact that Lombroso, first and foremost, pays such a great deal of attention to tattoos has everything to do with his belief that they are worn so extensively by criminals because they are a kind of hieroglyphs expressing not only feelings of vindictiveness, cynicism, and sensuality but also of fellowship, for example among members of criminal organisations such as the Camorra.[15]

The feelings of an atavistic human are, according to Lombroso, characterised on the one hand by a lack of physical sensitivity and a high pain threshold reminiscent of savages. On the other hand, this physical insensitivity is accompanied by moral insensitivity, by a marked lack of compassion, and by outright cruelty towards others. He goes on to say that it would be wrong, however, to think that criminals have no feelings or passions whatsoever. Most of these have indeed disappeared but some remain, in particular vanity and capriciousness, vindictiveness and cruelty, blindness in matters of love, alcoholism and addiction to gambling. In this regard too, Lombroso concludes that criminals closely resemble the mentally ill.

---

14 Lombroso 1895, 1, p. 123.
15 Caplan 2006.

The above summary of Lombroso's *magnum opus* shows how he came to the conclusion that atavistic criminals do exist and what, according to him, they look like, not only biologically but also psychologically. This summary demonstrates that although Lombroso always tried to distinguish between normal, civilised people and these criminals, he was nevertheless forced to recognise repeatedly that the distinction was not always as absolute as he had originally claimed. On the one hand, not all criminals exhibited atavistic features to the same extent and there were even criminals who did not exhibit any at all. On the other hand, such criminals often had much in common, physically and psychologically, with the mentally ill; they were not therefore so entirely "distinct". Lombroso's negative comparison of atavistic criminals and "savages" naturally demonstrates the cultural and political bias that also plays such an important role in the work of Darwin. Effective control of atavistic criminals therefore automatically takes on the character of a fight to defend Western civilisation.[16]

However, before considering Lombroso's ideas about combatting crime, it is important to point out how he further elaborated on his paradigm, especially under pressure from the large amount of criticism directed at *Uomo delinquente* both at home and abroad. In that sense, he acted entirely in accordance with Kuhn's theory regarding the structure of scientific revolutions.[17]

5.2.2. TYPOLOGICAL AND DIFFERENTIAL ELABORATION ON THE PARADIGM

One can say that Lombroso elaborated his paradigm in two ways. He did so in the first place by working out a general typology of criminals on the basis of the concept of the atavistic criminal. He did this above all in his *magnum opus*, *Uomo delinquente*, by dividing criminals up into ever more – and ever more refined – categories and subcategories. Second, he elaborated on his paradigm by dedicating separate studies to certain categories of criminal who already appear in *Uomo delinquente*. The most important and best known of these studies concern the political criminal and the female criminal. His book on human genius (1909) does occasionally refer to his criminological theory but only so marginally that it can be disregarded here.[18]

5.2.2.1. Development of a General Typology of Criminals

At the start of his discussion of the biology and psychology of the criminal in the first volume of his *magnum opus*, Lombroso laments the great difficulty of

---

[16] Becker (P.) 1995; Becker (P.) 2002, pp. 289–330.
[17] Fijnaut 2005a.
[18] Lombroso 1909; Gibson 2002, pp. 1–8.

finding data to be used as a basis for distinguishing between the born criminal, the habitual criminal, and the passionate criminal. In the course of his career, however, he collected so much material about these and other categories of the criminal that he was able to fill a second volume of *Uomo delinquente*. Entirely in line with the development of his research, that volume begins with a long exposition on individuals who are mentally ill, i.e. epileptic. This is followed by extensive discourses on three specific categories of offender: passionate criminals, mentally disturbed offenders, and opportunistic offenders.[19]

As regards the first of these discourses, we can be brief. Lombroso concludes it, in a rather satisfied manner, with the finding that also occurs so frequently in the first volume of the work, namely that his research shows that the criminal is simultaneously a savage and mentally ill. The first part of volume two was apparently intended primarily to give greater weight to his discovery of the born criminal by demonstrating, above all, that there is a strong similarity, structurally speaking, between the *fou moral*, the born criminal, and the epileptic. In this way, he was in fact positioning his revolutionary discovery within the existing psychiatric discussions and attempting, as it were, to normalise his new paradigm in academic circles. He goes on to do something similar with what he considers to be the essential similarity between the born criminal and the savage. After all, he asserts, someone who had read the first volume of his book will have become convinced of the large number of character traits that the savage has in common with the criminal.

In Lombroso's view, passionate criminals are, as it were, carried away by an irresistible inner psychic force. He believes that there are not many of them and that in general they look good in both body and mind. What is noticeable is that they are easily excited and excessively clingy. They commit their crime due to sudden anger, great love, or a feeling of honour. After committing the crime, they are highly emotional – even crazed – and often even commit suicide, which is quite different to ordinary criminals. What is also very different is that they do not attempt to conceal their crime but gladly admit what they have done in order, as it were, to assuage their grief and remorse.

Mentally disturbed criminals form a category which Lombroso considers to be common, believing that one can so conclude from all kinds of studies carried out in various places in Europe. It had become repeatedly apparent that criminals include many people with a mental illness such as monomania, dementia, imbecility, or idiocy. These criminals commit all kinds of crimes – crimes of violence, theft, sexual offences, and arson. The great majority are men aged between 20 and 30. In a number of respects, they exhibit not only physical similarities to born criminals but also psychological similarities. Criminals sometimes commit a crime in the form of a manic, impulsive act; similarly, in

---

[19]   Gibson 2002, pp. 18–30.

preparing and concealing their actions, the mentally ill regularly behave exactly like criminals. Like the mentally ill, criminals often exhibit no affection, no sympathy, no kindness, and no benevolence towards their victims.

Lombroso believes that opportunistic offenders also belong to a category that can be subdivided in various ways. He distinguishes between pseudo-criminals (a subcategory which he then further subdivides into pseudo-criminals, criminaloids, and habitual criminals), associations of criminals, latent criminals, and epileptoids.

By pseudo-criminals, Lombroso is referring primarily to people who commit crimes that do not demonstrate any kind of mental illness and that also do no harm to society. This means, in other words, actions that have been made punishable on the basis of a certain opinion or prejudice, and that can in short be referred to as contraventions of the law, for example traffic offences. Criminaloids, on the other hand, are people who already have a predisposition towards wrongdoing but in whom that predisposition only reveals itself in certain circumstances. Lombroso is thinking here, for example, of men in seminaries who develop into child abusers, accountants who embezzle from their company, and weak characters who allow themselves to be led astray by born criminals. Just how much these people differ from born criminals becomes apparent when they are imprisoned: they then display a genuine aversion to the latter. Finally, Lombroso also believes that habitual criminals cannot be placed on a par with born criminals, however much they sometimes resemble them in their behaviour. These are, after all, people who have come into contact with criminals because of a lack of education or support and who have learned from them how to make a living through crime.

He also has an outspoken opinion about criminal associations such as the Sicilian Mafia and the Neapolitan Camorra. In his view, such gangs are generally a mix of opportunistic and habitual offenders *"entraînés par quelque criminel-né de génie"* (incited by an ingenious born criminal). The aim of these associations (i.e. their members) is, on the one hand, of course to misappropriate other people's property and, on the other, to defend themselves more effectively – because they are more organised – against action by the authorities. Such gangs are usually led by a criminal who, like the chief of a savage tribe, has virtually dictatorial power. Very large gangs even have a veritable division of labour, with an executioner and a secretary, and even a priest and a doctor. They also have their own codes of conduct, contravention of which is punished severely. One of the worst contraventions is to steal for oneself, thus not allowing the gang to share in the proceeds.

Finally, there are latent criminals and epileptoids. The former subcategory, according to Lombroso, is made up of wealthy and/or influential people who owe their social position to the criminal behaviour that they exhibit in certain circumstances. In his eyes, the prototype of such latent criminals comprises people who have successfully carried on a political or social struggle. He does, however, make a clear distinction between real criminals who have thrown themselves into the struggle at a given moment (whom he does not mean here) and politicians who have emerged after the struggle as criminals (whom he does mean). Lombroso mainly presents the final subcategory, that of the epileptoids, to conclude his book by once more pointing out that criminal behaviour actually goes back to a "*substratum épilectique*" (epilectic substratum) and develops along with atavism. Right up to the end, Lombroso therefore maintains that crime is always also an illness and that criminology and psychiatry must therefore always go hand in hand.

5.2.2.2. Differential Application of the Paradigm to Female Criminals and Political Criminals

If one were to read only Lombroso's *magnum opus*, one would conclude that he takes it for granted that criminals are male. Both his theoretical reflections and his many examples focus, after all, on men. Nevertheless, it was Lombroso who, together with his son-in-law Guglielmo Ferrero, published a monograph in 1893 on the woman as criminal and as prostitute.[20] That study can, on the one hand, be viewed as being in line with those by Quetelet, who had, after all, established that gender was an important differentiating factor in explaining criminality. But quite unlike Quetelet, Lombroso and Ferrero associated the role of "gender" not so much with the social status of women but above all with the structure of their body and mind. Sociology and bio-anthropology were thus diametrically opposed on this point.

The 1893 monograph should be seen, however, as a defence of Lombroso against his critics and especially against their argument that female criminals do not exhibit any atavistic features, and that his theory of the atavistic criminal is therefore totally wide of the mark. In this sense, the aim of Lombroso and Ferrero was therefore to prop up their scientific paradigm. Making a distinction between both born and opportunistic female criminals and between born and opportunistic prostitutes fits in entirely with this rescue attempt. In this way Lombroso and Ferrero were in fact still attaching a certain influence to social factors in explaining certain forms of criminal behaviour and prostitution.[21]

The publication by Lombroso and Ferrero – the first comprehensive study of its kind – quickly created a furore, as is apparent from the translations that appeared, in 1894 into German and in 1896 into French: *La femme criminelle et la prostituée* [*The Criminal Woman and the Prostitute*]. This remarkable book consists of three parts. The first comprises a description of the normal woman and the second of the crimes committed by women, including prostitution. These descriptions form the background to the analyses that Lombroso and Ferrero

---

[20]   Lombroso and Ferrero 2004.
[21]   Uhl 2003, pp. 91–107; Gibson 2002, pp. 53–96.

present in the third part of the book of the anatomy, biology, and psychology of the female criminal and the prostitute.

As regards the anatomical features of these women, Lombroso and Ferrero naturally focus on the skull and the physique in general and on atavistic features in particular. They contend that it can be established, inter alia, that female criminals are not only smaller in stature and – especially in the case of thieves and prostitutes – have a smaller skull content than honest women but also exhibit more signs of degeneration than the latter. The authors refer, amongst other features, to the asymmetry of the face, the masculine appearance, and the size of the molars. They also assert that women who have murdered someone or committed arson generally exhibit more severe degeneration than women who have committed infanticide, for example. Prostitutes, according to Lombroso and Ferrero, often have excessive hair growth, hypertrophy of the genitals, and dental abnormalities.

In line with the latter findings, they make a distinction in their description of biological and psychological features between born female criminals and prostitutes on the one hand and their opportunistic counterparts, passionate criminals, and mentally disturbed prostitutes on the other.

Where the first category of female criminals is concerned, the authors' conclusion is that born female criminals are very similar to their male counterparts. They combine violent masculine characteristics with the worst female traits. The born prostitute does not therefore merely resemble the born criminal but is in fact exactly the same. Anatomically and psychologically they look the same, with the prostitute representing the female aspect of crime. Most female criminals are, however, opportunistic criminals. Such criminals can be divided into two categories, those who more closely resemble born criminals and those who are more like normal women. According to Lombroso and Ferrero, female criminals in the former category are much more likely to be guilty of crimes of violence and those in the second category of property offences.

It shows scientific determination and courage for Lombroso to defend his views on the atavistic criminal not only in relation to the distinction between man and woman but also to try it out on such a difficult category of criminals as political offenders. If the definition of what does or does not constitute crime and who is or is not a criminal is rather relative, then surely it is in the political field? In the book on political crime and revolutions that Lombroso published in 1891 together with the lawyer Rodolfo Laschi, he nevertheless attempted to apply such a definition. That work too was the object of a great deal of attention. A German translation appeared the same year and a French translation in 1892: *Le crime politique et les révolutions par rapport au droit, à l'anthropologie criminelle et à la science du gouvernement* [*Political Crime and Revolutions with regard to Law, to Criminal Anthropology and to the Science of Public Administration*].[22]

---

[22]   Lombroso and Laschi 1892.

The book consists of two parts. The first – probably written by Lombroso alone – deals with the anthropology and sociology of political crime and revolutions, while the much shorter second part – mainly written by Laschi – concerns the criminal law response to political crime and the means for preventing it. But the preface is also important. In it, the authors leave no room

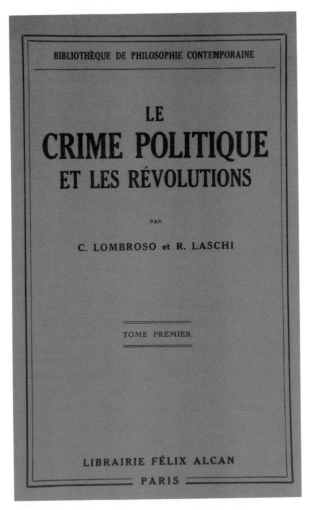

Cesare LOMBROSO and Rodolfo LASCHI, *Le crime politique et les révolutions par rapport au droit, à l'anthropologie criminelle et à la science du gouvernement*, Paris, Félix Alcan, 1892, 2 vol.

for any misunderstanding that their book was written against the backdrop of the political changes and conflicts in Italy and elsewhere in Europe. They therefore make no secret of the fact that it was written from a particular political standpoint. While able to understand the society for which republicans and socialists were striving, they adopted an outspoken position against communists and anarchists who had turned totally against the state. Similarly, they warned against attempts by born criminals to disrupt a prosperous society with a contented population under the guise of politics. One needs to remember in this connection that in the early 1880s Lombroso occupied a seat on the Turin city council on behalf of the socialist party.

His basic premise is that societies can only achieve social and moral progress via the path of gradualism. Attempts to bring about progress by force – however necessary they may be in the eyes of an oppressed minority – are anti-social and consequently a crime. And often, Lombroso adds, they are a useless crime because they are nullified by the response to them. A distinction can consequently be made between, on the one hand, gradual and necessary developments that under certain conditions are transformed into fruitful revolutions and, on the other hand, sudden, artificial, and violent revolts that lead nowhere. At the end of the first part of the book, Lombroso states plainly that rebellion is always a political crime but that revolution as such is not a criminal phenomenon.

As regards climate, Lombroso claims that hardly any revolutions or uprisings take place in very hot or very cold regions. In the first case, that is because the population is usually not very active, while in the second it is because people's imaginations are slower and less quickly stimulated. Where the role of geography is concerned, he points out that that factor can take many forms. Among mountain peoples, for example, there is only a slight tendency towards revolt, but that tendency is great among lowland peoples, namely because there is less oxygen in the mountains, thus increasing people's inertia, including from the political perspective. As regards food, Lombroso states, inter alia, that in countries where there is great poverty – as in Africa or for a very long time in Ireland – people's hunger prevents them from rising up, although they do rise up in urban areas where prosperity and wellbeing are relatively great.

In terms of race, Lombroso firmly believes that the more northern blonde races of Europe are more inclined to revolution than the more southern swarthy races. He attributes this not only to differences in their physique but also to important differences in culture. As regards other (social) circumstances, Lombroso believes, inter alia, that in societies in which power is concentrated in the hands of an elite (religious or economic), extremely violent revolutions can occur more easily than in societies where power is divided between a number of population groups. But poor governance of a country or an excessively unequal distribution of wealth may be the cause of revolution and revolt.

In the subsequent chapters (9–16) Lombroso discusses individual factors such as gender, age, status, and occupation. Women, for example, are not in general able to unleash or lead revolutions. He attributes the fact that in Russia they do often participate in revolutionary movements to the mystical-religious tendencies that there have been in that country in response to all kinds of economic horrors and dreadful natural disasters. The major role played by women in such movements in Russia and other Eastern European countries is above all, he says, the result of the relatively high intellectual level of Slavic women. Usually, however, it is young men who take the lead in revolutions: in their youth men are still impulsive, have not yet developed a very high moral awareness, and at that age are also still very altruistic.

In chapter 10, Lombroso raises the question of the extent to which atavistic criminals – born criminals but also *fous moraux* – are involved in political turmoil. In general, that is difficult to tell, but in the anarchist movement there are, he says, a lot of them. Their writings also show that many anarchists are in contact with born criminals and make no secret of it. As evidence of this, Lombroso cites, inter alia, the writings of a certain Panizza, in which it is stated that the thief is actually a victim and therefore has the right to steal. For Lombroso, there is no mystery as to why born criminals are so extensively involved in political revolutions: revolutions not only provide them with the opportunity to give full vent to their impulsive instincts but also to endow their crimes with the appearance of generosity. In that way, they even succeed in gaining influence over ordinary people, something that they greatly desire because they are extremely vain, even megalomaniacal.

In chapter 11, Lombroso goes into greater detail about mentally disturbed political criminals, both the mentally deficient and the disaffected who blame all their misfortunes on society and politicians. Chapter 12 is devoted to the role of mentally ill persons who behave as if they are geniuses or apostles and who, in politically volatile times, can gain a hold on masses of people through their appearance, their enthusiasm, their tenacity, and also their vulgarity. Opportunistic political offenders are featured in the brief chapter 13. By these, Lombroso means well-behaved citizens who due to circumstances – poverty, poor treatment – are forced to break the law or to join in with insurgents. The similarly brief chapter 14 deals with the phenomenon that people easily allow themselves to be swept along in political adventures if they are part of a crowd that, for whatever reason, allows itself to be incited. Following on from these two chapters, chapter 15 discusses impassioned political criminals: these exhibit no degenerative features but are afflicted by a certain fanaticism, however nobly intentioned that may be. Finally, Lombroso refers in chapter 16 to the very important role of real geniuses in revolutions, i.e. that of people with great intellectual and moral qualities. In mere revolts, one will seek them in vain.

5.2.3. SCIENTIFIC REVOLUTION AT AN IMPASSE: THE DIVERGING OF OPINIONS

The above descriptions of female criminals (and prostitutes) and of political offenders show how Lombroso, in the differential application of the paradigm of the atavistic criminal, utilised the general typology that he had developed on the basis of this type of criminal as a guideline. Doing so gives his scientific work more coherence and consistency, of course, than it has at first sight. For the same reason, it is not surprising that his ideas became so widely known in Europe and beyond: the typological elaboration and its differential application automatically strengthened the credibility of the underlying basic tenet. They in any case strengthened the authority of Lombroso's paradigm among his supporters, and his opponents could not therefore simply dismiss it. Lombroso's oeuvre confronted them with an onerous and difficult task. The "*choc des idées*" was therefore severe.

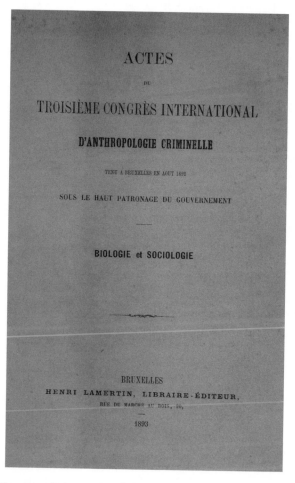

Actes du troisième congrès international d'anthropologie criminelle: biologie et sociologie, Brussels, Henri Lamertin, 1893.

Just how severe became apparent in 1891–92 in the discussion of the programme for the Third International Congress of Criminal Anthropology to be held in Brussels in August 1892. One of the conclusions at the Second Congress – which took place in Paris in 1889 and at which Lombroso had come under heavy fire from the founders of the French School – was that at the Brussels conference a committee of seven anthropologists would present the results of a comparative study of a hundred living criminals and a hundred respectable citizens. When it became clear that that study had not in fact been carried out, the Italians refused to attend the Brussels conference. In a letter to the organising committee, Lombroso, Ferri, Garofalo, and others explained their absence with the argument that a scientific conference should not just be a more or less brilliant machine for producing words but a venue for reporting on the latest scientific developments. And since the promised comparative analysis had not been produced, the upcoming conference would in their view lack the necessary basis for a truly scientific discussion.[23]

The scientific revolution that Lombroso had undeniably unleashed therefore found itself at an impasse. One could also say that that was when a parting of the ways occurred that is still apparent in criminology to this day, namely between the supporters of a more sociologically oriented criminology and those of a more (bio-)psychologically oriented approach.[24]

5.2.4. LOMBROSO'S VIEWS ON CRIMINAL LAW, THE CRIMINAL JUSTICE SYSTEM, AND THE COMBATTING OF CRIME

The battle of ideas in the emerging field of criminology was so fierce not only because the Lombrosian concept of the criminal was radically rejected by many, but also because of the far-reaching consequences that Lombroso and his followers attached to that concept as regards combatting crime in general and criminal law and the criminal justice system in particular.[25] For Lombroso, explaining crime and combatting it therefore went hand in hand. That was extremely clear in his final major work, published in 1899 and translated into German in 1902. An English translation followed a few years later in 1911: *Crime, its Causes and Remedies.*

It is unnecessary to look very deeply into the first part of that book, but we can certainly not ignore the second and third parts. Nowhere else did Lombroso explain more coherently his general thinking about the (preventive) battle against crime and the application of criminal law.[26]

In setting out his ideas on this matter, Lombroso distinguishes between general measures aimed at all forms of crime and special measures to control specific types of crime. As regards the latter category, he pays particular attention to the prevention of sexual offences, fraud, and political crime. It would be going too far

---

23   *Actes* 1893, pp. XVI–XVII.
24   Wright 1983, pp. 109–128.
25   Garland 1985.
26   See also Gibson 2006, pp. 137–151.

to deal here with everything that he has to say about the prevention of the latter categories of offences. It is difficult enough to summarise the general preventive measures that he proposes for controlling crime problems in Italy and elsewhere in Europe. One can say, however, that he expected the following to be very effective:

- strengthening of the (liberal) economy in Europe (smuggling would decrease, as would corruption among customs officials);
- reducing the gap between rich and poor in all areas – housing, education, employment, childcare, assistance with upbringing, etc. – and extension of social assistance (which would reduce crime in all areas);
- introduction of complete political freedom (fewer uprisings and less violent anarchism); and
- modernisation of personal and family law (a decrease in the number of abortions, child murder, and revenge-motivated offences).

Lombroso also advocates harsh measures to combat the barbarism which he saw as manifesting itself in all kinds of banditry and particularly in the Mafia and Camorra (deprive politicians associated with these gangs of all political rights, banish gang members to remote islands, restrict pardons for members of these criminal organisations). Lombroso also proposes drastic measures – even speaking of the possible need for a targeted neo-Malthusian policy – to prevent the formation of urban agglomerations that would need to contend with large-scale security problems: on the one hand, relocation of employment, but also all kinds of facilities (universities, reformatories), to small towns in rural areas; and, on the other, encouragement of emigration to the colonies and a crack-down on crime in the cities.

In the second part of this study, Lombroso makes no secret of the fact that he does not think much of the way the criminal justice system was organised at the time. He is critical not only of the cellular system in the prisons – both because it costs a great deal of money and does not in fact operate as intended, and because it produces only "defective automatons" – but also of the criminal justice system. He considers, for example, that the jury system is completely out of date for many reasons, including because juries are usually made up of illiterate individuals, which is one reason why their decisions tend to be based on instinct. In the light of modern psychological findings regarding memory, it is incomprehensible, he says, that judges and lawyers in general still attach so much importance to interrogations and witness statements.

It is only in the third part of his book, however, that Lombroso explains why he is so critical of the criminal justice system. That criticism clearly derives from his views on the personality of the born criminal, namely not someone who knowingly weighs up the pros and cons and then decides whether or not to commit crimes but someone who commits crimes because it is in his nature to do so. The implication of this view, Lombroso says, is that a criminal cannot be held responsible for his criminal conduct and cannot therefore be penalised in terms of personal guilt. But that does not mean – this much will be clear in the light of the above – that society should stand idly by and watch how criminals unleash their natural impulses.

On the contrary, he believes that society is fully entitled to defend and secure itself against crime and thus to take appropriate action against offenders. And the only measures that can be considered appropriate are those that are tailored as far as possible to the personality of the offender. Even the seriousness of the offence, says Lombroso, should not be taken into account when imposing measures because it is often a matter of chance whether a criminal commits a minor or a serious criminal offence.

Given all this, it is immediately clear why Lombroso was not very fond of the existing prison system, and certainly not of the cellular system. He did not agree with the fundamentals of that system, nor with the uniform and therefore impersonal way in which sentencing was implemented within it. He was in favour of individualising punishment and therefore of the indefinite duration of punitive measures; after all, one cannot know in advance when someone will have ceased to be a danger to society. This position did not mean for Lombroso that the prison system should be abolished entirely, but rather that prisons should form part of a varied system of custodial facilities: prisons, lunatic asylums, reformatories, agricultural colonies, etc. One of his great models in this regard was the reformatory set up in Elmira (in New York State) in the second half of the nineteenth century. Based on the concept of individualisation, he also argued for the introduction of non-custodial sentences. This naturally included fines, but also judicial warnings, payment of compensation, and house arrest. He also did not entirely exclude civilised forms of corporal punishment.

For born criminals, Lombroso believed that special prisons needed to be built and that these should be run by mixed committees composed of doctors and judges. He did not deny that these institutions could have a beneficial effect on some of these offenders, but he naturally did not assume that that would in fact be the case. Rather, he saw their establishment as a positive contribution to the evolution of the human race. Locking up the most violent individuals would after all benefit the process of selection.

5.2.5. FERRI AND GAROFALO, LOMBROSO'S ASSOCIATES IN THE ITALIAN SCHOOL

5.2.5.1. *The Sociology of Enrico Ferri*

Even before he came into contact with Lombroso, Enrico Ferri (1856–1929) thought that the Classical School in criminal law was based upon a fiction, namely the belief that people have free will and can therefore be held morally accountable for their deeds. He immediately viewed Lombroso as a kindred spirit. Soon after publication of the second edition of Lombroso's *Uomo delinquente* in 1878, Ferri sent him the thesis with which he had completed his law studies at the University of Bologna and in which he vigorously defended the position just mentioned. Lombroso is reported to have responded positively to this overture but immediately told Ferri that he was not a real positivist because his position was not based on empirical research.

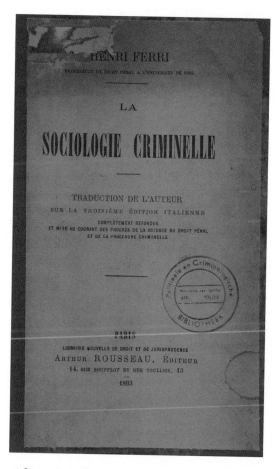

Henri Ferri, *La sociologie criminelle*, Paris, Arthur Rousseau, 1893 (translated by the author from the third Italian edition).

Irritated by this response, Ferri moved to Paris in 1878, where, inspired by Quetelet, he collected material for a study of the evolution of criminality in France. The following year he went to Turin to study with Lombroso and to familiarise himself with the latter's criminal anthropology. In 1880, aged 25, he was appointed professor of criminal law in Bologna. A year later, in 1881, he organised a comparative study of 700 criminals, 300 mentally disturbed persons, and 700 soldiers. He incorporated the results of that study into a monograph about murder and suicide which appeared in 1884.

However, Ferri established his scientific reputation above all with his inaugural lecture in Bologna in December 1880 on the future of criminal (procedural) law, the third edition of which he published in 1892 with the title *La sociologia criminale*.[27] In the preface to the French translation – *La sociologie criminelle* (1893); a German translation appeared in 1895 with the title *Das Verbrechen als sociale Erscheinung: Grundzüge der Kriminal-Sociologie* – Ferri wrote that the title of this book corresponded to the name of the science of crime and punishment that had been modernised by the application of the experimental method based on anthropological and statistical data.[28] His book could thus be regarded as a synthesis of all that he had produced so far.[29] It is therefore unsurprising that in the introduction he immediately distances himself from the classical study of the criminal law, dismissing this as a form of scholasticism which erroneously believed:

- that the offender has the same ideas and feelings as everyone else, whereas the organic and psychic, hereditary and acquired anomalies mean that he is in fact a special variety of the human species;
- that counteracting the increase in criminality is the main objective of punishment, but the evolution of criminality has nothing to do with the penalties listed in criminal codes and pronounced by judges; and
- that man has free will and is therefore morally responsible for his actions, whereas free will is in fact merely a subjective illusion.

Following on from this, Ferri highlights in his first chapter what criminal anthropology had produced so far. He does so in a remarkable, indirect manner. After discussing all the criticism of criminal anthropology, and in particular the ideas of Lombroso, he comes to the conclusion that crime is the necessary result of biological, physical, and social conditions. Ferri was well aware that with this conclusion he was distancing himself somewhat from Lombroso's original ideas. At the start of his argument, he makes clear in fact that he also thinks that Lombroso had, on the one hand, initially attached too much value to craniological and anthropometric data and too little to psychological data, and, on the other, had wrongly assigned all criminals to just a single category. However – based on his own research and that of others – Ferri had developed a classification of criminals that, he asserted, had ultimately been taken over to a significant extent by Lombroso.

---

[27]   Collin 1925, pp. 24–27; Sellin (T.) 1968; Vervaele 1990, pp. 284–296.
[28]   Ferri 1893, p. V.
[29]   Collin 1925, pp. 27–53.

That classification distinguishes between mentally disturbed criminals, born criminals, habitual offenders, opportunistic offenders, and passionate criminals. Ferri describes the main characteristics of each of these categories but comments at the end of the description that the difference is one of degree as regards the anthropological features of criminals and the influence of the physical and social environment. By anthropological (biological and psychological) factors, Ferri is referring to aspects such as physical condition, age, gender, occupation, social class, education, and mental condition. Physical factors include race, climate, and the weather. Social factors are the composition of the population, religion and public opinion, political and financial conditions, industrial development, and the quality of public administration.[30]

Ferri does not conclude from this description of the causes of crime and criminals that the criminal law should be set aside completely, but rather that priority should be given to the defence of society against crime, which should be organised in conjunction with other administrative measures. Just as floods cannot be prevented solely by constructing dykes, Ferri writes, but must be countered by means of reforestation of the river source regions, deepening of navigation channels, etc., so must we utilise different, more effective means than just the criminal law to defend society against crime. Further on in his argument – in chapter 3 – he makes this conclusion more specific in the sense that, in his opinion, the criminal law is essentially also a mechanism for defending society and that this mechanism must be deployed regardless of someone's responsibility or guilt. In other words, as soon as it is established that someone has actually committed a criminal offence, action may be taken against him because, as a member of a particular society, he is always responsible for any anti-social act he commits, i.e. for its social consequences.

In line with this, Ferri redefines criminal sociology as the science whose aim is to defend society against crime. That, he states, is why society's response to individual anti-social conduct can comprise four types of measures: preventive measures (aimed at removing the immediate causes), remedial measures (aimed at stopping the behaviour, undoing its consequences, and repairing the damage), repressive measures (to a large extent the existing penalties: imprisonment, fines, an occupational ban), and removal measures (such as the death penalty, institutions for incorrigible criminals, banishment).

Following on from this fourfold classification, Ferri goes more deeply into the consequences of his view of criminal sociology for the structure of the criminal justice system. He reduces this to two general principles: on the one hand, restoration of the equilibrium between the rights of the individual who is to be judged and those of the society which judges, and on the other hand,

---

[30]   Gibson 2006, pp. 151–157.

coordination of society's response to the more or less anti-social personality of the perpetrator of the offence.

In elaborating on the former principle, Ferri points out first of all that the rule of *in dubio pro reo* is in his view far too easily interpreted in favour of criminals, whereas there is often no real compensation for their victims. He also discusses the modernisation that criminal proceedings need to undergo in the framework of the defence of society. First, not only does the effectiveness of detection need to be improved with the aid of modern science but also the quality of the way evidence is furnished. In this context, Ferri speaks highly of *Bertillonnage*, the anthropological identification system developed by Alphonse Bertillon of the Paris police. Second, it is necessary to appoint experts to the offices of investigating magistrates so that the latter can perform their duties according to state-of-the-art scientific insights. And third, abolition of jury trials is unavoidable so as to ensure that the administration of justice could take on the character of a scientific study of the accused.

In elaborating on the latter principle, Ferri was dovetailing with the categorisation of criminals that we have already referred to: the defensive measures must be adapted to the various categories. For mentally disordered offenders, special institutions needed to be established – in line with initiatives already taken in various parts of Europe – with different regimes for those who had committed serious crimes and for those found guilty of less serious offences. Born criminals should either be permanently banished or locked up without the option of release. In line with his critical views on the death penalty, Ferri opposed cellular imprisonment, referring to it as one of the aberrations of the nineteenth century. Cellular confinement extinguishes the social feelings which criminals already only have to a lesser degree. In practice, it also fails to achieve the goal of moral isolation because inmates have countless to communicate with one another. It also merely reinforces their insanity and laziness. And because nothing changes in their domestic situation, their time in prison has no effect because once they are released they will necessarily continue in the same way as before. Partly for this reason, Ferri also considers imprisonment an unsuitable punishment for habitual offenders. Offenders of this type should be made subject to the same measures as born criminals.

Ferri then states, contentedly, that he has thus broadly outlined what a preventive and repressive system for defending society against crime and criminals should look like that is consistent with the findings of scientific research on crime as a natural and social phenomenon. He adds that this system should replace the doctrinaire classical criminal justice system, the basic principles of which no longer comply with what society so desperately needs and whose results are increasingly disastrous.

He dwells on what he means by this in his general conclusion, emphasising in particular that the Positive School is not seeking any kind of superficial alliance between the study of criminal law, criminal anthropology, and criminal statistics. No, the point is to develop a new science, a new criminal sociology, in which these subdisciplines should be integrated; they are the components of one and the same science. He does not believe in a dichotomy between the study of criminal law and criminal sociology: a crime is always a natural, social, and legal fact and must therefore always be studied from these three perspectives.

Ferri therefore could not agree at all with the ideas propagated by Franz von Liszt regarding the *gesamte Strafrechtswissenschaft* (integrated criminal science) because these, on the one hand, distinguished between the study of criminal law and criminology and, on the other, quite wrongly aligned criminal sociology with criminal policy (*Kriminalpolitik*). Ferri was in fact seeking to develop a fully integrated criminal sociology. He found it obvious that achieving that goal would be no easy matter; even after a century, the ideas of Beccaria still provoked many hostile responses. Nevertheless, he did not doubt for a moment that his own views would at some point come to be viewed as commonplace truths. Such a course of events was in his view an integral part of scientific progress.

This optimistic view of the future was derived, on the one hand, from Ferri's positivist view of science and, on the other, had a lot to do with his socialist convictions. Elected to the Italian parliament in the late 1880s, he initially aligned himself with the radical liberals but in 1893 he joined the socialist workers party, editing its newspaper *Avanti* from 1904 to 1908. Ferri did not believe in revolutionary socialism, however, and over the years he became increasingly moderate. He was in fact convinced that there was no contradiction between social Darwinian theory on the evolution of mankind on the one hand and Marxist theory on the development of society on the other. Quite the contrary, in his view these could be reconciled with one another if one accepted that social progress proceeded along an evolutionary path and not by means of revolutionary reversals, and if one also accepted that the inequality between people – in terms of their ability to adapt to their environment – need not necessarily be fought out to the bitter end ("the struggle for life") but could be offset by solidarity.[31]

5.2.5.2.   *The Criminology of Raffaele Garofalo*

In an appendix to his *Socialisme et science positive (Darwin – Spencer – Marx)*, Ferri turned against the third leader of the Italian School, Raffaele Garofalo. He noted for a start that, whereas he himself had always built on the full range of Lombroso's ideas, Garofalo – although always agreeing with both of them about the fact that crime is a criminal-pathological phenomenon – had quickly expressed different views on how crime should be combatted. Garofalo continued to believe, for example, in harsh criminal law repression and had

---

[31]   Ferri 1895; Ferri 1897.

little faith in poverty reduction as a means to combat crime preventively. Ferri went on to say that whereas Lombroso and he himself had increasingly taken the socialist path, Garofalo had instead sought refuge in reactionary circles and with *La superstizione socialista* [*Socialist Superstition*] had ended up taking an anti-socialist direction. And that – according to Ferri – had left him no choice but to combat the assertions in that book.[32]

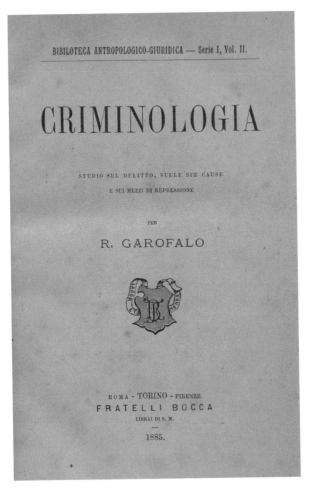

Raffaele GAROFALO, *Criminologia; studio sul delitto, sulle sue cause et sui mezzi di repressione*, Turin, Fratelli Bocca, 1885.

In that anti-socialist work, Garofalo does indeed fiercely attack the revolutionary socialists, setting himself the specific goal of tearing off the scientific mask that they had assumed. He therefore attempts first of all to demonstrate that there

---

is nothing scientific in the science of socialism, also sharply criticising Ferri's views, for example on the compatibility of Darwinism and Marxism. Garofalo then proceeds to attack the logic of socialism by demonstrating the lack of consistency between its political objectives and the methods for achieving them. Following on from this, he argues against the morality of socialism, saying that what it comes down to is preaching hatred of the bourgeoisie, which supposedly exploits the working class, and thus amounts indirectly – for socialists like Ferri do not directly encourage the workers to actually commit certain offences – to encouragement for all kinds of crime against their alleged exploiters. In support of his assertions, Garofalo refers to the murders and bombings perpetrated by anarchists, which he says have already transformed the social struggle into a violent battle against the upper classes and the government.

These writings for and against socialism amply demonstrate the extent to which Ferri's criminal sociology is permeated by his political views. The same is true, however, of the book *Criminologia* which Garofalo published in 1885 (with a second impression following in 1891). He provided his own French translation in 1905 and an English translation appeared in the United States in 1914.[33] In this study – notably the first introductory work in Europe with the title "Criminology" – Garofalo, clearly argues in favour of some reform of the social status quo and he ridicules the idea that a socialist transformation of society would lead automatically to the disappearance of crime because social injustice would no longer exist. In his view, every society must deal with forms of "natural crime", i.e. with behaviour that constitutes a significant breach of the average morality of society as particularly reflected in altruistic feelings of sympathy with others and of fairness in social interaction.

He therefore considers it important to define which offences should be placed in the category of "natural crime". Doing so would, after all, clarify what types of crime really do constitute a danger to society and thus which categories of criminals are genuinely dangerous and against whom, in particular, society needs to arm itself. Garofalo therefore chose to make an explicit distinction between "natural crime" and other – one would perhaps have to say "non-natural" – crime. With the latter category, he is referring to conduct which is criminalised more as a matter of the policy pursued by the authorities at a particular point in time with a view to ensuring the safety of society and that can be revised when there is a change in the political, economic, or social conditions. Garofalo even advocates including only forms of "natural crime" in the Criminal Code and assigning all other forms of crime to a separate code.

In the light of his definition of "natural crime", it is clear to Garofalo who is a true criminal: "necessarily a man in whom there is an absence, eclipse or weakness of these sentiments, one or both". And because such a man – marked as he is by his moral anomaly – is unable to adapt to the society around him

---

[33]   Garofalo 1885; Garofalo 1914.

in which these basic sentiments – compassion and sincerity – are considered indispensable, he constitutes a real threat to his surroundings and must thus be incapacitated. It must be possible to take forceful measures against someone of this kind and it is therefore essential to define precisely who is concerned and how he can be identified. Having arrived at this point, Garofalo does not turn squarely against Lombroso but he allows there to be no doubt that the latter has hitherto been unable to describe the physical form of the true criminal in an indisputable manner: "It has not been possible to fix a single constant characteristic which will enable us to distinguish him from the normal man." So far, according to Garofalo, Lombroso had merely managed to determine certain physiognomic features that make it possible to distinguish one group of offenders from another, for example murderers from thieves.

Garofalo himself considers the real criminal within a civilised society to be someone who distinguishes himself from the majority of his contemporaries and fellow citizens by his lack of certain essential feelings and thus his lack of morals. In his opinion, the lack of adequate research methods means that it is not possible to say whether this lack, this deficit, has an organic or a psychological basis. Nevertheless, real criminals can be classified, he says, into four categories: murderers, violent criminals, devious criminals, and lecherous criminals. Garofalo, incidentally, rejected Ferri's categorisation completely: "this classification is without a scientific basis and lacks homogeneity and exactness". Under Garofalo's categorisation, habitual criminals, for example, are either born criminals (i.e. their misdemeanours go back to innate instincts) or opportunistic criminals (i.e. their misdemeanours are the result of bad examples and other factors in their social environment); they do not, however, exist as a separate category of criminals. Garofalo therefore distanced himself from Lombroso's theory on the born criminal to a greater extent than did Ferri.

So did social factors have no influence at all on criminal behaviour? Was such behaviour solely the consequence of a personal lack of morality? Garofalo had no doubt that as the level of civilisation in a society increases – and not just in terms of material prosperity but also of upbringing and education – criminal behaviour also changes: it becomes less violent and more cunning. Crimes such as piracy, robbery, honour killings, and arson gradually decrease. He doubts, however, that crime also decreases as a result of cultural developments. He equally does not endorse the economic argument that if the distribution of scarce goods were more equal, the extent of crime would also decrease. In his view, that argument amounts, after all, to the reprehensible socialist idea that society is the original and actual villain and that crime will disappear entirely if society is organised in a less evil manner.

In Garofalo's opinion, the limited possibilities for preventing crime make the question of how to punish real criminals all the more important. His answer to this question is very Darwinian but is also entirely in line with the belief that society has the right to defend itself adequately against real criminals. What this comes down to is that true criminals should basically be removed from society, by means of the death penalty, banishment to the colonies, life imprisonment in their own country in a prison, an agricultural colony, or an asylum:

> In this way, the social power will effect an artificial selection similar to that which nature effects by the death of individuals inassimilable to the particular conditions of the environment in which they are born or to which they have been removed. Herein the State will be simply following the example of Nature.[34]

Garofalo thus rejects the penitentiary idea that punishment makes atonement by criminals and thus their improvement possible. In his view, that idea is based on the false assumption that criminals think and feel in the same way as the majority of people. He consequently also turns against the Classical School, in particular against both the proposition that one can only speak of crime if someone is morally responsible for his deeds and the proposition that the severity of the punishment should be proportionate to the seriousness of the crime. The point, according to Garofalo, is to determine how dangerous a particular criminal is to society and to fit the punishment to the degree of danger that he poses: "The aim is not to strike at misfortune, but to preserve society from new misfortunes whose advent is already foreshadowed."

He therefore recommends that judges receive training in modern anthropology so that they are able to assess how dangerous someone is. He in any case expressly opposes the imposition of prison sentences on "natural" criminals with the term being defined in advance. He believes that the duration of imprisonment should be wholly dependent on the progress that such criminals may perhaps make during their sentence. If there is no progress, then there must also be no end to their removal from society. He does see scope, in some cases, for penalties that oblige criminals to compensate the victim for the harm sustained and to pay a fine to the state. If they do not have the financial resources for this, then they should be able to earn the necessary amount by performing forced labour. Garofalo does in fact consider temporary imprisonment acceptable in the case of more serious forms of "non-natural" crime.

This sketch of the range of penalties which Garofalo wished to deploy in order to avert the serious danger posed by crime shows that his views on the criminal law response to crime were clearly in line with those of Lombroso and Ferri on a number of points. They shared his criticism of important principles of the Classical School regarding the purpose of punishment and the basis for sentencing, and all three believed that those principles needed to be reformulated in terms of the need to defend society. All three had a profound aversion to cellular detention but were at the same time fully convinced of the need to exclude real criminals from society by means of imprisonment (for life). And they also

---

[34]   Garofalo 1914, p. 220.

agreed on the need for some recognition of the victim in criminal proceedings. Their ideas clearly diverged, however, on the contribution that the criminal law could actually make to the process of human selection. This difference in how they valued the criminal law as a Darwinian selection mechanism was in a way a reflection of their very different attitudes towards socialism as the model for a better world: Garofalo's heartfelt aversion to socialism was diametrically opposed to Ferri's devotion to that political doctrine.

5.2.6. CRIMINOLOGY BECOMES A UNIVERSITY-LEVEL FIELD OF STUDY

We have already seen that Lombroso was appointed professor of criminal anthropology at the University of Turin in 1900. After his death in 1909 and at the initiative of professors at the Faculties of Law and Medicine, his chair was transformed into an Institute of Criminal Anthropology. The *Corso di perfezionamento in criminologia* (Course of Improvement in Criminology) organised by that Institute from 1911 covered not only criminal anthropology but also criminal law and procedure, psychiatry, forensic medicine, and scientific police investigation. An institute was established at the University of Bologna in 1913 – the *Istituto di studi criminali e di polizia scientifica* (Institute of Criminal Science and Police Science) – which did resemble the Institute of Criminal Anthropology in some respects but which on the whole was more like the institute set up by Ferri in 1911, with support from the Ministries of Justice and the Interior, at the Faculty of Law of the University of Rome, the *Scuola di applicazione giuridico-criminale* (School of Applied Criminal Law).

At the latter institute – officially opened with great ceremony in 1912 – Ferri taught criminal law and procedure, Salvatore Ottolenghi taught a course on the biological and physiological study of criminals, and Alfredo Niceforo was responsible for training in scientific investigation. The curriculum also included penitentiary policy, experimental judicial psychology, forensic medicine, clinical study of criminals, general judicial anthropology, and criminal policy from the perspective of comparative law.

Although this was a much broader curriculum than that in Turin, it fundamentally had a lot in common with it. It was also based, on the one hand, on the view that the criminal law should be practised in relation to other person-centred social sciences and, on the other, on the view that the result of this integrated research should promote a manner of applying the criminal law that was appropriate to the problems of crime as they actually presented themselves. Moreover, it was not only students who took the programme, but also judges, lawyers, police commissioners, physicians, and prison directors.

It is noteworthy that Ferri also founded a journal to function as the mouthpiece of his school and thus of the whole Italian School – *La Scuola*

Positiva nella Dottrina e nella Giusprudenza [*The Positive School in Doctrine and Jurisprudence*]. The instructors also formed the board of the *Società italiana di antropologia sociologia e diritto criminale* (Italian Society of Sociological Anthropology and Criminal Law), which was in turn the Italian branch of the International Association of Criminal Science.[35]

Alfredo NICEFORO, *Die Kriminalpolizei und ihre Hilfswissenschaften*, Gross-Lichterfelde-Ost, P. Langenscheidt, s.a. (introduced and extended by H. LINDENAU).

That these institutes devoted so much attention to "scientific policing" was largely because in 1902 Ottolenghi, at that time professor of forensic medicine in Siena, had established a *Scuola di polizia scientifica* (School of Scientific

---

[35]   Niceforo 1914; Niceforo n.d., pp. XLV–XLVIII.

Police) at the request of the Ministry of Internal Affairs in Rome.[36] That school – whose initial concept was clearly inspired by the identification service set up by Bertillon in the 1880s within the Paris police (see below) – quickly grew into an important national institution. That was on the one hand because it already gave courses from 1903 on the field of applied anthropology and psychology, criminal law, and police law. It was also because the institute housed the central identification agency that was the hub of all of Italy's regional and local identification services. It was therefore an obvious step for Ferri to bring in Ottolenghi to teach anthropology at the institute that he founded in 1912.[37]

5.3. OPPOSITION FROM FRANCE: ALEXANDRE LACASSAGNE, GABRIEL TARDE, AND ÉMILE DURKHEIM

5.3.1. SCHISMS BETWEEN THE ITALIAN AND FRENCH SCHOOLS

Initially, criticism of Lombroso in France was still expressed graciously, for example in Lacassagne's inaugural lecture (1881) – on the development of crime in France and the state of scientific understanding of criminals – at the opening of the academic year at the Faculty of Medicine of the University of Lyon. In his lecture, Lacassagne not only expressed high praise of Lombroso – "*mon savant ami*" (my learned friend) – but also Ferri, saying that these two had become leaders for the whole of Europe. He did wonder, however, whether Lombroso had not overlooked the fact that atavistic criminals formed only a minority of all the offenders who were brought before the courts.

Later in the 1880s, the criticism expressed by Lacassagne – and not only by him but also by Tarde – became much fiercer and more acerbic, and directly opposed to the Italian School. Their opposition became evident above all at the first two international conferences on criminal anthropology (in Rome in 1885 and in Paris in 1889) and led in 1892 – as we have already seen – to a veritable impasse in scientific discussion among the organisers of the third conference, in Brussels. It was, after all, the French who had turned the Paris conference into an anti-Lombroso conference.

The Paris anthropologist Léonce Manouvrier, in particular, had championed the view, at great length, that the hypotheses of Lombroso regarding the existence of the atavistic criminal had not been proven by in-depth research, and that even

---

36   Gibson 2002, pp. 135–161.
37   Niceforo 1907; Niceforo 1926; Ottolenghi 1903; Ottolenghi 1926; About 2005; Zaki 1929, pp. 120–122; Quinche 2011, pp. 226–232.

if such research had revealed differences between criminals and non-criminals, such differences said nothing about their positive or negative association with criminal behaviour. It was also Manouvrier who proposed carrying out a comparative study to determine the truth or otherwise of Lombroso's views. We do not know why exactly Manouvrier launched that proposal but when Lombroso accepted it unconditionally he naturally found himself facing a major problem. Manouvrier now needed to prove that Lombroso was wrong.

As we have seen, he did not manage to do so. That was why "the Italians" stayed away from the Brussels conference in 1892. At that conference, Manouvrier defended the fact that the research committee had never even met by arguing that the proposed study was not actually possible. This was because, for one thing, it was very difficult, if not impossible, to assemble a group of truly respectable citizens, and for another because detained criminals were not representative of the actual criminal component of the population. It will be clear that this defence did little to strengthen the position of Manouvrier and of French criminologists in general.[38]

To give physical expression to the special identity of the emerging French criminology, Lacassagne – together with a number of his colleagues at the Faculties of Medicine and Law at the University of Lyon – founded the *Archives de l'anthropologie criminelle et des sciences pénales* in 1886. In the preface to the first issue, the 1886 editors emphasised that the new movement in criminal science had manifested itself in Italy with the brilliant school of Lombroso and Ferri, and that France had merely followed that development critically from a distance. To further strengthen their own French voice, not only was the composition of the editorial board revised in 1893 but the title of the journal was also changed. From then on, the editors-in-chief were Lacassagne and Tarde (the former "*pour la partie biologique*" (for the biological part) and the latter "*pour la partie sociologique*" (for the sociological part)), while Bertillon and Manouvrier were included as associate editors. From that point on, the title included the term criminology: *Archives d'anthropologie criminelle, de criminologie et de psychologie normale et pathologique* [*Archives of Criminal Anthropology, Criminology and Normal and Pathological Psychology*]. In combination, these two changes also meant that the jurisprudential approach to crime disappeared from view.

The attitude to his views adopted by the French did not leave Lombroso unmoved. He had no trouble, in any case, in denouncing it in France too, as appears from a foreword that he contributed in 1901 to a book by Raoul de la Grasserie, the title of which was entirely in the French spirit: *Des principes sociologiques de la criminologie* [*On the Sociological Principles of Criminology*].[39] In his foreword, Lombroso emphasised that science basically "*n'a pas de patrie*

---

[38]   *Actes* 1893, pp. 171–182; Renneville 1994b, pp. 118–124.
[39]   De la Grasserie 1901, pp. VI–VII.

et ne connait pas de bornes politiques" (has no homeland or political borders) but that French scholars had nevertheless attempted to obstruct access to their country for new scientific developments that did not bear a French seal of approval and, when that proved not to be possible, had contested those developments with patriotic fanaticism. That was why, he said, he was so pleased that he had been invited – against the flow of the anti-scientific undercurrent – to write a foreword to this particular book. It showed, after all, that the view would perhaps be victorious again in France too that true science knows no boundaries.

Just how stubborn the desire of leading figures in France had been to put a French stamp on the invention of modern criminology is evident from the obituary of Lombroso that Lacassagne wrote in 1909.[40] Although he praised Lombroso in high-flown terms, he emphatically pointed out the French origins of his work:

- first, Lombroso had continued the work begun by Morel;
- second, Lombroso had applied the methods developed by Broca in the context of the *Société d'anthropologie* which was founded in 1859; and
- third, Lombroso was indebted to Gall.

In Lacassagne's inaugural lecture in 1881 there had been no question of this kind of "Gallicisation" of Lombroso.[41] In the lecture, Lacassagne did openly express doubts about the validity of Lombroso's initial ideas but he did not position them in a French perspective. However, he already left no doubt in that lecture that – in the wake of Quetelet, Guerry, and other statisticians – he attached great significance to the social factors that play an important role in the development and type of crime. What is even more important, viewed in retrospect, is that he already discussed the role of factors such as the weather, age, gender, etc. against the backdrop of a view of crime that went back, on the one hand, to the degeneration theory of Morel and, on the other, to the phrenology of Gall.[42]

In the lecture, he in fact defended the view that crime is only the outward manifestation of natural and anti-social conditions and that any change in the physical, biological, or social environment will necessarily have an impact on the total number of crimes. If we want to do something about the problem of crime, he says, we must exert a positive influence on the environment in which that problem can flourish.

In other words, although in this lecture Lacassagne did not yet explicitly criticise Lombroso's view of the true nature of the criminal from the perspective of his own view of the role of the "*milieu social*" (social environment) on crime

---

40   Lacassagne 1909.
41   Lacassagne 1881.
42   Debuyst 1998, pp. 343–356.

and the criminal, he did already lay the basis for his subsequent assessment of Lombroso's work. That is perfectly explicit from his obituary of his Italian adversary, in which he in fact defined criminal anthropology as the study of the offender by observation of the physical, psychological, and social influences that act on the organism of criminals. That definition shows that Lacassagne – unlike Lombroso, who, with Darwin, saw the atavisms (both physical and psychological) of true criminals as signs of backwardness in the evolution of the human species – considered these atavisms as signs of a standstill, if not decline, in the development of society. Both scholars therefore did agree – certainly towards the end of their lives – that there is such a thing as a "criminal type". At that point, Lacassagne even endorsed the existence of the incorrigible born criminal. However, their explanations for this finding differed greatly.

That difference was, incidentally, more than a disagreement between two individuals. It was rooted in a fundamental difference of opinion between "the Italians" and "the French" about the evolution of man and society. Where the former reasoned from a Darwinian perspective, the latter did so from a (neo-) Lamarckian perspective, in other words, from a perspective in which the social deterioration, i.e. degeneration, of parts of the population is attributed to increasing hereditary defects in their brain caused by the economic, social, and moral conditions in which they have to live from generation to generation. Lamarck took the view, after all, that people would by nature become ever more complex beings but that their natural development would come to a standstill if they constantly found themselves in poor social circumstances. This stagnation would have its effect, down the generations, on their hereditary makeup.[43]

5.3.2. ALEXANDRE LACASSAGNE: LOMBROSO'S POLAR OPPOSITE

As has become clear, Lacassagne was the primary French opponent of Lombroso. Born in Cahors in 1843, he studied medicine in Strasbourg and in 1880 was appointed to the chair of forensic medicine at the University of Lyon, the institution where in 1881 he gave the inaugural lecture already referred to. Lacassagne held his chair until 1913, dying in Lyon in 1924 due to a traffic accident.

In 2004, there was an exhibition dedicated to his life and work in the main building of the public library in Lyon, based on the personal archive that he had deposited there in 1921.[44] The catalogue of this exceptional exhibition conjures up the image of an extremely industrious individual.[45] Lacassagne not

---

[43]   Duesterberg 1979, pp. 244–290.
[44]   Artières and Corneloup 2004.
[45]   Gryphe 2004, No. 8.

only published numerous books, pamphlets, and articles in the field of forensic medicine but was also an avid collector of literature and press reports about the many issues in which he was interested. Criminal anthropology was, in other words, only one of his interests. It is therefore perhaps unsurprising that he – unlike Lombroso – did not write any comprehensive general criminological treatises or carry out substantial criminological research on specific matters. His major books are all in the field of forensic medicine and are above all manuals for use in actual practice, including the practice of criminal justice.

One should not forget, however, that Lacassagne promoted the development of criminal anthropology for many years as one of the editors-in-chief of the *Archives d'anthropologie criminelle*. Nor can we ignore the fact that his own involvement in this new research field found expression in a large number of pamphlets on highly specific topics, many short articles in journals, and a number of aphorisms.[46] His obituary of Lombroso is one of his important contributions to the *Archives d'anthropologie criminelle et de médecine légale et de psychologie normale et pathologique*.[47] It was largely his aphorisms, however, that for many years ensured that Lacassagne was not forgotten in the history of science. The best-known of these is probably:

> *Le milieu social est le bouillon de culture de la criminalité ; le microbe, c'est le criminel, un élément qui n'a d'importance que le jour où il trouve le bouillon qui le fait fermenter* (The social environment is the hotbed of the criminality; the microbe is the criminal, an element that is of no interest until the time that it finds the broth that ferments it).[48]

These and other aphorisms are not merely empty words. In their succinctness, they articulate extremely well the French (environmental) view of the causal relationship between society and crime and therefore the way in which crime should essentially be combatted. However, in the case of Lacassagne, the question is whether he did not in fact give more substance to these pithy expressions of his views. He was, after all, the undisputed leader of the French School. Did he not elaborate on its ideas, to some extent, in numerous pamphlets and articles? Various publications make it possible to answer that question.

We have already seen that Lacassagne already questioned Lombroso's views on the atavistic criminal as soon as he took up his appointment in Lyon in 1881. In order to substantiate his critical questions, he invoked both the research that he had carried out in his own laboratory on the skulls of beheaded criminals (only a few of which met the description given by Lombroso) and on the various different types of thieves – opportunistic thieves as opposed to professional thieves – distinguished by Vidocq. His conclusion was that it was obvious that

---

[46] Renneville 2004.
[47] Lacassagne 1909.
[48] Lacassagne 1913, p. 364.

not every offender met the description that Lombroso had outlined in his first publications. He then explained emphatically that in his view there were three types of criminals: instinctive and thus incorrigible criminals, opportunistic criminals who can still be improved by means of the criminal law, and mentally disordered offenders.

This tripartite categorisation is of course immediately reminiscent of the typology of criminals that Lombroso developed in his later work. The same applies to the penalties that Lacassagne considered most appropriate for the various categories. The first category should be transferred to a deserted region distant from society, which has simply progressed too far for them. The second category should be placed in prisons, while the third category should be confined to institutions for the mentally disturbed.

The question is of course whether Lacassagne stuck to his initial views on crime and punishment or whether he – like Lombroso – developed them further after setting himself up, in the 1880s and 1890s, as the leader of the French School.[49] In short, his categorisation of criminals did not evolve significantly.[50] Lacassagne also aligned himself emphatically with the Italian School as regards combatting crime: society was fully entitled – indeed obliged – to defend itself against crime. All this is quite clear from the report that Lacassagne and his successor Étienne Martin drew up in 1901 on the positive role that criminal anthropology could play in the drafting and application of legislation.[51] In that report, they distinguished between, on the one hand, the considerable number of degenerate and disturbed criminals and, on the other hand, anti-social criminals. We have already seen what Lacassagne believed should be done with the first category: they should be confined to institutions and prisons. As for the second category, the authors are very much in favour of the introduction of the aforementioned *Bertillonnage* because that system would make it possible to remove the recidivists from their social environment. In line with their explanation, they also press for extension of the child protection system and for amendment of the law to allow criminals who are capable of mending their ways to be reintegrated into society.

It seems highly likely that by the end of his academic career Lacassagne no longer saw much benefit in social action to prevent crime or in the rehabilitation of (real) criminals, but increasingly believed in the imposition of harsh penalties.[52] By that, not only did he mean the strict application of unconditional imprisonment, he also emerged as a fervent advocate of the death penalty and the introduction (or reintroduction) of corporal punishment. The social defence movement by then had him completely in its grip.[53]

---

[49]   Souchon 1974.
[50]   Laurent 1890; Laurent 1908.
[51]   Lacassagne and Martin 1901.
[52]   Lacassagne 1909; Renneville 2004.
[53]   Mucchielli 2006; Vervaeck 1924.

5.3.3. GABRIEL TARDE: ORIGINATOR OF THE IMITATION THEORY

Gabriel Tarde was born in 1843 in Sarlat and it seems likely that it was through his profession that he developed his interest in the emerging criminology: he was a judge in Sarlat for 25 years. It was in any case during the period when he

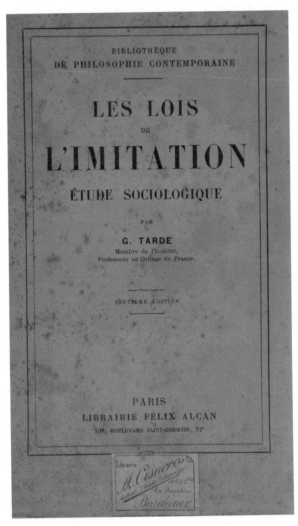

Gabriel TARDE, *Les lois de l'imitation: étude sociologique*, Paris, Félix Alcan, 1921.

held that position, the 1880s, that he wrote his main treatises in this field. In 1886, he published *La criminalité comparée* [*Criminality Compared*], followed four years later by *La philosophie pénale* [*Penal Philosophy*]. The ideas that he developed in these works on criminals, crime (and its causes), and criminal justice were clearly a consequence of the theory that he also published in 1890 in *Les lois de l'imitation* [*The Laws of Imitation*], namely that people's behaviour develops by their imitating others. In his later, more philosophical and political writings, for example *Les transformations de droit* [*The Transformations of Law*] (1893), he did return to his views on crime and punishment, although he did not develop them any further, let alone go into them more thoroughly or test them through research.

That is in itself more remarkable than it might seem. From 1894 to 1900 he was, after all, the head of the criminal statistics department at the Ministry of Justice in Paris. But Tarde was a solitary figure. He did no research, formed no school, and did not train any researchers.[54] In 1900 he was appointed to a professorship at the *Collège de France*. He died in 1904, a year after his great debate with Émile Durkheim about the scientific status of sociology. In that debate, Tarde defended the position that sociology always had to refer back to psychology because the social is inconceivable without the individual. Durkheim, on the other hand, defended the relative autonomy of sociology: the social can often not be traced back to the individual but has a nature of its own. As regards its object and method, sociology must therefore be viewed as an autonomous discipline.[55]

What Tarde's imitation theory essentially amounts to is that imitation – i.e. the interplay, the social interaction, between people – is the social fact par excellence and that sociology should study the laws that this interaction obeys.[56] The laws to which he himself attached great importance are, first, that imitation is determined by the frequency of the contacts that people have with others in a particular community. He distinguishes here between superficial contacts with many others in unstable urban communities and the numerous but close contacts with others in stable rural communities. In the first case, imitation manifests itself in the form of fashions; in the second in the form of traditions. The second law to which he devotes great attention is that imitation proceeds from the upper to the lower classes: people who enjoy social prestige are imitated by those with less or no prestige.

Tarde's promulgating of these laws might make one think that he had little regard for social change, but nothing could be further from the truth. As well as the imitation of behaviour, he distinguishes invention, i.e. new thinking, which leads to innovations in the way people behave. Inventions, he states, can come about in numerous ways but what they have in common is that they are essentially forms of adaptation to existing or changing social circumstances. For example, he saw the discoveries of the Ampère brothers in the field of electricity as a response to the growing needs for light and communication. And it was

---

54 Mucchielli 1994c; Wilson Vine 1960.
55 Geisert (M.) 1935, pp. 91–133; Van Ginneken 1983.
56 Tarde 1898, p. 37.

clear to him that the changes through imitation and invention would have an impact ever faster and on an ever-larger scale. The conditions for that to happen had been met in any case: the gradual waning of classes and nationalities, the reduction of distances by ever more rapid means of transport, and the density of the population.[57]

Given these views, it is not surprising that Tarde took a stand against Lombroso. In *La criminalité comparée*, he does not deny that there is such a thing as a criminal type of person – quite the contrary, such a type really did exist. Lombroso, however, had made the mistake, first of all, of providing a much too far-reaching biological interpretation of the characteristics of criminals. Existing research did not in fact allow for such an interpretation. On the one hand, too little research had been done worldwide to support the thesis of the born criminal, while on the other the small amount of research that had indeed been done had yielded only conflicting results. Second, Tarde considered that Lombroso's error had been to make the assertion – on the basis of this untenable theory –that criminals were biologically very different to other, normal people. Tarde did not immediately make clear, however, what exactly the criminal type of person that he had in mind was like.

Tarde himself initially came up with little more than peculiar generalisations, for example that the born criminal is not mentally disturbed or a savage but in fact a monster that – viewed in terms of the evolution of the human species – has regressive features. Elsewhere, he characterises the criminal as an *"excrément social"* (social excrement). But he did realise that if he characterised the criminal in such a way, he had to explain what he meant.[58] The explanation he provided remained vague, however. His point of departure was clearly very different and much more sociological than that of Lombroso. What it came down to was that criminals bear the imprint of the society in which they live. In line with that basic assumption, a distinction needed to be made between, for example, the rural and the urban criminal. These have grown up, after all, in very different criminal environments and have therefore imitated different groups of people. To make more specific what he means by imitation in the context of crime, Tarde resorts to providing examples, with one of his main examples being banditry.[59]

He gives a lengthy explanation of how banditry has always existed throughout rural Europe, but also how an urban banditry had evolved alongside rural banditry in the mid-nineteenth century. Based on the history of the Italian Mafia, he describes how in the late 1870s that organisation – as a result of forceful repression by the Italian government – had left the countryside and successfully established itself in the coastal cities, where it had reinvented and

---

57   Tarde 1890b, p. 399.
58   Tarde 1886, pp. 19–38, 46, 50; Tarde 1890a, p. 224; Geisert (M,) 1935, pp. 23–76, 89–90.
59   Tarde 1886, pp. 38–46; Tarde 1890a, pp. 270–294; Paramelle 2005, pp. 45–51, 72–84.

perfected its organisation and methods. He then warns – like Lombroso – that in politically uncertain times the Mafia can forge alliances with the organised working class and thus can grow into a dreadful sect in the heart of civilisations that makes the world bewildered. In normal times, such sects are combatted, if not destroyed, by the police, i.e. action by civilisation prevents a major criminal industry from arising. According to Tarde, however, that battle does not prevent veritable professional criminals from flourishing in the cities. In these groupings of professional criminals, small boys not only learn from one another that you can break the rules by committing all kinds of crime, but also learn the most effective ways of doing so.[60] They then learn from adult criminals, whom they imitate, how crime can enable them to live at the expense of society.

This explanation of the relentless growth of the underworld in cities demonstrates in particular how impossible it was for Tarde – given his basic theoretical position – to agree with the conventional explanations of the origin of crime. In this regard, he is strongly opposed not only to Lombroso but especially to moral statisticians such as Quetelet. He accuses them, first of all, of simply having confirmed the mistaken preconception that society is governed not by men but by the laws of nature.[61] Second, he argues that the regularities that they believe to have discerned in society are completely non-existent. The large fluctuations in both the crime rate and the birth rate in the course of the nineteenth century clearly demonstrate this. Third, he accuses them of not having any clear idea of the causes of crime.[62] On the latter point, Tarde said himself that he was far more in line with Ferri, who had at least produced a threefold categorisation of those causes: bio-anthropological, social, and physical. He was not very convinced, however, of the usefulness of that categorisation.

In his view, Ferri had made the mistake of placing the three categories of causes on the same footing and had failed to recognise that it was the social causes that played the greatest role in causing crime. Tarde therefore believed that it was not just a matter of determining the relationships between the various types of causes but also of determining the role of the social causes with greater precision. He does not dispute that bio-anthropological causes are involved but he assigns them a subordinate role in the emergence of criminal behaviour. As for the second point, he claims that at that time – due to the laws of imitation – crime was increasingly spreading from the big towns to the countryside, and that it was increasing in the big towns because it was irresistibly attractive to outsiders and villains in the countryside.

With a view to the future, Tarde considers it of the utmost importance to assign top priority to studying urban crime. This can best be done by investigating how all kinds of social conditions promote or prevent the spread of crime. Crime may

---

[60]   Geisert (M.) 1935, pp. 33–47.
[61]   Tarde 1890a, pp. 268, 320–323; Tarde 1890b, pp. 124–151.
[62]   Tarde 1890a, pp. 340–373; Beirne 1987b; Beirne 1993, pp. 145–186.

well be a particular social phenomenon but, all in all, it is a social phenomenon like any other.[63] That Tarde considers crime to be a social phenomenon like any other does not prevent him from also speaking of it as an anti-social phenomenon, one that acts like a cancer in the life of the organism and gradually kills it. For that reason, he believes that we must not resign ourselves to the development of crime; the threat posed to society by this pathological phenomenon is too great. He agrees with Lombroso and others that crime cannot be restrained solely by means of the criminal law. Doing so requires that we also work on the manifold causes of crime. The question, however, is how exactly that should be done; so far, only vague ideas have been developed.

He therefore concludes that for the present the battle against crime will mostly need to be waged by means of the criminal law.[64] He writes, for instance, that he is not against the cellular confinement of ordinary serious criminals but he does find that how such confinement is applied should be adapted to the social origin of the convicts and the nature of the offences they have committed. He also argues in this context for the introduction of the Irish regime in the prison system, i.e. the Crofton system, which made it possible for convicts to work, step by step, towards their (conditional) release. He resolutely rejected the banishment of criminals to the colonies; the disadvantages of this were far greater than the benefits.[65]

Tarde was therefore not very original when it came to modernisation of the criminal law and especially the penal system. His most significant contribution to the development of criminology lies mainly in the application of the imitation theory to the development and continuation of professional crime. His achievement in this regard was acknowledged in France, but at the same time was also fiercely contested, none more so than by Durkheim (as we will see below). In the United States, however, his theory received a lot of attention. That reception of his ideas across the Atlantic in the 1920s will be discussed in the next chapter.

5.3.4. ÉMILE DURKHEIM, A SOCIOLOGIST IN CRIMINOLOGY

Tarde engaged in debate with the representatives of the Italian School even less than Lacassagne, and Durkheim even less than Tarde. It is only here and there that the names of Lombroso, Ferri, and Garofalo occur in those of Durkheim's books that are most relevant in the context of the present study. However, Lacassagne does not appear at all, and nor do his ideas on crime and punishment. For this

---

63 Tarde 1890a, pp. 55–71, 383–405.
64 Tarde 1890a, pp. 418–425.
65 Tarde 1890a, pp. 487–572; Geisert (M.) 1935, pp. 162–192.

reason alone can it be said that Durkheim did not exactly present himself as a member of the French School in criminology. The fact that he repeatedly opposed the views of Tarde shows that Durkheim can at most be considered a surprising odd man out within that School. The only thing that Durkheim shared – very generally speaking – with Lacassagne and Tarde is that he too initially viewed crime as a social phenomenon and not as a bio-anthropological problem of individuals.

Durkheim was born in the town of Épinal in the Vosges in 1858 and died in Paris in 1917. All his books with which we are concerned here were written within just a few years. The first of these was his renowned dissertation *De la division du travail social* [*On the Division of Social Labour*], the first edition of which appeared in 1893. The second was his equally well-known methodological study, *Les règles de la méthode sociologique* [*The Rules of Sociological Method*] (1895) and the third his major study *Le suicide* [*Suicide*], first published in 1897. The reason for also discussing the first two books here is that – even though the titles do not suggest it – they deal extensively and authoritatively with the topic of crime and punishment. The authoritative character of Durkheim's observations is evident above all from the fact that, like those of Tarde, they have had a major influence on present-day criminology, mainly indirectly, namely through their impact in the American criminal sociology of the 1920s and 1930s.[66]

The fact that Durkheim already deals with crime and punishment in *De la division du travail social* is largely because in that work he assigned himself the task of studying the evolution and various forms of social solidarity through the rules of law that embody those forms.[67] This research led him to the realisation that in (so-called) primitive, undeveloped societies the law consists predominantly of criminal law – primarily offences against religious belief, against rites and ceremonies, against morality, and against authority – and that in developed societies criminal law has to a large extent given way to civil law. This finding then caused him to ask what actually constitutes a crime.

Contrary to the usual answer to that question – namely that it is an act that violates the collective or communal consciousness because it is criminal – Durkheim argues that the opposite is true: an act is criminal because it assails the core of the collective consciousness; that is why it is made punishable. Crime, in other words, is primarily a matter of social definition and not a question of the nature of a particular act or of the nature of the person who exhibits the behaviour concerned. Complementary to this, punishment is for Durkheim an impassionate response – but one organised by society – to a punishable violation of the criminal law rules of behaviour that are anchored in the collective consciousness. That response is by its nature driven by the need for revenge but

---

66   Lunden 1960; Martin, Mutchnick and Austin 1990, pp. 47–66.
67   Durkheim 1973, pp. 35–78.

can vary in severity depending on the nature of the offence, the intensity of the feelings that have been assailed, etc.[68]

Following on from these considerations, Durkheim looked more deeply at the different forms of solidarity. This closer investigation led him to conclude that a distinction needs to be made between mechanical solidarity and organic solidarity.

Émile Durkheim, *Les règles de la méthode sociologique*, Paris, Editions de Minuit, 1975 (new edition).

The first kind of solidarity is characteristic of primitive societies. In such societies, the individual is entirely incorporated into the group of people around him and individual consciousness is totally bound up with the collective

---

[68]   Gephart 1990, pp. 35–48.

consciousness. This kind of solidarity can be termed mechanical because the line connecting the individual with society is entirely analogous to that which connects a thing with a person. The second kind of solidarity is characteristic of societies that have become more and more complex due to the increasing division of labour.[69] Partly as a result of this, individual members of those societies acquire a certain degree of independence and freedom, not only towards one another but also towards society as a whole. In these kinds of societies, the law fulfils the function that the nervous system has in all higher organisms. It serves to control the various functions of the body so that they enable it to function harmoniously.

At this point, Durkheim clearly opposed Tarde for the first time.[70] According to Durkheim, Tarde had quite wrongly attributed such a development – from a primitive society organised around family relationships to a complex, highly organised society – to the laws of imitation. According to Durkheim, the forces driving this development are above all the increase in population, urbanisation, and the growth in the means of communication and transport. These not only make the transmission of traditions increasingly difficult but also make the individual less and less dependent on his fellow citizens. In these societies, the law is in other words primarily a "*droit coopératif*" (co-operative law) and its sanctions are pre-eminently aimed at restoring mutual relationships. The criminal law thus gradually decreases in importance, partly because religious crime disappears entirely. In some essential respects, however, it still retains its traditional integrative social function, for example as regards crimes against the person.

It should be noted in this connection that Durkheim – and this is one of the few times he did so – speaks out squarely against Lombroso. The latter had claimed somewhere that such crime is not the exception in primitive societies but the rule, and that crime there is not even regarded as crime at all. According to Durkheim, however, the evidence that Lombroso adduces in support of that statement is totally worthless, amounting to no more than a series of anecdotes. In his opinion, Lombroso completely fails to realise that the nature of crime is intimately linked to the type of society in which it manifests itself; every society gets the crime it deserves. Partly for this reason, Durkheim also opposes Lombroso's assertion that a large proportion of criminals are born criminals, even in the sense that the types of crime in which they engage are determined genetically. His main argument against this, however, is that the anatomical and physiological features that Lombroso attributed to them are not at all specific to supposedly "born" criminals. According to Durkheim, these features can also frequently be found in persons with neurasthenia; no sensible person would argue, however, that neurasthenia always inevitably leads to crime.[71]

---

69   Durkheim 1973, pp. 84–102.
70   Durkheim 1973, pp. 79–83.
71   Durkheim 1973, pp. 138–142, 305–310.

He concludes his observations on social solidarity with a discussion of the circumstances in which an abnormal, anomic form of the division of labour is found. The circumstances to which he refers in this context are those in which balanced coordination between the different social functions is lost as a result of rapid and profound social changes, such as mass unemployment caused by industrial mass production. In such circumstances, the division of labour does not generate any kind of social solidarity but in fact disrupts the regulated relationships between the associated social functions. Their relationships thus come to be in "*un état d'anomie*", i.e. a state of lawlessness.[72]

In his study of suicide, Durkheim applies his general ideas on the development and state of societies to a particular phenomenon.[73] He does not explain why he has chosen this topic for this test, but the purpose is clear: even in the case of something personal such as suicide there is not only a series of similar individual behaviours but also a self-contained social fact which is more than the sum of all suicides taken together, i.e. a fact *sui generis*. Durkheim then proposes a typology of suicides that is broadly in line with the results of his analysis of the development and circumstances of social solidarity.[74] His basic assumption is that suicide varies with the degree of integration of the social groups within which it occurs.

In social groups that are disintegrating – i.e. groups whose members set their personal interests and way of life above those of the group and thus lose their relationship with society as such – suicide essentially stems from this unbridled individualisation, and can consequently be classified as egoistic suicide. This type of suicide will naturally occur more readily in a group in which solidarity is organic in nature than in a group in which it has remained mechanical and which therefore still has a highly integrated way of life. In the latter group, suicide is of a very different nature. Here it is committed with a view to safeguarding the interests and values of the group; it can thus be categorised as altruistic suicide. As an example of this, Durkheim refers to societies that believe in a god embodied in humankind, in which elderly people therefore take their own lives to safeguard the vitality of that god.

In addition to egoistic and altruistic suicide, there is finally anomic suicide. This type of suicide occurs when a person's existence is totally disrupted as the result of some crisis – which may just as well be an economic crisis as a marital crisis – and that person sees no way out other than suicide. Durkheim notes, incidentally, regarding this tripartite categorisation, that the various types of suicide can sometimes overlap. He gives the example of someone who has been financially ruined and commits suicide because he does not know how his debts can be paid off but also wants to save his family the shame of bankruptcy.

---

72   Durkheim 1973, pp. 343–366.
73   Durkheim 1969.
74   Durkheim 1969, pp. 149–311.

In the final part of his study, Durkheim expresses his concern about the state of French society at that time. In particular, he found it worrying that more and more egoistic and perhaps even anomic suicides were occurring. Their number, in his view, was increasing even to such an extent as to constitute a highly threatening pathological phenomenon. It was in fact quite a step for Durkheim to speak of a pathological development. Was he not the one who had opposed the pathologising of social phenomena from the very start? He therefore understood perfectly well that he needed to explain himself. He did so by falling back on the problem of crime, the most eloquent obvious kind of immorality. That problem should not, indeed, be regarded simply as a pathological problem.

First, this is because every society has to deal with this problem in all kinds of forms; the moral standards of every population are assailed daily by crime. One can therefore only conclude that crime is inextricably linked with the foundations on which all known societies are organised; it is consequently a normal phenomenon. It therefore makes no sense in this connection to point out the shortcomings of human nature or to assert that an evil remains an evil even if it cannot be counteracted: that is the language of the preacher, not of the wise man.

The second reason why crime cannot be regarded simply as a pathological problem is that crime is not only necessary and normal, but can also be useful, at least when it is punished. Crime and punishment quite simply go hand in hand. Any abnormal weakening of the repressive system will therefore bring about an abnormal increase in crime. In fact, something similar is the case with suicide. It occurs everywhere and takes certain forms depending on the society. That is normal, but it becomes abnormal if the level of suicide in a society increases disproportionally. This in fact indicates that such a society is itself dysfunctional.

Durkheim had already tentatively expressed this view of the necessity, normality, and usefulness of crime in *De la division du travail social*. In *Les règles de la méthode sociologique*, however, he discusses this topic much more extensively, and in *Le suicide*, he also refers to it emphatically. Having stated in that work how social facts should be studied, he focuses entirely on the distinction between normal and pathological crime. He examines that distinction particularly on the basis of the kind of crime whose pathological character seems indisputable. He begins with a sweeping statement: those who agree on this should not have been so hasty in dealing with this problem.[75]

Crime is, first, a normal and even necessary and unavoidable phenomenon because it occurs in every society and cannot be entirely eliminated. For that to be done, it would be necessary, after all, for all members of society to have fully

---

[75]   Durkheim 1968, pp. 65–72.

internalised the feelings that are assailed by certain types of crime, and to have done so with the necessary strength to restrain conflicting emotions. But even if that were possible, the problem would not have been solved because other feelings would immediately lead to other behaviours being made punishable. The history of criminal codes makes that clear: it constantly includes new offences.

Second, crime – apart from being normal and necessary – is also useful. On the one hand, it is useful indirectly: by assailing collective feelings crime sometimes demonstrates that certain relationships within society need to be revised. On the other hand, it may be useful in a direct manner for the further development of society. Take the case of Socrates, for example: the boldness with which he spoke was undoubtedly punishable and he was justifiably condemned for it, but it was also a blessing for mankind.

Concluding this passage, Durkheim states that the foundations of criminology need to be revised. The criminal is not a strange parasite, as is commonly thought, but a normal participant in society. And crime is not simply an evil that must be minimised.[76] If crime drops below a certain level, for example, it undoubtedly indicates some disruption in society. In other words, crime is also a kind of yardstick for the quality of a society. If one wishes to study crime scientifically, one cannot immediately pronounce that it is abnormal, i.e. pathological. If one wishes to study such a phenomenon as a fact, as a thing, one must first define and explain its normal state.

5.3.5. APPLICATION OF CRIMINOLOGY IN POLICY AND PRACTICE

5.3.5.1. Role of Academic Criminology in Criminal Policy

As with the studies by the leaders of the Italian School, it is difficult to estimate the importance of the publications of Tarde and Durkheim in particular. Their major role in the intellectual history of criminology is indisputable, but what was their practical importance, i.e. their impact on the criminal policy and practice of the Third Republic? Research on the development and application of that policy suggests that their publications did indeed have some influence on certain basic principles of the policy pursued between 1871 (after the Franco-Prussian War and the fall of the Commune) and 1914 (the outbreak of the First World War), but that their impact on the effects of that policy, both positive and negative, was extremely modest.

One must not forget, of course, that it was only a few people, all in all, who made up the so-called French School and that these totally disagreed with one

---

[76] Durkheim 1968, pp. 71–72.

another regarding essential points; the differences between them were certainly as great as those between the leaders of the Italian School. One must also not disregard the fact that there was a great deal of opposition – especially on the part of the lawyers, both in the ministries and the judiciary and at the universities and in the political parties – to the ideas of Lombroso and his associates and therefore particularly to those of someone like Lacassagne.[77]

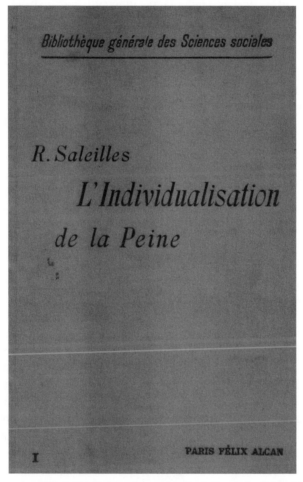

Raymond SALEILLES, *L'individualisation de la peine: étude de criminalité sociale*, Paris, Félix Alcan, 1898.

Not all lawyers were in fact all that radical in their rejection of criminal anthropology. A number of them agreed to an extent with the criticism of the Classical School and the uniform imposition of penalties. They sought a

---

[77]   Badinter 1992, pp. 97–224; Kaluszynski 1994a; Persell 1987.

compromise between that School and the Positive School. One of the best known of them was Raymond Saleilles. Saleilles acquired his reputation with the book *L'individualisation de la peine: étude de criminalité sociale* [*The Individualisation of Punishment: Study of Social Criminality*] (1898), in which – partly following Tarde – he called for greater differentiation in the range of penalties and measures so that sanctions could be applied more effectively which focused more on the personality of the offender, for different training of judges so that they would be better able to adequately handle a more differentiated range of penalties, and for the redesign of prisons, above all, so as to make possible the individualised enforcement of custodial sentences. For him, the major challenge in criminal law was therefore the classification of criminals and the individualisation of their treatment. Which criminals needed to be placed in an institution in order to cure them? Which of them needed to be removed from society permanently because there was no hope whatsoever of improvement?[78]

It was not in fact only the ideas of Lombroso and Lacassagne that were abhorred by some classically trained lawyers; those of Durkheim also came in for a great deal of criticism. For example, speaking at the first international conference (Monaco, 1914) on the establishment of a system of international criminal investigation, the dean of the Faculty of Law at the University of Paris, Ferdinand Larnaude, derisively stated – without mentioning Durkheim by name – that serious sociologists argued that crime was useful, even indispensable, for societies and that societies without crime would be intolerable. He then went on to give a lecture about the wave of crime which in his view threatened to engulf civilised countries.[79]

The views of Lacassagne, remarkably enough, did play a role in the enactment of the Act of 27 May 1885 that made it possible not only to continue to banish political offenders to the colonies (French Guyana and New Caledonia) but also to banish inveterate repeat offenders, who in his opinion were professional vagrants who repeatedly committed all sorts of criminal offences.[80] Sending them to the overseas territories would mean that they had been permanently removed from France, from French society, or at least removed for a long period. But that legislation was not enacted without a struggle. Such cleansing of France was perhaps useful but was banishment to the colonies not a measure that countries including the United Kingdom had abolished decades ago for all sorts of reasons? Ultimately, the French parliament nevertheless approved the legislation because the existing prison system was apparently unsuitable for counteracting the major problem of recidivism.[81] Unlike Tarde, Lacassagne was

---

[78] Saleilles 1898; Wright 1983, pp. 129–152. See also in this connection Ottenhof 2001, pp. 9–190.

[79] Larnoude and Roux 1926, p. 77.

[80] Wagniart 1999, pp. 115–142; Martin (B.) 1990; Duesterberg 1979, pp. 361–370.

[81] Kaluszynski 1998.

able to accept this measure precisely for that reason. He too considered the mass of habitual and professional criminals to be a serious danger to France.

This controversial measure was not a success, however, for one thing because judges were reluctant to impose it, considering it too severe. And so thousands of beggars and vagrants continued to be locked up every year in the traditional beggars institutions. Whereas the legislature expected that some 5,000 criminals – whether or not vagabonds – would be deported to the tropics each year, the annual average was in fact not even 1,000; between 1885 and 1893, the total came to 6,088. In about 1910, the number of prisoners in French Guyana was about 8,500. It was only in 1938 that banishment to the colonies actually came to an end. This punitive measure was only formally abolished in 1946.[82]

Lacassagne's ideas, but also those of Tarde and Durkheim, did indeed legitimise measures that did not exclude criminals from society who were capable of improvement but instead helped ensure their reintegration. If it was true that criminal behaviour was primarily caused by external social factors, then society should also be involved in the rehabilitation of the offenders concerned. In this view of matters, society was partly responsible, after all, for their misdeeds. Certainly in the case of those criminals who were capable of improvement, it was not enough merely to apply criminal law sanctions.

Such sanctions were indeed necessary but were certainly insufficient as regards the policy that a majority of the republicans had in mind. Criminals who had been sentenced had somehow to be effectively integrated into society by reinforcing their links with it in a wide range of areas – employment, education, social services, housing, etc. Obstacles to this – such as the need for regular police supervision and the negative effect of having a criminal record – needed to be overcome. The best way to organise the protection of society against crime was to pursue a policy of integration. In the view of the republicans, social solidarity and social defence against crime went hand in hand.[83] Voices were nevertheless occasionally raised in favour of allowing incorrigible, degenerate criminals to become extinct by means of eugenics, but these generally received little support.[84]

The first step in this direction was the statutory introduction – in addition to the conditional sentencing already introduced by the Act of 1885 – of conditional release in 1891. This important intervention in criminal law policy – prompted largely by the British example – in fact increased the options for controlled reintegration of criminals into society. The establishment of patronage associations throughout the country – usually composed of members of the affluent bourgeoisie and with the aim of putting this policy into practice – fitted in well with the ideas of the criminal sociologists. These associations, which concerned

---

[82]   Badinter 1992, pp. 267–276; Duesterberg 1979; Wright 1983, pp. 187–189; Mucchielli 2006, pp. 207–229.

[83]   Duesterberg 1979, pp. 319–348.

[84]   Mucchielli 2006.

themselves with the housing, income, etc. of paroled convicts and their families, were a clear example of the moral links between state and citizen which Durkheim was referring to when he spoke of the urgent need for achieving greater unity in French society with a view to controlling the pathological increase in crime.

Second, relatedly, one should not forget that the view that crime, in its most persistent forms, was rooted in the deplorable social, economic, and moral conditions in which people grew up from generation to generation also meant that fighting poverty and immorality became a priority in the domestic policy pursued by the republicans. All kinds of measures were developed via the *bureaux de bienfaisances* (bureaus of benevolence) for children who, for whatever reason, had been left to their social, moral, or economic fate or who were in danger: such children were housed in orphanages or put to work, parents were deprived of parental authority, families were placed under supervision, etc. The measures adopted in 1911 – after much discussion and a few isolated measures, such as the increase of the age of criminal responsibility from 16 to 18 in 1906 – to deal with the problem of juvenile offenders as a special problem from the criminal law perspective represented in a sense merely a tightening up of this general, more care-oriented policy. Following the American, British, and German examples, for instance, special juvenile courts were established and large-scale placement began of juvenile delinquents in penitentiary colonies in the country (mindful of the example of the colony at Mettray).[85]

That the emerging criminology did not play any prominent role in the formulation and implementation of republican policy on crime is evidenced by the fact that there was hardly any government investment in education and research in the field of criminology. Unlike in Italy, no special institutes or schools were set up in France before the First World War that offered a more or less extensive programme in criminal law, penology, criminology, forensic medicine, and scientific police investigation. Even at leading universities such as those in Lyon, Paris, and Montpellier, teaching was limited until 1914 to a course in one or more of these subjects. Tarde and Durkheim certainly had no successors of equivalent stature. In the wake of Lacassagne, however, there were a few people who were in fact better able than he was to put across his views on criminals and their treatment in a coherent and systematic way, for example André Lorulot, who published his overview *Crime et société: essai de criminologie sociale* [*Crime and Society; Essay on Social Criminology*] in 1923.[86]

It was not until 1922 that the University of Paris set up an *Institut de criminologie* (Institute of Criminology), under the auspices of the Faculties of Law and Medicine. The programme had a lot in common with that provided by Ferri's institute. Here too, criminal anthropology was taught in close combination

---

[85] Duesterberg 1979, pp. 371–374, 400–407; Martin (B.) 1990; Badinter 1992, pp. 347–374.
[86] Lorulot 1923.

with criminal law. The teaching therefore was mainly concerned with the needs of the criminal justice system, but this institute did not in any way continue the research of Tarde and Durkheim. There was therefore no illustrious continuation of the French School in the field of criminology. In the inter-war years, that School faded away completely. It also made no attempt to link up with the emerging American sociological research into such matters as the crime problems in major cities. The stifling annexation of French criminology by criminal law was reflected especially in the *Revue de science criminelle et de droit pénal comparé* [*Journal of Criminal Science and Comparative Criminal Law*], a journal founded at the University of Paris's institute in 1936.[87]

5.3.5.2. Practical Application of Criminology: Anthropometry, Dactyloscopy, and Scientific Police

By the end of the 1870s, the Paris police had assembled an enormous collection of photographs of suspects and convicts, estimated at 100,000. Because there was no proper system for classifying so many photographs with a view to identification, the collection was not particularly useful. In any case, the photos presented all kinds of problems in identifying suspects or convicts: they had not been taken from the same angle, they rapidly became out of date, etc. Alphonse Bertillon, who was appointed to a clerkship in the administrative department of the police in 1879, almost immediately took on the challenge of solving that problem. He sought the solution in anthropology, a field with which he was familiar because of his background. His father was a prominent member of the *Société d'anthropologie* (Society of Anthropology) in Paris, and he had often heard his father's friends speaking at length about the research of Quetelet, Broca, and Lombroso, and also of Lacassagne, and therefore about anthropometry, i.e. taking measurements of people in the context of anthropological research.[88]

Bertillon Jr quite quickly became convinced that this new branch of science could provide a solution to the problem faced by the police and judicial authorities in Paris and elsewhere in France, namely the identification of individuals. He believed that by systematically measuring a number of specific physical features of the bodies of suspects and convicts – who were adults and therefore fully grown – one could develop an identification system that was far more reliable than using the collection of photographs. He informed his superiors about this finding only a few months after being appointed, but he did not encounter much enthusiasm. Nevertheless, Bertillon began working with great energy and gradually developed an anthropometric method that could ensure the reliability of the identification system that he had in mind.

---

[87]   Kaluszynski 1994b; Muchielli 1994c, pp. 307–308; Muchielli 2004.

[88]   Bertillon (S.) 1941, pp. 103–131; Martin (B.) 1990; Lacassagne 1914; Rhodes 1956, pp. 71–129; Beavan 2001, pp. 76–93; Piazza 2011a.

In 1882, a new prefect of police gave him the scope he needed to prove the usefulness of his system within a period of few months by actually identifying suspects. Bertillon succeeded in doing this and was permitted to continue work on his newly devised method. This he did, and with increasing success: more and more suspects were identified using his method. The Act of 1885 on the banishment of criminals to the colonies further increased the importance of his finding. Application of the Act assumed, after all, that the judiciary and the prison system could determine clearly who – certainly in judicial terms – was a repeat offender and who was not. And of course Bertillon's method provided the means for making that distinction in a scientifically responsible manner. It was for that reason that anthropometry was introduced right across the French prison system between 1885 and 1887.[89]

It is not surprising that at the International Congress on Criminal Anthropology that took place in Paris in 1889 Bertillon received praise from all sides for his finding. After all, on the one hand, his method responded to the need of the police and judicial authorities to know exactly who they had before them and that of the judiciary and the prison system to identify repeat offenders among the inmates with real certainty. On the other hand, Bertillon's method could also greatly benefit bio-anthropological investigation in the field of criminology: it enabled investigators to trace born criminals more easily, more effectively, and more completely, or at any rate those offenders who were potentially most clearly destined for a life of crime. It is therefore understandable that it was said at the time that anthropometry, as applied by Bertillon, was the most practical application of bio-anthropological criminology.[90]

Bertillon was aware, however, of the weaknesses of his system: measurements were not always taken with the same precision, the skeleton changes as people get older, the system was unsuitable for identifying young offenders, and so forth. He therefore made it more complete and precise during the 1880s by adding three further components. First, he added a method for systematically describing the head in particular or, even better, the face ("*portrait parlé*"). The second addition was systematic description of unusual physical features (such as scars, tattoos, missing limbs, etc.). And third, he added a photo library. To increase the value of the latter, he developed a special methodology and an associated set of tools for ensuring that photos were taken as uniformly as possible and were therefore suitable for comparison. This whole system of identification methods gradually came to be referred to as *Bertillonnage*.[91]

---

[89] Von Hentig 1914; Beavan 2001, pp. 91–92; Renneville 2011.
[90] Kaluszynski 1994a; Valier 1998; Heilmann 1994.
[91] Bertillon (A.) 1893; Locard 1914; Kaluszynski 1987; Becker (P.) 2005a, pp. 65–88; Berlière 2005b; Quinche 2011, pp. 197–208; Berlière et Fournié 2011, pp. 53–70; About and Denis 2010, pp. 73–84.

In 1888, Bertillon was allotted his own *Bureau d'identité* (Identity Office), but his crowning achievement was the creation of the *Service d'identité judiciaire* (Department of Judicial Identity) in 1893. That service belonged to the *Préfecture de police* but was housed in the *Palais de justice*. All the above-mentioned collections were brought together within this department.[92] By that time, *Bertillonnage* had become world-famous, with people coming to Paris from all over the world to see the miracle that Bertillon had performed. His discoveries

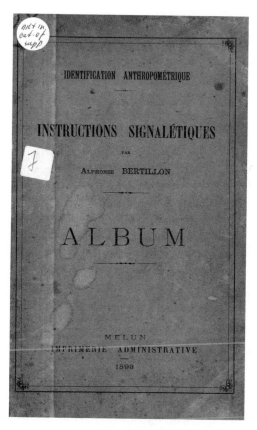

Alphonse BERTILLON, *Identification anthropométrique instructions signalétiques*, Melun, Imprimerie Administrative, 1893.

made such an impression on outsiders and foreigners that *Bertillonnage* quite soon began to be used in a number of countries, for example in the United States and Canada (1887), Argentina (1891), and the United Kingdom (1894). The rise of violent anarchism led to a decision being taken – at the secret international conference held in Rome in 1898 to agree on measures to control this European

---

[92]   Bertillon (A.) 1888; Locard 1890; Berlière 1993, pp. 212–218, 225–232; Berlière 2011, pp. 315–326.

problem – to introduce *Bertillonnage* in all the states of Europe. This was intended to enable the international exchange of comparable descriptions of anarchists between national police forces. A uniform identification system was necessary to increase the effectiveness of cross-border suppression.[93]

In 1898, *Bertillonnage* was still virtually unchallenged, but within just a few years the core of this method – anthropometry – was rapidly replaced throughout the world by dactyloscopy, i.e. identification by means of fingerprints. This counter-movement came primarily from the United Kingdom. Fingerprints had already been used in the British colonies in civil matters since the 1860s, particularly in India, including by William Herschel; they served the purpose of "signing" contracts. The idea that these prints could also be used to gain better control of known criminal groups arose in the 1880s, as it began to become clear that *Bertillonnage* was not suitable for registering and identifying large numbers of people, mainly because of the difficulties involved in taking the measurements. One of the officials concerned, Edward Henry, saw the replacement of *Bertillonnage* with dactyloscopy as highly promising but also knew that there was a major problem with the latter method, namely the lack of any classification system. In 1880, the Scottish physician Henry Faulds suggested in the journal *Nature* that fingerprint recognition could be used to identify criminals, but he too had no solution for the classification problem.[94]

That solution was provided by Francis Galton, a cousin of Charles Darwin, who had become greatly interested in anthropometry, partly from reading the works of Quetelet. While in Paris work on developing the Service d'identité judiciaire continued gradually, Galton – probably encouraged by Darwin, who had himself been alerted to the possibilities of dactyloscopy by Faulds – worked feverishly in his Anthropometric Laboratory to find a solution to the classification problem. In 1890, Galton gave a lengthy lecture on the progress of his research to the Royal Society in London. In 1892, he published his solution in a study with the snappy title *Finger Prints*, shortly followed by instruction manuals on how to take fingerprints.

These publications created such a stir that the French government established a commission in 1894 to investigate which identification system was to be preferred, *Bertillonnage* – and specifically anthropometry – or dactyloscopy. The committee expressed a clear preference for dactyloscopy but pointed out that applying the Galton system was still too complicated. Not long after, however, that problem was solved by Edward Henry. While working in Bengal and already corresponding with Galton, he developed a usable classification system that was officially introduced throughout India in 1897. When he was later appointed Assistant Commissioner of London's Metropolitan Police in

---

93   Cole 2001, pp. 51–53.
94   Beavan 2001, pp. 61–75; Cole 2001, pp. 60–96.

1901, he immediately set up the Central Fingerprint Branch within the Criminal Investigation Department. The classification system used by that department very quickly gained worldwide fame as the Galton–Henry system.[95]

By the mid-1890s, Bertillon had also become convinced that fingerprints could play an important role in identifying offenders. However, he viewed dactyloscopy primarily as a means of enhancing his own method and not

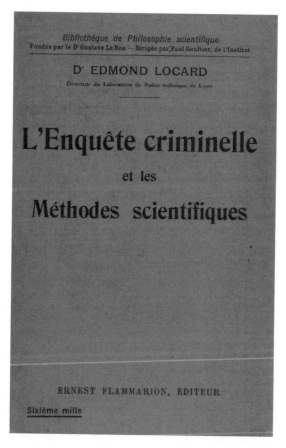

Edmond LOCARD, *L'enquête criminelle et les méthodes scientifiques*, Paris, Ernest Flammarion, 1933.

as an alternative to anthropometry. This explains why fingerprints were added to the data on identity cards in 1904 and why a special division of the identification service was entrusted in 1909 with the collection and comparison of fingerprints. Other experts in France made it perfectly clear, however,

---

[95] Heindl 1922a, pp. 19–108; Beavan 2001, pp. 94–111; Cole 2001, pp. 99–113; Gillham 2001, pp. 231–249; Davie 2004, pp. 75–84; Becker (P.) 2005a, pp. 114–135; Quinche 2011, pp. 209–211.

that Bertillon remained too attached to the system that he had developed.[96] In particular, Edmond Locard, at the time an up-and-coming specialist in the field of forensic medicine at the University of Lyon's Faculty of Medicine – i.e. someone associated with Lacassagne – emerged as one of Bertillon's most outspoken critics. In 1903, he published a lengthy work on how dactyloscopy had developed in the United Kingdom and Argentina, where Juan Vucetich had in the meantime developed his own very useful own classification system. In that publication, Locard had already pointed out that Bertillon's anthropometric description system had become too complicated and that more scope should be allocated to dactyloscopy in the identification of offenders. Locard wrote that he was convinced that dactyloscopy had a great future ahead of it; but whether it would replace anthropometry entirely was something that he did not wish to claim at that time.[97]

In 1912, however, Locard allowed for no misunderstanding that he believed that dactyloscopy was a better method of identification than anthropometry, openly asserting that France risked lagging behind compared to other civilised countries because dactyloscopy was being introduced so hesitantly. He did not mention Bertillon's name, but he clearly implied that Bertillon was the reason for the delay.[98] A committee of the *Académie des sciences* had in fact already decided in 1906 that dactyloscopy had many advantages over anthropometry and that there was therefore every reason for this new identification method to also be introduced in France.[99] By 1914, that had still not been done, however, and in that year Locard still found himself forced to advocate for the national introduction of dactyloscopy, at least within the brigades of the judicial police.[100]

In the meantime, Bertillon had in fact taken up dactyloscopy and had also published the results he had achieved in specific cases. He did not therefore reject this system on principle; however, he obviously had great difficulty in abandoning anthropometry, which had brought him worldwide fame.[101] It is fair to say that he was not entirely alone in his struggle to preserve anthropometry. Rudolphe Reiss, director of the *Institut de police scientifique* (Institute of Scientific Police) at the University of Lausanne, argued at the *Premier congrès de police judiciaire internationale* (First Congress of International Judicial Police) in Monaco in April 1914 that the *"fiche parisienne, dite anthropométrique"* (Parisian index card, called anthropometric) was still very useful, that it was not prudent, especially at an international level, to rely entirely on dactyloscopy,

---

[96]   Piazza 2005.
[97]   Locard 1903; Cole 2001, pp. 221–231; Rhodes 1956, pp. 139–159; Niceforo 1907, pp. 289–377.
[98]   Locard 1912a.
[99]   Dastre 1907.
[100] Locard 1914.
[101] Bertillon (A.) 1912a.

and that it was better to set up an international commission to investigate how to harmonise the existing identification methods and to introduce a unified system of identity cards. His proposal was that, until that had been done, anthropometric descriptions should continue to be used, and that they should be sorted according to a dactyloscopic classification system, namely that developed by Vucetich; he considered the Galton–Henry system too complicated.[102]

The half-hearted way that dactyloscopy was adopted in France was symptomatic of the lack of investment in the scientisation of criminal investigation. It was only after his death that Bertillon's department was gradually transformed into a laboratory for forensic science. Locard, with state aid, established a second laboratory in Lyon in 1910, and it was not until 1927 that a third laboratory was founded, this time in Marseilles. There was still no question of a national laboratory, nor of a national training programme for the police and judicial authorities in this field.[103] In 1907, Lacassagne argued that the neglect of forensic science in France was mainly because politicians and senior civil servants were lawyers and therefore not fully aware of the social importance of making criminal investigation more scientific; it was otherwise incomprehensible that no specific training programmes had been established at the various faculties of law.[104] It also had to do with the fact that there had been no figures in France like Ferri in Italy or Hans Gross in Austria or the German language area more broadly. In any case, Locard complained bitterly in 1937 of the inadequate state of his laboratory.[105]

5.4. CONCLUSION

If one considers Lombroso's entire oeuvre, one cannot help but be impressed by the enormous efforts he made to substantiate his paradigmatic ideas about the person of the criminal – including in the face of the great deal of criticism levelled at those ideas – by broadening and refining their content to take in more specific groups of offenders. But that was not the only reason why he succeeded in establishing criminology as a new and separate discipline. He was also successful because he gradually succeeded, to a certain extent, in integrating into his approach a number of important theories on the problem of crime proposed during the nineteenth century. That he relied more strongly in this regard on the biological, psychological, and psychiatric views that had been put forward in the previous decades is indisputable. Lombroso had little affinity with the

---

[102]   Reiss 1926.
[103]   Zaki 1929, pp. 97–118.
[104]   Lacassagne 1907; Locard 1912b.
[105]   Locard 1937.

more sociological perspective on crime problems and no sympathy at all for the revolutionary variants of such that perspective.

These disciplinary and ideological preferences and aversions make clear why, within the confines of his own Italian School, he disagreed on a number of points with the socialist Ferri and leaned more towards the rather bourgeois Garofalo. But these largely ideological differences should not obscure the fact that, despite all this, important similarities, or at least parallels, also developed in the course of time between their ideas on crime and the criminal. Those similarities include, for example, the extensive way in which the concept of the born criminal was put into perspective and the recognition of the role that geographical, economic, and social conditions play in the genesis of crime problems. Ferri's view that a proper understanding of crime requires a multi-disciplinary approach – anthropological, sociological, and legal – might therefore well be described as the ultimate principle of the Italian School.

The strong affinity between the ideas of the individual members of the Italian triumvirate is also reflected in their criticism of the criminal law and the criminal justice system. They were in broad agreement that the basic principles of classical criminal law did not correspond to the reality of crime problems and that the criminal justice system, which was largely based on those principles, needed to be radically redesigned. Anyone who accepts that, if society is to be protected, it is the personality of the offender and specifically the danger he poses – and not the severity of the crime he has committed and his responsibility for it – that must be the focus of the criminal law is inherently arguing not only for improving and strengthening detection, but also for alterations in the sentencing options, for targeted training of both prosecutors and judges, and for reform of the prison system. The effective individualisation of criminal justice and sentencing is otherwise impossible.

That this rather radical – to an extent also ideological – criticism of the existing criminal justice system was not immediately translated into policy across the board is understandable. It is therefore all the more remarkable that from 1900 onwards criminology was incorporated, bit by bit, into the university system. It should be emphasised, in particular, that the establishment of real criminology departments at the universities of Bologna and Rome was a first anywhere in the world. Together with the endowment of professorial chairs, the establishment of journals, and the production of textbooks, the creation of these departments set the seal on the institutionalisation of criminology in Italy. But not only in Italy: the institutionalisation of criminology in that country was the starting point for the massive development that criminology has since undergone worldwide.

However, this would not immediately have appeared to be the case given the way that criminology in France – despite the establishment of a similar institute in Paris in 1922 – failed to get off the ground after the First World War. Even the policing branch of this new discipline – which had caused such a furore through the agency of Bertillon and others before the war – failed to flourish during that period. But this should not make us lose sight of the extremely important socio-psychological and sociological contributions made to the emerging discipline by Tarde and Durkheim in particular. It is true that Lacassagne played an important role by emphasising the theoretical differences between the Italian and French Schools, but because he himself – unlike Tarde and Durkheim – did not develop any coherent and/or new system of ideas regarding crime and the criminal, he eventually disappeared from the criminological field of view. However, it must also be noted immediately that in his case the differences between the two Schools should not be exaggerated either. The picture of the criminal which Lacassagne repeatedly presented in fact had much in common with that of Lombroso and Ferri. The biggest difference was that Lombroso constructed that picture to a great extent from a Darwinian perspective while Lacassagne did so from the Lamarckian perspective that Morel had worked out so thoroughly.

The descriptions and explanations that Tarde and Durkheim presented, on the other hand, on the development of crime and, to a much lesser extent, on the personality of the criminal generally had little in common with the views of Lombroso, Ferri, and Garofalo on these matters. They were framed not only within a different, more sociological perspective but were also more related to certain specific issues and developments in the society around them. In that sense their theoretical insights were, and still are, not only easier to get across and to apply than those of their Italian opponents, but were also more eloquent and more convincing than the Italians' ideas. For that reason alone, it is not so surprising that the writings of Lombroso, Ferri, and Garofalo have largely been forgotten and that the studies by Durkheim and Tarde not only had a major influence on the development of criminal sociology, but are also still studied by anyone who wishes to become better acquainted with the origins of criminology.

CHAPTER 6

DEVELOPMENT OF CRIMINOLOGY IN GERMAN-SPEAKING EUROPE AND THE UNITED KINGDOM

6.1. INTRODUCTION

How Italian and French criminology were received elsewhere in Europe differed greatly from one country to another. In Germany, the Italian School, and particularly Lombroso, gained a considerable following thanks to the "missionary work" of a number of its protagonists. In the United Kingdom, opinions on the significance of Lombrosian criminology were more divided. This is apparent from the fact that at the beginning of the twentieth century a detailed study was initiated by Charles Goring of the validity of the views proclaimed by Lombroso in the context of that school regarding the born criminal. In Germany, there was no question of any such study. In both countries, hardly any attention was paid to the ideas promulgated in the context of the French School, with Lacassagne and also Tarde and Durkheim being ignored. In neither country did they play any recognisable role in public or academic debate on crime and the criminal justice system.

It is important to note that the development of criminology in Germany in around 1900 cannot be viewed in isolation from its development in the other main German-speaking countries, namely Austria and Switzerland. The developments in these countries are in fact very closely linked and will therefore be discussed in relation to one another. That said, it can also be noted that the development of criminology in these three countries – like its rise in Italy and France – was closely linked to major figures who carried out pioneering work. Those figures were, in particular: Franz von Liszt, a professor of criminal law, who, on his appointment at the University of Marburg in 1882, made an impassioned plea for the integration of criminology into the study of criminal law; Hans Kurella, who around the turn of the century was a tireless advocate of Lombroso and his criminal anthropology; Gustav Aschaffenburg, a psychiatrist who published a book in 1903 – *Das Verbrechen und seine Bekämpfung* [*Crime and its Repression*] – that gave him the same leading role in German-speaking Europe as Lombroso had in Italy and Lacassagne in France; and finally Hans Gross, a magistrate and later professor in Graz, who in the 1890s positioned himself with several large-scale studies as the founder of both modern criminal psychology and modern criminalistics.

It is therefore an obvious step to first discuss the work of these four main figures. We will take account as far as possible of the gradual split of Italian criminal bio-anthropology in German-speaking Europe in two different directions, one towards *Kriminalbiologie* and the other towards *Kriminalpsychologie*. In line with this, considerable attention will be paid to the application of criminology – in the broad sense of the word – in the actual operation of the criminal justice system, especially in detection, with particular reference to the work of Gross in the context of *Kriminalistik* (criminalistics). It is essential to realise immediately how *Kriminalbiologie*, in particular, permeated the work of the *Kriminalpolizei* in Austria and Germany if we are to understand what became of German criminology after 1933 in the Third Reich.

How very differently criminology developed in the United Kingdom! There, as already pointed out, the message of the Italian bio-anthropologists was received with more mixed feelings than in Germany and, as we shall see, criminology did not develop there in anything like the same way as in Germany. We will consider what happened in the United Kingdom before the First World War in two stages: first, and in detail, the reception of Lombrosian criminology in that country. It is important to go into this in some depth because doubts have been raised about the accuracy of the picture sketched by recent British writers. Second, we will discuss Goring's study of the validity of Lombroso's initial ideas regarding the born criminal. Why and how was that renowned study performed and what were its results? We will then consider the views expressed between the wars, against the background of that important study, on the problems of crime and punishment. Did the battle of opinions simply continue or did things also occur during that period which justify us in thinking that a certain degree of institutionalisation of criminology was also possible in the United Kingdom?

It is also important to point out immediately that discussion of the development of criminology in German-speaking Europe in this chapter stops in 1933, the year the Nazis came to power, a power that also allowed them to misuse criminology for political purposes. What happened in Germany between 1933 and 1945 is dealt with separately in Chapter 8, which concerns the fate of criminology in the two totalitarian police states – the Third Reich and the Soviet Union – that dominated a great deal of European history in the twentieth century.

The outline of the development of criminology in the United Kingdom in this chapter is extended until after the Second World War, with particular attention being drawn to the ironic fact that the post-war development of criminology in the United Kingdom was largely determined by scholars who had left Germany in the 1930s. These included such figures as Leon Radzinowicz, Hermann Mannheim, and Max Grünhut who, based at Cambridge University, the London School of Economics, and Oxford University respectively, did a great deal to promote research and education in criminology.

6.2. DEVELOPMENT OF CRIMINOLOGY IN GERMAN-SPEAKING EUROPE

6.2.1. THE PIONEER OF CRIMINOLOGY: FRANZ VON LISZT

What apparently caused Von Liszt to include criminology in the study of criminal law was his observation – openly expressed for the first time in his inaugural lecture at the University of Marburg in 1882, hence the name *Marburger Programm* – that the study of criminal law had become alienated from civic life and had become *Doktrinarismus* (doctrinarianism).[1] As an empirical science, criminology, he asserted, could rejuvenate that discipline and elevate it to a social science that really mattered. Von Liszt made no secret of why he was striving for the integration of these two disciplines. He was concerned, above all, with making the struggle against crime more effective, in particular against the criminal underworld. In his view, the criminal justice system needed to be better suited to controlling this social problem.

To convince others of the necessity of this change, Von Liszt founded the *Zeitschrift für die gesamte Strafrechtswissenschaft* [*Journal of Integrated Criminal Science*] in 1881. In 1888–89, in response to discussion throughout Europe of the reform of criminal law and the criminal justice system, he founded the *Internationale Kriminalistische Vereinigung* (International Association of Criminal Law), doing so in collaboration with Gerard van Hamel, professor of criminal law at the University of Amsterdam, and Adolphe Prins, director-general of Belgian prisons and a professor at the University of Brussels. The

---

[1]   Von Liszt 1883. On this lecture, see Naucke 1982; Baurmann 1984.

Association's *Mitteilungen* (Proceedings) show clearly how, until the First World War, it provided an important platform for criminal-political debate on the criminal justice system and the containment of crime in Europe.[2]

Von Liszt left no room for doubt, however, either nationally or internationally, that in the context of integrated criminal science, criminology should be

Franz Von Liszt, *Lehrbuch des deutschen Strafrechts,* Berlin, J. Guttentag Verlagsbuchhand-lung, 1908.

regarded as an ancillary science of criminal law. This position shows that he viewed the criminal law not only as an instrument of social control but also still as an important means of protecting the citizen against the state. The belief that the criminal law should be abolished was therefore foreign to him. It merely needed to be modernised, with the aid of criminology, in order to better fulfil its social function.

---

[2]   Radzinowicz 1991; Bellman 1994; Groenhuijsen and Van der Landen 1990.

But more had to be done. The criminal law, after all, could only affect the individual factors underlying the commission of crime, whereas the social causes of crime needed to be tackled by means of social policy. With this dichotomy, Von Liszt made clear just how far he was disassociating himself from the ideas that Lombroso had originally defended. His advocacy of targeted social policy was in line with the ideas of the many German doctors who, in the wake of the psychiatrist Abraham Baer, were more sympathetic to Morel's degeneration theory than the theories of Lombroso. It was, in particular, Baer's criticism in 1885 in his pamphlet *Der Verbrecher in anthropologischer Beziehung* [*The Criminal from an Anthropological Perspective*] that had brought about this counter-movement.[3]

In the opinion of Von Liszt, modernisation of the criminal law should focus on the range of penalties. He advocated, for example, the abolition of short custodial sentences and, parallel to this, the introduction of conditional sentences. With a view to the protection of society and the rule of law, however, incorrigible criminals should be rendered harmless (*Unschädlichmachung*) by permanently confining them in special institutions. In the case of criminals with potential for improvement, however, their criminal disposition should be extinguished by means of lengthy and severe punishment. Von Liszt was therefore definitely not in favour of mildness where adult criminals were concerned. Juvenile offenders should not be punished but put back on the right path by means of forcible education. To ensure the effective deployment of such a range of sanctions, it was necessary, moreover, for all those involved in the criminal justice system to be properly trained. They needed to be familiarised, in every respect, with the world of criminals.[4]

The fact that Von Liszt applauded the advent of criminology and was in favour of a far-reaching policy regarding crime had everything to do with his perception of the crime problems facing Germany. In his view, they were manifestly very serious, requiring both a major overhaul of the criminal law and the deployment of extensive social measures, both in the field of education and employment and in that of housing and social security. And in that assessment of the situation, he was by no means alone – quite the contrary!

Von Liszt's publications reflect extremely well the feelings of many citizens who felt very insecure in a Germany that after the Franco-Prussian War in 1870 – amidst all kinds of major social problems, such as massive urbanisation and an uncertain economic future – needed to rediscover itself under the leadership of its Emperor. The enormous increase in crime was widely seen as the best evidence of the lamentable state in which Germany found itself and of the impending dark future for its people. By hammering away at this growing

---

3   Wetzell 2000, pp. 49–52.
4   Von Liszt 1908, p. 78.

problem of crime, Von Liszt involuntarily played the same role in Germany as Tarde did in post-war France. He not only articulated the widespread feelings of insecurity and uncertainty regarding the issue of crime but also offered the prospect of a solution.[5]

In his Berlin inaugural lecture of 1899, Von Liszt elaborated on his views of the relationship between the criminal law and criminology. He presented *gesamte Strafrechtswissenschaft* (integrated criminal science) as a tripartite approach: education in the theory and practice of criminal law, criminological research on crime and criminal justice issues, and policy advice on the containment of crime. In his textbooks, Von Liszt showed that he was a true master not only in the field of criminal law but also in that of criminal policy.[6] However, he did not himself actually carry out criminological research, and his views on criminology gradually changed, although that did not affect his high opinion of Lombroso. He wrote that the latter had roused him and his colleagues – with a lot of tumult but also a great deal of success – from their metaphysical sleep and had liberated them from their rigid dogmatism.[7]

Even so, Von Liszt's critical attitude towards the existing criminal law sometimes cost him dearly because, despite everything, it nurtured the idea that he did not really believe in the criminal law and was slowly but surely digging the grave of that system of control. This feeling was trenchantly expressed in 1907 by Karl Birkmeyer, a professor at the University of Munich, in a pamphlet with the provocative title: *Was lässt Von Liszt vom Strafrecht übrig? Eine Warnung vor der modernen Richtung im Strafrecht* [*What of the Criminal Law Does Von Liszt Leave Untouched? A Warning against the Modern Direction in Criminal Law*]. According to Birkmeyer, the policy on crime advocated by Von Liszt would inevitably lead to the marginalisation of the criminal law because it was no longer the offence that had been committed and the criminal responsibility of the offender that were central to that policy but the offender's inclinations and his diminished or non-existent accountability. That marginalisation would result in the abolition of penalties in the true sense of the word and their replacement by all kinds of measures tailored to the degree to which the person convicted was or was not capable of improvement. This completely negated Von Liszt's argument that the criminal law must remain an important bulwark of the citizen against the state. Conversion of the criminal law into a system of corrective measures would mean, after all, that nothing would be left of the former other than some pathetic ruins.[8]

---

[5] Galassi 2004, pp. 81–138; Hett 2004; Evans 1998.
[6] Von Liszt 1908, pp. 115–294.
[7] Fijnaut 1986a, p. 14.
[8] Birkmeyer 1907; Wassermann 1909.

6.2.2. FROM CRIMINAL ANTHROPOLOGY TO CRIMINAL BIOLOGY

6.2.2.1. Hans Kurella: Tireless Champion of Lombroso

Von Liszt did therefore utilise Lombroso's ideas to reinforce the urgency and direction of reform of the criminal law that he envisaged, but he was certainly not a champion of those ideas. However, Hans Kurella, a mental asylum physician in Brieg (Brzeg, Silesia), was indeed – along with others – such a champion. In 1891, with Lombroso's assistance, he had already translated the latter's study of political offenders.[9] Two years later, in 1893, he published his own *Naturgeschichte des Verbrechers: Grundzüge der criminellen Anthropologie und Kriminalpsychologie* [*Natural History of the Criminal: Basic Principles of Criminal Anthropology and Criminal Psychology*].[10] In that work he embraced Lombroso's ideas to a large extent. He did not really find it problematic that those ideas were controversial, including in Germany. That merely emphasised just how daring Lombroso's views were from a scientific perspective in a world still ruled by out-of-touch lawyers, lawyers who, for example, were of the opinion that releasing a repeat offender into the community for the umpteenth time was the ultimate proof that they were living in the best of all possible legal systems. It was therefore fortunate, according to Kurella, that the purpose of the criminal law was now being questioned. In that respect, he was clearly in agreement with Von Liszt.[11]

Kurella thought that Lombroso's classification of criminals was not sufficiently clear and he thus refrained from discussing that typology in his *Naturgeschichte*; he was therefore not merely a blind disciple of Lombroso. Instead, he first described the anatomical variety that was to be found – in all kinds of forms: skull shape, development of organs, physical abnormalities, etc. – in true criminals, both male and female. Second, he explored the biology of criminals in depth, more particularly the biological factors that could account for their criminal behaviour, such as heredity and gender. Third, he elaborated on the psychology of true criminals, their character, their lack of adaptability, their dishonesty and mendacity, their cruelty, and their general lack of empathy.

What is typical of his time is of course the attention that Kurella paid to the world of professional criminals, especially gangs, both in Italy and Spain and in what he considered the more civilised European countries. No less typical is

---

9   Lombroso and Laschi 1891.
10   Kurella 1893.
11   Bondio 1995, pp. 101–118.

the fact that he made a link between real criminals and socialists; members of the first type, he asserted, had even collaborated on the development of socialist theories. What was totally outrageous was what he believed was happening in the area of anarchism. Its adherents were proclaiming that murder and robbery were legitimate ways of promoting their views, resulting in real criminals beginning to regard themselves as social reformers.

Given the above, it is not hard to understand why Kurella wished to go further in reforming the criminal justice system than did Von Liszt and his adherents. Besides measures including life imprisonment for incorrigible offenders, the introduction of conditional sentencing and the replacement of custodial sentences by forcible education in the case of juvenile offenders, he also favoured, for example, the introduction of banishment for true criminals, compensation for victims, and forced labour without internment. Kurella also supported the creation of patronage associations, believing that their members could do particularly good work with occasional criminals after their release. On the other hand, they were not suited to dealing with released habitual criminals and mentally ill vagrants.

After setting out his own views in this way, Kurella continued with his translation of Lombroso's and Ferri's writings into German. He published translations, for example, of Ferri's criminal sociology (1896), Lombroso's study of prisoners' graffiti (1899), and Lombroso's work on the causes and prevention of crime (1902).[12] Kurella was therefore unimpressed by the harsh comments that were levelled at Lombroso's ideas from time to time in Germany, for example by Eugen Bleuler in *Der geborene Verbrecher: eine kritische Studie* [*The Born Criminal: A Critical Study*] (1896). Bleuler felt that Lombroso had by no means established that the criminals he was talking about actually existed, or that degenerative characteristics of criminals should be regarded as signs of atavism.[13]

That was one reason why Bleuler himself found it more responsible to align himself with what he considered to be more tried and tested views such as Morel's degeneration hypothesis, and to work on the assumption, for example, that criminals included various different types of degenerates and that some of them could indeed be termed morally weak-minded. He therefore did not wish to go as far as Kurella in punishing offenders. One of his basic principles was that no more harm should done to them than strictly necessary. Therefore, he was of the view that dangerous habitual criminals (inter alia) should not be banished or subjected to lifelong solitary confinement, but rather that they should in all cases

---

[12]   Ferri 1896; Lombroso 1899; Lombroso 1902.
[13]   Bleuler 1896.

be detained in a humane manner. And to the extent that it might be possible to cure them, an attempt should be made in each case to achieve such a cure with the aid of psychiatric, educational, and health-related measures.[14]

In 1912, Kurella published his criminological swansong in the form of two essays, *Anthropologie und Strafrecht* [*Anthropology and Criminal Law*].[15] The first essay was a tribute to Lombroso, to his restless, creative, and productive quest for the personality of the offender and to his tireless crusade for a reform of the criminal justice system in line with his discoveries. This essay elaborates on the biography of Lombroso that he had published in 1910, *Cesare Lombroso als Mensch und Forscher* [*Cesare Lombroso as Man and Researcher*].[16] The second essay was a review of the Seventh International Congress of Criminal Anthropology in Cologne in October 1911. Based on the presentations at that conference, Kurella primarily explains at length why it had been so difficult for criminal anthropology to take root in Germany and other north-west European countries. According to Kurella, this was because it was at odds with strong criminal law traditions and had widely aroused the (erroneous) feeling that embracing that discipline would automatically lead to the abolition of the criminal law. In the essay, he therefore made his last strenuous attempts to dispose of that fatal prejudice.[17]

6.2.2.2. *Gustav Aschaffenburg: The German Counterpart of Lombroso and Lacassagne*

Gustav Aschaffenburg was born in Zweibrücken in 1866. He studied medicine at universities in both Germany and France, also working for a time with Richard von Krafft-Ebing in Vienna and with Emil Kraepelin in Heidelberg. He also worked as a prison doctor in Heidelberg and later in Halle. It is therefore unsurprising that he became interested in criminal bio-anthropology, retaining that interest after being appointed director of a psychiatric clinic in Cologne in 1904. After the First World War, the then mayor of Cologne, Konrad Adenauer, personally converted that appointment into a professorship at the re-established University of Cologne. In 1938, Aschaffenburg felt forced to leave Nazi Germany. He died, lonely and disappointed, in Baltimore in 1944.[18]

A year prior to his appointment in Cologne, in 1903, Aschaffenburg published a book that made him famous not only in German-speaking countries but throughout Europe: *Das Verbrechen und seine Bekämpfung*, with the subtitle

---

[14]   Galassi 2004.
[15]   Kurella 1912.
[16]   Kurella 1910.
[17]   Bondio 2006.
[18]   Von Hentig 1960.

Einleitung in die Kriminalpsychologie für Mediziner, Juristen und Soziologen: ein Beitrag zur Reform der Strafgesetzgebung [*Crime and the Fight against Crime: Introduction to Criminal Psychology for Physicians, Lawyers and Sociologists: A Contribution to the Reform of Criminal Legislation*].[19] The beginning of the

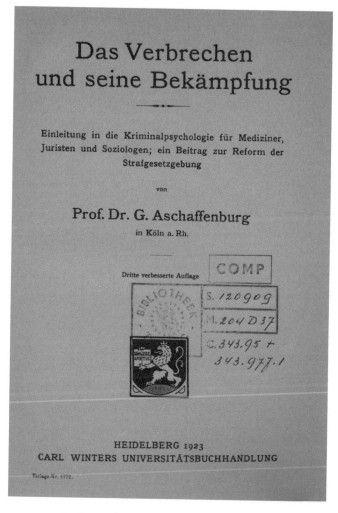

Gustav ASCHAFFENBURG, *Das Verbrechen und seine Bekämpfung,* Heidelberg, Carl Winters Universitätsbuchhandlung, 1923.

subtitle might suggest that the book is solely a treatise on bio-anthropology from a psychological perspective, but that is not the case. The structure and content of the study – the third and final improved edition of which was

---

[19]   Aschaffenburg 1923.

published in 1923 – in fact show that it was clearly an attempt to write a general, interdisciplinary introduction to criminology that went beyond the boundaries of medicine, law, and sociology.

That is probably one reason why it was successful both in German-speaking countries and elsewhere. Another reason is certainly that no such erudite overview of current criminology had hitherto been published. It would therefore be an injustice to both the book and its author if one were only to position it in the context of criminal psychology as it was beginning to flourish in German-speaking Europe at about that time. Aschaffenburg's study must be seen above all as a well-thought-out attempt to reconcile the bio-anthropological – rather atavistic – approach to crime and criminals with the bio-sociological approach, based more on the degeneracy thesis.[20]

The structure of the book is very clear. It consists of three parts, with the first two providing a picture of both the general and individual causes of crime. To the first category, Aschaffenburg assigns the time of year, race and religion, alcohol, economic crisis and war, and to the second such factors as age, gender, upbringing, and education. In that connection, however, he also discusses the teachings of Lombroso and, by extension, the physical and mental characteristics of criminals. Aschaffenburg distanced himself not only from the dogmatism with which Lombroso had spoken of the born criminal, but also from that idea itself: all attempts by Lombroso (and others) to demonstrate the existence of such a type of criminal had failed.[21] The third part of the book is entitled *Der Kampf gegen das Verbrechen* [*The Battle against Crime*]. In line with the first two parts, Aschaffenburg here defends the view that where the general causes of crime are concerned, the battle against crime should also focus, quite naturally, on eliminating or reducing those causes. But – as he immediately adds at the end of the second part of the book – the effect of those causes depends above all on the personality of the perpetrator. If that personality is strong, then those causes must be very strong in order to cause crime; if it is weak, then weaker causes are sufficient to do so. In other words, fighting crime should above all involve dealing with the personality of the offender.

At the beginning of the third part of the book, Aschaffenburg explains, in some detail, the contemporary situation regarding crime in Germany and neighbouring countries. Based on that presentation – one that is still interesting for us today – he then first shows how some problems could be prevented with the aid of a whole range of social, economic and political measures, ranging from alcohol control and job creation to decent housing, social assistance, and vigorous action by the police. As might be expected, where combatting crime is concerned, he is no great believer in imprisonment as traditionally imposed and

---

[20]   Wetzell 2000, pp. 60–68; Galassi 2004, pp. 184–225; Schneider 2004.
[21]   Bondio 1995, pp. 199–217.

carried out. Entirely in line with the views of Von Liszt, he sees greater benefit in the imposition of that penalty according to the personality of the offender: if he or she has potential for improvement, then imprisonment should be imposed according to an appropriate regime, but for incorrigibles there is no other option than life imprisonment. In this context, Aschaffenburg also advocates the introduction of conditional sentences, the payment of compensation to victims, and conditional release. He is also absolutely convinced that if such a transformation of the criminal justice system is to have any chance of success it will require the retraining of all those involved, from police officers to prison guards.

In all of this, one must not lose sight of the fact that in the third edition of his handbook Aschaffenburg also spoke positively about entirely different, drastic measures. He had apparently fallen under the influence of the eugenics movement. That movement had been initiated in about 1900 by Francis Galton – the same person who had campaigned for the introduction of dactyloscopy – and had received a great deal of attention in Germany in 1903 in response to a study by Wilhelm Schallmayer, *Vererbung und Auslese im Lebenslauf der Völker* [*Heredity and Selection in the Life-Process of Nations*]. The journal *Rassen- und Gesellschaftsbiologie* [*Racial and Social Biology*] was founded in 1904, followed in 1905 by a *Gesellschaft für Rassenhygiene* (Society for Racial Hygiene).[22] Given the reference in his book to the eugenic policies then being pursued in the United States, Aschaffenburg was apparently convinced that such a policy was fitting and feasible in Germany too. In 1923, he in any case considered it acceptable and even desirable to intervene in the reproduction of (in his eyes) inferior individuals such as incorrigible criminals. In his book, he argued for them not only to be prohibited from marrying but also to be castrated or sterilised. Whereas before the First World War Aschaffenburg still questioned such an approach to the problem of crime, in the 1920s he no longer found it objectionable.[23] Quite the contrary, he believed that those who were degenerate would soon be legally prohibited from reproducing. That such measures added an entirely different dimension to the "rendering harmless" advocated by Von Liszt is obvious. It no longer only a case of explaining and combatting individual criminal behaviour with the aid of Darwin's theory of evolution, but the active and radical application of a "social" version of that theory to whole population groups so as to rid the world, preventively and definitively, of the problem of crime. Aschaffenburg failed to consider where such a criminal policy – essentially a far-reaching policy consequence of the biologising of degeneration – might lead.[24]

---

22   Gillham 2001, pp. 336–337; Willems, 1995, pp. 207–216.
23   Wetzell 2000, pp. 377–414.
24   Weingart, Kroll and Bayertz 1992, pp. 121–125.

This radicalisation of Aschaffenburg's views on the containment of crime is not reflected in the title and subtitle of his principal work, which only express a desire for an interdisciplinary criminology and a firm commitment to reform the criminal justice system. And where that more limited objective is concerned, it is reasonable to place Aschaffenburg on a par with Von Liszt and, as we shall see, with Gross. It is therefore no surprise that, like them, he realised that in a country, in a language area, in which the classic criminal law was so entrenched both academically and socially, publishing a book was not enough to bring about reform of the criminal justice system. That would require, at the very least, the creation of a forum not only for discussion of such a revolution but where the building blocks for such a revolution could be assembled.

For that reason, Aschaffenburg – with the support of Von Liszt and others – established his own journal in 1904, the *Monatsschrift für Kriminalpsychologie und Strafrechtsreform* [*Monthly Journal of Criminal Psychology and Criminal Law Reform*]. In the first issue of that publication, he left no doubt as to its aim, namely to lay a solid scientific foundation for the reform of the criminal law that reckons with the personality of the offender and in this way serves the security of society. The intention was not to construct an edifice devoid of content but a solid structure that would ensure legal certainty for society.[25]

6.2.2.3. Return to the Roots: The Rise of Kriminalbiologie

In the third edition of *Das Verbrechen und seine Bekämpfung*, in 1923, Aschaffenburg mentioned in passing that a theory was being defended in Germany by Ernst Kretschmer which led in the same direction as the theory of the born criminal formulated by Lombroso. Aschaffenburg pointed out that Kretschmer himself rejected any similarity, but the idea that there was a correlation between a person's physique and his or her character was fundamentally highly reminiscent of Lombroso's original idea.

Kretschmer published the first edition of his famous book *Körperbau und Charakter* [*Physique and Character*] in 1921, with the nineteenth edition appearing in 1948 (in a run of no fewer than 5,000 copies). Particularly in the later editions, he devoted a great deal of attention to the correlation between physique and crime, allowing us to assess properly whether Aschaffenburg's comment was actually valid. In his study, Kretschmer distinguished between three body types: leptosomic, athletic, and pyknic. For each of these types he specified not only the bodily measurements – the leptosomic type was tall and thin, the athletic shorter and broad-shouldered, and the pyknic stocky and stouter – but also, as shown by the title of his book, the associated character.[26]

---

[25]   Aschaffenburg 1904–05, p. 7; Galassi 2004, pp. 274–284; Lamnek and Köteles 2004.

[26]   Kretschmer 1948; Baumann 2006, pp. 63–64.

Based on the correlation that he and others asserted as existing between these, Kretschmer believed that one could determine what type of person would tend to commit what type of crime. He was convinced, for example, that leptosomic types would tend to be found among thieves and swindlers rather than among violent or sexual offenders. Crimes of violence, against both property and persons, would mainly be committed by individuals with an athletic build. The pyknic body type would be represented mainly among perpetrators of all kinds of deception and to a lesser extent crimes of violence. In Kretschmer's opinion, this correlation between physique and crime was explained by the associated differences in character.

Although he undoubtedly viewed physique and character and – as a derivative thereof – the propensity to commit certain types of crimes as issues that had a great deal to do with heredity, he did not directly defend – in the vein of the early Lombroso – the proposition that committing particular categories of offences was innate in people with a certain body type and thus a certain character. He did not think in terms of such biological determinism. That idea was invoked, however, in 1927 in a study by Adolf Lenz, Gross's successor at the University of Graz: *Grundriss der Kriminalbiologie* [*Outline of Criminal Biology*]. According to the preface, that book – which was to an extent in line with Kretschmer's theory – was an attempt to apply a general theory of personality to criminals. Its basic assumption was that crime should be seen as the expression of someone's personality. According to Lenz, investigating that personality involved three elements: a study of the individual's lineage and life story, a study of his physique, and a study of his psychological structure.[27]

This tripartite division shows that Lenz was not a supporter of a biologistic view of criminals but in fact adhered to a bio-social view. This also appears from the way he explained in his book what he meant by the examination of one's personality. What it essentially came down to was the task of determining what features of their innate or acquired individual characters are very likely, under the influence of their environments, to manifest themselves in crime. The result of such examination would in the first place, as might be expected, be both a complex account of a person's high-risk features (including their criminogenic hereditary predisposition in the form of excessive aggression or excessive drinking) and a general analysis of their high-risk environment, in the form, for example, of a criminogenic environment marked by debauchery, prostitution, work-shyness, violence, etc. Second, he also set out how the interaction between predisposition and environment led, in specific cases, to crime. In this regard, he pointed out emphatically that this was not a mechanical interplay of forces but that this interplay developed within a setting in which all possible impulses but also inhibitions applied.

---

[27]   Lenz 1927; Simon 2001, pp. 73–76.

In 1928, Lenz was permitted by the Vienna police chief, Johannes Schober, to set up a *Kriminalbiologische Station* (Department of Criminal Biology) at police headquarters where, with the aid of specially trained police officers, he could implement his system of personality investigation on both juvenile and

GRUNDRISS DER
KRIMINALBIOLOGIE
VON
ADOLF LENZ

Adolf LENZ, *Grundriss der Kriminalbiologie: Werden und Wesen der Persönlichkeit des Täters nach Untersuchungen an Sträflingen*, Vienna, Verlag von Julius Springer, 1927.

adult suspects. According to the founders, compared to the *Kriminalbiologische Untersuchungsstelle* (Bureau of Investigation in Criminal Biology) set up the year before at Lenz's initiative at the prison in Graz, the *Kriminalbiologische Station* had the advantage that criminal-biological study could be done there on suspects who had not yet been altered by their pre-trial detention and conviction.[28]

A criminal-biological view of crime was also defended in a third controversial book published just before the Nazis' seizure of power in 1933: *Verbrechen als Schicksal [Crime as Destiny]* by Johannes Lange, professor of medicine and head of department at the renowned Kaiser Wilhelm Institut for psychiatric research in Munich. That work appeared in 1929 and became known worldwide via the English translation (1931) by Charlotte Haldane (wife of John Haldane, professor of physiology at the Royal Institute, who wrote a preface to the translation). In it, Lange reported on his study of 30 criminal twins whom he had identified on the basis of data held by the *Kriminalbiologische Sammelstelle* (Bureau for the Collection of Data in the Field of Criminal Biology) at the prison in Straubing (Bavaria), the same agency where Lenz had collected some of the material for his *Grundriss der Kriminalbiologie*.[29]

The *Sammelstelle* had been founded in 1924 primarily to provide scientific evidence for the classification of prisoners and thus for the individualisation of their prison regime, and in that way to put into actual practice progressive views on the reorganisation of the prison system and the gradual rehabilitation of offenders.[30] Totally different reasons also played a background role, however. There were, for one thing, the efforts of the middle classes and professional groups – amidst the revolutionary violence that plagued the Weimar Republic – to preserve a civil society that was not threatened by a criminal underclass. For another, there were the eugenically tinted concerns of the political and medical elites in Bavaria about the strength and health of the German people after the great losses that it had sustained in the First World War. At any rate, the head of the *Kriminalbiologische Untersuchungsstelle*, Theodor Vierstein, stated in 1926 that his research was also intended to gain an understanding of the criminal class that not only exerted such a negative impact on society and the economy but that also, by bringing forth criminal personalities, had such an impact on the hereditary foundations of the German race.[31] Similar anthropological research centres were established within the prison systems of a number of other German states.[32]

Trenchant criticism was indeed levelled within some German universities, particularly the University of Hamburg, at the validity of the theory and the methodology applied in research at the *Sammelstelle*, but that did not

---

28 Kalmann 1931; Erkens 1931, pp. 491–492; Simon 2001, pp. 144–148.
29 Lange (J.) 1929; Lange (J.) 1931; Wetzell 2000, pp. 153–167; Baumann 2006, pp. 64–66; Hohlfeld 2002, pp. 54–55.
30 Baumann 2006, pp. 57–69.
31 Simon 2001, pp. 69, 101–128.
32 Baumann 2006, p. 58; Simon 2001, pp. 128–144.

lead to the modification or discontinuation of that research.[33] The fact that eugenics and "racial hygiene" (*Rassenhygiene*) were emphatically linked with each other – leading to the risk that the one might become a means for achieving the other – could not prevent the flourishing of scientific and social interest in eugenics. It is therefore not surprising that in the mid-1920s leading *Rassenhygieneker* (racial hygienists) advocated the sterilisation of supposedly criminal families or at least of anti-social elements, whose criminal behaviour should be seen as demonstrating innate inferiority or hereditary defects.[34] On the contrary, interest in such matters was so great that Lenz and others were able to set up a *Kriminalbiologische Gesellschaft* (Society of Criminal Biology) in 1927, which quickly caused a furore in all kinds of circles – among scientists, policymakers, and the heads of services – thereby emerging as the main criminological society in Germany.[35]

Of the 30 pairs of twins that Lange studied, 13 were monozygotic (i.e. identical) and 17 dizygotic (i.e. non-identical). What he found striking was that in ten of the 13 identical pairs, both twins were punished for committing all sorts of crimes, while in the case of the remaining three pairs only one of each pair had been in trouble with the law. In the case of the 17 pairs of non-identical twins, the situation was entirely different, with only two cases in which both twins had been punished, while in the other 15 cases only one member of the pair had been sentenced. According to Lange, these findings led to the inescapable conclusion that in the existing social situation it was predisposition that played the dominant role in whether those concerned became involved in crime, or in any case a much greater role than hitherto assumed. He did not, however, exclude the influence of environmental factors – what else could explain that not all pairs of twins committed crimes – but for him it was beyond dispute that in this context such a thing as "biological destiny" was involved. Lange did not therefore go so far as to classify crime as a purely biological phenomenon.

This raised the question of whether the criminal behaviour of twins, and thus the results of Lange's research, was not essentially due to the fact that the twins had grown up in the same social circumstances and had therefore had the same experience. Lange did not dismiss the influence of these circumstances but ascribed their impact on criminals to the latter's inability to defend themselves against the negative influence of the environment in which they lived. He immediately added, however, that it was no accident that most pairs of twins were found in a wretched environment. They lived in such an environment because their predisposition rendered them unable to extricate themselves from it. This was something that was important for the *Milieutheoretiker* (environmental theorists) to realise. There was a close relationship and interaction between

---

33   Wetzell 2000, pp. 125–142; Liang 2006.
34   Weingart, Kroll and Bayertz 1992, pp. 239–246, 304–305; Baumann 2006, pp. 77–79.
35   Baumann 2006, pp. 66–69; Simon 2001, pp. 152–157; Willems 1995, pp. 216–220.

predisposition and environment. What Lange himself failed to realise was that with this conclusion he was not only very close to the views of Lombroso and the other members of the Italian School, but was also close to those circulating within the French School, especially the ideas of Lacassagne and Tarde. An individual might not have been born a criminal but his hereditary predisposition nevertheless made him susceptible, under certain circumstances, to exhibiting criminal behaviour.

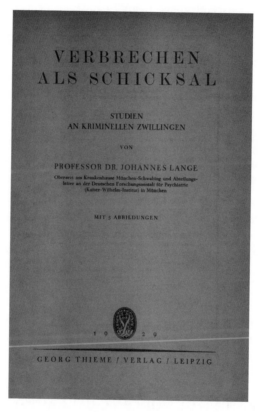

Johannes LANGE, *Verbrechen als Schicksal: Studien an kriminellen Zwillingen*, Leipzig, Georg Thieme Verlag, 1929.

The main consequence that Lange attached to the results of his research was that there was a dire need for *Prophylaxis*, i.e. measures taken to prevent people with an active criminal disposition from being born. That needed to be achieved – and it could be achieved – with the aid of "hygienic" measures in the area of reproduction. Lange did not specify precisely what those measures were because that would require further research, in particular genealogical investigation, into the hereditary predisposition of criminals. With that conclusion he nevertheless took German criminology a lot further than

Aschaffenburg had done, in the wake of the eugenics movement for which the *Kriminalbiologische Sammelstelle* in Straubing was one of the most important hubs. Within the eugenics movement, criminal personalities were viewed, after all, as a serious threat to the healthy and, in particular, racially pure development of society. *Kriminalbiologie* needed to make it possible to identify those dangerous personalities.

Needless to say, eugenicists made no secret of the measures that they found necessary to counter that threat, namely castration for men and sterilisation for women, etc. Unlike Aschaffenburg, neither Lange nor Lenz directly advocated the application of such measures to certain categories of criminals. Nevertheless, their studies paved the way for those who considered that applying a eugenics policy to (in their eyes) genetically predisposed criminals was indeed justified. Their work, like that of Aschaffenburg and Kretschmer, could all too easily be invoked as a justification for imposing a eugenic criminal policy. Leading figures in the eugenics movement had already argued in the mid-1920s that further study of the genealogies of criminals was needed, but they believed that it was an established fact that crime was a matter of innate inferiority. For them, there was therefore no longer any question as to whether it was appropriate to sterilise such anti-social persons once their deviant hereditary predisposition had been established. Doing so was an obvious step.[36] It needs to be made perfectly clear, however, that this view was not commonplace in criminal biology around 1930.[37]

We cannot say whether Von Liszt would have agreed personally with the imposition of these and other preventive measures; he died in 1917 in the middle of the First World War. What we can say, however, is that with his radical ideas about rendering incorrigible criminals harmless he was to some extent one of those who initiated discussion of whether criminals served any purpose at all. But as we have already seen, Von Liszt never moved towards the widespread application of eugenic measures in order to rid the German race of criminals and thus German society of crime.[38]

6.2.3. FLOURISHING OF MODERN CRIMINAL PSYCHOLOGY

Anyone who looks into the current major German criminology textbooks will find that they include only fragments of the history of criminal psychology in German-speaking countries.[39] This is certainly strange because psychology is

---

36 Simon 2001, pp. 53–160.
37 Simon 2001, pp. 79–81.
38 Weingart, Kroll and Bayertz 1992; Wetzell 2000, pp. 166–178; Baumann 2006, pp. 69–79; Simon 2001, pp. 95–97.
39 Kaiser 1996, pp. 115–121; Schneider 1986, pp. 94–97, 369–376.

still an important facet of German criminology today, namely in the form of witness psychology and interrogation skills.[40] Any proper attempt to outline what went on in German criminal psychology before the Second World War cannot but begin with a study of the available sources themselves.

When one consults them, one encounters a confusing amount of literature, in which it is no easy matter to identify movements and arguments. Every classification that one attempts to apply will have numerous deficiencies. Nevertheless, one classification that holds good, at least to a certain extent, is based on the distinction between the psychology of crime and criminals on the one hand, and the psychology of the criminal law and the criminal justice system on the other.

A second important distinction is between, on the one hand, movements in criminal psychology that ultimately called for the abolition of the criminal law and its associated institutions, and, on the other hand, movements that essentially concerned themselves with the reform, i.e. improvement, of the criminal justice system. In contrast to an abolitionist criminal psychology there was therefore clearly a reformist criminal psychology.

Further to this second distinction, we may also introduce a third distinction between psychoanalytic and non-psychoanalytic psychology – a distinction that not only makes sense from a theoretical perspective but also fits in with the previous, second, distinction between reformist and abolitionist criminal psychology. It is then logical to return to the first distinction and subsequently, from both the psychoanalytic perspective and the non-psychoanalytic perspective, to outline, on the one hand, the psychology of the crime and perpetrator and, on the other, the psychology of the criminal law and the criminal justice system.

6.2.3.1. Criminal Psychology from a Reformist Perspective

It makes sense to begin this account of German criminal psychology with a discussion of the reformist, non-psychoanalytically oriented literature. This literature is not only of an earlier date and the largest in scope, it also constitutes the literature that some psychoanalysts clearly disputed.

6.2.3.1.1. The Starting Point: The *Kriminalpsychologie* of Hans Gross

Criminal psychology had existed in German-speaking countries since the late eighteenth century. Here too, it developed in the wake of the views of Pinel, Esquirol, and Gall on the nature of mental illnesses and the treatment of people suffering from them. The central problems in *gerichtliche Arzneywissenschaft*

---

40   Arntzen and Michaelis 1970; Busam 1983.

(judicial medicine) – insofar as this emerging discipline had to do with the theory and application of the criminal law – included explaining the commission of crimes, criminal responsibility, and sentencing. In the first decades of the nineteenth century, these problems were thoroughly examined by, among others, Paul von Feuerbach.[41] Towards the end of the century, there was no one who dealt with them better than the Viennese psychiatrist Richard von Krafft-Ebing in his *Lehrbuch der gerichtlichen Psychopathologie* [*Textbook of Judicial Psychopathology*].[42]

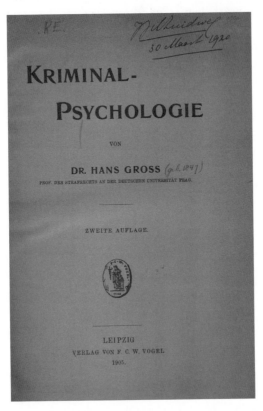

Hans GROSS, *Kriminalpsychologie*, Leipzig, Verlag von F.C.W. Vogel, 1905.

Against that background, it is not difficult to demonstrate how another famous Austrian, Hans Gross, revitalised the field of criminology in his 1898 book *Kriminalpsychologie*. The book no longer dealt only with problems in the area of responsibility and sentencing, but also presented a survey of all the psychological theories that a criminalist requires in his work. According to Gross, the book

---

41   Greve 2004, pp. 29–142.
42   Von Kraft-Ebing 1900.

aimed, in other words, to make psychology fully applicable to the criminal justice system. However, that was not his sole aim: the book arose out of his general concern of entirely modernising the practice of criminal justice – particularly investigation, prosecution, and adjudication – with the aid of the emerging social and natural sciences. Gross had already revealed that concern a few years previously, in 1893, in his *Handbuch für Untersuchungsrichter, Polizeibeamte, Gendarmen u.s.w.* [*Manual for Examining Magistrates, Police Officers, Gendarmes, etc.*]. In that work (which does not refer to "psychology"), he also touched – based on his extensive practical experience – on a few of the themes that would later be dealt with at length in his *Kriminalpsychologie*.[43]

This study, which clearly focuses on the work of the criminal judge, consists of two parts, the first dealing with the psychology of the judge and the second with the psychology of the person being questioned. The judge must, on the one hand, base his actions, and in particular his questioning, on the psychological method and, on the other, take full account of the insights gained via this method into human perception and the internal and external factors affecting it. Even though the structure of the book therefore clearly reflects the asymmetrical power structure of the criminal trial, that does not mean that the first part only indicates – on the basis of what were at the time highly influential philosophical and methodological writings – how the methodical scientisation of that process, and more specifically the work of judges hearing criminal cases, should be carried out.

What that scientisation involves is demonstrated by examples from the literature and from Gross's own experience. Gross discusses in detail the virtues that a criminal judge must possess, inter alia patience, confidentiality, discipline, and curiosity. The knowledge of human nature that is indispensable for his work is also dealt with at length, for example understanding of people's faults. Gross also devotes a great deal of attention to the understanding that the judge must have of argumentation, logic, and so forth. Nevertheless, it is noteworthy that the analysis of all of these conditions for making the criminal trial a scientific quest for truth and guilt is predominantly prescriptive. How criminal judges actually go about their work and what factors determine their findings and subsequent decisions are largely ignored.

The analysis in the second part of the psychology of the person being questioned is, as might be expected, essentially descriptive in nature. Gross first sets out in detail the contemporary, physiologically oriented theory of human perception, both in itself and in relation to the formation of thoughts, the operation of memory, and the functioning of speech. He then discusses the differential psychology of perception: the peculiarities of perception in men, women, children, and the elderly. Finally, he deals with all sorts of factors other

---

43   Gross 1893; Gross 1905; Grassberger 1960.

than age and gender which may affect perception, namely habits, prejudices, superstitions, delusions, etc.

The foregoing clearly shows that Gross's *Kriminalpsychologie* really did constitute a new kind of criminal psychology. It is an original, ground-breaking study. It is therefore not surprising that – if only for that reason – it had consequences. More specifically, this work became the basis for a tradition in German criminal psychology, namely the psychology of testimony (*Aussagepsychologie*) and the psychology of interrogation (*Vernehmungspsychologie*).

6.2.3.1.2. Criminal Psychology as the Psychology of Crime and the Criminal: Gustav Aschaffenburg, Max Kaufmann, and Erich Wulffen

Criminal psychology as the applied psychology of the criminal and his crime first took shape in Germany in the aforementioned book by Aschaffenburg, *Das Verbrechen und seine Bekämpfung*.[44] Although that title does not in itself say anything about his interest in criminal psychology, the subtitle does make that entirely clear: *Einleitung in die Kriminalpsychologie für Mediziner, Juristen und Soziologen; ein Beitrag zur Reform der Strafgesetzgebung* [*Introduction to Criminal Psychology for Physicians, Lawyers, and Sociologists: A Contribution to the Reform of Criminal Legislation*]. He was therefore concerned above all with the practical application of psychology in the criminal justice system. The book shows that when referring to criminal psychology, Aschaffenburg meant above all the study of the personality of the offender. In the first issue of the *Monatsschrift für Kriminalpsychologie und Strafrechtsreform*, he wrote that little was as yet known about what went on in the minds of people who committed crimes.[45]

Why he thought that the psychology of criminals needed to be studied can be deduced both from the subtitle of Aschaffenburg's book and from the title of that journal. Entirely in the spirit of the Modern Direction, he found it necessary to optimise the application of society's response to the personality of the criminal. That is also why the final chapter of his book is devoted entirely to the punishment of (juvenile) offenders and the provision of assistance for them. He calls in passing for measures to remedy the general lack of knowledge of psychology among the judiciary.

This call raises the question whether there was already so much useful knowledge available regarding that subject. In his book, Aschaffenburg himself does not provide any evidence for this. Entirely in line with Lombroso's views – without in fact sharing all of them – he only offers some reflections on, inter alia, the intellectual capacity, drives and emotions, language (including the

---

[44] Aschaffenburg 1923.
[45] Aschaffenburg 1904–05.

body language) of criminals, and the mental disorders that occur frequently among them – so frequently, in fact, that, according to Aschaffenburg, one can legitimately conclude that crime and mental illness are two plants that draw their sustenance from the same soil, namely physical and mental degeneracy.

A broader definition of what constitutes the criminal psychology of the offender was applied by the physician Max Kaufmann in his 1912 book *Die Psychologie des Verbrechens* [*The Psychology of Crime*].[46] According to that definition, criminal psychology comprises the study of all the circumstances and relationships that have led to a crime. In line with this definition, Kaufmann deals not only with the individual and general causes of crime and penal responses to it, as Aschaffenburg does, but, unlike the latter, also goes into detail regarding the concepts and methods of (criminal) psychology and the psychology of different types of criminals.

However, the most comprehensive conception of criminal psychology as the psychology of the criminal is presented by the public prosecutor Erich Wulffen[47] in his *Psychologie des Verbrechers: ein Handbuch für Juristen, Ärzte, Pädagogen und Gebildete aller Stände* [*Psychology of the Criminal: A Manual for Lawyers, Doctors, Educators, and Educated Persons of all Classes*] (1908).[48] In this two-volume work, Wulffen states that the field of criminal psychology includes not only the psychological features of criminals and crimes, as well as the individual and general causes of the specific criminal behaviour concerned, but also the normative, social, and ethical context of that behaviour.

It is also striking that this criminal psychology is entirely embedded in a scientific framework that comprises not only psychology, psychiatry, and characterology but also (criminal) anthropology. The criminal justice system itself is in fact dealt with at the end of this magnum opus but almost exclusively as a source of knowledge on the psychology of the criminal; the other actors are for the most part ignored.

That is not, of course, merely by chance. It stems from the fact that for Wulffen the real essence of criminal psychology concerns the inner life, imagination, and criminal inclinations of the individual criminal. In any event, Wulffen's second major general work was devoted entirely to this branch of criminal psychology: *Kriminalpsychologie: Psychologie des Täters* [*Criminal Psychology: Psychology of the Offender*] (1926).[49] The first part of this book is largely a repetition of what had already been presented regarding general psychology and anthropology in the author's main work.

Things only become interesting in the second part, in which Wulffen deals in great detail with numerous types of criminals – swindlers, robbers, arsonists,

---

[46]   Kaufmann 1912. See also Pollitz 1909.
[47]   Leistner 1999.
[48]   Wulffen 1913. See also Birnbaum 1921.
[49]   Wulffen 1926.

murderers, traitors, and so forth. He also discusses an extremely varied range of aspects of crime and criminal justice, but always in the context of the individual offender. His discussion includes, for example, the temptation and perception of crimes, the psychology of the methods by which crimes are committed, and criminals' awareness of the law.

This mix of stories of varying degrees of interest about all sorts of crimes and criminals mean that Wulffen's books are a kind of collection of criminological curiosities. But even viewed as such, his publications – incidentally, like those of Gross and others – are signs of the times. They reflect, on the one hand, the intense fascination that there was in Europe at that time for abnormal, bizarre, primitive and cruel behaviour, while on the other embodying, both directly and indirectly, a representation of what behaviour should be considered normal, ordinary, developed, and civilised.[50]

6.2.3.1.3. Criminal Psychology as the Psychology of Testimony, Confession, and Interrogation: Adolf Stöhr, Albert Hellwig, and Otto Mönkemöller

We have already seen that Gross's *Kriminalpsychologie* formed the start of a quite rich and influential German tradition in criminal psychology, namely the psychology of testimony and interrogation. Besides Gross, there were various other people who made a significant contribution to the flourishing of that tradition at the beginning of the twentieth century, not least Wilhelm Stern and Carl Gustav Jung. To show what their efforts led to in later years, it is appropriate to discuss a number of important books that were published at that time.

The first important survey of what had been achieved was presented in 1911 by the physician Adolf Stöhr in *Psychologie der Aussage* [*Psychology of Testimony*], parts 9–10 in the series *Das Recht: Sammlung von Abhandlungen für Juristen und Laien* [*The Law: A Collection of Essays for Lawyers and Laymen*].[51] If one compares this little book with the study by Gross, it immediately becomes apparent that, all in all, not very much more had in fact been achieved. Most of the topics are dealt with at the same level: the psychological, physical, and intellectual conditions that must be fulfilled if someone is to testify at all; the personal and other factors that influence the provision of testimony; and, very briefly, issues such as suggestion that play a negative or positive role in criminal interrogation. The only thing that is actually new is the account of the diagnostics with regard to the facts of cases (*Tatbestandsdiagnostik*). This refers to the tests performed, in particular by Wilhelm Stern and Carl Gustav Jung,

---

50   Becker (P.) 2002.
51   Stöhr 1911.

to measure people's psychological and physiological reactions – as if they formed unconscious, non-verbal testimonies – to stimuli, preferably words that can be associated with elements or aspects of a criminal offence that has been committed.

More important – being not only longer but also more innovative – was the major study published in 1927 by the magistrate Albert Hellwig: *Psychologie und Vernehmungstechnik bei Tatbestandsermittlungen: eine Einführung in die forensische Psychologie für Polizeibeamte, Richter, Staatsanwälte, Sachverständige und Laienrichter* [*Psychology and Interrogation Techniques in Investigations with regard to the Facts of Cases: An Introduction to Forensic Psychology for Police Officers, Judges, Prosecutors, Experts, and Laymen*].[52] The basic premise of this book is very similar to that of Gross's *Kriminalpsychologie*, namely that the judgment rendered by a court is the final outcome of a whole series of psychological actions by the perpetrator himself, but also by witnesses, experts, police officers, investigating magistrates, prosecutors, defenders, and of course judges. The rulings handed down by judges are in other words constructed from a highly complex chain of observations, assessments, and statements on facts. It is entirely in line with this premise that Hellwig, unlike Gross, deals not only with the psychology of the judicial examination by the court but also with the psychology of interrogation by police officers, experts, and others. Another important difference is that Hellwig systematically explains the techniques of interrogation, both in general and of defendants and witnesses in particular. The third major difference is that he does not develop a general psychology of the person questioned but clearly distinguishes the psychology of the accused from that of the witness. It is because of these differences that Hellwig's study can be termed innovative.

The final author to be dealt with here is Otto Mönkemöller, who in 1930 published the most comprehensive book on witnesses and interrogations in the period with which we are concerned, *Psychologie und Psychopathologie der Aussage* [*Psychology and Psychopathology of Testimony*].[53] The special feature of this book, however, is not so much that it demonstrates the author's wide-ranging experience and an almost unlimited knowledge of the German, French, and English literature. Rather, its significance is to be found, first, in the far-reaching (if somewhat muddled) detailed description and classification of all kinds of types and variants of normal and mentally disturbed adult witnesses: the ambitious witness, the garrulous witness, the stuttering witness, the manic-depressive witness, etc. Second, the book contains an impressive inventory of facts and circumstances that impede or prevent a focused and correct witness

---

[52]   Hellwig 1927.
[53]   Mönkemöller 1930.

statement, for example the complexity and rapidity of the events that the witness has experienced, the influence of the media, and cultural taboos.

Moreover, this synthesising study includes a lengthy chapter on testimony by children, constructed in more or less the same way as the chapters on testimony by adults. A wide range of types of juvenile witnesses are discussed, and numerous facts and circumstances are presented that can play a positive and/or negative role in the questioning of young children.

If one compares this exhaustive study with the original work of Gross, it is astounding to see how much practical insight and relevant knowledge on the provision of testimony and the conduct of interrogations had been acquired within just 30 years. In this respect, Gross's call for the criminal justice system to be made scientific had certainly fallen on fertile ground.

6.2.3.1.4.   Criminal Psychology as the Psychology of Criminal Law
              and the Criminal Justice System

In the light of the comments just made, the finding that the psychological study of criminal law and the criminal justice system remained the least developed branch of reformist criminal psychology during the period with which we are concerned is not that remarkable. It is perhaps better to say that this specialisation had not actually developed, given that it did not advance beyond some initial steps taken by only a few relatively unknown authors.

The first of these was Julius Friedrich, the author of *Die Bedeutung der Psychologie für die Bekämpfung der Verbrechen: zugleich eine Kritik neuerer Straf-, Strafprozess- und Jugendgerichtsentwürfe und der herrschenden strafrechtlichen Schuldlehre* [*The Importance of Psychology for Combatting Crime: also a Critique of Recent Drafts for Criminal Law, Criminal Prosecution, and Juvenile Courts and Prevailing Criminal Law Doctrine*] (1915).[54] As the title of this little book – a collection of lectures – shows, Friedrich examines the contributions that criminal psychology, in the two meanings examined above, can make to combatting crime, broadening the range of penalties and measures, and organising the criminal justice system. It does not, however, put forward much that is new.

Another author who should be mentioned is Karl Haff, who in 1924 published a work entitled *Rechtspsychologie* [*Forensic Psychology*] about, as the subtitle indicates, *Forschungen zur Individual- und Massenpsychologie des Rechts und zur modernen Rechtsfindung* [*Research on the Individual and Mass Psychology of Law and on the Modern Interpretation of Law*]. Following on from Friedrich's observations, those of Haff on freedom and guilt in civil and criminal law are certainly interesting.[55] What is more important, however, is his account of the

---

[54]   Friedrich 1915.
[55]   Haff 1924.

relationship between the logic of legal systems, people's sense of justice, and the legal intuition of judges, and within that discussion in particular his plea for the administration of justice, including in criminal cases, to be based more on psychological investigation and, conversely, for more psychological research to be carried out on the application of the (criminal) law. This is with a view to not only a less subjective but also a more objective criminal justice system, i.e. a system that can adapt itself better and faster to the extremely variable and changing needs of society.

6.2.3.2. Criminal Psychology from an Abolitionist Perspective

What one does not find in reform-oriented criminal psychology can be found to some extent in criminal psychology with an abolitionist tendency, namely criminal psychoanalysis. I say "to some extent" because this "alternative" criminal psychology did not really come to fruition, either before the Second World War or afterwards. However, a number of notable studies were published in the 1920s in German-speaking countries that to this day form the starting point for psychoanalytic views on crime, the criminal, and punishment. Those studies were by Franz Alexander, Hugo Staub, August Aichhorn, and Theodor Reik.

Imago, the official journal of the International Psychoanalytical Association published a special issue in 1931 on the topic of criminology, with contributions by Alexander and Staub, as well as an essay by Erich Fromm on the psychology of the criminal and the punitive society in which Fromm sought to link up with the views previously defended by Von Liszt. That special issue can be regarded as a token of the psychoanalytic movement's recognition of criminology. That recognition is also reflected, however, in the appearance of specifically psychoanalytic publications on the relevant themes outside the German language area. In France, for example, Georges Genil-Perrin published a clear overview of the ideas hitherto proposed in psychoanalytic circles on crime, criminals, and the criminal justice system.[56] What is more, he was not the only person in France who wrote about the contributions that psychoanalysis could make to the development of criminology.[57]

The German-language studies that form the foundation of criminal psychoanalysis also lend themselves very well to discussion according to the threefold classification we have been applying: reformist, abolitionist and psychoanalytical psychology. That classification will therefore be followed below.

---

[56]   Genil-Perrin 1934.
[57]   Muchielli 1994c.

6.2.3.2.1. Criminal Psychology as the Psychoanalysis of Crime and the Criminal: August Aichhorn, Franz Alexander, and Hugo Staub

At various times and in various works, Freud himself explicitly expressed an opinion on the background to criminal behaviour. In his important essay *Das Unbehagen in der Kultur* [*Civilisation and its Discontents*], for example, he wrote that the tension between the superego and the ego leads to a feeling of guilt, and that this in turn leads to a need for punishment.[58] It was mainly his students, however, who elaborated on this problem,

The foremost among them was the Austrian educator August Aichhorn. The book he published in 1925 about his experience as director of a correctional home for juveniles in Vienna made a huge impression throughout the world. That book, *Verwahrloste Jugend* (published in New York in 1935 as *Wayward Youth*), argues that the manifest neglect of children as expressed through anti-social or criminal behaviour can be traced back to latent neglect, which itself may have various primary causes.[59]

First, it may be the result of a disturbed emotional life in early childhood because the child's need for love was not sufficiently satisfied or in fact satisfied to excess. In such a case, there is an inner conflict within the neglected child between his ego (*Ich*) and his ego-ideal (*Ich-Ideal*), the superego; this inner conflict, as Freud had already asserted, evokes a feeling of guilt and a need for punishment that can be satisfied by exhibiting anti-social or criminal behaviour. Second, that latent neglect may result in the child growing up in an anti-social, criminal environment, in which case there is an external conflict in the neglected child, namely between the superego, which drives him to anti-social or criminal behaviour, and the community that disapproves of and rejects that behaviour.

This view of the origin and nature of criminal behaviour comprises quite a lot of criticism of certain trends in the criminal psychology of the time. Aichhorn, for example, explicitly distanced himself from theories that allude to people being predisposed to criminal behaviour. According to Aichhorn, the existence of criminal families can be explained even without postulating such a predisposition: the transfer of ego-ideals from father to son makes this entirely understandable. It is obvious, however, that Aichhorn's view involved a more radical critique of the criminal justice system than the criminal-psychological view adhered to by others. But that was not because Aichhorn considered any kind of punishment to be out of the question. From the perspective of protecting society, he did not consider punishment for neglected juveniles with an external conflict to be reprehensible: the threat of punishment would aid in the suppression of impulses to commit crime. But Aichhorn considered punishing

---

[58]   Freud 1971.
[59]   Aichhorn 1967.

internally conflicted neglected juveniles to be totally counterproductive. Doing so in fact met their perceived need. They ought actually to be approached in a non-repressive, loving manner.

Aichhorn's ideas were systematised and refined some years later by the German psychiatrist Franz Alexander and the German jurist Hugo Staub in their book *Der Verbrecher und sein Richter* (1929), which became very well known particularly in its later expanded American edition, *The Criminal, the Judge and the Public*.[60] Alexander and Staub assert, much more firmly than Aichhorn, that psychoanalysis is in fact the first and only branch of criminal psychology that can provide an understanding in specific cases of the motives that people have for committing a crime. Where "neurotic" criminals are concerned, for example, the authors differentiate between those whose ego has been significantly damaged by the effects of toxic or organic influences (i.e. alcoholics), and those in whom the ego has, as it were, lost the conflict with the super-ego and thus has also lost its grip on the id (*Es*), that huge reservoir of anti-social or criminal forces. They also acknowledge the existence of crime that is not based on either inner or external mental or psychosocial conflicts but is simply the result of fortuitous but extreme social conditions that overpower or overshadow the ego, as it were.

Alexander and Staub also go much further than Aichhorn in their criticism of the criminal law and the administration of criminal justice. They fundamentally question the meaning of such concepts as responsibility and freedom, and thus the meaning of functions such as those of the courts. They characterise the criminal justice system as an institution that both satisfies unconscious needs for punishment and channels all kinds of conscious aggression. In their view, that characterisation explains why the criminal justice system, and especially the prison system, are maintained even though these systems generally fail to provide an adequate response to the crime that is committed – quite the contrary. They believe that the prison system should to a large extent be converted into a network of psychiatric institutions.

6.2.3.2.2. Criminal Psychology as the Psychoanalysis of Testimony, Confession, and Interrogation: Theodor Reik

The critical view of the criminal justice system adopted by Alexander and Staub was to a large extent based on the ideas first expressed on the subject by Theodor Reik in his book *Geständniszwang und Strafbedürfnis* [*The Compulsion to Confess and the Need for Punishment*] (1925) and later, in about 1930, in *Psychoanalytische Studien* [*Psychoanalytical Studies*]. Reik went further than his followers, however, ultimately even advocating the complete abolition of

---

[60] Alexander and Staub 1962.

punishment of any kind.[61] He even accused his followers of wrongly wanting to sit in the judge's seat because he believed that psychoanalysis was entirely unsuited to answering questions regarding the material truth of an event and the guilt of a suspect. Seen in that light, it is no wonder that Reik was harsh about Gross, Wulffen, and Hellwig, accusing them of having a total lack of understanding of phenomena such as self-betrayal, confession of the accused, and the return of murderers to the scene of their crime.

Theodor REIK, *Geständniszwang und Strafbedürfnis: Probleme der Psychoanalyse und der Kriminologie*, Leipzig, Internationaler Psychoanalytischer Verlag, 1925.

Reik presented the ideas that brought him worldwide renown in his book about the need for punishment and the compulsion to confess. The basic premise of that work was to a large extent at odds with the current literature on confessions,

---

[61]   Reik 1925; Reik 1978.

which in fact deals with the psychological pressure that can be placed on the suspect during interrogations.[62] Reik's position has already been mentioned: a lot of people suffer from feelings of guilt and can only reduce the distress that those feelings trigger by actual atonement, i.e. by confessing the crime that they have committed and thus calling down punishment on themselves. Reik took this point further, however.

In particular, he asserts that it is only through confession that suspects, i.e. criminals, gain insight into the motives for their crimes and the personal significance of those motives. Complementary to this, by confessing before society, as it were, defendants distance themselves from their deeds and at the same time express to their fellow human beings that they wish to become part of that society once more. Conversely, confessing not only facilitates the application of the criminal law and makes judges milder, it also confronts society with the role that it has itself played in the occurrence of crime, for example by allowing poverty to continue to exist. Moreover, Reik says, confessing meets society's unconscious need for punishment and also makes it possible for society to identify with the criminal. In this way, it is possible to reconcile the two.

6.2.3.2.3. Criminal Psychology as the Psychology of the Criminal Law and the Criminal Justice System: Paul Reiwald

Much of what we have already dealt with is also to be found in a book that Paul Reiwald published in 1948, but which belongs entirely to the psychoanalytically oriented criminal-psychological literature of the 1920s, namely *Die Gesellschaft und Ihre Verbrecher* [*Society and its Criminals*].[63] In that study, it is not Reiwald's aim, however, to provide an analysis of the criminal and/or criminal behaviour, but rather a study of the punitive society.

In other words, he begins his study at the point where others conclude theirs. The reason for this is clear: in the same way as the criminal is inconceivable without society, so society cannot do without the criminal, whom it needs in order to vent its own subconscious emotions. In Reiwald's view, a full-scale psychology of criminal law must also include the psychology of the criminal with whom we are all involved.[64]

Reiwald ascribes the reason why such a psychology does not yet really exist to opposition from lawyers. So why do they resist its development? Because psychoanalysis would inform them of the similarity between their own impulses and those of an anti-social person, while, precisely because of their fear of that

---

62   Henschel 1914.
63   Reiwald 1948. See also Nolte 1928.
64   Reiwald 1948, p. 45.

identification, they do not wish to know who the offender actually is, and would rather retreat into the artificial and abstract world of legal language.[65]

In line with this premise, Reiwald demonstrates – on the basis, inter alia, of the symbolic function of the judge and the external features of the law as ceremonial – that there is a taboo on the criminal within the criminal justice system, as if he were a successor to the devil of the Middle Ages. We project our subconscious fears onto him. We need him in order to alleviate our own psychological distress. This, according to Reiwald, is strikingly expressed in police and detective fiction, but is also reflected in actual detection and particularly in the person and work of Gross; these testify to the obsessional neurosis lurking behind that projection.

Abolition of the criminal law seems to Reiwald to be desirable on rational grounds but virtually impossible on irrational grounds, for the simple reason that the criminal law is actually a form of sublimated aggression towards an anti-social person. It is only with the aid of the criminal law that peace can be established within a society.[66]

6.2.4. ACADEMIC, POLICY, AND PRACTICAL CONSEQUENCES OF CRIMINOLOGY

6.2.4.1. Denial of Criminology at the Universities

The above overview already suggests that even though criminology had some influential supporters in German-speaking countries inaround 1900 and even if an increasing amount of important literature was being published at that time, no special university chairs were established or special education programmes set up in the field of criminology. On the contrary, criminology in that period was and remained predominantly a field in which professors of criminal law, medicine, or psychiatry became involved as a "side-line".

Not that in all those years there were no proposals to set up chairs of criminology and courses in the subject, whether or not in the framework of the existing educational programmes. On the contrary, on more than one occasion proposals to that effect were defended and developed, not only by Von Liszt, Aschaffenburg, and Gross, but also by leading prison wardens and police chiefs, such as Heinrich Lindenau and Hans Schneickert. Their efforts were always in vain, however. They were in any case insufficient to overcome the strong resistance to such initiatives within the scientific community. That resistance had a lot to do, on the one hand, with the widespread lack of agreement on the theoretical

---

[65] Reiwald 1948, pp. 42–43.
[66] Reiwald 1948, p. 288.

foundations and practical usefulness of criminology: what did that science in fact stand for and who actually had a need for it in professional practice? On the other hand, resistance also stemmed from the traditional structure of the faculties into which criminology would need to be incorporated, those of law and medicine. Within those faculties, there was little room for innovation.

The result was that the practice of criminology in German universities remained limited, until the 1960s, to the occasional class or seminar taught by professors who, for one reason or another, had a personal interest in the subject. Thus, even as an ancillary science to criminal law, criminology failed to get off the ground within a university context, quite apart from it being possible, within or outside the universities, to set up separate institutes of criminology where professors from various faculties would collaborate on issues concerning crime and punishment.[67]

6.2.4.2.   Application of Criminology in Policy

The history of criminology in German-speaking countries between 1880 and 1933 also shows that during that period there was no lack of proposals to take the necessary steps to tackle the problem of crime and in particular the problem posed by incorrigible habitual criminals. These proposals mainly concerned those criminals within that category who, according to leading experts, should be considered of unsound mind or at the very least to have diminished responsibility because of their hereditary defects and/or their insufficient intellectual abilities. It had in fact been Von Liszt himself who had continually advocated the recognition of such a category of criminals in the Criminal Code and the acceptance of penalties or measures to protect the community against them by locking them up for a long time, if not permanently. We have already seen, however, that that advocacy led to him being attacked directly by the "pure" criminal lawyers, who questioned what part of the criminal law he would allow to remain. That attack was not without its effect, and the existing provisions regarding criminal responsibility remained unamended.

At the end of the nineteenth century, the ongoing debate on the need for reform of the criminal justice system with a view to combatting crime more effectively did lead to greater scope for conditional sentencing in a number of German states. That change was also introduced there to allow for a more appropriate means of dealing with occasional offenders: rather than immediately locking them up in prison – the classic approach at the time – they would be left at liberty, under certain conditions, thus giving them the opportunity – or indeed compelling them – to mend their ways.

---

[67]   Galassi 2004, pp. 286–338.

Where habitual criminals were concerned, the preliminary draft of a new Criminal Code provided in 1909 that their term of imprisonment could be extended considerably depending on the number of custodial sentences that they had already received. But Von Liszt and his associates wished to go further. In an alternative draft, they proposed that in the case of offenders who were capable of improvement, imprisonment should be followed by time-limited confinement in a workhouse; for incorrigible habitual criminals, on the other hand, the latter form of detention would not be subject to any time limit, with a view to "rendering them harmless". The state commission dealing with these matters included this proposal in its final report in 1913.

The commission stated, however, that not all measures were acceptable in the name of defending society. That certainly applied to the proposal of some asylum physicians, also defended by Gross and Von Hentig in around 1910, to impose long-term measures to combat crime by castrating or sterilising seriously degenerate offenders, and if necessary even making use of the death penalty. These eugenics-inspired ideas – which to some extent were defended on the basis of the policy pursued at the time in the United States – were rejected by most colleagues of Gross and Von Hentig not only on scientific grounds – which offenders would this involve? How could they be identified with certainty? – but also on moral and political grounds. What claim could criminal policy make to legitimacy if, as a matter of principle, it treated the interests of the community as being of greater importance than the interests of the individual? A few commentators drew attention to the risk that under certain circumstances a policy that did this systematically could turn into an outright policy of extermination. As we have already noted, at the time of the Weimar Republic the application of such a policy did, however, acquire a certain legitimacy through the agency of *Kriminalbiologie*.[68]

6.2.4.3. Hans Gross, Kriminalistik *and* Bertillonnage

Like his *Kriminalpsychologie*, Gross's *Handbuch für Untersuchungsrichter, Polizeibeamte, Gendarmen u.s.w.* was in line with the existing literature regarding detection and prosecution, for example Wilhelm Stieber's practical guidelines for detection. If those guidelines are compared with the *Handbuch*, however, some major differences are immediately obvious. Not only are far more topics discussed at greater length in the *Handbuch* than in the guidelines, but the way this is done is based to a much greater extent on the current state of scientific research. It is precisely that fact that makes the *Handbuch*, which was first published in 1893, such a remarkable and innovative book: it was a large-scale attempt at modernisation, i.e. the scientisation of criminal proceedings. That

---

[68]   Galassi 2004, pp. 378–414; Bondio 1995, pp. 220–240.

attempt was also so astonishing because it was undertaken not from within the academic world but by a magistrate who had established, through his work as an investigating magistrate and prosecutor in and around Graz, that his law studies had left him totally inadequately prepared for carrying out his duties.

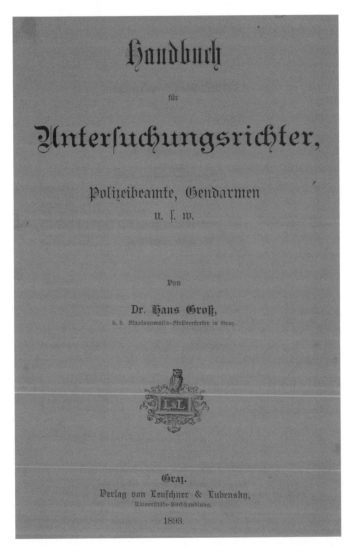

Hans Gross, *Handbuch für Untersuchungsrichter, Polizeibeamte, Gendarmen u.s.w.*, Graz, Verlag von Leuschner & Lubensky, 1893.

This discovery had not only led him to learn from his own and others' experience of detection but also from types of scientific research that were relevant to criminal investigation. Large parts of the *Handbuch* (a reference book totalling some 620 pages) are devoted to interrogation, examination of the crime scene, the use of experts in a number of fields, the world of professional criminals and gypsies, the features of the most frequent crimes, important types of clues (such as bloodstains and footprints, and how they should be dealt with), up to and including weapons and explosives. Nowhere else in the world was there such a thoroughly complete and practical handbook. That explains why Gross's book was a sensation throughout Europe, but also elsewhere, and was quickly translated into many languages, either in complete or abridged versions. Until his death in 1915, Gross published six successive revised and augmented editions.

If this book is viewed from the historical-criminological perspective, the first striking thing is that the first edition paid absolutely no attention to Lombroso, the Italian School, or criminal bio-anthropology in general. Later editions did do so, but very marginally, with only a mention in the section on the interrogation of the suspect, a mention that does not amount to much. The main message is in fact that although Lombroso had created an enormous sensation at the time, his ideas should, by the time the *Handbuch* was written, be regarded as obsolete. It is therefore rather remarkable that in 1898 Gross published the first issue of a journal entitled *Archiv für Kriminal-Anthropologie und Kriminalistik* [*Archives of Criminal Anthropology and Criminalistics*].

It may be that he gave it that name because – as is shown by the later editions of the *Handbuch* – he saw criminalistics as part of a *kriminologische Phänomenologie*, which in turn, together with *kriminologische Anthropologie* and *kriminologische Soziologie* formed the essential *Kriminologie*. This image of criminology at least creates the impression that, for Gross, anthropology and criminalistics could not be seen separately from one another and that some aspects, such as the interrogation of suspect, were interlinked.[69] That he used the term *Kriminalistik* in the title was not surprising because from its second edition onwards his manual was entitled *Handbuch für Untersuchungsrichter als System der Kriminalistik* [*Manual for Examining Magistrates as a System of Criminalistics*]. In the opening article of the first issue, Gross justifies the choice of title for the journal by stating that the two disciplines are associated in many respects, and that both are sciences ancillary to the criminal law.[70]

Given that Gross's *Handbuch* quickly became a worldwide sensation because it met a great need for understanding, knowledge, and information regarding investigative practice, one would expect that – at least in Germany or, more broadly, in German-speaking Europe – institutes of criminalistics would soon have been founded, especially since the police forces in major cities had already set up large-scale identification services at the end of the nineteenth century. That was not the case, however.

---

[69] Lindenau 1902.
[70] Gross 1998; Galassi 2004, pp. 265–273; Bondio 1995, pp. 150–181.

At the University of Graz itself, where Gross – having worked for years at the Universities of Czernowitz (Chernivtsi) and Prague – was appointed professor in 1905, a *Kriminalistisches Institut* was not founded until 1912, i.e. three years after the establishment of such an institute by Reiss at the University of Lausanne (1909). In Germany, at least in Prussia, it was actually only within the Berlin police force that a laboratory was set up, although until the 1930s it frequently

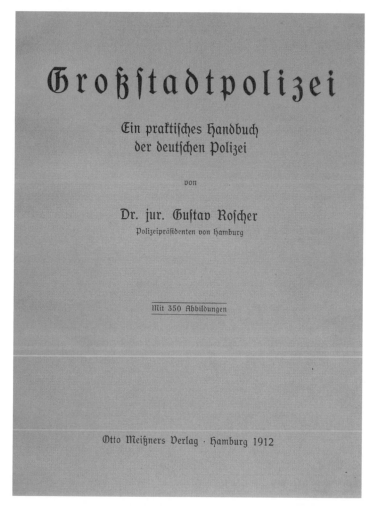

Gustav Roscher, *Großstadtpolizei: ein praktisches Handbuch der deutschen Polizei*, Hamburg, Otto Meißners Verlag, 1912.

had to rely on the cooperation of university institutes and private laboratories. Nor did proposals for the establishment of a large state institute for the whole of Germany or, in view of the associated drawbacks, for the setting up of such institutes in a number of different places come to anything; this was probably due to lack of funds.[71] What that meant was that the lack of infrastructure led to the actual practice of detection generally lagging far behind what was possible in theory.[72]

As mentioned previously, matters were very different as regards identification services. In the first edition of the *Handbuch* – which appeared in the same year as the Service d'identité judiciaire was founded in Paris (1893) – Gross had already expressed great appreciation for the achievements of Bertillon and explained the anthropometric and photographic elements of *Bertillonnage* in detail. No mention was yet made in that edition of dactyloscopy. Apparently, Gross – located of course in Graz – had not followed the discussion in the United Kingdom (or had perhaps been unable to follow it), and had failed to notice the publication of Galton's book on fingerprints (published just the year before, in 1892). He did of course discuss dactyloscopy in later editions, in each case comparing its capabilities and limitations with those of anthropometry. Gross eventually also came to the conclusion that dactyloscopy was in certain respects clearly a more suitable method of identification than anthropometry.

That was also the conclusion of the heads of the police forces of the major cities in the German language area. As in other European cities, those cities had also assembled impressive collections of photographs since the 1860s and 1870s so as to be able to identify suspects and convicts, distinguish occasional criminals from repeat offenders, etc.[73] And, as elsewhere, they found themselves confronted, sooner or later, by the problems involved in the application of judicial photography and the construction of such collections. To address those issues as well as they could, the major police forces switched over in the 1890s to *Bertillonnage* and more particularly to anthropometry.[74] But just like their counterparts in other countries, the police in Germany were quickly confronted by the question of whether it was not better to replace anthropometry as such with dactyloscopy.[75]

Here too, the answer was in the affirmative: in 1903, the Prussian police, at any rate, made the switch to dactyloscopy.[76] That certainly does not mean, however, that they abandoned use, for example, of the *Verbrecheralbum* (rogues' gallery) and the *portrait parlé*. In a sense, dactyloscopy was in fact simply a new method to be added to the overall range of methods for identifying people.[77] It is therefore no wonder that the identification services of the major police forces in Germany and Austria – those of Berlin, Dresden, Hamburg, and

---

[71]   Gross 1913; Strafella 1916.
[72]   Wagner (P.) 1996, pp. 77–148.
[73]   Zafita 1915.
[74]   Gruder 1898; Roscher 1899; Von Meerscheidt-Hüllesem 1900.
[75]   Paul 1903; Roscher 1904; Koettig 1908.
[76]   Schlinzig 2003.
[77]   Schneikert 1911; Wagner (P.) 1996, pp. 96–107; Roth (A.) 1997, pp. 92–110; Becker (P.) 2005a, pp. 114–135.

Vienna – expanded in time into extensive, complex bureaucratic identification machines.[78]

6.2.4.4. *The* Kriminalpolizei *under the Spell of* Kriminalbiologie

The basically organisational and technical transformation of the *Kriminalpolizei* in German-speaking Europe must not obscure the fact that both the development of criminology in a biological direction and the discussion of the application of its findings in combatting crime during the Weimar Republic influenced the organisation of the *Kriminalpolizei* in a very different way. It is also very important to point out that influence specifically with a view to a proper understanding of the role played by criminology in Nazi Germany.

Following on from what has already been said concerning the establishment of a criminal-biological department within the Vienna police in 1928, it should first be noted that a number of such offices were set up in the late 1920s within several major German police forces. It should also be borne in mind that in 1921 Arthur MacDonald, the ardent American champion of criminal anthropology, had already advocated the creation of anthropological investigation departments within the police in the *Archiv für Kriminalanthropologie und Kriminalistik*.[79] In 1929, the initiative was taken in Hamburg to have psychiatrists from the city's health service and detectives from the *Kriminalpolizei* cooperate in order to meet the pressing need for modern criminal-biological research. Such cooperation was also instigated in Kiel in 1930 in order to determine the personality of criminals in the spirit of Lenz. There were also emphatic calls for criminal-biological departments to be set up within the *Kriminalpolizei* throughout Germany. One of the arguments in favour of this was that the investigations carried out by such departments would make it possible to put security measures in place at an early stage, in addition to or instead of criminal law measures.[80]

These initiatives clearly show that during the 1920s discussion had again arisen in the Weimar Republic on the extent to which it was necessary, in the case of professional and habitual criminals, to impose custodial measures – whether or not temporary – for the protection of society (*Sicherungsverwahrung*) in addition to or as an extension of prison sentences. That debate resulted in 1925 in a bill which proposed that dangerous habitual criminals, after serving their actual sentence, should continue to be confined until they had mended their ways.[81] That compromise did not, of course, receive much support within the *Kriminalpolizei*.

---

[78]   Gross 1903a; Roscher 1912, pp. 210–239; Harster 1910; Harster 1914; Stieber 1921, pp. 28–38; Heindl 1922a, pp. 83–90; Heindl 1926, pp. 78–87.
[79]   MacDonald 1921.
[80]   Erkens 1931, pp. 491–498.
[81]   Thulfaut 2000, pp. 79–86.

The best proof of this is the book published by Robert Heindl in 1926 (reaching its seventh edition in 1929): *Der Berufsverbrecher: ein Beitrag zur Strafrechtsreform* [*The Professional Criminal: A Contribution to Penal Reform*]. Heindl asserted, based on an assortment of arguments, that Germany was contending with an extremely harmful class of professional criminals and that

Robert HEINDL, *Der Berufsverbrecher: Ein Beitrag zur Strafrechtsreform*, Berlin, Pan-Verlag Kurt Metzner, 1929.

the only remedy was life imprisonment for such individuals, not as a form of punishment but as a measure to protect society. That was necessary, he asserted, because their persistent malevolence resulted not from social circumstances or educational deficiencies in the enforcement of penalties but from the fact that, for whatever reason – personality, upbringing, etc. – they were quite simply incorrigible. According to Heindl, anyone who denied this and believed that other measures would be effective was guilty of self-deception.

In his view, professional criminals – by which he meant, for example, murderers, burglars, swindlers, robbers, and pimps – came in all shapes and sizes. They had various things in common, however: they operated for profit, they had their own specialisations and methods, and they sought one another's company in certain pubs, brothels, clubs, etc. In other words, professional criminals were well organised; indeed, they formed an organised power.[82] Heindl estimated the number of truly dangerous professional criminals in Germany at over 4,000. That number might not seem large, given an adult population of 46 million, but in view of the harm done to society and individual citizens by incorrigible criminals, he considered that they formed a great danger and that combatting them in the normal manner by the police and judicial authorities would also cost a great deal of money. Lifelong internment of these criminals was not only cheaper than a temporary sentence but would instantly achieve an almost unimaginable drop in crime, as foreign examples, according to Heindl, already showed. The conclusion, he wrote, was obvious: every society must defend itself against those who harmed it. A society that did not do so would be destroyed.

In all fairness, it should be added that Heindl's book – no matter how ominous his final conclusion sounded – did not advocate the application of eugenic measures such as the castration or sterilisation of criminals in order to save the country from destruction. This means that those who during the Nazi period put a eugenic spin on his strong views on combatting professional criminals were wrongfully invoking his book *Der Berufsverbrecher*.[83]

6.3. DEVELOPMENT OF CRIMINOLOGY IN THE UNITED KINGDOM

In the United Kingdom around 1900, criminology failed to get off the ground. The emergence of bio-anthropological criminology in Italy did provoke responses but did not lead to any similar movement such as there had been in Germany, nor did it bring about a counter-movement as in France. That it failed to do so is probably because it was not sufficiently aligned with the established views on crime and punishment in the United Kingdom, the responses regarding the scientific, practical, and policy-related value of this new discipline being too much divided.

---

[82] Dobler and Reinke 2009.
[83] Heindl 1929a, pp. 1, 7, 91–92, 105, 109–110, 139–140, 142, 148, 190–194, 198–199, 314–316, 392–394.

That does not mean, of course, that discussion regarding the personality of the criminal, and in particular regarding the structure of the prison system, fell silent in the United Kingdom at the end of the nineteenth century. It also does not mean that no interesting publications on these issues appeared there before the Second World War. That is certainly not true. But unlike in Italy, France and Germany, there was nobody in the United Kingdom during this period with the stature of a Lombroso, Ferri or Garofalo, of a Lacassagne, Tarde, Durkheim or Bertillon, or of a Von Liszt, Aschaffenburg or Gross.

Also relevant here is the fact that during this period no general introductions or treatises, etc. were published that constituted major points of reference for discussion of crime and punishment at the universities, among policymakers, and in everyday practice. Nor can one say that there were any special developments in the United Kingdom in particular subfields of criminology. Even a field such as criminalistics was not developed, either systematically or otherwise.[84] There was therefore no question of one or more specific criminological journals being founded, of university chairs of criminology being established, or of criminological societies emerging. During this period, there was simply no institutionalisation of criminology in the United Kingdom, in any form whatsoever. In many historical, biographical, and encyclopaedic summaries of criminology hardly any attention is therefore paid to the developments in that country at the time.[85]

A book that can nevertheless be regarded, to some extent, as a turning point in the development of criminology in the United Kingdom during this period is the report published by Charles Goring in 1913: *The English Convict*. That study was in fact the result of an extensive investigation, set up with the official support of the highest judicial authorities, to settle once and for all the debate that had been going on since the 1880s on the value of Lombrosian bio-anthropological criminology for the study and treatment of criminals. The research concerned did not act, however, as the intended litmus test and the accompanying report therefore failed to bring about any consensus on the issue. As a result, the literature on crime and criminals that appeared in the United Kingdom between the wars was just as divided on that point as the literature published around 1900.

6.3.1. MIXED RESPONSES TO ITALIAN BIO-ANTHROPOLOGY

At the end of the nineteenth century, the psychiatrist Henry Maudsley was still a widely read author on the topic of the personality of the criminal. And although

---

[84] Teignmouth Shore 1931; Emsley 2002, pp. 217–218.
[85] See for example Martin, Mutchnick and Austin 1990; Rock 1994; Hayward, Maruna and Mooney 2010.

since the 1870s he viewed the inadequate physical and mental development of criminals from a much more evolutionary Darwinian perspective than had previously been the case – thus attributing it far more to the hereditary transmission of characteristics – he still did not make the link to Lombroso in 1895 in one of his last familiar works, *The Psychology of Mind* – not even when he compared criminals with savages who, when they come into contact with civilised peoples, display nothing other than "low cunning, lying, stealing, treachery and crime".[86]

Two pages later, he explains why he did not make that link: criminals can only be understood by means of thorough investigation of their personality and of the circumstances in which they live.[87] It was, in other words, a certain aversion to categorical statements about "the criminal" that prevented Maudsley from embracing the paradigm as originally formulated by Lombroso. In keeping with the British tradition, he still apparently believed that generalisations were inappropriate in this field and that one always needed to consider, on a case-by-case basis, which factors had actually played a role in causing a crime and which had not. This is in any case one of the reasons invariably cited in the British literature to explain why criminal anthropology gained no permanent foothold in the United Kingdom. The other reason was apparently that the pronouncements that Lombroso and his followers sometimes made about the personality of the criminal were irresponsible and too bombastic for British ears. As Paul Rock has noted, "triumphal grand theorising" and such an "overblown manner" was not an approach favoured by his predecessors in criminology around 1900.[88]

To what extent these two arguments are in fact generally applicable is open to debate, however. They are in any case inconsistent with comparisons such as those made by Maudsley between criminals and savages. But they are also difficult to accept given that Lombrosian criminology was in fact embraced by a number of other authors and that the large-scale study by Goring was intended to determine the value of Lombroso's (initial) ideas. Why would one carry out such a study into ideas that do not in any case fit in with one's own theories and experiences? In other words, did that study demonstrate a defensive and complacent – perhaps even rather nationalistic – attitude towards a new paradigm of foreign origin that nevertheless had a certain following in one's own country? Or was it, on the contrary, precisely to provide this paradigm – against prevailing opinion – with greater legitimacy on the British side of the Channel? When one considers – as we will do below – the institutional framework within which the study was conducted, the answer to the latter question may well be positive, or at least more positive than we commonly think.

---

[86] Rafter 2004a, pp. 997–999, 1001–1003.
[87] Maudsley 1895, pp. 80–82; Davie 2005, pp. 79–86.
[88] Rock 2007.

Neil Davie has in any case shown that Lombroso's (initial) descriptions of born criminals had far more in common with his British contemporaries' views on habitual criminals than recent British authors such as Rock, as well as Roger Hood and David Garland, have claimed. Davie also indicates implicitly that it

Portrait of Francis Galton, in: R. Heindl, *System und Praxis der Dactyloscopie und der sonstigen technischen Methoden der Kriminalpolizei*, Berlin, Vereinigung Wissenschaflicher Verleger, 1922.

was precisely because of this similarity that the impact of criminal anthropology in the United Kingdom was greater than Rock, Hood, and Garland have suggested.[89] It was not, after all, only Havelock Ellis who spread the word of

---

[89]   Garland 1988, pp. 2–7; Garland 2002, pp. 29–33; Radzinowicz and Hood 1990, pp. 11–20.

Lombroso in the United Kingdom in his book *The Criminal* (1890). Galton – already referred to a number of times and who had shown, since the 1870s, an unparalleled interest in both the hereditary basis of human behaviour and the anthropometry of offenders – immediately praised Ellis's book, and thus also criminal anthropology, in *Nature*. And these were not Lombroso's only adherents.

In support of his assertions, Davie refers both to a number of articles on crime and criminals in leading British medical journals and to official reports on addressing crime problems in the second half of the nineteenth century. These, he states, refer in a positive way, either implicitly or explicitly, to Lombroso and criminal bio-anthropology, or in any case write in a Lombrosian manner about the role of hereditary factors in the causation of crime and the identification of criminals by certain external physical characteristics. Prison doctors certainly did not find Lombroso's description of the born criminal problematic. It is not surprising, therefore, that in the late 1890s Lombroso himself – also a prison doctor, after all – saw extensive similarity between his views on habitual criminals and the ideas about such criminals that appeared in leading publications in the United Kingdom.[90]

Among those publications was, for example, the fairly well-known book *Crime and its Causes* written by William Morrison in 1891. Referring to the many discussions that were raging on the continent about whether or not the born criminal actually existed, Morrison asserted that it could also be shown in the United Kingdom "that criminals, taken as a whole, exhibit a higher percentage of physical degeneracy than the rest of the community".[91] In *Crime: Its Causes and Remedy* (1889), Louis Rylands did not deal as thoroughly as Morrison with the discussion of the born criminal.[92] He argued – briefly – that the causes of crime could ultimately be traced back to two factors, namely heredity and environment, and that the negative impact of those factors was responsible for the existence of the criminal classes in major cities that posed such a great danger to the "security and prosperity of the State". To overcome this problem, one could no longer count on the deterrent effect of the criminal law because the low percentage of crimes that were solved and the relatively humane imprisonment penalties counteracted that effect. On the contrary, given the important role of the social environment in the development of criminal behaviour, Rylands believed that it was necessary, to begin with, to do everything possible – by means of upbringing and education in special institutions – to create an environment that would deter young people from the dangerous classes from pursuing a criminal career.

---

90   Davie 2004, pp. 123–147, 168–182; Davie 2005, pp. 74–75, 95–99, 126–131; Davie 2011.
91   Morrison 1891, p. 198.
92   Rylands 1889, pp. 4–5, 7–8, 16–19, 29–30, 35, 42–43, 46, 48–50, 53, 57–58, 65–67, 70–72, 78–80, 137–142, 152–153, 240, 247, 261–262.

He also advocated that adult prisons – which in practice functioned as sources of infection with crime – be transformed, according to the Belgian and German example, into institutions where adult criminals would be taught to earn their living by working. He was convinced that such an approach offered the prospect of getting rid of the criminal classes and of a significant drop in the number of offenders. It was not a solution, however, to the problem of criminals who were apparently incorrigible because of hereditary factors. Rylands thought that that problem could be solved in only two ways: life imprisonment or the death penalty. And because such imprisonment was not only extremely harsh but also very costly, the choice of the death penalty was obvious: "To keep a wild beast in a cage is cruel, death is more merciful and more effective."[93]

Morrison and Ryland's books show, moreover, that in the United Kingdom too the intense debate on the background and treatment of habitual criminals dealt with only part – an important part, nevertheless – of the crime problem as it was defined in many Western European countries at the end of the nineteenth century. An equally large part of the problem concerned the underworld that had formed in the major cities and that had become intermingled, as it were, with an underclass that was dangerous not only in terms of crime but also in terms of public order, security, and health. To bring that class under control, it was not enough to deter young people (using all kinds of measures) from taking to crime or to identify habitual criminals and imprison them for life or put them to death. As in Italy, Germany and France, progressive politicians and policymakers in the United Kingdom were convinced that, given the osmosis between the underworld and the underclass, an effective policy on crime must necessarily form part of a much broader political programme in order to bring about structural improvement – by reorganising education, housing, and healthcare – in the appalling conditions in which many people lived in the big cities, and which Henry Mayhew had portrayed so strikingly in the early 1860s in his *London Labour and the London Poor*.[94]

Garland has provided an excellent description of how four control programmes were implemented simultaneously in the United Kingdom. Besides programmes in the fields of social security, social work, and eugenics, there was also a criminological programme. The latter naturally had much in common in many respects with the proposals made in Italy, France, and Germany by criminal lawyers and criminologists. It involved technical improvement of detection, large-scale involvement of psychologists and psychiatrists in assessing criminal behaviour, greater differentiation within the prison system according to age and personality,

---

[93]   Rylands 1889, p. 252.
[94]   Quennel 1987; Levin and Lindesmith 1937; Chesney 1979; Tobias 1972; Garland 1986, pp. 40–53; Emsley 2002, pp. 207–211; Brunt 1987.

the introduction of conditional sentencing and conditional parole, and further development of the probation system.[95]

Needless to say, there were also major differences of opinion in the United Kingdom on aspects of this programme, and – as in other countries – it was not of course fully implemented across the board, although it was not limited to just a paper exercise. The real essence of the policy programme on crime that was in fact implemented was undoubtedly the Prevention of Crime Act 1908. That piece of legislation stemmed from the report published in 1895 by the Gladstone Commission (set up following all kinds of scandals in sentencing) on conditions within the prison system and how they could be addressed.[96] One of the report's conclusions was that judges should be able to impose sentences depriving offenders of their liberty for long periods or compelling them to work under less severe conditions. In the years that followed, this recommendation – which implied that Lombroso and his British allies were right in their belief that the hard core of criminals were incorrigible – won the support of senior officials within the prison system. In 1903, it was incorporated into a bill that – after a great deal of debate on the conditions in which the measure should be imposed – was adopted by Parliament in 1908.

On the one hand, that Act laid a more formal and solid foundation for the existing system of institutions and facilities to prevent juvenile offenders aged 16–21 from turning to crime (the borstal system). The idea was to have them serve their sentence in a special institution for juveniles and after their release to place them under the supervision of sympathetic volunteers with a view to their rehabilitation. The first experiments with that system began in 1900. According to its proponents, the results were so successful that the proposal for introducing it nationally in the following years could be piloted through Parliament with ease.[97]

On the other hand – with a view to protecting society – the Act did in fact introduce the preventive detention of habitual offenders who had already served their sentence. Such detention was therefore a measure intended to prevent them from continuing to commit crimes. The first convicts were made subject to this measure in 1909, and were confined in a separate facility at the famous Parkhurst Prison. It must be remembered, however, that the Act was fundamentally directed not only at habitual criminals who had become actual career criminals but also – to the annoyance, incidentally, of the then Home Secretary, Winston Churchill, in 1910–11 – at "habitual petty delinquents, i.e. the vast army of beggars, vagrants, drunkards, and disorderly people".[98]

---

[95] Garland 1986, pp. 89–109, 130–158.
[96] Radzinowicz and Hood 1990, pp. 576–588; Garland 1986, pp. 59–66.
[97] Radzinowicz and Hood 1990, pp. 384–397.
[98] Morris (N.) 1950, pp. 33–80; Grünhut 1948, pp. 386–394; Radzinowicz and Hood 1990, pp. 268–287.

Besides this important piece of legislation, Parliament passed numerous other Acts in about 1900 that all related in one way or another to groups of persons covered, directly or indirectly, by the discussion of the personality of the criminal and how to deal with him. They created an extensive and differentiated "penal complex" around the traditional prison system.[99]

These Acts included the Idiots Act 1886 – which the Lunacy Act 1890 extended to "idiots" and "persons of unsound mind" and which was incorporated into the Mental Deficiency Act 1913 – which enabled local authorities to establish special institutions for persons suffering from "mental deficiency" or "feeble-mindedness". The Mental Deficiency Act – which clearly had a basis in eugenics, namely the aim of preventing the persons concerned from procreating – relieved the prison system of a category of people for whom it was not in any way suitable.[100]

Another example was the Probation of Offenders Act 1907, which introduced social work in the context of the criminal justice system. On the one hand, its intention was as far as possible to prevent individuals, especially notorious delinquents, from offending again, while, on the other, it aimed to "empty" the prisons as far as possible. Special probation officers were appointed to implement those aims by means of social case work.[101]

6.3.2. CHARLES GORING AND *THE ENGLISH CONVICT*: A LITMUS TEST FOR LOMBROSIAN IDEAS?

The illustrious research carried out by Goring derived essentially from discussion of the value of Lombrosian bio-anthropology at the third international bio-anthropological conference in Geneva in 1896. The fact that that protracted discussion again produced no clear decisions, led Arthur Griffiths, an English physician who had attended the conference, to recommend that the Home Office order a conclusive investigation of the links between physical characteristics and crime by "subjecting a large number of prisoners convicted of certain similar offences to accurate measurements in order to ascertain whether these showed any deviation from what might be described as the normal i.e., non-criminal persons". The medical inspector of prisons was in favour, and in 1901 proposed that measurements should be systematically taken of all detainees at four large prisons. This led to the development of an observation form which was first used to measure inmates in June 1902. In 1903, this study came to the attention of the editors of the journal *Biometrika*, one of whom, Karl Pearson, was a close

---

[99]   Garland 1986, pp. 18–27.
[100]   Walker and McCabe 1973, pp. 22–25, 59–64; Radzinowicz and Hood 1990, pp. 316–338; Garland 1986, pp. 222–225.
[101]   Radzinowicz and Hood 1990, pp. 633–647.

associate of Galton. In 1904, *Biometrika* printed an article about the results of a comparison between 100 normal and 30 mentally disturbed prisoners. By 1908, however, 1,000 prisoners had already been measured and the question arose as to how and where the data would be analysed. In a way, the answer was obvious: at the Anthropometric Laboratory (or simply Biometric Laboratory) that Galton had set up at University College London in 1883 but whose daily management was in the hands of Pearson.[102]

Just how remarkable that location was in this context will be obvious, however, to anyone who remembers that Galton not only brought about a breakthrough in the debate on the use of fingerprints for judicial purposes but that he was also an advocate of criminal bio-anthropology as propounded by Lombroso. That Galton – whose interest in anthropometry was also prompted by the anthropometric studies of Quetelet – advocated Lombroso's bio-anthropology had a great deal to do with the fact that, under the influence of Darwin's *On the Origin of Species*, he had engrossed himself since the 1860s in the hereditary aspects of people's intellectual achievements and in that context had worked on developing a methodology for responsibly determining the role played by heredity in the transmission of those achievements.

This methodology not only assigned an important role to research on the development of identical twins, but also – referring to the theories of Lavater – considered photography to be a valuable means of recording both the outer and inner person. In the late 1870s, at the behest of the head of the prison system, Galton had even focused his photographic research for a time on thousands of detainees, and had concluded after analysing their photographs that although it was not possible to use photography to identify "certain natural classes" of criminals it was perhaps possible to use it to determine who was "liable to fall into crime". For the head of the prison system, that was nevertheless an important finding. It in fact opened up the possibility that one could determine while people were still young who was doomed to commit crime and who could perhaps be prevented from turning to crime by means of educational measures.[103]

Be that as it may, when analysis of the data began in 1909 the aim of the study was significantly broadened and – given the above – was elevated into a test of the validity of Lombroso's original views on the born criminal: "the refutation or confirmation of the various theories that had been promulgated concerning the existence of the criminal type". Whether the Anthropometric Laboratory was the most suitable location to test out the ideas of Lombroso, of all people, on the English prison population is a question that was not in fact raised! Apparently there was no reason to fear that this litmus test would almost inevitably turn out to the advantage of his views.

---

[102]   Goring 1913, pp. 6–7; Davie 2005, pp. 230–232; Gillham 2001, pp. 158, 211–212.
[103]   Gillham 2001, pp. 155–171, 187–194, 215–219, 250–259; Davie 2005, pp. 243–253.

In his report, Goring did not in any case comment on the scientific nature of this institution, as if it did not matter. Similarly, he did not mention the fact that in about 1900 Galton had increasingly emerged as a nationally and internationally renowned pioneer of the eugenics movement and had asserted more than once, from a social-Darwinist perspective, that eugenic measures

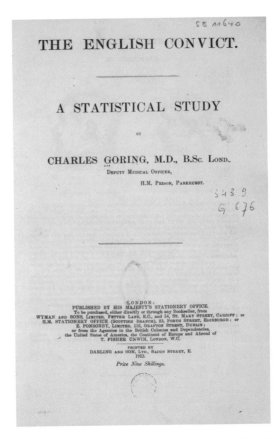

Charles GORING, *The English Convict: A Statistical Study*, London, His Majesty's Stationery Office, 1913.

were suitable and justified to maintain the hereditary qualities of the population or to improve it. More specifically, Goring did not point out that Galton had concretely noted in this context, for example, the possibility of isolating habitual criminals for a long period and in that way preventing them from "producing low class offspring".[104] One needs to be aware of this, however, if one is to fully

---

[104]   Gillham 2001, pp. 324–331; Hermans 2003, pp. 331–421.

understand the recommendations that Goring attached to the results of his research in 1913.[105]

He stated almost immediately in the introduction to his report that the investigation did not constitute a condemnation of Lombroso's original thesis that there is "a definite line of demarcation, an absolute difference in nature, as opposed to degree, between those human beings who are, and those who are not, criminal".[106] After all, without a hypothesis there could be no proper research. His study – he repeated once again – should not be seen as a direct attack on Lombroso's doctrine or on the results achieved by criminal anthropology but as an attack "against the methods by which they were reached".[107] Real, methodical scientific research was therefore needed in order to determine whether the criminal type was "a real thing" or not. Without such research, real scientists would always view belief in its existence as a form of "superstition of criminology". Goring thus reiterated that the aim of his research was therefore to clear away the remnants of the old criminology – a criminology "based upon conjecture, prejudice, and questionable observation" – but also "to found a new knowledge of the criminal, upon facts scientifically acquired, and upon inferences scientifically verified". In order to achieve that aim, data was collected at random on more than 3,000 male English convicts. Processing of that data "form[ed] a representative and unprecedented statistical portrait of those of our population who become convicts".

The basic premise of the study was that it was impossible, in the given circumstances, "to state dogmatically, on a priori grounds, whether the criminal is born or made".[108] It would take too long to explain how the research was conducted, both on the entire group studied and in various subgroups. It is important to note, however, that Goring did not really jump to conclusions but worked step by step towards a general evaluation. He established in the first part of the report, for example, that the investigation of physical differences between criminals and law-abiding citizens in general, and between categories of detainees, showed that there were indeed such differences but that if they were corrected for such factors as age, intelligence, and class they disappeared almost entirely. The unavoidable conclusion was therefore "that there is no such thing as a physical criminal type".[109]

However, according to Goring that did not mean that there were no differences on specific points. In relation to physique and weight, for example, he asserted that the study showed indisputably that all British criminals – except fraudsters – were "markedly differentiated from the general population" and

---

[105]   Beirne 1988; Beirne 1993, pp. 187–224; Mannheim 1966, 1, pp. 226–228.
[106]   Goring 1913, p. 15.
[107]   Goring 1913, p. 19.
[108]   Goring 1913, p. 26.
[109]   Goring 1913, pp. 139, 173.

that violent offenders were on average significantly stronger and healthier than other criminals and ordinary citizens. That therefore also meant that criminal anthropology was "not entirely without basis in fact; but fact perverted by credibility and fanaticism".[110]

In Goring's opinion, his study had demonstrated "that the one significant physical association with criminality is a generally defective physique; and that the one vital mental constitutional factor in the aetiology of crime is defective intelligence". And when it came to the influence of social, economic, and other "environmental conditions", the result of his study was that crime in his country was only marginally the product of social inequality or other adverse conditions.[111]

Finally, the study dealt – how could it do otherwise! – with the role of the fertility of criminals and the role of heredity in "the genesis of crime". On the latter issue, he pointed out that it was generally difficult to measure the role of heredity, because:

> germinal action is not a visible thing: its power cannot be directly appreciated by the senses. The existence of germinal influence is only known from its effect – from its effect in producing an organic relation of resemblance between generations.[112]

In order to determine "the influence of heredity in the making of criminals", the best thing in the given circumstances would be to commence a comparative statistical analysis of the histories of both criminal and law-abiding families. Goring immediately made clear, however, that the lack of general research into family histories and flaws in the investigation of criminal families meant that he too was unable to provide a sufficient answer as to the role of heredity in the genesis of criminal behaviour. He found that analysis of the data on the family histories of 1500 detainees had nevertheless shown "that, despite of education, heritable constitutional conditions prevail in the making of criminals; but they contain no pronouncement upon the extent to which the general standards of morality may have been raised by education".[113] The fact that Goring, in line with these conclusions, made recommendations that led step by step towards eugenics is unsurprising.[114] In individual cases, one first needed, he thought, to consider whether it was possible to alter the inherited criminal behaviour by means of appropriate educational measures. One could then decide whether it would be possible "to modify opportunity for crime by segregation and supervision of

---

[110] Goring 1913, pp. 200–201, 263.
[111] Goring 1913, pp. 263, 288.
[112] Goring 1913, pp. 337–338.
[113] Goring 1913, pp. 343, 372–373.
[114] Goring 1913, pp. 372–373.

the unfit". Third, it was a matter of "attacking the evil at its very root" i.e. of "regulat[ing] the reproduction of those degrees of constitutional qualities".

Goring's conclusions and recommendations were obviously not in all respects in line with the views about the born criminal that Lombroso had expressed at the start of his career and also in fact later. They did have a lot in common, however, with the bio-social ideas on crime and the criminal as later emphatically asserted by Ferri, but also advanced by Tarde and Aschaffenburg. The same can be said, in a sense, of Goring's recommendations for fighting crime at the root. In terms of social Darwinism and eugenics, those views went further than Lombroso and other criminologists had argued at that time, but they were in line with the generally positive responses to such proposals for maintaining or improving the genetic qualities of the population or "the race".[115]

It was probably partly for this reason that the head of the prison system, Evelyn Ruggles-Brise, was very pleased – according to the preface to the report – with the results of the study. Those results, it is true, had not provided the answer to the question of "whether a criminal is born or made, or whether he is a victim of heredity or environment" but they had demonstrated:

> that a considerably larger minority of persons with clearly appreciable mental defect, apparently of congenital nature, is found among convicted criminals than in the population at large […] that a significant proportion of them are of primarily defective mental capacity.[116]

He did not state what that conclusion meant for policy, for example regarding habitual and professional criminals, but that could not perhaps be expected at that juncture. That loose end does make it all the more understandable, however, that in the United Kingdom Goring's study, especially after the First World War, formed an important incentive to discuss the role of heredity in criminal behaviour and of the desirability and/or necessity of a eugenics policy in order to combat crimes committed by habitual criminals more effectively. Some, nevertheless, viewed Goring's study as confirmation of Lombroso's theory, while others considered it the death blow to that theory.[117] In other countries too – for example the developments in the Weimar Republic that we have already considered – Goring's study was utilised to take one's stand in the debate and was an incentive for the police and judiciary to carry out criminal-biological investigation of the personality of the criminal through their own agencies.

---

[115] Davie 2005, pp. 234–239.
[116] Goring 1913, pp. 7–9.
[117] Driver 1972, p. 346.

6.3.3. BIO-PSYCHO-SOCIOLOGICISATION OF THE CRIMINAL BETWEEN THE WARS

Three books appeared after the First World War that – in relation to Lombrosian bio-anthropology and especially the study by Goring – clearly reflect the diversity of views in the United Kingdom on the causes of crime, the personality of the criminal, and the treatment of offenders. We will ignore publications about criminology intended more for the general public, such as the short book by Horace Wyndham published in 1928.

The first of these three works, *Crime & Criminals: Being the Jurisprudence of Crime, Medical, Biological, and Psychological*, was published in 1918 by Charles Mercier, a highly experienced asylum doctor and well-known writer of psychological treatises in numerous fields. His book was an immediate sensation not only in the United Kingdom but also in the United States, where an American edition appeared in 1919.[118] In the preface itself, Mercier made no secret of his low opinion of criminology. He knew, he wrote, that crime had not been studied systematically in the United Kingdom, but he had an explanation for that: "the abhorrence of the English mind for general principles. The English genius is predominantly inductive […] Research has in this country scarcely any meaning beyond the discovery of fact." This lead-in made clear what he thought of Lombroso and his many followers: they had contributed "nothing of value" to science. The discourse that followed consisted of a collection of chapters on very diverse topics: the nature of crime and the explanation for it, the psychology of crime and the criminal, types of crime and criminals, and the prevention, detection, and punishment of crime.

In relation to the causes of crime, Mercier found it clear that in the commission of a crime the "internal factor" ("the disposition of the criminal") was as important as the "external factor" ("the circumstances that conduce to the commission of any crime"). He added that research generally considered only one of these two factors, and also forced that factor into the straitjacket of the researcher's own prejudices. He found that even Goring's study, "laborious and painstaking as it is, takes account solely of the disposition of the criminal, and leaves out altogether consideration of the circumstances that conduct to any crime".[119] Where the psychology of crime and the criminal was concerned, he adopted the position that there was no question of any special kind of psychology "in order to account for the commission of crime".[120]

These views entirely reflect Mercier's general criticism of criminology as it existed at the time. He expanded on that criticism especially – in line with his

---

[118]   Mercier 1918; Mercier 1919.
[119]   Mercier 1918, pp. 45–46.
[120]   Mercier 1918, p. 68.

remarks in the preface – in the chapter on criminals (Chapter VII), successively discussing the "doctrines" of Goring, Beccaria, Lombroso, et al. The common denominator in his discussion was that although one seemed to be dealing with "cast-iron facts with respect to the kind of persons who commit crime", one was in fact confronted by "fantastic suppositions, conjectures, and surmises". The outcome of his discussion was therefore obvious and immediately formed the essence of his personal view of the personality of the criminal:

> The difference between the criminal and the non-criminal is, in short, first in the combination in various degrees of qualities that both and all possess in common, and second that the criminal is subjected to temptation that, relatively to his combination of qualities, is excessive. It may be a temptation that would be no temptation to the average man.[121]

Building on that conclusion, he worked out his own typology of criminals in the next chapter. This consisted of two main types, namely the habitual criminal and the occasional criminal. Where habitual criminals were concerned, he distinguished between "instinctive criminals" who are forced from within, as it were, to commit crimes ("active criminal propensity") and persistent offenders who commit crime after crime because their "social instincts" are either weak or have not been cultivated or strengthened by their upbringing.[122] In his view, occasional criminals are "ordinary citizens of ordinary upbringing and rectitude who are allured into some crime by temptation of exceptional severity".[123]

It almost goes without saying, incidentally, that with classifications like this Mercier's views are more similar to those of Lombroso, Von Liszt, Aschaffenburg, and other continental criminologists who he detested than he himself realised or wished to admit. And that similarity is even more pronounced when Mercier discusses the possibilities for reforming criminals. Those possibilities are realistic in the case of occasional criminals but not in the case of habitual or professional criminals: "The reformation of other kinds of criminals is either hopeless or unnecessary."[124]

The second book we shall consider appeared in 1924: *Crime and Insanity* by William Sullivan, a doctor at Broadmoor Criminal Lunatic Asylum.[125] From the very beginning, Sullivan leaves no room for doubt about his position in the debate: crime is a bio-social issue in which intrinsic individual factors interact with "factors of nurture". He thus immediately dissociates himself from Lombroso's theory about the real criminal being "a separate species of the

---

[121] Mercier 1918, pp. 201, 231.
[122] Mercier 1918, pp. 232–239.
[123] Mercier 1918, pp. 248–249.
[124] Mercier 1918, pp. 252.
[125] Sullivan 1924.

race, characterised by an innate incapacity of adaptation to the conditions of life, and marked off from normal man by a number of distinctive anatomical and physiological traits". However, he also has many reservations regarding the theory propounded by Goring because he believed that, in essence, it had much in common with that of Lombroso. In both cases, the basic assumption was:

> that phenomena of social conduct can be directly referred to conditions of organic constitution, that criminality is the result of a specific biological predisposition and is not to any appreciable extent a product of environmental forces: the only point of difference is that in the later theory mental deficiency fills the role which Lombroso assigned to atavism or epilepsy or degeneracy.[126]

By saying this, he does not mean that he questions the role played by constitutional factors in people's behaviour. He merely wishes to refer to the commonplace view that criminal behaviour is the result of the interaction between biological and sociological factors. By adopting this position, Sullivan is thus expressing the traditional aversion of quite a few British psychiatrists to generalisations about deviant behaviour, whether or not pathological. This is also apparent from his assertion that "the only reliable method of investigating the biological factors of criminal conduct must be the slow and tedious way of clinical observation".[127] Accordingly, he discusses, chapter by chapter, the problem of crime in relation to certain psychiatric syndromes such as manic depression, alcoholism, epilepsy, hysteria, and imbecility.

Whereas these two "classic" books provide an introduction to the explanation and containment of crime from a psychiatric perspective, a third classic work – this time taking a psychological approach – is *The Young Delinquent* (1925) by the London developmental psychologist Cyril Burt (the fourth revised edition appeared in 1945).[128] It is well known that Burt's academic reputation was discredited in the 1970s when colleagues and journalists justifiably called into question the integrity of his research on identical twins, in particular his research aiming to determine the extent to which intelligence is a matter of "nature" (i.e. heredity) or "nurture" (i.e. upbringing). This is not the place to deal with the lengthy, heated debate that arose about the integrity of Burt's research on that matter.[129] It will suffice to note that the integrity of the research underlying *The Young Delinquent* has never been called into question. In histories of British criminology, that work is still referred to quite regularly.[130]

However, the interesting and important lecture that Burt gave in 1964 to the Association of Educationalist Psychologists on the subject of his research

---

126   Sullivan 1924, pp. 7, 9–10.
127   Sullivan 1924, pp. 13–14.
128   Burt 1925; Burt 1945.
129   Butler and Petrulis 1999.
130   Garland 1988, pp. 142–145; Garland 2002, pp. 37–38; Morris (T.) 1988, pp. 157–159.

career is generally ignored.[131] In that lecture, Burt makes no secret of the fact that in about 1900 – via his father, a doctor – he had spent several years in circles associated with the Anthropometric Laboratory and had met Galton ("or Frank as he was commonly called at his own home"). He had read Galton's books,

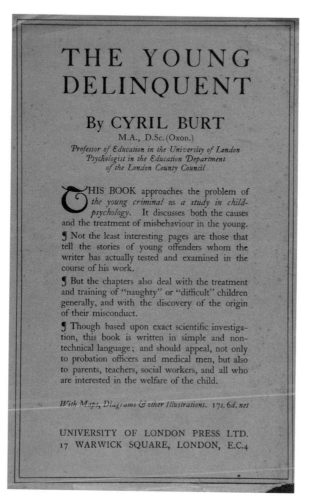

THE YOUNG DELINQUENT

By CYRIL BURT

M.A., D.Sc.(Oxon.)
Professor of Education in the University of London
Psychologist in the Education Department
of the London County Council

THIS BOOK approaches the problem of *the young criminal* as *a study in child-psychology*. It discusses both the causes and the treatment of misbehaviour in the young.

¶ Not the least interesting pages are those that tell the stories of young offenders whom the writer has actually tested and examined in the course of his work.

¶ But the chapters also deal with the treatment and training of "naughty" or "difficult" children generally, and with the discovery of the origin of their misconduct.

¶ Though based upon exact scientific investigation, this book is written in simple and non-technical language; and should appeal, not only to probation officers and medical men, but also to parents, teachers, social workers, and all who are interested in the welfare of the child.

With Maps, Diagrams & other Illustrations. 17s. 6d. net

UNIVERSITY OF LONDON PRESS LTD.
17 WARWICK SQUARE, LONDON, E.C.4

Cyril BURT, *The Young Delinquent,* London, University of London Press, 1925.

had heard him speak, and had been fascinated by his ingenious mathematical techniques. This explains why, when appointed school psychologist with the London County Council in 1913, he was immediately allocated funds to set up an agency, following the example of Galton's laboratory, to investigate children's intellectual abilities. This was the first Child Guidance Clinic in the United

---

[131]   The lecture was published in Rushton 2002.

Kingdom and possibly the world. It also explains why in *The Young Delinquent* Burt begins, right after the introduction, by explaining the role of heredity in people's criminal behaviour.

Burt's opinion on this point is not that "crime is inherited or at least inborn" but, in the wake of Lombroso and others, he believes that extreme forms of all kinds of deficiencies – emotional, intellectual, or physical – associated with the "hereditary constitution of the criminal" can have an indirect effect on someone's criminal behaviour. In his view, there is therefore no question of a "single and simple disposition to crime, inherited as such, but numerous underlying weaknesses of all degrees of gravity".

It may well be, moreover, that it is not only such innate weaknesses that are responsible for someone's criminal behaviour but that all kinds of other factors – "environmental, social, physical, and psychological" – also play a role. This means that if one wishes to determine the role of those innate weaknesses it must first be demonstrated that those other factors "are not enough to explain the known manifestations". In line with this view, Burt also considers it unjustifiable to systematically segregate criminals on the basis of eugenic principles, whether in their own interest or that of society and future generations. This is because no matter how strong the innate predisposition to criminal behaviour may be, "it is usually possible, by removing the delinquent from all ordinary opportunities for crime, to reduce his offences to a minimum".

In accordance with this principle, the following chapters not only discuss coherently what factors may be relevant as regards explaining criminal behaviour; they also explain how those factors can be taken into account when dealing with offenders. The factors concerned include: environmental factors such as the family, the use made of leisure time, and work; factors related to physical and mental health; intellectual factors such as morality and intelligence; and psychological factors such as instincts, emotions, sentiments, complexes, and neuroses. Burt's general conclusion is: "Crime is assignable to no single universal source, nor yet to two or three: it springs from a wide variety, and usually from a multiplicity of alternative and converging influences."[132] It is therefore impossible to attribute crime primarily to certain environmental factors or certain innate factors "while, with a large assortment of cases, both seem, on an average and in the long run, to be of almost equal weight". However, this does not affect the fact, he asserts, that research has shown that some factors are on average more important than others. The list of 15 factors is headed by "defective discipline", "specific instincts", "general emotional instability", "morbid emotional conditions", and "a family history of vice and crime". In terms of combatting crime, Burt considers that this ranking means that young people who exhibit delinquent traits should be treated, on an individual basis, as early and in as targeted manner as possible, within their own family, at school, or in

---

[132] Burt 1925, p. 599.

the framework of social work. In Burt's view, if we are to know exactly what factors cause criminal behaviour and what forms of therapy are more effective than others, it is necessary to organise research on these matters in the form of an "established criminological department".[133]

Such an institute was not set up, however, before the Second World War. Matters were confined during that period to the appearance of new general treatises on crime problems written by prison doctors and psychologists. The book that is said to best reflect the *communis opinio* in the 1930s on crime problems in the United Kingdom is *Medical Aspects of Crime* (1936) by the prison doctor William Norwood East. Large parts of that work concern the organisation of prisons and the enforcement of custodial sentencing. In relation to explaining criminal behaviour and the personality of the offender, Norwood East does discuss at length the development of the phrenological and anthropological debates through into the twentieth century but he ultimately states plainly that he sees no benefit in those discussions. He gives more credence to the possibilities that psychology can eventually offer for understanding the causes of criminal behaviour, even though attempts at this were currently still made difficult by the differences between the various schools within this discipline. It is therefore unsurprising that Norwood East calls for more impartial investigation of the validity of all the theories circulating in this connection.[134]

For a similar reason he was also hesitant regarding the use of sterilisation as a eugenic means for combatting crime. Nobody could assert, after all, that crime is transmitted by means of reproduction: eugenic sterilisation "as a means of combatting crime, appears to be previous [*sic*] and unwarranted". Norwood East thus indicated that he did not believe in any more or less general application of the radical ideas that had already been aired decades before within the eugenics movement. He referred here, incidentally, to the new legislation in Germany on the castration of sexual offenders, but he clearly did not consider this to be an example that deserved to be followed immediately. He did not assert that that development in Germany should be seen in light of the political upheaval of 1933, restricting himself to saying that it was too early to be able to assess the effects of the legislation concerned.[135]

6.3.4. "CONTINENTAL" STARTING POINT OF MODERN CRIMINOLOGY

We have already noted that no criminological institute was set up in the United Kingdom before the Second World War. In 1931, however, an Institute for the

---

[133] Burt 1925, pp. 606–612.
[134] Norwood East 1936, pp. 209–236.
[135] Norwood East 1936, p. 362; Garland 2002, pp. 34–35.

Study and Treatment of Delinquency was set up by psychoanalysts. To some extent, that institute manifested itself over the years as a research institute, but it still remained predominantly a training institute for the outpatient treatment of pathological delinquents.[136] That is not to say that the institute, which became part of the University of London in 1938, did not undertake any significant research initiatives. The most important of these was probably the establishment of the *British Journal of Delinquency* in 1950; this was renamed the *British Journal of Criminology* in 1960. Nor was it insignificant that the Scientific Group for the Discussion of Delinquency Problems that was set up in 1953 under the auspices of the institute, some few years later became – unintentionally – the cradle for the British Society of Criminology. That society was in fact founded by younger members of the discussion group who disagreed with the all too clinical and psychoanalytic orientation of the work.[137]

When we come to consider the progress of criminal biology in Germany after the Second World War, we will see that some leading criminal lawyers and criminologists were forced to flee that country in the 1930s for political reasons and took refuge in the United States or the United Kingdom. Of those who went to the United Kingdom, the most significant was undoubtedly Hermann Mannheim, a judge at the Berlin Court of Appeal, whose Jewish background meant that he was forced to leave Germany in 1934. The following year, 1935, he was appointed to an honorary part-time lectureship in criminology at the London School of Economics. He became a full-time lecturer in 1944 and reader in criminology in 1946, retiring in 1955.[138]

Mannheim is still regarded as one of the founders of modern criminology in the United Kingdom, especially because it was his teaching at the London School of Economics – particularly in the framework of the Institute for the Study and Treatment of Delinquency – that familiarised many young people with developments in the discipline. A number of his students were later appointed to professorships or readerships in criminology at British and overseas universities, for example Howard Jones, Norval Morris, and John Spencer. The first general introduction to criminology published in the United Kingdom – Jones' *Crime and the Penal System* (1956) – was strongly influenced by Mannheim's lectures. Mannheim was himself quite a prolific author – with works such as *Criminal Justice and Social Reconstruction* and *Comparative Criminology* – and also a very active member of the editorial board of the *British Journal of Delinquency*.[139]

Far less well known than Mannheim is Max Grünhut, who had been a professor of criminal law at the University of Bonn since 1928 but who was

---

[136]   Glover 1960, pp. 33–47, 51–52, 79–80; Mullins 1949, pp. 38–49.

[137]   Garland 2002, pp. 39–40; Martin (J.) 1988, pp. 169–170.

[138]   Radzinowicz 1988b, pp. 18–19; Mannheim 1946, pp. 219–237, 256–269.

[139]   Garland 2002, pp. 39–40; Morris (T.) 1988, pp. 155–156; Martin (J.) 1988, pp. 166–167, 171–172.

dismissed in 1933 because of his Jewish heritage. In 1940, after years of hoping in vain that the situation would improve, he also found himself forced to leave Germany, fleeing to the United Kingdom, where he found shelter at All Souls College (Oxford University). He lectured there and elsewhere on criminology and was involved in various research projects.[140] He left less of a mark on British criminology than did Mannheim and the third immigrant who earned his stripes in that respect, namely Leon Radzinowicz. Grünhut published a well-known book, *Penal Reform: A Comparative Study* in 1948. He died in 1964. In 1965, the University of Bonn brought out a commemorative collection in his honour.[141]

Radzinowicz was not in fact a victim of the Nazis, but nevertheless left Poland for the United Kingdom in 1939, where he spent some time as a fellow of Trinity College (Cambridge University).[142] Radzinowicz was more of an historian and theoretician than an empirical researcher. Above all, he was an institution builder.[143] In the late 1950s, he in any case pressed for the establishment of an Institute of Criminology at Cambridge and after striving adroitly for years for the creation of such an institute he was successful in 1959 in setting up such an institute, with the support of, inter alia, the Home Office. On the one hand, the institute was obviously intended to perform systematic research; on the other it was to improve the teaching of criminology, including by means of a post-graduate course in criminology and an advanced course in criminology for actual practitioners, but also through doctoral studies. The members of the institute also purposefully joined all kinds of local, national, and international committees in the field of criminal justice. Great efforts were also made to build up a modern library.[144]

The development of the Cambridge Institute of Criminology in fact shows that the flowering of criminology in the United Kingdom was not only the work of enterprising individuals, both British and foreign, at leading universities but also of a government that, in after the Second World War, began to consider criminological research important. The government expressed that attitude by creating scope within the Criminal Justice Act 1948 for the financing of criminological research. In 1957, the government again confirmed the importance of such research by setting up a research unit within the Home Office.[145]

---

[140]   Martin (J.) 1988, pp. 166–167.
[141]   Hood 2004; Hood 2013.
[142]   Martin (J.) 1988, pp. 166–167.
[143]   Radzinowicz 1966.
[144]   Radzinowicz 1988a; Martin (J.) 1988, pp. 42–44; Zedner 2003, pp. 209–210.
[145]   Garland 2002, p. 40.

6.4. CONCLUSION

The introduction to this chapter already pointed out the differences between Germany (in fact German-speaking Europe) and the United Kingdom as regards the reception of Italian criminal bio-anthropology. Having considered the development of that approach to criminology in these two countries, it is possible to highlight in a more thorough manner the differences between them on this point.

It is clear, first of all, that whereas bio-anthropology underwent significant further development in Germany in two directions – towards criminal biology and towards criminal psychology – there was absolutely no question of that in the United Kingdom. That is odd because, contrary to what well-known British authors claim, the ideas propounded by Lombroso were received quite positively in that country, certainly among anthropologists, physicians, and psychiatrists. There was of course criticism, sometimes fierce criticism, but there was also a great deal of approval. Just why that generally positive reception did not lead to the further development of a British version of bio-anthropology or to a French-style counter-movement is a question that goes beyond the remit of the present work. It is in fact all the more puzzling given that Goring's famous study produced conclusions that were not, it is true, entirely in line with Lombroso's initial ideas about the born criminal but that did have a lot in common with the bio-social ideas of Ferri and others regarding crime and the criminal. The results of Goring's study did have an impact on discussion of these matters between the wars, influencing in particular Burt's work on juvenile delinquency in London. They did not form the starting point, however, for the development of any type of criminology whatsoever.

Following on from the above, one can also refer, secondly, to the significant differences between the two countries in terms of the institutionalisation of criminology up until the 1930s. In Germany and the other German-speaking countries, that institutionalisation took the form not only of specialist scientific journals and an extensive scientific and practice-related literature but here and there also the form of separate professorial chairs or specialist courses of lectures. There was no question of any of this, however, in the United Kingdom. That absence can of course be explained by insufficient academic or policy-related interest in criminology. But the contrary may also be true: criminology failed to get off the ground because no scientific infrastructure was developed. It is remarkable in the case of both countries, but especially Germany, that not a single university established a criminological research and/or educational institution during that period, something that was in contrast done in Italy and France. It may indeed be the case – as suggested above – that in Germany that had to do with the conservative attitudes of the faculties that could perhaps have accommodated such an institute. After the Second World War, this form of institutionalisation did however get off the ground in the United Kingdom, through the efforts of a few enterprising "continental" professors.

Third, it should be noted that in German-speaking Europe, scientific policing did not get bogged down, as in France, in problems of judicial identification. Bertillon's achievements were certainly emulated but Gross was concerned with so much more, namely the scientisation of the entire course of events in criminal cases. That was in any case what he intended with his *Kriminalpsychologie* but also with his *Handbuch für Untersuchungsrichter u.s.w.* To what extent he actually succeeded is difficult to say, but there is no doubt that his publications contributed greatly to the professionalisation of the German police in the area of criminal investigation. The operational structure of the police forces of major cities in the early decades of the twentieth century leaves this in no doubt. When one compares this development in Germany and Austria, etc., with that in the United Kingdom, one can easily see that the differences between these countries were enormous. Strangely enough, no figure like Gross appeared in the United Kingdom, and there was also no far-reaching professionalisation of the police as regards detection. That is indeed strange given that it was the United Kingdom that led the way in applying fingerprinting for law-enforcement purposes.

What is not at all peculiar, finally, is that the British police did not become involved in any way in the application of any kind of criminal biology whatsoever with a view to combatting professional and habitual crime. This is not because that kind of crime was viewed as a problem in one country (Germany) but not in the other (the United Kingdom). In the United Kingdom too, that kind of crime was in fact placed on the agenda and drastic measures were devised to curb it. The big difference was that in the country of Darwin and Galton, bio-anthropological criminology did not develop, and certainly not in a biological direction.

CHAPTER 7

ESTABLISHMENT OF CRIMINOLOGY IN THE NETHERLANDS AND BELGIUM

7.1. INTRODUCTION

When one compares the development of modern criminology in the Netherlands and Belgium with its evolution in neighbouring countries, it is striking how in the Low Countries that discipline gradually became widely established in universities in the first half of the twentieth century and to some extent also in the criminal justice system. Why it developed in that way is not that easy to say. The fact, for example, that Von Liszt had such major allies, specifically in the Netherlands and Belgium in the persons of Van Hamel and Prins as regards innovation in the area of criminal law, suggests that he perceived a spirit of openness in those two countries that he did not immediately find elsewhere in Europe.

That openness will certainly have promoted the fruitful development of criminology in both countries but it cannot have been the sole cause of that success. Anyone who knows something of what actually happened in the field of criminology and the criminal justice system on both sides of the Belgian–Dutch border between 1880 and 1960 will realise that there are not only great similarities but also significant differences. It is highly likely that other factors also played an important role. But in any case, the history of criminology in the one country cannot simply be lumped together with that in the other.[1] In this chapter, the developments in each country will therefore be discussed separately.

A sketch will first be given of the rise of criminology, based on the bio-bibliography of the main driving forces behind it. Second, we will deal with the controversies that this led to in the scientific, political, and administrative worlds regarding the relationship between the principles of some variants of this new discipline and the foundations of the existing criminal law and criminal justice system. Third, we will discuss how criminology nevertheless had an impact,

---

[1] Fijnaut 2010a.

directly and indirectly, on certain aspects of the redesign of the criminal justice system and, more broadly, on the containment of crime. Fourth, an account will be given of how criminology became successfully established in universities in the 1930s. It in fact became so firmly established that the institutes and schools that were set up at the time survived the Second World War and were able to develop without major difficulties, until into the 1960s, on the model according to which they had been designed.

7.2. ESTABLISHMENT OF CRIMINOLOGY IN THE NETHERLANDS

7.2.1. DRIVING FORCES BEHIND CRIMINOLOGY: GERARD VAN HAMEL, ARNOLD ALETRINO, AND WILLEM BONGER

7.2.1.1. *Messenger of Criminology: Gerard van Hamel*

There is no question that the Amsterdam professor of criminal law Gerard van Hamel was the main driving force behind modern criminology in the Netherlands. At the beginning of his career, however, there were no signs to indicate that he would come to play that role. The dissertation that he defended in 1865 concerned a civil-law issue and his inaugural lecture at the University of Amsterdam in 1880 was in fact about the limits of the criminal law.[2] However, when preparing a talk on sentencing for the conference of the International Penitentiary Commission in Rome in 1885, he read the article by Von Liszt on *Der Zweckgedanke im Strafrecht* [*The Concept of Purpose in Criminal Law*] and thus became convinced, like Von Liszt, that the existing criminal law no longer corresponded to social reality and could – indeed must – be brought into line with the contemporary world by means of modern criminology. As he wrote at the time, this meant, inter alia, that a distinction needed to be made between incorrigible habitual criminals and those who were capable of improvement, and that – so as to protect society – lifelong deprivation of liberty should be included in the range of penalties available. In this way, he became the forerunner of what was later referred to in the Netherlands as the *Nieuwe Richting* (New Direction) in criminal law because it distanced itself in significant respects from the *Klassieke Richting* (Classical Direction).

In the years that followed – mainly due to his involvement with the International Association of Criminal Law – Van Hamel elaborated his views

---

[2]   Van Hamel 1865; Van Hamel 1912, 1, pp. 150–181.

on the role of criminology in relation to criminal law and the criminal justice system. On the one hand, he wrote repeatedly that criminal lawyers should concern themselves with more than just the dogmatics of criminal law. They should also delve deeply into the background to crime as a social phenomenon and also into the actual operation of the administration of justice and the implementation of penal sanctions. Everyone saw, after all, that the criminal justice system basically worked but that it had little or no social effect and was therefore in urgent need of reform. On the other hand, he also frequently distanced himself from what was asserted under the banner of criminology. He

Prof. Mr. G. A. VAN HAMEL   *Jan Veth pinx.*

Portrait of Gerard Van Hamel, in: Gerard VAN HAMEL (ed.), *Verzamelde opstellen*, Leiden, N.V. Boekhandel and Drukkerij E.J. Brill, 1912, 2 vol.

denied, for example, that there was a clear difference between criminals and non-criminals and he was very concerned about the erosion of criminal law principles – such as the protection of the individual freedom of the citizen from the authorities – by criminological doctrines. That does not mean, however, that – as Von Liszt asserted – he maintained close personal relations with both Lombroso and Ferri.[3]

---

3   Von Liszt 1917, p. 557; Bonger, Valkhoff and Van der Waerden 1950, 1, pp. 121–133.

What all this comes down to is that Van Hamel considered modern criminology to be a useful means for firmly criticising the existing criminal law and criminal justice system but that it should not go beyond that: criminology should continue to play an ancillary role with respect to criminal science. In his

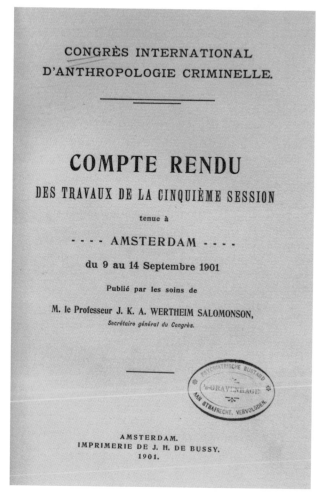

Johannes WERTHEIM SALOMONSON (ed.), *Congrès international d'anthropologie criminelle: compte rendu des travaux de la cinquième session tenue à Amsterdam du 9 à 14 septembre 1901*, Amsterdam, Imprimerie de J.H. De Bussy, 1901.

well-known *Inleiding tot de studie van het Nederlandsche strafrecht* [*Introduction to the Study of Dutch Criminal Law*] (1889), he defined criminal science as being on the one hand a form of jurisprudence which sharply defines concepts and principles, and on the other a social science, a doctrine regarding the causes and containment of crime. In that work, Van Hamel did not advocate the far-reaching integration of criminal science and criminology, let alone demonstrated how such integration could be achieved.[4] In his case too, integrated criminal science remained more a laudable goal than a genuine reality. In his obituary of Van Hamel in 1917, Von Liszt showed that he fully understood this, writing that Van Hamel was undoubtedly a tireless advocate of changes in the containment of crime and the criminal justice system but that he remained, above all, one of the leading dogmatists.[5] It should be noted that Van Hamel himself never carried out any (empirical) criminological research.[6]

In relation to the above, it should be noted that it is not only his interest in Italian and French criminology that makes Van Hamel the driving force behind modern criminology in the Netherlands. He also deserves that designation because of his role as editor of the *Tijdschrift voor Strafrecht* [*Journal of Criminal Law*], which – in the absence of any specific journal like those in Italy, Germany, and France – served for many years as the main distribution channel for national and international criminological news in the Netherlands, as the supervisor (or additional supervisor) of a number of important criminology dissertations and studies – for example those by Arnold Aletrino, Joseph van Kan, and Bonger – and as an advocate for the adaptation of the criminal justice system to the ideas of the New Direction in the study of criminal law. In 1896, for example, he founded the Pro Juventute juvenile welfare organisation in Amsterdam and from 1909 to 1917 he defended his ideas, for example on the suspended sentence, with enthusiasm and success in the Lower House of the Dutch Parliament.[7]

7.2.1.2. Champion of Criminal Bio-Anthropology: Arnold Aletrino

A more outspoken advocate than Van Hamel – or rather, a fanatical proponent of modern criminology, in particular bio-anthropology – was Arnold Aletrino, a doctor and man of letters who emerged in the early 1890s as a supporter of modern criminology.[8] Acting far more assertively than Van Hamel, he used that discipline, throughout his life, to question the principles of criminal law, the functioning of the criminal justice system, and conventional legal training. He demonstrated his positive attitude to criminology and his aversion to the criminal law for the first time and at considerable length in *Twee opstellen over crimineele anthropologie* [*Two Essays on Criminal Anthropology*] (1898) and in the inaugural lecture *Over ontoerekenbaarheid* [*On Lack of Responsibility*] that he gave when appointed to a lectureship at the University of Amsterdam

---

4   Van Hamel 1889.
5   Von Liszt 1917, p. 563.
6   Fijnaut 1984a; Fijnaut 1986a, pp. 14–15; Vrij 1951, pp. 372–378.
7   Fijnaut 2003b.
8   He wrote, inter alia, the novel *Zuster Bertha*. See Aletrino 1982.

in 1899.[9] In these two publications, he adopted the position that a person's life is determined by the interaction of predisposition and environment. He – like others – therefore basically saw no essential difference between the views of the Italian School of criminology and those of the French School.

In his opinion, however, it was extremely important for criminals to be treated in a manner that was suited both to them as individuals and to the interests of society. This, he believed, meant that the existing penal system needed to be reformed because it was still based on the view that people were free to decide what they will or will not do, whereas criminal-anthropological research had shown that they did not in fact have that freedom. In Aletrino's view, reform of the penal system should, above all, involve imprisonment being devoted entirely to the improvement of the detainee so that he or she could become a useful member of society once more. What that actually meant was that prisoners should be viewed as being ill and should therefore be treated as such. A few years later, in 1906, Aletrino published a very sharply worded pamphlet against imprisonment, a penalty which, he stressed, was not only in many ways inhuman but also counterproductive.[10]

Aletrino's most important publication was his lengthy *Handleiding bij de studie der crimineele anthropologie* [*Manual for the Study of Criminal Anthropology*], the first part of which appeared in 1902, but no further parts of which ever appeared. That work met a need because – unlike in Germany and France – no Dutch translations were available of the well-known books on criminal anthropology. All that appeared at that time were a few slim volumes in Dutch that presented the ideas of Lombroso, Ferri, and Gross in a very rudimentary manner.[11] Aletrino's book, however – after a historical introduction – set out not only the theories of the Italian and French Schools but also went into detail regarding the anatomy, physiology, and psychology of certain categories of criminals. The table of contents already made clear where Aletrino stood in the ideological struggle within criminology. In line with what he had written a few years previously, he stated that there was no reason to choose one direction to the exclusion of the other.[12]

Contrary to which is sometimes thought or suggested, Aletrino was therefore not just a kind of Dutch Lombroso. That does not alter the fact, however, that the more sociological approach to the problems of crime and punishment was introduced in the Netherlands not by Aletrino but by Willem Bonger.

---

[9]   Aletrino 1898; Aletrino 1899; Joosse 1986; Van Weringh 1982; Mayet 1902, p. 109.
[10]   Aletrino 1906, p. 79.
[11]   Gross 1903b; Lombroso n.d.; Soesman 1901.
[12]   Aletrino 1902, p. 111.

7.2.1.3. Proponent of a Marxist Criminology: Willem Bonger

During the 1899–1900 academic year, the Faculty of Law at the University of Amsterdam – apparently at the instigation of Van Hamel – held a competition for a systematic and critical review of the literature on the impact of economic circumstances on crime. Two students took up the challenge, Van Kan and Bonger, with the former winning first prize and Bonger's study being awarded an honourable mention. That Bonger's essay lost out to that by Van Kan was and is understandable. Van Kan's study was considerably more coherent than Bonger's in terms of both its structure and its content. Bonger had restricted himself to comments – some only brief and others longer – on excerpts from a (systematically classified) series of books and articles.

Van Kan then immediately took the trouble to translate his study into French. It was published by A. Storck in Paris in 1903 as *Les causes économiques de la criminalité: étude historique et critique d'étiologie criminelle* [*The Economic Causes of Crime: Historical Study and Critique of Criminal Aetiology*].[13] Bonger, on the other hand, continued his research and published a two-part study, also in French, *Criminalité et conditions économiques* [*Crime and Economic Conditions*] (1905).[14] The first part of that work consisted of the essay that he had submitted to the competition in 1900; the second – and according to the foreword more important – part had been added in the subsequent years. Both Van Kan and Bonger gained their doctorates at the Faculty of Law on the basis of the studies that they had submitted for the competition.

Comparing the two books makes it clear why Van Kan won. It is therefore all the more remarkable that Van Kan's book – despite its clear structure and rich content – has since been forgotten, with Bonger's work in fact still playing a role in the international criminological literature. There are three reasons for this. First, an English translation of Bonger's book appeared in 1916 in the prestigious *Modern Criminal Science Series*, with an abridged version being brought out by Austin T. Turk as late as 1969.[15] The second reason is closely related to the first. Why was Bonger's work in fact translated into English, thus making it – unlike Van Kan's – accessible worldwide? The answer is that in the second part of his study Bonger elaborated – in a well-thought-out but also combative manner – a Marxist view of the problems of crime. The third reason, I believe, is that in the 1960s a "neo-Marxist" movement emerged within criminology that truly appreciated his book.[16]

The first part of Bonger's study comprises an overview of what had been asserted in the literature of the time regarding the connection between

---

[13]   Van Kan 1903.
[14]   Bonger 1905.
[15]   Bonger 1916; Bonger 1969.
[16]   Peters 1966.

economic conditions and crime.[17] The analysis of that connection was in fact the core question in the competition, to which the study provided a reply. Bonger therefore orders the literature by author according to the then-existing schools of criminology or the perspectives from which they studied crime. The fact that he deals with in excess of 50 authors testifies to an extensive knowledge of the literature, but the discussion of the selected passages is unbalanced. Some authors

Willem BONGER, *Criminalité et conditions économiques*, Den Haag, Martinus Nijhoff, 1905.

are discussed in detail and at length, while others are hardly dealt with at all. In some cases, Bonger fiercely contests the author's views, while in others those views are accepted without comment. But the fact is that when Bonger disagrees fundamentally with a particular author, he does not disguise his criticism but expresses it forcefully regardless of who that author is.

---

[17]   Regarding the dissertation, see Van Heerikhuizen 1987, pp. 63–146.

When dealing with the authors who are regarded as belonging to the Italian School, he asserts more than once that Lombroso's arguments on poverty as a source of crime do not stand up to scrutiny. Where Garofalo is concerned, Bonger states that when considering economic circumstances he refers only to people's poverty while totally ignoring the system that causes that misery. Ferri is not spared criticism either. After a relatively detailed discussion of his theory of crime, Bonger concludes that Ferri too interprets the term "economic

Willem BONGER, *Criminality and Economic Conditions*, Bloomington, Indiana University Press, 1969 (abridged and with an introduction by A. TURK).

conditions" far too narrowly, limiting its significance to the circumstances that may have a direct influence on the development of criminal behaviour. He thus fails, like many other authors, to appreciate the relations of production from which these conditions and thus that behaviour arise. It is striking that Bonger accuses Ferri of opposing Marxist theories with which – in Bonger's opinion – he is not properly familiar or in any case misunderstands.[18]

---

[18]   Bonger 1905, 135, 144, 171, 180–181.

The French School, in particular Tarde, also comes in for almost as much criticism.[19] Bonger more or less demolishes the imitation theory, saying that it may perhaps be new but it is not correct, and to the extent that it is correct it is not new. Bonger considers, in particular, that this theory does somewhat explain how social phenomena spread within a society but does not provide any explanation at all for the emergence of new social phenomena. And as regards, for example, the role of economic crises in the development of crime, Bonger notes that Tarde fails to provide any viable explanation for the occurrence of such crises; nor does he coherently explain their impact on crime. Bonger does not hold back in his final conclusion either. Tarde, he says, did put forward a lot of original ideas but he did not contribute much to solving what Bonger considers to be the relevant problems.[20] On the other hand, Bonger does not discuss the views of Lacassagne, merely repeating, several times, the leader of the French School's motto that societies have the crime that they deserve.[21]

Bonger finishes the first part of his book with a number of conclusions. One of the primary conclusions – having regard to the second part – is undoubtedly that most of the authors had wrongly failed to examine the nature of the system of production and the consequences it has for the organisation of society. After all, it is economic conditions that are the foundation, he believes, of every social system. He refers here explicitly to what Marx and Engels had written in their treatise *Zur Kritik der politischen Ökonomie* [*A Contribution to the Critique of Political Economy*], namely that the relations of production determine the economic structure of a society and that that structure in turn forms the basis for the legal and political superstructure.[22]

In the light of this conclusion, it is not surprising that in the first long chapter of the second part Bonger goes into detail regarding the existing economic system and the consequences it has for the various classes of society in all kinds of fields, as much in the field of marriage and the family as in prostitution and alcohol abuse. In his second chapter, he first makes a number of general remarks about the problems of crime and punishment. He then discusses various categories of offences: economic offences (including vagrancy and begging, theft, extortion, criminal bankruptcy, and foodstuffs fraud), sexual offences, crimes of passion, political offences, and pathological offences. He finally sets out his conclusions at length.[23]

It is interesting that at the beginning of Chapter 2 Bonger deals in particular with the (legal) definition of crime, concluding that the criminalisation of certain behaviour is ultimately a matter of power, namely the power to define

---

19   Bonger 1905, pp. 206–216.
20   Bonger 1905, pp. 211, 214–216.
21   Bonger 1905, pp. 204–205.
22   Bonger 1905, p. 306.
23   Van Weringh 1986, pp. 43–54.

a certain act as a crime and to punish the offender.[24] That does not alter the fact, Bonger continues, that where crime must be regarded as an egotistical act the question arises as to which forces cause people to commit offences; after all, people are naturally endowed with social instincts that, under favourable circumstances, prevent egotistical thoughts leading to egotistical deeds. It is particularly important, he concludes, to investigate – with a view to the aetiology of crime in general – whether the existing society forms an obstacle to the vigorous development of social instincts.[25] In a sense, asking the question is tantamount to answering it. Bonger goes on to do this at the end of the second part of his book, deciding that it can rightly be said that economic conditions play a dominant and even decisive role in crime.

Bonger adds that the existing economic system has reinforced people's egotistical tendencies and weakened the moral strength that normally counteracts their tendency towards egotistical deeds and consequently towards crime. Where everyone's economic interests constantly battle with those of everyone else, a great deal of morality naturally disappears and people care little about the views of others. What keeps people on the right path are the hope for reward and the fear of punishment. But because reward and also punishment fail to occur, many people take the risk and perpetrate offences.[26]

This general theory of the causation of crime did not come out of the blue. Bonger had already joined the Social Democratic Workers' Party in 1987 and in 1898 he became the first president of the Socialist Reading Society founded in that year.[27] In any case, in the subsequent chapters he applies Marxist theory to certain categories of crime. The way he does so is not always easy to follow and it is certainly not substantiated anywhere in detail; his sources are generally rather limited. Nevertheless, he arrives at findings that, while not always consistently new across the board, do often reflect his own Marxist perspective on certain types of crime. He states, for example, that the majority of economic crimes result, on the one hand, from absolute misery and frenzy of greed caused by the existing economic system, and on the other from the moral neglect and poor upbringing of children in the impoverished social classes. Professional criminals who are guilty of these offences usually come from the circle of occasional offenders who fall ever lower, socially speaking, after their release. And fraudulent bankruptcy is so closely intertwined with the existing economic system that in another system it could not even be committed.

But it is not only these offences that are an expression of the existing capitalist system. The same applies, according to Bonger, to sexual offences. The fact that

---

[24] Bonger 1905, p. 435.
[25] Bonger 1905, p. 458.
[26] Bonger 1905, pp. 589–590.
[27] Harmsen 2004; Van Heerikhuizen 1987, pp. 21–62.

the existing organisation of society means that divorce is hardly possible leads to adultery. Sexual offences against adults are mostly committed by paupers who have grown up in an environment without sexual morality and who thus view sex primarily from its animalistic side. Bonger believes that political crime is also very clearly a consequence of the existing economic system, just like the degeneration that is also responsible, in turn, for a great deal of crime.[28]

It is striking, finally, that in the overall conclusion of his dissertation Bonger asks what would happen if the social and economic conditions were to disappear that, according to his research, directly and indirectly constitute so many sources of crime. The answer is that if the structure of society were to be based on common ownership of the means of production – because that is the point – then material misery would largely disappear and with it the majority of economic crime, prostitution, and alcohol abuse. In such a society, moreover, civilisation would no longer be the privilege of just the happy few. As a result, various other categories of crime would also decrease significantly, namely revenge crimes as well as sexual offences. It is possible that crime by women would increase for a while, but over time it would ultimately disappear by itself.

In the final paragraphs of the general conclusion, Bonger's optimism becomes extreme. Where the existing society turns people into egoists, the society that he has in mind will in fact arouse their altruism and thus lead to a society in which crime – in the true sense of the word – will no longer exist. Offences will still be committed by pathological individuals but these should then be treated by doctors and not by lawyers. Bonger concludes his study, incidentally, with a quotation from Quetelet. That is not just by chance, because he saw himself in a certain sense as the heir to Quetelet. "*C'est la société qui prépare le crime*" (it is society that prepares the crime). That maxim strengthens Bonger's hope that it must be possible for mankind "*de se délivrer un jour d'un de ses plus hideux fléaux*" (to free itself some day from one of its most dreadful scourges).[29]

Against the background of this influential dissertation of 1905, it is rather strange that in the decades that followed Bonger did not publish any more large-scale studies in the field of criminology. In general, his criminological work in all that time was limited to a few briefer studies on issues that he had already dealt with, more or less, in his dissertation.[30] These included, for example, his study on *Geloof en misdaad* [*Faith and Crime*], in which he took particular aim at crime among the Catholic part of the Dutch population, and his more internationally oriented study on *Ras en misdaad* [*Race and Crime*] in which he repeated – very clearly in opposition to the racist policies of the Nazis towards the Jews – that

---

[28]   Bonger 1905, pp. 723–724.
[29]   Bonger 1905, p. 726.
[30]   Van Heerikhuizen 1987, pp. 147–252; Kempe 1957, pp. 72–74.

nobody comes into the world as a criminal and that speaking of criminal races is "*klare onzin*" (arrant nonsense).[31]

His appointment as professor of sociology and criminology at the University of Amsterdam in 1922 was an iconic event in the history of Dutch criminology: he was the first professor in this field. His inaugural lecture contained passages on the impact, in particular, of the First World War on Dutch society that are very much worth reading. His appointment did not lead, however, to any revival of his criminological research. The main fruit of his labours was the *Inleiding tot de criminologie* [*Introduction to Criminology*], which he published in 1932[32] but which was in fact not much more than a highly abridged and updated version of his dissertation.

The reason why Bonger's criminological *oeuvre* is so limited is definitely not the result of any lack of diligence. He in fact worked night and day. As a social democrat through and through, he devoted himself heart and soul to the cause of the Social Democratic Workers' Party and thus to advancing the interests of the people and institutions which that party supported. From 1916 to 1939, for example, he was the editorial secretary, without a break, of *De Socialistische Gids* [*The Socialist Guide*] and he was several times involved in the work of committees both significant and less significant. It is typical of him that in 1911 he became chairman of the Central Committee for Workers' Development and during the First World War chairman of the Amsterdam Rent Committee, attempting to keep rents under control.[33]

Just as noteworthy is the intellectual resistance he offered in the 1930s to the totalitarian police states that had become established in Russia, Germany, and Italy and about which he was quite rightly very concerned. That concern led in 1934 to his impressive publication *Problemen der democratie* [*Problems of Democracy*]. He explained just how great his concern was in the preface to the second edition:

> Where the path of democracy is abandoned, reign lies and violence. They are threatening the old Europe with destruction. Only the efforts of all forces will enable democracy to avert that calamity.[34]

On 14 May 1940, Bonger and his wife drew the ultimate conclusion from their abhorrence of dictatorship and committed suicide. In his farewell letter, Bonger explained their decision by saying: "I see no future for me, and I cannot bow to the scum that will now rule."[35]

---

[31] Bonger 1917; Bonger 1939.
[32] Bonger 1922; Bonger 1932.
[33] Van Heerikhuizen 1987, pp. 168–175; Harmsen 2004.
[34] Bonger 1934.
[35] Harmsen 2004.

7.2.2. PROPONENTS AND OPPONENTS OF THE NEW DIRECTION

The ideas of Van Hamel and certainly those of Aletrino caused a lot of commotion in and around Dutch criminal science and the criminal justice system. A number of people at the universities sided in one way or another and in varying degrees with their views. But there were also militant opponents from very varied perspectives, from a conservative-liberal but also a religious – both Protestant and Catholic – angle.

Unlike Van Hamel, and to some extent unlike Aletrino, Bonger had no successors, either in the Netherlands or elsewhere. His work was read a great deal – and still is – but there has never been a researcher who really followed in his footsteps. To be perfectly clear, Bonger was not a supporter of the New Direction in the criminal law. He did show an interest from time to time, however, in certain aspects of the criminal justice system, for example the prison system.[36]

7.2.2.1. Proponents of the New Direction

The proponents of the New Direction were mainly associated with Van Hamel. A number of them are worthy of our attention.

The first to be considered here is Jan Simon van der Aa, who made his name in 1890 with a dissertation on the state reform institutions (*rijksopvoedingsgestichten*) in the Netherlands.[37] Initially, this dissertation gives an extremely legal impression: it deals mainly with the existing arrangements for the placement and confinement of young people in these institutions. What follows, however, are critical considerations regarding the relevant government policy, with a number of proposals for revising that policy. These considerations and proposals are clearly inspired by the new broader concept of the criminal law that had manifested itself over the preceding years. According to contemporary views, science had also, after all, to concern itself with the prevention of crime and with more targeted policy for suppressing it. That ambition could be achieved more effectively by focusing on juvenile delinquents and seeking ways to prevent them becoming common criminals. It is therefore unsurprising that a few years later, in 1892, this very practically minded lawyer was appointed inspector and later chief inspector of the prison and reform system at the Ministry of Justice and, in 1898, was appointed to represent the Netherlands on the International Penitentiary Commission. In 1906, Simon van der Aa was appointed professor of criminal law in Groningen. A few years later, in 1910, he was elected Secretary-General

---

36 Bonger, Valkhoff and Van Waerden 1950, pp. lxxxix–xcii.
37 Simon van der Aa 1890.

of the International Penitentiary Commission, a position to which he devoted himself full-time from 1926 to 1938.[38]

The second proponent of the New Direction whom we will consider was David Simons. In his inaugural lecture (1897) on accepting a professorship at the University of Utrecht, and in the comments that he published the same year on the views of Von Liszt, he adopted a favourable position regarding the new, anthropological, or sociological direction in the field of criminal law. However – perhaps backed up by his experience as a lawyer – he repeatedly emphasised above all the dangers that this direction posed for the organisation of criminal proceedings. He was thinking here mainly of the danger that the rights of the state and society would prevail over the interests of the individual.[39] He was also extremely apprehensive about the "ruthless action against the habitual criminal" on the part of the Italian School. In his opinion, the more one realised that criminals are largely victims of their birth and predisposition, of innate features and physique, the more one would be compelled to conclude that one must not ignore the individual with whom one was confronted.[40] Certainly when it came to the position of the accused in criminal proceedings, Simons had great difficulty with the fact that individual freedom did not occupy such a prominent place in the New Direction because protecting society was the higher priority.[41] Under the pressure of social and scientific developments, he did gradually come to accept that the criminal law needed, more than hitherto, to be made to support the protection of society, but he certainly did not wish to therefore abandon the rights of the individual.[42]

The third and most influential criminological follower of Van Hamel was undoubtedly Jacques de Roos,[43] a lawyer who published his dissertation *De strafmiddelen in de nieuwere strafrechtswetenschap* [*Penalties in Modern Criminal Science*] in 1900.[44] That discipline, he wrote, seeks the causes of crime in the organism of the offender and in the circumstances that influence that organism. On the other hand, it develops scientific measures for combatting crime and investigates whether those measures are able to fulfil a dual purpose, namely reducing crime and protecting society against it. What he attempted to do in his dissertation – and did in fact achieve – was to discuss coherently the significance of the individual measures which this new science had proposed. Based on the existing literature, he then reviewed a wide variety of means for reducing crime: the death penalty, indeterminate sentencing and conditional release

---

[38] Van Bemmelen and Pompe 1945, pp. 1–6; Remmelink 2000, pp. 28–30.
[39] Fijnaut 1986, pp. 15–16.
[40] Simons (D.) 1897, pp. 25–27.
[41] Pompe 1931, no. 12246.
[42] Simons (D.) 1911, pp. 33–34.
[43] Kempe 1957, p. 67.
[44] De Roos 1900.

(i.e. release on probation), short custodial sentences, the cellular system, education and reform of children and the elderly, deportation, and indefinite detention. What is rather unusual is that De Roos did not conclude this study with a set of recommendations in which he summed up its results.

In the same year, i.e. 1900, De Roos was appointed head of the Judicial Statistics Department at the Ministry of Justice. A few years later, partly due to his work in that capacity, he began writing an *Inleiding tot de beoefening der crimineele aetiologie* [*Introduction to the Practice of Criminal Aetiology*].[45] In this book, just as systematically as in his dissertation, De Roos first discussed views on the causes of crime and then dealt with all the factors that were considered to be of any relevance: the physical and mental features of criminals (signs of degeneration, mental retardation), insanity and suicide among criminals (frequency of psychoses, numbers and causes of suicide), the influence of age and gender, the role of living conditions and education, family composition, occupation and social position, the geographical distribution of crime, and the nature and extent of recidivism. De Roos concluded this exceptional criminal-statistical study – the first in the Netherlands – with a summary in which he summarised his findings into a number of conclusions. Among other things, for example, he formulated the conclusion that crime has a less favourable environment for development if the psychological state and the living conditions of the population are normal.

It is important to point out that De Roos was not the only person in about 1900 who carried out more empirical research on the nature of crime problems and the best ways to tackle them. Students of the renowned Groningen psychologist Gerard Heijmans, for instance, produced dissertations on the psychology of the criminal. One of the most relevant of these is undoubtedly that by Willem Pannenborg (1912) on the psychology of the arsonist, based on a biographical analysis of arsonists' varying motives, such as dissatisfaction with their environment, revenge, despair, homesickness, greed, and concealment of another offence.[46] Heymans did not himself build up an *oeuvre* in this field but he was interested in it, as was made clear by the trenchant criticism that he wrote in 1901 on the views of Aletrino concerning criminal bio-anthropology.[47]

Unlike in Germany, but similarly to France and the United Kingdom, the psychology of testimony and interrogation failed to get off the ground, let alone the psychology of the criminal justice system. There was nevertheless some interest in the problems associated with testimony, and not only in the legal sense.[48] In his dissertation at the medical faculty of the University of Amsterdam (1914),

---

[45]   De Roos 1908; De Roos 1914.
[46]   Pannenborg 1912.
[47]   Van Weringh 1986, pp. 55–63; Pompe 1956, pp. 420–425.
[48]   Bonhomme 1893.

Chris van Geuns reported on his experimental contribution to the psychology of testimony. That contribution consists of a detailed description of the literature on testimony in pathological cases and on the influence of drugs and stimulants on testimony. It also gives a detailed and critical account of the design and results of three experiments with human subjects.[49]

7.2.2.2. Opponents of the New Direction

The opponents of the New Direction in criminal science came from a variety of backgrounds. Apart from quite a few older professors of criminal law, they came on the one hand from among the more conservative liberals and on the other from church circles, both Protestant and Catholic.[50] It should be noted that not all established professors opposed the reform movement. In the address that he gave as rector of the University of Leiden in 1879, the highly regarded professor of criminal law Anthony Modderman, for example, did refer to the consequences of all kinds of new developments in the discipline for the way it should be practised, but he also completely ignored the developments taking place in Italy in his own field.[51]

One of the professors who a few years later did indeed oppose with all his might the changes that were manifesting themselves in study of the criminal law due to criminology was Meinard Pols. In an address in 1894 about the new directions in criminal science, he sharply attacked criminology. Pols stated that he feared that the change in this science instigated by this new discipline would wipe out the positive changes that had been made since the end of the eighteenth century in the criminal law and penitentiary system. He abhorred, in particular, the rejection of people's individual responsibility for their actions and the demise of the idea that the penalty imposed should be proportionate to the crime.[52]

He was also far from impressed by the fact that criminal anthropology could count on a great deal of approval at international conferences. At all such meetings, positively phrased motions had been adopted with acclamation or without significant opposition, he stated, but when the texts were examined more deeply, it became clear that the unanimity the participants demonstrated in fact related to extremely vaguely worded so-called questions of principle or so-called facts that were taken to be indisputable without any proper investigation or only on the basis of very superficial research. Pols was ready to admit, however, that criminal sociology was far more moderate than criminal anthropology as regards the personality of the criminal. The supporters of that direction in criminology fortunately considered offenders more as victims of social injustices than as

---

49   Van Geuns 1914.
50   De Vries (C.) 1986; Pompe 1956, pp. 350–384.
51   Modderman 1879.
52   Pols 1894, p. 14.

misbegotten moral monsters. But that did not alter the fact that in the case of criminology, too, he was apprehensive about the undermining effect of these kinds of ideas on the existing institutions of criminal justice. Those institutions were perhaps imperfect but they were still not so powerless in the face of existing crime problems as supporters of the New Direction at the very least suggested. Partly because of this, Pols stated in conclusion that there was every reason to vigorously combat the emerging errors in the area of criminal law.

Pols' arguments against the New Direction in criminal science were largely related to the objections raised to it in conservative-liberal circles, with one of the main figures being Reinhart van der Mey, who in 1904 published a short work in which he gave short shrift to the foundations of the New Direction.[53] Specifically, he attacked the radical determinism that, in his opinion, dominated it. In line with that criticism, he was not only totally opposed to abandoning the classic requirement that the severity of the penalty should be in proportion to the extent of the guilt, he was also adamantly opposed to the introduction of a system of indeterminate custodial sentences. He totally rejected the argument of proponents of such penalties that it is dangerous for society to release criminals before one can be sure that they have reformed because it was diametrically opposed to the classical theory of punishment. He also believed that application of that argument would encourage arbitrariness. How could it be determined objectively within a prison whether someone had mended his ways?[54]

In 1911, the Jesuit Frans Tummers published a thorough, far-sighted commentary on the so-called New Direction.[55] Starting from the observation that the approach was gaining increasing control over the operation of the criminal justice system, he considered it high time to subject it to critical examination. Like other critics, he was very much disturbed by the fact that practitioners of criminal anthropology denied the existence of free will and were thus striking at the roots of the existing criminal law. Tummers also considered the impact that consistent application of the ideas of people like Van Hamel and Aletrino would have on the legal system and on society in general. In his view, those consequences would be appalling because the so-called New Direction – seen from a political perspective – was essentially a theory of power in which "the community is all and the individual is nothing". After all, abolishing the criminal law and replacing it with a system of mere protection of the community would give political leaders the power to mould the members of society in the way that in their opinion benefited the common interest ("artificial adaptation") or to eliminate them from society as being worthless ("artificial selection"). In other words, that theory would result in the most intolerable absolutism of individuals

---

[53]   Van der Mey 1904. See also Levy (J.) 1901.
[54]   Van der Mey 1904, pp. 21–24, 52, 58–59, 65, 73, 75, 79.
[55]   Tummers 1911.

or the even more dangerous despotism of a majority, or of a minority that was able to maintain its position by force.[56]

Following on from this he was especially critical – unsurprisingly – of the views of Von Liszt and his supporters regarding the lifelong institutional confinement of incorrigible criminals as well as the countless others whose supposed psychological inferiority meant that they could all too easily be considered as such, or worse, the termination of their lives – as was already being done in some American states – in a quick and painless manner. Tummers was referring here, in somewhat veiled terms, to the application of eugenic methods to promote social selection within the population.[57] The overall conclusion of his book comes as no surprise: little good was to be expected of the New Direction in criminal science.[58] With the wisdom of hindsight, one cannot deny that Tummers foresaw all too well the scenario that became reality after 1933 in Nazi Germany, when those in power also made use to some extent of certain criminological theories to justify aspects of their murderous criminal policy.

7.2.3. IMPACT OF THE NEW DIRECTION IN THE CRIMINAL JUSTICE SYSTEM

In later years, De Roos described the influence of modern criminology on criminal law and criminal justice in the Netherlands, above all thanks to the forerunner of the New Direction, Van Hamel.[59] In doing so, he pointed out that the confrontation had in general led to a search for more rational solutions to problems. He noted immediately, however, that in this quest to combat crime effectively, the theoretical differences between the doctrines of retribution and defence did not really play much of a role in policy and actual practice.[60] It had thus become possible to implement a number of reforms in the Netherlands that in other countries were still controversial.

However, that statement is something of a simplification of what had actually happened. The great scientific – and certainly also political and religious – divisions over crime prevention and criminal justice had meant that all such reforms could be introduced only after years of difficult and sometimes fierce debate. It therefore often took years before the facilities were created that made the proper implementation of the measures in question possible.

The fundamentally difficult transition from theory to policy and practice will be illustrated below with three examples: how dangerous criminals were dealt with, elimination of cellular confinement, and the scientification of detection.

---

56   Tummers 1911, pp. 120, 124.
57   Tummers 1911, pp. 127–142; Van Embden 1901, pp. 413–419.
58   Tummers 1911, p. 148.
59   De Roos 1911; De Roos 1917.
60   De Roos 1917, p. 471.

7.2.3.1. First Example: The Treatment of Dangerous Criminals

A good example is the approach to the issue of the insane offender, sometimes described as the criminal psychopath.[61] After much debate, the *Wetboek van Strafrecht* (Criminal Code), which was adopted by the Dutch Parliament in 1881 and came into force on 1 January 1886, stipulated that imprisonment was the main penalty and that for the first five years of the sentence it would take the form of cellular confinement. This means that the Code did not provide for the introduction of the communal system, let alone the "Irish" or progressive system. Such a policy change would never have been accepted, under any circumstances, by the conservative grouping in the Lower and Upper Houses; they already considered the limitation of solitary confinement to a maximum of five years to be a radical innovation.[62] The effect of the principled choice of cellular imprisonment was that in the years that followed panopticon prisons, among other types, were built in a number of places, for example Breda and Haarlem, to implement a penitentiary policy which – as was made clear by the associated *Beginselenwet voor het gevangeniswezen* (Penal System (Framework) Act) and *Gevangenismaatregel* (Prisons Order) – was permeated by the spirit of repression.[63] Only the introduction of the possibility of placing totally insane offenders in an asylum represented a small step in another direction.[64]

That this policy would be challenged by supporters of the New Direction was obvious. After all, it was not compatible in any way with their idea that the criminal law should be applied according to the personality of the offender and not according to the seriousness of the offence. That specifically demanded the individualisation of punishment and thus differentiation of the regime within prisons. And since this view of what needed to be done was in particular fuelled by the belief of psychiatrists such as Lombroso that many criminals, although not born criminals, are professional or habitual criminals, there was quickly a call for the greater involvement of psychiatrists in the administration of criminal justice, both to provide information to the courts and in the context of the prison system. However, the demand for psychiatric supervision in prisons to be improved also arose from the psychological problems with which many detainees had to contend, whether or not as a result of the pitiless regime to which they were subjected. There was good reason why as early as 1893 inspectors within the *Staatstoezicht op Krankzinnigen* (State Inspectorate of the Insane) argued for the creation of a separate institution with a view to the treatment of insane criminals.[65] In 1895, their proposal received support from a committee of the

---

61   Van der Landen 1992, pp. 238–261.
62   Franke 1990, pp. 315–335.
63   Franke 1990, pp. 339–411; De Wit 1986; Petersen 1978, pp. 451–455.
64   Haffmans 1984, pp. 1–2.
65   Haffmans 1984, p. 3.

Nederlandse Maatschappij tot Bevordering van de Geneeskunst (Dutch Medical Association), of which not only Van Hamel was a member but also Simon van der Aa and the renowned psychiatrists Gerbrand Jelgersma and Cornelis Winkler.[66]

Because such proposals failed to find sufficient support, discussion of the acceptability of solitary confinement continued.[67] The discussion concerned not only the sustainability of this penitentiary model as such but also a controversial issue that was closely linked to it, namely the disruptive effect that work in prisons could have on work in the rest of society.[68] In response to this complex debate, a state commission was appointed in 1902 to explore ways to arrange for the treatment of both detainees who were, to a greater or lesser extent, insane and persons consigned by a criminal court to an insane asylum. The commission – whose members, besides Simon van der Aa, also included Simons – concluded in 1904 that psychiatric supervision within the prison system needed to be extended and that, in addition to a central observation clinic in Utrecht, there needed to be psychiatric annexes in a number of prisons. A state insane asylum should be built in the centre of the country.[69] These proposals led in turn to a wide range of discussions as to what was desirable, necessary, and possible. As a result, it was only in 1911 that the government submitted a proposal for "psychopath legislation" to the Lower House.[70]

The creation of the *Psychiatrisch-Juridisch Gezelschap* (Psychiatric-Legal Society) by Van Hamel et al. in 1907 therefore did not arrive out of the blue. That organisation was intended as a forum where psychiatrists and lawyers could learn how to talk to one another, from their different disciplinary perspectives, about the nature of the psychological issues that manifested themselves in the successive phases of the criminal justice system, as well as how to tackle them.[71] Just how difficult this practice-oriented interdisciplinary discussion in fact was is already apparent from the fact that, right up to the 1950s, there were still references to the need to improve the level of forensic psychiatry not only from the criminal law and criminology perspective but also in terms of understanding the operation of the prison system and the treatment institutions.[72] Conversely, there were also references to the major importance of education and training of the judiciary in these areas because at the time the rules in the field of criminal procedure were becoming increasingly sophisticated, as was the organisation

---

[66] Visser 1896, pp. 84–96; Franke 1990, pp. 410–450.
[67] De Vries (J.) 1901, pp. 55–72, 133–147.
[68] *Verslag* 1897, p. 38; De Bonvoust Beeckman 1892; De Jonge 1994, pp. 32–37.
[69] *Rapport* 1902, pp. 92–96.
[70] Hafmans 1984, p. 5.
[71] Willekes MacDonald 1885, p. 9; Piepers 1907; Domela Nieuwenhuis and Van der Hoeven 1908; Feber 1932, pp. 74–80.
[72] Havermans 1954.

of the system of services that were involved in one manner or another in prosecution, adjudication, and sentencing.[73]

The essential aim of the 1911 bill was to develop a system of penalties and measures – in particular detention under a hospital order (*"tbs"*) – for persons who were suffering from a disturbance or from impaired development of their mental capacity when they committed the offence. The bill received considerable support from psychiatrists but in legal circles it was highly controversial. Supporters of the Classical Direction were not exactly enamoured of a measure that was apparently motivated by the doctrine of the need to defend society, while supporters of the New Direction considered that psychopaths should fundamentally not be punished.[74] This discussion meant that the bill immediately became a *casus belli* in the more general debate on sanctions and security measures prompted by the emergence of the New Direction. An astute analysis of the matter was provided in Willem Pompe's dissertation in 1921.[75]

The bill, introduced by Edmond Regout, was the subject of ever more new objections, both from the successive ministers of justice and from members of the Lower House, and was thus mothballed. It was only in March 1925 that the House approved the much-amended bill. The corresponding acts did not come into force until 1 November 1928 because the implementing act was delayed for all sorts of reasons. The essence of the arrangement was, and remained, that courts were empowered to confine persons who had committed a crime to an insane asylum if impaired development or a pathological disturbance of their mental capacity meant that they could not be held responsible. Moreover, courts could now order persons who were psychologically disturbed when they committed a serious crime to be detained under a hospital order, either conditionally or unconditionally, in the interest of public order.[76]

In 1928 and 1929 state asylums for psychopaths was also set up within a number of existing institutions. The capacity of these asylums – just a few dozen places in all – was insufficient to cope with the influx of patients, meaning that a much larger state asylum had to be opened in 1931. The influx of patients continued, however, confronting the government with the need to decide whether capacity should be greatly expanded. The government decided in 1933 not to do this, and it had the Lower House adopt a *Stopwet* (Stop Act) to limit the increase in the number of patients. This was not only because of cost considerations – in the midst of the major economic crisis in those years – but also to prevent too many people being labelled "abnormal".[77]

---

[73]   Lamers 1954b.
[74]   Haffmans 1984, p. 6.
[75]   Pompe 1921, pp. 42–66; Van Maanen 1912; Van der Landen 1992, pp. 219–278.
[76]   Feber 1932, pp. 24–48; Patijn 1938, pp. 311–321; Petersen 1978, pp. 467–468; Haffmans 1984, p. 9.
[77]   Van Bemmelen 1957, pp. 12–13.

After the Second World War, however, it was not so much the repeal of the Stop Act which caused a flood of committals under a hospital order but above all the further dissemination of New Direction ideas within the judiciary and among psychiatrists. The problems that this development entailed ultimately led to the opening in 1949 of the *Psychiatrische Observatie Kliniek voor het Gevangeniswezen* (Psychiatric Observation Clinic for the Prison Service) that the state commission had already requested in 1902. The clinic was intended to make it possible, by providing expert advice to the judiciary, to apply committal under a hospital order in a more responsible and therefore more selective manner.[78] This attempt to channel the influx of patients was not an unnecessary luxury: in the 1950s about half the 2,000 persons so sentenced were held in an institution, often under conditions in which there could be no question of treatment. The rest were either on probationary release, had been conditionally discharged, or were absent without leave.[79]

7.2.3.2.   Second Example: The Elimination of Cellular Confinement

Another preoccupation of the New Direction was the elimination of cellular confinement. From the very start, advocates of this direction were greatly in favour of the widespread use of conditional sentencing and release on probation. Following lawyers who had been greatly impressed by the developments in England and Ireland, they advocated these measures in order – specifically in the case of short prison sentences – to counter the adverse psychological and social effects of cellular confinement but also so as to give prisoners a serious chance of returning to society in a responsible manner.[80] The Criminal Code of 1886, however, had only made a cautious start on introducing release on probation. Prisoners could only be released in this way after serving three quarters of their sentence and they also had to have spent at least three years in prison.[81] This very rigorous arrangement was of course not much used. Of the 370 prisoners who were theoretically eligible for this measure between 1886 and 1891, for example, only five (four men and one woman) were actually freed.

For supporters of the New Direction, figures such as these naturally provided an additional reason not only to advocate greater scope for release on probation but also to introduce the kind of conditional sentencing already practised in many other countries.[82] Their arguments aroused a great deal of resistance in conservative scientific and political circles. Opponents viewed such changes to the penal system as an outright subversion of the cellular prison system.

---

[78]   Lamers 1954a, pp. 60–65.
[79]   Haffmans 1984, pp. 16–17.
[80]   Claringbould 1881, pp. 119–146; Van Duyl 1881, pp. 166–191, 220–233.
[81]   Van Duyl 1881, pp. 321–322; Franke 1990, pp. 335–338.
[82]   Patijn 1938, pp. 282–300.

They feared – not without cause – that introducing such measures would be the beginning of the end. The vehemence of the discussion at the beginning of the twentieth century between experts and associations regarding the overall sustainability of the cellular prison system was indeed justification for this fear.[83] The consequence of this sometimes furious debate was that it took until 1915 before those proposals could be transformed, to some extent, into legislative measures: extension of release on probation to prisoners who had served two thirds and at least nine months of their sentence and introduction of conditional sentencing in the case of sentences of one year or less. The extension of the probation system meant that the number of prisoners released annually subject to this measure increased almost twenty-fold compared to previous years.[84]

In the years that followed, more breaches were made in the regime of solitary confinement. At the end of the First World War, for example, specifically in 1918, the prisons were so overcrowded with smugglers that emergency legislation had to be introduced to put an end to the deplorable conditions. That legislation empowered the Minister of Justice to order that prison sentences be served within the community. He immediately used this power to establish an "open air prison" at Veenhuizen (in the east of the country) for over 1,000 smugglers, thus unintentionally carrying out a real-life experiment to prove that the communal regime did not have the terrible consequences that had always been invoked as an argument in favour of cellular confinement.[85]

It was not until after the Second World War that the cellular system was really abandoned. Three things were then decisive: first, the developments that had already occurred before the war and shown that solitary confinement was not an acceptable penal method; second, the experience of imprisonment endured during the war by members of the Dutch Resistance and others who had been forced to go into hiding; and third, the problems that had arisen after the war with the confinement of thousands of political prisoners.[86] The work of drafting the unavoidable shift in policy was entrusted in 1946 to a commission chaired by Willem Fick, vice-president of the *Hoge Raad* (Supreme Court). The commission's report (1947) formed the basis for the *Beginselenwet gevangeniswezen* (Prison System (Framework) Act) that was adopted by Parliament in 1951.

That act more or less put an end to solitary confinement in the Netherlands. The penalties and measures were in future to retain their intrinsic character but were above all intended to prepare the detainee for his or her return into society, as this "socialisation" of the criminal sanction system was described in section 26.[87]

---

[83]   Franke 1990, pp. 478–520.
[84]   De Vlugt 1930, pp. 119–132; Franke 1990, pp. 524–531; Patijn 1938, pp. 301–304, 396–400; Tjaden 1954; Pompe 1954; Fijnaut 2003b.
[85]   Franke 1990, pp. 540–542, 553–557; Petersen 1978, pp. 479–481; De Vlugt 1930, pp. 133–149.
[86]   Franke 1990, pp. 632–641.
[87]   Eggink 1958, pp. 262–263.

But even when there was a fundamental change in attitudes, there was not automatically a change in the conditions at the relevant facilities. After 1951, it was, in other words, a real challenge to implement the necessary adjustment in facilities so as to bring the structure of the prison system into line with the new Framework Act. The provision in section 11 of the Criminal Code that, depending on the personality of the convicted person, the sentence should be served in a general or restricted communal setting or in isolation was not really implemented until the 1960s. Passing laws is one thing; creating the conditions to implement them properly is quite another.[88]

7.2.3.3. Third Example: The Scientification of Criminal Investigation

In his overview of what had been achieved in the first decades of the twentieth century, De Roos completely ignored the impact of the New Direction on the scientification of investigation in the context of regular policing. It is true that that modernisation was not as fast, relatively speaking, as in major German and French cities – for example, Dresden, Hamburg, and Lyons – but in a number of places, particularly Amsterdam and Rotterdam, it was well in line with developments there. This was largely due to progressive, Europe-oriented police chiefs such as the Rotterdam police chief Willem Voormolen. They were well aware of what was happening elsewhere in Europe and, as far as possible, introduced those developments within their own force. However, one can search in vain for police officers, magistrates, or scientists of the calibre of Bertillon, Reiss, Gross, Locard, or Heindl.[89]

In tracing the emergence of criminalistics and scientific policing, it should first be noted that in around 1900 various professors, prosecutors, magistrates, investigative judges, and also police officers began to write about overseas discoveries in periodicals such as the *Tijdschrift voor Strafrecht* [*Journal of Criminal Law*], the *Nederlands Tijdschrift voor Geneeskunde* [*Netherlands Journal of Medicine*], and the *Politiegids* [*Police Guide*]. Their subjects included, of course, photography, *Bertillonnage*, and dactyloscopy, but also the role of scientific research in the collection, analysis, and interpretation of clues.[90] In the early twentieth century, in line with this, important works by luminaries such as Gross, Bertillon, Roschner, and Reiss were also translated into Dutch in the form of pamphlets and manuals.

There was also a good reason for this second stage in the developments in the Netherlands. Since the late nineteenth century, criminal investigation departments had been set up within the police forces of major cities, in line with

---

88 Lamers 1954a, pp. 13–19, 34–46; Petersen 1978, pp. 908–919.
89 Fijnaut 1985.
90 Lignian 1894; Bijleveld 1899; Trivelli 1908.

foreign models, so as to improve the quality and effectiveness of investigation both nationally and internationally. This meant that instructional materials were needed to train the detectives who were to man these departments. It is striking, incidentally, that their publications show that prosecutors and investigating magistrates were also very much interested in the scientific approach to investigation that was being pursued in other countries.[91]

In conjunction with these first two steps, there was also a third step in the developments, which began with the enlistment of external experts such as the Amsterdam pharmacist Christiaan van Ledden Hulsebosch and the director of the *Warenkeuringsdienst* (Commodity Inspection Service) in Arnhem, Willem Hesselink, for forensic investigation of serious criminal offences. In 1914, this resulted in the appointment of a part-time lecturer at the University of Amsterdam, Herman Roll, to teach forensic medicine and police science.[92] It was then finalised in 1916 with the permanent appointment of Van Ledden Hulsebosch in the Amsterdam police force.[93] A few years later, in 1923, he was also appointed to a part-time lectureship at the University of Amsterdam. Van Ledden Hulsebosch did not have a specialised laboratory at the university, however, and nor did the pathologist Jan Hulst, who was appointed to a part-time lectureship in criminalistics at Leiden University in 1929. It was only after the war that a start was made – in the framework of the then *Rijksrecherchecentrale* (Central Criminal Investigation Department) – on the development of what is now the *Nederlands Forensisch Instituut* (Netherlands Forensic Institute).[94]

7.2.4. ESTABLISHMENT OF THREE UNIVERSITY INSTITUTES

When one considers the developments in criminology between the two world wars, the main figure remains Bonger. Despite his preoccupations as a professor, journal editor, and administrator, he still found time during this period – as we have already seen – to write his famous introduction to criminology and to dedicate himself to completing a certain amount of criminological research. He did not, however, make use of his appointment at the University of Amsterdam to get a criminological research institute off the ground. He thus remained a solitary figure whose main work was rediscovered in the 1960s.

After some time, a number of other universities did attempt – in the context of the New Direction – to place criminological research on an institutional footing. This implementation of the New Direction occurred mainly at the Universities of Leiden, Utrecht, and Groningen, where it took the form, to a greater or lesser

---

91 Fijnaut 1985, pp. 35–38; Fijnaut 2007, pp. 292–301; Meershoek 2007, pp. 105–112.
92 Fijnaut 1985, pp. 36–37.
93 Meershoek 2007, pp. 182–183.
94 Kempe 1948, pp. 100–101.

extent, of veritable institutes for the practice of criminology. That is not to say, however, that everyone connected with one of these institutes was committed to exactly the same ideas or applied them in the same way. As in the Italian and French Schools, there were also major differences of opinion at the Dutch institutes on a wide range of subjects.[95]

7.2.4.1. Leiden Institute

The institutionalisation of criminology – in the strict, almost literal sense of the word, i.e. the establishment of institutes – began at Leiden University, where the *Vereniging het Leidse Criminologisch Instituut* (Association of the Leiden Institute of Criminology) was founded in 1933. A few years later, the research centre received a donation that allowed it to amass an outstanding library. Oddly enough, the centre did not really get off the ground, either before or after the Second World War, in terms of empirical research.[96] It was nevertheless officially renamed the *Strafrechtelijk en Criminologisch Instituut* (Institute of Criminal Law and Criminology) in 1959.[97]

In 1933, however, a decision was immediately taken, entirely in the spirit of the New Direction, to launch a series of books entitled *Strafrechtelijke en Criminologische Onderzoekingen* [*Studies in Criminal Law and Criminology*], published by Martinus Nijhoff in The Hague. By 1940, ten books on a wide variety of topics had been published in the series.[98] The editorial board comprised Bonger, Muller, Pompe, and Van Bemmelen; it was in fact an inter-university initiative.

Among the books that appeared in the series were legal studies by Jacob Patijn on probation and by Bernard Röling on legislation on professional and habitual criminals. From an empirical perspective, the statistical studies by Leonardus Drukker on sexual crime in the Netherlands from 1911 to 1930 and by Johan van Sandick on sentencing in the years 1913 and 1929 are the most relevant. However, the most remarkable of all is the 1933 study by Herman Pippel in this series on the legal possibilities for permitting sterilisation in the Netherlands. Even more than that by Röling, this study shows how strong the influence was in the Netherlands, certainly in the early 1930s, of the debate in Germany on the containment of crime.[99]

As late as the 1950s, the image of the Leiden Institute was determined by Jacob van Bemmelen, who was appointed to the chair of criminal law in 1931. In his inaugural lecture on that occasion, on the significance of criminal law,

---

95 Van Eck 1940; Kempe 1948, pp. 104.
96 Kempe 1957, pp. 83–84.
97 Fijnaut 1986a, p. 21.
98 Kempe 1957, p. 84.
99 Van Weringh 1986, pp. 122–123.

he referred repeatedly to foreign criminological publications to clarify the conditions under which the criminal law can in practice perform its functions in the area of special and general prevention.[100] This approach was certainly understandable for someone who had been supervised by Simon van der Aa at the University of Groningen. The same can be said of the programme that he proposed to implement, namely to see clearly the difficulties involved in the theory of criminal law and in its application in practice, and to investigate how much effort it would take to master the normative character and empirical character of the discipline.

The initiatives just referred to demonstrate that Van Bemmelen immediately attempted to implement this programme, greatly inspired as it was by the New Direction. For unknown reasons, however, he did not manage to convert the programme into a real research programme. At the end of his career, Van Bemmelen made it clear that he had tried in various places to bridge the gap between criminal science and criminology because these two disciplines had remained too separate, but it had not been possible to make any progress because integrating those disciplines was such a difficult undertaking: not all criminological research could be applied in the criminal justice system and criminal law research is also not always suited to such application.[101]

This finding is in any case in line with the way in which his more important publications fulfilled the task that he had taken on, namely not to mix up his publications in the field of criminal law, so to speak, with those on criminology. In 1936, for example, with Leonard van der Plas, he published a *Leerboek van het Nederlandsche strafprocesrecht* [*Textbook of Dutch Criminal Procedure*] and in 1953–54, with Willem van Hattum, a *Hand- en leerboek van het Nederlandsche strafrecht* [*Manual and Textbook of Dutch Criminal Law*], in which criminology plays no significant role. In between, in 1942, his *Leerboek der misdaadkunde* [*Textbook of Criminology*] appeared, which largely omitted the criminal law and criminal procedure. Van Bemmelen nevertheless argues in that book that not only criminal psychology but also criminal sociology is relevant to the criminal law and the criminal justice system. He does not explain, however, what that relevance actually is.[102] That does not alter the fact that, to this day, Van Bemmelen has been the only Dutch professor to write introductions to both the criminal law (and criminal procedure) and criminology.

In the early 1960s, Willem Nagel took on the role played by Van Bemmelen in the field of criminology, certainly in the eyes of the general public. Shortly after completing his renowned study at the University of Groningen on serious crime in the town of Oss (North Brabant) since the end of the nineteenth century,

---

[100]   Van Bemmelen 1931.
[101]   Fijnaut 1986a, p. 23.
[102]   Van Bemmelen 1958; Fijnaut 1986a, pp. 22–23; Fijnaut 1986c, pp. 78–80.

he was appointed to a senior lectureship under Van Bemmelen and in 1956 to the chair of penology and criminal sociology.[103] In terms of criminological research, his professorship was not very fruitful. Apart from a few shorter works, his larger-scale research was essentially limited to a lengthy summarising study of the international literature on predicting criminal behaviour – a study that was not, incidentally, very hopeful. Its conclusion was in fact that a great deal of research needed to be done before, for example, courts could be provided with methods for basing their judgments, in part, on reference data predicting criminal behaviour among offenders.[104]

In a certain sense, it is also interesting to note that the aforementioned study by Nagel regarding crime in Oss was still very much in line with the New Direction and thus with integrated criminal science, but that his later writings are increasingly sceptical as to the possibility of bringing criminology to fruition in that context. In his farewell address in 1975, for example, he wrote that criminal science had launched criminology, as it were, but that the latter would not complete its flight. For him, that meant that criminology should depart from the faculties of law – or at least that those faculties should no longer be the only or the primary faculties where the discipline could be accommodated. Its further development, in other words, should be sought in the direction of the behavioural sciences.[105] He himself did not make that transition. That was probably because as a writer in many fields he had numerous interests (and conflicts) and moreover – as evidenced by the contributions to his *liber amicorum* – a large international academic network.[106]

7.2.4.2. Utrecht Institute

A year after the establishment of the institute at Leiden University, i.e. in 1934, a "primitive institute" of criminology was set up at Utrecht University on the initiative of Pompe (appointed professor of criminal law in 1928) and Röling (appointed to a part-time lectureship in penology and penitentiary law in 1933). They used the funds that had been made available to them by the *Stichting tot Werkverruiming voor Academisch Gevormden* (Foundation for Work Extension for Academics) and established a "working community in the criminological field" in three rooms in Utrecht's then-vacant prison.[107] Unlike what had happened at Leiden University, they started to carry out criminographic research almost immediately. A few years later, the publishing house Dekker & Van de Vegt also launched a series of books so that they could publish the

---

103   Schuyt 2010, pp. 229–230, 328–329; Fijnaut 1986c, pp. 80–82; Fijnaut 1986a, pp. 22–23.
104   Nagel 1965, pp. 235–241.
105   Nagel 1977b, p. 76; Kempe 1948, p. 106; Fijnaut 1986c, pp. 82–83.
106   Jasperse, Van Leeuwen-Burow and Toornvliet 1976.
107   Kempe 1948, pp. 102–103.

results of their investigations. The official title of the series was *Criminologische Studiën* [*Criminological Studies*] but it was referred to informally as the *Groene reeks* [*Green Series*] because of the colour of the cover. In the mid-1950s, this series was replaced by a *Nieuwe reeks* [*New Series*] of *Criminologische Studiën*, published by the Gorcum & Comp. in Assen.[108]

The first criminographic study carried out by the two initiators – in 1934–35 – was an investigation into crime in the Utrecht judicial district. Similar studies were subsequently performed on crime in the municipality of Utrecht, by Bert Jens, and on crime in the province of Drenthe, by Gerrit Kempe and Jan Vermaat.[109] This tradition was continued after the Second World War by the impressive empirical study by Hilarius van Rooy of crime in Nijmegen and its environs in 1910–35. That study was published in 1949, two years after Van Rooy had been appointed to a lectureship in criminology at Utrecht University.[110] A year later, in 1950, Jan Stachhouwer published a study of crime, prostitution, and suicide among immigrants in Amsterdam; the study is very concise and is still relevant today.[111] The criminographic research tradition was completed by the 1957 study by Rijk Rijksen of serious forms of crime committed during the German occupation in the Utrecht judicial district and the categories of offenders who had committed the offences in question. This was published in the *Nieuwe reeks*.[112]

The most controversial non-criminographic piece of research appeared only after the war, namely Rijksen's study of the views of prisoners on the criminal justice system. Opposition by the Ministry of Justice to publication of the results meant that the study could not be published until 1961. This study – an original one from both the theoretical and methodological perspectives – was based on letters from no fewer than 901 detainees, distributed fairly systematically across the country, about their experience of the system and their views on it. Based on excerpts from those letters, this still readable study brings together what are often unpleasant memories of crucial moments in criminal proceedings: the police investigation, the appearance before the public prosecutor and the examining magistrate, pre-trial detention, the hearing, etc. It would be well worth repeating that study today.[113]

It was in fact no coincidence that the study took place in Utrecht. One needs to bear in mind that when appointed to his chair there in 1928, Pompe – referring to the classical thinkers in the field of criminal law but also, repeatedly, to Lombroso – had placed the emphasis on the individual offender in criminal

---

[108]   Kempe 1957, pp. 84–85.
[109]   Jens n.d.; Kempe and Vermaat 1939.
[110]   Van Rooy 1949; Van Rooy 1947; Litjens 1953; Dercksen and Verplanke 1987; *Rapport* 1951.
[111]   Stachhouwer 1950.
[112]   Rijksen 1957.
[113]   Geisert (H.) 1930.

law: "It is the actual offender who is now going to dominate criminal law".[114] Pompe foresaw that abstract classical legal considerations regarding the offender would increasingly be intertwined with the insights of the New Direction regarding the actual offender, and no longer in order to determine to what extent the crime could be attributed to him or her but also to establish what treatment would be most appropriate. It was therefore for a good reason that he advocated continuing research on the personality of the offender.

He was later joined, incidentally, by such formidable allies as the psychiatrist Pieter Baan, who – first in his public lecture (1947) and later in his inaugural address (1952) – sharply criticised the fact that many judges, prosecutors, and lawyers applied the criminal law without making any attempt whatsoever to truly understand the individual concerned. He attributed this to the incorrect and automatic use of their power in interpersonal relationships.[115] It was for good reason that the title of the famous paperback published in 1968 by Jacob Kloek – extraordinary professor of forensic psychiatry at the Institute of Criminal Law and Criminology since 1957 and director of the Psychiatric Observation Clinic for the Prison Service since 1958 – was *Dialoog met de criminele psychopaat* [*Dialogue with the Criminal Psychopath*].[116]

In that sense, Rijksen's study can still be seen as applying the credo of Pompe. What was innovative about his study, of course, was that it presented statements not from all sorts of experts and professionals, on the subject of the offenders they dealt with in the criminal justice system, but from the perpetrators themselves, who had the opportunity to speak frankly about themselves and their actions. This was unprecedented in the Netherlands. That this reversal of the usual research perspective fitted in with the programme formulated by Pompe is also apparent from the writings of other members of the Utrecht School, in particular Kempe's publications about the probation system.[117] These very strongly express the view that effective functioning of the criminal justice system requires not only expert and honest action on the part of the officials and magistrates involved, but also recognition of the interests and needs of suspects and convicts.

Moreover, it should be recalled that in 1959 the leading members of the Utrecht School – Pompe, Baan, and Kempe – together with a number of other authors also promulgated the mission of the institute in French. In his foreword to the booklet in question, the editor, the famous French criminal lawyer Jacques Léauté, wrote that, according to the Utrecht School, the criminal is a man like any other and the only difference between him and his peers is that he

---

114   Pompe 1928.
115   Fijnaut 1986a, pp. 28–29.
116   Kloek 1968.
117   Kempe 1958.

has committed a criminal offence.[118] The broad international orientation of the research carried out at the Institute of Criminal Law and Criminology is also evident from the fact not only that many of its empirical studies made reference to German, French, and Italian publications, but also, even before the war, that criminographic publications were already citing American studies, above all of course those on the socio-geographic spread of crime that were carried out by members of the Chicago School. In particular, the names that appear include researchers such as Clifford Shaw and Henry McKay, whose work will be discussed in the next chapter. Stachhouwer's study of crime, prostitution, and suicide in Amsterdam made use of Edwin Sutherland's *Principles of Criminology* (1934).

Finally, it should be emphasised that in Utrecht and elsewhere in the Netherlands – in contrast to countries such as Italy and, as we shall see, Belgium – the establishment of criminology institutes was not accompanied by the introduction of teaching programmes in criminology. Before the war, training in criminology in the Netherlands remained confined to the attention paid to it by criminal law professors during their lectures, to lectures by part-time lecturers, and to symposia organised with varying regularity for interested parties. After the war, there was a structural change to that situation, due in particular to Pompe. Pompe saw to it that the new higher education regulations provided that professors who taught criminal law should also offer a minor in criminology.[119] Not everyone was happy with this. Some feared that such a link would stifle the development of criminology, while others considered that their fear was unwarranted.[120]

7.2.4.3. Groningen Institute

In the first few decades of the twentieth century, the University of Groningen did not remain inactive in the field of criminology. There was the renowned psychologist Gerard Heymans, for example, who concerned himself with that discipline from time to time. For a number of years, the internationally equally acclaimed Simon van der Aa was also associated with the Groningen Faculty of Law. But no real tradition of specifically criminological research developed at that time.

Even after Maarten Vrij was appointed professor of criminal law in 1928, it took several years before criminological research began. That is actually somewhat curious because, in his inaugural lecture, Vrij – entirely in the spirit of the New Direction – had expressed himself so positively about the great

---

[118]   Léauté 1959, p. 16.
[119]   *Rapport* 1946, pp. 187–204.
[120]   Kempe 1948, p. 77.

importance of criminology for the foundations of the criminal law and the functioning of the criminal justice system, especially with a view to a balanced trial for the accused: "Criminology called the criminal law to reality."[121]

The appointment of Synco van Mesdag as a part-time lecturer in criminal biology and psychology in 1935 did nothing to change the situation. That was probably because – judging by his inaugural lecture – his main aim was to use his lectures to make prospective lawyers aware of developments in the fields concerned.[122] He was thinking in particular of the great importance of biological and psychological knowledge for the proper trial of offenders. On that issue, Van Mesdag was therefore in agreement with Vrij. How could judges properly assess the individual offender and his conduct without such knowledge? He considered it impossible. Lombroso and his followers had indeed overestimated the significance of anatomy and physiology for an understanding of the offender, but it was important to keep in mind that the essence of Lombroso's hypothesis had been revived in another form and some people were again assigning relevance to the biological features of the offender. This revaluation of Italian bio-anthropology and the explicit appreciation of German *Kriminalbiologie* did not lead, however, to the development of research in the field of what was at that time already such a controversial discipline, either in Groningen or elsewhere in the Netherlands, not before and certainly not immediately after the war. This was probably partly due to the fact that Van Mesdag had died in 1941.[123]

In any case, it officially took until 1943 before an Institute of Criminology was set up by Vrij with the aid of Nagel. The fact that he had to go into hiding from the German occupiers shortly afterwards meant that it was obviously impossible to build up that institute. Nor did it happen after the war, because in 1947 Vrij left to become a member of the Supreme Court.[124] He in fact made no secret of this failure in his farewell address. On that occasion, he pointed the finger at others – the board of the university and certain funds – who he felt had not provided him with the means to really get criminological research off the ground. It was only after the liberation of the Netherlands that he was allowed a certain degree of leeway to develop various sorely needed activities in this field.[125]

That is not to say, however, that no interesting research was carried out in Groningen during the years when Vrij had full responsibility.[126] One of the most interesting criminal-sociological studies carried out in the Netherlands is in fact Nagel's previously mentioned study of crime in the town of Oss. The levels of violence that crime had reached there in the mid-1930s was in fact a reason for

---

[121]   Vrij 1928, pp. 20–21.
[122]   Van Mesdag 1935.
[123]   Kempe 1948, p. 104.
[124]   Kempe 1957, pp. 87, 96.
[125]   Vrij 1948, pp. 24–26.
[126]   Nagel 1966.

Vrij, with a number of his students, to conduct an investigation of this notorious criminal phenomenon.[127] Those students included Nagel, who actually went to Oss, talked to a large number of those involved, and amassed a large number of criminal files. However, the war and in particular his own activities in the Resistance meant that he did not have the opportunity to work out his findings immediately. He was only able to do so after the war.

The results of his diligent work were not published until 1949.[128] What is noteworthy about his study is not only how he collected and analysed so much biographical data about the criminals involved, but also the way in which he interpreted their crimes, which he also described in detail. This was the first time in the Netherlands that use was made, almost exclusively, of the theories on criminal gangs that had been developed in the United States in recent decades by Frederic Thrasher, Hans von Hentig, Edwin Sutherland et al. In that sense, Nagel's study indicated in its own way the post-war shift of Dutch criminology towards the United States and away from the Italian, German, and French Schools.[129]

7.3. ESTABLISHMENT OF CRIMINOLOGY IN BELGIUM

7.3.1. FORERUNNERS OF CRIMINOLOGY: PAUL HEGER AND ADOLPHE PRINS

There can be no doubt that the cradle of modern criminology in Belgium was the *Université de Bruxelles*. There, the renowned criminal lawyer Adolphe Prins and the equally renowned physiologist Paul Heger became extremely interested in the 1880s in Lombroso's views on criminals and his ideas about how they should be treated.

Equally important is that it was not only in the context of their lectures that they propagated their own ideas about the emerging modern criminology, about a more suitable approach to crime problems, and about the consequences for the criminal justice system. Starting in 1889–90, they also organised exchanges of views on these matters in the framework of a *Cercle de criminologie*. This study circle was the forum in which many of those who would later play an important role in French-speaking Belgium both in academic discussion of crime problems (and how to tackle them) and in policymaking with regard to reform of the criminal justice system first became aware of international developments in

---

[127] Smeets 2001.
[128] Nagel 1949, pp. 6–12.
[129] Schuyt 2010, pp. 212–214.

these fields. They included, for example, Louis Vervaeck, Henri Carton de Wiart, and Emile Vandervelde.[130]

The establishment of a socialist-oriented shadow university in Brussels in 1894 – the famous *Université Nouvelle*, funded by the Freemasons – as a result of serious political conflicts within the *Université de Bruxelles* was detrimental to the functioning of that exceptional study circle. On the other hand, it gave a boost to criminological debate in Brussels because it led to such figures as Ferri and Niceforo regularly coming to lecture at this remarkable institute.[131]

Finally, it should also be noted that Prins et al. founded the *Revue de droit pénal et de criminologie* in 1907, thus creating a vehicle for the dissemination of their ideas and those of their followers.

7.3.1.1. Bio-Anthropological Insights of Paul Heger and Jules Dallemagne

The physician Heger had strong views on the personality of criminals and on how they should be treated. He did not, however, become a leading bio-criminological researcher. Nor did he himself play any major role in formulating and developing a criminal policy that would be consistent with the views that were circulating in modern criminology. He and others did go to great lengths, however, to get anthropometric research on criminals onto the agenda of the Brussels Société d'anthropologie.[132]

Heger first publicised his views on criminals in 1881, when, together with his co-worker Jules Dallemagne, he published a study of the criminological features of the skulls of executed murderers. That study shows that Heger did not blindly follow Lombroso's ideas and therefore did not believe that criminals formed a certain distinct branch of the human race. But that did not mean that he did not adopt a bio-anthropological view of the personality of the criminal.[133] What that view came down to was that criminals should be regarded as being ill.[134]

For many years afterwards, Heger remained silent in this field. He made himself heard once more at the International Congress on Criminal Anthropology that took place in Brussels in 1892. That Congress has already been mentioned because it was boycotted by Lombroso and the other Italians in protest against the fact that the French, in their eyes, had not fulfilled their promise of designing and conducting a study to test Lombroso's ideas. Heger was the general rapporteur for the conference and in that capacity played the role, to a greater or lesser extent, of conciliator between the two camps.[135]

---

130   Durviaux 1990.
131   Vervaele 1990, pp. 360–364.
132   Beyers 2003, pp. 43–50; Mayet 1903, pp. 85–89.
133   De Ruyver and Goethals 1993a, pp. 128–129.
134   De Moor 1935, pp. 166–167.
135   *Actes* 1993, pp. 469–477.

In his summary of the reports and discussions at the end of the conference, he stated, inter alia, that none of the conference participants still wished to defend the concept of the "born criminal"; however, he said, that did not alter the fact that everyone was aware that the fruitful exchanges of the previous few days were ultimately thanks to the organisers of the Rome conference, in other words to Lombroso and his associates, without whom, he wrote, none of them would be in Brussels. He also pointed out that disputes between different scientific schools are inevitable; they are comparable to people's growing pains. Fortunately, however, the conflict between the Italian and French Schools had been resolved, as could be seen from the approval for the conciliatory proposals that were based on mutual respect and aimed to achieve consensus. He therefore considered that the conference had been a success. The barricades had been torn down and all the participants wanted just one thing: the improvement of society.[136] Subsequently, Heger did not publish anything very special in the field of criminology.

One of his followers took over the helm in the years that followed, namely the man with whom Heger, in 1881, had published the famous piece on the skulls of Belgian criminals who had been condemned to death, Dallemagne. Unlike Heger, Dallemagne, a doctor, did still publish pieces from time to time on the personality of criminals. At the above-mentioned third international criminal-anthropological conference in Brussels, for example, he presented a report on the *Étiologie fonctionnelle du crime* [*Functional Aetiology of Crime*] in which he defended the position that biological factors do indeed play the main role in the causation of criminal behaviour but that the importance of the environment in which a criminal grows up cannot be denied. That environment, according to Dallemagne, played a (secondary) role in the sense that it gave a certain colour to a crime, a certain cachet, a certain allure.[137] According to him, the biological factors which, however, formed the core of the problem were those associated with diet, with reproduction (in particular heredity), and with intellectual capacity.

However, Dallemagne also published various studies on the stigmata of crime and how they should be interpreted. To a significant extent, he summarised those studies in 1896 in a handy little paperback of 185 pages, *Stigmates anatomiques de la criminalité* [*Anatomical Stigmata of Crime*].[138] In the general introduction, he left no doubt – despite all the criticism of criminal anthropology – that he had not lost his faith in that discipline: its method, its purpose, its technique, and even its spirit were, he asserted, undisputed. In that same spirit, he went on to describe, in as factual a manner possible, the results of all the research carried out in Europe up to that point on the skeletons of criminals, their organs and senses,

---

[136] See also De Moor 1935, pp. 170–171.
[137] *Actes* 1893, pp. 140–152.
[138] Dallemagne 1896.

their limbs, their weight, and their stature. His main conclusion from that survey was that criminals admittedly displayed far more stigmata than normal people but that that still did not justify the suppose existence of a "criminal type" of human. But what those stigmata actually meant was something that Dallemagne was unable to say.

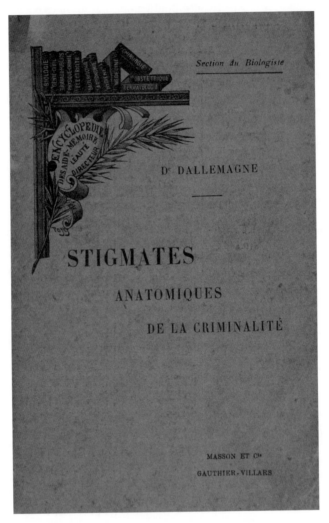

Jules DALLEMAGNE, *Stigmates anatomiques de la criminalité*, Paris, G. Masson, 1896.

7.3.1.2. Development of the Criminal-Political Programme of Adolphe Prins

Unlike Heger, Prins gradually emerged as the figure who, in Belgium around 1900 and also in subsequent years, managed to transform international developments in the field of criminology and criminal justice into specific criminal policies. He acquired that role as a pivotal figure not only as a professor at the University of Brussels but also as the Inspector General of Prisons (1884–1917), and also – together with Von Liszt and Van Hamel – as one of the founders of the International Association of Criminal Law in 1888. Although never a Member of Parliament, he was also a leading figure in the liberal movement. Even more so than Von Liszt and Van Hamel, Prins therefore had some major advantages when it came to turning his ideas into practical policy, both directly and indirectly.

Prins first publicised his views on the emerging Italian criminology and the consequences it would have for the structure of the criminal justice system in 1880, in an article entitled *Essai sur la criminalité d'après la science moderne* [*Essay on Crime according to Modern Science*].[139] In that essay he made no secret of his belief that criminology could not be a reason to do away with traditional criminal law or to merge the latter into criminology. He did believe, however, that criminology offered sufficient reason to liberate the criminal law from the fictitious, conceptual world in which it had ended up, and to give it a useful role in society once again.

In determining that role, he did not go along with the idea that every criminal was born as such, although he was willing to accept that professional criminals had an almost irresistible inclination towards crime. Rather, his idea was basically that many criminals – just like non-criminals – had a degree of freedom to organise their lives in a particular manner and that the way in which criminals had used their freedom of choice was just as closely linked to the conditions in which they had grown up and lived as in the case of ordinary people. Take a look, he wrote, at the major cities, at the poverty in those urban centres and at the physical and moral deterioration of the people who vegetate there in total misery. That made it clear, did it not, that crime should in the first place be combatted preventively, i.e. by improving housing, utilities, nutrition, education, and morality? In the control of crime, the criminal law and criminal justice system could play only a secondary role.

The article left no room for doubt that it was written by a progressive-liberal politician whose ideas on crime prevention and criminal justice were part of a much broader political programme. That was noted more than once in contemporary analyses of Prins' work: his ideas on those matters were from the outset strongly determined by his general views on the condition and future of Belgian society. Indeed, his views – at first glance so progressive – were essentially determined to a large extent by his great concern for preserving political order in the country.[140] Just why he was so concerned from the outset about the stability of Belgium is not in fact so hard to understand. Like many other members of

---

[139] Fijnaut 1983b; Wodon and Servais 1934; Vervaele 1990, p. 382.
[140] Tulkens 1988a, pp. 10–11.

the country's political elite, he was very apprehensive about the revolutionary potential among the working population in the industrial centres. At the end of the 1860s, that potential had already erupted in a number of very violent confrontations with the gendarmerie and the army, and there was a deep-rooted

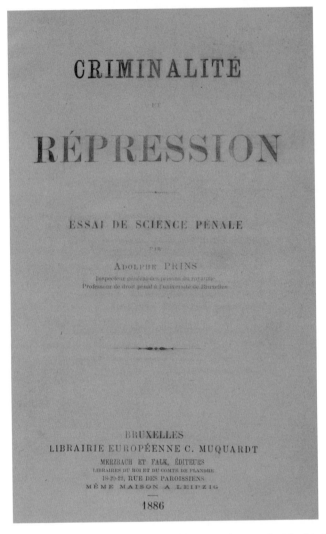

Adolphe PRINS, *Criminalité et répression: essai de science pénale*, Brussels, Librairie Européenne C. Muquardt, 1886.

fear that that scenario could repeat itself with even more violence. That fear was not unwarranted. In 1886 – *l'année terrible* – there were again very serious disturbances in Wallonia which had to be crushed using military force.[141]

---

141   Dupont-Bouchat 1986.

These events explain why Prins wrote the book *Criminalité et répression: essai de science pénale* [*Crime and Repression: Essay on Criminal Science*] in 1886 – of all years! – in which he argued even more forcefully not only for reform of the criminal justice system but in that connection specifically also for social reforms.[142] In that work, he reiterated that the criminal law should not be mere sterile scholasticism but a social science based on anthropological, medical, and sociological research. And even though the advent of industrial society had been accompanied by new forms of crime, in particular all kinds of fraud, the worst crime problems still occurred among the lower classes. They, after all, had long been living in economic conditions that naturally brought forth criminals. There was thus no reason to question the personal responsibility of criminals – everyone is to a certain extent a free man – and even less reason to abolish the criminal law. Quite the contrary: society was in fact fully entitled to defend itself against crime. And that social defence – Prins wrote – was essentially a struggle for the preservation of public order that should be conducted by the competent authorities using the criminal law in proportion to the seriousness of the dangers that threatened it.

This meant, on the one hand, that both the criminal law and the criminal justice system needed to be reformed in order to fulfil that function more effectively. Prins was thinking here specifically of the abolition of solitary cellular confinement.[143] The belief that this was a beneficial method of punishment was, after all, no more than an article of faith. The introduction of the cellular system had not in every case yielded the results that had been predicted. In other words, the prison system was in dire need of reform based on a regime that could be tailored to the needs of the individual detainees. At the same time, Prins thought the system of patronage towards ex-prisoners should be tightened up, perhaps by means of more and better supervision by the state, although he believed it would be better to improve the upper classes' patronage of the lower classes. On the other hand, the concept of social defence entailed doing far more to prevent crime by means of social reforms: recognition of trade unions, the establishment of labour exchanges, subsidies for emigration and for deportation of criminals to the Congo, protection of neglected children, and construction of reformatories.

In the years that followed, Prins published a number of articles in which he held fast to the idea that the emergence of modern criminology was a major reason to implement all kinds of social reforms with a view to preventing crime and also to radically reforming the criminal justice system, but certainly no reason to abolish the criminal law, despite the contentious nature of many of its insights. That was also the basic principle behind the impressive standard work that he published in 1899, *Science pénale et droit positif* [*Penal Science and*

---

[142] Tulkens 1988b, pp. 42–46; Tsitsoura 1990, pp. 109–112.
[143] Stevens 1878.

Positive Law]. Criminal science – he asserted – on the one hand is and remains a legal science but on the other, in the form of anthropological and sociological criminology, is also a social science. And the underlying principle in this twin science is the theory of social defence. That is in any case the theory that is nowadays used – according to Prins – to justify the right to punish.

When compared with the views of Von Liszt and Van Hamel on the relationship between criminal science and criminology, these principles show that Prins too did not believe in a radical version of integrated criminal science (*gesamte Strafrechtswissenschaft*). That is also clear from the structure and contents of *Science pénale et droit positif*, which – generally speaking – are very conventional. What is new about this book is mainly the fairly consistent application of more offender-focused thinking to the organisation and functioning of the criminal justice system. He calls more than previously, for example, for the far-reaching individualisation of the enforcement of penalties, certainly imprisonment. He also stresses the importance of the establishment of juvenile courts more strongly than before. And of course he repeatedly suggests that a number of social reforms are needed.

Prins' final book on criminal law appeared in 1910, namely *La défense sociale et les transformations du droit pénal* [*Social Defence and Transformations of Penal Law*]. That book was to a large extent a summary of the 15 articles he had published over the past ten years. The thrust of those articles is that it was extremely important to preserve the existing social order. That order was certainly not perfect and still needed improvement in many respects but it should also be vigorously defended, first and foremost against the "criminal forces" that threatened it. Prins was thinking here not only of the army of unemployed, degenerate vagrants and the infirm, but also of the professional criminals who formed, as it were, the shock troops of the "army of evil" in the major cities and who always emerged, whenever an opportunity arose, as the leading troublemakers. This justification of the theory of social defence is naturally also an important part of the book. The book also deals in more detail than his previous books with the struggle against repeat offenders, especially professional criminals.

What is new is, in particular, that Prins now called for drastic measures against this category of criminals, even if they had not yet committed an offence; the measures he had in mind basically involve long-term, indefinite imprisonment. This argument was based on his assessment of the intrinsic danger posed by these criminals, and also on his disappointment at the fact that many social reforms which he had previously advocated had since in fact been put into effect but had failed to bring about a decrease in crime. Where the latter point is concerned, he even argued that it might be necessary to take drastic action against the extreme fertility of women with defects and the large number of illegal births among them.

Clearly, Prins' latter recommendation placed him among the social Darwinists who, as in other countries, claimed they were defending the health of their own race. He did not make clear, however, just what measures he considered desirable or acceptable in this regard. Sterilisation? A marriage ban? Intense patronage?

7.3.2. OPPONENTS IN THE PARLIAMENTARY, ACADEMIC, AND JUDICIAL WORLD

Before dealing with the policies of the government ministers who advocated implementation of the aforementioned criminal-political programme – in particular Jules Lejeune (1887–94) but also, following on from him, Carton de Wiart (1911–18) and Vandervelde (1919–21) – it needs to be emphasised that in Belgium, too, the new views on the criminal justice system and on combatting crime were not acceptable to everyone.

The analysis by Donald Weber of the parliamentary debates on crime and criminal justice between 1830 and 1940 clearly shows that the ideas defended with so much fervour by figures such as Heger and Prins encountered quite strong resistance in Parliament from various parties.[144] Conservative Catholics – unlike progressive Catholics – were suspicious of those who strove for recognition of limited criminal responsibility on the part of criminals and, by extension, for the need to reorganise the prison system by reducing solitary confinement. Liberals could generally agree to the pro-change policy as defended by successive ministers of justice. The socialist party was often very much divided, with some of its members in full agreement with the plans set out by Prins and others totally opposed. Discussions between the two factions sometimes became so heated that they could only be kept under control by forcefully imposing party discipline. A common party-political denominator in all the debates was the fear that the lawyers within the parliamentary groupings felt regarding the psychiatrisation of the criminal and their aversion to the power that implementing all sorts of plans would allocate to judges.

In university circles, the innovators could count on a certain amount of opposition but not on such a large scale or as ardent as in some other countries. That is perhaps because until long after the First World War, modern criminology was not an important topic at Belgian universities other than the *Université de Bruxelles*. The practice of that discipline and debate about its consequences for reform of the criminal justice system and other social reforms was in fact – and for many years remained – largely a Brussels matter. This was actually stated explicitly by Lucien Mayet in 1903 in his description of the state of criminal anthropology in Belgium at that time.[145]

---

[144] Weber 1996, pp. 108–110.
[145] Mayet 1903, pp. 91–99.

There were of course professors of criminal law here and there at other universities who did not think much at all of criminologically inspired modernism. One of the best-known opponents of it was undoubtedly Albéric Rolin, professor of criminal law in Ghent.[146] With all his might, Rolin opposed the undermining of freedom and thus criminal responsibility by more or less deterministic theories about the personality and behaviour of criminals. In line with this, he also disagreed completely with the replacement of penalties with security measures. He found the introduction of such measures unacceptable for several reasons, including the fact that he considered them to be contrary to the principles of elementary justice.

The famous sociologist Hector Denis was not only a well-known professor at the *Université de Bruxelles* but also a prominent figure in Freemasonry and the socialist movement.[147] It is necessary to know this if we are to understand the thrust of his most important criminological article, *Le socialisme et les causes économiques et sociales du crime* [*Socialism and the Economic and Social Causes of Crime*], which he published in 1901 in the proceedings of the Fifth International Congress on Criminal Anthropology, held in Amsterdam that year.[148] What this conference contribution basically comes down to is that there had certainly been a decrease in the level of misery in which most Belgian people lived at that time but that many of them were still teetering on the edge of poverty, meaning that the slightest disturbance of economic life – and thus of their living conditions – caused their genetic predisposition to crime to manifest itself.

Denis did not therefore wish to explain the problem of crime from an economic or socialist perspective but sought in his own way – to some extent following in the footsteps of Quetelet – to reconcile the anthropological and sociological schools in modern criminology: people already have a certain predisposition to commit crime – whether or not because of their ancestry – but that innate tendency manifests itself only when their existence is at stake. According to Denis, the consequence of this was that controlling crime required society to be organised in such a way that the material resources would be more evenly distributed, with people living in more or less similar circumstances, with the judicial institutions not magnifying the differences and contradictions between the classes, with there being a certain equilibrium between production and consumption, and with solidarity prevailing between people.

It should be clear that Denis' ideas on the causation of crime were to a certain extent in line with those of Prins. But that comparison cannot conceal the fact that Denis, on principle, assumed a far more egalitarian society than Prins, who was very apprehensive about democracy and wanted to hold fast to the

---

[146]   Rolin 1907.
[147]   Vervaele 1990, pp. 364–367
[148]   Denis 1901; Vandekerckhove 1993a.

class-based society as far as possible.[149] In this respect there was a far greater similarity between Denis' views on the nature, extent, and evolution of crime problems and those that Bonger would express a few years later in his *Criminalité et conditions économiques*.

In addition to the opponents in the political and academic world, there were also those in the professional world. Judges in particular wondered how they should deal with the ideas and proposals of people like Heger and certainly Prins. In 1908, the assistant public prosecutor in Brussels, Raphael Simons – in a series of articles in the *Revue de droit pénal et criminologie* on the theory of social defence – when still discussing basic principles nevertheless warned against undermining the foundations of the criminal law. If that were to occur, he stated, it would have devastating social consequences: "the law impotent and crime sovereign".[150] The Procurator General in Ghent, Alexis Callier, was less restrained in his address at the start of the 1909 judicial year, *La défense sociale par la justice* [*Social Defence by Justice*]. Right from the start, he mocked the innovators. They asserted, he said, that crime had increased and that society was therefore in great danger, but that was not true. The figures showed – contrary to what the know-alls of the Italian School and the readers of the popular news reports believed – that crime was not increasing but in fact decreasing. And that was despite the fact that new means of transport had led to an enormous increase in interactions between people and in opportunities to commit crime. How should that paradoxical trend be explained? According to Callier, it was due to the increased morality within society and, as a component of that, of the moderate and humane application of the criminal law. In other words, there was no reason whatsoever for any radical reform of the existing criminal law.

7.3.3. CRIMINAL JUSTICE POLICIES OF JULES LEJEUNE, HENRI CARTON DE WIART, AND EMILE VANDERVELDE

There is good reason why Jules Lejeune is renowned as a great Minister of Justice.[151] It was he, after all, who gave concrete shape, from 1887 on, to the criminal-political programme whose outlines had been mapped out by Prins in the preceding years. That does not mean that Lejeune also managed to accomplish all their plans during his time as minister. The manifold differences of opinion regarding the future structure of the criminal justice system made that impossible. Even someone with the engaging personality and great charisma of Lejeune could not overcome the opposition across the board.[152]

---

[149] Prins 1884; Prins 1905; Prins 1918.
[150] Simons (R.) 1908, pp. 736–737.
[151] Christiaensen 2004.
[152] Biermé 1928.

The fact that he had his plans approved, as it were, by embedding them in the resolutions of major national and international conferences that he himself organised in Belgium will certainly have helped to make them more acceptable to Belgian parliamentarians. These illustrious gatherings failed, nevertheless, to yield that little extra that was apparently necessary for him to implement his entire programme within just a few years. In 1890, Lejeune organised a major international conference in Antwerp on the patronage of prisoners and the protection of neglected children.[153] Two years later, in 1892, the famous international conference on criminal bio-anthropology took place in Brussels,[154] and in 1893 Lejeune organised a national conference in Mons in order to endorse the introduction of patronage.[155]

But what Lejeune himself was unable to achieve as a minister was implemented, wholly or partly, in the decades that followed by successors who hailed from the same academic school as he did. As the *Journal des Tribunaux* [*Journal of the Courts*] wrote when he was forced to give up his ministerial post, the seed had been sown and the harvest would germinate.[156] It should be noted that, as a member of the Senate from 1894 to 1901, he also did everything he could to ensure implementation of the policy that he had helped design. Moreover, it goes almost without saying that some of the new ministers, Carton de Wiart and Vandervelde, added their own points to the programme that Prins and Lejeune had got underway in around 1890.

All in all, that programme was dominated in the 1930s by five aims:

- introduction of the suspended sentence and release on probation, combined with strengthening of the role of patronage committees;
- increased options for offering a helping hand to neglected and delinquent juveniles;
- systematic abolition of imprisonment in the form of solitary confinement;
- modernisation of criminal investigation and prosecution; and
- indefinite confinement of mentally ill offenders.

By way of example, we will briefly discuss three of these programme points: the introduction of conditional sentencing and release on probation, the introduction of child protection legislation, and the professionalisation of criminal investigation and prosecution.[157]

---

[153]   *Congrès international* 1891; Ugeux 1955, pp. 27–28.
[154]   *Actes* 1893; Ugeux 1955, pp. 36–37.
[155]   Ugeux 1955, pp. 39–41.
[156]   Ugeux 1955, p. 44.
[157]   Ugeux 1955; Dupont 1988; Tsitsoura 1990.

7.3.3.1.   Introduction of the Suspended Sentence and Release on Probation

One piece of legislation that has made Lejeune immortal, so to speak, is that on the suspended sentence and release on probation. He had already succeeded in 1888 in getting these two changes – ground-breaking at the time – into prosecution, adjudication, and sentencing policy through Parliament.[158] The suspended sentence was intended to make it possible to suspend the serving of a custodial sentence for six months, subject to certain conditions. Release on probation could only be applied after a prisoner had served half his sentence. In the light of the parliamentary debates, that period was subsequently shortened to one third of the sentence. The bill was approved on 16 May 1888 by 73 votes to eight (with four abstentions).[159]

This was undoubtedly the first major piece of legislation to be based on the theory of social defence. Lejeune vigorously refuted accusations in Parliament that these measures meant a softening of the criminal justice system: the criminal law should not be applied if it served no purpose.[160] The suspended sentence was intended to counteract short terms of imprisonment with their negative effects on prisoners. The purpose of release on probation was to separate criminals with potential for improvement from incorrigible ones and to give them the opportunity to gradually return to society. This was not in fact the progressive system that Prins was aiming for but it was an important step in the right direction. But for incorrigible criminals – especially repeat offenders – Lejeune believed that the prison system could hardly be tough enough. They should simply serve out the sentence they deserved.

An important component of the policy regarding release on probation was the creation of patronage committees.[161] The intention was that these, in collaboration with the prison management, would provide support for convicts while they were still detained, as well as assistance with their reintegration into society. We have already seen that Prins, with his elitist view of society, favoured a system of patronage in which representatives of the upper classes would concern themselves with "fallen" members of the lower classes; he in any case ascribed all sorts of objectives to such a system. Prins knew that Lejeune was on his side in this regard. Lejeune, in turn, was very much in favour of this means of mitigating the class struggle. But in actual practice the system was a great deal more problematic than in theory. In 1908–09, for example, there were only three people in Liège willing to visit the hundreds and hundreds of inmates in the local prisons.[162]

---

[158]   Tulkens 1988a, p. 40.
[159]   Christiaensen 2004, pp. 239–358; Ugeux 1955, pp. 6–10; Weber 1996, pp. 116–125.
[160]   Ugeux 1955, pp. 9–10.
[161]   Christiaensen 2004, pp. 359–499; Ugeux 1955, pp. 13–16.
[162]   Mary 1990, pp. 173–175; Dupont 1988, pp. 83–85.

In conjunction with his initiative for arrangements to organise the release of prisoners on probation, Lejeune also succeeded in getting the Belgian Parliament to vote in 1891 on a law to combat vagrancy and begging. That legislation was also designed in part to reduce the problem of short prison sentences. First, it made it possible to organise institutions that were intended solely for people who, for whatever reason, were guilty of begging, as well as for pimps. Second, the act arranged for hostels for unfortunates who because of age and/or infirmity were no longer able to earn their own livelihood. And third, the act introduced a system of charity schools for beggars and vagrants under the age of 18. The bill was passed without major changes by the Lower House in August 1891 and approved unanimously by the Senate in the following November.[163]

Here too, the question arises of what actually happened as regards implementation of the legislation. In his dissertation on the containment of begging and vagrancy in Belgium, Wim Depreeuw notes a number of reasons why we cannot really know. Those in favour pointed to the neutralisation of many vagrants, beggars, and pimps, whereas opponents continued to say that the act merely treated the symptoms. For that reason alone, it is not surprising that Vandervelde set up a committee in 1919 specifically to prepare an amended version of the act regarding the problem of vagrants.[164] The American John Gillin, professor of sociology at the University of Wisconsin, who visited a number of Belgian establishments in the late 1920s – specifically Merksplas, Hoogstraten, and Wortel – in any case praised them in his study *Taming the Criminal*. He said of the Belgian labour colonies that "while not a part of the penal system [...] [they were] of the very greatest importance and significance" for American policy on begging and vagrancy.[165]

7.3.3.2. Introduction of Child Protection Legislation

Lejeune introduced a bill in 1889 with a view to the protection of children who were left to their fate – materially and morally – in cities, industrial areas, and commercial centres: victims of the environment in which they found themselves by birth. If society tolerated this situation, Lejeune wrote in the explanatory memorandum, it would be responsible for the evils that these children would sooner or later undoubtedly perpetrate. The bill was therefore based, on the one hand, on the belief that when children grow up in decent conditions they will not become involved in crime. On the other hand, it was also motivated – certainly implicitly – by the idea that that objective could not be achieved through penal

---

163   Ugeux 1955, pp. 29–32; Weber 1996, pp. 128–131; Prins 1899, pp. 569–589.
164   Depreeuw 1988, pp. 364–370, 453–458.
165   Gillin 1931, pp. 190–215.

repression but only by educational means.[166] He also objected very much to the fact that he still came across children during his prison visits. They simply did not belong there. Children should go to school, not to prison.[167]

Among the bill's provisions were that parents could be deprived of parental authority, that prosecutions could no longer be brought against children aged under ten, that a juvenile court could place children under the age of 16 in special reform institutions or with farmers or craftsmen, and that infringements of penal provisions that served to protect the physical and moral integrity of children would be punished more severely. All sorts of reasons not connected with the actual substance of the bill – including the revision of parts of the Civil Code – meant that on two occasions it was not subjected to parliamentary debate. As a result, Lejeune's successor had to attempt to get the bill passed, but without success.

That is why the bill was reintroduced only in 1904 and, due to various circumstances, was only dealt with in 1910. In 1912, under pressure from the new Minister of Justice, Carton de Wiart, it was finally passed by Parliament, with various amendments.[168] Recent empirical research on the reform of "incorrigible juvenile delinquents" in Ghent around 1900 makes clear, incidentally, that it is must have been no small task to apply this legislation in an orderly manner. Nobody, it would seem, was in any case prepared for the turnaround that it was intended to bring about in tackling the problem of juvenile delinquency. Moreover, the outbreak of the First World War naturally made it almost impossible to commence implementation of the act; that was only done to some extent in around 1920.[169]

That does not mean that the Child Protection Act did not attract considerable attention abroad. Lucie van den Bergh, for example, published a legal analysis of the act, comparing it with the Dutch legislation on juveniles that had been introduced a few years earlier.[170] Conversely, the application of that legislation aroused curiosity in Belgium as to how special facilities for juvenile offenders were organised in other countries and how they actually worked. In 1919, Minister Vandervelde instructed a committee to investigate the situation in the United Kingdom.[171]

7.3.3.3. Professionalisation of Criminal Investigation and Prosecution

As far back as the 1870s, Prins and others had been highly critical of the state of criminal investigation and prosecution in Belgium, which they considered

---

[166] Dedecker and Slachmuylder 1990.
[167] Christiaens 1999, pp. 183–194; Weber 1996, pp. 146–153.
[168] Ugeux 1955, pp. 19–25. See also Verhellen 1988, pp. 36–41; Mary 1999, pp. 179–186.
[169] Christiaens 1999, pp. 195–270, 303–342.
[170] Van den Bergh 1915.
[171] Office de la Protection de l'Enfance 1920.

to be lacking in organisation and expertise.[172] Their analysis did not, however, result in any improvement whatsoever in the situation. This is one of the reasons why the need for action was discussed in Parliament on several occasions in the ensuing decades, but always in vain. Typical of this is that a billon setting up a separate judicial police in addition to the gendarmerie and the urban and rural local police was introduced three times before the First World War.[173]

It should be noted in this context that – compared to developments in other countries – it also took a long time before the Ministry of Justice took action to create the central facilities that were absolutely necessary for the uniform and thus efficient application of the new identification methods.[174] Not that there were no experts who could have done that. Eugène Stockis, a forensic physician in Liège, and Ernest Goddefroy, a police officer in Ostend, knew very well what such services should look like.[175] And there were also numerous critics in around 1910 who repeatedly referred publicly to the way Belgium was lagging behind in the field of scientific policing and criminalistics. These people argued forcefully that it was not sufficient merely to establish a judicial identification service within the Ministry of Justice, as had been done in 1908, but that it was just as necessary to establish a school for training police and judicial personnel, like those in other countries.[176] The fact that action had been taken locally here and there to learn about the new methods of identification was a good thing, but it was not nearly enough.[177]

It was therefore no coincidence that in 1913 the Minister of Justice, Carton de Wiart – who had been influenced by Prins – instructed a judge of the Brussels court, Raymond De Ryckere, to write a report on the training of the police and judiciary in Paris, Lausanne, and Rome. In the lengthy report that De Ryckere submitted to the Minister in May 1913, he made no specific proposals as to what action should be taken in Belgium.[178] He had not in fact been asked to produce such proposals, but he apparently wondered whether it would be possible to set up a school in Belgium, on the lines of those in other countries, for the in-service professionalisation of the police and judicial authorities in criminal investigation and prosecution. He concluded his report, with good reason, by asking whether such a school could in fact be established in a country dominated by a spirit of mockery and scepticism. He did not know the answer to that question, he said, but he thought that an attempt should

---

172   Prins and Pergameni 1871.
173   Fijnaut 1995, pp. 27–28.
174   See in this connection Thomas 1978.
175   Stockis 1908a; Stockis 1908b; Stockis 1908c; Stockis 1910; Goddefroy 1914. See also the texts by Stockis, De Ryckere, and others included in Quinche 2006.
176   Ruttiens 1910a; Ruttiens 1910b; Ruttiens 1910c.
177   Coopman n.d.
178   De Ryckere 1913.

at least be made. The outbreak of the First World War meant that Carton de Wiart did not have the opportunity to test this out, but in 1919 his successor Vandervelde immediately took decisive action.

First, Vandervelde succeeded – partly in the light of the major criminal investigation problems that manifested themselves at the end of the First World War – in convincing Parliament that the time really had come to set up the judicial police, under the aegis of the Public Prosecution Service, that people had been demanding for decades. Its organisation and functioning were broadly defined in an Act of 7 April 1919. The arrangement basically meant that a judicial police unit would be set up within each branch of the Public Prosecution Service, with it being directed by the public prosecutor and supervised by the procurators general. There was no provision for nationwide coordination between these units, let alone for central control. It was only in 1936 that the post of commissioner-general of judicial police was created to meet the need for cooperation to some extent, a need that had in fact been inherent to the tasks of the judicial police from the outset. It was intended, after all, not only to carry out criminal investigation in more complicated criminal cases but also in the event of offences that transcended the boundaries of a judicial district.[179]

In 1920, in addition to the judicial police, Vandervelde set up the School of Criminology and Criminalistics within the Ministry of Justice in order to bring police officers and magistrates up to date.[180] He did not rush into this. In 1920, as in the case of the report ordered by Carton de Wiart in 1913, he dispatched a number of persons to Lausanne, Lyon, Paris, and Rome to ascertain the latest state of affairs regarding the training of the police and judicial authorities in criminalistics and criminology. It was apparently the example of Rome that most impressed his researchers.

In any case, the establishment of the school was ordered by a Royal Decree of 19 October 1920, with the ceremonial opening taking place on 17 January 1921. Almost from the start, training was provided at two levels, secondary and advanced. The secondary level was mainly for lower-ranking police officers, with the advanced level being for magistrates and officers of the gendarmerie. From the outset, the intention was to set up a coherent network of police laboratories on the basis of existing local initiatives, although actually doing so turned out to be problematic. The larger branches of the Public Prosecution Service and the School of Criminology and Criminalistics gradually set up police photographic laboratories.[181]

---

[179] Servais 1921; Fijnaut 1995, pp. 31–35.
[180] Constant 1957, pp. 198–200; Quanten 1979; Depreeuw 1988, pp. 502–503.
[181] Quanten 1979; Zaki 1929, p. 122; De Rechter 1929.

Needless to say, these two developments – the creation of the judicial police and the establishment of a school – reinforced one another. This is demonstrated by the fact that the most high-profile works in the professional literature in the 1920s and 1930s were produced by members of the judicial police. Florent Louwage – commissioner and subsequently chief of the judicial police in Brussels and in 1936 the first commissioner-general of the judicial police – was the epitome of this interconnection. In the 1930s and 1940s he wrote several books on the technique and tactics of criminal investigation, the methods and techniques of thieves and swindlers, and the psychology of various types of crime and categories of criminals.[182] Those works show that Louwage was fully au fait with the international literature in these and other areas, something that is not in itself surprising given his increasing involvement, from 1925 on, in the work of the International Criminal Police Commission. In 1932, he became one of the permanent rapporteurs for the Commission. After the Second World War, he was closely involved in the creation of Interpol.[183]

7.3.4. ESTABLISHMENT OF FOUR UNIVERSITY SCHOOLS

We have already seen that, at the end of the nineteenth century the *Université de Bruxelles*, with professors such as Prins and Heger and its *Cercle de criminologie*, could without hesitation be described as the institutional cradle of modern criminology in Belgium. We also saw that the programme that was developed in Belgium by the pioneers and implemented by Lejeune had been more or less accomplished in many respects by 1930. It was about the same time, namely in 1929, that a professor of criminal law at the Catholic University of Leuven, Louis Braffort, set up a School of Criminal Sciences at the university's Faculty of Law. Or was that less surprising in his case than it seems?

On the one hand, one should not lose sight of the fact that part of his law studies had been with Von Liszt in Berlin and with Van Hamel in Amsterdam, meaning that he was thoroughly familiar with the evolution of the intense discussion on the integration of criminal law and criminology. In this context, it should also be emphasised that from 1919 on he was a member of the editorial board of the *Revue de droit pénal et de criminologie*. On the other hand, one needs to know that Braffort was also one of the best-known defence lawyers in Brussels and in that capacity knew a great deal about the practical side of the criminal justice system and, partly because of that, was highly critical of the Act of 1930 in particular.[184] Therefore, it is not that astonishing that at that point

---

[182] Louwage 1932; Louwage 1939; Louwage 1945; Lechat 1950–51.
[183] Fijnaut 1993a.
[184] Braffort 1931.

he apparently wanted more than merely to offer students a handful of courses in criminology, namely to provide them with a fully coherent educational programme in criminal law and criminology. Such a programme scarcely existed anywhere in Western Europe at the time.

In any case, within just a few years the Leuven example found numerous followers. In 1936, the *Université de Bruxelles* – specifically through the action of Léon Cornil, professor of criminal law and Advocate General at the Court of Cassation – set up an *École des sciences criminologiques* (School of Criminological Sciences). Two years later, in 1938, the universities of both Ghent and Liège set up a school of criminology. What these various schools had in common was that they were intended initially and primarily as an institutional framework within which up-to-date training could be provided in criminal law and criminology.[185]

7.3.4.1. Leuven School

In 1929, Braffort published a pamphlet explaining why he thought that the Catholic University of Leuven needed to set up a School of Criminal Sciences.[186] He gave three reasons. First, because the training provided by the university was not sufficient to produce good criminal lawyers. It focused too much on the principles of the Criminal Code and did not take enough account of the reality and complexity of the problem. In order to remedy that deficiency and in particular to bridge the widening gap between legal studies and the continuous flow of scientific discoveries, it was necessary as a matter of urgency to get other sciences involved in legal education as ancillary sciences.

Second, a School of Criminal Sciences was needed because the training of lawyers and of other scientists and scholars was too one-sided, meaning that when analysing criminal cases they could not speak each other's language and could only collaborate with difficulty. What needed to happen was therefore obvious: both the lawyers and the other scientists and scholars needed to be trained less exclusively and in a more harmonised manner so as to make the necessary close cooperation possible.

And third – given the changes in the criminal law that affected people and society so directly – it was certainly the intention to train researchers who would explore the many issues methodically that had arisen due to all those changes. The results of their work should be published in a journal. This approach would gradually enable the doctrine to be developed that would give direction to the operation of the School.

---

185   Constant 1957.
186   Braffort 1929.

More specifically, Braffort stated that research at the School should initially concern the most varied physical, individual, and social factors that affect someone's decision to commit an offence. A better understanding of these factors was also important in order to develop a policy to prevent crime. The

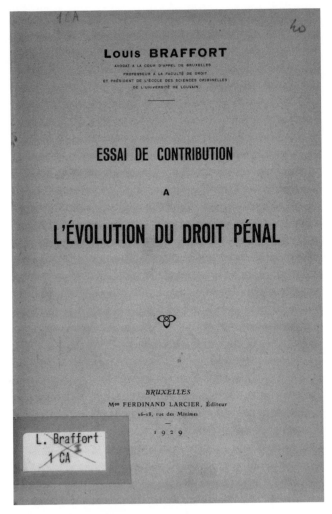

Louis BRAFFORT, *Essai de contribution à l'évolution du droit pénal: mémoire pour la fondation d'une Ecole des Sciences Criminelles à l'Université de Louvain*, Brussels, Ferdinand Larcier, 1929.

methodology applied within the School would consist primarily of studying specific cases, as well as demonstrating those cases for students during lectures. An attempt would then be made, based on such cases, to acquire a more general understanding, inductively, of the nature of criminal behaviour and its underlying causes. Finally, crime problems would need to be analysed with the aid of that understanding, both theoretically and practically. Braffort emphasised that research at the School would be carried out with full academic freedom.

In line with this programme, he sketched the broad outlines of the criminal policy that he had in mind. In doing so, he devoted considerable attention, inter alia, to the high degree of abstraction of the criminal law and the criminal justice system, the lack of criminal response modalities, the overwhelming importance of preventive policy, the relationship between criminal law and morality, the adaptation of penalties to the requirements of social defence, the importance of an adequate typology of criminals, the application of security measures to mentally disturbed criminals and juveniles, and the abolition of jury trials.

He concluded by noting that the Catholic University of Leuven, with its wide range of faculties, had the professors needed to implement an appropriate educational programme. It also had the clinics, prisons, and laboratories in its environs that were important for carrying out scientific research.

The programme included a number of mandatory subjects, some optional courses, seminars, and lectures. The mandatory subjects included criminal law and criminal procedure, psychology and psychiatry, forensic medicine and scientific policing, and international criminal law. These subjects were mainly taught by professors from the faculties of Law, Literature and Philosophy, and Medicine. It is notable that – entirely in line with what Braffort had in mind – case studies were dealt with in both some of the compulsory subjects and the optional courses. Braffort himself taught most of the criminal law subjects, as well as a criminal law seminar.[187]

The fact that Braffort gave a new boost to the practice of criminology in Belgium at a point when the reform programme of Prins and Lejeune, inspired by modern criminology, had spent its force, is evidence of his great strength of mind and determination as attested by many contemporaries. For unknown reasons, Braffort unfortunately did not set out his ideas on the criminal law and criminal justice in larger treatises or systematic studies.[188] It is obvious that the undoubtedly high-pressure combination of work at both the university and in court made that impossible.

It is therefore all the more important for the present work to emphasise the courageous and principled stance that Braffort adopted towards the Nazis during the Second World War. As dean of the Brussels Bar, he refused, amongst other things, to provide the Germans with the names of Jewish lawyers, and protested formally against the arrest of the lawyers who had called the validity of some decrees into question. It goes without saying that such actions did not make

---

187   Casselman 2012.
188   Hutsebaut 1993a.

him any friends among the German authorities or their henchmen. Numerous people warned Braffort in 1944 that he should go into hiding but he refused to do so. On 22 August 1944, that principled bravery proved fatal. Three Belgian collaborators (members of a "Rexist" militia) apprehended him at his home and threw him into a clandestine prison somewhere in Brussels.[189] Early on the morning of 24 August 1944, they took him to open country outside the city and murdered him in cold blood with four pistol shots to the neck as he knelt with a rosary wrapped around his hands.

This terrible event meant the chairmanship of the School had to be taken over by Étienne De Greeff. This was an obvious step because in previous years – in fact from as early as 1929 onwards – he and Braffort had jointly guided the School through the difficult 1930s and 1940s. Like Braffort, De Greeff was a man involved in both criminal law practice and scientific research. In 1926, he had been appointed to the post of assistant physician at a psychiatric clinic and also physician-anthropologist at the central prison in Leuven, and in 1929–30 he taught two courses in the programme of the School of Criminal Sciences; substituting for Professor Fernand D'Hollander, he taught a course on criminal anthropology as well as a course on the human organism.

De Greeff's bibliography as included in Joris Casselman's biography of him (2010) shows that this successor to Braffort was extremely active in a variety of scientific and philosophical fields. Moreover, he wrote several widely read and translated novels.[190] One of his most important larger publications in the field of criminology is undoubtedly his *Introduction à la criminologie*. This was the first introduction to criminology to be written in Belgium. The first edition appeared in 1937 and the last in 1946. Reference should also be made in this context to *Amour et crimes d'amour* [*Love and Love Crimes*] (1942) and *Ames criminelles* [*Criminal Souls*] (1949).

Together with a number of highly original articles in scientific journals, these publications gradually made De Greeff famous within the international, particularly francophone, world of criminology.[191] That recognition was very much evident from the acclaim that his ideas received in 1950 at the Hague Congress of the International Society for Criminology. In 1955, a major international conference was held in in Leuven in honour of his 25 years as a professor.[192] The contributions of an array of international speakers, including Pompe, were published in 1956 in a two-volume *liber amicorum, Autour de l'œuvre du dr. E. de Greeff*. On 21 July 1961, De Greeff – to the great dismay of the many people who had worked with him or been his students – died suddenly of a

---

[189] Sassarath 1940–46, pp. 363–365.
[190] See, inter alia, De Greeff 1949b; De Greeff 1962.
[191] De Greeff 1935; De Greeff 1956b.
[192] Knibbeler 1962.

heart attack.[193] Since then several lengthy studies – in addition to the biography by Casselman – have been published dealing with the central concepts in his work on the psychological sentiments and processes in people who commit serious (capital) crime within their own circle of friends and relatives, for example *le passage à l'acte* and *le sentiment d'injustice subie*.[194]

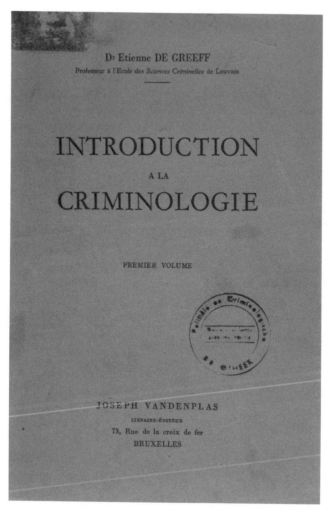

Étienne DE GREEFF, *Introduction à la criminologie*, Brussels, Joseph Vandenplas, 1946.

Broader analysis of De Greeff's criminological studies shows that he was above all interested in subjects that can be classified as belonging to the domain of

---

[193]   Casselman 2010; Van Rooy 1961.
[194]   Ley 1961; Pinatel 1967; Digneffe 1989; Debuyst 1994; Tange 2001; Pinatel 1980; Debuyst 1993; Mary 1999, pp. 72–95.

criminal psychopathology.[195] However, the way in which he studied those subjects was undoubtedly highly innovative. The instinctive and dynamic relationship between the offender and the world around him was central. And being open-minded, De Greeff examined that relationship from all possible angles, making his criminological works seem sometimes phenomenological and at other times psychoanalytic. What ultimately drove him was his wish to gain an understanding of the offender as he or she really was. One might also say that he was a gifted innovator in criminal anthropology. The ideas he developed can be classified under two headings. On the one hand, they mainly concern the personalities of individual perpetrators, and on the other the processes that underlie the crimes they commit.

De Greeff's premise was that criminals are not totally different people to non-criminals. He therefore had extremely serious doubts about anatomical and physiological studies that dogmatically assert that there is in fact such a difference: One should take note of these studies but not become trapped in all-too-easy explanations. For De Greeff, a criminal also has an "ego" that must constantly attempt to maintain a delicate balance between its inner forces and its relationship with its surroundings. Nevertheless, after his years of experience De Greeff concluded that the personality of criminals does have certain typical features – features that clarify why he or she commits a certain offence while others do not. Those features include a high degree of aggression towards others, strong self-centeredness, a far-reaching inability to organise life in a stable manner, and affective indifference to other people.

It is important, however, that he does not consider the profile of any offender to be a natural and established fact but rather to be the end result of a dynamic process of interaction. In his *Introduction à la criminologie*, he demonstrates this with particular reference to the violent bands of thugs who infested Belgium after the First World War. He had had lengthy contact with some of them in the prison at Leuven and had thus seen how they developed from minor delinquents into criminals who could only achieve their ends by means of murder. In addition, he had seen how lengthy prison sentences led to their feeling more and more excluded from society. In peacetime, De Greeff wrote, the number of criminals who developed in that way was relatively limited, but in times of war and revolution their number increased rapidly. He even went so far as to say that Belgium had had extremely high levels of crime during the Second World War, indeed at one point so high that it was comparable to the crime in some cities in the United States.

Given this outline of his ideas, it is understandable why De Greeff had such a great interest in the process that occurs in people between the point at which they

---

[195]   Fijnaut 2000b.

imagine a particular crime ("*la criminalité imaginaire*") and the point at which they actually commit it ("*la criminalité réelle*"). He referred to that process as "criminogenesis". What is peculiar to this process is that perpetrators gradually come to see their crime as an acceptable and successful solution to problems in the world around them (i.e. in their relationship to it). Depending on the type of crime and the type of perpetrator, the process certainly has its variants. A liquidation, for example, is different to a murder committed in a fit of passion. In both cases, however, the victim is reduced to an abstraction.

De Greeff pays particular attention to two components of this process. First, he notes repeatedly that many criminals are afflicted with *le sentiment d' injustice subie*, i.e. the feeling that a great injustice has been done to them and that their crime is justified to rectify that injustice. That feeling is often the starting point for criminogenesis. It is not a cheap, superficial feeling, but rather a deep-seated resentment that informs their whole personality: they constantly feel they are the victim of their surroundings. Second, he devotes a great deal of attention to the culmination of the criminogenesis process, namely the *passage à l'acte*, i.e. actual perpetration of the offence. De Greeff describes, strikingly, how at that point many (violent) offenders fall prey to highly ambivalent feelings, often to such an extent that they are no longer in control of themselves. Some ultimately shrink back from committing the intended offence, or only half-commit it. Others, by contrast, carry it out with terrible force and surrender themselves completely to committing violence.

It should be noted that De Greeff's intriguing research also had its limits. Numerous kinds of serious crime, for example in the realm of economics, are not dealt with in his studies. He strangely enough also ignores the just as interesting sociological research carried out in the United States in the 1930s on individual perpetrators, for example *The Jack-Roller* by Clifford Shaw (1930) and *The Professional Thief* by Edwin Sutherland (1937). De Greeff was apparently uninterested in sociology, a discipline that was also not on the curriculum of the School of Criminal Sciences. Given the interdisciplinary premise of the School, however, these innovative American studies could have played a major role in the design and development of his own analyses.

7.3.4.2. Brussels School

The *École des sciences criminologiques* at the *Université de Bruxelles* was ceremonially opened on 23 October 1936 by Cornil, professor of criminal law and Advocate General at the Court of Cassation, who had been the driving force behind the establishment of the School. In his address, Cornil rightly referred to the role that people like Prins, Lejeune, Vervaeck, Heger, and others had played in the development of the country's policy on crime, not least as a result of the confrontation between the traditional criminal law and modern criminology. The time had now come, however, to go a step further and break through the isolation in which the lawyers, anthropologists, and sociologists had continued to work. The motto should no longer be confrontation but cooperation.

In designing the School, Cornil and others had been inspired by what was going on in Paris and the United States, but also by the establishment of the School at the Catholic University of Leuven. He was therefore gratified that Braffort was present. He then noted, rather mysteriously, that there would be rivalry between the two Schools but that it would be limited to cordial and fruitful scientific competition.

He announced that the curriculum would comprise subjects such as (comparative) criminal law and procedural law, forensic medicine, psychiatry, philosophy, criminology and anthropology, penology, and psychology. Criminalistics would not play any major role because the School was seeking to be paired with the School of Criminology and Criminalistics within the Ministry of Justice.[196] It is striking that Cornil, unlike Braffort, did not present any preview of the research programme envisaged by the founders. The question is therefore whether they actually had such a programme or considered it necessary. In 1945, the School was named after its founder, Cornil, precisely in order to express the aim of closer cooperation between lawyers, anthropologists, and sociologists.[197]

If one browses through Cornil's bibliography one will note, however, that he personally never achieved that cooperation in his research. Here, his position as Advocate General and later Procurator General at the Court of Cassation and his administrative functions at the Ministry of Justice probably meant that he did not have, or create, the necessary opportunity. In his publications, he in any case turned out to be primarily a commentator on current legal and policy discussions and developments in the area of criminal procedure and sentencing.[198] That does not of course detract from the courageous role that he played during the German Occupation. Walter Ganshof van der Meersch recalled in 1972, with great respect, how in 1941–42 – in his capacity as vice-chairman of the central office of the university – Cornil radically and systematically opposed every attempt by the German occupiers to strengthen their grip on the university. The opposition by Cornil and other members of the central office led to their being arrested by the Germans on 9 December 1941 and imprisoned in the citadel at Huy. They were held there until 3 February 1942 and subsequently prohibited from holding any public position.[199] Cornil survived the war but retired from the university in 1954 for health reasons. He died on 19 November 1962 and was succeeded by his nephew Paul Cornil. The latter was appointed professor of criminal law at the *Université de Bruxelles* in 1946 and in 1962 professor

---

[196]   Cornil (L.) 1936.
[197]   Screvens 1963, pp. 740–742.
[198]   Snacken 1993.
[199]   Ganshof van der Meersch 1972.

of penology at the new *Vrije Universiteit Brussel*.[200] For Paul Cornil too this was actually only a part-time position, with his main appointment being that of Secretary-General at the Ministry of Justice from 1946 to 1968.

One should note in that connection that, unlike in the case of the Leuven School, nobody emerged during this period at the Brussels School who – like De Greeff – developed, on the basis of their own original research, into a recognised international authority in the field of criminology. That finding must be put into perspective, however, by referring to Aimée Racine, who in the 1920s spent some time in the United States and apparently came back with ideas on how to carry out empirical research on juvenile delinquency. As early as 1929, she began analysing 300 case files at the Brussels juvenile court. Ten years later she published a remarkable study on juvenile delinquency among the wealthy. In that context, she came across a "dark number" that made it abundantly clear how selective the criminal justice system was in actual practice.[201] After the Second World War, she too ended up in all kinds of administrative positions but nonetheless remained active as a researcher. From 1959 on, for example, she published several studies on the work of the juvenile courts. These publications were drawn up under the auspices of the *Centre d'étude de la délinquance juvénile* (Centre for the Study of Juvenile Delinquency) that was set up at her initiative in Brussels in that year. In the context of that institute, she and her staff also carried out research in the 1960s on a number of contemporary problems such as sexual abuse of children, the behaviour of hooligans, and counterculture "provos".[202]

7.3.4.3. Ghent School

The fact that in May 1938 the state universities of Ghent and Liège were given the official green light to set up a School of Criminology was to no small extent down to two Ghent professors.[203] One of these was Nico Gunzburg, who had studied law at the *Université de Bruxelles* in about 1910 and had worked with Prins for a time. In 1923, he was appointed lecturer in private law at the Ghent Faculty of Law, being promoted to the chair of general legal principles a few years later. However, he had not abandoned his earlier interest, and in the first half of the 1930s began once more to write about the connections between criminal law and criminology. The other was Jules Simon, who had also studied at the *Université de Bruxelles*, and subsequently built up a judicial career in the courts in Leuven and Brussels. In 1924, he was appointed professor of criminal procedure at the Ghent Faculty of Law, while retaining his position in the judiciary. In 1932, he

---

[200]   Eliaarts 1993.
[201]   Racine 1939.
[202]   Somerhausen and Walgrave 1993.
[203]   De Clerck 1978; Cools and Ponsaers 2013; Cools and Daems 2013.

was appointed a judge of the Brussels Court of Appeal and in 1946 of the Court of Cassation.

In 1936, these two professors took the initiative of setting up a School of Criminology at the State University of Ghent. In this they were inspired not only by the establishment of such institutions in Leuven and Brussels but also by similar initiatives in other countries. They also made clear why they also wished to establish a School in Ghent, namely to train all those professionally involved in the containment of crime: future magistrates, lawyers, prison wardens, and senior civil servants at the Ministry of Justice. Their list did not include police officers. Like elsewhere, the academic staff would be recruited not only from the Faculty of Law but also from the faculties of Medicine and Literature & Philosophy.

The proposal was confirmed by the Faculty Board on 19 December 1936 and by Royal Decree in May 1938. As early as 22 June 1938, Gunzburg, at that time the dean, called a meeting to discuss how they would tackle the task of setting up the School. Things then moved quickly, with instructors being appointed on 30 September 1938, Simon elected chairman on 10 November 1938, and lessons starting with ten students on 1 December 1938. The programme, based on the Royal Decree, was almost exactly the same as that in Leuven and Brussels: (comparative) criminal law and criminal procedure, criminology and penology, psychology and (forensic) psychiatry, forensic medicine and criminalistics, and juvenile protection law. Gunzburg taught criminology and juvenile protection law, with Simon dealing with criminal law and criminal procedure. The course in forensic medicine was entrusted to the internationally renowned forensic physician Frédéric Thomas.

On the outbreak of the Second World War, Gunzburg's Jewish heritage forced him to leave Belgium and his work with the Allies led him on an incredibly adventurous life across much of the world. After almost unimaginable peregrinations, he returned to Ghent and in 1946 became chairman of the School of Criminology. He was accorded emeritus status in 1952.

7.3.4.4. *Liège School*

The *liber amicorum* presented to Jean Constant on 29 November 1971 reflects very well the important role of this leader of the Liège School in post-war European criminal law.[204] Jescheck, Van Bemmelen, Radzinowicz, and so on – all of them contributed to the *liber amicorum*. Like his counterparts in Brussels, Constant had had a successful career with the Public Prosecution Service before the war and he also held two parallel positions after it, namely as Procurator

---

[204] *Revue de droit pénal et de criminologie* 1971, pp. 593–612.

General at the Liège Court of Appeal and professor at the Faculty of Law of the University of Liège, specifically at its School of Criminology.[205]

Unlike the two Cornils in Brussels, Constant – in addition to a significant number of articles on a great variety of criminal matters – published two textbooks setting out his views on both criminal law and criminology. Both these works appeared in 1949, with one being a three-part commentary on the Criminal Code and the other what he referred to as a workbook, *Eléments de criminologie*.[206]

The latter, which amounted to more than 200 pages, was largely based on a number of foreign introductions to criminology – German, Italian, Dutch, French, and American. It deals in a very orderly manner with the history of criminology, the phenomenon of crime from a legal and criminological perspective, the personality of the criminal, and the social and economic factors that foster criminal behaviour. It concludes with a discussion of a number of current issues: narcotics, the role of the cinema, the continued effects of the war, and –given the length of the book, very extensively – prostitution.[207]

Because Constant was familiar to some extent with several areas of criminology, it is not surprising that he clearly demonstrated that familiarity in some of his more important articles by taking a position on some key criminal-political issues. One of the best examples of this is his article on the training of criminal court judges, in which he urged specialisation, not only because the individualisation of sentencing demanded it, but also because of the way crime was developing: it was occurring in more and more areas and becoming increasingly professional.[208]

7.4. CONCLUSION

As in other Western European countries, the history of criminology in Belgium and the Netherlands goes back to the invention of criminal bio-anthropology in Italy. The fact that the controversial ideas of Lombroso in those two countries marked the starting point of that history has a lot to do, at first sight, with the receptiveness of some leading criminal lawyers to those ideas. On closer inspection, however, it becomes apparent that their sympathy for Italian bio-anthropology was above all based on its potential to call into question the operation and thus the foundations of the criminal law and the criminal justice system, and in that way also the political and economic developments in the two countries. What one should not lose sight of is that – especially in the case of

---

[205] *En hommage* 1971, pp. XXIII–XXV.
[206] Kellens 1993.
[207] Constant 1949.
[208] Constant 1947.

Prins but also of Van Hamel – those involved were politically engaged and very much policy-oriented professors who were well connected in political circles and who thus had the opportunity to get their innovative insights on how to tackle crime, whether or not by means of the criminal law, onto the political agenda at the highest level. It is otherwise difficult to explain why a significant number of their proposals were implemented, to varying degrees, over the years. Their ideas obviously found enough people at that level who were prepared to listen to them.

But the fact that these proposals were not accepted unquestioningly and were not, so to speak, implemented immediately shows that they were more controversial at the time than they seem in retrospect. And they were controversial not only in political and – given, for example, the Vervaeck–Bertrand controversy – administrative circles; in scientific circles too opinions on the proposals were mixed. There were also mixed reactions among criminal lawyers. But one must not lose sight of the divided views among criminologists either. It was not, after all, the case that, towards the end of the nineteenth century, only a single type of criminology developed in the two countries. Quite the contrary: there were numerous versions, with a wide variety of views, ranging from socialist or Marxist interpretations of crime problems to bio-anthropological or biological explanations of criminal behaviour. What is striking is that – unlike in some other countries – the adherents of the various tendencies in criminology did not fiercely battle one another but were generally very tolerant of one another. That is perhaps one reason why in the countries concerned criminology as such could play such a constructive role in reform of the criminal justice system.

Moreover, one might suggest that that role perhaps also partly explains why criminology could become so firmly established through the establishment of schools and institutes at the two countries' universities in the 1930s. In other words, did its positive role in that reform perhaps mean that it had acquired the social and scientific legitimacy needed for this important kind of academic institutionalisation? That possibility definitely cannot be excluded. It is more likely, however, that the acquisition of that prestige and thus the establishment of those centres also had to do with the fact that those who set them up were generally enterprising figures with the necessary influence in the political, academic, and professional worlds and who could therefore get something like that done. In addition, it is very probable that competition between the universities played a role, in the sense that they did not want to be inferior to one another in this regard and that their boards therefore agreed quite readily with plans to set up a school or institute.

The broad academic institutionalisation of criminology in Belgium and the Netherlands involved the risk not only that the qualitative differences between the pioneers of criminology in the two countries would be lost sight of, but also that the substantive differences between the institutions set up in the two countries would be levelled out too.

On the first point, it is in any case appropriate to note that whereas Van Hamel's and Prins' handbooks and other writings show that they were at the top of the criminal law profession in their time, both nationally and internationally, the publications of Bonger and De Greeff undeniably place them in the same leading position in criminology, however different their views otherwise were scientifically speaking. They stood head and shoulders above contemporaries who were engaged in criminology, whether or not in an academic context. Partly for that reason, it is unsurprising that they were the first professors in the two countries with significant academic duties in the field of criminology. For the same reason, it goes almost without saying that they enjoyed renown both nationally and internationally.

The second point is to some extent complementary, namely that the academic parallel – similarity even – between Bonger and De Greeff should not cause us to overlook the fact that until the 1960s there was a fundamental difference between the institutes that were set up in the Netherlands and the schools that were founded in Belgium. The establishment of the Dutch institutes primarily involved the promotion of scientific research, while that of the Belgian schools had more to do with the provision of university education. That is evidenced not only by the differences in the curricula of the two types of institutions but also by the differences in their research programmes. These differences also explain why in the Netherlands – in contrast with Belgium – numerous criminological theses were quickly defended, specific series of books came onto the market, and – to put it in contemporary terms – "contract research" was carried out. It should be noted, however, that introductions to criminology were produced on a larger scale and more research was carried out in the Netherlands than in Belgium right from the beginning, i.e. from the end of the nineteenth century. In that sense, the Dutch institutes might be expected to have a different, more research-oriented mission that did the Belgian schools. Since the 1960s, those differences have gradually decreased, first as regards research and in the past few years also as regards training. The Belgian schools have in fact since increasingly developed into research centres, while the Dutch institutes have expanded their limited range of criminological training into full-scale training programmes in criminology.

Finally, it must also be pointed out that the establishment of the Third Reich had a serious impact on criminology in both Belgium and the Netherlands. The events that unfolded were, on the one hand, directly responsible for the suicides of Bonger and his wife and, on the other, indirectly responsible for Braffort's murder. The negative impact of the totalitarian police state on the development of criminology was not therefore confined to criminology in Germany. The devastating effect that it had in the latter country will be dealt with in the next chapter.

CHAPTER 8

IDEOLOGISATION OF CRIMINOLOGY IN THE THIRD REICH AND THE SOVIET UNION

8.1. INTRODUCTION

The history of criminology in the twentieth century is marked very much by its extreme ideologisation in the two totalitarian police states that dominated Europe during that century, namely the Third Reich and the Soviet Union. However, most introductions to criminology, entirely wrongly, have ignored its evolution under those regimes. But to understand how the far-reaching Americanisation of criminology took place in Western Europe after the Second World War, one needs to have some understanding of the demise of criminology under those dictatorships.

The demise of the rather successful German criminology was the consequence of its extreme ideologisation during the Third Reich. In particular, its ruin created a vacuum that after the Second World War was in many European countries largely filled by the type of criminology that had developed in the meantime through the reception of European criminology in the United States.

The criminology that had developed in Russia, and later in the Soviet Union, obviously could not fulfil that role. This is not only because it was historically not very highly developed, and thus had little or no appeal to scientists in other countries, but also because after the Second World War it remained a totally ideologised activity, with the Cold War making it even less attractive for Western researchers than was already the case.

8.2. NAZIFICATION OF CRIMINOLOGY IN THE THIRD REICH

During our discussion of the development of criminology in the Weimar Republic, it was pointed out that not only criminology itself but also the criminal justice system – or at least the police and prison system – fell increasingly under the spell of a type of *Kriminalbiologie* that was indebted to eugenics and that was considered useful in preserving the purity of the (German) race. Our explanation of its development also devoted the required attention to the view of the crux of the crime problem – *das Verbrechertum* – that had become rooted within the *Kriminalpolizei* and the views of Heindl on combatting that problem by means of the lifelong internment of dangerous professional criminals.

The present chapter will first consider how, after the Nazis' seizure of power in 1933, high-ranking Nazi police chiefs almost immediately and systematically linked *Kriminalbiologie* and *Kriminalpolizei* with one another to decisively shape their party's policy on crime. Second, we will investigate how that policy was further radicalised in two stages – first mainly by means of the central integration of the police with the *Schutzstaffeln* (SS) in 1936, then specifically due to the start of the Second World War in 1939 – and how it was also implemented on a large scale. Following this historical sketch of the Nazis' criminal policy, we will consider, third, the role that criminology – or rather *Kriminalbiologie* as reformulated by criminal lawyers in particular – played in that history. The chapter concludes by looking at how criminology fared after the Second World War in West Germany.

8.2.1. NATIONAL SOCIALIST HIJACKING OF DISCUSSION IN THE WEIMAR REPUBLIC

The Nazis' seizure of power in 1933 had two initial effects. On the one hand, the *Gewohnheitsverbrechergesetz* (Habitual Criminals Act) of 24 November 1933 implemented the criminal legislation that had been debated fruitlessly for so long during the Weimar Republic: the introduction of *Sicherheitsverwahrung* (detention for security reasons) and other measures for the *Sicherung und Besserung* (security and improvement) of dangerous convicted habitual criminals and sex offenders. Those other measures involved, inter alia, the admission of alcoholics to an alcohol treatment clinic and the castration of dangerous sex offenders. On the other hand, however, far-reaching custodial measures were introduced almost immediately – out of the view of the judicial authorities – in order to get rid of both political opponents (*Schutzhaft* (protective detention), used by the Gestapo) and inveterate professional criminals (*Vorbeugungshaft* (preventive detention), used by the *Kriminalpolizei*) by imprisoning them in concentration camps.[1]

Why the Nazis made use not only of the criminal law to put into practice their ideas on combatting serious (non-political) crime but also of police law has everything to do with the fact that, in totalitarian police states, the police, for all sorts of reasons, is in any case the principal body used by those in power to actually implement the core of their political mission. The head of the *Kriminalamt* (Criminal Investigation Bureau) in Chemnitz, Albrecht Böhme, interpreted this independence of the police in the Third Reich in 1933 by saying that criminal investigation, i.e. the *Kriminalpolizei*, should not by handled by the judicial authorities but was a matter for the administrative authorities.[2] Why an emphatic decision was immediately taken to introduce a radical form of *vorbeugende Verbrechensbekämpfung* (preventive crime control) specifically by the *Kriminalpolizei* was explained, brazenly, by National Socialist police and justice officials in the years that followed. In their comments, they emphasised that the new policy was a response to the supposed inability of the police in the Weimar Republic to take decisive action against serious crime.[3]

The Reich Minister of Justice, Franz Gürtner, clarified matters only slightly in an article in the *Archiv für Kriminologie* in 1933.[4] Referring to Heindl's book *Der Berufsverbrecher*, he stated that tightening up the criminal law was not a sufficiently effective method for combatting hardened recidivists, but that the new law against dangerous professional criminals would be. That law provided for the lasting protection of the German people against criminals who were unable, or who did not intend, to adapt to the rules of law and society. It would enable the battle against habitual and professional criminals to be conducted with greater success than hitherto because the existing legislation did not allow – beyond penalising individual criminals – society to be defended in an active manner against persons who endangered its security.

---

[1]   Werle 1989, pp. 499–521; Müller 1997, pp. 30–44; Baumann 2006, pp. 80–89; Vanhoudt 1940, pp. 189–281.

[2]   Böhme 1933.

[3]   Wagner (P.) 1996, pp. 193–203.

[4]   Gürtner 1933.

Kurt Daluege, however, at that time lieutenant-general of police as well as head of the Police Department at the Reich Ministry of the Interior, together with Erich Liebermann von Sonnenberg, produced a pamphlet in 1936 setting out in detail how the Nazis intended to combat serious crime.[5] What that came down to was destroying the hard core of the underworld, i.e. the legion of professional criminals. This meant that criminal investigation would no longer involve the prosecution of these criminals but almost mechanical prevention of their crimes, thus safeguarding the *Volksgemeinschaft* (national community) from the harm that it would suffer as a result of those crimes. "Professional criminals" was taken to mean persons who, according to the *Kriminalpolizei*, derived most of their income from the proceeds of crime.[6]

The foregoing descriptions of and justifications from the "new" approach to the old problem of habitual and professional criminals in fact prove that the Nazis were guilty, right from the start, of the political perversion or functionalisation of the views that Von Liszt and others had advocated, to the effect that that category of criminals should not only be penalised but should also be the object of security measures.[7]

8.2.2. RADICALISATION OF NAZI CRIMINAL POLICY AFTER 1936

The fusion of the police and the SS in 1936 led gradually to the further radicalisation of criminal policy. That was apparent not only from the promulgation in 1937 of new guidelines for placing habitual criminals, sex offenders and, much more broadly, anti-social elements under indefinite police supervision, but also from the way in which existing measures were applied.[8] Whereas in 1937 and 1938 *Sicherheitsverwahrung* had been applied in 765 and 964 cases, respectively, in 1939 it was applied in 1,827 cases, in 1940 in 1,916 cases, and in 1941 in 1,651 cases. That increase was partly due to a certain level of competition between the judicial authorities and the police. After 1936, all kinds of individuals – known or suspected criminals as well as members of all kinds of marginal groups – were not only placed under police supervision on a fairly large scale but were also put into *Vorbeugungshaft* by the *Kriminalpolizei*. At the end of 1938, 12,921 persons were being held in *Vorbeugungshaft* and 3,231 were under police supervision.[9]

---

5   Daluege and Liebermann v. Sonnenberg 1936.
6   Werle 1989, pp. 40–51, 86–108.
7   Vogel 2003, pp. 662–664; Höpfel 2003, pp. 918–919.
8   Werle 1989, pp. 492–499; Ayasz et al. 1988, pp. 75–88; Wagner (P.) 1996, pp. 258–265.
9   Wagner (P.) 1996, pp. 294–298, 300.

This sharp increase in the number of people dealt with in one way or another by the *Kriminalpolizei* shows a radicalisation in the application of the supposed preventive measures, fuelled by the observation that crime had still not completely disappeared.[10] Radicalisation at that time was also increasingly due to a racist extermination policy that was justified using criminal-biological arguments by policymakers whose ultimate aim was to eradicate the *biologische Brutstätten* (biological breeding grounds) of crime.[11] In 1939, this was justified in a pamphlet published by the Reichskriminalpolizeiamt (Central Criminal Investigation Bureau) with the argument that someone who criminally harmed the person or property of a *Volksgenosse* (fellow member of the German people) was not worthy of being considered such a member himself. It was the task of the *Kriminalpolizei* to determine the predisposition and character of such criminals. Biology quite simply showed that criminal behaviour was not a disease but a defect of character.[12]

When considering all this toxic rhetoric, we must not forget that, especially after the Second World War had begun, this new policy was also intended to increase the number of workers available for the businesses – controlled by the SS – in the concentration camps. This was partly to use their work to finance the wretched operation of those camps, and partly to keep the war industry and war economy running. The murderous regime in those work camps has been described in detail in numerous publications.[13]

In any case, a special campaign by the *Kriminalpolizei* in March 1937 – in the framework of the battle against professional criminals – deprived 2,000 people of their liberty, with the victims being detained in concentration camps. In May–June 1938, there were similar purges of anti-socials (for example, vagrants, beggars, and pimps) and Jews with a criminal record, i.e. all male Jews who had been sentenced to at least one month's imprisonment. In this way, the term "criminal policy" was of course stripped entirely of its traditional meaning, gradually taking on more and more the meaning of a policy that must be labelled as literally criminal.[14]

What is remarkable in all this is that the leadership of the *Reichskriminalpolizeiamt* continued to officially defend its murderous policy of internment as an application of *Kriminalbiologie*. This went so far that a decision was taken in December 1941 – with a view to a more methodical approach to *vorbeugende Verbrechensbekämpfung* (preventive crime control) – to set up a *Kriminalbiologisches Institut* within this central body. The leadership of this

---

10   Wachsmann 2001, pp. 176–177.
11   Werle 1989, pp. 726–732; Wagner 1996, pp. 262–279; Baumann 2006, pp. 106–113; Roth (T.) 2009, pp. 543–545.
12   Reichskriminalpolizeiamt 1939, pp. 18, 21–22.
13   Lofti 2003, pp. 114–128, 210–237, 279–292. For an example, see Wagner (J.-C.) 2009.
14   Müller 1997, pp. 53–57; Wagner (P.) 1996, pp. 256–258, 279–280; Werle 1989, pp. 522–532; Dobler and Reinke 2009.

supposed scientific research institute was entrusted to the psychiatrist Robert Ritter, lecturer in *Kriminalbiologie* at the University of Berlin and head of the centre within the Reichsgesundheitsamt (Central Health Authority) that carried out pseudo-scientific research in the field of racial hygiene and demographic biology. It is by no means surprising that Ritter was given charge of the institute: in 1936–37, including in his *Habilitationsschrift* (professorial dissertation), he had defended the proposition that crime prevention called for research on the entire anti-social and criminal population of Germany.[15]

The start of the Second World War encouraged the further radicalisation of the policy against potential enemies of the people, in particular the intensified use of the criminal law against habitual and professional criminals.[16] This was not immediately clear in the ordinances of 5 September 1939 against *Volksschädlinge* (public vermin) (including looters and saboteurs) and of 5 December 1939 against violent offenders. However, internal instructions from the *Reichskriminalpolizeiamt* from 1939–40 allow for no misunderstanding as regards this development. They state unequivocally that wider use should be made of preventive police detention with a view to protection of the home front.

The amended version of the Criminal Code in September 1941 even went a step further, making it possible for habitual and professional criminals to be executed if, inter alia, the security of the "national community" required it. That these and other measures were intended not only to promote security behind the front lines but also to promote racial purity is indisputable. In a letter to the judiciary regarding this amendment, the then Minister of Justice referred to dangerous habitual criminals as parasites on the population, adding that the criminal law, along with other measures to protect the German race, also had a major "hygienic" duty to fulfil on behalf of the German people.

Where that policy would ultimately lead became apparent when, in the autumn of 1942, more than 12,600 of those sentenced to *Sicherungsverwahrung* were transferred to concentration camps with a view to their being exterminated through work (*Vernichtung durch Arbeit*). A large number of them did in fact die there. In the latter half of 1943, these camps contained 22,500–29,000 people who were interned in the context of either *Vorbeugungshaft* or *Sicherungsverwahrung*. In late 1943, Heinrich Himmler, the *Reichsführer-SS*, stated that there were a total of 70,000 anti-socials.[17]

---

[15]   This decision in included in *Monatsschrift für Kriminalbiologie und Strafrechtsreform*, 1942, vol. 33, nos. 3–4, pp. 57–58. See also Wagner (P.) 1996, pp. 270–279, 378–384; Luchterhandt 2000, pp. 123–137, 227–234; Willems 1995, pp. 237–246.

[16]   Werle 1989, pp. 233–224; Wachsmann 2001, pp. 177–181; Roth (T.) 2009, pp. 566–569.

[17]   Ayasz et al. 1988, pp. 88–92; Wagner (P.) 1996, pp. 331–333, 336–343; Müller 1997, pp. 89–94; Roth (T.) 2009, pp. 563–566.

Three communities that were particularly hard hit by Nazi racism and thus also by the aforementioned criminal law and police measures were of course the Jewish community and the Sinti and Roma communities.[18]

As we have already seen, the new police measures were specifically declared in 1938 to apply to convicted Jewish men. But that was not the only action against the Jewish community in that year. Far better known in any case is the *Kristallnacht* that took place that same year. From then on, matters proceeded directly towards the Holocaust. The attempt by the Nazis to completely eradicate the Jewish people in Europe was above all driven by political hatred rooted in the centuries-old persecution of European Jewry, which was stirred up and exploited by Hitler from the beginning of the 1920s.[19]

This persecution was therefore not derived – at least definitely not directly – from a particular kind of racist criminology. Certainly, criminological treatises before 1933 in Germany too did sometimes devote special attention to crime in Jewish circles or crime committed by Jewish people. And it is likely that even during the Weimar Republic this interest, in the eyes of some, provided additional legitimation for anti-Jewish policies. But the primary rationale for the Holocaust was not any kind of racial-purity-drenched *Kriminalbiologie*.

The Sinti and Roma had long been considered in many European countries, and certainly in Germany, as communities on the margins of society that were guilty of all kinds of property crime. In Germany, *Zigeuner* (gypsies) were traditionally described as a kind of social plague that needed to be combatted by all kinds of means.[20] After the Nazis' seizure of power in 1933, they became the immediate target of the "new" detention practices; more specifically, they were brought together right from the beginning in special caravan camps.[21] In 1936, however, police control of these communities became tighter and more centrally organised, with the *Reichszentrale zur Bekämpfung des Zigeunerunwesens* (Central Office for Combatting the Gypsy Menace) being set up within the *Reichskriminalpolizeiamt*.[22]

A few years later, in 1938, Himmler explicitly labelled the Sinti and Roma as an alien race that should be banished from the German national community. It is true that this racist change of direction, which gradually came to be supported by "racial biology" research carried out by the aforementioned Ritter at the *Reichgesundheitsamt* and the *Kriminalbiologisches Institut*, was not fully embraced in police circles. Nevertheless, it resulted in May 1940 in an aggressive police campaign in which some 2,300 Sinti and Roma were detained and deported to Eastern Europe.

---

[18]   Müller-Hill 1984, pp. 26–68.
[19]   Weingart, Kroll and Bayertz 1992, pp. 374–376.
[20]   Luchterhandt 2000, pp. 19–36; Ayasz et al. 1988, pp. 19–20.
[21]   Luchterhandt 2000, pp. 37–59, 68–71.
[22]   Milton 2001, pp. 214–216, 218–221.

In 1942–43, almost all the "gypsies" still living in Western and Central Europe were deported to various concentration camps, but in particular to Auschwitz-Birkenau. Some 20,000 were murdered in that camp alone.[23]

8.2.3. NAZI CRIMINOLOGY AND CRIMINAL POLICY: EDMUND MEZGER, FRANZ EXNER, WILHELM SAUER, AND HANS SCHNEICKERT

It is generally assumed that criminology, as largely reformulated in criminal-biological terms by Nazi-minded criminal lawyers such as Edmund Mezger and Franz Exner, played an important legitimising role in the development and application of the Nazis' increasingly murderous criminal policy after 1933, in the framework of a radically racist policy in the service of what they conceived of as a racially pure *Volksgemeinschaft*.[24] Criminal biology was no longer intended to make individualisation of punishment and treatment of offenders possible, but rather above all served to identify those members of the population who – because of their genetic and racial characteristics – constituted a supposed serious danger to the community and who therefore needed to be systematically eliminated. That no room was left in this *Kriminalbiologie* for the traditional criminal law, with its legal safeguards for the individual offender, almost goes without saying. Some authors gradually even incorporated the criminal law as such into that totally politicised *Kriminalbiologie*.[25]

In this National Socialist ideologising of *Kriminalbiologie*, it was appropriate that, right from the start, the *Kriminalbiologische Gesellschaft* (Society of Criminal Biology) became the primary mouthpiece of Nazi criminology in the Third Reich and that the title of the well-known periodical *Monatsschrift für Kriminalpsychologie und Strafrechtsreform* was changed in 1935 to *Monatsschrift für Kriminalbiologie und Strafrechtsreform*. Parallel to this – along the lines of organisations established in the 1920s in Bavaria and some other German states – a *Kriminalbiologische Untersuchungsstelle* (Bureau of Investigation in Criminal Biology) was set up within the prison system in all states in 1936–37 and, as noted above, a *Kriminalbiologische Reichssammelstelle* (Central Criminal Biological Collection) was set up within the Reich Ministry of Justice in 1941, followed by a *Kriminalbiologisches Institut* (Institute of Criminal Biology) within the *Sicherheitspolizei* (security police).[26]

---

[23]   Ayasz et al.1988, pp. 20–32; Luchterhandt 2000, pp. 83–94, 100–122, 139–226, 235–306; Lewy 2000, pp. 36–55,135–198; Roth (T.) 2009, pp. 539–540; Milton 2001, pp. 216–217, 222–226; Willems 1995, pp. 253–271.

[24]   Dölling 1989, pp. 210–225; Weingart, Kroll and Bayertz 1992, pp. 518–532; Streng 1993, pp. 154–155; Baumann 2006, pp. 91–98.

[25]   Dürkop 1984, pp. 112–120.

[26]   Simon 2001, pp. 161–200; Wetzell 2000, pp. 179–185, 289–294; Hohlfeld 2002, pp. 56–63.

The criminal lawyer who, immediately after the seizure of power in 1933, brought criminology and criminal policy into line with Nazi ideology was Edmund Mezger, a renowned professor of criminal law at the University of Munich.[27] He made clear where he stood in the opening lines of the preface to

Hans EICHLER (ed.), *Römischer Kongresz für Kriminologie; Kameradschaftsarbeit von Teilnehmern und Mitarbeitern am Ersten Internationalen Kongresz fúr Kriminologie in Rom – Oktober 1938*, Berlin, R. v. Decker's Verlag, 1939.

his study *Kriminalpolitik auf kriminologischer Grundlage* [*Criminal Policy on a Criminological Basis*], which he completed in October 1933 and published in 1934. Germany, he wrote, was undergoing an enormous political and spiritual

---

[27]   Wetzell 2000, pp. 209–213.

revolution. The new total state was founded on the two basic concepts of race and nation. That revolution would also bring about radical changes in the criminal law. The new criminal law would be based on two principles, the idea that the individual is accountable to his nation and the idea of racial improvement of the nation as a whole.[28]

The book's table of contents does not immediately reveal how all this was to be effectuated. The titles of the various chapters appear relatively normal, even for that time, referring, for example, to the anthropological, psychopathological, and sociological concepts of crime. It is only when one actually reads these chapters one by one that one realises that in this work a different wind is blowing, so to speak, than in the introductions to criminology published in Germany before 1933.

Mezger's chapter on criminal anthropology and the ideas of Lombroso tells us, for example, that the existence of the born criminal has admittedly not been proved but that given the causal explanations for the manifestation of criminal behaviour, it is imperative to eradicate criminal strains of people. Combatting degeneration must, in other words, become a central task of criminal policy. The born criminal must be excluded from the community before he has the opportunity to commit a crime.[29]

In the chapter on the biological view of crime, the longest chapter, Mezger discusses in detail both the research carried out in recent decades by Kretschmer and Lange, for example, and the development and operation of the criminal biology research centres in the various German states. The conclusion that he draws from his reflections is that genetic research on criminals is a prerequisite for treating them. The biological concept of crime would become the cornerstone of the future criminal law in Germany.[30]

What is also noteworthy is that in his chapter on the sociological interpretation of crime Mezger concludes that extreme environmental theories are incompatible with the principles of the "Total State" precisely because that state assumes that people are responsible to the nation for what they do. And according to the conclusions of the final chapter, on a dynamic view of crime, that means – given the pillars on which the National Socialist state rests, i.e. nation and race – that the highest goal of the criminal law will in future be to restore the responsibility of the individual towards the national community and remove those elements from the community who are tainted by heredity.[31]

It will be clear that in these views on the adaptation of traditional criminal policy to the advent of the "Total State", the Nazi rulers found a convenient justification for the radical policy that they designed immediately after the

---

[28]   Mezger 1934.
[29]   Mezger 1934, pp. 21–22, 24.
[30]   Mezger 1934, pp. 138–139.
[31]   Mezger 1934, p. 203.

seizure of power and began applying to habitual criminals, sex offenders, and entire population groups. Mezger's views – including his radical terminology, e.g. "eradication", "improvement" – were in any case very close to those expressed by Nazi members of the police and judiciary after 1933.[32] And gradually in the Third Reich it was not only the parallel between his thinking and the ideas of ardent Nazis that became ever stronger, but also the congruence between his ideas and their eradication practices. In the long run, his writings came to form an outright legitimisation for those practices. Given his previous enthusiasm for the Nazi transformation of criminal law it is therefore in no way surprising that he formally joined the *Nationalsozialistische Deutsche Arbeiterpartei* (National Socialist Workers' Party) in 1937.[33]

The second professor who a short time later, in 1936, expressed in print what the task of criminology would be in the new Reich was Franz Exner, since 1 April 1933 also a professor of criminal law at the University of Munich.[34] Exner did this in an article in the *Monatsschrift für Kriminalpsychologie und Strafrechtsreform* that immediately set the "new" tone.[35] Criminology, he wrote, is an applied science that can certainly provide some job satisfaction but the real value of which depends on whether it is given the opportunity to prove itself in practice and make its results beneficial to the nation and the state. What that actually means is explained a little further on. Given that all criminal law is inherently warlike law, and it is therefore crucial – in the framework of combatting the *Verbrechertum* – to know one's opponent through and through, it is the task of criminology to disseminate that knowledge. According to Exner, this involved in particular predicting future criminal behaviour, not only of major criminals such as murderers and traitors but also of more ordinary criminals. Insight into their personality was important in order to prevent the recurrence of criminal behaviour.

The research essential to acquire that knowledge was genetic research. Exner considered, however, that this type of research was, unfortunately, not very far advanced. But that was not the only reason why he advocated such research. It also had to do with the fact that heredity would play a major role in the new criminal policy, and with the fact that, in his opinion, judges would eventually only be able to hand down adequate judgments if they had been able to gain an idea of the significance of hereditary predisposition in the specific case concerned.

Nevertheless, he also considered it advisable for criminological research to focus on the effects that the enormous social changes resulting from the triumph of National Socialism would have on the behaviour of those persons with whom

---

32 Rebbein 1987, pp. 200–202; Thulfaut 2000, pp. 227–263.
33 Baumann 2006, pp. 98–107.
34 Wetzell 2000, pp. 213–219.
35 Exner 1936.

the criminal courts had to deal as being dangerous individuals. The changes that Exner had in mind were the new sense of community in Germany, the sharp fall in unemployment, and the integration of young people into party militias and the armed forces. In fact, Exner's article was to some extent surprising. In a detailed report on his study trip to the United States in 1935, there is only one important point – the explanation for the high degree of aggression concealed in crimes such as hold-ups and kidnappings – when he strikes a criminal biology note; otherwise he presents a fairly faithful account of his trip.[36]

Exner's preoccupation with *Kriminalbiologie* became fully clear in 1939 when he published his lengthy *Kriminalbiologie in ihren Grundzügen* [*Principles of Criminal Biology*].[37] Although that treatise is not dominated entirely by criminal biology as practised until then, and therefore allows scope for the interaction of predisposition, environment, and personality in explaining criminal behaviour, it is nevertheless striking that Exner views criminal anthropology, criminal psychology, and criminal sociology as all constituting components of *Kriminalbiologie* in the broad sense.[38] In concrete terms, that view means, for example, that although Exner asserts that someone's hereditary predisposition determines his character traits, he also states that whether this is likely to lead to a life of crime depends not only on those traits but also on the person's experience over the course of his life.[39]

In line with this view is, inter alia, his comment that there are essentially no criminal pedigrees or criminal families but only pedigrees, i.e. families within which criminals and vagrants figure frequently and for all kinds of reasons. Similarly, his discussion of the criminological research on twins displays the necessary critical attitude to both the findings presented and the methods used to determine whether it was the hereditary predisposition and not the environment that was decisive. That is also why it is not surprising that he sometimes refers to studies conducted in the United States, such as the geographical studies by Shaw in Chicago.[40]

The introduction nevertheless also has a National Socialist slant, specifically as regards the role of heredity and race.[41] To be honest, however, he is more moderate on these two points than Mezger. Exner states, for example, that it is not easy in Germany to connect the "race" factor with crime problems because, where race is concerned, Germans are quite simply not a single nation but an historically determined mix of nations. That does not alter the fact, however,

---

36   Exner 1935.
37   Exner 1939.
38   Exner 1939, p. 20.
39   Exner 1939, p. 151.
40   Exner 1939, pp. 55–56, 153, 169–170.
41   Pfennig 1996, pp. 254–255.

that he forcefully poses the question of whether what "we" generally term the individual character of the Jewish race is reflected in the criminality of the Jews. After various digressions, he says that it is and that in their case it is likely that their criminality is caused by their race. The Jew, he says, is generally not a strong

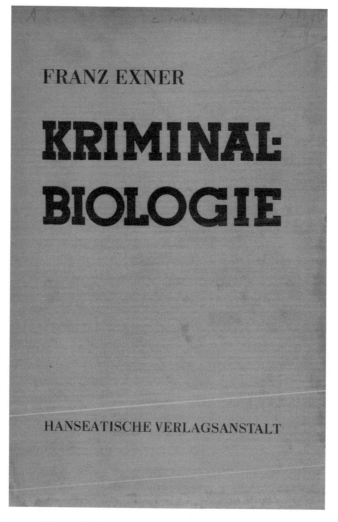

Franz EXNER, *Kriminalbiologie in ihren Grundzügen*, Hamburg, Hanseatische Verlagsanstalt, 1939.

person and therefore tends to commit offences such as defamation and slander rather than crimes of violence. The pursuit of profit dominates everything he does and causes him to pursue his material interests without any scruples.[42]

---

[42]   Exner 1939, pp. 59, 69–71.

It is notable that in this study Exner, implicitly or explicitly, writes approvingly about the practices that had arisen in Germany as a result of the Nazis taking power. He does not in any case question them. He concludes the book by remarking that it is disgraceful that there are so few *Frühprognosen* (predictions of criminal behaviour) even though such forecasts are extremely important for putting far-reaching measures in place to combat such behaviour. How much suffering for victims, how much trouble for society, and how much expense for the state could be averted if men who at the age of 30 are ripe for having security measures imposed on them and/or being castrated could have been identified ten years earlier.[43]

Besides Mezger and Exner, there were other less prominent authors in the field of criminal law and criminology who approved of Hitler's seizure of power and who strove to reformulate criminology on a National Socialist footing. One of the best known of these is Wilhelm Sauer, a professor at the University of Königsberg. In the latter half of 1933, Sauer published a very extensive work on *Kriminalsoziologie*, writing in an afterword (July 1933) to the original preface of July 1932 that he could not have imagined when finishing off his manuscript that the change he had advocated in the criminal justice system would be accomplished so rapidly.[44]

Far better known than Sauer in police and judicial circles was Hans Schneickert. After the seizure of power in 1933, Schneickert was first appointed lecturer in auxiliary criminal law sciences at the University of Berlin and subsequently lecturer in criminalistics and criminal psychology.[45] In one of his first studies, *Einführung in die Kriminalsoziologie und Verbrechensverhütung* [*Introduction to Criminal Sociology and Crime Prevention*] (1935), he adopted the position that combatting crime presupposes that certain behaviour has been criminalised but that the essential thing is to tackle crime at its roots. In that regard, it was hardly surprising that in his view *Kriminalbiologie* offered the most opportunities, in particular in the form of eugenics. Eugenics made it possible, after all, to prevent people from procreating whose descendants would certainly, or probably, emerge to become parasites on the national community.

Schneickert was therefore entirely in favour of the measures that had been taken in 1934 against habitual criminals. Later in this study, he also made no secret of the fact that he would like to go a step further and eradicate whole criminal families by means of sterilisation and other methods. As one might expect, such views are also defended in the *Leitfaden der kriminalistischer Charakterkunde* [*Guide to the Criminalistic Study of Character*], which he published in 1941.[46]

---

43   Exner 1939, p. 359.
44   Sauer 1933, p. VIII.
45   Schneickert 1935; Schneickert 1941.
46   Schneickert 1935, pp. 11, 59, 65–67.

8.2.4. DISAPPEARANCE OF *KRIMINALBIOLOGIE* AFTER THE FALL OF THE THIRD REICH

Further to the above discussion of the legitimising role of criminology in Nazi criminal policy, it needs to be emphasised first of all that in the mid-1930s a number of well-known professors of criminology and criminal law were forced by the Nazis to relinquish their chairs and found themselves compelled to leave Germany.

The most significant example was Gustav Aschaffenburg, whose Jewish heritage led in 1934 to his being ousted as professor and director of the psychiatric clinic at the University of Cologne. In 1935, aged 70, he was also forced to relinquish his editorship of the *Monatsschrift für Kriminalpsychologie und Strafrechtsreform*, which he had founded. In 1939, he emigrated to Switzerland and from there to the United States, where he was on the faculty of Johns Hopkins University in Baltimore, as mentioned earlier in Chapter 6, until his death in 1944.[47]

As also recounted in Chapter 6, the founder of today's criminology in the United Kingdom, Hermann Mannheim, was forced in January 1934, because of his Jewish heritage, to abandon his position as extraordinary professor of criminal law at the University of Berlin and his position as a judge of the Berlin Court of Appeal. He left Germany, settling in the United Kingdom the same year. The next year, i.e. 1935, he was appointed to a part-time lectureship in criminology at the London School of Economics. In 1944, that appointment became full-time and two years later, in 1946, he became reader in criminology.[48]

Hans von Hentig was forced to step down from the editorial board of the *Monatsschrift* in 1934 for political reasons. His opposition to the Nazis then led in 1935 to his being dismissed from his chair of criminal law at the University of Bonn. In 1936, he had no choice but to leave Germany and to flee to the United States, where he held positions at a number of universities and with the Justice Department in Washington. In America, Von Hentig became known primarily as the director of the *Colorado Crime Survey*. His global fame is mainly due to his developing the discipline of victimology. After the collapse of the Third Reich, he was reappointed to a chair at the University of Bonn in 1951.[49]

Against the background of these events it is truly remarkable that after 1945 the professors whose writings had legitimised the criminal practices of the Nazi regime – Mezger and Exner above all – were able to continue their academic career without any major problems. It should be noted, however, that they were certainly not the only ones who were then able pursue their career unaffected. Many members of the *Kriminalpolizei* continued to work as if they had not had

---

[47]   Wetzell 2000, pp. 186–187.
[48]   Radzinowicz 1988b.
[49]   Wetzell 2000, p. 186; Middendorff 1976.

any part in the murderous practices of the Nazis. A significant number of top officials at the new Bundeskriminalamt (Federal Bureau of Criminal Investigation) had worked at the Reichssicherheitshauptamt (Central Security Office).[50]

In October 1945, Mezger was dismissed by the Americans from his chair at the Faculty of Law of the University of Munich, but not for long: in 1948, he was permitted to resume his position. He was accorded emeritus status in 1952, being celebrated not only with a *Festschrift* but also praised by prominent colleagues and major newspapers such as the *Süddeutsche Zeitung* as one of the leading criminal lawyers of his time. It is therefore no wonder that he also served from 1954 to 1959 on the Strafrechtsreformkommission (Criminal Law Reform Commission), which was tasked with the preparation of the revision of the Criminal Code, and that in 1957 he was one of the principal members of the German delegation to the conference of the International Association of Penal Law in Athens.[51] In 1961 he was appointed honorary president of the *Kriminalbiologische Gesellschaft*, which had been re-formed in 1951. When he died in 1962, he was described in an obituary as, among other things, a criminologist who had carried out pioneering work.[52] That praise may perhaps be due to the fact that he published an introduction to criminology in 1951, which, although differing greatly in structure from his *Kriminalpolitik* of 1934, had a lot in common in some respects with the latter publication in terms of its actual content. It is striking that that book pays no special attention to what had happened between 1933 and 1945, never mind Mezger discussing his own role in those events or at least showing any willingness to account for his part in them.[53]

Exner was relieved of his duties at the University of Munich due to illness in 1944, but he continued to work on a new edition of his *Kriminalbiologie*. When he died in 1947, that work was continued by one of his pupils and the new edition, entitled *Kriminologie*, appeared in 1949. That second edition broadly resembled the 1939 edition, but those passages were deleted that, in Exner's eyes too, had become totally untenable.[54] The most striking of these is the passage on the criminality of the Jewish community, which was deleted from the 1949 edition. A more subtle amendment was, for example, the deletion of the term "*Entmannung*" (emasculation, i.e. castration) where the book is dealing with the benefits of prognostic investigation in criminology for the state and society.[55]

Finally, it should be noted that some resistance emerged in around 1960 to the strongly criminal-biological slant of the prevailing criminology of Mezger

---

50   Bundeskriminalamt 2008; Wildt 2002, pp. 731–846; Schenk (D.) 2001.
51   Mezger, Jescheck and Lange 1957.
52   Thulfaut 2000, pp. 16–24; Baumann 2006, pp. 159–162.
53   Mezger 1951; Thulfaut 2000, pp. 322–334.
54   Thulfaut 2000, pp. 322–334.
55   Baumann 2006, pp. 151–154; Exner 1949, pp. 51, 318.

and Exner.[56] In that same year, a *Deutsche kriminologische Gesellschaft* (German Society of Criminology) was founded under the leadership of Armand Mergen as an alternative to the *Kriminalbiologische Gesellschaft*.[57] At the initiative of Thomas Würtenberger, the name of the latter was changed in 1967

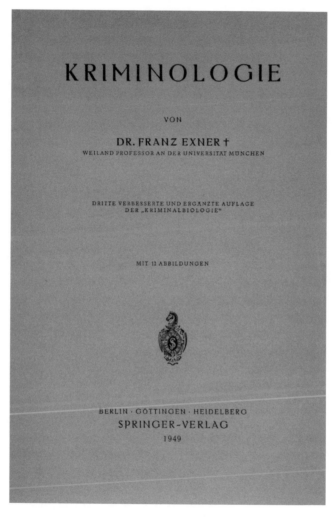

Franz EXNER, *Kriminologie*, Berlin, Springer-Verlag, 1949.

to *Gesellschaft der gesamten Kriminologie* (Society of Integrated Criminology). It was only then that the problem of the role of *Kriminalbiologie* in the Third Reich was raised within the Society.[58] At the symposium in Cologne on

---

56   Baumann 2006, pp. 193–201, 222–232.
57   Thulfaut 2000, pp. 332–333.
58   Hohlfeld 2002, pp. 63–64; Baumann 2006, pp. 244–268.

13–16 October 1967, Würtenberger – who as late as 1953 had written a piece in the *British Journal of Delinquency* referring without a single critical comment to the new editions of the books by Exner, Mezger, and Sauer – said in his opening address, inter alia, that the dark years of National Socialism had been ones of adversity for the Society too.[59] *Kriminalbiologie* could in fact easily be used to support the delusional ideas of that time. From then on, there had been a dark shadow over the Society and it had lost its international standing. The lesson to be learned from this painful experience, said Würtenberger, was that criminology and criminal policy always had the danger that the individual would be reduced, under the guise of science, to an object without rights and that his essential moral value would be sacrificed.[60]

A short time later, a criminological movement developed in Germany too that reacted quite radically to criminology as practised until the 1970s. Partly for that reason, it is strange that until late in the twentieth century, the leading German textbooks by Kaiser and Schneider quite definitely failed to deal in much depth or very critically with the history of German criminology during the Third Reich. It was as if there was still a taboo on that part of its history.[61]

8.3. BOLSHEVISATION OF CRIMINOLOGY IN THE SOVIET UNION

In Chapter 4, we saw what Marx and Engels thought about the issues of crime and punishment and how in their view the establishment of a communist society would, of its own accord, lead to the decline of crime and the disappearance of the police and judicial authorities. In Chapter 5, it was noted that these ideas played an important role in the views of Ferri on the development of crime issues and were a source of strong disagreements with Garofalo. The latter was horrified by the thought that the proletariat might emerge victorious from the struggle with the propertied classes; the day that happened would mark the beginning of the end of civilisation. Garofalo ridiculed the idea that a socialist transformation of society would automatically lead to the disappearance of crime because social injustice would no longer exist.

That discussion, however, is not the only reason why we need to pay some attention to the fate of criminology in the communist utopia founded by the Bolsheviks in Russia after the 1917 revolution. Did crime problems in fact disappear of their own accord and did criminology cease after a while to have any right to exist? Or did matters turn out entirely differently? The second reason

---

59   Würtenberger 1953–54, pp. 28–29.
60   Würtenberger 1968, pp. 4–5.
61   Kaiser 1996, pp. 128–138; Schneider 1987, pp. 131–137.

why we cannot ignore the history of criminology in the Soviet Union is because a "neo-Marxist" criminology emerged in the West in the 1960s. The questions raised by this development are what ideas were propagated by the proponents of the latter version of criminology, and how those views related both to the ideas of Marx and Lenin and to the history of criminology in the Soviet Union.

Unlike in the case of the Nazification of criminology in the Third Reich, there has not been much research on the Bolshevisation of criminology in the Soviet Union. There has also been little research either on how that process actually continued until the 1960s in relation to the overall development of the Soviet Union or on the history of criminology or, in that context, on the history of the criminal justice system in Tsarist Russia, with the exception of the prison system to some extent. We will therefore deal first only with how criminology flourished after the founding of the Soviet Union and with its elimination during the 1930s. Second, we will deal with how criminology came back to life, to some extent, during the 1950s after the death of Stalin in 1953.

We will not consider the development of criminology in the major satellite states of the Soviet Union after the Second World War, for example the German Democratic Republic. It is in itself quite important to consider the extent to which its development in that "other Germany" also involved the expectation that in a communist utopia crime will automatically decrease and the police and judicial authorities will eventually become redundant. The literature needed to answer that question is in fact available, both in the form of textbooks written by leading scientists and civil servants in that country and in the form of scientific analyses by outsiders of the actual evolution.[62] However, it is beyond the scope of the present work to discuss the evolution of criminology in this and other satellite states between 1945 and the fall of the Iron Curtain in 1989.

8.3.1. BLOSSOMING OF CRIMINOLOGY IN THE 1920s

There can be no doubt that late nineteenth-century Tsarist Russia, particularly as regards policing, can be described as a modern police state. To a great extent, the ever-larger Department of Police that was established in 1880 formed the top tier of that state. The security sections – the *Okhrannoye Otdelenie*, commonly abbreviated to Okhrana – that were added to that department from 1883 on, under the command of senior officers of the Gendarmerie, were a real symbol of the Russian police state of about 1900. These sections were not only responsible for gathering political intelligence but also carried out campaigns to combat political crime and, in particular, to prevent strikes and demonstrations.

---

[62] Buchholz, Hartmann, Lekschas and Stiller 1971; Lekschas, Harrland, Hartmann and Lehmann 1983; Mulder 1980; Rode 1996; Schmelz 2010.

Their most notable action was probably the creation of governmental unions to take the wind out of the sails of more revolutionary movements of workers. In 1883, the equally notorious Foreign Agentura was established within the Department of Police, with its base in Paris and the aim of combatting political opposition in Western Europe.[63]

The development of a modern police state in Russia did not prevent the practice of modern criminology. That is clear both from contemporary reports about the development of criminological debate in that country and from the contributions of Russians at the international conferences on criminal law and criminology that took place in Europe at the time. And it is also not surprising that in Russia too discussion was fuelled by a certain dichotomy between supporters of the Italian (Bio-anthropological) School and supporters of the French School, i.e. the Sociological School. As an extension of the latter, a "leftist" group of criminologists emerged at the beginning of the twentieth century who – like Ferri – were influenced by socialist ideas and devoted particular attention to a socio-economic explanation of the origin and development of crime. It was probably because this form of criminology was certainly greatly distrusted by the government that no real criminological research institutions were set up at that time, either attached to the universities or to one or more state institutions.[64]

That situation gradually changed after the successful Bolshevik coup in October 1917. In the course of only a few years, criminology institutes were established centrally and in a number of cities. The principal institution was the State Institute for the Study of Crime and the Criminal, founded in 1925 mainly under the auspices of the Ministry of the Interior but also supported by the Ministries of Justice, Health, and Education. Its first director, the Marxist Evsei Shirvindt, justified the creation of the institute by arguing that Marxists had hitherto paid little attention to crime problems because according to the Marxist theory they would disappear in any case. That, however, had been a false premise. In his opinion, studying those problems in depth was the only way to work out a rational policy on crime for the Soviet Union during the transition period. This close ideological connection between research and policy explains why Shirvindt's institute carried out studies, inter alia, on all kinds of categories of detainees.[65]

However, the person-focused orientation of penological research at the institute did not take place in a vacuum. Quite the contrary: it reflected the fact that in the early 1920s the individual perpetrator was still very much central to criminological research. Such research largely concerned itself with the

---

63   Zuckerman 1973, pp. 1–23; Pospielovsky 1971; Abbott 1971. See also Andrew and Gordievsky 1990, pp. 38–106.
64   Kowalsky 2003, pp. 369–371.
65   Solomon 1974, pp. 572–573.

personality of offenders and the psychological profile of different categories of criminals. On the other hand, it frequently examined the influence exerted by socio-economic structures and developments on the phenomenology of crime and on the criminal activities of individual offenders. There was, for example, extensive research on the social, psychological, and physical features of criminals and on the social conditions in which they grew up and lived. However, systematic attention was also paid to groups of offenders – murderers and swindlers – who formed, as it were, the criminal face of the socio-economic problems caused by the revolutionary developments in Russia, namely the economic crisis in large parts of the country and the social uprooting of many members of the population.

These same reforms were in fact also an important source of criminological research in themselves. Attempts were in any case made, in all kinds of ways, to clarify the impact of these reforms on the quantitative evolution of crime. This involved both studying the impact that the post-war famines had on the overall development of crime and investigating the effects of the different policy on the role of women in society. Given the collectivisation of agriculture, the changes in the socio-geographic patterns of crime were also an important topic.

8.3.2. ELIMINATION OF CRIMINOLOGY IN THE 1930s AND 1940s

The revision of the Criminal Code in 1926 led not only to the concept of "punishment" being systematically replaced by that of "social defence", but also to scope being created for the conditional sentencing of offenders and their release on probation. It also led to a great deal of research on the development and use of alternatives to imprisonment such as socio-pedagogical measures for both younger and older delinquents.[66]

Moreover, this adaptation of research to new developments in and around the criminal justice system also clearly shows how the practice of criminology in the early years of the Soviet Union was strongly influenced by the policies of the Bolsheviks, as was the research just mentioned on crime perpetrated by women. An overly bio-anthropological orientation of research on this problem was politically just as impossible as a socio-economic interpretation of such crime given the major economic problems encountered by the new state in the 1920s. Any suggestion that many women probably prostituted themselves as a means of trying to escape grinding poverty was out of the question.[67] The Bolshevik limiting of criminological research therefore severely restricted across the board

---

[66]   Shelley 1979a, pp. 391–394; Shelley 1979b; Vanhoudt 1940, pp. 10–12, 21–43.
[67]   Kowalsky 2003.

not only what could be studied but also the manner in which research could be carried out.

It is probably superfluous to point out that the research totally ignored the organisation and functioning of the regular police force, which after 1917 had been converted into a large militia with a view to bringing the proletarian revolution to a successful conclusion. There was certainly no room for research on the security police, the Cheka, which had been founded by Lenin in December 1917 and which in subsequent years was gradually forged by Felix Dzerzhinsky into the merciless weapon that the Bolshevik regime deployed to break every kind of opposition – real or suspected – to the revolution in a preventive or repressive manner.[68]

Towards the end of the 1920s, however, a definitive end was put to the relative freedom that criminological research – like all sorts of other types of scientific research – had until then enjoyed in spite of everything done by the party and the government. Research came to be focused more and more on the large-scale political and economic crime which the country, according to its communist leaders, was facing. The fact that this mainly involved resistance on the part of the somewhat wealthier peasantry to the radical collectivisation of agriculture and the resistance of Asian population groups to the suppression of their ancient Muslim traditions was ignored in that increasingly politicised research. Research restricted itself to analysing the crimes allegedly committed and thus provided an undisguised justification for the mass extermination of the *kulaks* and the destruction of those traditions.[69] This no longer involved any traditional form of criminology or any more traditional means of combatting crime. It was determined entirely by the objectives of criminal law as laid down in 1919 in a number of basic principles and subsequently embodied – partly under the influence of the parliamentary bill developed by Ferri in Italy – in the Criminal Code of 1922 and its successive amendments. The main objective of criminal law was the protection of the dictatorship of the proletariat against its class enemies and should in this framework particularly be used a means of combatting all that remained of the former legal order.[70]

In the light of these objectives, crime comprised all acts or omissions that were aimed directly at the Soviet Union or that were contrary to the system of law created by the leaders of the workers and peasants for the period during which the communist regime needed to be established. And some of the most severe "penalties" included in the Criminal Code were just as "combative": a declaration that those convicted were enemies of the proletariat, deprivation of liberty in work camps in far-distant areas, and expulsion from

---

68   Shelley 1996, pp. 19–37; Leggett 1981.
69   Lindeboom 1937, pp. 104–123.
70   Lindeboom 1937, pp. 58–64.

the Soviet Union.[71] What all this meant in actual practice soon became clear in 1918, when construction began on a special system of concentration camps for opponents of the regime, which eventually became known to the world, terrifyingly, as the "Gulag Archipelago". At the end of 1919, there were 21 such camps but by the end of 1920 that number had increased fivefold to 107. This archipelago of camps, constructed to some extent parallel to the regular prison system, was managed by the Cheka and – after that organisation was disbanded in 1922 – by its successors, the GPU and the OGPU. To get some idea of the extent of the archipelago, one can note that, between 1930 and 1933 alone, more than two million *kulaks* were banished to the gulags because they allegedly opposed the radical collectivisation of agriculture as implemented by Stalin as part of a new five-year economic plan.[72] A version of criminology that in such circumstances concerns itself solely with the "crimes" of the masses of people imprisoned in such concentration camps serves – like criminology in the Third Reich a few years later – merely as a means of justifying the kind of totalitarian police state that the Soviet Union undoubtedly was at that time.

The embedding of criminological research in the political regime was formalised in 1929 through the initiative of two leading members of the Communist Academy, in particular Evgeny Pashukanis, to turn over management of the existing research institutes to persons who were doctrinally sound from a Marxist perspective. These people attacked the theoretical departures from Marxist doctrines that they claimed still dominated these institutes. There was, on the one hand, the theory advocated by Lombroso: this was completely at odds with Marxist views on the social causes of crime problems. On the other, there was the positivism adhered to by lawyers and sociologists. In the view of the newly appointed managers, this did not reflect devotion to Marxist ideology but was clearly driven by a desire for "objective social science". The objection that the research was still at the very least "useful" from a policy perspective was immediately brushed aside by these ideological diehards, who argued that this had not so far become apparent. However, the efforts of the State Institute for the Study of Crime and the Criminal to nevertheless continue to carry out research and to have a say on major issues of criminal policy was quickly nipped in the bud. As late as 1929, two Marxist legal scholars were appointed to the Supervisory Board to prepare its reorganisation. Shirvindt was forced to resign in early 1931. A few months later, the sections that dealt with biopsychological research and police matters were closed down. The remaining sections were told that they were no longer permitted to engage in formulating theory. In order to reinforce these changes, the name of the institute was changed

---

[71]   Shelley 1979a, pp. 394–395; Shelley 1979b; Vanhoudt 1940, pp. 13–19; Lindeboom 1937, pp. 7–26, 78–103.
[72]   Applebaum 2003, pp. 4–57.

the same year to the Institute of Criminal Policy, with the management being entrusted to a Bolshevik warhorse, Nikolai Krylenko.[73]

In 1936, the name was changed again to the All-Union Institute of Juridical Sciences. That new name marked the end of all criminological research at the

Danzig BALDAEV, *Drawings from the Gulag*, London, FUEL, 2010.

institute and thus in fact throughout the Soviet Union. There were obvious reasons why, in the mid-1930s, the institute was reformed to turn it into a Marxist agency intended mainly to aid and abet the Ministry of Justice as well

---

[73]   Solomon 1974, pp. 573–577.

as – for example by publishing handbooks and comparative law studies – to uphold the international appearance of the Soviet Union as a normal state under the rule of law.

What is so remarkable in all this is that until late in the 1930s foreign observers still viewed the criminology pursued in the Soviet Union with a certain benevolence. One good example is an article on the topic by Nathan Berman and Ernest Burgess in the *American Sociological Review* in 1937.[74] The authors were apparently well aware of the revolutionary changes that were taking place in Russia but seemingly did not realise what the associated repression meant for large parts of Russian society. They in any case described with a certain admiration how much was being studied and published in the Soviet Union in the field of the criminal justice system. There is nothing to show that they were aware of the legitimising role that criminology was then playing – apparently with success, including towards foreign countries.[75]

8.3.3. REVIVAL OF CRIMINOLOGY IN THE 1950s

Apart from the ideological disputes within the Communist Party, there were two reasons that played a decisive role in the elimination of criminological research in the mid-1930s. The first is that according to party ideologues criminological research was incompatible with the theory and practice of a Marxist utopia: if crime was rapidly disappearing, there was no need to carry out any research; the fact that research was nevertheless being carried out meant that crime had not in fact disappeared. The second reason that is sometimes advanced is that, according to its opponents in the 1930s, criminology was not necessary to address the major crime problem at that time, namely that of the class enemies who were resisting the collectivisation and industrialisation of the economy.

In other words, there was no need for criminologists to provide an explanation in the context of the increasing terror against *kulaks* and "saboteurs"; ideologists were far better able to do so. And when we consider how terror was applied on an ever-increasing scale, including in the ranks of the Communist Party itself and within the state apparatus, until the early 1940s, and how from 1942 the country was engaged in a life-and-death struggle with the Third Reich, then we can easily understand that there was not much room in that period for starting any discussion of the usefulness of criminological research.[76] To give an indication of the nature, scope, and development of the domestic terror, it must suffice here to note that even just between 1 October 1936

---

[74]   Berman and Burgess 1937.
[75]   Beermann 1961–1962.
[76]   Solomon 1974, pp. 381–382; Solomon 1978, pp. 19–32.

and 1 November 1938 several million people were arrested and a large number of them sentenced to death by various courts.[77]

Despite everything, an initial attempt was made in 1945 to breathe new life into criminology in Russia but it was an attempt that quickly petered out. The situation then remained the same until after Stalin's death in 1953, apart from some publications by the staff of various legal research institutes during that period in which Western, in particular American, criminology was described as a bourgeois, if not fascist, pseudo-science that served only a single purpose, namely to prove that crime was not the consequence of social conditions but the outcome of hereditary defects, and which thus led to the application of eugenic methods such as sterilisation to eradicate crime.[78]

It was only in 1954–55 that the former director of the State Institute for the Study of Crime and the Criminal, Shirvindt, attempted to bring the importance of criminological research up for discussion again. It was not until the twentieth congress of the Communist Party in 1956, however, that there was the necessary scope for such discussion. The fact that the new leader, Nikita Khrushchev, publicly denounced the crimes of Stalin created the possibility of addressing the usefulness and necessity of criminological research. This development is clearest if we consider an editorial in the party magazine *Kommunist*, which encouraged initiatives of that kind.

Shirvindt grasped that opportunity immediately, organising a number of conferences in the field of criminology and penology in 1956–57, doing so together with various supporters, in particular Aleksei Gertsenzon. In 1957, Gertsenzon even succeeded in establishing a department of criminal law at the All-Union Research Institute of Police Science within the Procuratura (Public Prosecution Service), which could once more carry out criminological research. In 1960, that department was transferred to the Institute of State and Law within the Soviet Academy of Sciences.[79]

All this meant that criminology – or at least a limited version of it – was back in favour. One of the limitations was that the ideas developed should be compatible with Marxist views on crime; there was no scope at all for dissenting criminology. The other limitation was that the research conducted had to support the criminal policy pursued by the regime. It should certainly not question it. Rather, it had to propagate its successes, not only, for example, by means of statistical studies demonstrating the positive achievements of the Soviet Union as regards crime and punishment, but also by writing critical studies of the

---

[77] Jansen and Petrow 2002, p. 103; Montefiore 2004, pp. 201–306; Albats 1995, pp. 70–111; Andrew and Mithrokin 1999, pp. 68–88; Kizny 2013.

[78] Grygier 1950–51.

[79] Solomon 1974, pp. 383–386; Solomon 1970.

policy pursued in the West. The revival of criminology in the Soviet Union in the 1960s cannot therefore be viewed separately from the Cold War.

Reassessment of the role that not only criminology but also other social sciences could play in the development and implementation of policy, and

Enrich Buchholz, Richard Hartmann, John Lekschas and Gerhard Stiller, *Sozialistische Kriminologie: ihre theoretische und methodologische Grundlegung*, Berlin, Staatsverlag der Deutschen Demokratischen Republik, 1971.

particularly in the preparation of legislation, led in 1963 to the decision to house criminological research within the principal judicial bodies of the Soviet Union. To that end, the All-Union Institute for the Study and Prevention of Crime was set up that same year under the auspices of the Public Prosecution Service and the Supreme Court.[80] In the years that followed, the staff of that institute were in fact involved, in an advisory role, in all kinds of legislative projects and policy initiatives in the area of crime prevention and criminal justice.[81]

8.4. CONCLUSION

The foregoing discussion of the fate of criminology in the totalitarian police states that dominated the history of Europe for most of the twentieth century leaves no room for doubt that this was an important chapter in the history of criminology and that the usual introductions to criminology err in paying little or no attention to it. It was no small matter, after all, that criminology in these countries either was eliminated because it was contrary to the prevailing ideology and thus the interests of the regime, or was only tolerated to the extent it was consistent with that ideology and those interests, or was totally ideologised so as to serve as justification for inhuman practices on a large scale.

It goes without saying that it was not only criminology that was dealt with in this way in the Third Reich and the Soviet Union: in totalitarian police states no field at all can evade the grip of the regime. It should be clear, however, that in such states criminology can all too quickly find itself facing problems because the regime easily proceeds to criminalise the political opposition (or perceived opposition) or certain population groups so as to be able to tackle them in an extremist manner; the regime can then also easily be tempted to use criminology – i.e. to abuse it –to legitimise such practices.

This was well understood by a number of authors during the rise of modern criminology, whether or not as part of the New Direction. In the Netherlands, for instance, Tummers and others were in fact wary of criminology – certainly to the extent that it focused solely on the efficiency and effectiveness of the struggle against crime – because they thought that it could easily be turned into an instrument of oppression. In hindsight, they were in fact very perceptive. The example of Germany shows that such abuse is not easy to prevent in police states, if only because prominent party members knowingly and willingly organise that abuse and because in such circumstances leading professors – for whatever reason, for example because they agree with the new rulers or because they owe their appointment to them – become collaborators in the ideologising of their discipline.

The fact that in Germany it was leading professors of criminal law, among others, who were also involved clearly failed to prevent such a development. That is in fact understandable because the field of law is not by definition immune

---

[80] Solomon 1974, pp. 587–593.
[81] Solomon 1978, pp. 52–64.

to the influence of totalitarian ideologies on its principles and practices. The important lesson to be drawn from this is that criminologists need to be alert to the abuse of insights and outcomes in both the short and longer terms, and must constantly ask themselves what risks some research perspectives or research fields involve in this respect. Seen in this way, the concern expressed by certain authors, including in Germany, about present-day criminal biology is understandable, especially when that approach to criminology is practised by people who know – or appear to know – little or nothing about what occurred in that field in the Third Reich and the Soviet Union.[82]

Another side of the story is that the demise of criminology in those totalitarian states has also had consequences for its longer-term development, not only in Germany and Russia but also internationally. Not only was German criminology largely discredited after 1945 and destroyed at an individual level by the forced emigration of some of its main figures, but its demise also meant the loss of a strand of criminology that was the European and international leader in a number of areas. The consequence of this was twofold. On the one hand, the interaction that had been taking place in the preceding decades between European and American criminology came to a halt. On the other, this led to American criminology being easily able to fill the gap in Europe that had been inadvertently caused by the paralysis of German criminology.

Finally, it would be misguided for the conclusion of this chapter to consider only the consequences that can be traced to the fate of criminology in the Third Reich. It is definitely equally important to examine the consequences of its fate in the Soviet Union. First, it is obvious that one must dismiss the claim of Marx and his followers that in a communist society there can no longer be any question of crime. That is not only because achieving that goal involves an appalling amount of crime, but also because every society, whether communist or non-communist, must set boundaries between what it considers acceptable and unacceptable, and thus – let us remember Durkheim – must also impose standards on people's behaviour, including standards subject to criminal sanctions. In other words, a crime-free society does not exist and is also inconceivable.

It is partly for that reason that it is so strange that, in the 1960s and 1970s, a criminological neo-Marxism was able to emerge in the United States and the United Kingdom that took absolutely no account of what had happened in the Soviet Union between 1917 and the 1960s. Did these Anglo-Saxon pioneers of critical criminology not know what had occurred during that period in that totalitarian police state in the field of criminology? That is hardly plausible, but it may be that they did not wish to allow their academic discussion to be dominated by the Cold War which then had East–West relations in its grip. Be

---

[82] Thulfaut 2000, pp. 341–343; Hohlfield 2002, pp. 224–226.

that as it may, it is all the more curious that this so-called critical criminology attracted quite a lot of attention in Western Europe, as we will see in Chapter 10. Those involved should certainly have known what had happened on the other side of the Iron Curtain. It is highly likely that they did in fact know, but that that historical knowledge was outweighed, for example, by their aversion to the former German criminology.

CHAPTER 9

RECEPTION OF EUROPEAN CRIMINOLOGY IN THE UNITED STATES

9.1. INTRODUCTION

The history of criminology in the United States has so far received little attention from either criminologists or historians. No more or less cohesive, lengthy, or detailed and thorough history has yet been written. There are, of course, all sorts of separate publications in which certain developments or certain episodes are discussed to a greater or lesser degree. There are also editions of sources that are useful for getting an idea of this history. This serious lack of historical-criminological research is in fact recognised in the United States itself.[1]

This means that it is doubly difficult to deal with the history of criminology in the United States until the 1960s in the framework of an introduction in which one is attempting not only to do justice to the transatlantic dimension in the history of the criminology, but also to explore the interaction between criminology, the criminal law, and the criminal justice system in that country. It is nevertheless very important to attempt to obviate that lack and one-sidedness of the standard European and American introductions to criminology.

In the previous chapters of the present work, attention was repeatedly drawn to the interaction between developments in Europe and the United States as regards the criminal justice system. Until late in the nineteenth century, that interaction mainly involved the design of the prison system. There was, for example, the discussion in Europe in response to the conflicting views in the United States as to whether the Pennsylvania or Auburn system was preferable. Similarly, one should not overlook the conference on penitentiary matters in London in 1872 – organised by Enoch Wines, the head of the New York Prison Association – which was the first in a long series of transatlantic conferences under the auspices of the International Penitentiary Commission.

Moreover, we have already seen that in the first half of the twentieth century European researchers and policymakers cited not only European but also American literature in support of their views and proposals. Until into the 1930s, a few of them even crossed the Atlantic specifically to take an on-the-spot look at certain developments in the United States. Familiar examples include the study trip by Grassberger and Exner in the early 1930s with the aim of investigating not only the problem of organised and professional crime but also the state of

---

[1] Laub 2004; Rafter 2010.

criminological research.[2] But there were study trips in the opposite direction too, with one well-known example being that by Raymond Fosdick. He came to Europe shortly before the outbreak of the First World War to study the police system and in 1916 published a study on his experiences that even today is still impressive.[3]

In the light of the above, it is not surprising that researchers and policymakers from the United States attended not only the international meetings of the *Internationale Kriminalistische Vereinigung* but also the bio-anthropological conferences that took place around 1900. The conference in Brussels in 1892 was attended, for example, by Arthur MacDonald (in fact as the Honorary President of the conference), William Round, representing the Prison Association of New York, and Thomas Wilson, curator at the Division of Prehistoric Archaeology of the National Museum in Washington.[4] At the Amsterdam conference in 1901, there were eight participants from the United States, including the director of the famous Elmira Reformatory, Zebulon Brockway.[5] It probably goes without saying that these conference participants included precisely those persons in the United States who were promoting the spread of bio-anthropological criminology.

This immediately brings us to the first issue discussed below: how did the views of Lombroso and his followers become known in the United States, and who played a role in disseminating those ideas in that country?

Following on from this, the second issue to be considered is whether the rise of their version of criminology in the United States at the end of the nineteenth century led to a movement aimed – through an innovative interaction between criminology and the criminal law – at developing ideas for improving the criminal justice system and, in general, for a better approach to combatting crime. Dealing with this second issue will involve a detailed discussion of the national conference on that issue organised by John Wigmore at Northwestern University's School of Law in Chicago in 1909.

Third, we will consider the development of criminal biology at Harvard University in the 1920s and 1930s. This return to criminal bio-anthropology was, on the one hand, due mainly to Earnest Hooton, but it was also promoted by the famous researchers Sheldon and Eleanor Glueck. Their publications will be discussed in some detail. For some researchers in America and Europe, the studies by Mr and Mrs Glueck, in particular, represented the epitome of the criminological innovation that had been achieved in the United States.

The fourth issue to be considered in this chapter is how, and in what ways and what areas, criminal sociology underwent innovation in the 1920s, 1930s,

---

2 Grassberger 1933; Exner 1935; Lenz 1908.
3 Fosdick 1916.
4 *Actes* 1893, pp. XXIV and XXXI.
5 Wertheim Salomonson 1901, pp. XII and XXIII.

and 1940s by researchers who were mainly affiliated, in one way or another, with the Department of Sociology at the University of Chicago. We will deal first with the innovations mainly in socio-geographic and biographical/autobiographical research on the development of juvenile delinquency and professional crime. As well as this new encouragement of empirical criminological research, we will consider the innovative insights into the causation of criminal behaviour – the differential association theory, the anomie theory, and the culture conflict theory – developed by Edwin Sutherland, Robert Merton, and Thorsten Sellin. Third, we will give an idea, on the one hand, of the beginning of political-sociological research on organised crime in the 1920s and, on the other, of the inquiries by Congress that followed in the 1950s. To round off, we will deal, fourth, with the redefinition of the object of criminology brought about by Sutherland in 1949 with his book *White Collar Crime*.

Because advocates of criminology in the United States too were very much focused on modernising the criminal justice system, we will consider, fifth, the extent to which the reformers succeeded in their aims regarding the police and prison systems in the latter half of the nineteenth century and the first half of the twentieth.

As in the chapters on the European countries, discussion of the various developments in the present chapter will be extended as far as possible into the 1950s and 1960s. That is not only because the innovation that commenced in the 1910s in the area of criminological theories and criminological research by and large continued – especially on the part of the persons who began it – until in the 1950s and 1960s. It is also because this allows us to demonstrate why the innovation that criminology had undergone in the United States was so very refreshing – theoretically, methodologically, and thematically – and thus attractive for interested parties in Europe that it was relatively easy after the Second World War for it to fill the large gap that had been created in European criminology by the demise of criminology in Nazi Germany and the Soviet Union, its decline in countries such as Italy and France, and its limited revival in the United Kingdom and the Benelux countries. That remodelled criminology was an obvious alternative within the imperial power structure that had arisen in the world since 1945.

9.2. CRIMINAL ANTHROPOLOGY CROSSES THE ATLANTIC

9.2.1. RICHARD DUGDALE AND OTHER PRECURSORS OF CESARE LOMBROSO

In 1877, Richard Dugdale published *The Jukes* (subtitled: *A Study in Crime, Pauperism, Disease and Heredity, Also Further Studies of Criminals*), which refers not only to born criminals but also highlights the important role of heredity in causing criminal behaviour. That little book immediately attracted a great deal of attention in the United States and later in Europe as well.[6]

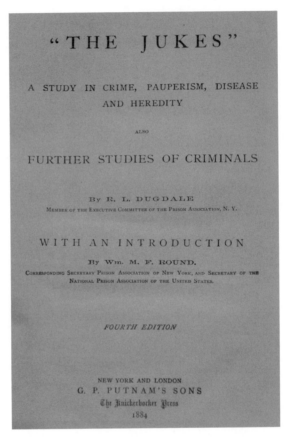

"THE JUKES"

A STUDY IN CRIME, PAUPERISM, DISEASE
AND HEREDITY

ALSO

FURTHER STUDIES OF CRIMINALS

By R. L. DUGDALE
MEMBER OF THE EXECUTIVE COMMITTEE OF THE PRISON ASSOCIATION, N. Y.

WITH AN INTRODUCTION

By Wm. M. F. ROUND.
CORRESPONDING SECRETARY PRISON ASSOCIATION OF NEW YORK, AND SECRETARY OF THE
NATIONAL PRISON ASSOCIATION OF THE UNITED STATES.

FOURTH EDITION

NEW YORK AND LONDON
G. P. PUTNAM'S SONS
The Knickerbocker Press
1884

Richard DUGDALE, *"The Jukes": A Study in Crime, Pauperism, Disease and Heredity: Also Further Studies of Criminals*, New York, G.P. Putnam's Sons, 1884 (with an introduction by M. ROUND).

In it, Dugdale set out the findings of a study of the causes of the repeated criminal and, more broadly, amoral activities (such as prostitution) of what was essentially a single large family – of Dutch origin, incidentally – which he had come across in just one New York county during the inspection that he carried out in 1874 and 1875, as a member of the executive committee of the Prison Association, at 13 prisons in New York State.

---

6   Dugdale 1884; Dugdale 1994; Rennie 1978, pp. 79–83; Fink 1938, pp. 179–187.

Based on statistical-genealogical and criminal-statistical research, Dugdale believed that he could assert that a significant portion of that family – which, over five generations, consisted of a total of 1,200 members, 719 of whom were classified as Jukes – were trapped in "a process of atrophy, physical and social" due their biological ancestry and their living conditions. Dugdale explained the dynamic interaction between these factors as follows: "environment tends to produce habits which may become hereditary, especially so in pauperism and licentiousness, if it should be sufficiently constant to produce modification of cerebral tissue".[7]

According to Dugdale, that process could only be reversed by the application of methods that eliminated the constraints that inhibited the growth of the brain or that led, through successive generations, to a modification of behaviour as the cumulative effect of training.[8] He believed that those methods should primarily involve the removal of juveniles from their family environment because it was that background that very largely determined someone's path in life. Second, there should be considerable investment in reforming juveniles who were at risk. That meant not only that they should learn an occupation ("industrial training"). It in fact involved the overall development of all their faculties: touch, hearing, sight, smell, and taste. The use of these methods would ultimately lead to their criminal way of life being replaced by a virtuous one.

In this way, Dugdale was in fact immediately giving a damning verdict on the existing system of "punitive and reformatory institutions" in New York State. That system was not the result of wisdom but rather the cumulative result of neglect, indifference, and incompetence.[9] Moving on from that criticism, he then developed a number of ideas as to how children who were growing up in miserable circumstances should be educated and how prisons for hardened criminals should in future operate. He observed, without any reticence, that it was no easy matter to put forward convincing proposals because he had come to the conclusion that not enough reliable research had been done on crime and the criminal classes. Such research should be built up from the very beginning, he believed.[10]

Despite that lack of basic research, he nevertheless asserted that criminals could in principle be reformed if they were treated in the right manner. He therefore welcomed the fact that New York State had recently decided to put an end to the "political mismanagement of our state prisons". Dugdale did not, therefore, believe that every criminal was a born criminal. But that does not mean that he thought that all criminals could be reformed. Criminals who, by whatever route, ("forecast by hereditary transmission or induced by miseducated

---

[7]   Dugdale 1884, p. 66.
[8]   Dugdale 1884, pp. 11–15, 26, 55.
[9]   Dugdale 1884, pp. 61–62, 112.
[10]   Dugdale 1884, p. 71.

childhood") had become "crime capitalists" who regarded crime as "legitimate business" were in his view incorrigible and were of service to the State only "as examples of the austerity of her justice".[11] With "contrivers of crime, criminal capitalists and panders", he wished to go much further: if they could not be reformed individually, then the extinction of their race must be organised by imprisoning them for life.[12]

At no point in the book, which came as a bombshell in the United States, does Dugdale refer to the pioneering work of Lombroso, although he does refer to that of the English psychiatrist Henry Maudsley, for example. This does not mean, however, that Lombroso played no role in *The Jukes* being written. What is in any case striking is that in the preface to the third edition in 1877, Dugdale writes that the reason for his study could be traced to a question posed by Martino Beltrani Scalia, then the inspector of prisons in Italy:

> What is crime in those who commit it? Until we shall have studied crime in its perpetrators and in all its relations and different aspects, we will never be able to discover the best means to prevent or to correct it, nor can we say that penitentiary science has made any great progress. Convicts must be studied in their outward manifestations, because, by examining all the surrounding circumstances, we shall discover what we aim at – truth.[13]

Was it perhaps the case that when he wrote this Beltrani Scalia was aware of the initial studies in which Lombroso was engaged? The latter was, after all, a prison doctor in Turin. It is impossible to say, and in a certain sense it does not really matter. What is just as important is that Dugdale's publication fitted in, on the one hand, with a psychiatric tradition in the United States in which – just as in Europe – it was not unusual to assert that the commission of crime had biological causes. On the other hand, Dugdale's little book confirmed that position in such a systematic manner that it seemed almost impossible to doubt any longer the importance of the role that heredity, interacting with the social environment, played in the development of criminal behaviour. It is otherwise inexplicable that until late in the twentieth century Dugdale's study was cited by some criminologists and policymakers as an authoritative source of wisdom regarding degeneration problems in American society.[14]

Where that tradition is concerned, it should be noted that the phrenology developed by Gall in the first half of the nineteenth century also had ardent supporters in the United States in the person of, among others, Charles Caldwell. The latter was firmly convinced that crimes that disrupted the social order to

---

[11] Dugdale 1884, p. 111.
[12] Dugdale 1884, pp. 114–115.
[13] Dugdale 1884.
[14] Rafter 1997, pp. 37–39.

the greatest extent – such as burglary, crimes of violence, and sexual offences – were the result of five uncontrolled animal traits in humans, for example destructiveness and belligerence. Caldwell claimed that people do not have any specific "organ of crime" but that they do have certain organs which, if misused or abused, supposedly lead to crime. And matters went beyond merely expressing such opinions: a number of prisons actually commenced measuring the brains of deceased inmates. The annual reports of the Eastern State Penitentiary in Philadelphia around 1860 invoke phrenological concepts to explain the criminal behaviour of prisoners.[15]

It must also be emphasised in relation to this that one of the leading American psychiatrists of the nineteenth century, Isaac Ray, published a *Treatise on the Medical Jurisprudence of Insanity* in 1838 in which he argued, inter alia, that people who he referred to – in the terminology of the time – as idiots and imbeciles were by nature "criminalistic", i.e. inclined to engage in all kinds of criminal behaviour, whether sexual offences or property crime. Nor should we forget that statements such as these were confirmed not only by the views of someone like Maudsley but also by the psychiatrist James Thompson, who had worked for many years in the Scottish prison system and who also enjoyed great prestige in the United States. Thompson asserted unequivocally in the early 1870s that habitual criminals constitute a separate class, one made up of moral imbeciles who are "born into crime", and that the only effective remedy capable of preventing the survival of that class was to prevent its members from procreating by confining them for life.[16] The solution chosen by Dugdale did not therefore come out of the blue.

9.2.2. ACTUAL TRANSMISSION OF CRIMINAL BIO-ANTHROPOLOGY

Upon its appearance in the United States in 1876, *L'uomo delinquente* did not receive a great deal of immediate attention. Dugdale did not in any case devote attention to it. And while that is perhaps understandable because his research dated from 1874–75, it is less understandable in the case of the booklet published by Richard Vaux in Philadelphia in 1879: *Some Remarks on Crime-Cause.*[17] In that work, Vaux does cite Maudsley in reference to the almost overriding role played by heredity, together with the influence of certain social circumstances, in the development of the criminal behaviour of individuals or even entire population groups, but he also disregards Lombroso. The same is true of the 1889 study by

---

[15]   Fink 1938, pp. 1–19.
[16]   Rafter 1997, pp. 80–82.
[17]   Vaux 1879.

Sanford Green, a leading Michigan judge: *Crime, its Nature, Causes, Treatment and Prevention*.[18] That book refers to a number of familiar individuals – Howard, Gall, Morel, Maudsley et al. – but not to Lombroso.

9.2.2.1. Pace and the Overall Content of the Message

This does not mean, however, that the views of Lombroso and other European bio-criminologists were not generally well received in the United States specifically through publications such as those by Ray, Thompson, Dugdale, and Vaux. Those views already became more or less familiar there in the 1880s by various other routes, for example the 1881 translation of the book by the Austrian Moriz Benedikt on the brains of criminals and a handful of articles in subsequent years on criminal anthropology in a wide variety of periodicals.[19]

It was not until 1889, however, that a number of authors – above all the aforementioned MacDonald, but also Henry Boies, Charles Henderson, August Drähms et al. – began to write books that discussed the ideas of Lombroso, Garofalo, and Ferri extensively and systematically, whether or not along with those of their allies and opponents in Europe, with parts adapted to the American context.[20] However, the importance of this rather slow but insistent transatlantic transmission of Italian criminal bio-anthropology is hard to overestimate. It ensured – as Clarence Jeffery asserted in 1959 – that criminology in the United States has traditionally had a strong focus on the individual offender.[21]

In the early 1990s, Nicole Rafter summarised the essence of this Americanised criminology.[22] In her opinion, it means, first, that these authors concerned all assumed that there was such a thing as a criminal class. Some, however, were thinking of a non-cohesive collection of all kinds of criminals, others far more of the lower class in general; the latter formed a dangerous class, by definition, as it were.

Second, she considers that it was commonplace for these authors to recognise that there was in fact such a thing as the born criminal, but that they – like Dugdale – saw such persons' criminal predisposition as lying in the long-term social degeneration of the families or population groups from which they came.

Third, she emphasises that American bio-anthropologists, following on from Lombroso, continued to accept that there were other criminal types besides the born criminal, ranging from the fortuitous first offender to the mentally ill or instinctive criminal as well as the "gentleman criminal".

---

18   Green 1889.
19   Rafter 1992, pp. 528–531; Rafter 1997, pp. 113–116; Fink 1938, pp. 99–114.
20   Rafter 1997, pp. 116–118.
21   Jeffery 1959, p. 4; Jeffery 1972.
22   Rafter 1992, pp. 531–542; Rafter 1997, pp. 118–125; Rafter 2006.

Fourth, a number of these writers – in the spirit of Dugdale – were in fact very much in favour of eugenic measures against more hardened, incorrigible criminals, believing that those measures could take the form of life imprisonment, sterilisation, castration, or a prohibition on marrying.[23]

9.2.2.2. *Thomas Wilson: Curator at the Smithsonian Institution in Washington*

In the context of the present introduction, the above summary is insufficient and it is necessary to pay particular attention to the publications of some of the authors referenced. To start with, it was not MacDonald who – as Rafter indicates – was the first (in 1892) to devote an extensive publication to European criminal bio-anthropology but in fact Thomas Wilson. For the 1890 annual report of the Smithsonian Institution, Wilson, curator at the Division of Prehistoric Archaeology at the National Museum, wrote a detailed report entitled *Criminal Anthropology* on the Second International Congress of Criminal Anthropology that took place in Paris in 1889.

His report was published in 1891 as a separate study.[24] Wilson first explains, in an structured manner, the topics around which the Congress was organised and who the various participants were. He then discusses in some detail both the content of the contributions that were submitted and the key points addressed during the discussions. The fact that in many places he reports in considerable detail on the exchanges between all the leading criminologists of the time means that the reader of his report is given a very good picture of the state of criminological discussion at that time, a picture that is still valuable today.

Wilson tells us, for example, that it was not only Lacassagne who disagreed with the ideas of Lombroso regarding the born criminal, but that Garofalo, Benedikt, and Ferri also did not share his views on that issue. Likewise, he makes absolutely no secret of the strong disagreement between Lombroso and Manouvrier about the possibilities of distinguishing and separating criminals from non-criminals. That Wilson recognises the importance of the discussion on whether born criminals do or do not exist appears from his postscript to this part of the programme:

> The importance of this question or the value of its discussions in this congress cannot be overestimated, for while the substance may have been argued pro and con in years past, yet here for almost the first time the scientific men of the world were assembled in an international congress for its discussion, with full opportunity for preparation, and with the knowledge that they were here to be brought face to face with their opponents or those who held different opinions from themselves, and here they were to appear with what arguments, reasons, statistics they might have in defense of the position which

---

[23]   Fink 1938, pp. 188–210.
[24]   Wilson (T.) 1891.

they claimed to be right. Accordingly as this question shall be decided, so should there be a change in the fabric of our criminal jurisprudence. If men are born criminals then they are not to be punished as they would be if otherwise. If, on the other hand, they are educated to be criminals, then ought our system of education to be seriously and radically changed. I repeat my impression of the profound importance of this science.[25]

Wilson is an acute observer on other points too, including the issue of release on probation, the responsibility of the state for children, the complex interplay between a predisposition to criminal behaviour and the social conditions in which people grow up, the classification of offenders based on psychological criteria, and the right to perform biological research on the corpses of criminals.

He also devotes a relatively large amount of attention to the state of anthropometry and in particular *Bertillonnage*, describing in detail the visit he and other conference participants paid to the *Préfecture de police* in Paris to see for themselves how the system worked in actual practice. He is pleased to report that the system is so perfect that even foreigners who have no prior experience with it are able to apply it successfully. It is therefore unsurprising that he concludes that there is every reason for "giving to the labors of M. Bertillon and their practical utilization, the publicity they merit".[26]

9.2.2.3. Arthur MacDonald: A Transatlantic Missionary for Criminal Bio-Anthropology

The fact that Wilson was the first American to present criminal anthropology in book form in the United States does not diminish the fact that Arthur MacDonald was actually far more important than him from a transatlantic perspective. That is not only because in 1892 this pedagogue wrote the first American introduction – entitled *Criminology* – to what was then predominantly European criminology, but also because he devoted his life, on both sides of the Atlantic, to the development and application of criminal bio-anthropology.[27] That Lombroso viewed him as a defender par excellence of that approach is apparent from the foreword he wrote to *Criminology*. In that foreword, Lombroso writes rather bitterly about the criticism levelled at him by Paul Topinard regarding the criminal type that he had identified, although he immediately adds that once that problem has been resolved it would no longer be possible to deny the organic basis of crime.

At the end of his foreword, Lombroso returns to that point, noting that his School had already become deeply rooted in the United States and had also borne practical fruit, as the Elmira Reformatory proved. That made him very

---

25   Wilson (T.) 1891, pp. 633–634.
26   Wilson (T.) 1891, p. 682.
27   MacDonald 1892.

hopeful because if the new ideas could not count on understanding in the Old World and died out there, they would nonetheless find those in the New World who would develop and apply them. We will see below to what extent these prophetic words became reality, but we can already say that they did not prove entirely unfounded. For the present, we must briefly turn our attention to the contents of MacDonald's rather bulky book. The work consist of three parts:

- a general part on the development of crime, on the anatomy, psychology and intelligence of criminals, and on criminal partnerships, criminal contamination and recidivism;
- a special part on investigation in specific cases and especially various types of murder and robbery; and
- an extensive bibliography.

It should be understood that this book is not merely a summary of the ideas that Lombroso had advanced up to that point: it also contains numerous references to other authors. But where the approach to the problem of crime is concerned and the description of the hard core of crime, Lombrosian criminology is undoubtedly the starting point. That is apparent not only from the numerous references to Lombroso's work but also from the description of what criminals basically look like:

> The criminal, as to aesthetical physiognomy differs little from the ordinary man, except in the case of women criminals, who are most always homely, if not repulsive; many are masculine, have a large, ill-shaped mouth, small eye, large, pointed nose, distant from the mouth, ears extended and irregularly implanted. The intellectual physiognomy shows an inferiority in criminals, and when in an exceptional way there is a superiority, it is rather of the nature of cunning and shrewdness. The inferiority is marked by vulgarity, by meager cranial dimensions, small forehead, dull eyes. The moral physiognomy is marked in its lowest form with a sort of unresponsiveness; there is little or no remorse; there is sometimes the debauched, haggard visage. In the lesser forms of crime there is difficulty in making out much that is special, as the individual is capable of concealing his motives and impulses. Lombroso gives the results of his study of 220 men and 204 women of different nationalities.[28]

9.2.2.4.   August Drähms: The Idiosyncratic Follower of Lombroso

A few years later, in 1900, Lombroso once more wrote a brief foreword, this time to another book that caused a sensation in the United States: *The Criminal*

---

[28]   MacDonald 1892, p. 40.

by August Drähms.[29] Lombroso praised the author, saying that he had never previously come across a writer "who so thoroughly understands my ideas and is able to express them with so much clearness, as the author of this book".

But that did not prevent Lombroso from immediately wanting to straighten something out. Drähms had written that "the American criminal differs in physiognomical type from his European contemporary". According to Lombroso, that was correct insofar as the majority of occasional criminals were concerned, i.e. "criminals made so by environment or circumstances, and in whom degeneration is not so universal and pronounced as in the congenital criminal". He went on to say that the latter category of criminals very much resembled numerous other categories of degenerate types of people even though they were born in countries that were far distant from one another.

After reading that preface, the reader naturally knows what to expect: a kind of history of the "criminal man"; a discussion of the concept of the born criminal in which Drähms does in fact distance himself from the uniform description that Lombroso had provided; the possibilities for allocating criminals to certain categories on the basis of specific criteria; a detailed discussion of the three categories of criminal that Drähms considers plausible ("the instinctive criminal", "the habitual criminal", and "the single offender"); and finally the consequences that this analysis of the problem must have for the punishment and prevention of crime, in particular the design of the prison system.

Drähms believed that the "instinctive criminal" constitutes the congenital criminal par excellence ("with predisposing bent toward innate criminal wrong-doing, whose instinctive proclivities lead him preternaturally to immoral overt acts and into anti-social environment"), and that the "habitual criminal" ("the criminal by instinct is born, not made; the criminal by habit is made, not born") is above all the product of "social degeneration in conjunction with low mental, moral and physical standards". It was therefore obvious to him that the prison system should no longer be based on principles such as retribution and the punishment of crime but on the idea of reforming the criminal. In the previous century, the introduction of the Pennsylvania and Auburn systems had been a remarkable achievement but now the next progressive step in the treatment of offenders needed to be taken: "the substitution of moral agencies and the scientific spirit in place of brute force and coercive measures".[30]

That meant, according to Drähms, that practices needed to be abandoned such as those in Florida where detainees ("mostly negroes") were publicly sold, or around the Mississippi where they were rented out to the highest bidder. Drähms knew what was needed to replace these practices, at least for occasional offenders: a prison regime like the one increasingly being applied in European

---

29   Drähms 1900.
30   Drähms 1900, pp. 56–57, 144–147, 194.

countries such as Ireland, Germany, Denmark, the Netherlands, and Belgium, in which prisoners were divided into classes and in which they had a kind of right to promotion on the basis of "good conduct and industrial labor, regulated by a scientific credit system of marks for merit and demerit".

However, Drähms had entirely different plans in store for the "instinctive criminal" and the "habitual criminal": these dangerous offenders needed to be imprisoned for life "under a just and humane system of detention". Unlike others, however, he did not go so far as to argue that they should be put to death in order to defend society. Such a solution would go "beyond the limits of reasonable necessity" and was thus a kind of barbarism "at the expense of civilization". For the same reason, he was also opposed to sterilisation and castration.[31]

9.2.2.5. Henry Boies: The Criminal Justice System as the Defence of Society

Where Drähms, even more than MacDonald, addresses the potential consequences of criminal anthropology for combatting crime and for criminal justice, Henry Boies goes considerably further than Drähms in his 1901 study of the problem of crime. The title of his book already makes that clear: *The Science of Penology: the Defence of Society against Crime*.[32] In his preface, he explains why he has written the book: "Notwithstanding our tremendous expenditure of effort and money, crime continues undiminished, and popular apprehension unrelieved. The laws don't protect." Later in his book, Boies tightens up his definition of the problem to be considered, somewhat in the terms that Quetelet had used, although he does not refer to him. In his opinion, penology is extremely important because the criminal class are terrorising society and causing security costs that are disproportionate to their number.[33]

As regards improving the protection of society – indeed its defence – against crime, Boies first discusses in some detail the crime problems facing the country and the options for identifying criminals. He then deals with the existing criminal law provisions for combatting these problems: the criminalisation of behaviour, the system of sanctions, and in particular indeterminate sentences. He then looks at the main components of the criminal justice system: the prison system – including the treatment of mentally ill, "instinctive", and "habitual" offenders – and the police system. Finally, he devotes several chapters to the upbringing of delinquent, neglected, and abandoned children specifically, because it is from their ranks that the majority of the criminal class derive. He argues that potential criminals must be tackled and rendered harmless before they can become active:

---

[31]　Drähms 1900, pp. 339–340, 345–349, 357, 361–362, 365.
[32]　Boies 1901.
[33]　Boies 1901, p. 7.

"the constant reinforcement and recruiting of the criminal class must be checked at its source".[34]

In describing the composition of the criminal class, Boies refers not only to the aforementioned American authors, but also very clearly to Lombroso and Ferri. In his opinion, the impact of "moral depravity" on the physique, physiognomy, and behaviour of individuals – apart from the crime itself – is the only reliable indicator of membership of that class.[35] He does recognise, however, that causes of crime are also involved that are separate from the person of the offender: the satisfaction of all kinds of material needs, the proliferation of criminal legislation, the lack of upbringing and education of children, the concentration of masses of people in large cities "with the consequent impairment or destruction of domestic privacy and family life", and the birth of "defective, depraved and criminally disposed children" to parents who are themselves the same.

But regardless of exactly what factors play a role in the development of criminal behaviour, it is according to Boies important first and foremost, from the perspective of the protection of society, for "every person infected with the disease of criminality" to be identified. At this juncture, he recommends not only the large-scale application of the method developed by Bertillon, but also – referring to a motion adopted by the National Association of the Chiefs of Police in Atlanta in 1896 – the establishment of a national office in Washington "for the collection of the signalments of all the criminal class in North America". The director of that agency, Boies believes, should be guided by a "commander-in-chief of operations against the criminal class".[36]

Like other reformers, Boies also strongly supported the introduction of the "reformatory system" within the prison system modelled on the Elmira Reformatory ("a new era in the development of penology in the United States"). He considered the first director of that institution, Brockway, to be a true genius, comparable to Howard.[37] Boies naturally recognised that the transformation of the prison system in that direction would encounter great difficulties in terms of both the lack of funding and opposition from conservative politicians. Nevertheless, those obstacles could be overcome. The great objective was in fact the indefinite confinement of all criminals until they had been cured because, according to Boies, "the prognosis of the disease of criminality is quite as hopeful as that of any of the serious diseases which afflict humanity".[38]

Boies did not hold back either as regards the reorganisation of the police. In essence, he proposed that municipal police forces should be transformed into military state police services. The latter would be more suitable – in any case

---

[34]   Boies 1901, p. 14.
[35]   Boies 1901, p. 24.
[36]   Boies 1901, pp. 60–69.
[37]   Boies 1901, pp. 137, 159–173.
[38]   Boies 1901, p. 160.

more suitable than the army – not only for the prevention of crime and the detection of criminals, but also for the maintenance and restoration of public order.[39] Nor was he reticent as regards the role of the legal profession within the criminal justice system. Criminal lawyers are themselves often members of the criminal class and, Boies adds, are in fact "its most dangerous and pestiferous element".

According to him, it is partly for that reason that the judiciary should be given the power to have anyone physically removed from the courtroom who was guilty of improper practices that genuinely run counter to "the facts and the law". Such a policy, he says, would in fact benefit the entire profession because its members would then think twice about "[winning] victory at the expense of fidelity and honor".[40]

9.2.2.6. Charles Henderson: Criminal Sociology along the Lines of Enrico Ferri

It goes without saying that other studies around the turn of the century also referred to the consequences of criminal anthropology for the police and prison systems and for juvenile protection. A good example is the 1901 book by Charles Henderson, professor of sociology at the University of Chicago, on the "dependent, defective and delinquent classes" within society.[41] In terms of its content, that study has a lot in common in several respects with those of MacDonald, Drähms, and Boies. Nevertheless, there are a number of significant ways in which it differs clearly from them.

First, a comparison of the titles of their books shows that Henderson views the problem much more widely than the other authors. He does not discuss only people who commit offences due to poverty or need. Rather, he deals with anyone who, for whatever reason, must rely on assistance from others to maintain himself or herself.

Second, and in this respect more important, is the fact that the title of his fourth chapter is "An Introduction to Criminal Sociology". With that title, Henderson clearly indicates that he does not wish to consider the problem of the delinquent classes from a bio-anthropological perspective but rather from a sociological one. Coming from a sociologist, this different perspective was naturally not surprising, but seen against the background of the entirety of the literature that existed at that time, it in fact represented a new and different approach. It should immediately be noted, however, that Henderson – following on from Ferri – applies a broad definition of criminal sociology: like his illustrious Italian predecessor, he treats biologically oriented criminal anthropology as part

---

39   Boies 1901, pp. 317–323.
40   Boies 1901, pp. 420–425.
41   Henderson 1901.

of criminal sociology. The first section of this chapter is thus devoted completely to this essential component of his criminal sociology.

In all of this, it is noticeable that Henderson considers criminal sociology entirely as serving for "improvement in the actual system of treating crime, whether by legislation, public custom, or by voluntary action". In general, he is guided by what Von Liszt had called "criminal politics": "a systematic study of principles by which juristic order is defended against crime by means of penalty and other agencies". As regards the role of criminal sociology, he adopts the position that it must devote itself to systematically studying the social conditions that demand legal regulation. In that way, it can lay the foundations "for modification of law".[42] Henderson was thus not without a certain missionary zeal.

The survey of criminal anthropology that Henderson provides in the first part is a fairly faithful reflection of what had been written at that time, mainly in Europe, about the anatomy, physiology, and psychology of the criminal and about the classes to which criminals can be allocated, including the discussion of the "born criminal" that was going on in the United States. Where the causes of crime are concerned, Henderson believes that there is a kind of mysterious interaction between the personality of criminals and the environment in which they grow up and live: "The causes of crime are factors of personality and of environment, and of the reaction of personality upon environment in the formation of habits and new nature."[43]

He then discusses the causes that he has in mind in this definition, ranging from climate to personality traits. More interesting, however, is section 3, in which he specifies not only the "institutional mechanism for the treatment of antisocial classes" but also "the bearing of criminal sociology on criminal law". Specifically, he states here that criminal sociology should focus on discovering the effects that a legal system has on the criminal and on society. And based on these findings he is entitled to criticise substantive criminal law and criminal procedure.[44]

What then follows is not all that interesting, being largely limited to an explanation of formal and substantive criminal law, including in comparison with other branches of the law. More interesting is case his discussion in section 4 of "elements of prison science", i.e. the discipline that concerns itself with "the entire system of punishment and reformation". In this part of the book, he deals in a balanced manner with the development of the prison system in the United States and the ongoing discussions about it. Noteworthy here is, on the

---

[42]   Henderson 1901, pp. 212–213.
[43]   Henderson 1901, p. 238.
[44]   Henderson 1901, p. 263.

one hand, his uncompromising defence of the status quo as regards the entire range of sanctions as such. When discussing the debate on the death penalty, for example, he writes – without batting an eyelid – that even those who oppose the death penalty generally recognise that robbers and rioters should be shot dead by the police or the army if that is necessary to preserve life and limb or public order.[45]

On the other hand, he has no problem, for instance, with the criticism of the continued imposition of solitary confinement at the Eastern Penitentiary, nor with recognising that the prison system at county level has been struggling with major problems for decades. However, his proposals for what should be done are rather meagre: "There should be district houses, under state control, in various parts of the state, to meet this demand." He is referring here to the idea that wider use should be made of the suspended sentence.

In section 5, he discusses preventive measures for combatting crime. He begins firmly: the application of *Bertillonnage* must be perfected nationwide in the United States too because people will do everything they can to avoid being registered in a system from which there is no escape. He goes on, however, to discuss less repressive methods of preventing crime, for example financial assistance for the families of detainees. But he is definitely no less in favour of a rigorous application of the old idea that it must be clear to all that crime will certainly be detected and punished ("swiftness and certainty in the legal procedure and the penal process"). He believes strongly that to achieve that goal as effectively as possible, a proper policing system is an absolute requirement, as are police officers who are rewarded just as much for preventing crime as for arresting criminals and bringing them to justice.[46] Henderson therefore realised full well that the state of the police at that time was lamentable.

9.2.2.7. Maurice Parmelee: The Advocate of the Integration of Criminology and Criminal Science

The study which must be explicitly mentioned in this context is the monumental 1908 study by the New York sociologist Maurice Parmelee: *The Principles of Anthropology and Sociology in their Relations to Criminal Procedure.*[47] With hindsight, that study can in fact be seen as the bridge between the initially not very criminal law-oriented transmission of criminal anthropology and its subsequent incorporation into the American version of integrated criminal science.

---

[45]   Henderson 1901, p. 277.
[46]   Henderson 1901, p. 315.
[47]   Parmelee 1908.

The study begins by reporting on the development and substance of, above all, Italian criminal anthropology. It goes on, however, to concern itself mainly with the consequences that branch of anthropology can have, or must have, for criminal proceedings. On the one hand, he considers potential implications for criminal proceedings, in particular for the various forms of evidence and the furnishing of evidence. On the other, he discusses the potential consequences for the institutions involved in the application of the criminal law: the police, the prosecution service, the defence, the judiciary, and the jury. Parmelee does not entirely ignore substantive criminal law. In that connection his focus is, above all, on the impact of the individualisation of sentencing for certain principles of substantive criminal law and for the system of sanctions.

It would be going too far to discuss the whole of this remarkable study here. Rather, we must limit ourselves to a few points that clearly demonstrate the special role, including from a European perspective, that it played in developments in the United States. One of those points is that Parmelee saw it as his task to bring two things together: on the one hand, the "new science of criminology" that had emerged in Europe and, on the other, the practical reforms that had been implemented in the United States in the previous decades (the establishment of the Elmira Reformatory, release on probation, the establishment of juvenile courts). The work of the "continental criminologists" needed to form "the scientific basis of our study".

In line with this starting point, he first discusses criminal anthropology and then criminal sociology. In doing so, he makes no secret of his appreciation of the views of Lombroso and Ferri, saying that they had demonstrated that "a large number of criminals are not normal, many of them being very abnormal", that "the rational treatment of the criminal" therefore requires an understanding of criminals' type and character, and that effective criminal proceedings must make it possible to treat them in an appropriate manner. Where defending society is concerned, the point, according to Garofalo, is not, after all, to punish the crime through the criminal but to ensure that "the criminal will be judged and punished in his crime". In other words, criminal proceedings should from now on be viewed as a "practise of social defense".[48]

Parmelee also makes clear that this other view of the function of criminal justice did not leave the principles of criminal law and criminal procedure untouched. There is good reason why later in his book – referring to Von Liszt, Prins, Saleilles, and other progressive European criminal lawyers – he deals, for example, with the discussion regarding the balance between: first, the principle of *nullum crimen sine lege, nulla poena sine lege,* and the need for society to be protected effectively against dangerous criminals; second, the debate on

---

[48]   Parmelee 1908, pp. 6, 47, 128.

reinterpretation of the attempt doctrine (should the objective interpretation be replaced by a subjective interpretation?); and third, the discord regarding the extent to which criminal proceedings should be based on the adversarial principle. Parmelee devotes more attention, however, to the institutions responsible for applying the criminal law. Unlike previous authors, he naturally focuses – given the theme of his book – mainly on the organisation and activities of the police, the prosecution service and defence lawyers, and the judiciary. He ignores the structure of the prison system almost entirely.

As regards the police, Parmelee discusses not only the powers that it should be possible to apply in the investigation stage, but also how police officers should be equipped so as to exercise those powers in a modern manner. The issues he deals with in this context concern, inter alia, the general lack of training for the police and especially the lack of scientific training in the proper gathering of evidence in criminal cases. He elucidates the latter point particularly with a discussion of the schools and laboratories in Rome, Lausanne, and Paris and by means of extensive references to *Bertillonnage* and the advent of dactyloscopy. This shows, incidentally, that he was well aware of the publications by Gross, Locard, Reiss, Niceforo, and other European luminaries.

As regards the legal profession, it is interesting that he proposes the development of a system of public defenders. One reason for this would be to dispense with the self-interested opposition of lawyers – who fear a significant curtailment of their room for manoeuvre – to reform of the criminal justice system. On the other hand, it would create greater institutional balance within that system because prosecution and defence would then both be in public hands. One could of course go a step further and entrust both functions to one and the same public body, a step that Parmelee considers to be the best option from the perspective of social defence. However, that ideal could not of course be achieved as long as one adhered to the adversarial principle, something that he in fact understood.

Finally, it is relevant to point out that Parmelee extends the criminal law consequences of modern criminology through to the trial stage. He points out, in particular, that the judiciary is not only being increasingly confronted by all kinds of new forms of technical evidence but that it should also be given the means for ordering a further investigation of the personality of the offender. How else would it be possible to implement the individualisation of sentencing? He also points out that the emerging psychological research in Europe – whether or not experimental – on people's perception of events, on memory, on the reliability of witness statements, on the veracity of confessions, etc., will have important implications for the furnishing of evidence in criminal cases. It probably goes without saying that Parmelee emphasises in this connection that investment is urgently needed in the scientific training of the judiciary, and not just of the police. Nor is it any wonder that he believes that the jury system should be abolished, if only because jurors "are greatly hampered by their ignorance".

9.3. A GROUND-BREAKING CONFERENCE ON CRIMINAL LAW AND CRIMINOLOGY: CHICAGO 1909

9.3.1. BACKGROUND AND OUTCOME OF THE CONFERENCE

Unlike in Europe, there were initially no professors of criminal law or judicial officials among the advocates of European criminology in the United States. The explanation for that difference is probably that in the United States at that time there were no criminal lawyers of the stature of Von Liszt, Prins, or Van Hamel who almost immediately viewed modern criminology as an excellent means of bringing about innovation in significant aspects of the dogmatics of the criminal law and of more effectively matching the criminal justice system and the combatting of crime to contemporary crime problems.[49] That difference in any case explains why the reception of Italian criminal bio-anthropology in the United States at the end of the nineteenth century as regards the criminal law and criminal procedure was very different to its reception in countries such as Germany, Belgium, and the Netherlands.

In 1909, however, there was a radical change. To celebrate the fiftieth anniversary of the Northwestern University Law School, the enterprising dean John Wigmore – inspired in particular by the bio-anthropological congresses in Europe and his visit to Lombroso in Turin in July 1907 – invited a few hundred people to Chicago for the First National Conference on Criminal Law and Criminology on 7–8 June 1909.[50] In his welcoming speech, the equally famous jurist Roscoe Pound made clear why it had been decided that the conference would concern the "administration of punitive justice in this country", namely because "there [was] a general and in many ways a well-grounded public dissatisfaction" with the way in which that process operated. It was not only criminologists and sociologists who complained about this but also ordinary citizens, who knew that – despite their paying taxes for the maintenance of the criminal justice system – crime went unpunished and society was not in fact protected.

Wigmore and Pound had therefore clearly realised that after 20 years of discussion, the time had come for a more comprehensive initiative to modernise the organisation and operation of the criminal justice system on the basis of scientific research. Pound realised of course that this was not something that could be achieved overnight. It was for good reason, therefore, that he pointed out that there are naturally always difficulties, conflicts, and dilemmas in applying the law, but he added immediately that such problems did not justify refraining from an investigation of what could or must be changed in a legal system.

---

49   Mueller 1969, pp. 67–77.
50   Mueller 1969, pp. 78–81.

A more specific task in this case was to facilitate dialogue between critics of the existing criminal justice system and, in particular, to ensure that psychiatrists, sociologists, lawyers, etc. – instead of all dealing with issues separately – were prepared to combine the sum total of their wisdom regarding the criminal

Proceedings of the First National Conference on Criminal Law and Criminology, Chicago, Illinois, June 7 and 8, 1909, Chicago, Northwestern University, 1910.

justice system. With a view to achieving that objective, the conference focused on three major topics: the treatment of offenders, the appointment and training of officials, and the state of the criminal law and criminal procedure. General sessions took place to discuss a number of motions and recommendations.

Those discussions led to resolutions on the following matters:

- the establishment of an American Institute of Criminal Law and Criminology with a view to "the scientific study of crime, criminal law and procedure, to formulate and promote measures for solving the problems connected therewith";
- translation of "important treatises on criminology in foreign languages";
- the establishment of a journal, because although some 25 journals already existed in Europe, there was none in English "devoted to the scientific study of criminal law and criminology";
- promotion of collaboration with other organisations such as the International Prison Congress, the Union internationale de droit pénal, and the International Congress of Criminal Anthropology;
- the appointment of a committee to develop proposals for a system of appropriate national criminal and judicial statistics.

In addition, the various sections also discussed a number of separate recommendations, for example setting up a system of laboratories "for the systematic study of convicted criminals with a view to determining methods of treatment and reform based on a scientific knowledge of the criminal himself". Another recommendation considered the treatment of suspects held on remand: "We disapprove the so-called third degree or sweating process as an infringement of personal liberty and of the rights of the prisoner guaranteed by the constitution." Also interesting is the recommendation regarding the parallel use of *Bertillonnage* and dactyloscopy and the need for a central identification agency to be set up in Washington.[51]

9.3.2. FRUITS OF THE CONFERENCE: TRANSLATIONS, A JOURNAL, AND LABORATORIES

The American Institute of Criminal Law and Criminology was indeed set up and functioned quite effectively for a number of years. It faded away in the 1930s, however, amongst other things because of changes of perspective in criminology, but also due to a lack of financial resources. Before that happened, however, it held annual meetings – in some cases together with the conferences of international organisations, for example in 1910 that of the International Penitentiary Commission – and a number of committees carried out a great deal of important work. Partly because of the Institute, two major laboratories were set up: in 1914 the Psychopathic Laboratory at the Municipal Court in

---

[51]   *Proceedings* 1910, pp. 1–3, 29, 52–53, 219–222.

Chicago to diagnose offenders, and in 1929 the first National Crime Detection Laboratory at Northwestern University.[52]

The translation project – led by such figures as Wigmore, Pound, and Parmelee – produced translations of a total of nine books within just a few years (1911–17) in the framework of the Modern Criminal Science Series. These naturally included the major treatises by Lombroso, Ferri, and Garofalo, but also those by Gross, Tarde, Aschaffenburg, and Bonger. In the general introduction to the translation of Garofalo's main work, the editorial committee noted that the reason for the series was to show the "community at large [...] that criminal science is a larger thing than criminal law". It emphasises in particular that "the great truth of the present and the future" is the individualisation of punishment and that that truth demanded the reconsideration of existing ideas about the causation of crime and how to combat it. In Europe, the editors wrote, all this had been under discussion for 40 years, but in the United States many people, especially the legal profession, were completely unaware of this evolution or were indifferent to it, thus blocking progress in criminal justice.[53]

The journal that was set up and that first appeared in May 1910 is still one of the most important journals in the field in the United States. Originally entitled *Journal of the American Institute of Criminal Law and Criminology*, it is now the *Journal of Criminal Law and Criminology*, after for a time also including *Police Science*. This title is a very good illustration of the original purpose of the 1909 conference: to create an American variant of integrated criminal science (*gesamte Strafrechtswissenschaft*) by uniting criminal science with criminology and in this way compose a repository for research in the social and natural sciences in relation to the criminal justice system and, more generally, the combatting of crime. Given that in his first editorial the first editor-in-chief, James Garner, explicitly refers to the Belgian *Revue de droit pénal et de criminologie*, it is not impossible that the title of the American journal was derived from that of the Belgian journal (which was established in 1907).[54]

Referring to the conference, Garner emphasises again how important cooperation between lawyers and scientists was in Europe in improving the criminal law and criminal procedure, and how important their cooperation would be – "in the interest of justice and social security" – in the United States in achieving the high level of civilisation in the criminal justice system as had already been achieved in other areas. He believed in any case that the journal would appeal not only to those working in the field who were interested in the progress of "a scientific criminal law" but also to a very wide range of officials concerned, either directly or indirectly, with the criminal justice system, as well as to the large number of researchers working in the neighbouring fields of sociology, anthropology, psychology, etc.

---

[52] Devroye 2010; DeLine and Crosley 2010, pp. 1–6.
[53] Garofalo 1914, pp. VI–VIII.
[54] Garner 1910, p. 6.

It would of course be interesting to determine the extent to which the journal managed to achieve that objective in actual practice, but it would be going too far to do so in the present work. It is important to note, however, that the journal leaned strongly towards Italian criminal anthropology even though that was

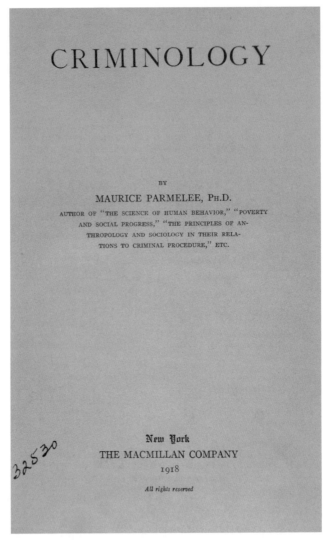

Maurice PARMELEE, *Criminology*, New York, The Macmillan Company, 1918.

not stated in so many words in the first editorial. This connection in any case explains why in the first issue Adalbert Albrecht paid resoundingly paid homage to Lombroso, who had died in Turin the year before, on 19 October 1909.[55]

---

[55]   Albrecht (A.) 1910.

Given the present state of historical research, it is difficult to say what effects Wigmore's great initiative in 1909 had, directly and indirectly – through the conferences, the series of translations, and the journal – on the practice of criminal science and criminology in the United States. If we consider the widely used introductions that were published in these two areas after the First World War, we must conclude that those effects cannot be underestimated. Their tables of contents alone show clearly that – perhaps following the example of Parmelee's 1908 book, but in any case following that of the translation of the introductory work by Aschaffenburg (*Crime and its Repression*, with a foreword by Parmelee) – they attempted systematically to integrate knowledge of crime and criminals with insights into the criminal law and criminal procedure, the criminal justice system, and the combatting of crime.

Honesty requires one to note that that integration in fact took place in a manner, and also on a scale, that hardly occurred in Europe, either before or after the First World War. The introductory works that should be mentioned here are not only Parmelee's new book, *Criminology* (published in 1918 and frequently reprinted), or that brought out in 1932 with the same title, *Criminology*, by Robert Gault – then already for many years editor-in-chief of the *Journal of Criminal Law and Criminology*.[56] They also include those by John Gillin (*Criminology and Penology*; first edition 1926), Philip Parsons (*Crime and the Criminal*; first edition also 1926), Fred Haynes (*Criminology*; first edition 1930), Nathaniel Cantor (*Crime, Criminals and Criminal Justice*; first edition 1932), and Albert Morris (*Criminology*; first edition 1934).[57]

9.3.3. TRANSFORMATION OF IDEAS INTO EMPIRICAL RESEARCH: WILLIAM HEALY AND AUGUSTA BRONNER

Another question is whether Wigmore's 1909 initiative also bore fruit, directly or indirectly, in terms of empirical research in the area of crime, the criminal justice system, and the combatting of crime. One must not, after all, lose sight of the fact that the criminological literature – at least as concerns the personality of the offender – had up to that point been based mainly on European research. There was one important exception, namely the anthropological study published by Frances Kellor in 1901 about the "experimental" field research that she had carried out as a student, under the inspiring guidance of the aforementioned Henderson at the University of Chicago, into – in short – the anthropological, psychological, and sociological differences between, on the one hand, groups of

---

[56] Parmelee 1918; Gault 1932.
[57] Gillin 1926; Parsons 1926; Haynes 1930; Cantor 1932; Morris (A.) 1934.

male and female, white and black students and, on the other, groups of male and female, white and black criminals, specifically in the Southern states.[58]

However, the revealing results of this very enterprising and bold research never actually became part of the discussion of criminal anthropology.

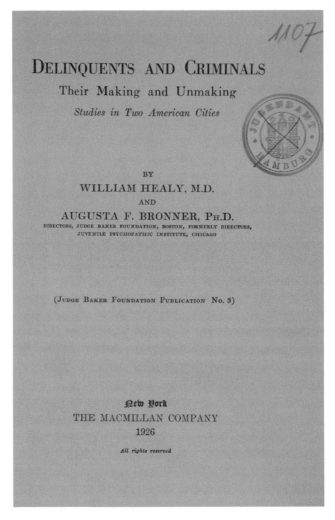

William HEALY and Augusta BRONNER, *Delinquents and Criminals: Their Making and Unmaking: Studies in Two American Cities*, New York, The Macmillan Company, 1926.

The results were probably not very politically correct in the progressive America of the time. Kellor wrote, for example, that the crime problems within the black population were largely due to the miserable conditions under which they had

---

58   Kellor 1901.

had to live during slavery. Her finding that in the six years prior to her study, nearly 900 African Americans had been lynched in the Southern states for committing a crime did not, of course, fit in very well with the self-image of the policymakers, priests, professors, etc. who gathered in Chicago in June 1909 to talk about the scientification of the criminal justice system.[59]

Kellor's name has been forgotten. That is not the case, however, for William Healy and Augusta Bronner. Healy, a psychiatrist, carried out his initial research at the Psychopathic Laboratory set up in 1914 at the Municipal Court in Chicago. Based on data collected by Hickson at the laboratory, Healy published his first study in 1915: *Pathological Lying, Accusation and Swindling*.[60] However, it was another book published in the same year that made him almost instantly world-famous, namely *The Individual Delinquent*.[61] That work was the result of an original and comprehensive psychological-psychiatric study of some 1,000 juvenile delinquents aged 15–16. It was still rooted in the bio-anthropological views of the Italian School – Healy was an ardent admirer of Lombroso – but it was mainly conducted using "mental tests and psychological analysis" that were considered modern at the time. The reason why he subjected the young repeat offenders to psychological testing was quite simply the belief that their delinquent behaviour was closely linked to their "mental abnormality" and thus not to "peculiar palates, or insensitive fingertips, or queerly-shaped heads".[62] As Arthur Fink wrote in 1938, Healy therefore clearly shifted the focus "from the anatomical to the psychological and the social".[63]

Healy was hesitant about formulating general conclusions regarding the "mental life underlying delinquency" because that could be very different from case to case. Nevertheless, he listed a number of "bases of delinquency", in particular all kinds of dissatisfaction, rather obsessive images of crimes, misdemeanours as responses to living conditions, and temporary psychoses or psychotic reactions, self-images in which other people are always enemies.[64] The big question for him was of course how these disorders originated. To identify the causes, Healy developed a complex multidisciplinary analysis grid in which, inter alia, family history and individual development were assigned just as much weight as inherited mental and physical weaknesses, biological defects in the family, and social conditions. How relevant these and other factors were (or had been) in the development of delinquent behaviour therefore had to be investigated on a case-by-case basis.

---

[59]   Kellor 1901, pp. 131–158.
[60]   Devroye 2010, p. 24.
[61]   Healy 1918; Mueller 1969, pp. 86–95.
[62]   Healy 1918, pp. 14–30; White 1933.
[63]   Fink, 1938, pp. 149–150.
[64]   Healy 1918, pp. 31–32.

In addition to this conclusion, Healy formulated, as a kind of mirror image, his recommendations for tackling juvenile delinquency.[65] The lack of self-control of many delinquents was no reason not to punish them, but the punishment needed to be useful, and certainly not harmful. According to Healy it was totally wrong to imprison them en masse or uniformly subject all of them to short prison sentences. On the contrary, special juvenile courts should investigate, on a case-by-case basis, what treatment was necessary or desirable at the physical, psychological, social, and institutional levels. Individualising sentencing was therefore the way to go in the case of juvenile delinquency too. Partly due to this conclusion, casework really took off right across the criminal justice system. The manual published by Pauline Young in 1937 shows this convincingly.[66]

It will be clear that this original empirical study was the embodiment of the integrated criminal science that Parmelee, Wigmore, and others attending the 1909 conference had in mind. It was to be expected that the follow-up studies that Healy and Bronner subsequently published on the causes of juvenile delinquency and the treatment of juvenile offenders could certainly count as on as much approval as the ground-breaking study of *The Individual Delinquent*.[67]

Moreover, Healy and Bronner did not merely repeat the earlier study but built on it, adding new emphasis. In the study that they completed in 1936 at Yale University's Institute of Human Relations, for example, they referred with greater emphasis to the fact that in a number of cases delinquent behaviour should be viewed as a form of rational behaviour, a form of self-expression, that gave meaning to the young person's life.[68] It is also still relevant that their investigation into the root causes of juvenile delinquency had taught them that it is difficult to put a stop to a delinquent career once it has started.[69] And knowing how popular genetics was in some circles in this field, they warned that little was yet known about the role of genes and chromosomes in the transmission of criminal behaviour.[70]

Healy and Bronner did not indicate who exactly that warning was intended for, but it may well be that it was in fact aimed at a number of Harvard professors who were developing an American version of *Kriminalbiologie* on the basis of criminal bio-anthropology.

---

[65]   Healy 1918, pp. 166–182.
[66]   Young (P.) 1937; Cooley 1927, pp. 207–278, 369–388.
[67]   Healy and Bronner 1926.
[68]   Healy and Bronner 1936, pp. 200–205.
[69]   Healy and Bronner 1936, p. 216.
[70]   Healy and Bronner 1936, p. 39.

9.4. REVIVAL OF BIO-ANTHROPOLOGICAL CRIMINOLOGY AT HARVARD UNIVERSITY

Nicole Rafter asserted some years ago that in the 1930s a criminological "school" had developed at Harvard University, with the core members being Hooton, the Gluecks, and William Sheldon. At that time, they more or less shared "a set of beliefs, principles and goals" concerning the biological causes of criminal behaviour and the eugenic options for combatting crime.[71] Also in this case, the designation "school" must be viewed as a very relative term, however.

Sheldon's contribution to bio-anthropology did not remain limited to a few publications comprising general ideas about people's physique based largely on the views of Kretchmer. In the late 1940s, he tried those ideas out on juvenile delinquents, publishing a book on the matter, *Varieties of Delinquent Youth*, in 1949.[72] More important, however, is that these ideas were used by Hooton and the Gluecks when assembling, analysing, and interpreting their data on (juvenile) offenders. This in itself was quite remarkable because Sheldon's ideas consist of little more than that people could be classified according to their physical form into three somatypes (mesomorph, endomorph, and ectomorph) and that these (hereditary) types were supposedly accompanied by specific character traits and patterns of behaviour. Sheldon himself was something of an intellectual vagabond who in any case never published any substantial research of his own in the field of crime and punishment.[73]

There is no question that in their major studies the Gluecks devoted considerable attention to biological factors, but almost always did so in the context of a multi-factor view of that behaviour. In this sense, the well-known research by this married couple in fact has much in common with that of Healy and Bronner; in some respects, it can even be seen as a continuation of that research. Moreover, this affinity is also reflected in the acknowledgments in their books; the Gluecks thanked Healy and Bronner for their support on more than one occasion.

The criminal biology developed at Harvard between the two World Wars was undoubtedly truly embodied by Hooton.[74] It should be noted, however, that Hooton's research is somewhat reminiscent not only of Dugdale's *The Jukes* but also the immensely popular 1912 book by the psychologist Henry Goddard, *The Kallikak Family*. In that work Goddard aligned himself with the then popular belief that a large proportion of criminals are feeble minded but also defended the view that that feeblemindedness is the source of their crime and that, since

---

[71]   Rafter 2004b, pp. 758–761; Davie 2005, pp. 276–281; Walby and Carrier 2010.
[72]   Mannheim 1966, 1, pp. 236–241.
[73]   Rafter 2004b, pp. 758–761; Martin, Mutchnick and Austin 1990, pp. 119–138.
[74]   Rafter 2004b, pp. 739–758; Jones (D.) 1986, pp. 108–125; Hohlfeld 2002, pp. 69–73.

that condition was inherited, their crime could be regarded as innate. With that assertion, he was endorsing discussion of eugenic solutions to crime problems.[75]

9.4.1. ERNEST HOOTON: THE BIO-ANTHROPOLOGY OF THE AMERICAN CRIMINAL

As a young assistant at Harvard in 1916, Hooton became interested in Italian bio-criminology, and in particular the work of Lombroso, when he had to lecture on "criminal anthropology and race mixture". He then transferred his interest for several years to the physical phenomenology of the Irish. In the 1920s, however, he returned to his initial interest and set up a large – one might in fact say gigantic – bio-anthropological study of American criminals, publishing two books on the topic in 1939. The first of these – *The American Criminal: An Anthropological Study* – comprises three volumes. In it he deals exhaustively with the development, implementation, and findings of his study (and also defends it with gusto). His second book – *Crime and the Man* – was a summary of his first, but this time intended for the general public, and was largely spin-off from a series of lectures he had given at the Lowell Institute.[76]

That in itself shows that, between the two World Wars, Hooton's views were considered less bizarre in certain circles than they may appear to us today. If one reads, for example, what the Chief Judge of the Municipal Court in Chicago, Harry Olson, claimed in 1923 at the annual meeting of the Eugenics Research Association, one will realise that supporters of the eugenics movement must have welcomed his research. Olson was profoundly convinced that criminal behaviour ("the secret of crime in the *criminal himself*") had a genetic basis and that the majority of (juvenile) offenders displayed one or more defects in psychological or psychiatric terms. In his opinion, this indicated that natural selection no longer operated adequately in the northern races, and – since killing and castrating "all our defectives" was no longer acceptable – the only solution was to confine them all in the protected environment of colonies controlled by the state.[77]

A great deal of criticism was levelled at Hooton's research, and that criticism definitely did not hold back. In his books, Hooton attributed this more than once to the fact that he was going against the prevailing sociological and psychiatric paradigms in criminology and politics and that that had probably also played a role in the fairly broad rejection of his work. But if one reads his books for oneself, it is difficult not to conclude that the basic principles, the composition of the subpopulations of criminals and non-criminals that are compared, and the

---

75   Rafter 1997, pp. 133–148; Barnes 1927, pp. 349–351.
76   Hooton 1939a; Hooton 1939b; Hooton 1994.
77   Olson 1925; Schlapp and Smith 1928.

processing and interpretation of the research results, are highly questionable in many respects. Even so, it is important for us to look briefly at his publications because the "biological temptation" in criminology is considerable and thus new "biological tempters" constantly arise again from time to time.[78]

In his preface to *The American Criminal*, Hooton states almost immediately what his research is about, namely "to ascertain whether criminals differ physically from law-abiding citizens of the same race, nationality, and economic status, and if so, why". And right after that he also allows no misunderstanding as to the societal relevance of his research: if criminals constitute a biologically inferior group, then there are no sociological measures that can mitigate the terror that organised malefactors inflict in the United States. He also writes that he knew in advance that his study would make him the object of "a bristling array of hostile spears", but that Glueck had convinced him by suggesting that he commence his intended criminal-anthropological research as a sociological and psychiatric study within the department of the State of Massachusetts' psychiatric service that was responsible for examining detainees.

He had followed Glueck's advice and had then gradually expanded his research into a comparative anthropological study of prison inmates in ten states who, racially and ethnically, best reflected the population of the country as a whole. Ultimately, anthropological data – including a great deal of morphological data on, inter alia, the skull, hair, eyebrows, cheeks, nose, ears, lips, teeth, chin, neck, and shoulders – was collected on 17,077 individuals, including 3,203 who were not prisoners, i.e. ordinary citizens.[79] That mass of data was processed using the Hollerith Electric Card Sorter.

In his introduction, Hooton also made absolutely no secret of the fact that his research was rooted in the criminal-anthropological tradition initiated by Lombroso. He also made clear that his research was essentially designed to test Lombroso's core thesis. There had, after all, been a great deal of criticism of Lombroso's ideas, and the manner in which Lombroso had substantiated those ideas, according to Hooton, was indeed full of errors to varying degrees. But those ideas, wrote Hooton, had still not been adequately rebutted.[80] Goring had attempted to do so in the United Kingdom in 1913, but that attempt was so biased against Lombroso that it must be considered unsound.

It is impossible in the scope of this work to follow Hooton's ramblings through his three thick volumes packed with research data and comments. Of necessity, we must restrict ourselves here to the general summary of results. However, just the summary in volume 1 of *The American Criminal* takes up some 60 pages; we will therefore pass on to Hooton's second book about his research, *Crime and the Man*, in which everything is presented more succinctly.

---

[78]   Rafter 2004b, pp. 753–754.
[79]   Hooton 1939a, 1, pp. 32–36.
[80]   Hooton 1939a, 1, p. 17.

First, Hooton asserts, without much in the way of reservations, that American criminals who come from an "authentic" American family, are, on average, morphologically different in some respects from non-criminals from the same background.[81]

Second, it has been found that there are also significant differences between, on the one hand, American criminals born in America to foreign parents and those born outside the United States (for example in Poland or Italy) and, on the other, non-criminals from those population groups. Here he mentions, inter alia, them being shorter in height with a narrower chest, wider head, and shorter nose.[82]

Third, Hooton addresses the particularly sensitive issue of the possible connection between race and crime. In that context, he first of all makes clear that he wishes to have nothing – absolutely nothing – to do with "all the trash about Nordics and Aryans which has been trumpeted by the dictators of the Fascist states and by their kept professors". In his view, all that is lies. As regards race, his own data prove entirely that crime is not attributable to the race of the perpetrator. What he has discovered, however, is that within each race the biologically inferior portion of the population is responsible for the majority of the crimes committed.[83]

In line with that finding, Hooton finally speaks about the possible differences between "Negro and Negroid criminals and civilians". In his view, differences certainly exist, for example "the Negro criminals are probably shorter than college Negros and the Negroid criminals are certainly shorter than Negroid collegians."[84]

Based on all these findings, Hooton ultimately concludes that Lombroso had definitely not been foolish:

> There are in modern societies a considerable number of persons who are too ignorant and too stupid to understand the complicated and highly artificial codes of behavior, the infraction of which may be punishable by imprisonment. A large part of modern civilized populations is in precisely this state of befuddlement. Sometimes we call these confused individual morons.[85]

What all these findings ultimately meant scientifically remains vague. According to Hooton, Lombroso was right to a significant extent. But what would the significance of that be? Hooton does not answer that question. But he had obviously thought about the possible consequences of his findings for criminal policy. Following Olson, he too in fact believes that habitual criminals ("hopeless

81   Hooton 1939b, pp. 127–128.
82   Hooton 1939b, p. 195.
83   Hooton 1993b, pp. 248–252.
84   Hooton 1939b, p. 353.
85   Hooton 1939b, p. 362.

constitutional inferiors") should be permanently imprisoned and must certainly not be given the chance to reproduce.[86] For the rest he places his hope in the wider opportunities that man will probably have at some point in the future to control and predict genetics.[87]

This seems to him to be extremely important from the perspective of preserving democracy, because that form of government quite simply has the greatest potential for human happiness if the majority of people are healthy in mind and body. But it is also true, he writes, that ongoing biological degradation inevitably leads to anarchy and dictatorship. The lesson he drew from this was that if humanity wanted to save itself, more needed to be known about "human parasitology and human entomology" so that artificial and scientific selection could be applied rationally.[88]

These concluding lines of *Crime and the Man* show that Hooton's criminal anthropology was also motivated by political anxiety about America's future.

9.4.2. SHELDON AND ELEONORA GLUECK: PREVENTING AND COMBATTING JUVENILE DELINQUENCY

A broad twofold division can be made in the research carried out by the Gluecks. Initially, that research concerned in particular the effectiveness of the treatment of juvenile delinquents; later it increasingly focused on the causes, prevention, and prediction of delinquent behaviour.

The study that best represents their first period of research is undoubtedly *500 Criminal Careers* (1930).[89] In it, they noted that of the 510 young men held at the Massachusetts Reformatory in the period 1911–22, five to 15 years later, i.e. in 1926–27, about 80 per cent had again committed a crime of one sort or another, and had thus simply continued their criminal career to a greater or lesser extent. To determine how this "failure" could be explained, they not only explored the personal, social, and criminal background of the offenders concerned, but also looked in depth at the actual operation of the reformatory and the actual implementation of the suspended sentence in their cases. Remarkably, their research involved not only analysing all kinds of files and interviewing the staff of the reformatory and departments concerned, but also asking ex-prisoners for their opinions on the positive and negative effects of the institution.

This comprehensive, in-depth investigation revealed that this manifest failure of the system could be attributed to a whole range of causes.

---

86   Hooton 1939b, pp. 392–393.
87   Hooton 1939b, p. 396.
88   Hooton 1939b, pp. 397–398.
89   Glueck and Glueck 1930.

On the one hand, it had a lot to do with the background and personality of the detainees, many of whom came from totally broken and marginalised families, most of which, in turn, had a criminal record. Before being placed in the Massachusetts Reformatory, a large number of them – whether or not because of delinquency – had already spent much of their life in all kinds of institutions, and most had no trade or profession, found themselves constantly in bad company, and had developed all sorts of bad habits (for example drinking and gambling).

On the other hand, the causes could also clearly be traced to the nature of the regime at the reformatory and the limited resources for enforcing that regime effectively. Among other issues, inmates were not adequately categorised and thus they were not treated in a sufficiently differentiated manner, the methods to successfully treat juveniles – casework included – were insufficiently developed, the school activities and work in which the young people had to engage were not sufficiently in line with their background and skills, and the institutional bureaucracy was counterproductive (it had become a sport among the inmates to thwart it as much possible). There were similar problems in the context of release on probation.

The Gluecks naturally provided numerous recommendations for redressing the situation at this and other comparable reformatories. Some of those recommendations were in fact surprising, for example the proposal to allow a kind of self-government by the detainees and to teach them in a realistic manner how to coexist peaceably with others. But at the same time the Gluecks realised that what was being demanded of the institutions concerned was virtually impossible and that it was therefore unfair to level overly harsh criticism at them. They had to attempt, after all, to make something of the lives of the juvenile delinquents in question after all the other institutions – home, school, and church – had failed to do so.

This explains why in 1936 they organised a ground-breaking symposium on the prevention of crime at which the speakers included not only representatives of the reformatories but also people with experience of social work with young people in disadvantaged neighbourhoods, speakers on the design and implementation of local programmes to educate maladjusted juveniles, probation officers, and representatives of the special crime prevention sections set up by the police in New York and Berkeley. The message of the symposium was clear: given the complexity of the problems in the area of juvenile crime – "the interplay of biologic handicaps, subtle human motivations and often unmeasurable social and economic factors" – only a timely, targeted, and coordinated approach by all the parties involved could offer solutions.[90] That was also the message, in many respects, that the Gluecks derived from the grim results of the study

---

[90] Glueck and Glueck 1936.

that they had carried out in the intervening years – for some parts of which they were assisted by Healy, Bronner, and others – on the treatment of 1,000 juvenile offenders by a special juvenile court and a specialised juvenile clinic in Boston.[91]

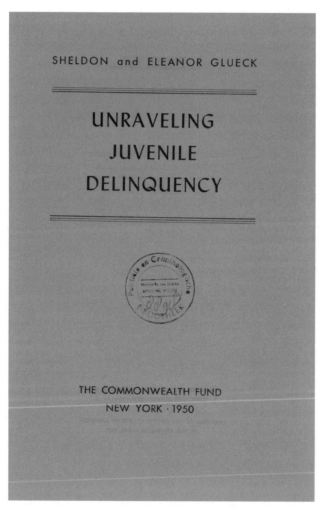

SHELDON and ELEANOR GLUECK

UNRAVELING JUVENILE DELINQUENCY

THE COMMONWEALTH FUND

NEW YORK · 1950

Sheldon and Eleanor GLUECK, *Unraveling Juvenile Delinquency*, New York, The Commonwealth Fund, 1950.

That study, which embodied the second period of their career, was published in 1950 with the challenging title *Unraveling Juvenile Delinquency*.[92] In 1952, they summarised the results of this large-scale study in the short book *Delinquents*

---

[91] Glueck and Glueck 1934; Carr 1941.
[92] Glueck and Glueck 1950; Sampson and Laub 1995, pp. 25–63.

in the Making: Paths to Prevention.[93] In the preface to the former work, they wrote that, since 1939, they had shifted their attention from research on the effectiveness of various types of treatment on juvenile delinquency to research on the causation of delinquent behaviour, "with a view to determining the bases for truly crime-preventive programs and effective therapy". This study comprised a large-scale comparison between 500 delinquent and 500 non-delinquent boys aged between five and 16 on such issues as their family circumstances, experiences on the street and at school, intelligence, character and temperament, physical characteristics, and body type.

Precisely these latter two studies show how much the Gluecks still believed in the value of criminal anthropology and therefore in the notion that in some respects criminals are different people to non-criminals, as Hooton had phrased Lombroso's thesis some years previously. In those studies, they fell back not only on the dubious somatypes that Sheldon had postulated based on the theories of Kretchmer, but also on typical Lombrosian bodily characteristics such as height, weight, teeth, nose, eyes and ears, as well as the skin, belly, abdomen, and genitals. But just why they wanted to gather data about all these factors was something that the Gluecks were not really able to explain. In attempting to do so, they went no further than writing: "Comparison of the bodily morphology of the delinquents and non-delinquents should, we felt, prove especially fruitful in view of the fact that the two groups were matched in respect to both age and ethnic-racial deviation."[94]

After completing their research, they concluded that the differences between the two groups – in terms of their physical characteristics – were not great, and certainly not statistically significant. They were therefore unable to explain the significance of these findings: "The possible significance of these findings is that they may relate to differences in types of physique among the two groups."[95] As regards the physique of the juveniles in the two groups, they came to the conclusion that delinquents were generally of more mesomorphic build than non-delinquents. Here too, the Gluecks were unable to explain what that finding meant in terms of the delinquents' behaviour.[96] The conclusion, which should have consisted of an integration of their findings into a coherent picture of juvenile delinquency, in fact contained no such effort. They merely stated:

> The foregoing summation of the major resemblances and dissimilarities between the two groups included in the present inquiry indicates that the separate findings, independently gathered, integrate into a dynamic pattern which is neither biologic nor exclusively sociocultural, but which derives from an interplay of somatic, temperamental, intellectual, and socio-cultural forces.[97]

---

[93] Glueck and Glueck 1952.
[94] Glueck and Glueck 1950, pp. 54–55.
[95] Glueck and Glueck 1950, p. 181.
[96] Glueck and Glueck 1950, p. 196.
[97] Glueck and Glueck 1950, p. 281.

In the summary of the study that they published in 1952, they did go a bit further, however, in interpreting their findings, but not really that much further. They in fact wrote that their finding that delinquent boys are mainly of mesomorphic build was a striking conclusion. But after that bland remark they immediately throttled back a bit: "Of course, the relationship of body types to motivations, attitudes, and behavior tendencies has not been clarified."[98]

The Gluecks published more details of their research a few years later in *Physique and Delinquency*. According to the summary in their retrospective look at a lifetime of research, this more detailed analysis of their data did not really produce much that was new. They in fact clarified only a little bit of what they had meant to say in general, namely that significant features – such as aggressiveness and a sense of adventure – of boys who become caught up in delinquent behaviour are not tied to a particular body type. And the fact that many delinquents are mesomorphs could perhaps mean that they have certain features "that equip them readily for a delinquent role under pressure of unfavorable sociocultural conditions; while endomorphs, being less energetic and less likely to act out their 'drives', have a lower delinquency *potential* than mesomorphs."[99]

One of the "most influential studies in the history of criminological research" therefore actually ended up being insignificant, or at least went no further than Healy's study of the individual delinquent, merely concluding that, in general, there is little one can say about the development of delinquent behaviour; the point is to analyse the delinquent's history on a case-by-case basis. There are, nevertheless, researchers who believe that a more rigid analysis – theoretical and methodological – of the data collected by the Gluecks can achieve a more meaningful result.[100]

Finally, it is appropriate to point out that, after the Second World War, the Gluecks considerably moderated their views on the biological basis of criminal behaviour. That is also apparent from the above presentation of their studies. In their later publications, they no longer referred to the physical characteristics which they had considered so relevant in the 1940s that the collection of data on those characteristics formed an important part of *Unraveling Juvenile Delinquency*. They had apparently become more aware of the political abuse of *Kriminalbiologie* by the Nazis. A certain Werner Landecker – then a lecturer in sociology at the University of Michigan – had published a lengthy article in 1941 in the *Journal of Criminal Law and Criminology* that already referred emphatically to that abuse and its consequences.[101]

---

[98] Glueck and Glueck 1952, pp. 102–103.
[99] Glueck and Glueck 1974, pp. 73–75.
[100] Laub and Sampson 1988.
[101] Landecker 1941.

Moreover, one should not forget in this context that, in 1943–46, Sheldon Glueck pressed strongly for the establishment of an international tribunal to try war crimes and crimes against humanity, and in 1945 had attended the conference which led to the Nuremberg Tribunal.[102]

9.4.3. JAMES WILSON: THE REVIVAL OF BIOLOGICALLY ORIENTED CRIMINOLOGY

In the light of these facts, it is therefore all the more remarkable that at the same university new life was being breathed into a moderate version of biologically oriented criminology in the 1970s in the framework of a multi-factorial perspective on the causes of crime. In a seminar on crime and criminal justice that started out from an interest in "individual differences in criminality", James Wilson and Richard Herrnstein also discussed the work of their Harvard predecessors who had carried out research on the biological bases of criminal behaviour, namely Hooton, Sheldon, and the Gluecks. They supplemented the findings of these predecessors with, inter alia, a Danish study of twins and, in their book *Crime & Human Nature* (1985), concluded unreservedly but cautiously:

> The average offender tends to be constitutionally distinctive, though not extremely or abnormally so. The biological factors whose traces we see in faces, physiques, and correlations with the behavior of parents and siblings are predispositions toward crime that are expressed as psychological traits and activated by circumstances. It is likely that the psychological traits involve intelligence and personality, and that the activating events include certain experiences within the family, in school, and in the community at large, all large topics in their own right and dealt with in chapters of their own. The existence of biological predispositions means that circumstances that activate criminal behavior in one person will not do so in another, that social forces cannot deter criminal behavior in 100 percent of a population, and that the distributions of crime within and across societies may, to some extent, reflect underlying distributions of constitutional factors. Perhaps the simplest thing to say at this point is that crime cannot be understood without taking into account individual predispositions and their biological roots.[103]

Wilson and Herrnstein were not the first people after the Second World War to again put research into the biological bases of criminal behaviour on the research agenda. They were preceded, not only in Scandinavia but also in the

---

102   Hagan and Rymond-Richmond 2009, pp. 35–43.
103   Wilson and Herrnstein 1986, pp. 102–103.

United States, by a large number of psychological and medical researchers.[104] They did, however, have far greater influence in America than these researchers. That was not necessarily because they claimed to have found a simple answer to everything ("the definitive study of the causes of crime") but mainly because their book bore the Harvard stamp of quality and Wilson was a leading authority on policy, at least in Republican circles. The book that he had published a few years earlier, *Thinking about Crime* (1975), had given him great prestige in those circles.[105]

For that reason alone, it is not surprising that ever since the publication of *Crime & Human Nature*, biologically oriented research on criminal behaviour has again acquired a certain legitimacy in the United States. Moreover, the flourishing of genetics, in particular, has strengthened the legitimacy of biological research, whether or not in the context of a bio-socially oriented criminology. This is clear from more recent publications in this field.[106] It does not mean that the criticism already levelled at the "new Lombrosians" in the 1970s is not still worthy of attention. That criticism includes, for example, the accusation of disregarding the political, legal, social, and moral dimensions in matters of crime and punishment, and of underestimating the risks involved in taking drastic measures against people – eugenic measures, etc. – due to the bio-medicalisation of crime.[107]

What is also noticeable in many of today's Lombrosian publications is that the authors apparently fail to realise that crime is ultimately a matter of defining behaviour and not of genetics. Moreover, they generally take no account of the overall spectrum of criminal behaviour. By doing so, they make themselves immune to the question of whether their argument also applies in the case of white-collar crime, for example.

9.5. THEORETICAL, METHODOLOGICAL, AND THEMATIC INNOVATION IN SOCIOLOGICALLY ORIENTED CRIMINOLOGY

The further development of biologically oriented criminal anthropology in the 1930s and 40s at first remained largely limited to the multifactorial study of juvenile delinquents in particular and to the comparative biological study of criminals in general. The way sociologically oriented criminology developed,

---

104   Cortés and Gatti 1972; Mednick and Shoham 1979.
105   Wilson (J.) 1985.
106   Wasserman and Wachbroit 2001; Walsh and Beaver 2009.
107   Moran 1978; Platt and Takagi 1979.

however, was more manifold in various respects. It was in fact Clifford Shaw and Henry McKay, in particular, who paved the way for socio-geographical research on juvenile delinquency, while Frederic Thrasher and John Landesco did the same for political-sociological research on that topic.

It should also be borne in mind that not only were various new theoretical initiatives developed or implemented regarding these two approaches, but new research methods were also tested. The former, for example, involved application of the differential association theory as developed by Sutherland as an extension of Tarde's imitation theory. A good example of the latter is the targeted use of the biographical/autobiographical method by Shaw but also by Sutherland to clarify the structure of a criminal career.

We will examine this many-sided development in four ways. We will deal first with socio-geographic and biographical/autobiographical research on the development of juvenile delinquency and professional crime. We will then discuss the innovative insights into the causation of crime developed in the 1930s not only by Sutherland but also by Merton and Sellin. Those insights will be dealt with here because those of Sutherland and Sellin, in any case, relied to some extent on, inter alia, the research carried out by Shaw and McKay. Subsequently we will focus on the political-sociological research on organised crime that took place in Chicago in parallel with research on juvenile crime. We will then deal with the redefinition of the object of criminology brought about by Sutherland in 1949 with his book *White Collar Crime*.

Finally, it is appropriate to emphasise that the innovation in criminal sociology was mainly the work of professors and researchers who were affiliated for a lengthy period, in one way or another, with the Department of Sociology at the University of Chicago. This has sometimes led to the references to the "Chicago School of Sociology" and even the "Chicago School of Criminology". As with the "Italian School" or "French School" of criminology, these designations are not perhaps inappropriate in some respects, but here too they tend very much to conceal the major differences in theory and research practice between the various members of this School. We will therefore not use those terms any further.[108]

What one can say, however, is that 1927–49 were the "golden years" of sociologically oriented criminology in the United States. Within that period, there appeared not only a number of empirical studies that still act as reference points for scientific research, but also a number of related theoretical initiatives that are still relevant.

---

[108]   Harvey 1987; Short 2002.

9.5.1. SOCIAL GEOGRAPHY AND BIOGRAPHY/ AUTOBIOGRAPHY OF JUVENILE DELINQUENCY AT THE UNIVERSITY OF CHICAGO

9.5.1.1. *The Founders: Robert Park, Ernest Burgess, Georg Mead, and William Thomas*

This is not the place to deal in detail with the ideas of the pioneers at the University of Chicago's Department of Sociology, which was such a bastion of innovative thinkers and actors in the first three decades of the twentieth century. Reference has already been made to the stimulating role that Henderson played at the university in the context of the impressive field survey by Kellor. And although Henderson was also the professor whose lectures at the University of Chicago aroused Sutherland's interest in criminology, he was still in fact a Lombrosian criminologist, as Kellor's study shows. Innovation in criminology originated elsewhere.[109]

Insofar as they are relevant to the research discussed below, the first names that need to be mentioned are those of Robert Park and Ernest Burgess.[110] They were sociologists who researched cities – first and foremost Chicago itself, at that time one of the world's most dynamic cities – from an organic perspective, and therefore considered cities the "natural" biotope in which people and businesses must live and survive. From this perspective – also referred to as the "ecological" perspective – they viewed the city, or at least Chicago, as developing outward from the centre in a pattern of concentric circles. In relation to the ideas of Tarde and other Europeans on the development of crime in modern society, the way Park and Burgess linked the problem of crime largely to the urbanisation of society was not particularly innovative. What was new, however, was the circles theory and its application to the problem of crime by Shaw and McKay.

From an American perspective, the methodological complement of this was certainly also new, namely statistical long-term research on the socio-geographical distribution of crime (and the official response to it) based on government data. Such research had so far not been done. From a European perspective, such research was new to the extent that, in the Old World, such detailed and extensive research had never been carried out at the level of a single large city. However, it was not a new approach to carry out socio-geographical research on the development and distribution of crime and on the operation of the criminal justice system in the same area. There had been the studies by Von Mayr and Quetelet, for example.[111]

---

[109] Williams III and McShane 1988, pp. 33–46; Jones (D.) 1986, pp. 164–168.
[110] Martin, Mutchnick and Austin 1990, pp. 93–118; Chapouli 2003; Bovenkerk 2010.
[111] Levin and Lindesmith 1937.

Second, some of the ideas of Mead and Thomas must be mentioned in this context. They devised what is sometimes referred to as "symbolic interactionism". This version of sociology is based on the idea that people's behaviour is to a large extent determined by their interaction with other people and especially by the images that they have (or think that they have) of one another and which they share with one another within that interaction in all kinds of ways. Thomas, in particular, stated that people's perception of themselves or others is heavily dependent on the situation in which they find themselves. In other words, it is very important within an interaction to define appropriately the situation in which people find themselves and to coordinate behaviour with that definition, and therefore with that situation. This explains the famous "Thomas Theorem": how people define a situation determines how real it is for them.

By extension, it is pertinent to point out that Thomas was not only more of an empirical researcher than Mead, but was also a researcher who drew methodological conclusions from his theoretical perspective.[112] This means that in his studies he deliberately allowed his subjects to speak for themselves at length so that they could explain how they did or did not allow themselves to be guided by the images that others had of them and how they defined all kinds of situations and acted according to those definitions.

An excellent example is provided by Thomas' 1923 study *The Unadjusted Girl*.[113] In that study he discussed the behavioural development of this type of young woman not only in terms of his important theorem that human behaviour is determined by four "wishes" (the desire for new experience, the desire for security, the desire for response, and the desire for recognition) but above all on the basis of quotations – sometimes lasting for pages – from the interviews he had conducted or the statements that the women concerned had given in another context. It is clear that he thus laid the basis for the autobiographical research that was conducted in subsequent years by Shaw, Sutherland, and others. It is for good reason that their publications frequently refer to his.

9.5.1.2. *Surviving in the Wilderness: Frederic Thrasher's 1,313 Gangs*

Even though socio-geographic research is usually associated mainly with Shaw and McKay and their associates, one should not forget that Thrasher's remarkable study of Chicago gangs appeared (in 1927) two years before the first two publications on that topic by Shaw and McKay and their associates (in 1929).[114]

In his foreword to the original edition of Thrasher's book in 1927, Park does not make it very clear why he and his colleagues were interested in the gang

---

[112]   Mead 1918.
[113]   Thomas 1924.
[114]   Thrasher 1963.

scene in the city, but he does indicate how they viewed that phenomenon. They saw gangs as a particular type of society, and one that was very interesting: "they are, in respect to their organization, so elementary, and in respect to their origin, so spontaneous". It was as if he wished to say that gangs embody the most rudimentary form of human society that we know today. And anyone wanting to study gangs needed to do so "in their peculiar habitat: they spring up spontaneously, but only under favoring conditions and in a definite milieu". What milieu was that in this case?

> It is the slum. The city wilderness, as it has been called, which provides the city gang its natural habitat. [...] The slum includes also the areas of first settlement to which the immigrants inevitably gravitate before they have found their places in the larger urban environment.[115]

In writing this, Park was of course anticipating the findings of Thrasher, who had counted no fewer than 1,313 gangs in contemporary Chicago, with a total of some 25,000 members. Thrasher stated that the habitat of most of these gangs was indeed "that broad twilight zone of railroads and factories, of deteriorating neighborhoods and shifting populations, which borders the city's central business district on the north, on the west, and on the south". And as though dealing with primitive tribes, Thrasher – like a true explorer – then described what the gangs were like in those three "natural areas" and how they engaged in continual "feudal warfare" with one another: the number of gangs, their size and status, their territories, their national origin or composition, their relationships, their illegal activities, etc. This survey of the "location and distribution" of the gangs led him to conclude that "gangland" Chicago "represents a geographically and socially interstitial area in the city", i.e. a large and complex border region within the overall structure, or the transition "to the more settled, more stable, and better organized portions of the city [...] a region characterized by deteriorating neighborhoods, shifting populations, and the mobility and disorganization of the slum", and in that sense "a phenomenon of human ecology".[116]

Thrasher went on to describe how the children in those densely populated transition areas of the city spontaneously formed play groups, the "gangs in embryo" that constantly disappeared from the scene and then reappeared. How did this remarkable phenomenon originate? The gangs, Thrasher writes, "represent the spontaneous effort of boys to create a society for themselves where none adequate to their needs exists". And those needs included "the thrill and zest of participation in common interests, more especially in corporate action, in hunting, capture, conflict, flight and escape", in a world characterised by disintegrated families, bad schools, meaningless religions, corrupt local

---

[115] Thrasher 1963, p. IX.
[116] Thrasher 1963, pp. 20–21.

politics, unemployment and low wages, and a lack of leisure facilities. Under those circumstances, the gang fulfilled two functions: "It offers a substitute for what society fails to give; and it provides a relief from suppression and distasteful behavior."[117]

The gangs therefore automatically knew the places within the city where they could get their hands on valuables or where they could at least have a laugh. They were guilty of all kinds of thefts and loved gambling, but they also liked playing sports. And of course, each gang had to constantly fight to maintain "its play privileges, its property rights, and the physical safety of its members" in the face of other gangs. That was one reason why *esprit de corps* was so important within the gang: "Effective collective action and continued corporate existence require that the gang controls its members."[118] The latter was in turn one of the reasons why the gangs were usually not very large. If a gang became too large, it became difficult to keep control of its activities and also to maintain "intimate contacts and controls".[119] The leader was the member who "goes where others fear to go. He is brave in the face of danger."[120]

Not all the gangs were in fact the same. If the circumstances were such that they could survive, then they could go through all kinds of developments. Some grew into true criminal gangs, but most took more conventional forms and became, for example, a kind of a sports club or society. Some made common cause with party-political groupings and were subsumed, so to speak, into a kind of federation. But many gangs disappeared again over the course of time. They succumbed in clashes with rival gangs or were decimated by campaigns against their practices by local residents, the police, and sometimes their parents. Some adapted to their environment in a more peaceful manner and simply ceased hostilities.

Given the prominent role played by *La Cosa Nostra* in the American and international literature on organised crime, it is also important to note that the Chicago gangs at the time were of very varied and often very mixed origin as regards race and nationality. In Thrasher's overview, almost 40 per cent of the gangs (351) were mixed in terms of national origin. In the second place were the Polish gangs: 148 or 16.82 per cent. Italian gangs were in third place (99 or 11.25 per cent), followed by Irish gangs (75 or 8.52 per cent) and, lagging somewhat behind, Jewish gangs (20 or 2.27 per cent). There were 63 gangs made up of African Americans, i.e. 7.16 per cent. Thrasher also found 8 German gangs, accounting for not even one per cent of the total (0.91 per cent). He did note,

---

117 Thrasher 1963, pp. 32–33.
118 Thrasher 1963, pp. 194–195.
119 Thrasher 1963, p. 221.
120 Thrasher 1963, p. 239.

however, that in some cases – measured by the size of the various population groups – the number of gangs whose members shared their nationality was disproportionately large, particularly the Polish, Irish, and Italian gangs. The number of German gangs was disproportionately small. He was unable to estimate the number of Chinese tongs.[121]

Thrasher's descriptions of certain types of gangs are also fascinating in this context, giving a taste of the atmosphere in the city's transition zones. One example is his characterisation of the Irish gangs:

> Among the Irish, fighting has been described as a sort of national habit. Bricks are popularly known as "Irish confetti". The Irish make good politicians and good policemen. It is said that the Jews own New York, but the Irish run it. Irish gangs are probably the most pugnacious of all; not only do they defend themselves, but they seem to look for trouble. Irish names are the favorites for Jewish and Polish "pugs" who assume them for prize fighting. Irish athletic clubs are probably the most numerous and most vigorous in Chicago.[122]

Finally, it is also relevant that Thrasher found that gangs with somewhat older members were naturally well aware of the activities of the underworld in their area and that the transition of their members to the organised crime gangs went very smoothly: "The gang boy sees lawlessness everywhere and in the absence of effective definitions to the contrary accepts it without criticism."[123] And if gangs were able about their activities undisturbed, then they continued along the path of "demoralization in the direction of more serious criminality. Their end product is the slugger, the gunman and the all-round gangster."[124]

9.5.1.3. Disorganisation, Conflict, and Inequality: Clifford Shaw, Henry McKay, and their Associates

Shaw, McKay, and their associates published not just one report in 1929 on the problem of juvenile delinquency in Chicago – as is commonly thought – but two.[125] The first of these, *The Juvenile Delinquent*, was published by Shaw and Earl Meyers as part of the renowned *Illinois Crime Survey*; the second was published separately by Shaw and his associates under the title *Delinquency Areas*.[126] It is

---

[121]   Thrasher 1963, pp. 130–131, 144–149.
[122]   Thrasher 1963, p. 149.
[123]   Thrasher 1963, p. 186.
[124]   Thrasher 1963, p. 274.
[125]   Gelsthorpe 2010.
[126]   Shaw and Meyers 1968; Shaw, Zorbaugh, McKay and Cottrel 1929.

not clear which of the two reports appeared first. Given the way they overlap, it is in any case preferable to read them in conjunction, as well as in fact in conjunction with Thrasher's report on the gangs, because in some respects they have a lot in common with that report.[127]

ILLINOIS ASSOCIATION FOR CRIMINAL JUSTICE (ed.), *The Illinois Crime Survey*, Montclair, Patterson Smith, 1968.

9.5.1.3.1. *The Juvenile Delinquent*: The Personification of Social Disorganisation

The Juvenile Delinquent reports on what was certainly a very large study for the time. It covered, generally speaking, all the cases brought to the attention of the

---

[127] Reiss, Jr 1987.

police or the juvenile court in 1920–26 and also the many thousands of cases dealt with during the longer period of 1900–27 by the juvenile court in Cook County. It is possible to get an idea of the numbers involved from the fact that, for example, in the former period a total of 118,177 cases were investigated by police probation officers, an average of more than 16,000 a year.

Further investigation of the cases reported in 1926 showed that the majority of the juveniles concerned lived in the neighbourhoods surrounding the centre, the Loop, and the associated industrial districts along the Chicago River, among other areas. In other words, these were the neighbourhoods that according to Thrasher – and Shaw and Meyers also refer to his study – formed the transitional areas between the centre and the residential areas on the outskirts of the city. The neighbourhoods where most juvenile delinquents lived were quite simply those that were characterised by:

> physical deterioration, poverty and social disorganization. In this area the primary group and conventional controls that were formerly exercised by the family and the neighborhood have largely disintegrated. Thus delinquent behavior, in the absence of the restraints of a well-organized moral and conventional order, is not only tolerated but becomes more or less traditional. Surrounding the area of deterioration there is a large area of disorganization, populated chiefly by immigrant groups. In this area of confused cultural standards, where the traditions and customs of the immigrant group are undergoing radical changes under the pressure of a rapidly growing city and the fusion of divergent cultures, delinquency and other forms of personal disorganization are prevalent.[128]

This passage shows that Shaw and Myers considered that the problem of juvenile delinquency in Chicago was not one that must be attributed to the anatomy, physiology, and/or psychology of the juvenile suspects but one that arose primarily, if not exclusively, from the social conditions in which they grew up. Shaw and Myers put it like this:

> These findings seem to suggest that the problem of delinquency is to a certain extent a community problem. [...] The study of detailed life stories of delinquents reveals that the experiences and behavior trends of offenders reflect the culture and the spirit of the community in which they have lived.[129]

This immediately reveals that their statement of the problem to be considered was of a very different order to the multifactorial problem statement of Healy and Bronner and worlds apart from that of the Gluecks, to say nothing about that applied by Hooton.

---

[128] Shaw and Meyers 1968, p. 652.
[129] Shaw and Meyers 1968, p. 662.

Privately, Shaw was in fact prepared to go a major step further and to state explicitly that the social disorganisation which he was discussing and which he defined almost as a kind of natural phenomenon was actually the direct, and certainly also indirect, consequence of the thoroughly capitalist policies pursued by Chicago's political and economic elite. There was therefore nothing at all "natural" about that phenomenon. He could not afford, however, to announce that view publicly because the institute at which he worked – the Institute for Juvenile Research – was funded by the same elite.[130]

Later in the report, Shaw and Meyers discuss how the gap had been closed, so to speak, between the circumstances in which the juvenile suspects had grown up and the illegal activities of which they were guilty. To put it in their terms: how "the diffusion of delinquent patterns of conduct" took place:

> From a study of life histories of delinquents it appears that delinquent patterns, particularly those of stealing, are transmitted from one individual to another and from one group to another in much the same manner that any cultural form is disseminated through society. This process of transmission takes place largely through the medium of social contacts.[131]

In other words, delinquent behaviour is behaviour learned in interaction with others; it is not therefore something that is naturally inherent in someone. That fact, say the authors, has major implications for those who wish to do something about the problem of juvenile delinquency. The problem should not therefore be viewed in isolation but in the context of the social and cultural world in which it has originated.[132]

In their recommendations, they therefore advocate a "program of community treatment for the prevention of delinquency". The main components should be a minimum income for vulnerable families, proper housing for impoverished households, play opportunities for young people, measures to protect children from exploitation by street vendors, etc., the reorganisation of (vocational) training for young people, and the integration of a whole range of support services into the life of the neighbourhood.[133]

9.5.1.3.2.   *Delinquency Areas:* "Nature Reserves" with a Different Culture

After reading the above account, one will realise that there is not much that is actually new in the 1929 study that Shaw – with the collaboration of Frederick Zorbaugh, Henry McKay, and Leonard Cottrell – published on the delinquency

---

[130]   Snodgrass 1976, pp. 9–12, 14–17.
[131]   Shaw and Meyers 1968, p. 663.
[132]   Shaw and Meyers 1968, p. 663.
[133]   Shaw and Meyers 1968, pp. 728–729.

areas in Chicago.[134] It too deals with the geographical distribution of individual delinquents and the distribution of the cases brought before the juvenile courts across the city. In a certain sense, the study's introduction and conclusion are in fact more interesting than the intervening chapters.

The introduction, or at least Chapter 1, is interesting specifically because the research is placed in the context of "the cultural approach to the study of delinquency". To make clear what this means, they refer primarily to Thomas and Parks. As regards Thomas, we are told that in his work he "pointed out how patterns of behavior and character and attitudes of whole populations arise in social interaction and become social patterns or definitions". Referring to the work of Park, the authors add that the habits, attitudes, and ways of thinking of people in modern industrial society differ greatly from those of people living in more primitive societies, and that that difference between those societies must be seen as "a difference in cultural worlds". When applied to a large city like Chicago, these two facts mean that that city must be divided into:

> local communities and neighborhoods each of which develops characteristics peculiar to itself. [...] The selective and segregative processes which bring together "natural" social groupings also distribute them in "natural areas".[135]

This "natural" division of the population into communities and areas implies that their social standards and attitudes also differ and that their character reflects the character of the individual communities and individual areas. That means: "If the community is disorganized and weak in its control, it will be easy for the institutions to disintegrate and behavior will not be controlled by conventional standards." It is in communities of this kind that play groups can develop into:

> delinquent gangs with persistent delinquent patterns and traditional codes and standards which are very important in determining the behavior of the members. Some gangs become so powerful in their hold on members that the patterns persist and actually dominate the community.[136]

But this does not yet make clear, the authors say, how the social conditions are associated with the behaviour of the persons involved. That requires a sociological analysis that takes account not only of their social contacts but in which an important role is also played by "the inner personal world of the subject, his attitudes and wishes, his interpretation of the situation, and his conception of himself". This description of the analysis ultimately leads them to a kind of concentric structure of the world of the juvenile suspects in Chicago:

---

134 Shaw, Zorbaugh, McKay and Cottrell 1929.
135 Shaw, Zorbaugh, McKay and Cottrell 1929, pp. 3–5.
136 Shaw, Zorbaugh, McKay and Cottrell 1929, pp. 6–7.

Behavior of a delinquent may be in part a reflection of a family conflict which drives him into a gang in which delinquency is a traditional group pattern. The delinquent gang may reflect a disorganized community life or a community whose life is organized around delinquent patterns. The local community in its turn reflects the processes of cultural conflict and social disorganization incident to the expansion of the city and the movement and segregation of its population.[137]

Where the conclusion of this study is concerned, it is striking that the summary of findings does not in fact differ from that in the study in the *Illinois Crime Survey*. The opposite would have been rather remarkable! The interesting point that thus remains is that Shaw and his associates point out the great importance that life stories have in order to be able to make the link between the conditions in the neighbourhoods concerned and the development of delinquent behaviour. It is only then that one can properly understand what happens there when commercial life and industry intrude into a community and that community no longer functions – can no longer function – as an effective means of social control: "Traditional norms and standards of the conventional community weaken and disappear." That definitely happens when European immigrants and African Americans from the South move into those neighbourhoods, because they have social and cultural backgrounds that are very different from those of the established communities. And that then means that:

> Delinquent and criminal patterns arise and are transmitted socially just as any other cultural and social pattern is transmitted. In time these delinquent patterns may become dominant and shape the attitudes and behavior of persons living in the area. Thus the section becomes an area of delinquency.[138]

A not insignificant factor in the above is, finally, that Shaw and his associates point out that Healy had in the meantime also acknowledged that situational factors were important in addition to individual factors. They also note that to ascertain the relative importance of the various factors, a thorough study comparing offenders and non-offenders from similar groups would be required. That clearly foreshadowed the research that the Gluecks would carry out years later.

What is not insignificant is that in this study no reference at all is made to Sutherland or Sellin. These apparently exerted no influence on the design or performance of the study or the interpretation of the results. This is an important point because the theories that the latter proposed a few years later did in fact have quite a lot in common with significant aspects of what Shaw and his associates had written.

---

[137]   Shaw, Zorbaugh, McKay and Cottrell 1929, pp. 9–10.
[138]   Shaw, Zorbaugh, McKay and Cottrell 1929, pp. 204–206.

9.5.1.3.3. Juvenile Delinquency: A Tradition in Unequal Social Circumstances

In 1942, Shaw and McKay rounded off their socio-geographical study of the distribution, etc. of juvenile delinquency in Chicago with the study *Juvenile Delinquency in Urban Areas*.[139]

In that study they repeat, on the one hand, the findings and insights from their previous studies, with all kinds of nuances. In particular, they state more succinctly than in their previous publications that a combination of three factors is responsible for the development of social disorganisation: low economic status, ethnic heterogeneity, and high residential mobility.

On the other, they also opt for a somewhat different approach – one focusing more on inequality of opportunity – to explain the crime problems in transition areas. They now argue, for example, that even in areas where many juvenile delinquents live, "conventional traditions and institutions are dominant", but that in those areas:

> delinquency has developed as a powerful competing way of life. It derives its impelling force in the boy's life from the fact that it provides a means of securing economic gain, prestige, and other human satisfactions and is embodied in delinquent groups and criminal organizations, many of which have great influence, power, and prestige.[140]

In other words, in those areas two rival systems of standards and values operate that provide fairly equal opportunities "for employment and for promotion". Every boy who grows up there is thus confronted by the conflicts between those two systems and must make choices one way or another. Or, as Sutherland puts it, they now add that in those areas there is "differential association". What can then be established, according to Shaw and McKay, is that areas with a (high) concentration of juvenile delinquents are usually also areas where a (proportionately) large number of juvenile delinquents have traditionally lived. And that, they say, means:

> that delinquent boys in these areas have contact not only with other delinquents who are their contemporaries but also with older offenders, who in turn had contact with delinquents preceding them, and so on back to the earliest history of the neighborhood. This contact means that the traditions of delinquency can be and are transmitted down through successive generations of boys, in much the same way that language and other social forms are transmitted.[141]

Just how that process actually operates is shown by their life stories:

> These stories indicate how at early ages the boys took part with older boys in delinquent activities, and how, as they themselves acquired experience, they initiated others

---

[139] Shaw and McKay 1994.
[140] Shaw and McKay 1994, p. 193.
[141] Shaw and McKay 1994, p. 195.

into the same pursuits. These cases reveal also the steps through which members are incorporated into the delinquent group organization.[142]

What Shaw and McKay now emphasise more strongly than before, however, is that when it comes to making choices between rival systems of standards and values, not everyone is in the same position. Quite the contrary: there are large differences between people and groups in that regard. They are all, it is true, exposed at school and in church to the same ideas of equality, freedom, and entrepreneurship and therefore all develop the desire for "acquiring material goods and enhancing personal status", but in the case of young people in low-income neighbourhoods those goals are difficult to achieve legitimately due to limited access to the necessary facilities and opportunities. That discrepancy consequently means that:

> where there exists the greatest disparity between the social values to which people aspire and the availability of facilities for acquiring these values in conventional ways, the development of crime as an organized way of life is most marked. Crime, in this situation, may be regarded as one of the means employed by people to acquire, or to attempt to acquire, the economic and social values generally idealized in our culture, which persons in other circumstances acquire by conventional means [...] The power and affluence achieved, at least temporarily, by many persons involved in crime and illegal rackets are well known to the children and youth of the community and are important in determining the character of their ideals.[143]

Comparing the foregoing explanation for juvenile delinquency with the explanations presented in the earlier books, on the one hand a number of parallels can be seen. On the other hand, that explanation unmistakably involves a reinterpretation of how juvenile delinquency comes about in poor neighbourhoods. Unlike formerly, its genesis is now attributed to the wide discrepancy between people's general aims in life and the means for achieving those aims.

What is noteworthy here is the fact that – unlike in the case of the operation of "differential association" according to Sutherland – there is now no reference to Robert Merton, who only a few years previously, in a famous article, had characterised this situation as a state of anomie, as we shall see below. I do not know why there is no reference to Merton, but it is certainly strange.

9.5.1.4. Biographical/Autobiographical Studies of Clifford Shaw and Associates and Edwin Sutherland: The Jack-Roller, Brothers in Crime and The Professional Thief

Thrasher, Shaw, and McKay argued more than once – following Thomas – that the life stories of juvenile delinquents are indispensable to bridging the gap between

---

142   Shaw and McKay 1994, p. 196.
143   Shaw and McKay 1994, p. 199.

the conditions in which they grew up and their criminal behaviour, whether or not in groups. That is why the publications discussed above frequently allow their subjects to have their say and to explain what goes on in their life and that of their fellows.

Shaw, the main figure, went a step further in 1930 with *The Jack-Roller: A Delinquent Boy's Own Story*.[144] There is a lot that can be said about this autobiography. Why, for example, was Shaw not more critical when listening to the story that "Stanley" told him? To what extent and in what ways was, and is, this ego document an illustration – a demonstration, evidence perhaps – of the soundness of the explanation given by Shaw and his associates of the nature, extent, and development of juvenile crime in Chicago in the 1920s?

It should be noted that many of these questions were only posed much later, from the 1960s on. Nevertheless, ever since its publication, *The Jack-Roller* has been read and re-read in academic circles. That is probably because it is in fact a brief, interesting, and well-structured narrative which – quite apart from the events themselves and certainly also the way it is told – can be viewed as an important illustration of the way youngsters develop a delinquent career. As Burgess puts it in his postscript to *The Jack-Roller*:

> This one autobiography of a delinquent career is a concrete and dramatic exemplification of what a case-study may reveal about the causes and treatment of delinquency that can never be arrived at by more formal techniques like statistics, which must depend very largely upon external data.[145]

That is not the only reason, I believe, why this little book is still read so frequently and so enthusiastically. This was also the first time that it was not police officers, judicial officials, or academics writing about professional and habitual criminals – that had been going on, after all, since the French Revolution – but such a person himself. Stanley, indeed, told the story of his social life and his criminal occupation to Shaw, who wrote it down.[146]

In any case, the story of the jack-roller – i.e. a boy who joins with others to rob drunks and homosexuals, if not in the street then in their own homes – is a rather fascinating tale. That is not only because the reader is taken, in a compelling way, into the world in which Stanley grew up, but also because the reader learns through Stanley why it is very tempting for a boy like him to enter into a criminal career and engage in all kinds of illegal activity in order to live (and survive) in his world. In particular, Stanley's account of what goes on in prisons is highly instructive. It enables us to understand fully why incarceration – including because of its

---

144 Shaw 1966.
145 Shaw 1966, p. 185.
146 Shaw 1966, pp. V–XVIII; Maruna and Matravers 2007; Sampson and Laub 1995, pp. 204–242.

stigmatising effect – is not necessarily a beneficial means of combatting juvenile delinquency, certainly not if it is the only means of doing so.

The literature often ignores the fact that, a few years later, Shaw published another autobiography of a young male recidivist: *The Natural History of a Delinquent Career*. Better known is in any case the sequel to these two

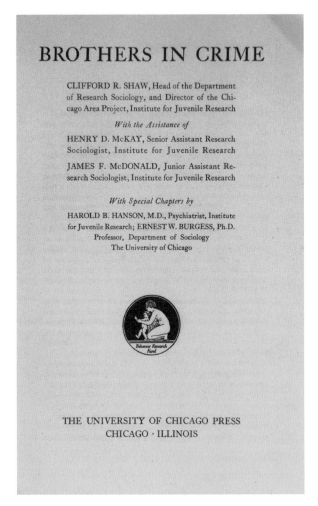

BROTHERS IN CRIME

CLIFFORD R. SHAW, Head of the Department of Research Sociology, and Director of the Chicago Area Project, Institute for Juvenile Research

With the Assistance of

HENRY D. McKAY, Senior Assistant Research Sociologist, Institute for Juvenile Research

JAMES F. McDONALD, Junior Assistant Research Sociologist, Institute for Juvenile Research

With Special Chapters by

HAROLD B. HANSON, M.D., Psychiatrist, Institute for Juvenile Research; ERNEST W. BURGESS, Ph.D. Professor, Department of Sociology The University of Chicago

THE UNIVERSITY OF CHICAGO PRESS
CHICAGO · ILLINOIS

Clifford SHAW, Henry McKAY and James McDONALD, *Brothers in Crime*, Chicago, University of Chicago Press, 1938.

monographs, *Brothers in Crime*, published in 1938, this time together with Henry McKay and James McDonald, and again with a postscript by Burgess, among others.[147] In the preface to this book on the delinquent activities of five

---

[147] Shaw, McKay and McDonald 1938.

brothers, Shaw himself explains what it is about: "Their cases are published to suggest the relationship between delinquency and the culture conflicts which often confront the immigrant family in the physically deteriorated and socially disorganized communities in large American cities."

Part 1 of the book deals with the criminal careers of the brothers, while Part 2 examines their social background. Part 3 comprises the life stories of the five brothers. In Part 4, Burgess comments comparatively on these stories. In Part 5 the authors give an account of their research. There is a lot that one could say about this book, but we will need to restrict ourselves. Nevertheless, with a view to discussion of the theories dealt with below, it is important to highlight the following points.

First, Shaw emphasises that the crimes the boys have committed were no more and no less than an attempt "to secure certain common human satisfactions in the particular situation in which they lived", i.e. a matter of meeting their needs. That does not change the fact, however, that the brothers gradually progressed to committing more serious crimes, and that this was no accident but rather the result of "a continuous process of education, habituation, and increasing sophistication in the art of stealing".[148] And that is only one of the important conclusions that Shaw draws from the study:

In the cases of the brothers, as in numerous other cases, the initial acts of theft were part of the undifferentiated play life of the street. Gradually, however, stealing became a more distinct and specialized practice which required appropriate skills, insights and knowledge. At the outset these were provided by the gang and the more experienced delinquents with whom the brothers had personal contact in the community and in juvenile institutions. The delinquents not only furnished the fund of appropriate knowledge but they provided the stimuli, the encouragement, the incentives, the approvals, and the necessary sanctions. From the simple forms of stealing the brothers progressed to more complicated, more serious, and more specialized forms of theft.[149]

In other words, building a criminal career clearly involves a learning process, but not one that could have taken place just anywhere.

Second, the social conditions in which the brothers grew up facilitated that process. Many young people, after all, did not have the ability to systematically earn a living in the world of business and industry, and (organised) crime gave them the opportunity to nevertheless gain a minimum level of economic security. According to Shaw and his associates, the choice that a boy eventually makes in those circumstances – i.e. whether or not he becomes a delinquent – depends in many cases on the worlds with which he is most familiar.

As a result – and this is the third point – a boy who has a career as a delinquent is regarded in his own social world as a "right guy", but "from the standpoint of the

---

[148] Shaw, McKay and McDonald 1938, pp. 49, 61.
[149] Shaw, McKay and McDonald 1938, p. 355.

court he is regarded as a law-violator and a delinquent". And the world with which the boy is most familiar is not a small one. Shaw and his associates calculated that, during the period when they were fully engaged in crime, the brothers concerned were in contact with more than 250 known juvenile delinquents and criminals. It was precisely that larger network that "provided the morale, the *esprit de corps*, and moral sanction necessary to sustain their interest in crime and the market for their loot. […] In short, their delinquencies may be regarded as an adjustment to the social world in which they lived."[150] That interplay between their world and their crimes was not in fact free of obligations. The brothers' close ties with numerous delinquent and criminal groups in their community meant that it was almost impossible for them to escape their fate.[151]

As regards, specifically, the issue of cultural conflict, Shaw and his associates refer to the major differences between the culture of most immigrants' countries of origin and the culture of the United States. Those differences also tore apart the brothers' family. The attitudes and sentiments of their parents reflected the culture of the Old World. Their children, however, were incorporated "into the street crowds, play groups, and gangs of children in the community, where they acquired the language of the New World".[152] The end of the tale was that the responses of the brothers to the cultural differences in their neighbourhood were ultimately the product of their experiences in the delinquent environment and the coercive measures that many institutions utilised to induce them to behave according to standards that were not consistent with the values of their own world.[153]

A year prior to the appearance of *Brothers in Crime*, i.e. in 1937, Sutherland published *The Professional Thief: By a Professional Thief* (the Philadelphia protagonist of which used the pseudonym "Chic Conwell"). Did Sutherland also view the problem of professional crime as one that had arisen from a culturally imposed learning process within a disorganised society? In his introduction, Sutherland in fact already indicated the conclusions that he drew from the story of the professional criminal.

His first conclusion was that professional thieving involved more than "isolated acts of theft frequently and skillfully performed", namely "a group way of life and a social institution". His second was:

> that professional thieves constitute a group which has the characteristics of other groups and that these group characteristics are in no sense pathological […] No one is a professional thief unless he is recognized as such by other professional thieves. Tutelage of professional thieves is essential for the development of the skills, attitudes, codes, and connections which are required in professional theft.[154]

---

[150]   Shaw, McKay and McDonald 1938, p. 119.
[151]   Shaw, McKay and McDonald 1938, p. 126.
[152]   Shaw, McKay and McDonald 1938, p. 135.
[153]   Shaw, McKay and McDonald 1938, p. 140.
[154]   Sutherland 1967, p. VIII.

Unlike *The Jack-Roller*, *The Professional Thief* is not based on a broad empirical study of crime in a big city like Chicago, let alone the entire United States. That does not mean, however, that Sutherland did not view the life story of Chic Conwell as a demonstration of his differential association theory – in fact he did so categorically. In the final interpretive part of the book, it is for good reason that he discusses Conwell's story at length in terms of that theory, stating in that regard, for example, that:

> The differential element in the association of thieves is primarily functional rather than geographical. Their personal association is limited by barriers which are maintained principally by the thieves themselves. These barriers are based on their community of interests, including security or safety. These barriers may easily be penetrated from within; since other groups also set up barriers in their personal association, especially against known thieves, the thieves are, in fact, kept in confinement within the barriers of their own groups to a somewhat greater extent than is true of other groups. On the other hand, these barriers can be penetrated from the outside only with great difficulty. A stranger who enters a thieves' hangout is called a "weed in the garden". When he enters, conversation either ceases completely or is diverted to innocuous topics.[155]

What this passage also shows, however, is that Sutherland is here imbuing the term "differential association" with a meaning that is somewhat different to that in his general version of that theory as published in 1939. Here, it is not in fact used to explain how criminal behaviour is learned, but rather to show how a group of professional criminals maintains itself in a hostile environment. It goes without saying that using the same term to mean different things can cause confusion.[156]

Moreover, in the context of the reception of European criminology in the United States, it should be noted that – as is shown by the bibliography and notes in *The Professional Thief* – Sutherland was aware both directly and indirectly (through translations and references) of the important German literature on professional criminals, in particular the books by Friedrich Avé-Lallemant, Wulffen, and Heindl, but also that by Grasberger on organised crime in the United States. But to what extent these books influenced his views on professional crime is difficult to say. In any case, Chic Conwell's story of how professional thieves are organised, about the various specialisations in the profession, about the benefits and burdens of the work, on relationships with wives and girlfriends, and on the corrupt relationships with the police and judicial authorities, is certainly as fascinating as that of *The Jack-Roller*.

---

155   Sutherland 1967, pp. 206–207.
156   Cohen (A.) 1967, pp. 28–29.

9.5.2. DIFFERENTIAL ASSOCIATION THEORY, THE ANOMIE THEORY, AND THE CULTURE CONFLICT THEORY

It is remarkable that within just two years in the late 1930s, three theories were published that are not only based – or seem to be based – on the findings of the studies discussed above but that also have a great deal in common with each other. These theories are: the differential association theory (already presented by Sutherland in rudimentary form in 1934 but not in detail until 1939 in his *Principles of Criminology*), Merton's anomie theory (presented for the first time in 1938 in an article in the *American Sociological Review*), and the culture conflict theory (presented by Sellin in 1938 in a report for the Social Science Research Council in New York).

9.5.2.1. Edwin Sutherland: The Differential Association Theory

Sutherland is generally viewed as one of the leading American criminologists of the twentieth century.[157] That designation is thanks, in particular, to the aforementioned theory that he developed gradually in the framework of his *Principles of Criminology*. The first edition of that book appeared – with the title *Criminology* – in 1924. Sutherland, who had studied sociology (and other subjects) at the University of Chicago with Henderson and Thomas, and who became acquainted with criminology from their lectures, wrote the book for the Lippincott Sociological Series at the invitation of Edward Hayes, then his colleague at the University of Illinois at Champaign-Urbana. The book was well received in sociological circles, not least by sociologists in Chicago, the hub of Sutherland's old boys network.[158]

The 1924 version did not yet deal, however, with his personal theory of the causation of crime, although he did note even then that:

> The essential reason why persons become criminals is that they have been isolated from the culture of the law-abiding group, by reason of their residence, employment, codes, native incapacity, or something else. Consequently, they are lacking in the experiences, feelings, ideas, and attitudes out of which to construct a life organization that the law-abiding public will regard as desirable.[159]

The good relationship that he already had with Shaw had therefore not yet left its mark on this introduction. That would probably have been difficult because his investigations had only begun in the early 1920s. But what was immediately clear was that for Sutherland crime was not a matter of heredity, anatomy, or physique.

---

[157] Martin, Mutchnick and Austin 1990, pp. 139–176.
[158] Gaylord and Galligher 1988, pp. 1–70.
[159] Gaylord and Galligher 1988, pp. 71–72; Bruinsma 1985, pp. 23–25.

In terms of its structure, this book was in fact similar to various others that had already appeared in recent decades: a limited part was dedicated to the "causes of crime" and "crime causation", with by far the majority of the work being about the institutions of the criminal justice system, i.e. the police, the prison system, etc.[160]

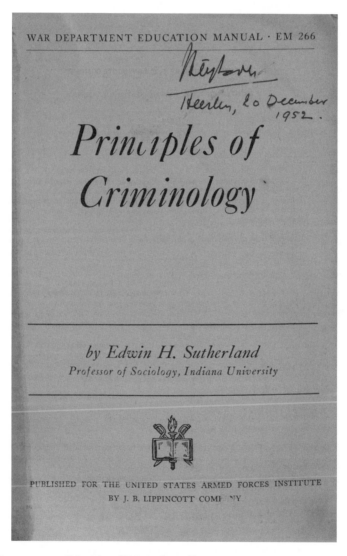

WAR DEPARTMENT EDUCATION MANUAL · EM 266

Heerlen, 20 December 1952.

Principles of Criminology

by *Edwin H. Sutherland*
Professor of Sociology, Indiana University

PUBLISHED FOR THE UNITED STATES ARMED FORCES INSTITUTE
BY J. B. LIPPINCOTT COMPANY

Edwin SUTHERLAND, *Principles of Criminology*, Chicago, J.B. Lippincott, 1939.

After some peregrinations, Sutherland returned in 1929 as a research professor in the Department of Sociology at the University of Chicago. He tackled a number of research projects there, both large and small, but in the first half of

---

160   Sutherland 1924.

the 1930s still managed largely to finalise the manuscript of *The Professional Thief.* In 1934, he also published the second edition of his *Criminology*, this time with the title *Principles of Criminology.*[161] In the preface to that edition, he wrote that the change of title was "because the changes made in the revision are many and fundamental". One of those changes definitely concerned the "general thesis" of the book, namely:

> that crime is a response to the general culture which has been developing during the last two centuries. The local agencies which were effective in social control when interaction was confined largely to local communities have disintegrated and, even where they are best preserved, are relatively ineffective in controlling the behavior in the wider areas to which interaction has extended.[162]

It is also significant that in the preface Sutherland emphasised how important he had found the studies by Shaw, McKay, and Landesco. He recommended them in any case as "supplementary reading".

It is immediately apparent from the table of contents that the first part presents a multifactorial view of the causes of crime: physical and physiological factors, psychopathy, race, nationality, culture, family, and relatives. Again, the majority of the introduction is devoted to the criminal justice institutions, in particular the prison system. But even so, the book is genuinely different in a number of important respects. In terms of Sutherland's theory, there are two things that need to be pointed out.

First, the footnotes and bibliography make clear that he had taken note of a number of by then classic European works on criminology by Bonger, Garofalo, and Tarde. Where Tarde is concerned, he refers only to a statement in the English translation of *La philosophie pénale* to the effect that criminals are in fact no more than the refuse of society.[163]

Second, he already makes very clear at the end of the first chapter where he stands, namely on the side of Thrasher and Shaw: "Crime is a symptom of social disorganization and probably can be reduced appreciably only by changes in the social organization."[164]

He does not go any further down that route in Chapter 3 ("Causes of Crime: General"), but he does in Chapter 4, on "Crime and the Social Process". In that chapter, he writes that the crime problems of his time are a reflection of a state of "social disorganization" which is itself the result of a process of "mobility, competition and conflict" that began with the colonisation of America. More specifically, that state is characterised by the existence of all kinds of conflicting

---

[161] Gaylord and Galligher 1988, pp. 109–114.
[162] Sutherland 1934, p. V.
[163] Sutherland 1924, p. 14.
[164] Sutherland 1924, p. 22.

cultures and thus by confusion as to standards of behaviour and even by disintegration.

Against that background, it is easier to understand why in Chapter 3, after discussing a number of theories on the causes of crime, Sutherland states that the general hypotheses of his book are the following:

- "First, any person can be trained to adopt and follow any pattern of behavior which he is able to execute";
- "Second, failure to follow a prescribed pattern of behavior is due to the inconsistency and lack of harmony in the influences which direct the individual";
- "Third, the conflict of cultures is therefore the fundamental principle in the explanation of crime"; and
- "Fourth, the more the cultural patterns conflict, the more unpredictable is the behavior of a particular individual".[165]

It should be pointed out immediately that it is indeed not so difficult to link these four fairly abstract propositions to what Thrasher and McKay and their associates had written more specifically in about 1930: criminal behaviour is learned behaviour, it has to do with culture and cultural conflict, etc. The fact that Sutherland follows up these four propositions by writing that crime arises when the desires of people cannot be satisfied by legitimate means is certainly not inconsistent with this conclusion. After all, that remark can very well be construed as a reference to the function that Thrasher says the gangs fulfilled for juveniles from the disadvantaged neighbourhoods of Chicago. It can in fact also be understood as foreshadowing what Merton would write a few years later in the framework of his anomie theory regarding crime as a response to the discrepancy between aims and means in a society, as we will explain below.

It is not clear whether Sutherland – trying in the 1934 edition to cast his theory about the origins of criminal behaviour in the form of four propositions – was prompted by the highly critical report on the state of criminology in the United States written in 1932–33 by Jerome Michael and Mortimer Adler at the request the New York City Bureau of Social Hygiene.[166] It is clear, however, that the further elaboration of his theory was largely a response to the criticism in that report to the effect that criminological research up to that time did not amount to much, that the low quality of the research was the result of "incompetence of criminologists in science", that the conventional criminological research methods needed to be abandoned, and that scientists needed to be "imported into criminology from other fields". Sutherland himself, for all kinds of reasons,

---

[165] Sutherland 1924, pp. 51–53; Gaylord and Galligher 1988, pp. 111–120.
[166] Michael and Adler 1971; Mueller 1969, pp. 104–108.

was enormously offended by the report but he did admit a few years later that it had prompted him to devote his attention to "abstract generalizations".[167]

It was probably for personal reasons that in 1935 Sutherland's appointment at the University of Chicago was not renewed and he was forced to seek refuge at Indiana University.[168] Ultimately, however, that move did not turn out badly for him. In 1937, *The Professional Thief* was published, followed in 1939 by the third edition of *Principles of Criminology*.[169] This time, partly on the recommendation of McKay, he placed his views on the causation of crime in the form of seven propositions at the front of the book, in Chapter 1, entitled "A Theory of Criminology".[170] He did so, however, with considerable caution:

> The principles of this theory should be regarded as tentative and hypothetical and should be tested by the factual information which is presented in the later chapters and by all other factual information and theories which are applicable.

The seven propositions are:

"1. The processes which result in systematic criminal behavior are fundamentally the same in form as the processes which result in systematic lawful behavior;

2. Systematic criminal behavior is determined in a process of association with those who commit crimes, just as systematic lawful behavior is determined in a process of association with those who are law-abiding;

3. Differential association is the specific causal process in the development of systematic criminal behavior;

4. The chance that a person will participate in systematic criminal behavior is determined roughly by the frequency and consistency of his contacts with the patterns of criminal behavior;

5. Individual differences among people in respect to personal characteristics or social situations cause crime only as they affect differential association or frequency and consistency of contacts with criminal patterns;

6. Cultural conflict is the underlying cause of differential association and therefore of systematic criminal behavior;

7. Social disorganization is the basic cause of systematic criminal behavior."

In conclusion, Sutherland summaries his theory as follows: "Systematic criminal behavior is due immediately to differential association in a situation in which culture conflicts exist, and ultimately to the social disorganization in that situation."

Incidentally, it is important to emphasise that Sutherland had not entirely dismissed other theories of criminal behaviour. In the accompanying

---

[167] Laub 2006, pp. 238–239.
[168] Gaylord and Galligher 1988, pp. 119–120.
[169] Sutherland 1939.
[170] Gaylord and Galligher 1988, pp. 132–141.

"considerations in a theory of criminal behavior", he writes explicitly that theories regarding individual differences between people remained important for understanding their specific criminal behaviour, as did theories relating to "situational or cultural processes": "All of these must be considered and most of them included in a final organization of thought regarding criminal behavior."

Nevertheless, he became the object of a considerable amount of criticism, for example concerning the fact that he viewed the city, almost by definition, as a disorganised part of the world. Just how critical he himself was is evident from the fact that in the 1947 edition he significantly altered his seven propositions.

The first proposition now read straightforwardly: "Criminal behavior is learned", followed by a new proposition 2: "Criminal behavior is learned in interaction with other persons in a process of communication"; a new proposition 3: "The principal part of the learning of criminal behavior occurs within intimate personal groups"; and a new proposition 4: "When criminal behavior is learned, the learning includes (a) techniques of committing crime [...] (b) the specific direction of motives, drives, rationalizations, and attitudes". Proposition 6 is similar to the former proposition 4: "A person becomes delinquent because of an excess of definitions favorable to violation of law over definitions unfavorable to violation of law", at least in combination with the new proposition 7: "Differential association may vary in frequency, duration, priority, and intensity."

One of the criticisms of Sutherland's book had been that differential association was no more than a restatement of Tarde's imitation theory. Sutherland's defence against that criticism was supposedly that "differential association" involved not only imitation but all kinds of learning processes, for example the temptation to engage in illegal sexual conduct. To emphasise this, he supposedly phrased proposition 8 as follows: "The process of learning criminal behavior by association with criminal and anti-criminal patterns involves all of the mechanisms that are involved in any other learning."[171]

This defence by Sutherland was not exactly a powerful one. He was familiar with the English translation of Tarde's *Penal Philosophy* and therefore knew that when Tarde spoke of "imitation", he was referring not to the simple mechanical and uniform imitation of other people's criminal behaviour, but to a complex set of "laws" concerning the transfer of deviant standards of behaviour in which learning processes play a major role. That is even shown by the table of contents of Tarde's book, for example the heading to section 64(II) et seq.:

The laws of imitation. Men imitate one another in proportion as they are in close contact. The superior is imitated by the inferior to a greater extent than the inferior by the superior. Propagation from the higher to the lower in every sort of fact: language, dogma, furniture, ideas, needs. The great fields of imitation; formerly aristocracies, today capitals. [...] Application to criminality. Vices and crimes were formerly

---

171   Gaylord and Galligher 1988, pp. 149–150.

propagated from the nobles to the people. [...] At the present time they are propagated from the great cities to the country.[172]

Unfortunately, Sutherland died unexpectedly of a stroke on 11 October 1950 and therefore did not live to bring out a new edition of his *Principles*. That task was taken on by his loyal associate, Donald Cressey.[173]

9.5.2.2.　Robert Merton: The Anomie Theory

The article published by Merton in 1938 caused a sensation. That was not only because – very unlike Sutherland – he had never before involved himself in crime problems, but also because in that article he dealt succinctly with a number of problems and developments that had previously only been brought up in disparate publications by various authors.[174]

The statement of the problem in this concise article is based on the distinction between, on the one hand, "culturally defined goals, purposes, and interests" and, on the other, "the acceptable modes of achieving these goals" or "permissible and required procedures for attaining these ends". Aims and means, however, are not always in equilibrium and it is that lack of equilibrium that can lead to deviant behaviour: "Aberrant conduct, therefore, may be viewed as a symptom of dissociation between culturally defined aspirations and socially structured means." If that dissociation goes so far that, increasingly, "the technically most feasible procedure, whether legitimate or not, is preferred to the institutionally prescribed conduct", then "the integration of society becomes tenuous and anomie ensues".

At the beginning of his article, Merton states that what he wishes to demonstrate with this analysis is that tensions in the social structure of a society can create conditions in which violating social codes constitutes a "normal" response. He omits to note that he was in fact borrowing that proposition – and particularly the term "anomie" – from Durkheim. Not only does note 3 in his article show, however, that he was familiar with the latter's work on precisely that point, but later publications also show that Durkheim was here the source of his wisdom.[175] The fact that Merton does not acknowledge this plainly in his article is perhaps an ironic example of the theory that he develops in it: in his unrelenting pursuit of academic success, he conceals his primary source so as to appear far more original than he really was.

Be that as it may, the way he then elaborates on "the social genesis of the varying rates and types of deviate behavior characteristic of different societies" is interesting and original. In his view, there are five "logically possible, alternative

---

[172]　Tarde 2001, pp. 322–342; Manouk 2011, p. 6.
[173]　See Sutherland and Cressey 1955; Cressey 1964.
[174]　Jacoby 1994, pp. 178–187; Martin, Mutchnick and Austin 1990, pp. 207–235.
[175]　Cullen and Messner 2007, pp. 20–22; Merton 2000.

modes of adjustment or adaptation *by individuals* within the culture-bearing society or group". Those five are:

- conformity: aims and means are both accepted;
- innovation: aims are accepted but means are not;
- ritualism: aims are rejected but means are not;
- retreatism: aims and means are rejected; and
- rebellion: aims and means are rejected with a view to a new social order.[176]

When applied to problems of crime such as those in Chicago, this fivefold division means, first, that these problems occur above all when there is:

> differential access to the approved opportunities for legitimate, prestige-bearing pursuit of the cultural goals. The lack of high integration between the means-and-end elements of the cultural pattern and the particular class structure combine to favor a heightened frequency of antisocial conduct in such groups.[177]

Second, those problems will occur if achieving the goals by legitimate means:

> is limited by the fact that actual advance toward desired success-symbols through conventional channels is, despite our persisting open-class ideology, relatively rare and difficult for those handicapped by little formal education and few economic resources. The dominant pressure of group standards of success is, therefore, on the gradual attenuation of legitimate, but by and large ineffective, strivings and the increasing use of illegitimate, but more or less effective, expedients of vice and crime. The cultural demands made on persons in this situation are incompatible.[178]

Merton adds that the equilibrium between ends and means is highly unstable "with the progressive emphasis on attaining the prestige-laden ends by any means whatsoever". In such a situation, he says:

> Capone represents the triumph of amoral intelligence over morally prescribed "failure", when the channels of vertical mobility are closed or narrowed *in a society which places a high premium on economic affluence and social ascent for all its members* [Merton's italics].[179]

It is not therefore the lack of opportunities as such that is decisive for the development of deviant behaviour. Rather, it is caused by the lack of opportunities in relation to the prescribed aims:

> It is only when a system of cultural values extols, virtually above all else, certain *common symbols* of success *for the population at large* while its social structure rigorously

---

[176] Merton 1938, p. 676.
[177] Merton 1938, p. 679.
[178] Merton 1938, p. 679.
[179] Merton 1938, pp. 679–680.

restricts or completely eliminates access to approved modes of acquiring these symbols *for a considerable part of the same population* that antisocial behavior ensues on a considerable scale [Merton's italics].[180]

At the end of the article, Merton points out its brevity and that it has therefore ignored some important issues. He refers in particular to "the various structural elements which predispose toward one rather than another of the alternative responses open to individuals". That is in fact interesting, because when Merton was honoured by the American Society of Criminology with the Edwin H. Sutherland Award in 1996, he emphasised in his acceptance speech that the anomie theory and differential association theory are essentially complementary. That was, briefly, because:

> [T]he theory of differential association holds that individuals learn to engage in criminal behavior by associating with others, principally in face-to-face groups, who prefer and practice such behavior. Thus, the key question in this theory centers on the sociocultural transmission of criminal patterns: it inquires into the processes of socialization and social learning through which such patterns are learned from significant others.

> [T]he theory of anomie-and-opportunity-structures [...] holds that rates of various types of deviant behavior (not only crime) are high in a society where, as with the American Dream, the culture places a high premium on economic success and upward mobility for *all* its members, although in brute social fact large numbers of people located in the lower reaches of the social structure have severely limited access to legitimate resources for achieving those culturally induced or reinforced goals. Since the key question in this theory focusses on the socially structured sources and consequences of deviant behavior, it says next to nothing about the social mechanisms for transmitting such patterns of behavior or about the ways in which individuals' initial departures from the norms crystallize into deviant careers.[181]

In line with this comparison, Merton correctly pointed out in 1996 that, in the 1950s and 1960s, their students – Albert Cohen, Lloyd Ohlin, and others – had almost automatically incorporated this complementarity into their research on the formation and operation of criminal juvenile gangs.

9.5.2.3.   *Thorsten Sellin: The Culture Conflict Theory*

Compared to Sutherland and Merton, Sellin can hardly be called a productive and innovative researcher. Rather, he was a kind of scientific bookkeeper, i.e. someone who mainly keeps track of what others write.[182] That first became apparent in the 1930s in the research memorandum about crime during the

---

[180]   Merton 1938, p. 680.
[181]   Merton 1997.
[182]   Lejins 1987; Melossi 2010.

Depression that he wrote for the Social Science Research Council in 1937. Although that document demonstrates a certain familiarity with the literature on the impact of economic conditions on crime problems, it does not in any way demonstrate any research of Sellin's own on what had happened in the United States in previous years on that issue.[183]

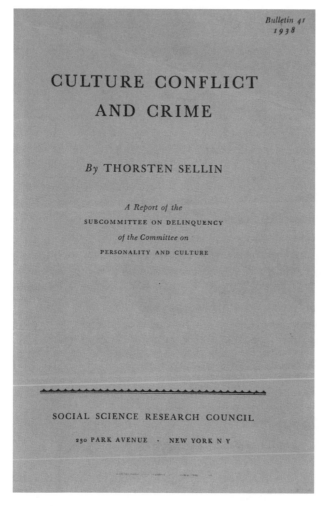

Thorsten SELLIN, *Culture Conflict and Crime*, New York, Social Science Research Council, 1938.

Sellin's 1938 report for the Council on "culture conflict and crime" is also mainly a long-winded, abstract, and somewhat internationally oriented review of the literature on the setting of standards, on conflicts between standards, on types of

---

[183]   Sellin (T.) 1937.

conflicts, etc. What is striking in the report is not only that at crucial moments he strongly invokes the research by Shaw and his associates but that throughout the study he – himself an immigrant – closely links the problems of cultural conflict with the problems of the integration of all kinds of immigrant groups in the United States.[184]

That link therefore greatly determines the altogether meagre conclusion that he draws at the end of his study. This comes down to there being, in his view, two kinds of cultural conflicts: on the one hand, primary cultural conflicts, and on the other, secondary culture conflicts. The first category of conflicts applies, he says:

> If the immigrant's conduct norms are different from those of the American community, and if these differences are not due to his economic status, but to his *cultural origin* then we can speak of norms drawn from different cultural systems or areas.[185]

This type of conflict concerns, for example, the freedom to carry arms: where that freedom is strictly regulated in one country but is not subject to restrictions in another. The result is that immigrants from the latter type of country can easily get into trouble in the former because they quickly break the law. Another example in this context is the very varied regulation of games of chance.

The second category of cultural conflicts, Sellin states, are conflicts arising from the process of social differentiation that is characteristic of the evolution of one's own culture. He provides no clear and therefore convincing examples. This in itself raises the question of the extent to which the dichotomy between primary and secondary cultural conflicts is in fact a meaningful distinction.

That question is naturally also justified because in the case of a multicultural country like the United States, it is difficult to imagine that a homogeneous internal culture exists that could be said to clash in significant respects with foreign cultures.

9.5.3. IMPACT OF THE "GOLDEN YEARS" OF 1927–49 IN CRIMINOLOGICAL RESEARCH

The innovative studies by Thrasher, Shaw, and McKay – whether or not coloured to any extent by the views of Sutherland, Merton, and sometimes Sellin (or variations of those views) – continue to this day to affect American criminological research on the causation, manifestation, and control of certain forms of crime. This can easily be demonstrated with a number of examples.

In the 1950s, 1960s, and 1970s, a considerable number of empirical studies were carried out in cities across America on the relationships between juvenile

---

[184] Sellin (T.) 1938.
[185] Sellin (T.) 1938, p. 104.

crime and social class at neighbourhood level. That research considered not only those relationships as such, but also the soundness of the official sources of information on the social spread of juvenile crime, such as police databases. Shaw and McKay had already frequently expressed their concerns about social bias in such databases – resulting from the social selectivity of police action – but in the 1960s those concerns were presented with much more forceful arguments. The result was that widespread doubts arose about the reliability and validity of the findings in studies that uncritically took data from such sources.[186]

Nevertheless, that issue was no reason to refrain from this kind of criminographic neighbourhood-oriented research, but it was a reason to carry it out differently and, inter alia, to enhance it by incorporating surveys of victims. That does not mean, however, that disputes did not continue until the 1990s – and even later – as to how such social disorganisation can or must be detailed in operational terms in order to determine to what extent and in what way it is reflected in the nature, scope, and development of (juvenile) crime.[187]

Whereas this development can still, from the theory perspective, be related directly to the research conducted in the 1920s and 1930s, an entirely different development has taken place since the 1970s in the context of research on the spatial development of crime. That development was heralded in 1972 by Oscar Newman's *Defensible Space*. In that book, Newman argued forcefully, on the basis of numerous examples, that crime can be prevented by designing cities differently – or at least important nodes such as residential areas, shopping centres, industrial estates, etc. – both physically and socially.[188]

This idea was not necessarily at odds with the ideas of Shaw and McKay about how social disorganisation and thus crime can be combatted, but its one-sidedness distanced it greatly from them; no proposals to achieve this objective through social action are mentioned in Newman's book. That did not, however, prevent "ecological criminology" as originally developed in Chicago developing into "environmental criminology". This is thus a type of criminology that focuses on defensive crime prevention by designing cities (or parts of cities) physically in such a way that they provide minimal opportunity for all kinds of traditional forms of – in the main – property crime (whether or not violent): theft, burglary, mugging, robbery, etc.[189] A very important precondition for achieving this is the availability of a detailed, well-qualified criminography of cities as regards these forms of crime. Attempting to comply with that precondition encouraged the development of crime mapping.[190]

---

186   Braithwaite 1979, pp. 24–63.
187   Reiss, Jr 1983; Sampson and Groves 1989; Schwendinger and Schwendinger 1997; Veysey and Messner 1999.
188   Newman 1972.
189   Brantingham and Brantingham 1991; Brantingham and Brantingham 1998.
190   Weisburd and McEwen 1998.

However, not only do the studies by Thrasher, Shaw, and McKay, and the subsequent theories of Sutherland, Merton, and Sellin, still form the starting point for research on the evolution of crime in urban areas, they have also led to the development of a fairly extensive body of literature regarding the phenomenon of (juvenile) gangs in American cities. Three books that in the 1950s and 1960s greatly encouraged research on that phenomenon were Albert Cohen's *Delinquent Boys: The Culture of the Gang* (first edition 1955), Richard Cloward and Lloyd Ohlin's *Delinquency and Opportunity: A Theory of Delinquent Gangs* (first edition 1960), and Lewis Yablonski's *The Violent Gang* (first edition 1962).[191] The titles of these three well-known publications indicate that they deal selectively with topics that had not only received much attention in the books by Thrasher, Shaw, and McKay, but that also play an important role in the theories propounded by Sutherland, Merton, and Sellin. It is obvious that the way these three "classic" studies deal with this empirical and theoretical heritage is in itself a source of discussion, and remains so. Francis Cullen, for example, pointed out in the 1980s – correctly in my view – that many readers of the book by Cloward and Ohlin too readily view that study only in the context of Merton's anomie theory, wrongly overlooking how much that book also depends on the research by Thrasher, Shaw, and McKay.[192]

Because the problem of (juvenile) gangs is still a major problem in many American cities, it is not surprising that they continue to be an object of research. A good sense of the research that has been carried out is provided in the publications by Scott Cummings and Daniel Monti's *Gangs* (first edition 1993), Clarence Huff's *Gangs in America* (first edition 1993), and Malcolm Klein's *The American Street Gang* (first edition 1995).[193] Not only do these publications shed light on the theoretical discussions that took place in the second half of the twentieth century on the circumstances in which gangs emerge and on their internal and external social effect, they also clarify the legal and illegal activities in which these gangs engage in order to survive in the tough world in which they must operate. Among the interesting points are the (increasing) violence of many gangs, their extensive involvement in the distribution of narcotics, and the difficulties involved in combatting the problem of gangs effectively.

It is worth noting that the anomie theory, in particular, not only influenced research on the development of juvenile gangs, but is still regarded, including in a much wider context, as an important theoretical aid to investigating the origin, nature, extent, development, etc. of deviant, in particular criminal, behaviour in general.[194] That does not mean, of course, that that theory has been tested, so to speak, automatically, for example on the distribution of crime across urban

---

[191]   Cohen (A.) 1967; Cloward and Ohlin 1969; Yablonsky 1967; Miller 1958; Matza 1967.
[192]   Cullen 1988, pp. 214–240.
[193]   Cummings and Monti 1993; Huff 1990; Klein 1997.
[194]   Messner and Rosenfeld 1997.

neighbourhoods or on the manifestation of certain types of criminal behaviour in tense social relationships. Quite the contrary: its application has always been accompanied by critical discussion of the strengths and weaknesses of its claims, specifically as these become apparent in practice.[195] In addition, the actual application of the anomie theory has also led to proposals for refining or broadening some of its components.[196] One example of this is the attempts to give a clear place in the theory to the intense psychological feelings that arise through the frustrating effect of a situation in which one does not have sufficient opportunity to achieve centrally shared objectives.[197]

It should be noted in relation to this that, around the turn of the twentieth century, the differential association theory no longer held as much sway as the anomie theory. Not that it has disappeared completely, nor that components of it are not still respected or applied in a different way than was previously the case, but it has clearly lost much of its appeal.[198] For many years now, no individual studies or collections of articles have been devoted to this theory. It is difficult to say why that is so. It may be that this theory has to a significant extent been absorbed by new theories on the causation of criminal behaviour. What may also play a role, however, is that it is not as well suited to large- or small-scale quantitative research and has therefore fallen out of favour for that reason.

Finally, it may be noted that the biographical/autobiographical method has also been followed on a relatively limited scale. Partly in view of the success of *The Jack-Roller* and *The Professional Thief*, it is not surprising that similar monographs have been produced, based on the story of only a single criminal. These include, in particular, the studies by Carl Klockars and Darrell Steffensmeier on the "fence" (i.e. professional receiver of stolen goods).[199] Since the 1950s, there have also been some probing studies of certain categories of criminals. Good examples are that by Cressey, Sutherland's right-hand man, on fraud and fraudsters,[200] and that by Edwin Lemert on cheque forgers.[201]

9.5.4. SOCIOLOGY OF ORGANISED CRIME: FREDERIC THRASHER AND JOHN LANDESCO

The literature published in the United States since the 1960s on the history of organised crime could easily create the impression, both there and in other

---

195 Agnew 1999; Bernburg 2002; Baumer 2007.
196 Murphy and Robinson 2008; Clinard 1964a; Ortmann 2000; Adler and Laufer 2000; Smith and Bohm 2008; Agnew and Kaufman 2010.
197 Konty 2005.
198 See, for example, Matsueda 1988; McCarthy 1996; Matsueda 2006.
199 Klockars 1974; Steffensmeier 1986.
200 Cressey 1953. See also Polsky 1971; Irwin 1987; Hobbs 1995.
201 Lemert 1967, pp. 99–134.

countries, that organised crime in America was not only a form of crime perpetrated mainly by *La Cosa Nostra* but also crime the emergence of which was linked to the Prohibition of the 1920s. Both those assertions are entirely incorrect.[202]

From the late nineteenth century, gangs of various origin in the major American cities were in fact engaged in racketeering (i.e. extortion of individuals, businesses, and industries), prostitution and illegal gambling, and in resolving violent conflicts between employers and workers. These included Italian gangs, of course, but also Chinese, Jewish, and Irish gangs. That is in fact also shown by the study by Thrasher already referred to.

Given their past, by around 1920 many of these gangs had the infrastructure, manpower, and skills – but also the corrupt links to politicians, the police, and the judicial authorities – that enabled them to operate successfully in the illegal production and distribution of alcohol. These strengths also were very useful in acquiring dominant positions in legal markets such as construction, textiles, and food supply.[203]

9.5.4.1. *Frederic Thrasher's* The Gang: *The Eye-Opener*

The point, however, is that until the late 1920s criminologists and criminal lawyers paid little or no attention to the problem of organised crime. The first time it became an issue for them was in 1927, when Thrasher's book about Chicago gangs devoted several sections to the links between the gangs and organised crime.[204] Thrasher begins his main observations on this topic with the proposition: "The seriousness of modern crime grows largely out of the fact that it has been ceased to be sporadic and occasional and has become organized and continuous."

For anyone somewhat acquainted with the literature on the gangs that had emerged in Europe in the eighteenth and nineteenth centuries, that would of course have been a rather odd basic assumption, but let us not digress. What is more interesting is that Thrasher describes how in Chicago the juvenile gangs and the gangs belonging to the hard core of organised crime could not be separated but in fact merged into one another, as it were: the former supplied manpower for the latter and sometimes gradually even took on the form of a gang itself, they operated to a large extent within the same territory and the same contested sectors of the economy, they worked together from time to time in all kinds of fields, etc.

---

[202]   Fijnaut 2013a.
[203]   Nelli 1976; Asbury 1990; Fried 1993; Durney 2000; Kavieff 2000; McIllwain 2004; Reppetto 2005; Critchley 2009; Lombardo 2010.
[204]   Thrasher 1963, pp. 281–359.

If one considers organised crime in isolation, Thrasher writes, then one sees not "a vast edifice of hard and fast structures" but a "surprising amount of organization of a kind in the criminal community":

> there is a certain division of labor manifesting itself in specialized persons and specialized groups performing different but related functions. There are, furthermore, alliances and federations of persons and groups, although no relationship can be as fixed and lasting as in the organization of legitimate business.[205]

He goes on to say that not every gang was structured the same. Some were able to maintain themselves on the outskirts of town on their own, while others were dependent for their survival in the inner city on political and administrative support. There were also others that had political connections and were violent towards opponents but that were successful mainly because their illegal activities were very efficiently organised using a business model. The latter type – the "master gangs" – formed, as it were, the top echelon because such a gang was a "more permanent and powerful group which has great resources in money, political influence, and intelligence". It was also the case that gang members could quite easily switch from one gang to another. They did so because for the "new type of gangster" the pursuit of profit was the main reason for joining a gang. In other words, such people went where the most money could be earned.

Needless to say, it was precisely these "master gangs" that caused great harm to society. Not only did they make a lot of money with their illegal activities, but they were also quite prepared to murder people in defence of their interests, thus terrorising whole communities. This was precisely why bosses, both political and others, quickly proceeded to strike deals with them. Gangs could in fact be used to break strikes or to protect them. According to Thrasher, there was absolutely no doubt that this enabled them to increase their political influence. Political bosses, in particular, were happy to make gangs part of the political machine that they needed in order to win or retain power in the city. One way of disguising that link was to conceal gangs within sports clubs.

9.5.4.2. John Landesco: Chicago in the Grip of Organised Crime

The above observations by Thrasher can be regarded as the prelude to the extensive study on organised crime in Chicago carried out by John Landesco in the late 1920s in the framework of the *Illinois Crime Survey*. In just under 300 pages, Landesco describes the organisation, operations, criminal activities, and political and business links of, in particular, the Torrio–Capone syndicate in the city. He deals with how that syndicate operated in the fields of prostitution, gambling, and naturally the market for alcohol. He also discusses their racketeering in

---

[205] Thrasher 1963, p. 286.

connection with laundries and food markets. And he explains how that was to a large extent made possible not only by their breaking resistance within the relevant market by means of a great deal of violence, but also by their building up and maintaining close corrupt relationships at the level of the city authorities.[206]

ORGANIZED CRIME IN CHICAGO

By

JOHN LANDESCO

ILLINOIS ASSOCIATION FOR CRIMINAL JUSTICE (ed.), *The Illinois Crime Survey*, Montclair, Patterson Smith, 1968, Chapter XVI–XXVII: John Landesco: *Organized Crime in Chicago*, p. 815–1090.

The beginning of Landesco's study reads as if it were the conclusion:

> It discloses a startling and amazing story of the interlocking interests of gambling, bootlegging, vice, and politics. Back of this organized crime and this organized corruption is syndicated vice, syndicated gambling, syndicated prostitution and syndicated liquor selling. [...] Not the least of the disclosures that have been made are those of the permanence of the reigns of the lords of the underworld and the introduction of the capitalistic system into their operations. [...] The illegal liquor business furnishes a stable means of livelihood for many of our confirmed robbers and burglars, and these captains of the underworld have been able to rally to their support the suffrages of a large portion of our population. By becoming political powers, they have been able not only to secure immunity for themselves, but in a large measure to make our city government itself a partner in crime.[207]

---

206   Landesco 1968.
207   Landesco 1968, pp. 815–816.

Landesco then deals in detail with the topics listed above (too many to discuss at length here). However, the conclusions to the successive chapters are still eye-openers as regards the crime situation that prevailed in Chicago in the 1920s. Where prostitution is concerned, Landesco concludes, for example, that it was deeply rooted in the city's social and political order. This had led, inter alia, to enforcement of the relevant legislation taking place subject to the political protection that the brothels enjoyed. And when Prohibition came into force, it was precisely those who had built up a strong position in the prostitution market who saw an opportunity to take over "the systematic organization of this new and profitable field of exploitation".[208] In that connection, some paragraphs on the beer wars in the conclusion to the chapter speak volumes:

> In the war of rival factions which followed [after the collapse of the policies pursued by the administration of Mayor William Dever], the gang code of silence and personal vengeance rather than legal redress was so compelling that of the two hundred fifteen murders of gangsters during four years of armed strife, only a handful of arrests and no convictions were secured by the law enforcement agencies. But the police, forced apparently to resort to shooting it out in running battle, succeeded in killing one hundred sixty gangsters during this same period. While the heavy casualties of the beer war did not lead to the extermination of the gangsters, as many law-abiding citizens optimistically expected, they did induce the leading gangsters, for different reasons, to agree to peace terms which defined the territory within which each gang or syndicate might operate without competition and beyond which it should not encroach upon the territories of others.[209]

In his chapter on the use of bombs to settle conflicts, Landesco indicates, however, that such a geographical peace agreement in the Chicago underworld was not sufficient to bring organised violence under control right across the city. Conflicts about acquiring political office, conflicts between whites and blacks, and between employers and trade unions still provoked a great deal of armed violence. It was noteworthy that all parties hired "strong-arm gangs" and "professional bombers" in order to gain or maintain the upper hand in such conflicts. As a result, these "gunmen, bombers and gangsters" were able to turn their violence into a business and could thus develop into racketeers who intervened, sometimes on their own initiative and sometimes by invitation, in the violent resolution of conflicts.[210]

Landesco then describes how racketeering had become fully incorporated into the economy:

> In "racketeering" the gunman and the ex-convict have seized control of business associations and have organized mushroom labor unions and have maintained or

---

[208]   Landesco 1968, p. 863.
[209]   Landesco 1968, pp. 930–931.
[210]   Landesco 1968, pp. 974–975.

raised price and personal profit. The rule of violence now controls scores of business fields, according to Mr. Walter G. Walker, formerly of the state's attorney's office. The entrance of the gangster and gunman into the field of business and industry in Chicago seems to be due to two factors: 1. A situation of cutthroat competition among small business enterprises [...] 2. A tradition of lawlessness and violence in Chicago.[211]

Finally, it is appropriate to return to the introduction to Landesco's study, and in particular to his comments on the enormous importance of political protection in the commission of organised crime. He sums up what that actually meant in the conclusion to the chapter on that cynical relationship, particularly as regarded the specific links between Al Capone and politicians. In Capone's case:

> Neighborliness and friendly relations recede to the background. Operations in crime and political protection from its consequences are no longer local but city-wide. Immunity is no longer obtained by friendship, but from graft. Organized crime and organized political corruption have formed a partnership to exploit for profit the enormous revenues to be derived from law breaking.[212]

That analysis of the situation in Chicago was confirmed, as it were, in the mid-1930s by an equally famous study as that by Landesco, namely the investigation by William Whyte of the environment in one of the Italian slums in Boston, which he first published in 1943 under the title *Street Corner Society*.[213]

Equally important, however, is the fact that that study showed that, after Prohibition, the gangsters had pursued their further collective wellbeing in the large-scale organisation of illegal gambling: casinos, slot machines, horse racing, illegal lotteries, etc. In that way, they also gained a great deal of influence over the businesses involved in selling lottery tickets. The gangsters then used the money earned through gambling to invest in legitimate businesses. And it was not only in Chicago that legitimate businesses were infiltrated in this way. That is shown not only by studies such as that by Humbert Nelli that were carried out much later in order to understand the development of organised crime in the 1930s, but also by publications dating from that period itself.

There was, for example, the National Commission on Law Observance and Enforcement, the (George) Wickersham Commission. In its final report, the Commission did not go very deeply into the role played by Prohibition in the development of organised crime as such, but its conclusion that it was better to abolish that legislation and to regulate the alcohol issue differently spoke volumes.[214] Matters were made clearer by a number of presentations at

---

[211]   Landesco 1968, pp. 996–997.
[212]   Landesco 1968, p. 1021.
[213]   Whyte 1955; Whyte 1993.
[214]   *Enforcement* 1931.

a 1934 conference organised by the United States Attorney General on topics including organised crime and how to combat it. At the conference, the New York State Attorney General said that: "commercial racketeering in the United States is one of the most revolting forms of modern organized crime. It constitutes not

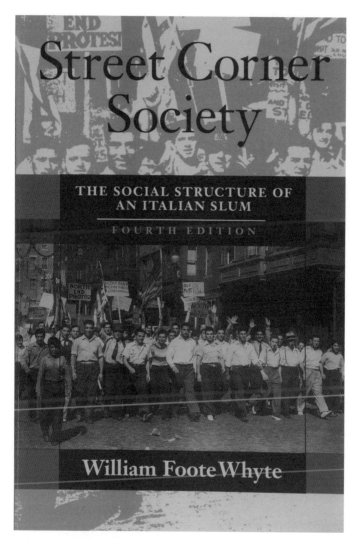

William WHYTE, *Street Corner Society: The Social Structure of an Italian Slum*, Chicago, University of Chicago Press, 1993.

only a menace to society, but a challenge to legitimate business everywhere." He explained how racketeering operated in actual practice by referring to the laundry sector. In 1932, that entire sector in New York had fallen into the hands of a "notorious racketeer with a long criminal record". Criminal investigation into his role in that sector was no simple matter because the closer prosecutors got to him, the more they were confronted by the "code of silence".[215] The Attorney General referred hardly at all – perhaps understandably, given his position – to the role of politicians in the success of organised crime, something that was naturally rather strange.

In 1934, Sutherland in any case stated – in the second edition of his *Principles of Criminology* – that the powerful position of organised crime was due in the first place to the fact that, since at least the end of the nineteenth century, political parties – or powerful politicians at any rate – had for various reasons collaborated closely and systematically with influential criminals in their area. Second, he ascribed that powerful position to the fact that since then corruption within the police, judicial officials, and administrators had reached endemic proportions. As a result, criminal gangs in many American cities had free rein to organise their illegal activities within both black and legitimate markets. Sutherland wrote: "Protection against arrest and conviction is a necessary part of organized crime. [...] The techniques of fixing crimes are much more important than the techniques of executing crimes."[216]

What we must certainly not overlook in relation to this is *The Police and Modern Society*, published in 1936 by August Vollmer, a scholarly but highly experienced police chief who will be dealt with in more detail below. In that book, Vollmer in fact provides a crystal-clear explanation – very much in the vein of Landesco – of how the problem of organised crime had infected the country's illegal and legal economy and its politics system, and how difficult it would be to curb it. In one section after another, he describes the nature of that problem in various sectors: how criminal gangs had penetrated into every part of society, how racketeers had made themselves masters of whole areas of commerce, how they had turned kidnapping into a full-scale industry, and how they had gained control of prostitution, gambling, alcohol distribution, and the sale of narcotics.

It is interesting, incidentally, that Vollmer was sceptical about the enforcement of the relevant legislation by the local police. Given all the problems with corruption, he was very concerned about police integrity and therefore professionalism.[217] However, responsibility for this police task could not simply be transferred to the state police, let alone to the federal police services such as the Federal Bureau of Investigation (FBI), the Secret Service, or the Intelligence Unit at the Internal Revenue Service, no matter how important the role of the latter had been in the arrest and conviction of Al Capone.[218]

---

[215]   *Proceedings* 1934, pp. 46–49; MacDougall 1933.
[216]   Sutherland 1934, pp. 189–190.
[217]   Vollmer 1936, pp. 65–118; Lynch (D.) 1932; Reckless 1950, pp. 129–160; Tannenbaum 1938.
[218]   Millspauch 1937.

9.5.4.3. Congressional Investigations: Estes Kefauver, John McClellan, and Robert Kennedy

Despite the problem of organised crime having taken on such huge proportions, it was no easy matter to gain Congressional approval for a rigorous federal approach to that problem. To a certain extent, the road towards such an approach was opened up in 1951 by the United States Senate Special Committee to Investigate Crime in Interstate Commerce, chaired by Estes Kefauver. For anyone familiar with the analyses produced in the 1930s, the committee's appalling conclusion was not unexpected:

> There is a sinister criminal organization known as the Mafia operating throughout the country with ties to other nations in the opinion of the committee. The Mafia is the direct descendant of a criminal organization of the same name originating in the island of Sicily. In this country, the Mafia has also been known as the Black Hand and the Unione Siciliano. The membership of the Mafia today is not confined to persons of Sicilian origin. [...] The Mafia is the binder which ties together two major criminal syndicates as well as numerous other criminal groups throughout the country.[219]

That conclusion was already controversial as soon as it was presented. On the one hand, its empirical basis was disputed and, on the other, it was seen as a party-political statement.[220] That does not alter the fact, however, that the conclusion was to an extent supported by the reports from the 1930s as well as by all kinds of reports drawn up in the early 1950s. It is therefore not surprising that the views of the Kefauver Committee were echoed in the reports of various Senate committees, chaired by John McClellan and Robert Kennedy, which, around 1960, investigated racketeering within the trade union movement and illegal drug dealing.[221]

They were echoed even more in the 1968 report of the President's Commission on Law Enforcement and Administration of Justice: *The Challenge of Crime in a Free Society*.[222] The first line of the chapter on the problem of organised crime allowed no misunderstanding as to the seriousness of the situation: "Organized crime is a society that seeks to operate outside the control of the American people and their governments". This was an entirely clear reference to *La Cosa Nostra*, with its "families" in many large cities and its national coordinating structure.

Beginning from that presentation of the problem, it is not surprising that the commission proposed implementing tough measures to avert that danger, namely increased powers for the police and prosecution authorities to infiltrate

---

[219]   United States Senate 1951, p. 2; Kefauver 1952; Caldwell 1956, pp. 72–111; Barnes and Teeters 1959, pp. 17–37; Von Hentig 1959.
[220]   Moore 1974; Bloch and Geis 1970, pp. 190–217.
[221]   Jacobs (J.) 2006, pp. 13–15; Kennedy 1960; Tyler 1962.
[222]   *Challenge* 1968; Clark 1970, pp. 56–100.

and to wire-tap, the establishment of special investigation units in cities and states, the introduction of the option for the accused to become a crown witness, witness protection, etc. It took until the 1980s before this offensive had its full effect in actual practice, but it was then in fact highly successful,

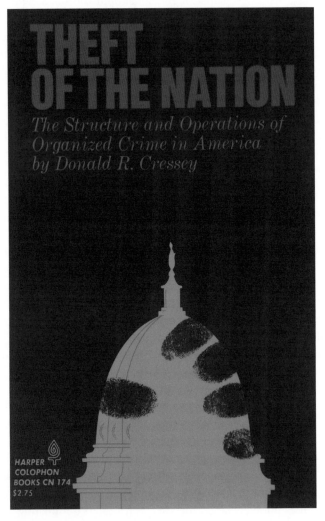

Donald CRESSEY, *Theft of the Nation: The Structure and Operations of Organized Crime in America*, New York, Harper & Row, 1969.

as James Jacobs and his colleagues have demonstrated in a number of books.[223] It is also certain that on a number of occasions things went badly wrong. One of the most notorious cases is the far too extensive cooperation between an FBI

---

[223] Jacobs, Panarella and Worthington 1994; Jacobs, Friel and Radick 1999; Kelly 1999; Woodiwiss 2001.

agent and the boss of the Irish underworld in Boston, James "Whitey" Bulger, in exchange for information about *La Cosa Nostra* in that city.[224]

Finally, it is also relevant to note that one of the most famous American criminologists of the time, Cressey, was responsible for the picture of organised crime in the United States outlined in the latter report.[225] That involvement led

James JACOBS, Coleen FRIEL and Robert RADICK, *Gotham Unbound: How New York City was Liberated from the Grip of Organized Crime*, New York, New York University Press, 1999.

to his being caught up in the crossfire of an academic and journalistic debate about the nature of organised crime. That debate concerned not only the way *La Cosa Nostra* was portrayed as a kind of foreign power that was attempting to gain a hold on the United States, but also the way all the other forms of serious (organised) crime in the country were disregarded.[226]

---

224 Lehr and O'Neill 2000.
225 Cressey 1969; Cressey 1972.
226 Kenney and Finckenauer 1995, pp. 242–255; Smith (D.) 1975; Chambliss 1988.

9.5.5.   EDWIN SUTHERLAND: *WHITE COLLAR CRIME* OR THE REDEFINITION OF CRIMINOLOGY

Sutherland owes his prominent place in the history of criminology not only to *Principles of Criminology* and *The Professional Thief* but also to *White Collar Crime*, which was published in 1949. This is a revolutionary book, one that comprises

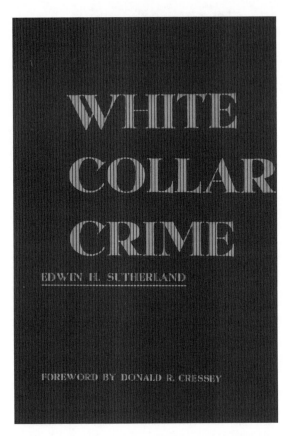

Edwin SUTHERLAND, *White Collar Crime*, New York, Holt, Richard and Winston, 1961 (foreword by D. CRESSEY).

nothing more nor less than a redefinition of the essential object of criminology: what is crime? The book does not concern itself with theft, burglary, rape, and other categories of traditional property crimes and crimes of violence but with extremely drastic and very harmful misdeeds by 70 of the largest US companies in several key sectors of the legitimate economy. And those crimes can hardly be explained by means of bio-criminological theories regarding the person or the family of the perpetrator, nor by criminal-sociological theories in which, for example, physical deterioration and social disorganisation play a crucial role at a neighbourhood level.[227]

It is consequently understandable that the manuscript was not immediately welcomed with open arms. The anxiety of the publisher and the board of Indiana University about costly civil actions brought by the relevant white-collar criminals led not only to their names being deleted from the text but also to a number of case studies being removed. In his preface, Sutherland did not say that that was the reason for those changes. Rather, he stated that other scientific books also concealed the identity of criminals and that anonymising them was in this case more suited to the scientific objective of the study.[228] The introduction by Gilbert Geis and Colin Goff to the "uncut version", however, shows that these were to some extent specious arguments.[229] The fact that Sutherland felt forced to cooperate in this concealment was in fact all the more evidence for one of his propositions in the book: the companies concerned, and others, had not only the power to prevent their misdeeds from being the object of criminal penalties, but also the power to prevent those practices from being revealed through lawsuits, press releases, etc.

No revolution is ever total, but there are always portents that herald a radical change. It was not only Sutherland who in the foregoing decades had more than once criticised all kinds of practices by big business that he considered highly reprehensible.[230] Other authors had already to such practices as far back as the late nineteenth century. Sanford Green, for example, in his aforementioned book on the nature and causes of crime, had also strongly denounced "the aggressions of capital upon the rights of the people". From a moral perspective, according to Green, practices such as those in which thousands of workers were treated like slaves "who inherit neither wealth nor privilege", and who – if it suited the owners for the sake of increasing their profit – were sacked out of hand and condemned to grinding poverty, were on a par with piracy and robbery. In his view, such companies should be tackled immediately because they constituted a serious threat to the good governance of the country: "Our danger does not arise from our great national prosperity, nor the increased production of material wealth, but from allowing it to be grasped by a few, instead of benefiting the many."[231]

The undertone of *White Collar Crime* is certainly one of similar political and moral outrage at what was happening in corporate America. But that outrage is not so strong as to make the book a kind of political pamphlet. Quite the contrary, the book is in fact the result of years of laborious research, conducted

---

227   Sutherland 1983, pp. 5–9.
228   Sutherland 1961, pp. XIII–XIV.
229   Sutherland 1983, pp. X–XIII.
230   Sutherland 1983, pp. XIV–XXI.
231   Green 1889, pp. 301–311.

together with students, into the white-collar crime perpetrated by major American companies in the previous decades.

Sutherland sets out the book's thesis on pages 9 and 10, namely:

> that persons of the upper socio-economic class engage in much criminal behavior; that this criminal behavior differs from the criminal behavior of the lower socio-economic class principally in the administrative procedures which are used in dealing with the offenders; and that variations in administrative procedures are not significant from the point of view of causation of crime.

He goes on to define what constitutes white-collar crime: "White collar crime may be defined approximately as a crime committed by a person of respectability and high social status in the course of his occupation."

As is made clear later in the book, what Sutherland really meant by "administrative procedures" was that much of the criminal behaviour in the higher socio-economic class was not in fact defined in criminal legislation and was not dealt with by usual criminal proceedings.[232] He goes on to say that that did not mean, however, that it was not in fact genuine crime.

According to Sutherland, the point is in fact that the socio-economic class concerned has the power, if not to prevent its misdeeds being criminalised in legislation but at least to prevent their being curbed via the civil and administrative law and thus to prevent those misdeeds being stigmatised as crimes. In their case, moreover, the criminal behaviour concerned is extremely harmful to society. Not only does it cause great financial damage but, more importantly, it also profoundly violates social relations within society:

> White collar crimes violate trust and therefore create distrust; this lowers social morale and produces social disorganization. Many of the white collar crimes attack the fundamental principles of the American institutions. Ordinary crimes, on the other hand, produce little effect on social institutions or social organization.[233]

In Chapters 5–13, Sutherland then discusses the "criminal records" of 70 companies (in Chapter 3 of the unabridged version, including the three "case histories"). The misconduct denounced here includes forms of unfair competition through the formation of cartels, circumvention of patents and copyrights, unfair regulation of labour relations, violation of environmental legislation, and manipulation of financial regulations.

The final part of the book is largely a recapitulation of the topics already dealt with in the introductory part. The first question is whether white-collar crime can be considered to be organised crime. Sutherland answers that

---

232   Sutherland 1961, pp. 29–55.
233   Sutherland 1961, p. 13.

question primarily by comparing white-collar crime to professional theft, seeing both similarities and differences. Among the similarities, he says, are that big companies, like professional thieves, are notorious repeat offenders, that they also have a great antipathy to the authorities, particularly the police and judicial authorities, and that they also genuinely organise their misconduct. The main difference is that white-collar criminals, for all kinds of reasons, do not view themselves as criminals. They are not dealt with by means of the same (criminal) proceedings and they do not move in circles in which one defines oneself as a criminal. Nor are they regarded as criminals within their circle of acquaintances.

Sutherland points out, moreover, that companies use all sorts of methods to conceal the criminal nature of their conduct. In the first place, they often commit crimes for which they have little to fear from the victims because the latter are "scattered, unorganized, lacking in objective information as to the qualities of commodities". Second, they often chose to perpetrate crimes that are difficult to prove. And third, when the pressure is on, businesses – like professional thieves – engage in "fixing", i.e. they not only attempt to avoid prosecution but also try to prevent the law being enforced and even try to ensure good will towards them on the part of the general public.

For these and other reasons, Sutherland concludes at the end of this chapter:

> the violations of law by corporations are deliberate and organized crime. This does not mean that corporations never violate the law inadvertently and in an unorganized manner. It does mean that a substantial portion of their violations are deliberate and organized.[234]

It is striking, finally, that in Chapter 14 – the chapter on the theory of white-collar crime – Sutherland states:

> white collar crime has its genesis in the same general process as other criminal behavior, namely, differential association. The hypothesis of differential association is that criminal behavior is learned in association with those who define such behavior favorably and in isolation from those who define it unfavorably, and that a person in an appropriate situation engages in such criminal behavior if, and only if, the weight of the favorable definitions exceeds the weight of the unfavorable definitions.

Sutherland goes on to say that anyone who reads the biographies or autobiographies of businessmen and is familiar with documents like for example letters and confidential reports of meetings that reveal how criminal practices become disseminated among them, will know that this hypothesis also applies to such businessmen. White-collar criminals too – just like professional thieves – learn from other white-collar criminals how to perpetrate white-collar crime. The

---

[234]   Sutherland 1961, p. 233.

spread of illegal practices is encouraged, on the one hand, by the centralisation of sectors by investment bankers and, on the other, via the conferences for companies organised by commercial associations. That white-collar criminals can go their own merry way is made possible by the fact, inter alia, that neither the media nor the authorities like to be tough with them in public.

One might add here that white-collar criminals in the United States (and elsewhere) do not usually have much to fear from academia. That may be a strange statement to make in relation to such a challenging and important book, but it is a fact. In the second half of the twentieth century, there was some research here and there, but more or less original projects were very rare.[235] This naturally raises the question of why that was the case. Was it because of a fear of the power that large companies can exert at the expense of researchers? Was it because researchers did not usually have sufficient technical knowledge to fully comprehend the illegal practices concerned? Was it because institutions whose task it was to finance research did not wish to devote funds to such criminological research? Or was it a combination of all of these reasons?

9.6. INFLUENCE OF CRIMINOLOGY ON THE CRIMINAL JUSTICE SYSTEM

It has been made abundantly clear in the foregoing that, from the 1910s on, criminological research was applied in some major American cities – led by Chicago and Boston – in particular as a means of gaining a better understanding of the personality of the juvenile delinquent, of how he should be dealt with both intramurally and extramurally, and of how juvenile delinquency should in general be prevented and combatted. This raises the question, however, of what was done with the insights and proposals propounded in the major criminological treatises of around 1900 about the prison system in particular, but also about the police and to some extent the judiciary. An attempt will be made below – without any claim to completeness – to give a broad answer to that question.

9.6.1. TRANSFORMATION OF THE PRISON SYSTEM

Dugdale, who had been so critical of the prison system in the State of New York in 1877, had at the same time been very enthusiastic about the creation of the Elmira Reformatory: together with the radical shift in the entire penitentiary

---

235   Geis and Meier 1977; Hochstedler 1984; Coleman 1985; Pearce and Snider 1995.

policy, that institution, he found, had already brought about legal and organisational changes "which give great promise". At the end of his book he moderated that enthusiasm somewhat – "[s]hall the Elmira Reformatory be this opportunity and become a new departure, or be a base repetition of the present failure?" – but he nevertheless considered the construction of that prison to be a major step forward.[236] Nor was he the only one who thought so.

Green, who in 1889 – as has been mentioned – was able still to write a book about the nature and causes of crime without reference to Lombroso, agreed. In that book, he was in any case very critical of the prison system in the United States. In particular, he criticised the "leasing" of detainees to private individuals and businesses "to work in the fields, on railroads, or in the mines". Those parties had only a single interest in leasing them, namely "to get the greatest possible amount of work from them, at the least possible expense to themselves". Reforming the detainees in question was the last thing on their minds. Those who wanted to achieve such reform needed to replace the infamous "nurseries of crime" with a system of reformatories with an appropriate regime, personnel, facilities, etc.[237]

It was not just these two individual authors who, after the Civil War, were highly critical of the prison system and in particular the prisons that had been set up between 1820 and 1830 in the States of New York and Pennsylvania. In the mid-nineteenth century, a whole range of publications had criticised the unhealthy construction of the prison complexes, the negative effects of the regimes on the mental health of the detainees, the total lack of any individualisation of treatment, and, in that connection, the lack of opportunities for accused persons to be sentenced and/or released conditionally. Needless to say, the proponents of these penal systems did everything possible to ward off this criticism; however, they constantly struggled to counter one particular argument, namely that there was absolutely no evidence that the systems were effective in preventing recidivism.[238]

This led to the gradual emergence in political circles of more and more support for a fundamentally different approach. This became most clearly apparent in the State of Pennsylvania from the fact that all kinds of changes in the regime essentially represented an increasing shift away from permanent solitary confinement. That was in fact unavoidable because the overcrowding in the prisons meant that the system was simply no longer manageable. In 1913, the Eastern Penitentiary formally abandoned this form of detention entirely. The fact that the relevant legislation did not arouse any debate adequately demonstrates that the system in fact no longer existed. Two years previously, in 1911, an

---

[236] Dugdale 1884, pp. 114, 120.
[237] Green 1889, pp. 167–175, 218–219; Alschuler 2003.
[238] Pisciotta 1994, pp. 8–13.

amendment had already made release on probation possible for adult detainees. The creation of the facilities necessary to implement this measure properly was finalised in 1927 with the establishment of the State Probation Bureau.[239]

9.6.1.1. Elmira: The Demise of a Puritanical Ideal

New York State did not wait that long; legislators were already willing to break with the existing system in the early 1870s. That had a great deal to do with the resolutions adopted by the International Penitentiary Congress held in Cincinnati in October 1870. The Congress in fact adopted a *Déclaration des principes de discipline pénitentiaire*, which formed the basis for large-scale innovation in the prison system in the United States and other countries.[240] The declaration comprised no fewer than 51 principles, some of them only brief, but others often of considerable length. They included, for example:

- the penalty must aim to prevent recidivism; indeterminate sentences should be introduced everywhere with a view to reforming detainees;
- the treatment of offenders is intended to protect society; in essence, the interests of society and of the detainee coincide;
- the highest purpose of a prison regime is the moral improvement of criminals and not their physical chastisement in a spirit of retaliation; systematic persuasion must replace coercion and compulsion; violence perhaps makes for good prisoners but it does not create free, loyal, and industrious citizens;
- the problem of reforming offenders has not yet been resolved: a small number of them are changed by their imprisonment; the vast majority, however, leave prison just as callous and dangerous as when they went in;
- in all prisons, a progressive classification of prisoners should be introduced, based on improvements in their behaviour; proper work is of great importance to achieve this goal;
- the prison system must be kept free of political interference and must focus entirely on education, discipline, and religion; all prison staff must be specially trained to achieve this; and
- the state has a duty of care towards ex-prisoners: it must support them, inter alia, by providing them with work and must encourage them to take their place within society once more.

It should be noted in relation to this summary that the declaration in its entirety reveals a very religious mood. Religion is even referred to in principle 10 as the main means of reforming detainees; that principle goes on to state that measures that are not based on religion cannot in fact be effective. Moreover, the Congress

---

[239]   Barnes 1927, pp. 288–310, 367–374.
[240]   Ver Loren van Themaat 1911, 2, pp. 346–380; Lewis 1917, pp. 26–27.

was also very much concerned with combatting the consumption of alcohol. In the view of a number of speakers, alcohol was one of the main causes of crime and other social problems. For that reason too, it can be said that the meeting had a very puritanical character.[241]

Where America was concerned, those principles meant, in practical terms, that reformatories had to combine three elements: the imposition of indeterminate sentences with a view to the personality of the offender, the introduction of a progressive ("Irish") regime in the prisons aimed at reforming the prisoners, and the introduction of release on parole.[242] The prison where all these new principles were put into practice for the first time was the Elmira Reformatory in New York State. The decision was already taken in 1869 to build an "industrial reformatory" for detainees aged 16–30, and building was completed in 1876.[243] Right from when it was opened, the prison was publicised, with a major public relations campaign, as the prison of the future. News of the prison spread quickly, and like the prison in Leuven in 1860, the Elmira Reformatory aroused interest worldwide and was visited by prison experts and prison reformers from all over the world. It was also replicated not only in other American states but also in many other countries.[244]

At the 1870 Congress, the high-profile first director of the Elmira Reformatory, Zebulon Brockway, not only gave lectures but was also closely involved in drawing up the declaration of principles.[245] There was therefore nobody better suited to making the institution a success. In addition to regular religious meetings, Brockway organised a system of school classes (for beginners and advanced pupils) and workshops (for woodworking, iron casting, etc.) in order to turn those whom he termed worthless people into valuable people. Partly because of this, the detainees were subjected to harsh discipline. They rose each morning at 5.15 am, cleaned their cell, had breakfast, worked (for a pittance) until noon, had lunch, and then continued working until 4.30 pm. The early evening was devoted to schooling. In the 1880s, the facilities at Elmira were expanded to include a school for art education. In 1888, all the detainees – on the pattern of the United States Military Academy at West Point – were divided into companies that paraded each day with dummy weapons, accompanied by a band.

To determine how the regime should be applied in each particular case, every new detainee was not only given a bath and measured for a uniform but also had a personal interview with Brockway. A decision was then taken, mainly on

---

[241]   Jenkins 1984b.
[242]   Barnes 1927, pp. 315–316; Simon (J.) 1993, pp. 24–59.
[243]   Pisciotta 1983, p. 614.
[244]   Pisciotta 1994, pp. 81–103.
[245]   Barnes 1927, pp. 334–335.

the basis of the interview, on which school class the inmate should be placed in and which trade he would learn. In the second phase, depending on his progress he was then awarded points for the things he did well each day at school or in the workplace. Conversely, if he misbehaved in some way, points were deducted from his total. If he earned sufficient points, he was then promoted to the third phase, namely parole. This phase not only meant a relaxation of the internal regime at Elmira – the inmate would no longer be required, for example, to walk in lockstep and had greater freedom to write letters – but also meant placement, subject to certain conditions, with a local employer. If an inmate or parolee did not comply with the conditions and failed, for example, to remain for six months with the same employer or behaved badly in the town where he was allowed to live, he was brought back to Elmira and had to remain imprisoned there longer as a punishment.[246]

But even though the Elmira Reformatory was already based on the optimistic idea that detainees are basically open to reform and thus are not doomed – by physical characteristics (whether or not inherited) – to commit crime, the institution was gradually unable to ignore the advent of Lombrosian criminology. In the course of the 1880s, one of the doctors, Hamilton Wey, in any case began to think that, although there was no question of a "criminal brain", certain physical and mental features – for example, certain abnormalities of the skull and the small (or indeed large) size of the heads of the various categories of prisoners – indicated that they belonged to a criminal class within society, and thus essentially constituted a special type of people, namely criminals. In order to determine more effectively how to deal with such people within the institution, detailed anthropometric data began to be collected on each prisoner.[247]

Even though this change in the regime reinforced the idea at the time that the Elmira Reformatory was a progressive institution, the reality was fundamentally quite different. In response to complaints by prisoners and ex-prisoners about ill treatment, an investigation was launched in October 1893 into what was really going on there. The investigating committee interviewed 200 witnesses and worked its way through around 1,000 letters. The unanimous conclusion was that the complaints, particularly those regarding Brockway himself, were indeed justified. He had frequently exceeded his remit, with "cruel, brutal, excessive and unusual punishment of the inmates". He apparently considered that it was only ultimately by force, or at any rate the threat of force, that order could be maintained within the institution. A host of witnesses reported how he had beaten them in all kinds of ways in an isolated washroom. He apparently also inflicted punishments such as prolonged solitary confinement and a

---

[246] Pisciotta 1994, pp. 18–22.
[247] Fink 1938, p. 115; Pisciotta, 1983, p. 619; Pisciotta 1994, p. 24.

bread-and-water diet. Many prisoners and ex-prisoners also reported that the so very important points system was applied extremely arbitrarily.

Although these findings did not put an end to Brockway's career, they still completely destroyed the image of Elmira as an almost "scientific prison" that operated entirely according to the principles of the Cincinnati Declaration.[248] Probably as a result, proposals were made, right into the twentieth century, for changing the regime at Elmira and elsewhere in one way or another. It should be noted that those who made such proposals also included staff members of this formerly model prison.[249]

9.6.1.2. General Fiasco of the Prison System

The demise of the Elmira Reformatory should not make us lose sight of the fact that more was going on in the American prison system around 1900 than just the proliferation of this kind of reformatory. There was increasing differentiation in the prison system around that time, involving not only the establishment of asylums that also accommodated mentally disturbed criminals, but also the construction of special prisons for women and juveniles. One particularly noteworthy example of the latter was the institution for male juvenile delinquents opened in Glen Mills, Pennsylvania, in 1891. Twenty years later, in 1910, a special facility for female juvenile delinquents was established in the same state at Sleighton Farms.[250]

Nevertheless, the prison system did not receive good press in the decades that followed. There was, for example, the criticism voiced in 1911 by Hendrik Ver Loren van Themaat in his book about the care of convicts.[251] As a member of the Dutch delegation to the Congress of the International Penitentiary Commission in Washington in 1910, Ver Loren van Themaat had taken the opportunity, along with some other attendees, to visit a number of prisons, in particular reformatories, and including that at Elmira. Their impressions after that tour were in general rather negative. The boys at Elmira, for example, performed all kinds of exercises on the parade ground with great precision, but whether they were being properly re-educated in decent conditions was questionable. It was not only the fact that the whole institution was surrounded by a high wall, in some places with watchtowers full of armed guards, that aroused considerable reservations about the alleged success of the reformatory, but also the fact that in a number of respects the cells were far from meeting the applicable standards. Moreover, all the visitors wondered whether the overpopulation of the institution

---

[248] Pisciotta 1983, pp. 620–626; Pisciotta 1994, pp. 33–59; Rafter 1997, pp. 93–109.
[249] Masten 1909.
[250] Barnes 1927, pp. 330–346.
[251] Ver Loren van Themaat, 2, pp. 703–733.

in fact allowed the staff to get round to ensuring the personal re-education of each inmate.

Equally important is of course the fact that in the 1920s a number of prominent American authors were critical – sometimes very critical – of the state of the prison system. In his book *Wall Shadows*, for example, Frank Tannenbaum – based on his personal experience of being incarcerated in a number of prisons – described such matters as the violent nature of the policy applied in many prisons, the systematic efforts of prison wardens to maintain order by isolating the detainees from one another as much as possible, the poor architectural and hygienic conditions, the utter lack of differentiation in the regimes, the severe shortage of meaningful daytime activities, and the systematic absence of education and training.[252]

One might perhaps be tempted to say that this negative assessment was motivated by resentment, but publications by a number of university professors confirmed Tannenbaum's depiction of the situation. In 1926, Harry Barnes wrote, rather more academically than Tannenbaum: "Our present institutions obviously fail to achieve this result of reforming the criminal. Instead of reforming criminals, they are in reality institutions for the training of more efficient and determined criminals."[253] After touring the world and visiting all kinds of prisons, including the colony at Merksplas in Belgium, John Gillin came to the conclusion that the prison system, particularly in the Southern states, must be considered a failure if measured by its own objective, namely to turn detainees into fellow citizens who could take care of themselves in the proper manner.[254] The conclusion of the Wickersham Commission in 1931 was devastating: the current prison system, wrote the Commission, "is antiquated and inefficient. It does not reform the criminal. It fails to protect society. There is reason to believe that it contributes to the increase of crime by hardening the criminal."

Arthur Beeley, a professor of sociology at the University of Utah, elaborated on this "judgment" on the prison system. In 1935, following on from his predecessors, he discussed at length the major problems confronting the prison system at that time, such as the way solitary confinement could drive prisoners insane, the miserable living conditions in many prisons, and the lack of training opportunities and meaningful work for prisoners.[255]

The studies of the American prison system by his successors in the 1950s, 1960s, and 1970s are much less ideological and far more empirical than the academic publications referred to above. They give the impression that not much had changed since the 1930s in the central prisons of the individual states in

---

[252] Tannenbaum 1922.
[253] Barnes 1926, p. 375; Barnes and Teeters 1959, pp. 426–439.
[254] Gillin 1931, p. 291.
[255] Beeley 1935, pp. 32–50.

a number of respects, and that in any case not much was happening in those prisons to achieve the old ideal of reforming detainees. One example is Gresham Sykes' *The Society of Captives*, a study of the maximum-security prison in the State of New Jersey.[256]

The publication of that study in 1958 showed that reform of detainees was still on paper the objective of prisons, but that that in practice that objective had been largely ousted by the overriding concern of the management and staff of ensuring the safety of everyone and everything within the walls of what was – from the viewpoint of quality of life – a wretched building. The central aim of policy was to prevent escapes and riots. It was therefore not surprising that most of the prisoners confined in this – for them totalitarian – institution experienced it as "depriving or frustrating in the extreme". The riots that broke out in the 1950s were mainly a form of resistance to the extremely harsh conditions in which they had to manage to survive.[257]

Another example is the study by James Jacobs in the early 1970s of the operation of Illinois' Stateville Prison in Chicago. In that prison, which was opened in 1925, the enforcement of order had priority over all other functions and activities, partly in response to the riots and violence that had occurred in the first years of both the old and the new prisons. In 1936, Joseph Ragen, a former sheriff, was made warden of Stateville. He transformed the institution into an "efficient paramilitary organization famous and infamous throughout the world" and successfully directed it, in an authoritarian manner, until the early 1960s. Ragen apparently understood, however, that to a certain extent a prison can only function properly with the support – at least passive and informal – of the detainees. It was therefore important to keep up the morale not only of the guards but also of the detainees. He therefore scrupulously ensured that they were given good food, clean clothing, and decent cells. For the same reason, a blind eye was turned to the small-scale smuggling of all kinds of important goods and services.

After the departure of Ragen, the existing system was put to the test, especially because new criminal legislation made it possible for many more prisoners than previously to become eligible for parole, and they fully exploited that opportunity. This required a major change in the organisation and operation of the prison. But that – for all kinds of other reasons – was not the only change. It was in fact the prelude to a new transformation of Stateville, this time in the direction of a professionally managed bureaucracy.[258]

The more general study by Daniel Glaser, in the early 1960s, of the effectiveness of the prison system and of parole in fact indicated that one needed, generally speaking, to deal cautiously with the results of case studies

---

[256]   Sykes 1971; Goffman 1970.
[257]   Sykes 1971, pp. 25, 31, 63.
[258]   Jacobs (J.) 1977; Jacobs (J.) 1983.

such as those discussed above. One could not simply generalise from them. The success of imprisonment, for example, could be measured, with the necessary caution, in terms of recidivism, but – for a fair and appropriate assessment of the operation of the prison system – it was extremely important for recidivism rates to be linked to the offences committed by the detainees concerned, to the life they had led before and after their detention, to the conditions to which they had been subject in prison, etc.[259]

9.6.2. PROFESSIONALISATION OF THE POLICE

9.6.2.1. An Arduous Task in Two Stages

In the mid-nineteenth century, the police departments in many American cities underwent a major change, partly based on the model of the system in London. That change consisted of proper police forces being formed by merging the existing police services and placing the new force under a single commander. This was intended, on the one hand, mainly to enforce a more orderly state of affairs in the public domain and, on the other, to maintain public order in the event of strikes, demonstrations, etc., and, if necessary, to restore order decisively. Preventing and investigating crime did play a role in the theory underlying this transformation but it was on precisely these two points that the new uniformed police forces easily fell short for lack of any appropriate specialisation, especially in the case of crime at a regional level.[260]

This explains why numerous private investigation services sprang up during the same period, both locally and nationally. For a variety of reasons, the best known of these – not to say the most notorious – was that headed by Allan Pinkerton. One reason why the Pinkerton agency became notorious was its role in strikebreaking. Another more positive reason was that – even before the regular police forces in New York and Boston, for example – it began building up a nationwide collection of photographs of criminals, but also applied *Bertillonnage* so as to increase the effectiveness of its investigation work.[261] One should not forget that at that time there was no federal investigation service. It was not until 1865 that the first federal police force was founded, namely the Secret Service, intended, inter alia, to combat counterfeiting of the dollar.[262]

In a number of respects, the establishment of proper police forces was not exactly viewed as a success in the eyes of the progressive middle classes, not to mention in the eyes of the reformers of urban government in their midst. The

---

[259] Glaser (D.) 1969.
[260] Richardson 1974, pp. 3–34; Fogelson 1977, pp. 40–92; Papke 1987, pp. 1–18.
[261] Papke 1987, pp. 143–180; Mackay 1997; Johnson (B.) 1976.
[262] Glaser (L.) 1968, pp. 102–117; Marx 1988, pp. 27–29.

close ties with the ruling political parties meant that corruption was rampant within these police forces. Their highly decentralised nature meant that police officers identified more with the people in their neighbourhood than with the force's management. It should also be borne in mind that these forces were generally very badly housed and only minimally equipped. The education and training of police officers was usually non-existent. Towards the end of the nineteenth century, broad general dissatisfaction with the way the police functioned generated a movement aimed at professionalising the police. That movement wished to make urban police forces more independent of local politics by means of internal bureaucratisation, to make them specialised, in terms of tasks and equipment, in combatting crime and solving traffic problems, and to man them with police officers who, after a decent prior education, would be trained at separate police academies.[263]

In practice, it proved no easy matter to bring about this professionalisation of the police in large American cities. For influential reformers such as Raymond Fosdick, that was perfectly obvious. Shortly before the First World War, he had toured police forces in major European cities and had seen how many of them conformed to a large extent to the model that he and others had in mind. In the account of that journey that he published in 1916, he made his admiration of the quality of the forces concerned clear.[264] When, shortly after the First World War, he looked into the situation of American police forces, he made plain his disapproval of the deplorable state in which they often found themselves. The final conclusion of the book that he published on this matter in 1920 begins as follows: "To an American who has intimately studied the operation of European police systems, nothing can be more discouraging than a similar survey of the police in the United States."[265]

It should be noted, however, that in that book Fosdick not only ignored the situation of the Secret Service, but also paid no attention to the Federal Bureau of Investigation, which had been set up in 1907–08 at the suggestion of a US Attorney General with the perhaps rather ominous name of Charles Bonaparte.[266] He also ignored the fact that, since the end of the nineteenth century, more and more states had set up state police forces – often modelled on the Royal Irish Constabulary and the Royal Canadian Mounted Police. That movement was largely a response to major problems in maintaining order, particularly during strikes, and countless problems in the enforcement of all kinds of special

---

263   Richardson 1974, pp. 62–85; Fogelson 1977, pp. 93–140; Monkkonen 1981, pp. 129–147; Harring 1983; Monkkonen 1992; Lane 1992.
264   Fosdick 1916.
265   Fosdick 1920, p. 379.
266   Lowenthal 1950, pp. 3–9.

legislation outside the cities. In some states, however, establishing these police forces was also intended to support and improve local criminal investigation.[267]

9.6.2.2.   Criminology as a Means of Police Reform

As regards the last remark, it is important to note that those who advocated the professionalisation of urban police forces saw the emerging criminology – at least modern criminology in the form of *Kriminalistik* and *police scientifique* – as a means for achieving that objective. They worked on three fronts to thus bring about a scientific approach to policing in the United States: the introduction of a modern identification system, the establishment of police laboratories, and the development of national police and judicial statistics.[268]

As regards the first of these points, it took a great deal of time in the United States, as in many European countries, before a certain consensus was achieved at national level regarding the implementation of *Bertillonnage* or dactyloscopy. There had been experiments with both those systems in many places in around 1900, but it was difficult in a federal country like the United States, which also has a strong local tradition, to make real decisions at national level regarding such a sensitive issue as the identification of individuals.[269] This is illustrated, for example, by the fact that in 1907 and 1910 *Scientific American* still juxtaposed *Bertillonnage* and dactyloscopy as two equally valid alternatives.[270] More significant is of course the fact that the National Bureau of Criminal Identification – established in 1896 at the initiative of the International Association of Chiefs of Police, first in Chicago and later in Washington – only gradually abandoned *Bertillonnage* after 1904.[271]

Remarkably, however, Fosdick still found it necessary in 1915 – in an article in the *Journal of the American Institute of Criminal Law and Criminology* – to call upon the police chiefs of America no longer to maintain two systems but to opt for dactyloscopy, no matter how regrettable that choice might be for Bertillon (who had died the previous year).[272] In 1924, the National Bureau of Criminal Identification was transferred, together with the identification agency of the federal prison system, to the Federal Bureau of Investigation. The establishment of the National Division of Identification and Information apparently brought about such an operational revitalisation that after a while even the smallest police forces switched over to dactyloscopy. By 1929, the Federal Bureau of

---

[267]   Bechtel 1995; Smith (B.) 1969, pp. 47–80, 203–227; Mayo 1920.
[268]   Walker (S.) 1983, pp. 1–28.
[269]   Cole 2001, pp. 119–167, 235–258.
[270]   Boyer 1907; Shepstone 1910.
[271]   Smith (B.) 1940, pp. 292–293.
[272]   Fosdick 1915. See also Upson 1929, pp. 124–125.

Investigation had more than 1.7 million fingerprint records and that same year it used dactyloscopy to identify almost 90,000 persons.[273]

As regards the second point on the reformers' agenda, we can note that it took until 1930 before – at the initiative of Wigmore and with the support of Vollmer, among others – a scientifically oriented periodical was created for the American police, namely *The American Journal of Police Science*. According to Wigmore's editorial in the first issue, that journal was intended mainly to bridge the gap that had developed between the police in the United States and the police in Europe regarding the application of scientific methods and techniques in solving crimes. Nevertheless, he had every confidence that that would be possible:

> It is plain that we in the United States have yet scarcely made a start, in comparison with Europe. But this is the most inventive country in the world, as well as the most practical. In many fields of applied knowledge we have been slow in starting; but when we once started with a will, we soon caught up, and surpassed the early starters.[274]

It is probable that this initiative needs to be seen in conjunction with the establishment of the first National Crime Detection Laboratory at Wigmore's own institution, Northwestern University in Chicago, the year before, i.e. 1929. We should also note that, in the meantime, attempts had been made in other parts of the country to set up police laboratories, whether or not at universities. As early as 1916, for example, at the initiative of the progressive police chief Vollmer – who had become acquainted with the work of Gross in about 1910 – a Scientific Crime Laboratory was established for the police in Berkeley, the first local laboratory of its kind in the country.[275] It is also relevant to note that in the 1920s the Federal Bureau of Investigation set up its own Technical Laboratory and in 1933 made it available to all police and prosecution services in the country. In 1938–39, the Technical Laboratory dealt with more than 5,500 studies of more than 39,000 pieces of evidence.[276]

As regards the third point, it is noteworthy that the National Police Association already took the initiative in 1870 – following a resolution adopted by Congress earlier that year – to deal with the registration of crime reports in a uniform manner and to manage the associated data nationally. However, it proved not only technically difficult to develop such a system, but also very difficult to implement effectively any system whatsoever within a divided police system. As a result, nothing actually came of the initiative.

---

[273] Hoover 1929; Smith (B.) 1940, pp. 294–295; Callan and Stephenson 1939, pp. 250–311.
[274] *American Journal of Police Science*, 1930, p. 2.
[275] Carte and Carte 1975, pp. 27–28.
[276] Smith (B.) 1940, pp. 300–301; Türkel 1929; Heindl 1929b; Callan and Stephenson 1939, pp. 195–245.

That was certainly one of the reasons why it was so strongly emphasised at the conference in 1909 that the problem of the national judicial and police statistics finally needed to be solved. Just how necessary that was became clear from the concise but probing study of that problem that was published by Louis Robinson in 1911. It was for good reason that he urged that serious measures be taken to finally organise a system of proper criminal statistics. One of his arguments was that if the situation did not improve, one could not assume that the United States would soon have "criminal statistics comparable in value to those of European nations". In the same little book, he explained in detail how that improvement could be achieved.[277]

It nevertheless took until 1927 before the International Association of Chiefs of Police, together with various other bodies, once more began working to set up a commission tasked with organising an appropriate and workable system of Uniform Crime Records. In 1929, the commission came up with a proposal for Uniform Crime Reporting that was put into practice almost immediately. By 1 January 1930, 400 police departments in 43 states had already submitted their statistics to the Federal Bureau of Investigation. After that, things moved fast and by 1939 the great majority of the country's police departments were systematically involved.[278]

Why matters moved so smoothly this time was probably, for one thing, because in the 1920s many states had set up crime commissions, which, among other things, had pressed for the most effective possible collection and analysis of figures on reported and solved crimes. Some states – for example California in 1917, with this also being at the initiative of Vollmer – had already gone a lot further and had set up their own Bureau of Criminal Identification and Investigation.[279] On the other hand, the federal authorities, in particular the Federal Bureau of Investigation, had in the preceding decades attempted in all kinds of ways to improve the national police and judicial statistics.

It was also the case that more and more scientists had urged the establishment of a system of national crime statistics because such statistics were quite simply extremely important for carrying out all kinds of criminological research and for developing proper criminal policy in certain areas.[280]

9.6.2.3. August Vollmer: Founder of the School of Criminology in Berkeley

Finally, it is certainly not unimportant in the history of criminology in America that one of the most influential police reformers in the first half of the twentieth century, Vollmer, made enormous efforts within many urban police

---

[277] Robinson 1911.
[278] Upson 1929; Smith (B.) 1940, pp. 312–315.
[279] Carte and Carte 1975, pp. 29–30; Moley 1926.
[280] Robinson 1934.

forces – first, that in Berkeley and later those in Chicago and Los Angeles, inter alia – and national police commissions towards the professionalisation of police operations and the professional reorganisation of the police system as a whole. He was invited no fewer than three times to teach and carry out research in criminology at leading universities.[281]

From 1916 to 1931, for example, he gave summer courses in criminology at the University of California that of course focused almost predominantly on the phenomenology of crime and on the limits and available options for the police during investigation. It is interesting that in these courses he brought in professional criminals to give guest lectures on the ins and outs of their profession.[282]

In 1929, he was the first person appointed to the brand new professorial chair of "research in police administration" at the University of Chicago.[283] That appointment was a result of a report that he had written in 1928 for the Illinois Commission for Criminal Justice on the state of the police of Chicago. Together with the renowned sociologist Burgess, he lectured at the university until 1931 on how the American police could be improved organisationally and operationally. He also helped design the Illinois State Identification Bureau.

From an academic perspective, his third appointment was in fact the most important. In 1933, he was invited by the University of California, Berkeley to take up the position of research professor at in the Bureau of Public Administration within the Department of Political Science, with funding coming from the Rockefeller Foundation. In that position, it was not enough for Vollmer merely to teach courses on the organisation and functioning of the police. In 1933, he and others set up a course in criminology that would later, in 1951, become the renowned Berkeley School of Criminology, the first school of its kind in the country.[284] In the meantime, however, Vollmer had already left Berkeley (in 1937). The first dean of the school was one of his best-known students, Orlando Wilson, author of highly influential textbooks on the organisation and management of urban police departments.[285] In 1955, Vollmer chose to end his own life with his service weapon at the age of 79 because he no longer wished to live with the effects of Parkinson's disease.[286]

It probably goes without saying that he not only wrote important reports but also published more in-depth studies, both alone and with others. We cannot discuss them all here. His best and most influential book was *The Police and Modern Society*, which was published in 1936 by the Bureau of Public

---

[281] Carte and Carte 1975; Smith (B.) 1940, pp. 324–327.
[282] Carte and Carte 1975, pp. 27–28.
[283] Merriam 1929, p. 117.
[284] Carte and Carte 1975, pp. 68–71.
[285] Wilson (O.) 1973.
[286] Carte and Carte 1975, pp. 74–83.

Administration at the University of California, Berkeley.[287] In that book, Vollmer deals mainly with the problems facing the police: on the one hand – besides the relatively large number of minor offences – especially the problem of organised crime and of other more politically oriented subversive movements, and on the other the large numbers of traffic deaths and injuries. From a more internal perspective, he denounces the organisational division of the policing system, the corrupt relationships between politicians and racketeers in cities like Chicago, the inadequate training of police officers at all levels, the neglect of the task of prevention by not taking the lead in "community programs", and the pathetic equipment available to police departments. At one point, he disconsolately writes:

> No marked degree of improvement can be expected from the police setup. It is defective internally because its functions are too often discharged by amateurs, and the lack of coordination among the separate, independent police agencies make it even less effective. Law enforcement necessarily suffers when it is halted at every political boundary line.[288]

He then discusses the various issues in greater detail. It is still particularly instructive to read what he writes about organised crime in the context of public morals in terms both of the extortion of legitimate businesses and of illegal markets. His detailed observations are still well worth reading: on the role of juvenile gangs in the activities of organised crime, on the symbiotic relationships between gangsters, the political system and the major business community, and on the impossibility for the police to properly – i.e. both effectively and honestly – enforce all kinds of morality legislation which, in the context of gambling, prostitution, alcohol or narcotics, is at odds with what many people want or at least will tolerate. These observations testify to Vollmer's extensive experience, great erudition, and far-reaching insights.

9.6.3. DEVELOPMENT OF INTERROGATION AND TESTIMONY PSYCHOLOGY

Even before Gross's main works were translated into English, his views on criminal psychology were to some extent already familiar in the United States, as were those of Wundt, Von Liszt, and Aschaffenburg. They were distributed in 1908 by Hugo Münsterberg, who in the same year assembled a number of his more informal articles on witness memory, false confessions, and other

---

[287]   Vollmer 1936.
[288]   Vollmer 1936, p. 4.

relevant topics in a collection entitled *On the Witness Stand*.[289] Münsterberg had familiarised himself with this branch of psychology while still living in Germany.

Despite the fact that Münsterberg's introduction has been frequently reprinted, my strong impression is that this version of psychology failed to flourish in the United States in the same way as in Germany. In the United States, it quickly became focused entirely on the psychology of interrogation and testimony, and then above all to the extent that it was (and is) relevant in the framework of the criminal investigation. The fact that this version of psychology was initially practised mainly at the Scientific Crime Detection Laboratory at Northwestern University in Chicago and at the University of California, Berkeley may perhaps have played a major role in this.

It is notable in any case that leading authors in this field – unlike Münsterberg, who was based at Harvard – were attached (or had been attached) to those institutions, in particular John Larson and Fred Inbau. In 1962, the latter, together with John Reid, published *Criminal Investigation and Confessions*. With numerous revisions, this was for decades the main textbook on police interrogation.[290] More academic treatises, such as those produced in Germany after 1900 by Störig, Hellwig, and Mönkemöller, were not published in the United State in the first half of the twentieth century.

Larson wrote in 1929 that there were four major issues in forensic psychology/psychiatry: What does the crime scene tell us about the perpetrator? What can psychology offer the investigator to help track down the suspect? Can psychology be useful in obtaining a statement from a suspect? And how can it help investigate the validity of that statement?[291] All four were perhaps the most important issues in theory, but in actual practice most attention was focused on the first two. Interest in profiling, for example, only came much later.

The first major issue was that of the propriety of interrogation methods, not only in the light of the abominable interrogation practices at many American police stations, especially in the South, but also in the light of the Amendments to the Constitution (in particular 5 and 14) that entitle an accused to the presumption of innocence and to the right against compulsory self-incrimination. That issue led to a certain amount of research on how interrogation actually took place and on which kinds of methods were considered acceptable.[292] The research showed that it was not easy to achieve a proper balance between the rights of the accused and the pressure – specifically also psychological pressure – that was (or at least could be) exerted on him through all kinds of methods and techniques.[293]

That finding meant that the Supreme Court, in a long series of decisions, had to increasingly determine the legal framework within which the interrogation

---

289 Münsterberg 1949.
290 Inbau and Reid 1962; Kidd 1940.
291 Larson 1929.
292 Larson 1925.
293 Sowle 1962.

of suspects, at least, had to take place.[294] That series of decisions culminated in 1966 in the famous decision by the Warren Court in *Miranda v Arizona*:

> The prosecution may not use statements, whether exculpatory or inculpatory, stemming from custodial interrogation of the defendant unless it demonstrates the use of procedural safeguards effective to secure the privilege against self-incrimination. By custodial interrogation, we mean questioning initiated by law enforcement officers after a person has been taken into custody or otherwise deprived of his freedom of action in any significant way.

What that meant in practice was that suspects must be advised of their rights prior to the start of interrogation. In addition – based on the idea that the "equality of arms" could be ensured right into the interrogation room if the suspect were assisted during police questioning by counsel – one of those rights was the right to have counsel present at the interrogation.

The irony of that decision was that it was not based on any elaborate empirical analysis of the interrogation practices at American police stations at that time, but rather for the most part on the textbook by Inbau and Reid. That was because, as Chief Justice Earl Warren (incidentally, a very good friend of Vollmer) argued, if matters proceeded in practice as those authors proposed, then that would be within an atmosphere controlled by the police to such an extent that suspects could all too easily make self-incriminating statements without having been informed of their constitutional rights. This meant that Warren was disregarding the argument by opponents that strengthening the legal position of the suspect in the police phase of criminal proceedings would reduce the clear-up rate and would thus therefore run counter to effectively and efficiently combatting crime. *Miranda* thus became a *casus belli* in the debate in America about the models that needed to be applied when organising the criminal justice system. In the words of Herbert Packer in his well-known book *The Limits of the Criminal Sanction*, should the due process model or the crime control model be decisive here?[295] Those familiar with the book by Beccaria know, of course, that that is a misleading question. The criminal law must pursue both goals in a balanced manner.

The second major issue was related to the first. It involved the question of whether or not it was possible to determine objectively that a suspect was telling the truth or at least determine that he was lying about the truth and was making a false statement. "Objectively" referred specifically to the technical recording of observable physiological reactions when certain facts were presented to the suspect or when he was asked certain questions. Two questions quickly provoked

---

[294]   Fijnaut 1987b, pp. 137–279.
[295]   Packer 1968, pp. 149–204. See also Sykes 1963.

discussion: what reactions is it most appropriate to record and how should those reactions be recorded?[296]

That discussion ultimately led to the construction of the "lie detector". The invention and increasing use of that device – including outside the criminal justice system, i.e. in the private commercial sector – did not in fact put an end to the debate regarding its ability to measure what one wishes to know. That issue was hotly debated not only in the 1930s and 1940s, but also into the 1950s and 1960s. By then, leading researchers not only had serious doubts about the functionality of the device, but were also afraid of its being used selectively, improperly, or incorrectly.[297]

9.7. CONCLUSION

The above overview of the reception of European criminology in the United States since the second half of the nineteenth century allows no room for doubt that in the space of just a few decades criminology did indeed find its way – in its entirety and in an accessible manner – to the United States, but that that process was in some respects more diverse and proceeded more gradually than is commonly thought. What is particularly remarkable is that that transfer was at first effectuated mainly by social reformers. Like their contemporaries in a number of European countries, they apparently saw the real potential of the emerging modern criminology for the criminal justice system and, more broadly, the organisation of society in general.

Analysing the reception process at the theoretical level reveals that it was initially, in around 1900, bio-anthropological criminology that became accepted in the United States, and only secondarily, in around 1915–1920, socio-anthropological criminology. There are three important caveats to this, however.

The first caveat is that the transmission of biologically oriented criminology did not immediately lead to the development of studies by American researchers from that perspective. Such research only got underway, to some extent, in the 1910s, reaching its peak in the 1930s and 1940s in large-scale research at Harvard University, and then largely disappearing from the university scene. It did not in fact disappear for good, because in the 1970s and 1980s it returned to the international criminological forum in new variants via the same university, and has since continued to play a still controversial but overall modest role.

The second caveat is that although American criminal-sociological research only got going in the 1920s, it then enjoyed such a boom in the 1930s that in the 1950s and 1960s it dominated the world's impression of criminology in the

---

[296] Inbau 1934; Trovillo 1939.
[297] Burack 1955; Skolnick 1961.

United States. That is clear not only from various bibliographical surveys but also from the structure and content of the important textbooks that were used during those years.[298]

The third caveat is that the research done in the United States was indeed inspired by the criminology that had developed in Europe, but was not an imitation of it. Where bio-criminological research is concerned it is striking – in spite of everything – that attempts were made to study, in a more systematic manner than had ever been done in continental Europe, the extent to which biological properties or physical characteristics (also) play a role in the causation of criminal behaviour. As regards criminal-sociological research, it can be concluded firstly that it was from a methodological point of view that socio-geographic and autobiographical research was carried out that had not been performed so thoroughly and on such a large scale in Europe up to that point. Secondly, it must be underlined that existing ideas about the causation of criminal behaviour were not only developed more methodically but also were applied to new areas. The development and implementation of the differential association theory is the best illustration of this conclusion.

Furthermore, we should note that although innovation in criminal sociology did not take place at Northwestern University, it did still take place in Chicago, namely at the University of Chicago's Department of Sociology. Chicago can therefore be seen in general as the focal point in the reception of European criminology in the United States

Caveats are also necessary in relation to that conclusion, namely that the reception of European criminology clearly advanced along two distinct paths. On the one hand, there was innovation in biologically oriented criminal anthropology via Northwestern University's School of Law and, on the other, innovation in sociologically oriented criminal anthropology via the Department of Sociology at the University of Chicago. The extent to which those innovation processes took separate paths is apparent, for example, from the fact that the work of the Chicago lawyers was hardly ever cited in the works of the Chicago sociologists, and vice versa. In that sense, there was little in the way of integrated criminal science, at least in Chicago.

The second necessary caveat is that the objective of creating an integrating criminal science was not achieved at national level either, although the Wigmore symposium in 1909 did in fact focus on it. Because criminal-sociological research increasingly flourished and was mostly practised within sociology faculties, criminology as pursued in the United States in the mid-twentieth century took on a predominantly sociological character and has since remained separate from criminal law studies in most places. One significant exception has for many years been the School of Law at New York University. At the School's Center for Research

---

[298]   Lunden 1935; Sellin and Shalloo 1935; Pollak 1952–55; Clinard 1957; Cressey and Ward 1969.

in Crime and Justice, directed by Jacobs and Skolnick, the two disciplines are in fact interconnected in numerous ways, both theoretical and institutional.

The intention of the foregoing observations is definitely not to say that there was absolutely no interaction between sociologists and lawyers in Chicago in the 1920s and 1930s. A third caveat is therefore necessary, namely to point out that such interaction did take place. In 1924, for example, the editors of the *Criminal Science Monograph*, a supplement to the *Journal of the American Institute of Criminal Law and Criminology* published Thomas's renowned study *The Unadjusted Girl*. Nor should we forget that Wigmore acted as editor-in-chief of the famous *Illinois Crime Survey* (1929), which included the innovative reports of both Shaw and McKay and of Landesco. Shaw and McKay, moreover, referred repeatedly in their reports to studies by Healy and Bronner. That is not surprising of course. Both pairs of researchers not only worked alongside one another for a long time in the same location, but also actually studied some of the same individual cases.

If the reception of European criminology in the United States in the period concerned is then considered at institutional level, the first thing to note is that, here too, the changes in the police and prison systems were not of course determined solely by beliefs that could be attributed to criminology since the 1880s. That caveat does not alter the fact, however, that some of the ideas that had been developed specifically in Europe concerning the redesign of those two important components of the criminal justice system also played a role in their reorganisation in the United States.

As regards the prison system, one can refer both to the discussion about differentiation of that institution according to categories of convicts and also to changes in the application of imprisonment through the introduction of the suspended sentence and release on probation. Where the policing system is concerned, it is absolutely clear that the scientific approach to detection was encouraged in several respects by developments in Europe, for example the introduction of anthropometric methods, the application of technical and scientific research, and the use of interrogation psychology.

It is no easy matter to find an explanation for the phases and manners in which European criminology was adopted bit by bit in the United States. My impression is that European criminology was able to help formulate an answer to two problems in the existing criminal justice system. That system no longer fitted in with the views of the urban and national political elites concerning sound, modern governance of the country. Moreover, it no longer offered a comprehensive and therefore appropriate response to some of the crime problems facing the country. Attention must also be paid, of course, to the major role played by a number of people in the expansion and application of European criminology in the United States. There are five who are head and shoulders above the others, namely Wigmore, Healy, Shaw, Sutherland and Vollmer. Without them and their supporters, the reception of European criminology would certainly not have been so successful as it has been.

CHAPTER 10

TRANSATLANTIC INTEGRATION
OF CRIMINOLOGY

10.1. INTRODUCTION

This chapter aims to reconcile the past with the contemporary development of criminology. It does so primarily to help the reader understand the transition from the history of criminology as recorded in this book and its current state. It is therefore not the intention of this chapter to deal with the overall development of criminology as a whole since the 1960s as extensively as has so far been the case for certain periods and certain countries. For the same reason, it largely ignores the interaction between criminology and the criminal justice system. This chapter is intended mainly to act as a bridge between criminology past and present. Any broader aim would have necessitated writing a book within a book, so to speak.

In line with the distinction made so far between the history of criminology in relation to the criminal justice system in the United States and that history in a number of European countries, we will first consider the turmoil in the 1960s, 1970s, and 1980s in American criminology, which was due not only to the emergence of Marxist, radical, or leftist criminology, but also to the development of equally radical neo-classical but rightist criminology. In conjunction with this analysis, the spread of interactionist criminology will also be considered.

Consideration will then be given to how that discordant reform movement manifested itself in the development of criminology in most of the European countries dealt with in this book. We will look first at what happened in the United Kingdom. Subsequently, the focus will be on the impact of the movement on the continent, namely in Germany, France, Belgium, and the Netherlands, omitting only the evolution of criminology in Italy during the period concerned.

It should be noted that the structure of this chapter is not based only on the division applied in the previous chapters. Developments in the United States are this time explained prior to those in Europe because what took place in the former during the period concerned had much more influence, generally speaking, on developments in Europe, rather than vice versa. That was indeed to such an extent that it is no exaggeration to speak of a certain Americanisation of European criminology.

10.2. TURMOIL IN THE UNITED STATES

We have already seen in the previous chapter how both theory and research in America continued into the present century along lines laid out in the 1920s. We thus deliberately ignored the changes – some radical, some less so – that took place from the 1960s on in scientific discussion and research.

These changes were intertwined with one another in all sorts of ways and are therefore not easy to unravel. On the one hand, they involved changes in the perspective on problems of crime and the administration of criminal justice and, on the other, changes in the study of those problems. Moreover, the changes were often associated in one way or another with political trends in the country.

10.2.1. UNREST IN THE COUNTRY AND THE BREAKTHROUGH OF POLICE RESEARCH

On the one hand, it should be borne in mind that in the 1960s America was not only confronted by the murder of prominent political leaders (the brothers John F. Kennedy and Robert F. Kennedy and Martin Luther King), but was also frequently the scene of fierce protests by African Americans against racism, by protesters against the war in Vietnam, and by students against a wide variety of situations both within and outside the universities. The unrest assumed such proportions that President Johnson found it necessary in 1967 to set up a National Advisory Commission on Civil Disorders, which reported its findings a year later.[1]

On the other hand, in the mid-1960s the Republican Party, in particular, radically politicised the crime problem or, more broadly, the issue of law and order.[2] That politicisation led in 1965 to the establishment of the Commission on Law Enforcement and Administration of Justice (already referred to in a previous chapter), which published its influential report *The Challenge of Crime in a Free Society* in 1967.[3] In 1969, the *Politics of Protest* report also appeared. This was written by Skolnick at the request of the National Commission on the Causes and Prevention of Violence with the aid of a number of leading sociologists.[4]

Skolnick was not just anybody. He was the author of a book that – when it first appeared in 1966 with the title *Justice without Trial: Law Enforcement in Democratic Society* – immediately caused a sensation not only in the United

---

1   *Report of the National Advisory Commission on Civil Disorders* 1968.
2   Finckenauer 1978.
3   *The Challenge of Crime in a Free Society* 1968.
4   Skolnick 1969.

States but also elsewhere, and which has since continued to be avidly read.[5] Skolnick's book is the outcome of a field study of a small local police department, dealing with how not only the social and institutional environment of the police but also their social role and internal culture affect the way police officers use

The Challenge of Crime in a Free Society: A Report by the President's Commission on Law Enforcement and Administration of Justice, New York, Avon Books, 1968 (introduction and afterword by I. SILVER).

their discretionary powers to give form and content to their work, in particular their investigative activities, for example controlling prostitution and combatting drug trafficking.

---

5   Skolnick 1967; Skolnick and Bayley 1986.

Skolnick was not in fact the only social scientist in the 1960s who – in the footsteps of Westley, who had already studied police culture in the 1950s[6] – investigated the way local police departments actually operated.[7] Partly under the influence of the disturbances in the country, other researchers had also

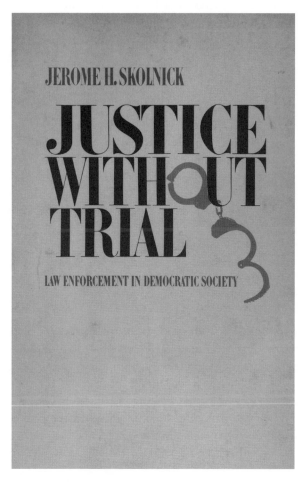

Jerome SKOLNICK, *Justice Without Trial: Law Enforcement in Democratic Society,* New York, John Wiley & Sons, 1967.

investigated, for example, the relationship between the police and the population, especially minorities, and the different policing styles used in America's towns and cities depending on the social context.[8] A few had also ventured to carry out

---

6   Westley 1970.
7   Bordua and Reiss, Jr 1967; Sherman 1974.
8   Bordua 1967; Bayley and Mendelsohn 1969; Wilson 1970; Reiss, Jr 1971; Bittner 1990; Goldstein 1977; Cicourel 1968; Greenwood, Chaiken and Petersilia 1977; Muir 1977; Manning 1979; Reuss-Ianni 1984.

probing research into the way the police in cities like New York made use of their powers and in particular how they made use of physical force.[9] For the well-known sociologist Gary Marx, the active role of the police in the disturbances was a reason to launch a research programme into undercover policing.[10]

Referring to the empirical research that had been done in the 1960s and 1970s into the actual operation of central prisons in the United States, this flourishing of empirical research on the activities of urban police departments meant that there came to be greater balance in sociological research on the American criminal justice system. It in fact meant that the controversial institutional "front line" of the criminal justice system, or more broadly the "thin blue line" in society, became the object of academic interest.

Not everybody was happy about this, however, and certainly not with the fact that not only Skolnick's research, but also that by some other policing researchers, was used by the aforementioned commissions to analyse problems and develop proposals for their approach to how matters should be tackled. As soon as that happened, the proponents of a Marxist shift in criminology became highly vocal, persons who according to their writings were entirely averse to such involvement on the part of social scientists – criminologists, sociologists, etc. – in the policy pursued or to be pursued.[11]

10.2.2. RISE OF MARXIST CRIMINOLOGY

Richard Quinney and Tony Platt – two of the leading proponents of a Marxist, socialist, radical, or leftist criminology – adopted the position, for example, that the aforementioned commissions, given their tasks and composition, were fundamentally doing only one thing: "provid[ing] the ruling class with one more means of protecting the existing order". Skolnick and his associates were personally accused of having simply legitimised the final reports of the commissions. In the eyes of the Marxist criminologists, their reports were in fact part of the problem rather than a solution:

> The liberal, reformist response to contemporary experiences is bankrupt. Following obsolete theories of government, law and social order, we are unable to act in a way that would begin to solve our problems. The only reaction of those who govern and those who advise is one of manipulation, control and repression.[12]

This criticism of the role of Skolnick and others in the commissions was of course the expression of an entirely different view of the existing criminology

---

9   Chevigny 1969; Niederhoffer 1969.
10   Marx 1988; Chevigny 1972.
11   Sykes 1974.
12   Quinney 1973, pp. 43–46, 68–75; Quinney 1969; Quinney 1970.

and social sciences in general. In the book from which the preceding passages are taken – *Critique of the Legal Order: Crime Control in Capitalist Society* – Quinney stated bluntly that criminology had up to then served but a single purpose: "legitimation of the existing social order". He continued:

Richard QUINNEY, *The Social Reality of Crime*, Boston, Little, Brown and Company, 1970.

The major theoretical perspective in criminology is that of the socialization of the law violator. [...] There is little in this perspective that will allow the criminologist to examine the process by which the person becomes defined as criminal by the state. And there is no room for questioning the rightfulness of the laws that are imposed on the citizen. The value of justice traditionally falls outside the realm of criminology. The result is that criminologists have become the ancillary agents of power. They provide the kinds of information that governing elites use to manipulate and control those who threaten the system.[13]

In 1979, he reinforced that position by writing that the value of the work of criminologists is to be found solely in "reproducing the formal structures of capitalism and maintaining capitalist production relations". It was therefore clear to him that an ideological battle was in fact raging in American criminology "between those members who openly defend or tacitly accept the interests of the capitalist class and those who defend the interests of the working class".[14]

This position fitted in completely with the programme that Platt had drawn up in 1974 for a radical criminology in the United States.[15] In that programme, he turned outright against all "liberals" in criminology because – no matter how different their basic positions perhaps were – they still accepted the authorities' definition of crime and criminals, wished primarily to reform people and systems, had no regard for the general relationships within society, lacked a historical perspective regarding the criminal justice system, and mainly carried out research that served the vested interests of parties and institutions.

By contrast, what radical criminologists should do was break with the "liberal" past of criminology, return to its socialist roots, and redefine its object, i.e. study the "real criminals", namely those who violate people's rights or exploit other people politically or economically.[16] And, it must be said, matters did not stop at mere words. In the years that followed, "radical" studies appeared on the police and prison systems in America. The periodical *Crime and Social Justice* became the leading vehicle for the movement.[17] Interestingly, this "radicalisation" of American criminology was driven by the School of Criminology that had been founded at Berkeley by Vollmer. Even simply in the light of that historical fact, it is not entirely incomprehensible that the school was closed down by the authorities of the University of California in 1976. As can be seen from the "radical" description of the fierce battle that accompanied the closure, two different worlds were in violent collision with one another.[18]

The "radical" Marxist position adopted by Platt gave rise in criminological circles to sharp and sometimes relentless criticism. Given the history of criminology in the United States as described above, that criticism was not at all surprising. Had Shaw not explicitly shown how disastrous the impact of the unrestrained capitalism of those days had been for large parts of the

---

13 Quinney 1973, pp. 26–27.
14 Quinney 1979, p. 450.
15 Platt 1974.
16 Bonger 1969.
17 Center for Research on Criminal Justice 1977; Platt and Takagi 1982.
18 Editorial 1976, pp. 1–4.

population of Chicago? Had Landesco not convincingly denounced the corrupt interrelationship between crime, the economy, and politics in that city? And had not Sutherland plainly defined the top echelon of American business as a collection of serious white-collar criminals?

Strangely enough, the contemporary critics of Quinney, Platt, and his associates did not usually pose those questions. Nevertheless, their questions were effective. Was radical criminology more than simply ideology? Why did the radical criminologists say nothing about the large-scale violations of human rights in the Soviet Union, Cuba, and other parts of the world where the Marxist utopia had supposedly been made a reality? Were robbery, rape, etc. not forms of crime with which criminologists should also concern themselves in the interest of the victims and potential victims? And so forth.[19] Discussions between radicals and their opponents sometimes deteriorated into academic mudslinging.[20]

In the course of the 1980s, that battle of opinions did die down to some extent. That can be inferred, for one thing, from the fact that by the year 2000 extensive collections – under the heading of Marxist or radical criminology – had appeared, with articles on all kinds of subjects, as much on theoretical issues as on certain types of crime. Apparently, a fairly broad range of researchers had gradually formed in the United States who still based their work, to a greater or lesser extent, on the principles that had been formulated in the 1970s.[21]

10.2.3. FLOURISHING OF INTERACTIONIST CRIMINOLOGY

However, that is certainly no reason to ignore the largest group of "liberal" criminologists against whom Richard Quinney, Tony Platt, William Chambliss and their supporters had turned so decisively in the 1970s: those who, from the 1960s on, had begun working more and more from an interactionist perspective.

The striking thing about this group was, on the one hand, that their supporters largely turned away from "aetiological" criminology (i.e. criminology that aimed to discover the causes of individual criminal behaviour) as practised from the 1910s on. On the other hand, however, they were not only the object of harsh criticism from the radical Marxist, "leftist" criminologists, as we have just seen, but were also attacked by those on the right (whom we will deal with shortly). The spokesman for this faction was undoubtedly Wilson, referred to a number of times in the previous chapter, including as one of the rediscoverers of bio-anthropological criminology.

---

19 Turk 1975; Meier 1977; Akers 1979; Klockars 1979.
20 Chambliss 1989.
21 Greenberg 1993; Lynch (M.) 1997.

The interactionist approach to criminology was promoted by a small but influential group of sociologists, with one of the leading figures undoubtedly being Howard Becker. In his books – *Outsiders: Studies in the Sociology of Deviance* and *The Other Side: Perspectives on Deviance* – Becker explained what

Howard BECKER, *Outsiders: Studies in the Sociology of Deviance*, New York, The Free Press, 1966.

that approach involved.[22] In *Outsiders*, which first appeared in 1963, he writes succinctly that where deviance is concerned, the crux of the issue is how one defines behaviour as being deviant:

> it is created by society. […] I mean, rather, that social groups create deviance by making the rules whose infraction constitutes deviance, and by applying those rules to

---

[22]   Becker (H.) 1966; Becker (H.) 1967.

particular people and labeling them as outsiders. From this point of view, deviance is not a quality of the act the person commits, but rather a consequence of the application by others of rules and sanctions to an "offender". The deviant is one to whom that label has successfully been applied; deviant behavior is behavior that people so label.[23]

Becker goes on to state that although rules are "the creation of specific social groups", there are great differences between groups as regards the power they – thanks to their position in society – have to create rules and apply them to others:

> those groups whose social position gives them weapons and power are best able to enforce their rules. Distinctions of age, sex, ethnicity, and class are all related to differences in power, which accounts for differences in the degree to which groups so distinguished can make rules for others.[24]

In his introduction to *The Other Side*, Becker states that interactionism has two aspects. First, interactionists are opposed to the usual way in which criminal behaviour – or more broadly, deviant behaviour – is studied. Research usually

> focuses on the deviant himself and has asked its questions mainly about him. Who he is? Where did he come from? How did he get that way? Is he likely to keep on being that way? The new approach sees it as always and everywhere a process of interaction between at least two kinds of people: those who commit (or are said to have committed) a deviant act and the rest of society, perhaps divided into several groups itself. The two groups are seen in complementary relationship.[25]

One of the consequences of this different view is that crime should not be seen as a characteristic of individuals. What behaviour is or is not labelled as criminal is a matter of definition:

> that we become much more interested in the process by which deviants are defined by the rest of society. We do not take for granted, as has sometimes naively been done, that a given action is deviant simply because it is commonly regarded so. Instead, we look to the process by which the common definition arises. This is, with increasing frequency, referred to as the process of labeling. People attach the label "deviant" to others and thereby make them deviant. […] The deviant is one to whom that label has successfully been applied; deviant behavior is behavior that people so label.[26]

Another consequence of this different view is:

> that we are able to correct false impressions fostered by earlier theoretical assumptions. For instance, if we assume, as has often been done, that deviance is somehow a quality

---

23   Becker (H.) 1966, pp. 8–9.
24   Becker (H.) 1966, p. 18.
25   Becker (H.) 1967, p. 2.
26   Becker (H.) 1967, pp. 2–3.

of the person committing the deviant act, we are likely to suppose without looking any further into the matter that the person who commits the deviant act is somehow compelled to do so and will continue to do so. On the other hand, if we view deviance as something that arises in interaction with others, we realise that changes in interaction may produce significant changes in behavior.[27]

Second, Becker states that the new interactionist approach to deviant behaviour is characterised by a "lack of sentimentality". By this he means that supporters of this approach do not let themselves be guided by the usual images of reality that they investigate because those images may well be completely wrong and may mask the actual reality. Quite the contrary: they are prepared "to question received opinion".[28]

If we remember what Durkheim wrote about criminal behaviour being behaviour that is defined as such, we will immediately realise that the interactionist perspective, as outlined above with reference to Becker, is not at all new. The fact that Becker does not refer to Durkheim in his publications raises important questions (as in the case of Merton in relation to Durkheim and Sutherland regarding Tarde) concerning – to put it cautiously – the completeness of his sources. Be that as it may, American interactionism is essentially little more than an elaboration of Durkheim's basic ideas on the phenomenon of crime and punishment in modern society.

That origin becomes more apparent in Kai Erikson's essay in *The Other Side* on the basic assumptions of the sociology of deviant behaviour – namely where he writes that deviant forms of behaviour can sometimes be highly beneficial for society. That is precisely what Durkheim wrote regarding the normality and usefulness of criminal behaviour. What is interesting, however, is the Erikson's addition to the effect that it sometimes seems – surprisingly so – that deviant behaviours are legitimised by the same institutions whose task it is to suppress those behaviours. Are these institutions not in fact designed precisely to preserve such behaviours?

Let us take prisons as an example. Defendants are first pressed – by means of a showy, ritualistic criminal trial – into the role of a deviant, a criminal. And when they eventually leave prison, the label, the stigma, of having been a prisoner is not removed from them. Rather, they retain that label; it is in any case not erased by means of a similar ritual, with all the associated consequences.[29] On the one hand, ex-convicts have few options for making a living other than resuming their criminal activities. On the other hand, the reluctance of society to receive them back into its bosom is understandable because it is well known that many

---

27   Becker (H.) 1967, p. 3.
28   Becker (H.) 1967, pp. 2–6.
29   Matza 1969; Goffman 1963.

of them revert to deviant behaviour. This circular process thus involves a self-fulfilling prophecy.[30]

Another important refinement was provided by Edwin Lemert, who introduced the important distinction between "primary deviation" and "secondary deviation". Primary deviation is the aberrant behaviour that people develop in a certain context relative to the standards prevailing therein. That behaviour – according to Lemert – usually has few if any consequences for the person concerned or for his surroundings. Problems arise only at the point when primary deviation becomes secondary deviation due to other people's reactions to the primary deviation:

> Secondary deviation is deviant behavior, or social roles based upon it, which becomes [a] means of defense, attack, or adaptation to the overt and covert problems created by the societal reaction to primary deviation.[31]

This is why not only Lemert but also, for example, Edwin Schur calls emphatically for caution, restraint, and variety in determining formal responses, especially via the criminal law, to primary deviant, criminal behaviour. The uncontrolled, indiscriminate application of sanctions can inadvertently exacerbate the initial problem rather than reduce it. It is therefore sometimes better, even much better, to refrain from intervening formally or officially as regards primary deviant behaviour.[32] Lemert, Schur and others refined, as it were, the view on deviant behaviour that Becker had developed and therefore remained interested in the causes of primary deviation: why do people defy the rules? What does that say about them as individuals and about their immediate surroundings, as well as about the larger society in which they grow up and try to survive?[33]

The interactionist approach led to a large number of studies, not only on the creation and enforcement of criminal legislation by the police and other institutions but also on the development of deviance and, more narrowly, on people's criminal careers, specifically because of the formal and informal forms of labelling to which they are subjected in the course of their lives. Famous examples include Becker's own studies on "moral entrepreneurs" who emerge as "rule creators" and "rule enforcers", and about how people start to smoke cannabis.[34] Leslie Wilkins developed proposals for evaluating policy from an interactionist perspective.[35]

One can naturally ask – partly in the light of these and other examples – whether the interactionist approach to criminal behaviour was as new as it

---

30 Erikson (K.) 1967, pp. 15–17.
31 Lemert 1967, pp. 17–18, 40–64.
32 Schur 1973.
33 Schur 1969, pp. 55–157.
34 Becker (H.) 1966, pp. 41–58, 147–164; Becker (H.) 1967; Rubington and Weinberg 1969.
35 Wilkins 1964.

appeared, even by American standards. Hadn't Sutherland and others shown how people become professional criminals through interaction with their environment? Hadn't Sutherland, in particular, shown that a great deal of white-collar crime is not covered by the criminal codes because white-collar criminals have the power to influence the creation of criminal legislation and can thus prevent their misconduct being labelled legally as "criminal"?

Similarly, it is justifiable to ask how far – and in any case on which points – the interactionist approach differs from the approach adopted in radical or Marxist criminology. Take the creation of criminal legislation, for example: In both approaches, the possession of power or influence plays a crucial role. Someone who does not possess power is unable to convert his values and interests into criminal law provisions (or ensure that they are so converted). However, the interactionists generally failed to criticise the overall power relationships within American society and the role of the criminal justice system in this context.[36]

Finally, it is interesting that the sometimes heated discussions about the major problems of public order and security in American society and the ways in which those issues could be viewed and needed to be addressed led to a revival of interest in the old question of the "interplay of legal theory and social policy" or, more narrowly, the question of the interaction between criminal science and criminology. In their influential pamphlet *Law and Society in Transition: Toward Responsive Law* (1978) Philippe Nonet and Philip Selznick came to the conclusion already expressed in the subtitle: the law – as already argued at the time in the "legal realism" and "sociological jurisprudence" of people like Pound and Wigmore – must "embrace knowledge of the social contexts and effects of official action", with "responsive law" being clearly distinguished from "repressive law":

> In repression, the integration of law and politics abridges the civilizing values of the rule of law, that is, legality conceived as fairness and restraint in the use of power. In a responsive legal order, the reintegration of law and government is a way of enlarging the meaning and reach of legal values from a set of minimal restrictions to a source of affirmative responsibilities.[37]

10.2.4. RISE OF NEO-CLASSICAL CRIMINOLOGY

It is generally known that after the 1960s there was an extraordinarily repressive response to crime problems in the United States and that that repressive development manifested itself mainly in two ways: on the one hand, the development and systematic implementation of a mainly police-enforced

---

[36]   Black 1976.
[37]   Nonet and Selznick 1978, pp. 73–74, 117.

zero-tolerance policy to crime, coupled with a quality-of-life policy, and on the other, the large-scale use of imprisonment and, in line with this, the development of a gigantic prison system.

The zero-tolerance/quality-of-life strategy was developed rapidly in New York City in the 1990s by the renowned Mayor Rudy Giuliani and the equally well-known police chief William Bratton as a means of bringing public order and safety back to a tolerable level and, in that context, of putting a stop to the city's enormous level of violent property crime and especially murder and manslaughter. It was thus the police department that was at the forefront of implementing that policy, systematically focusing its day-to-day activities in various ways on repressively combatting misbehaviour and crime.[38]

That shift in policing policy did not take place without a struggle within the police department. Its offensive nature also aroused a great deal of resistance within some sections of New York society.[39] The point, however, is that the overall (recorded) crime rate – particularly the number of murders – almost immediately began to decline much more sharply than before the arrival of Giuliani and Bratton. In 1993, for example, the number of murders was almost 2,000, but by the end of the 1990s it had dropped to well below 1,000; according to *The New York Times*, it had fallen to 515 in 2011 and to 414 in 2012.[40]

The question was and remains, however, just what the causes were of that decline, all the more so because the crime figures also began to fall elsewhere in America during that period. Was it the mobilisation of the police department against street crime that made the difference? Or did it have to do with the changing composition of the population? The change in the market for drugs? The parallel social measures that were introduced? The increased large-scale application of imprisonment, including for many minor offences? Or the fact that more and more people were taking steps themselves, technically and socially, to increase their personal safety? And so forth.[41]

Where prison policy is concerned, however, the statistics on the imprisonment of offenders, often for relatively minor offences, speak volumes. Depending on the period in question and the sources consulted, those statistics vary somewhat, but according, for example, to Elliot Currie, David Garland, Norval Morris and Michael Tonry, whereas fewer than 200,000 convicts were held in federal and state prisons in 1971, by 1996 there were 1,200,000, and by 2001 more than 2,000,000. Expressed per 100,000 inhabitants, there were 93 per 100,000 in 1972, 427 in 1996, and 450 in 2001. Those figures take no account of convicts who received a conditional sentence or were released on parole; they amounted in 1990, for

---

[38] Bratton and Knobler 1998, pp. 143–164; Silverman 1999, pp. 73–124; Parenti 1999, pp. 70–89.
[39] McArdle and Erzen 2001.
[40] Ruderman in *The New York Times*, 28 December 2012 ("414 homicides in '12 is a record low for New York"); Maple and Mitchell 2000, pp. 66–67.
[41] Blumstein and Wallman 2000.

example, to more than a further 2,500,000.[42] It is therefore not surprising that Currie wrote in 1998 that "[t]he prison has become a looming presence in our society to an extent unparalleled in our history."[43]

According to many qualified researchers looking back at the penitentiary developments in the United States at the end of the 1990s, the phenomenon of mass imprisonment cannot of course be attributed only to the third new movement in criminology that appeared in the country at the time, namely neo-classical criminology, which was just as radical as Marxist criminology but on the conservative or right wing of the political spectrum. That phenomenon also involved to a significant extent the sharp rise in (recorded) crime in the 1970s and 1980s, the increasing concern among large parts of the population about safety in the streets and at home, and party-political exploitation of these two developments, not only by Republicans but also by Democrats.[44] And in so far as this new criminology promoted these penal developments, it could only exert that influence because its message matched the circumstances that we have just referred to. In addition, however, it should be emphasised that the criminology of the 1960s developed no meaningful and actionable proposals for managing the increasing crime problems. It thus largely created the intellectual and political scope for a completely different kind of criminology.[45]

It is indisputable that the standard-bearer of this third new approach to criminology was the aforementioned Wilson, although he was not alone and was also not the first. He had in 1967 immediately been extremely critical of the report *The Challenge of Crime in a Free Society*. As a matter of fact, he tore it to pieces in an article in the periodical *The Public Interest*. In his opinion, the problem of crime had not only been misrepresented but also underestimated. Moreover, the remedies proposed by the commission for dealing with that problem did not amount to much. Just what had all those youth care centres, job creation projects, initiatives for family support and so forth that the commission talked of actually – and demonstrably – delivered? And although the commission had been insufficiently concerned with the possibility of preventing all sorts of crimes, Wilson thought that was not really a problem: after all, burglary, robbery, mugging, and car theft are quite simply hard to prevent.

He then came to the issue of imprisonment: "Should criminals spend more time in jail?" In his view, the answer was simply that they should. Someone who is behind bars cannot commit any more crimes. For Wilson, that principle applied especially to repeat offenders, most of whom were at the time sentenced

---

[42]   Currie 1985, pp. 28–29; Morris and Tonry 1991, pp. 9–13; Currie 1998, pp. 12–13; Garland 2001, p. 1; Tonry 2004, pp. 21–22.

[43]   Currie 1998, p. 21; Parenti 1999, pp. 163–244.

[44]   Currie 1998, pp. 37–79; Jacobs (J.) 2001, pp. 165–169; Garland 2001, p. 179; Tonry 2004, pp. 23–61.

[45]   Currie 1985, pp. 14–16.

conditionally or released on probation. His truly cynical conclusion was that "the major accomplishment of the President's Commission is that it existed". He thought, nevertheless, that the fact that the federal government would be spending some money, via the Law Enforcement Assistance Agency, on the local enforcement of criminal legislation was a good thing. Not that that money would provide greater safety for citizens in the streets, but it would demonstrate "to local judges, police and correctional authorities that they are not being left alone and unaided while they cope with society's most refractory problems".[46] This disparaging conclusion almost heralded the publication in 1975 of his highly influential book *Thinking about Crime*, a revised edition of which appeared in 1983.

The ideas that he set out in that little book in terms of how to tackle crime – expressly only street crime, in other words primarily violent property crime (mugging, robbery, burglary) in which the physical and psychological integrity of the citizen is assailed by an unknown third party – had in part already been defended by the well-known but rather psychologically oriented author Ernest Van den Haag. In his book *Punishing Criminals*, for example, the latter stated that it was not only high time to retaliate against crimes in terms of their seriousness but that imprisonment was also an appropriate means of doing so.

In the same eighteenth-century manner, Van den Haag repeated what Montesquieu, in particular, had already asserted, namely that in principle crime must always be punished and the punishment should follow as soon as possible after the crime if its specific and general preventive purposes are to be achieved. In more contemporary terms, he invoked the economist Gary Becker who – in the spirit of the economist Beccaria – had argued repeatedly since the 1960s that criminals are essentially just calculating citizens and that, given the choice as to whether or not to commit a crime in which the advantages outweigh the disadvantages, a positive balance will be decisive in their decision to commit it. A contemporary version of the rational choice theory thus made its arrival in criminology.[47]

Unlike Van den Haag, Wilson was someone whose in-depth empirical research into the functioning of the police departments in a number of cities not only made him familiar with the crime problems facing the country but also with the problems involved in the approach to be taken by the authorities. This partly explains why in 1982 he and George Kelling published a famous article in the *Atlantic Monthly* setting out the "broken-windows theory". Essentially, that theory states that petty crime and nuisances create feelings of insecurity

---

46   Wilson (J.) 1967.
47   Van den Haag, 1975, pp. 20–23, 49–50, 78–80, 153–191, 241–261; Singer 1979; Von Hirsch 1986; Von Hirsch and Ashworth 1992.

in neighbourhoods which in turn, on the one hand, lead to citizens in those neighbourhoods withdrawing from the public domain or simply going to live somewhere else, and on the other, make those neighbourhoods more attractive to perpetrators of more serious crimes, with such neighbourhoods thus ending

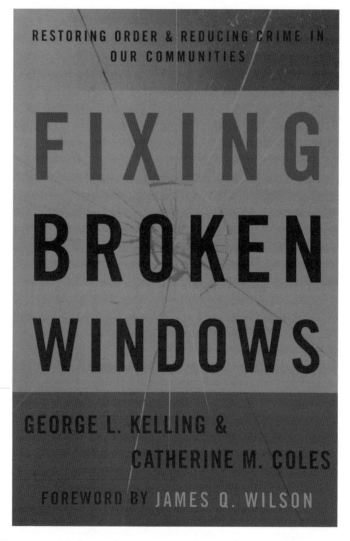

George KELLING and Catherine COLES, *Fixing Broken Windows: Restoring Order & Reducing Crime in our Communities,* New York, Martin Kessler Books, 1996 (foreword by J. WILSON).

up in a spiral of decline. If the police want to stop such a development, they must gain the support of residents; on their own, they will be unable to reverse such a trend. In the 1990s, this theory formed the starting point for the zero-tolerance/ quality-of-life policy in New York City that has already been mentioned and which was subsequently imitated in many major cities in the United States and elsewhere.[48]

Because Wilson's *Thinking about Crime* is such a concisely written book, it cannot really be summarised. Its four salient points are, however, set out in the following.

First, criminology has monumentally failed to develop a well-considered policy and appropriate policy alternatives to control crime. Criminologists have provided recommendations, but their criminology "could not form the basis for much policy advice". A serious analysis of the problem calls for measures that make it possible to change behaviour, and the only instrument available to society in that regard in the short term requires us to accept the view "that people act in response to the costs and the benefits of alternative courses of action" as well as the idea "that the criminal acts *as if* crime were the product of a free choice among competing opportunities and constraints. The radical individualism of Bentham and Beccaria may be scientifically questionable but prudentially necessary".[49]

Second, the police have allowed themselves to be confined too much to investigating individual cases, with all the legal complications that entails. They need to pay far more attention once again to the maintenance of public order at neighbourhood level; because they cannot do that alone, they must as far as possible reinforce the informal control mechanisms which already exist in neighbourhoods: "Just as physicians now recognize the importance of fostering health rather than treating illness, so the police – and the rest of us – ought to recognize the importance of maintaining, intact, communities without broken windows".[50]

Third, surveying all the existing theories regarding prevention, "the wisest course of action for society is to try simultaneously to increase both the benefits of noncrime and the costs of crime, all the while bearing in mind that no feasible changes in either part of the equation is likely to produce big changes in crime rates". Under certain conditions, that increase in the costs of crime can in general best be achieved through "incapacitation", i.e. more focused and large-scale confinement of high-risk offenders. The consequent need to expand prison capacity must be accepted as part of the bargain.[51]

Fourth, it must be accepted that "wicked people exist" and that for many citizens the response to those people is a clear signal:

> When we profess to believe in deterrence and to value justice, but refuse to spend the energy and money required to produce either, we are sending a clear signal that we

---

[48]   Kelling and Coles 1996, pp. 11–37.
[49]   Wilson (J.) 1985, pp. 50–51, 54.
[50]   Wilson (J.) 1985, p. 89.
[51]   Wilson (J.) 1985, pp. 143, 145–161.

think that safe streets, unlike all other great public goods, can be had on the cheap. We thereby trifle with the wicked, make sport of the innocent, and encourage the calculators. Justice suffers, and so do we all.[52]

Unsurprisingly, this book evoked mixed reactions in the world of criminology, even after Wilson toned down a number of points in the revised 1983 edition. In that edition, he expressed himself more moderately about socially oriented programmes for combatting juvenile delinquency. But in that edition, he was also much more vehement in his support for the view that in the case of many people a great deal of crime arises simply from their lack of self-control. Until the early twentieth century, the efforts of families, churches, and schools had focused on "the need for self-control, the delay of personal gratification, and the management of social relations on the basis of mutual restraint". All sorts of changes in the structure and culture of American society had led, however, to that ethos disappearing, with "self-control" being replaced by "self-expression".[53]

On the one hand, Wilson could more or less count on support from those criminologists who believed that "strain theories" – especially theories based on explanations in terms of social disorganisation and anomie – had had their day. In their view, it was really only control theories that offered a reasonable explanation for the crime problems facing the United States and that therefore provided an adequate basis for a rational and effective policy on crime. In that context, such authors as Travis Hirschi, together with Michael Gottfredson, posited a "general theory of crime" in 1990 with great aplomb.[54] That theory basically argues that the offender:

> appears to have little control over his or her own desires. When such desires conflict with long-term-interests, those lacking self-control opt for the desires of the moment, whereas those with greater self-control are governed by the restraints imposed by the consequences of acts displeasing to family, friends, and the law.[55]

Unsurprisingly, this so-called theory became the object of fierce criticism regarding its principles and pretensions, not only in the United States but also, for example, in Germany. All kinds of research showed, for example, that the benefits that people can obtain are certainly as important as self-control when the opportunity arises to commit an offence. Another important point is that in order to prove the general applicability of their theory, Hirschi and Gottfredson provide a picture of white-collar crime that is not really suited to this purpose.[56]

---

52   Wilson (J.) 1985, p. 260.
53   Wilson (J.) 1985, pp. 223–249; Wilson (J.) 1995; Currie 1985, pp. 21–50.
54   Farrington, Ohlin and Wilson 1986; Wilson and Petersilia 1995.
55   Gottfredson and Hirschi 1990, p. XV.
56   Reed and Yeager 1996; Fetchenhauer and Simon 1998; Schulz (S.) 2006; Buker 2011.

On the other hand, Wilson was fiercely assailed by Marxist and interactionist criminologists. The Marxists Tony Platt and Paul Takagi, for example, attacked Wilson and other "new realists" not for having brought up the problem of street crime, but for having ignored the social developments that had led to that problem assuming such major proportions. They also stressed that Wilson, Van den Haag, and others had been highly critical of the functioning of the criminal justice system but that, when it came down to it, they believed only in the blessings of capitalism and the power of the state to ensure law and order. In the wake of this criticism, the proponents of the neo-classical criminology were blamed for their willingness to work out a policy agenda for a more forceful law and order policy.[57]

Currie, one of the representatives of the interactionist faction, recognised that, in recent years, criminology had failed by not recognising crime problems or by minimising them, and by almost blindly adhering to the old ideal of reforming criminals by means of conditional sentencing, intramural programmes, and release on probation. However, he also immediately argued that Wilson had wrongly ignored factors that could be responsible for the increased crime problems: the increased inequality in American society, the marginalisation and exclusion of large groups of people, the rise in unemployment, the collapse of whole neighbourhoods due to the loss of jobs and migration of residents, and the diminishing welfare for individuals and persons who could hardly take care of themselves on their own in the face of the profound economic and social changes that were taking place. Currie was therefore of the opinion that the policies set out by Wilson did not constitute an answer to the prevailing problems. In his view, a meaningful anti-crime strategy needed to:

> Adopt a more coherent and consistent set of premises. It should take pathology seriously. It should, whenever possible, emphasize prevention rather than repression. It should address itself to maintaining the integrity of communal institutions of socialization, livelihood, and support. And finally, it must be tough-minded enough to confront unflinchingly the larger social and economic forces that now weaken and strain those institutions.[58]

More specifically, he advocated, inter alia, "full and decent employment", which he said was "the keystone of any successful anti-crime policy". He also argued, in particular, for "credible sanctions short of incarceration" – i.e. "middle-range sanctions" – because offenders, he wrote, were now incarcerated either for a very long – often unnecessarily long – time or were abandoned to their fate, "oscillating between alienating harshness and sheer neglect". A penalty to which

---

57   Platt and Takagi 1977.
58   Currie 1985, pp. 224–229; Currie 1998, pp. 124–147.

he drew special attention was community service. Although he knew that reform and support programmes for juvenile delinquents had fallen into disrepute, he felt that they were nevertheless indispensable in a significant number of cases and should therefore be retained, perhaps in a different guise.[59]

Currie was not in fact the only person who advocated a more differentiated criminal policy. Similar views were also defended by Tonry, for example.[60] It is striking, incidentally, that this group did not advocate the development of a more appropriate victimology. Until the 1960s, that relatively new discipline had remained mired in Von Hentig's view that victims are functionally partly responsible for what happens to them.[61] A modern view of that discipline would in fact be able to shed a different – probably sharper and more nuanced – light on the expectations that victims of crime have as regards both the authorities and offenders.

Finally, one should not ignore the fact that some veteran American criminologists were horrified by what both Wilson and his radical opponents were claiming. One very strong response came from Cressey,[62] who wrote that he had never expected that "criminology would become more and more concerned with increasing the efficiency of the punitive legal apparatus and less and less concerned with trying to discover the processes generating the criminals to be punished and the laws and personnel doing the punishing" or that the "typical modern criminologist [would be] a technical assistant to politicians bent on repressing crime, rather than a scientist seeking valid propositions stated in a causal framework".

Wilson, Van den Haag, and their associates were accused of apparently being satisfied "with a technological criminology whose main concern is for showing policy makers how to repress criminals and criminal justice workers more efficiently".

It should be noted that this aversion to the right-wing/realistic policy that Wilson had so strongly outlined was expressed not only in the United States but was also noticeable in Europe.[63] That does not of course alter the fact that the relative success of the zero-tolerance/quality-of-life policy raised important questions about the tenability of all kinds of conventional views in criminology, for example the generally preventive effect of a systematically implemented operational criminal policy.[64]

---

[59] Currie 1985, pp. 233–234, 263–267, 275–276.
[60] Morris and Tonry 1990, pp. 111–241; Tonry 2004, pp. 141–228.
[61] Schafer 1968.
[62] Cressey 1978. See also Glaser 1978.
[63] Ortner, Pilgram and Steinert 1998.
[64] Hess 1998, pp. 51–55.

What is interesting in the context of the present work, however, is that Cressey was also not enamoured of the alternative at the opposite extreme, namely the "new criminology" recently promulgated in the United Kingdom by Ian Taylor, Paul Walton, and Jock Young. In his opinion, these people looked as though they, in their own way, had an aversion to science and were losing themselves in "broad intellectualizing, accompanied by political proselytizing" instead of pursuing research involving "studies designed to secure comprehension of the conditions under which criminal laws are enacted, enforced and broken".

10.3.   TURMOIL IN EUROPE

That quotation from Cressey brings us to the turmoil stirred up in Europe in the 1960s, 1970s, and 1980s by the new criminologies. Developments in the United Kingdom will be discussed first because – definitely in part due to their interfaces with those in the United States – they were in general the most significant on this side of the Atlantic. We will then look at those in Germany and France, followed by the Netherlands and Belgium. The developments will be dealt with country by country because for all sorts of reasons – the history of criminology, the institutional embedding of criminological research, general political trends – they are after all very varied. We must also bear in mind that language differences still make it very difficult for many people in Europe to take note of what is happening in neighbouring countries.

10.3.1.   FURTHER EUROPEANISATION OF CRIMINOLOGY IN EUROPE

The fact remains that, in the light of the past, it is almost superfluous to mention that the developments in the various European countries were not only directly influenced, of course, by those in the United States but that there was also a certain cross-border interaction between those developments themselves.

As in the distant past, that reciprocal influence still operates today, on the one hand on an incidental and individual basis, through cognisance of the relevant literature (books, journals, newspapers), through attendance at national and international meetings, and through joint research projects. On the other hand, we must not forget that since the 1950s new frameworks have been created within which cooperation takes place on a more systematic basis. The pre-war European frameworks have to a significant extent disappeared. The international anthropological congresses and the congresses of the International Union of Penal Law were no longer organised after the First World War. The work of the International Penal and Penitentiary Commission was taken over after the Second World War by the United Nations, while the remit of the International

Society of Criminology and the International Association of Criminal Law had gradually shifted from Europe to the world as a whole.

These new frameworks involve, on the one hand, the international organisations in Europe within which not only the national but definitely also the cross-border problems of crime and criminal justice are an important concern. This involves the Council of Europe and also increasingly, since the Maastricht Treaty of 1992, the European Union. In recent decades, comparative and empirical research concerning these problems and how to tackle them has been carried out within these two institutions, in all kinds of fields.[65] Moreover, their involvement with these issues has certainly also encouraged such research indirectly. One example is the research carried out in the past ten years by a small Belgian–Dutch research team on developments in the border areas of the Netherlands, Belgium, and Germany, especially in and around the Meuse–Rhine Euroregion.[66] This was largely the result of initiatives already taken at the Catholic University of Leuven and the Max Planck Institute for Foreign and International Criminal Law in Freiburg with a view to studying the problems of (organised) crime and cross-border cooperation at European level.[67]

On the other hand, one must bear in mind that since the 1960s independent initiatives have also gradually been taken by researchers and research institutes to give shape to their cooperation at European level. For example, adherents of the critical, Marxist, and interactionist criminology from the United Kingdom, Italy, Germany, France, the Netherlands, and other European countries – inspired by the ideas developed in Berkeley – set up a European Group for the Study of Deviance and Social Control in 1972–73, which from the outset proclaimed itself as the leftist and progressive alternative to established criminology in Europe.[68] In the mid-1970s, with the support of a large number of European researchers and research institutes the director of the *Centre d'études sociologiques sur le droit et les institutions pénales* in Paris, Philippe Robert, set up the *Groupe Européen de recherches sur les normativités*. The journal *Déviance et société*, which appeared for the first time in 1977, became its intellectual forum.[69] In the 1990s, members of this network also occasionally published comparative studies on, for example, the development of relevant scientific research and on problems in the area of law enforcement, crime prevention, and judicial reform.[70] A counterpart to the

---

[65]   Fijnaut 2001.

[66]   Fijnaut and Spapens 2005; Fijnaut and De Ruyver 2008; Fijnaut, Van Daele, Kooijmans, Van der Vorm and Verbist 2010.

[67]   Fijnaut, Goethals, Peters and Walgrave 1995; Fijnaut and Paoli 2004.

[68]   See the group's *Manifesto* published in *Crime and Social Justice* 1975, p. 47. See also Ciacci and Simondi 1977, pp. 109–117; Van Swaaningen 1997, pp. 82–84.

[69]   Bailleau and Groenemeyer 2007.

[70]   Robert and Sack 1994; Van Outrive and Robert 1999.

American Society of Criminology – the European Society of Criminology – was later set up and the *European Journal of Criminology* was founded.

In addition to the newsletters, working papers, and journals that these partnerships published (and continue to publish) separate publication channels were also established to promote the exchange of ideas and research results at

European Group for the Study of Deviance and Social Control, *Terrorism and the Violence of the State,* Hamburg, 1978.

European level, and thus also at transatlantic and global level. One example is the *European Journal of Crime, Criminal Law and Criminal Justice,* which was founded in 1992 by members of the Department of Criminal Law and Criminology of the Faculty of Law of the Catholic University of Leuven and the

Max Planck Institute for Foreign and International Criminal Law. The title of that journal reveals the intention to continue to view the problems of crime and punishment from the double perspective of criminology and criminal science and thus to link up with the European tradition in this field.[71]

One important step in this direction was certainly also the publication of collections and handbooks with a distinctly European stamp. This important development commenced at the end of the 1980s, for example with the publication of the proceedings of the European colloquiums on crime and criminal policy organised by, among others, the aforementioned Max Planck Institute, the Dutch Ministry of Justice's Research and Documentation Centre in The Hague, the *Centre d'études sociologiques sur le droit et les institutions pénales* and the Centre for Criminology at Oxford University.[72] Over the years, this form of cooperation has resulted in book projects in all kinds of fields. The *Handbook of European Criminology* published in 2013 under the editorship of Sophie Body-Gendrot, Klara Kerezsi, Mike Hough, René Lévy, and Sonja Snacken represents the crowning achievement so far of this development.[73]

10.3.2. AMERICANISATION OF BRITISH CRIMINOLOGY

At the end of Chapter 6, we saw how – in particular due to refugee or immigrant professors from mainland Europe, such as Mannheim, Radzinowicz, and Grünhut – a number of British universities and the Home Office created facilities for the practice of criminology, in terms of teaching, research, and advice on policy matters. If we then consider the development of the literature in that discipline in the mid-twentieth century, we see, on the one hand, the disappearance of the more traditional British literature on such matters as juvenile delinquency and the prison system. A good example of that "old" literature is provided by the collection of essays on reform of the criminal justice system that was published in 1974 by Louis Blom-Cooper.[74] On the other hand, developments in American research found their way, in various ways and in various areas, into the British literature. Given what follows, it is important to first deal with this influence at somewhat greater length.

10.3.2.1. *Americanisation of Research*

First, a group of researchers emerged who – influenced by the research carried out in Chicago and at Harvard on social disorganisation and crime problems, the

---

71   Albrecht and Klip 2013.
72   Kaiser and Albrecht 1990.
73   Body-Gendrot, Kerezsi, Hough, Lévy and Snacken 2013.
74   Blom-Cooper 1974.

causes of juvenile delinquency, the functioning of subcultures, and white-collar crime – began to write about crime problems in disadvantaged neighbourhoods, developments in the area of juvenile delinquency, and, more broadly, deviant behaviour among young people and crime in the business sector.[75]

Among the publications that stand out are those of Howard Jones and Donald West on juvenile delinquency problems. Their studies were marked by interdisciplinary efforts to understand the social and personal background to that behaviour, but they were also evidence of a critical stance towards the ways in which the problems of young people were responded to, particularly by the criminal justice system. It is remarkable that these and other studies did not immediately result in a sequel. They stood alone, as it were, and apparently did not fit into any particular research programme. Similar research generally took place only years later. Interest in white-collar crime only became apparent in the late 1970s with the in-depth study by Michael Levi of serious fraud in business: how was it perpetrated and what was the criminal law response?[76]

Second, there was research on the structure, etc. of British police forces and prisons, partly under the influence of American examples such as that by Sykes on life in a maximum-security prison and that by Westley, Wilson, and Skolnick on the functioning of police departments. Mention may also be made of both the well-known study by Terence and Pauline Morris on the notorious Pentonville prison and the books by Michael Banton and Maureen Cain on the interaction between police forces or police officers and the social environment in which they operate.[77] The comparative observational study that Banton had carried out of police forces in America and the United Kingdom was also an eye-opener in Europe and was an incentive, including in the Netherlands, for the start of empirical research in that area. The study by Dick Hobbs in the 1980s on the way detectives in the East End of London attempted to carry out their work successfully is to some extent a continuation of the studies by Banton and Cain.[78]

Third, in the course of the 1960s, American interactionism found its way into British criminology, with the first clear demonstration of this being Dennis Chapman's *Sociology and the Stereotype of the Criminal* (1968).[79] This influence was also apparent, although less obviously so, from the circumspect discussion of interactionism in the widely read *Key Issues in Criminology* (1970) by Roger Hood and Richard Sparks, and from the application of interactionism

---

[75] Morris (T.) 1957; Mays 1963; Downes 1966; Jones (H.) 1965; Fyvel 1966; West 1968.
[76] Levi 1981.
[77] Morris and Morris 1963; Banton 1964; Banton 1973; Cain 1973; Galtung 1967; Mathiesen 1972.
[78] Hobbs 1988.
[79] Chapman 1968.

by Keith Bottomley in his study *Decisions in the Penal Process* (1973).[80] In the meantime, however, a group of young sociologists emerged who embraced American interactionism not only in order to shape their own research differently but also as a reaction to what they called establishment criminology in Britain.

One of the leading figures in that group, Stanley Cohen, later explained where that sometimes almost visceral opposition originated.[81] He gave several reasons. Two of these were that they could not live with the pragmatism of British criminology and its striving for interdisciplinarity. Viewed from a more sociological perspective, another important factor was that they believed that sociology had been deliberately excluded from the current scientific and policy-related discourse on issues of crime and punishment. They felt that they had been treated as outsiders and almost as outcasts, as if they constituted a threat to the monopoly apparently claimed by psychiatrists, psychologists, prison governors, and ministry officials regarding these issues.[82]

Be that as it may, from 1968 on resistance increasingly took shape at the annual National Deviancy Symposium at the University of York, and it involved more than just what was expressed at those events. Critical discussion of innovation in criminology was in general fuelled by treatises on American interactionism and its significance for criminology. These included *Deviance, Reality & Society* by Steven Box (first published in 1971) and *Deviant Behaviour* by Paul Rock (1973).[83] Detailed studies were also published, however, on compelling issues showing what effect the application of this perspective could also have in the British context. A number of these studies appeared in the familiar series of Penguin paperbacks. Cohen's *Images of Deviance* appeared in 1971,[84] followed in 1973 by Ian and Laurie Taylor's *Politics and Deviance*.[85] The latter collection has an undeniably more radical tone – including praise of social control in Cuba – than the former.

A fourth point to note in relation to the Americanisation of research is that in some fields the Home Office Research Unit – which in the late 1970s expanded to become by far the largest research institute in the United Kingdom, with 50 researchers – very much followed the lines of American neo-conservative research on the effectiveness of the criminal justice system and the techno-preventive approach to tackling crime. The Research Unit produced studies, for example, on the role of the police in preventing and investigating crime, on the possibilities of using the physical design of neighbourhoods and residential areas, and on the technical security of cars in combatting crime problems in

---

80   Hood and Sparks 1970; Bottomley 1973.
81   Cohen (S.) 1974.
82   Cohen (S.) 1974.
83   Box 1981; Rock 1973.
84   Cohen (S.) 1971.
85   Taylor and Taylor 1973.

the context of social safety.[86] In the course of the 1980s, the orientation of the Unit was clearly towards application of the rational choice theory in its research on, inter alia, shoplifters' and muggers' choices of victims.[87] The person at the Home Office who most embodied this kind of Americanisation of British criminological research in the eyes of the outside world was Ron Clarke.

Stanley COHEN (ed.), *Images of Deviance*, Harmondsworth, Penguin Books, 1971.

Fifth, one should not overlook the fact that in 1964 a well-known professor of psychology, Hans Eysenck, published *Crime and Personality*, which ran counter to the trends, arguing – briefly – "that it is the person who fails to

---

86   Clarke and Heal 1979; Clarke and Mayhew 1980.
87   Cornish and Clarke 1986.

develop conditioned moral and social responses, due to his low conditionability and his extraversion, who tends to become the psychopath and the criminal". To properly understand Eysenck's argument, there are two things that we need to note. First, Eysenck had asserted earlier in the book "that heredity is a very strong predisposing factor as far as committing crimes is concerned" and in particular that the features of "low conditionability and [...] extraversion" are determined by heredity. Second, he stated that research had shown "that strong emotions make normal integrative behaviour more difficult and make it more likely that a given person will behave in a manner which is not, over the long run, in his own best interests". The research to which he was referring was, inter alia, the bio-anthropological research carried out at Harvard in the 1930s and 1940s by Sheldon, Hooton and the Gluecks, but Burt's research on juvenile delinquents was also a source of inspiration for him.

Adopting this position naturally presupposed that in order to combat crime effectively a method of treating criminals was needed that was entirely different to that attempted within all sorts of institutions. That new method should focus on conditioning or reconditioning children who "by virtue of their poor conditionability, are predestined to become criminals and delinquents". Eysenck was thinking, for example, of advice to parents on how they should raise such children and the administration of drugs to ensure that people would become "much more amenable to discipline and much more socialised in their pattern of activities".[88]

Unsurprisingly, this very different but also very challenging position attracted enormous attention – not only in the United Kingdom – but it achieved little or no acceptance on a wider scale. If there was anything that the criminological *Zeitgeist* in the United Kingdom was not ripe for, it was this message, especially after the breakthrough achieved in 1974 by a group of Marxist criminologists in scientific research and public debate.

10.3.2.2. Rise and Fall of Marxist Criminology

It was not only the aforementioned collection of essays published by Taylor and Taylor in 1973 but also other publications that suggested that further radicalisation of some young, sociologically oriented criminologists was in the offing. The high point, however, was *The New Criminology: For a Social Theory of Deviance*, published in 1973 by Ian Taylor, Paul Walton and Jock Young.[89]

That book nearly demolished what they considered to represent classical and positivist criminology, and completely tore to shreds the biological variations of the latter approach. The authors held that the adherents of that discipline had

---

[88]   Eysenck 1964, pp. 74–75, 102–103, 110–111, 120–121, 126, 166–167, 172–174, 195–196, 204.
[89]   Taylor, Walton and Young 1973; Taylor, Walton and Young 1974.

disregarded the social conditions in which people are designated as criminals and in which such an oppressive apparatus as the criminal justice system functions. They had also ignored the ideological and therefore legitimising role that criminologists play within those relationships.

Ian TAYLOR, Paul WALTON and Jock YOUNG, *The New Criminology: For a Social Theory of Deviance*, London, Routledge & Kegan Paul, 1973 (with a foreword by A. GOULDNER).

Taylor, Walton, and Young also strongly criticised the successors to Durkheim and the American criminal sociologists: they too had largely ignored the "structures of power, authority and control" within a society organised on a capitalist basis. The interactionists did not fare much better. They were accused, inter alia, of ignoring the origin of deviant behaviour and the cause of society's response to it, thus becoming fixated "upon the important, but limited, questions of the outcome of societal reaction on a deviant's further behaviour".

In their view, "any description of the social totality we assert to be productive of deviance" was the crux of the issue. Did not Marx himself and Bonger provide such a description? No, because Bonger had seen things entirely wrongly. With his "environmental determinism" he was essentially, in his own way, a kind of positivist: "In a social structure encouraging of egoism, the obstacles and deterrents to the emergence of the presumably even-present 'criminal thought' are weakened and/or removed." The basic assumption ought in fact to be: "crime as human action, as reaction to positions held in an antagonistic social structure, but also as action taken to resolve those antagonisms". That was in any case what Marx had suggested but had not worked out in detail. But it was what Taylor, Walton, and Young did in the conclusion to their book, which dealt with the requirements to be met by a "fully social theory of deviance", i.e.:

> a theory that can explain the forms assumed by social control and deviant action in "developed" societies (characterized – as we have argued – by the domination of a capitalist mode of production, by a division of labour involving the growth of armies of "experts" […] who have been assigned a crucial role in the tasks of social definition and social control, by the necessity to segregate out – in mental hospitals, prisons and in juvenile institutions – an increasing variety of its members as being in need of control.[90]

That theory should be based on six factors: "the wider origins of the deviant act", "immediate origins of the deviant act", "the actual act", "immediate origins of social reaction", "wider origins of social reaction", and "the outcome of the social reaction on the deviant's further action". Furthermore, criminology should break entirely with anything that smacked of positivism and "correctionalism", and should commit itself to striving for "the abolition of inequalities of wealth and power, and in particular of inequalities in property and life-chances". This was because if one wanted to abolish crime one must also fundamentally change the social relations within which that phenomenon was viewed as problematic. Ultimately, the aim was "to create a society in which the facts of human diversity, whether personal, organic or social, are not subject to the power to criminalize".

Taylor, Walton, and Young were not the only ones in the 1970s who propagated this Marxist – also referred to as left-idealistic – view of criminology and society. Theoretical treatises and publications appeared with a more applied perspective, one of the best known being *Policing the Crisis* on the phenomenon of mugging.[91] Moreover, this radical approach enjoyed support, to a certain extent, from feminists: criticism of sexist criminological literature on women

---

[90]   Taylor, Walton and Young 1973, p. 269.
[91]   Pearce 1976; Hall, Chritcher, Jefferson, Clarke and Roberts 1978.

as offenders, the resistance of more and more women to domestic violence and street violence, and the invisibility of the role that women play in the criminal justice system. The primary object of opposition was the traditional perspective within which women were made guilty, or at least co-responsible, for the crimes committed by men against them. Carol Smart's *Women, Crime and Criminology: A Feminist Critique* (1976) was an eye-opener and still remains worth reading,[92] as does Frances Heidensohn's 1985 book on this and other issues.[93]

But how the Marxist message came to be generally well received in the United Kingdom – even in the light of what had happened and was still happening in the Soviet Union – was later explained by Young.[94] In 1988, he ascribed its success, on the one hand, mainly to the fact that the academisation of higher education created great scope for research by radical criminologists and, on the other, to the fact that in many parts of the country those criminologists received the support of leftist political groups and left-oriented public authorities. He nevertheless bemoaned the fact that his version of criminology had still not become generally accepted, as he and his comrades had hoped.

One of the reasons will certainly have been that the criminological establishment did not simply surrender to the blissful prospects offered by Marxist criminology. In the introduction to his critical criminology (1987), Nigel Walker wrote that Marxist criminology was over-simplified and came to grief on its own ideology:

> This chapter is not meant to do justice to the good intentions of politicians, feminists or criminologists. What it should have demonstrated is that ideological reasoning is not confined to politicians; and that where criminology and penology are concerned it leads up false trails, sheep-tracks, and abandoned paths. The warning signposts erected by less ideological historians and social scientists are overlooked, brushed aside, or even torn down.[95]

The rather paternalistic response by Radzinowicz was not very favourable either. Perhaps inspired by his own turbulent life before the Second World War, he wrote in 1977:

> Radical criminology has not been alone in going to extremes. All new movements, in their first flush of enthusiasm and their determination to achieve the maximum impact, begin by distorting or denying the achievements, reversing the values and emphases, of their predecessors. All attitudes towards crime have their periods of challenge and eclipse. Yet they tend to persist, sometimes reappearing in fresh guises, under new names. Often they have to learn to co-exist within a single system. They are perforce

---

[92] Smart 1976.
[93] Heidensohn 1995; Morris (A.) 1987; Daly and Maher 1998.
[94] Young (J.) 1988.
[95] Walker (N.) 1987, pp. 186–193.

modified by their own experience, by mutual influences and antagonisms, and by the changing climate of the times.[96]

The interactionists naturally had their say too. Rock, in particular, made short work of the Marxists on a number of occasions. In 1979, he wrote that they dealt extremely carelessly with what had been achieved by a variety of academic disciplines and reduced it all, entirely wrongly, to conservative or "liberal" criminology. Conversely, they themselves used sententious terms such as "social totality" without indicating what they were referring to in the real world, they pushed aside all forms of realism, reality, and empiricism etc., believing solely in the metaphysics that they had themselves created, and they systematically distrusted what others – definitely police officers, judges, probation officers, etc. – had to say about crime, criminals and victims, and indeed discredited it. In his view, the gap between the interactionists and the Marxists was therefore virtually insurmountable:

> Radical criminology searches for the roots and essences of social life: it is directed at the discovery of an absolute society which subtends all the mundane appearances of experience. Distrusting all that may be sensed, it eschews every exploratory use of the senses. It places reality in a realm which can only be intuited by a consciousness which is ideologically attuned.[97]

In 1982 – together with David Downes – Rock cynically summarised these and other criticisms of the "Marxist model of deviance and control" as follows:

> It is axiomatic that capitalism is criminogenic, as are all societies based on exploitation and oppression. The only form of society which in principle holds out any possibility of being crime-free is a society embodying the principles of "socialist diversity". "Socialism" entails an absence of material differences, and a willed commitment to equality. It removes the rationale for crimes against property, the bulk of offences in any capitalist society.[98]

But it was not only Rock who denounced the basic principles of British Marxist criminology. That approach was also the subject of a fairly devastating discussion by Currie in 1974 in *Crime and Social Justice*, the favoured journal of the American Marxists.[99] Currie found, for example that the analysis offered by the British Marxists of existing criminology was "shallow and derivative, taking us little beyond the liberal critique already offered by Leon Radzinowicz and others". He noted the lack not only of a thorough analysis of the existing theories,

---

[96]   Radzinowicz 1979, pp. 84–86.
[97]   Rock 1979.
[98]   Downes and Rock 1986, pp. 206–207; Heidensohn 1989, pp. 63–84.
[99]   Currie 1974.

particularly those of Bonger, but also of any thorough understanding of the social implications of those theories for people in the real world. He also had great difficulty with the often inaccessible style of *The New Criminology*, "occasionally falling into complex and almost incomprehensible jargon". Currie continued in this vein, finally concluding that the book, methodically and stylistically, was in essence a normal academic book but that "its main theoretical assumptions [are] a bit confused and fundamentally misleading".

What finally really finished off Marxist criminology and deprived it to a large extent of its scientific and political credibility was that in the early 1980s a number of its leading figures made the switch from a "left-idealistic" radical criminology to a "left-realistic" radical criminology.

That ideological reversal – or perhaps, rather, conversion – was on the one hand primarily due to the discovery that in large cities "real" crime problems were increasingly occurring, that those problems also had "real" victims, especially in those communities in whose name they claimed to be acting, and that the Labour Party had virtually no answer to those issues because it had turned away from "rightist" issues and had left them to the Conservative Party.

On the other hand, that conversion was definitely reinforced by the violent disturbances in some cities, such as the Brixton riots in London in 1981, and by the lengthy and equally violent clashes between the police – deployed by the Conservative Prime Minister Margaret Thatcher – and the strikers, supported by a militant trade union movement, in the struggle over the future of the British mining industry.[100] Moreover, there were major problems in the prison system from time to time, not only in England, Wales, and Scotland, but specifically in Northern Ireland. In the latter part of the United Kingdom, the problems were of course closely entangled with that of dealing with terrorists, or suspected terrorists, whether Republican or Unionist.[101]

This is not the place to deal with the inexhaustible discussion regarding this reversal on the part of the Marxist vanguard.[102] What is interesting is that this time the converted left-realists did not get mired in ideological discussions but committed themselves, in particular, to assisting the Labour Party in the development of non-conservative but nonetheless credible forms of crime policy, whether or not based on their empirical research, especially on crime and safety problems at local level.[103] Quite a lot of examples of this can be found in the criminological literature.[104]

---

[100] Scarman 1982; Cowell, Jones and Young 1982; Fine and Miller 1985; Jefferson and Grimshaw 1984.

[101] Fitzgerald 1977; Stanley and Baginsky 1984; Maguire, Vagg and Morgan 1985; Pointing 1986; Rutherford 1986; Stern 1987.

[102] Steinert 1985; Matthews and Young 1992; Young and Matthews 1992; Lowman and MacLean 1992; Walton and Young 1998.

[103] Taylor (I.) 1982b.

[104] Taylor (I.) 1982a; Kinsey, Lea and Young 1986; Jones, MacLean and Young 1986.

The best-known of these is *What is to be Done About Law and Order? Crisis in the Eighties*, the paperback published by John Lea and Jock Young in 1984. In that programmatic pamphlet, the authors attempted not only to identify and explain problems of street crime, both quantitatively and qualitatively, but also presented recommendations for, inter alia, a proper discussion of the entanglements between race and crime, as well as for an effective and efficient policing policy that could continue to rely on sufficient support from the British population. At the end, they described the reasons why the left, specifically, should also concern itself with crime problems and the problems of both offenders and victims. They concluded:

> For too long the politics of law and order have been the monopoly of the right. Yet the left has every reason materially, politically and ideologically to intervene in this area. We are too paralysed by our own preconceptions easily to take up the challenge which is demanded of us. The opportunities for an initiative from the left are enormous; we must not shirk the task.[105]

It goes without saying that this *mea culpa* allowed scope for a certain rapprochement between the "positivists," the interactionists, and the (former) Marxists within British criminology. In my view, that scope was in fact utilised, on the one hand, to share ideas – on a more common footing and in a more balanced manner – on a number of important issues that arose from the 1980s on,[106] for example the position of the victims of crime and their role within the criminal justice system.[107] A more acute and pressing issue was that addressed by Robert Reiner in a well-known book published in 1985, namely *The Politics of the Police*.[108]

On the other hand, it is my impression that that scope also created more opportunities for pursuing empirical research that, for example, had its roots in traditional socio-geographic research on the development, distribution, etc. of traditional forms of crime, but with the framework also being based on contemporary criminology and victimology.[109] One of the best examples is *Crime and Social Change in Middle England: Questions of Order in an English Town* (2000) by Evi Girling, Ian Loader, and Richard Sparks.[110]

---

[105]   Lea and Young 1984, p. 272; Cohen (S.) 1985, pp. 236–272.
[106]   Jefferson and Shapland 1991.
[107]   Maguire and Pointing 1988.
[108]   Reiner 1985.
[109]   See for example Smith (S.) 1985.
[110]   Girling, Loader and Sparks 2000.

10.3.3. TRADITION, CONFLICT, AND RECONCILIATION IN GERMAN CRIMINOLOGY

In Chapter 8, we saw that it was not until the 1960s that there was open discussion of the role played by the *Kriminalbiologie* in the Third Reich. We noted that that belated recognition of its dubious role was not an isolated matter but part of the overall silence that prevailed in Germany until long after the Second World War regarding the role played by scientists, police officers, judges, and others under the Nazi regime. But was there not also a specific reason in the case of *Kriminalbiologie*? In my opinion, that cannot be ruled out entirely.

10.3.3.1. Continuation of Pre-War Criminology

One should not forget that in Germany – unlike in the United Kingdom – there was no Americanisation of criminological research in the 1950s and 1960s. At the time, hardly any attempt was made to link up with the criminal-sociological research that had begun in Chicago in the 1920s and 1930s, nor with the research that was increasingly carried out in America from the 1950s onwards on the police and prison systems. In other words, it was only perhaps in the 1960s that a more specific demand arose in Germany for disclosure regarding the role of *Kriminalbiologie* under the Nazis because, despite everything, that approach to criminology still matched up to some extent with the criminology as generally practised until in the 1960s.

Be that as it may, when we look at the post-war criminological literature, we see that not only were the works of the advocates of *Kriminalbiologie* republished (omitting the most "wrong" passages), but that until the late 1970s literature continued, in general, to build on pre-war criminology as if nothing had happened. The same applies just as much to the general introductions to criminology as to the treatises regarding specific perspectives and specific subfields.

Those general introductions included Fritz Bauer's *Das Verbrechen und die Gesellschaft* (1957), Ernst Seelig's *Lehrbuch der Kriminologie* (1963), Armand Mergen's *Die Wissenschaft vom Verbrechen* (1961) and *Die Kriminologie* (1967), Hans Göppinger's introduction *Kriminologie* (1971), and Rüdiger Herren's criminology handbook *Die Verbrechenswirklichkeit* (1979). All these introductions focus on the criminal, together with the causes, manifestations, investigation and prosecution, and treatment of his criminal behaviour. That is not to say that there are no references to the developments in criminology in America since the 1920s. Such references are scarce, however, and serve primarily as a supplement to what had traditionally been written by German criminologists.[111] These developments did not therefore lead in any way

---

111   Bauer (F.) 1957, pp. 33–34, 44–46, 201–203; Mergen 1967, pp. 7–12, 166–177; Hacker 1964, pp. 171–254.

whatsoever to a different presentation of, let alone to a different approach to, introductions to criminology as such.

Where publications from certain theoretical perspectives are concerned, it is striking, on the one hand, the considerable extent to which they build on the bio-anthropological, criminal-biological, and criminal-psychological research performed in the 1920s.[112] On the other hand, it is also naturally striking that – apart from the reprinted book by Sauer – no new sociological introductions to criminology were published. The latter fact clearly demonstrates that during this period there was no question of the Americanisation of criminology in Germany.

It should also be noted that until the 1970s studies were indeed published on the application of imprisonment and thus also on the prison system, but that until then none were published concerning actual life in prison or the actual functioning of the police – certainly not along the lines of those by Westley, Skolnick, Wilson, Banton, and others.[113] For this reason too it is not surprising that – for example at a seminar on combatting juvenile delinquency at the *Bundeskriminalamt* in Wiesbaden in 1954 – the relevant American literature was referred to only sporadically in order to identify or explain certain developments in Germany in that area.[114]

One should also bear in mind that it was only in 1959 that a separate chair for criminology was established at Heidelberg University, and only in 1962 that a separate criminological research institute was established at the University of Tübingen. It should be noted that the professors involved were jurists and psychiatrists, and therefore not researchers in the empirical sense of the word. They did, however, appoint psychologists and sociologists because, on the one hand, they were advocates of an interdisciplinary criminology and, on the other, foresaw criminology increasingly becoming an empirical science.[115]

It will be clear, however, that these few psychologists and sociologists – also in view of the hierarchical relationships at German universities, certainly at that time – could not immediately take a different approach to criminological research in Germany. Nor did they in fact do so. That does not alter the fact, however, that the initiatives taken in Heidelberg and Tübingen fitted in with a more general discussion of the need to revive German criminology.

This became evident at the international colloquium on the role of criminology in reforming criminal law held in and around Freiburg in 1957 to mark the 500th anniversary of the University of Freiburg and organised by the

---

[112]   Seelig and Weindler 1949; Walder 1952; De Landecho 1964; Bott-Bodenhausen 1965; Dechêne 1975.
[113]   Mittermaier 1954; Kaiser, Schöch, Eidt and Kerner 1974.
[114]   Bundeskriminalamt 1955, p. 203.
[115]   Göppinger 1971, p. 49; Baumann 2006, pp. 303–307.

renowned professors Hans-Heinrich Jescheck and Thomas Würtenberger. At that colloquium, the speakers included not only German professors and senior civil servants, but also professors well disposed towards criminology from the Netherlands (Bernard Röling, Jacob Van Bemmelen), Denmark (Stephan Hurwitz), and Switzerland (Erwin Frey, Jean Graven). Remarkably, Mannheim and Grünhut also attended. This was obviously a gesture of reconciliation to the former exiles on the part of the organisers, especially Würtenberger, who – as we saw in Chapter 8 – would argue a few years later for an open discussion of the role of *Kriminalbiologie* in the Third Reich.[116]

How courageous that was can already be seen from the fact that, in 1960, the well-known professor Richard Lange warned against a criminology whose adherents – in the name of more effectively combatting crime – were calling for radical preventive measures that in his view amounted to the abolition of the criminal law, without his actually mentioning the word *Kriminalbiologie*. In particular, he was apprehensive about the implementation of drastic measures in respect of young children based on the results of deterministic forecasts using what he considered to be flawed methodologies, such as those developed by the Gluecks and propagated by their European followers.[117]

Honesty requires one to add that this controversial stance provoked a debate during which the view was also expressed that the traditional, retribution-based criminal law was not automatically the most appropriate instrument for persuading offenders to live a more responsible life and that, in other words, criminology was important in developing a system of criminal law in which punishment could indeed fulfil that function.[118]

10.3.3.2.   Fritz Sack: Critical Criminology and Criminal Science

Against that background, it is understandable that the publication of *Kriminalsoziologie* by the Cologne sociologists Fritz Sack and René König in 1968 created shockwaves.[119] That was, on the one hand, because suddenly 20 key European but above all American sociological criminology texts – ranging from Durkheim to Sutherland, Cohen, Merton, and Cressey – were made widely available in German. On the other hand, it was because in his concluding chapter Sack outlined the new perspectives in criminology that had until then remained virtually unknown in Germany. He was referring generally to the interactionism that was developing in the United States and in particular to the labelling theory.

Unlike in traditional aetiological criminology, Sack wrote, that in interactionist theory crime was not defined as an intrinsic feature of the

---

[116]   Jescheck and Würtenberger 1958; Baumann 2006, pp. 235–268.
[117]   Lange (R.) 1960.
[118]   Brauneck 1963.
[119]   Sack and König 1968.

behaviour concerned but as a label that people attached to one another in their relationships. In line with that distinction, he pointed out its consequences, for instance for the assessment of crime statistics. From this new perspective, the familiar flaws in those statistics were viewed not as technical deficiencies of the

AKADEMISCHE REIHE

AUSWAHL REPRÄSENTATIVER TEXTE · SOZIOLOGIE

Kriminalsoziologie

Herausgegeben von

F. SACK · R. KÖNIG

AKADEMISCHE VERLAGSGESELLSCHAFT·FRANKFURT A.M.

Fritz SACK and René KÖNIG (eds.), *Kriminalsoziologie,* Frankfurt am Main, Akademische Verlagsgesellschaft, 1968.

relevant collections of data but as consequences of the ways in which norms are created, complied with, and enforced. What is equally important is that in his concluding remarks he pointed out that this new criminology was based on entirely different principles to traditional criminology. For example, it rejected almost by definition the idea that criminals are essentially different people to non-criminals.

What is very remarkable is that in his concluding remarks Sack not only argued that the sociology of deviant behaviour which he had outlined represented an enrichment of the existing criminology, but also pointed out that the new criminology could reduce the gap between criminal science and criminology. That was, first, because it focused strongly on how criminal justice was actually administered and, second, because in the distant past the existing criminology had also arisen from discussions about the functioning of the criminal justice system at that time. Why, in other words, should one not now re-engage with the issues that had played such an important role in its inception?

It is obvious that those concluding remarks – like the collection itself – did not arrive out of the blue. Quite the contrary: they were the result of Sack's rather lengthy period at Berkeley in the mid-1960s, where he had met Aaron Cicourel and other sociologists, or at least had become acquainted with their work. Moreover, his stay in the United States was in fact partly the result of his dissatisfaction with the existing criminology in Germany and the discussions taking place in criminological circles.[120]

Sack was not the only criminologist who had difficulty with criminology as practised and discussed in Germany in the 1960s – that dissatisfaction with the existing situation was shared by dozens of young researchers and in 1969 it made itself fully apparent. That year saw the founding of the *Arbeitskreis Junger Kriminologen* (Young Criminologists' Working Group) and their new publication, the *Kriminologisches Journal*. The other main figures included Günther Kaiser, Erhard Blankenburg, Liselotte Pongratz, Karl-Dieter Opp, and Manfred Brusten. These trailblazers of *kritische Kriminologie* formed a small but heterogeneous group.[121]

For that reason alone, it was obvious that, although they were fairly clear as to what they were rebelling against, their views varied greatly as to what exactly constituted – or should constitute – the substance of their version of criminology. The members of the working group shared a certain aversion to traditional criminology – although without directly or explicitly problematising *Kriminalbiologie* – and they agreed that their criticism of criminology was also a form of ideological criticism. They all adhered to a leftist political perspective and believed that the practice of their critical criminology should also have a leftist slant. The disagreements played out within a spectrum bounded at the one end by researchers such as Opp, who wished to integrate the labelling approach into the more conventional sociological explanations for criminal behaviour, and at the other by researchers adhering to a Marxist view of crime and how to

---

[120]   Löschper and Von Trotha 1996; Sack 1998, pp. 49–57.
[121]   Baumann 2006, pp. 310–318.

combat it.[122] However, none of these more radical or extreme positions gained the upper hand within the *Arbeitskreis Junger Kriminologen*.[123] That explains why Sack's attempt in 1972 to reconcile the interactionists and the Marxists attracted not only a great deal of attention but also a lot of support.[124]

This was in itself an indication of what would happen in the course of the 1970s, namely that most "young" criminologists, including Sack, would generally opt for the golden mean. This is apparent from the introductions to criminology that were produced largely from the "new" perspective, for example Wolfgang Keckeisen's *Die gesellschaftliche Definition abweichenden Verhaltens* (1974), Bernd-Rüdeger Sonnen's *Kriminalität und Strafgewalt: Einführung in Strafrecht und Kriminologie* (1978), and Klaus Lüderssen's textbook *Kriminologie: Einführung in die Probleme* (1984). These and other introductions clearly distance themselves from traditional aetiological criminology and from the traditional legal approach to criminal law and criminal justice. But despite all the criticism and despite all the differing views, they still do not adopt the position that the labelling of crime is purely a matter of promoting the interests of the ruling classes and that the administration of criminal justice is solely a tool used by those classes to defend those interests. It is also notable that although these introductions devote considerable attention to the interests of victims, the victimological perspective is not presented as such. The eye-opener in that regard came from Hans Schneider. In 1979, he published a paperback in which, strongly influenced by Von Hentig and Schafer, he not only referred to the functional link between offenders and their victims but also discussed the options for having the former compensate the latter for the harm sustained.[125]

Sack himself never wrote his own introduction to criminology, but in the 1970s he did remain true to his 1968 position that the labelling theory made it possible to bridge the gap between criminology and criminal science. In 1975, to investigate whether that really was the case, he published – together with Lüderssen – a two-volume collection of German and other contributions on deviancy, concluding with fundamental reflections on the possibilities for cooperation between the two disciplines.[126] He did not dismiss the existence of such possibilities, but he did constantly wonder what conditions were necessary for them to be effective. One of those conditions was in any case that criminologists should delve more deeply into the dogmatic issues that play such an important role in the field of criminal law, in the same way as lawyers should make greater efforts to acquaint themselves with criminological theories and

---

[122]   Opp 1974; Werkentin, Hoffenbert and Baurmann 1974.
[123]   Baumann 2006, pp. 330–335; Schumann 1975; Plack 1974.
[124]   Sack 1975; Sack 1985; Smaus 1996.
[125]   Schneider 1979.
[126]   Lüderssen and Sack 1975.

studies. In subsequent years, following on from this experiment, Lüderssen and Sack organised highly focused dialogues between lawyers and criminologists on a number of topics, including on the question of guilt in the criminal law and the criminalisation of certain kinds of behaviour.[127]

This unique experiment yielded no conclusive results, but that did not prevent Sack from attempting to implement the conclusion that he had formulated in 1975 at the end of the first experiment, namely that it was probably necessary to institutionalise the dialogue between criminology and criminal science by developing training programmes in which both professions could participate on an equal footing. In 1984, he joined with a number of like-minded individuals at the University of Hamburg to establish a two-year postgraduate course in criminology which was for many years the sole university programme in criminology in Germany.[128] Options for the further institutionalisation of criminology in Germany were discussed at an international symposium in Hamburg in 1986 on the basis of various foreign examples (in Belgium, the United Kingdom, and North America). This broad debate did not result, however, in any major initiatives at other universities to launch a separate programme in criminology or to establish a criminological research institute.[129]

That is not really surprising when one considers that in Germany criminology had to flourish within the faculties of law, which did not view it very favourably in around 1980. Quite the contrary: responses to both contemporary criminology and the possible interaction between criminology and criminal science were in fact sometimes outright hostile or incredibly sceptical.[130] There was also disagreement as to whether there had in the past actually been such a thing as *gesamte Strafrechtswissenschaft* (integrated criminal science).[131] When the faculties of law were reformed in 2003, criminology remained as an optional subject at most of them – as it already was in many cases – and was made part of a section or specialisation along with more criminal law-oriented subjects. Nowhere was criminology made independent in any form whatsoever. The programmes that were developed were much more like the criminal justice programmes offered at many American universities.[132]

10.3.3.3.   Günther Kaiser: The Max Planck Institute and Empirical Criminology

In 1970, after years of discussion in scientific, political and administrative circles, an eight-member *Kriminologische Arbeitsgruppe* (Criminological Working

---

[127]   Lüderssen and Sack 1980; Jäger 1980.
[128]   Sack 1998, pp. 60–61.
[129]   Löschper, Manke and Sack 1986; Jehle 1992.
[130]   Lange (R.) 1981; Leferenz 1981; Schultz 1980; Sack 1987; Kaiser 2004.
[131]   Baratta 1980; Fijnaut 1984b.
[132]   Dessecker and Jehle 2003.

Group) was set up at the Max Planck Institute for Foreign and International Criminal Law in Freiburg im Breisgau. The intention was not only to promote empirical research in criminology, but also to encourage the much-needed interaction between criminal science and criminology. Leadership of this department was entrusted to Kaiser, a member of the Arbeitsgruppe Junger Kriminologen, who for a number of years had carried out research at the criminological institute of the University of Tübingen and who was generally regarded as an adherent of the golden mean.[133] That impression is confirmed by his lecture notes on *Kriminologie*, which were first published in 1971 and in 1997 reached their tenth (completely revised) edition.[134] Besides a general explanation of criminological theories and their development, that book includes reflections on the perpetrators and victims of particular forms of crime, current criminal penalties, and the possibilities and limits of criminal policy.

The *Kriminologische Arbeitsgruppe* came in for a great deal of criticism from the perspective of critical criminology. Sack, Brusten, and others wrote that the criminology advocated at that institution would inevitably result in a form of *Staatsforschung* (state research). It would become a criminology that would not develop its own critical theories and would all too easily serve as legitimation of the existing criminal law and the prevailing criminal justice system.[135] Kaiser took that criticism seriously, but did not allow it to divert him from his intention of establishing an up-to-date research programme.[136] Key basic principles were, inter alia, that criminological research needed to link up with international developments and should keep to the middle ground between criminology oriented towards the personality of the offender and critical criminology as practised by Sack. Thematically, the research would focus on the issue of the "dark number", the operation of the police and the Public Prosecution Service, economic crime and private justice in the business sector, and criminal sanctions such as fines and the application of imprisonment.[137]

Kaiser kept his word. All kinds of surveys in fact show that the themes referred to were in fact very successfully tackled by researchers and that the results of their studies were widely appreciated, not only in Germany but also elsewhere.[138] Moreover, one can easily come to the conclusion that the setting up a special research group at the Max Planck Institute suddenly led to greater recognition and a higher profile for empirical criminology in Germany. This may be inferred, for example, from the extensive surveys of research published in 1983 on the occasion of the congress of the International Society of Criminology in

---

[133] Kaiser 1985, pp. 1037–1047.
[134] Kaiser 1997a.
[135] Hirsch 2006, pp. 32–38.
[136] Kaiser 2006.
[137] Kaiser 1997b.
[138] Göppinger and Kaiser 1976.

Vienna under the double title *Deutsche Forschungen zur Kriminalitätsentstehung und Kriminalitätskontrolle/German Research on Crime and Crime Control*.[139]

These surveys, later followed by the release of more integrated reflections on a number of theoretical, policy-focused, and research-oriented topics, give the impression, in any case, that German criminology had arisen from the ashes, as it were, and had not only left behind its dubious past but had also overcome (*quod non*, as we have just seen) its internal theoretical, ideological, and disciplinary quarrels. There were in any case countless topics on the agenda. These included not only polemical contributions on the institutional development of criminology and reflections on certain contradictions between criminological theories but also socio-geographic or socio-economic studies regarding crime in certain cities, studies of the self-images of juvenile delinquents and the careers of terrorists, how to combat economic crime, and the effectiveness of conditional sentencing and release on probation.[140]

Partly for this reason it was not so strange that in 1983 – when a new co-director, Albin Eser, joined Kaiser – the criminological programme at the Max Planck Institute was redefined. Themes that were now highlighted included environmental crime, money laundering, sentencing, and compensation by offenders. A number of long-term studies were also initiated: one on the evaluation of social therapies in prisons and one on the long-term development of criminal careers.[141] A 1988 overview shows that the research programme had been revised. It in fact shows that both victimhood among foreign minorities and fear of crime had also become important research topics.[142]

When Kaiser retired from the Max Planck Institute in 1997, his successor, Hans-Jörg Albrecht, immediately announced how the institute's criminological research would be reoriented.[143] The topics that the research group would focus on under his leadership included the impact of the development of black markets on the application of criminal law, the problems of organised crime and terrorism, the influence of social modernisation on the ways in which crimes are committed, the increasing interconnectedness of criminal law with other forms of social control, and the long-term incarceration of dangerous offenders.

He also referred in his statement to the impact of the fall of the Berlin Wall and the collapse of the Soviet Union on criminological research at the Max Planck Institute and elsewhere in Germany. These major events meant that it was not only at the institute, but also in other places, that research would be conducted on crime – in all its forms (economic offences just as much as extremist political violence) – and on all kinds of victimhood in East Germany

---

[139]   Kerner, Kury and Sessar 1983.
[140]   Brusten, Häusling and Malinovski 1986.
[141]   Kaiser 1988b; Kaiser 1997b, pp. 27–30.
[142]   Kaiser and Geissler 1988.
[143]   Albrecht (H.-J.) 1997.

and Central Europe. Research was also initiated on crime problems among immigrants and on feelings of insecurity among citizens in Germany.[144]

Kaiser's major handbook – *Kriminologie: ein Lehrbuch* – the third and last edition of which was published in 1996, and also Schneider's handbook (1986) clearly demonstrate the boom that there had been in criminology in Germany

Günther KAISER, *Kriminologie: ein Lehrbuch*, Heidelberg, C.F. Müller Verlag, 1996.

since the 1960s, in spite of its relatively poor institutionalisation.[145] They not only give a nuanced picture of the theoretical perspectives and current research methods in criminology, but also deal in detail with all kinds of crime and all kinds of criminals and victims. They also paid quite a lot of attention to the prevention of crime and the criminal law's response to it, ranging from the

---

144   Albrecht and Boers 1999; Boers, Ewald, Kerner, Lautsch and Sessar 1994; Ewald 1997.
145   Kaiser 1996; Schneider 1986.

introduction of criminal legislation to the application of penalties. Compared to the textbooks published at the time in other countries, they are very similar in structure to the better American textbooks, and are head and shoulders above the textbooks published during that period in the United Kingdom and elsewhere in Europe.

It is striking, finally, that – unlike in the United States – nobody like Wilson emerged in Germany who, from a neo-classical position, advanced a different "rightist" criminology in that country or advocated a systematic toughening up of penal repression. Nor – unlike in the United Kingdom with people like Young – was there any radical shift within critical criminology, in the sense that some of its supporters switched sides and, with a great deal of political enthusiasm, exchanged left-wing idealism for left-wing realism. I am not aware of any clear explanation of these two differences. Does the first difference perhaps have to do with the chequered history of German criminology? And does the second relate once more to the low status of criminology at the faculties of law?

10.3.3.4. *Freiburg Memorandum: A Communal Cry of Distress*

When we consider the development of criminology in Germany in the 1980s and 1990s, it is hard to avoid the impression that the adherents of *kritische Kriminologie* were not only permanently at odds with themselves but were also very disappointed by what that version of criminology had managed to achieve at the universities and in the actual practice of criminal justice.[146] The assessment that Sack made in 1998 reads in any case like a kind of academic testament.[147]

This version of criminology, he wrote, has not even produced a body of publications suitable for university education. That was certainly due to the fact, he wrote, that this type of education – in any case outside Hamburg – had completely failed to flourish. But that, in turn, had a lot to do with the fact that in Germany – unlike in the United Kingdom – criminology remained embedded, as we have seen, within law faculties and was taught there by professors whose remit also included teaching criminal law. In that context, moreover, one should not forget the harmful effect of the internal divisions among critical criminologists. Perhaps, Sack wrote, one also needed to regret the fact that the adherents of critical criminology had not addressed the role played by traditional criminology during the Nazi era. That would perhaps have given critical criminology greater legitimacy.

However, the important role that *kritische Kriminologie* undoubtedly played in Germany in the modernisation of criminology had still not been entirely played out by the 1990s. A number of true devotees continued in any case to

---

[146]   Van Swaaningen 1997, pp. 84–91; Quensel 1989.
[147]   Sack 1998.

believe in the usefulness of the by then fairly predictable discussions of the differences of opinion, the relationship to traditional criminology and criminal law, and current criminal policy. That was not really strange: views that have been defended for years are not simply abandoned. Moreover, changes were taking place around them that also demanded that they comment, whether that was the impending privatisation of parts of the criminal justice system or the changes that British critical criminology was going through at that time. It is striking that some of them apparently became so disillusioned over the course of the years that they proceeded to advocate the outright abolition of the criminal law or the prison system.[148]

There seems to me to be no doubt that with views like that, critical criminology was placing itself on the fringes of the criminological debate that was going on in Germany at the time. That can be inferred from the introductions to criminology that appeared in the first few years of the present century, in which critical criminology undoubtedly plays an important role, both implicitly and explicitly, but which make hardly any reference to abolitionism.[149] Even the authors of introductions which – subject to the influence of critical criminology – propound highly critical views on criminal law and the criminal justice system do not go so far as to embrace abolitionism. That would, for the rest, be difficult for authors who believe that a critical independent criminology should be dedicated worldwide to defending the rights of the citizen. How could that task be accomplished without the criminal law to provide sanctions against those who wrongfully violate those rights?[150]

Karl-Ludwig Kunz, in his *Kriminologie* – one of the most authoritative and critical introductions to criminology in the German language area – does in fact discuss abolitionism. Kunz considers it to have failed and does not call for anything like the abolition of the criminal law. Kunz does, however, recognise that criminological research can and will erode the legitimacy of the criminal law. Similarly, he is also aware that in quite a few countries criminological research institutes had been established in the 1960s in order to optimise the functioning of the criminal justice system.[151]

In an article in the *Monatsschrift für Kriminologie und Strafrechtsreform*, Kunz asserts that since the 1990s German criminology has developed into an independent scientific discipline which, although strongly focused on the pursuit of criminal policy, comprises a very wide range of topics and methods. He adds, however, that in Germany criminology has become an extremely varied whole without sharp contours and that its scientific independence in relation to its basic

---

[148] Schumann, Steinert and Vosz 1988; Stangl 1988; Van de Boogaart and Seus 1991; Bussmann and Kreissl 1996; Cremer-Schäfer and Steinert 1998.
[149] Albrecht (P.-A.) 2005; Meier 2007.
[150] Albrecht (P.-A.) 2005, p. 48.
[151] Kunz 2004, pp. 37–62; Sack 2006.

disciplines has not yet been clarified. Indeed, he points out that where German criminology has historically always been highly dependent on general social and scientific developments, it is not possible to predict its further development, let alone its future. It can still go in all sorts of directions.[152]

His remarks fell on fertile ground at the colloquium on 28–30 June 2012 at the Max Planck Institute to discuss the state of criminology in Germany, compared with its situation in the United Kingdom and Switzerland in particular. It was attended by most of the leading German and German-speaking professors of criminology and led to the drawing up of the *Freiburger Memorandum zur Lage der Kriminologie in Deutschland* (Freiburg Memorandum on the State of Criminology in Germany).[153]

The memorandum states that criminology in Germany has increasingly profiled itself in diverse ways, but mainly through the research performed in recent decades, as an independent scientific discipline with its own theories, research fields and forms of teaching, a discipline which is increasingly internationally connected, but which – measured by its contributions to international developments – has also increasingly fallen behind. It has lost ground in that way because almost all German universities have done away with study programmes such as "the sociology of deviance" or "social problems" and many universities have also abolished their chairs of criminology. German criminology is thus in danger of withering away, and there is a major risk of negative consequences: it would forfeit its link to international developments, especially in the English-speaking world; the interaction between criminology and criminal science would cease; research and thus knowledge of important problems would disappear; commissioned research would gradually supplant basic research; the recently introduced Master's degree programmes in criminology would need to be terminated; and it would become impossible to train the researchers of the future.

The memorandum therefore ends with a cry of distress: instead of running down criminology any further, there in fact needs to be investment in its further development. An indication is given of what needs to be done: university education in criminology should be expanded and there should be greater integration of research into the programmes; interdisciplinary research at institutions such as the Max Planck Institute should be reinforced; and there should be increased funding for research into traditional forms of crime and social control as well as into combatting various forms of macro-crime, i.e. economic crime, organised crime, political crime, and corruption.

What the memorandum does not explicitly address, but what it implies, is that the post-war conflict regarding the direction of German criminology has to

---

[152] Kunz 2013.
[153] The memorandum is available from the Max Planck Institute.

a large extent already been fought and most of the parties have been reconciled. However, that does not mean that criminology has not benefited from that conflict. On the contrary: it has become far richer than it was initially. That, presumably, was fundamentally why reconciliation has been possible.

10.3.4. TRADITION, INNOVATION, AND CONFLICT IN FRENCH CRIMINOLOGY

It was noted in Chapter 5 that there were a number of important initiatives following the end of the First World War aimed at pursuing the developments that had taken place in France in the field of criminology and the criminal justice system prior to the war. The main initiatives were the establishment of the Institut de criminologie and the founding of the *Revue de science criminelle et de droit pénal comparé*. However, one's impression is that the reform movement, of which those initiatives were the expression, fell silent in the interwar period.

This makes it understandable why it is often argued in France itself that criminology from the end of the Second World War until the late 1960s was a fairly lifeless affair, certainly when compared with its development in the other countries dealt with in this book. But did French criminology in fact feed on the past – indeed the distant past – during that period? That matter will be considered in the first section below.

We will then deal with how Philippe Robert, and later with him the *Centre d'études sociologiques sur le droit et les institutions pénales* in Paris, livened up French criminology. What was new about that? And was Robert the only one who attempted to bring about innovation in French criminology?

Finally, it is important to sketch how in the past few years there has been an enormous conflict in France between the proponents of academic criminology and those who – in their eyes – are defending the political criminology practised by the "Bauer Gang" that is threatening to gain a place within the university system.

10.3.4.1. *Divided Continuation of a Criminological Tradition*

When one considers the post-war history of criminology in France, one encounters a discipline which was not only highly fragmented, both theoretically and thematically, but which was also not anchored institutionally anywhere, either at one or more state institutions or at one or more universities. The law faculties of a few universities outside Paris had set up an Institut de sciences criminelles or an Institut de criminologie et des sciences pénales, but at those institutes it was usually isolated loners who concerned themselves mainly with some form of criminology in the context of an educational programme; they conducted little if any empirical research, certainly not systematically.[154] In other words, criminology was at the time mainly a matter of isolated individuals working at a faculty of law or a faculty of medicine, or at the Ministry of Justice or a court in Paris.

In the post-war period, the link with the distant past, especially with Durkheim, was to some extent maintained by Lucien Lévy-Bruhl, a legally trained sociologist at the Sorbonne. But Lévy-Bruhl did not carry out any empirical or other criminological research himself, although his writings show that he did have personal views on various matters. In 1955, for example, he devoted a socialist-tinted essay to how crime should be combatted, concluding with the lament that the defence of society should not comprise policing methods that serve solely to create disquiet in the minds of decent citizens and that in fact, under the guise of promoting safety, disrupt the safety of us all.[155] Among criminologists, however, Lévy-Bruhl was known mainly through the work of his pupil André Davidovitch, who since the 1950s – in the footsteps of the nineteenth-century statisticians – devoted himself, inter alia, to the analysis and interpretation of the crime statistics, the numerical calculation of the decisions taken by the Public Prosecution Service, and the statistical distribution of crime in urban areas.[156]

Lévy-Bruhl's criticism of social defence was not just a shot in the dark. It was in fact clearly directed against the "new" social defence movement that was launched in Italy in 1945 under the inspiring leadership of Filippo Gramatica and propagated in France by Marc Ancel, a judge at the Court of Cassation.[157] Ancel did not, however, go anywhere near as far as Gramatica. The latter proclaimed categorically that the criminal law, or at any rate the criminal responsibility of individuals, should be abolished. It should then be replaced by a duty on the part of the state to socialise every citizen and a duty on the part of every citizen to take responsibility for the harm he has caused through his behaviour; penalties should be replaced by preventive, educational, and curative measures. It would also be better to rename criminology "anthropology" because it should henceforth only investigate the causes of crime and the ways to tackle it and develop methods to classify offenders on the basis of anthropo-psycho-sociological research.[158]

In his study *La défense sociale nouvelle* (1956), Ancel, by contrast, distanced himself clearly from Gramatica's radical abolitionism.[159] He denied emphatically, for example, that there was any association between the aims of the movement and the criminal policy pursued by Nazi Germany, amongst others. He pointed

---

[154] Robert 1986.
[155] Lévy-Bruhl 1955, p. 162.
[156] Robert 1994, pp. 431–432; Mucchielli 2004, pp. 225–227.
[157] Kinberg 1957.
[158] Gramatica 1964, pp. 1–9, 265–278.
[159] Ancel 1966, pp. 22–25, 35, 121–132, 272–281.

out explicitly that he adhered to the principles of the criminal law, to the institutions of criminal justice, and to criminal science. In his view, the fact that he believed that "decriminalisation" of the behaviour concerned should be considered in cases where the criminal law was ineffective did not detract

Jean PINATEL, *La criminologie*, Paris, Spes, 1960.

from this. What he was ultimately concerned with was solely the prevention of crime and the treatment of offenders with a view to achieving genuine judicial humanism. Ancel was still defending these views several decades later, in 1985, but by then he could point to some trends that in his view had resulted partly from "his" movement. He referred, on the one hand, to the decriminalisation of traffic law and economic law in a number of countries and, on the other, to the international emergence of victimology and increasing compensation of victims by offenders.[160]

Better known than Ancel, especially outside France, was – and still is – Jean Pinatel, who in the 1950s, 1960s, and 1970s played a leading role in the International Society of Criminology. When discussing the work of De Greeff, we already mentioned that Pinatel was an ardent supporter of his ideas. That is understandable when one reads his *Criminologie*, which was first published in 1960.[161] This concise introduction in fact focuses on *criminologie clinique*, an approach to criminology aimed at formulating recommendations as to the (future) behaviour of the offender and his treatment. It was therefore characterised entirely by the aim of using biological, psychological, and sociological research to determine the danger posed by criminals and on that basis to decide what treatment they should receive. For Pinatel, *criminologie clinique* was therefore the link between general criminology and penology. He had previously explained in the *British Journal of Delinquency* how this approach to criminology had been an important basic principle in reform of the prison system after the Second World War.[162]

It is perfectly clear that he found it difficult in the 1980s to keep up with the innovations in criminology that were taking place in the United States and Europe, although he did not dismiss them out of hand. He realised that they had positive aspects, writing, for example, that it was not impossible that criminology would become a stage for different and more satisfactory developments.[163] Honesty compels one to add that in the general section of his introduction, Pinatel not only devotes attention to the main currents and figures in European criminology, but in some places also refers to studies and researchers in the United States. Shaw and McKay, Healy, Sutherland, the Gluecks, Sellin, Merton, and Cohen are all discussed, if only briefly. It could of course be said that that was only to be expected of a man who belonged to the inner circle of the International Society of Criminology, but it is a good thing to note that Pinatel was clearly in fact quite familiar with the developments that American criminology had gone through into the 1950s. That fact is sometimes forgotten, including in France itself. This is to some extent understandable when one considers that many of his kindred spirits in France largely ignored international developments or specifically those in the United States.[164]

---

[160]   Ancel 1985, pp. 99–120.
[161]   Pinatel 1960.
[162]   Pinatel 1952.
[163]   Pinatel 2001, p. 105.
[164]   Marquiset 1964; Grapin 1973.

That also applies to the psychiatrist who set the tone in the 1960s regarding the problems of juvenile delinquency, namely Georges Heuer.[165] One of the few American studies referred to in his renowned study *La délinquance juvénile* was that by the Gluecks.[166] But that naturally does not mean – especially not in the light of the criticism targeted at the Gluecks' research – that Heuer's book is not an interesting one. His remarks regarding the personalities of the young people concerned, about their motives for committing violent crime and property crime, for becoming vagrants or turning to prostitution, and the ways they do all those things, testify after all to profound insight into the problem of juvenile delinquency. The same is also true of other publications of the time, for example that by Jean Chazal on the environment, personality, and behaviour of juvenile delinquents (1952), that by Robert on the phenomenon of juvenile gangs (1966), and that by Jean-Pierre Lauzel on the personality of juvenile thieves and the kind of thefts they commit (1974).[167]

It is remarkable, of course, that juvenile crime, and especially that committed by juvenile gangs, was at that time the only major topic in French criminology. Apparently, it was broadly viewed as a major problem by society as a whole. Otherwise, the Ministry of Justice would not have established a research centre in that field in 1958, namely the *Centre de formation et de recherche de l'éducation surveillée*, based in Vaucresson in the western suburbs of Paris. Within a few years, the centre developed an important research programme focusing not only on the problems of juvenile delinquency but also on the possibilities and difficulties in the re-education of juvenile offenders.[168]

Publications show that researchers at the centre were very familiar with the research on juvenile delinquency carried out in the United States, both at Harvard and in Chicago.[169] That familiarity with American research explains why the study by Herbert Bloch and Arthur Niederhoffer was translated into French in 1969.[170] Partly in view of the international orientation of the research in Vaucresson, it is difficult for outsiders to understand why the research centre was closed down in the late 1970s – juvenile crime problems were certainly not decreasing at the time. The available literature does not indicate why the centre disappeared. During the years of its existence, it was in any case the only major criminological research centre in France.

It should be noted in this connection that Davidovitch, Piaget, Ancel, and Heuer were not the only ones to work in criminology – in a personal capacity, one might almost say – or to advocate a particular criminal policy. It is

---

[165] Lefaucheur 1994, pp. 313–332.
[166] Heuyer 1969.
[167] Chazal 1952; Robert 1966; Lauzel 1974.
[168] Mucchielli 2004, pp. 28–29.
[169] Szabo and Normandeau 1970, pp. 196–240.
[170] Bloch and Niederhoffer 1969.

appropriate to also refer to the celebrated psychoanalyst Angelo Hesnard, who eruditely attempted in his *Psychologie du crime* (1963) to reconcile the clinical criminology of De Greeff with psychoanalysis and phenomenology.[171] The 1988 introduction *Criminologie* published by Raymond Gassin – a professor in Aix-en-Provence and later in Marseille – can certainly be described as the best introduction published in France at the time.[172] It deals extensively not only with the development of criminological theory and the methodological aspects of criminological research but also with the phenomenology of crime and the typology of the criminal, as well as with the possibilities for combatting crime both preventively and repressively.

The fact that Gassin's introduction ignores the criminal justice institutions almost completely does however demonstrate that the author had largely ignored the more recent developments in American, British, and European criminology. In that sense, his introduction can be seen as the culmination of traditional criminology in France.

10.3.4.2.   Renewal of Criminology by Philippe Robert

There is no doubt that Robert was the scientist who brought about the renewal of criminology in France. It was in any case he who published an article in *Année sociologique* in 1973 in which he stated that the traditional aetiological theories in criminology had had their day. According to him, it was high time to change course towards the social response to criminal behaviour and in particular to pursue research into the impact of criminal stigmatisation for the development of such behaviour.[173]

That article demonstrated a remarkable change in Robert's thinking about crime and society's response to it. In the late 1960s, he was in fact still writing articles about crime and juvenile delinquency which were very traditional in tone and content, and which did not in any way indicate familiarity with the research that was being done in these areas in the United States. Even the work of the earlier great French criminologists – Tarde and Durkheim – was not mentioned in the contributions that he wrote on these two issues for a collection on contemporary crime problems published in 1968 by Roger Merle, the director of the *Institut de criminologie et de sciences pénales* in Toulouse.[174]

Robert himself attributed his developing a different perspective on matters to his participation in the meetings of the Council of Europe on crime problems and his contacts at the *Université de Montréal* in Canada. Via those two routes he had become aware of the developments occurring in the United Kingdom and in

---

[171]   Hesnard 1963.
[172]   Gassin 1988; Larguier 1985; Négrier-Dormont 1992.
[173]   Mucchielli 2004, p. 32; Robert 2007.
[174]   Robert 1968a; Robert 1968b.

North America.[175] And he will, of course, have also read – after all, it contained a short text from his hand – the collection published by Denis Szabo and André Normandeau in 1970 with the interactionist-sounding title of *Déviance et criminalité*. For many francophone students, this was their first transatlantic encounter with modern criminal sociology.[176] That collection – which is rather similar to that published in Germany two years earlier (1968) by König and Sack on the new developments in *Kriminalsoziologie* – comprises 20 texts (if necessary translated into French) by writers including Marx, Durkheim, Sellin, Sutherland, Merton, Davidovitch, Robert, and Szabo himself.

Be that as it may, in the late 1960s Robert was first associated with the *Service d'études pénales et criminologiques*, which was established at the Ministry of Justice in 1968. Partly because the universities showed no interest whatsoever in taking under their aegis research centres that had been founded by the state, that service – like the centre in Vaucresson – acquired a dual status within a few years. On the one hand, they remained under the responsibility of the Minister of Justice, while on the other they were integrated into the structure of the overarching umbrella *Centre national de recherche scientifique*. The difference between the two centres was that in the 1970s the research centre in Vaucresson – as already noted – gradually disappeared into the background, enabling the *Service d'études pénales et criminologiques* increasingly to spread its wings. In 1983, the latter was renamed *Centre d'éudes sociologiques sur le droit et les institutions pénales*.[177]

This change, naturally enough, was primarily because of the entrepreneurial spirit of the people involved at the centre, led by Robert, but a few years later also by Lévy. The success of this centre can also be attributed, however, to the fact that it was not only able to develop its own basic principles for a research programme, but also to select a number of strategic research themes that were socially relevant and also appealed to the imagination.

As regards the first point, reference must be made to the aim – inspired by French pioneers, by the developments in America and Britain, and also by Foucault's historical study *Surveiller et punir* [*Supervise and Punish*] – of developing the centre's own sociological paradigm concerning crime. It focused in the mid-1990s on investigating the circumstances in which penal norms arise or are amended and also on the parties who influence these processes, for whatever reason.[178] There was therefore no question of a sort of imitation of the interactionist – let alone Marxist – research that was advocated in the United States and Britain. That kind of research was considered far too confined, not to say narrow-minded.

---

175   Robert 1994, pp. 432–433.
176   Szabo and Normandeau 1970.
177   Robert 1986, pp. 127–128; Mucchielli 2004, p. 33.
178   Robert 1994, pp. 432–441.

This perhaps explains why there have been no radical shifts in France in the criminological discourse of leftist idealism towards leftist realism; the debate was simply not conducted in those terms. It may also be the case that, at the end of the twentieth century, the nuanced approach to varied research on crime

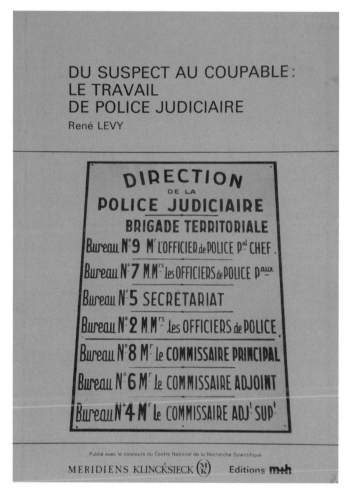

René LÉVY, *Du suspect au coupable: le travail de police judiciaire*, Geneva, Méridiens Klincksieck, 1987.

and the criminal law prevented the advent in French criminology of someone like Wilson who – forcefully, and with arguments – would have advocated a return to aetiological, specifically bio-sociological research and a shift in the policy concerning the administration of criminal justice towards a classical, i.e. neo-classical, direction.[179]

---

[179] Van Swaaningen 1997, pp. 93–97.

As regards the second point, the research initially had a strong focus, on the one hand, on statistical analysis of the data on the functioning of the institutions of the criminal justice system and, in particular, on their interaction with one another, for example that between police and the Public Prosecution Service. Lévy carried out thorough empirical research on this in the early 1980s.[180] On the other hand, a great deal of attention was paid to the ideas concerning the criminal justice system that exist within society and which, as it were, form the hidden powers – as Robert and Claude Faugeron term them in a book on that topic – that exert great influence on the operation of that system, from the creation of criminal legislation right through to its implementation.[181]

Researchers also increasingly sought contact with historians. This resulted in the first instance in research – together with Michèle Perrot – on the history of the prison system, but it also led, years later, to a considerable amount of research on the history of the police. The latter research culminated in 2011 in *Histoire des polices en France* by Lévy and Jean-Marc Berlière, with Jean-Noël Luc the leading French historian of the police.[182]

Later there was increasing cooperation with sociologists and political scientists working at other research centres within Paris and beyond, for example on research on police matters and on people's feelings of insecurity. As regards the former type of research, there was a link with Dominique Monjardet who in 1984, with others, published a labour-sociology study of the functioning of the police in Paris and in the French provinces and who emerged as the leading sociological police researcher in France.[183] The latter type of research first took the form of large-scale victim surveys by Renée Zauberman. It was later expanded to include more qualitative studies by, among others, Hugues Lagrange and Sebastian Roché, but also by Robert himself, about crime, insecurity, and feelings of insecurity on the one hand and the limited options on the part of government for implementing policies regarding those problems on the other.[184] The study by Lagrange is particularly interesting because it falls back on research by the Chicago School to interpret the problems in the suburbs of major French cities. Body-Gendrot raised the study of the problems of insecurity in major cities to the international level.[185]

Around 2010, research at the centre was grouped around seven main themes: statistical analysis of crime in all its manifestations; the sociology and history of deviant behaviour; the sociology and history of the institutions of criminal justice (in particular the police); the sociology and history of the criminal

---

[180]   Lévy 1987.
[181]   Robert and Faugeron 1980.
[182]   Perrot 1980a; Berlière and Lévy 2011; Luc 2002.
[183]   Chauvenet and Ocqueteau 2008; Monjardet, Chauvenet, Chave and Orlic 1984.
[184]   Lagrange 1995; Robert 1999; Roché 2005.
[185]   Body-Gendrot 2012.

justice system (in particularly the judiciary); the creation of penal norms and the safety policy of public institutions; criminal law penalties and measures; and the history of sociological theories of crime and deviant behaviour in general.[186] At that point in time, there were about 50 researchers.

10.3.4.3. University Institutes Up in Arms about the "Bauer Gang"

Following on from the above, it must be pointed out first and foremost that in recent decades the *Centre d'études sociologiques sur le droit et les institutions pénales* has not been the only centre at which relevant criminological research is carried out on a somewhat larger scale. Since the 1980s, some French universities have set up small research centres that perform systematic research in areas that are also highly relevant from the criminological perspective. One good example is the *Centre d'études et de recherches sur la police* which forms part of the *Institut d'études politiques de Toulouse* at the University of Toulouse. In recent decades, members of that institute have published very important studies on both the civil police and the *gendarmerie*.[187]

That does not alter the fact, however, that many institutions which one would expect – if only because of their name: *Institut de criminologie et de droit pénal, Institut de sciences criminelles, Institut de sciences criminelles et de la justice* – to have engaged in criminological research in recent decades have hardly done so, if at all. This becomes clear from a look at the websites of such institutes at universities in major French cities. Most institutes do publish in the field of criminal law and criminal procedure but hardly at all in the field of criminology. Some do organise limited introductory courses of a criminological nature or hold occasional seminars on topics that also appear to be criminological. But that is about all.

It is therefore not so strange that in recent years there have regularly been headlines in national newspapers about the "revalorisation" of criminology in France. On 28 January 2013, there was even a multidisciplinary conference of criminological centres in Lyon to discuss how that should be done. On 13 May 2011, representatives of many of these centres endorsed a statement to express their dissatisfaction.[188] In it, they opposed a potential decision by the Conseil national des universités to set up departments of "*criminologie, diplomatie, polémologie, stratégie*" within the universities. They viewed that decision as an attempt – in line with a report by Alain Bauer in 2008 – to officially categorise criminology as an independent scientific discipline, something that they considered unacceptable, at least in France, where it had been seen from the very start as a crossroads of numerous different disciplines.

---

[186]   Mucchielli 2009.
[187]   Susini 1983; Del Bayle 1988; Dieu and Mignon 1999; Del Bayle 2006; Dieu 2008.
[188]   See Jean-Baptiste Thierry's website (sinelege.hypotheses.org).

The manifesto went on to state that this attempt should be seen as an instrumentalisation of criminology for political purposes, which also failed to do justice to France's rich history in that discipline. It recognised that education in criminology was highly fragmented and not very visible, and that in many places research had in fact come to a standstill. As regards the aforementioned institutions, it was stated directly that some were still operating, others had disappeared, and yet others had become dormant. What clearly needed to be done – according to the signatories to the manifesto – was in fact clear: revalorisation of both education in criminology and criminological research at the existing institutes. That is why the meeting of directors was held on 28 January 2013.

It would of course be going too far to explain here the fierce controversy on the future of criminology in France, which has continued a number of years. It is necessary, however, to know that it was to a large extent instigated by the Bauer report and involved not just the actual content of that report but also its author as an individual. Although an important adviser to successive governments from both sides of the political spectrum, Bauer, like some of his direct supporters, was vilified by many in academic circles for what – in their eyes – were reprehensible scientific and political views and unacceptable links to the security industry and the police and intelligence services. Mathieu Rigouste published a short, scathing book about him and his supporters in 2011 with the title *Les marchands de peur: la bande à Bauer et l'idéologie sécuritaire* [*The Merchants of Fear: the Bauer Gang and the Ideology of Security*]. That title says enough.[189]

For his part, Bauer defended himself in every possible way. He gave interviews, for example, in which he said that he wished that France would – after 50 years of bickering – take its place alongside all the developed countries in the field of criminology. In academic terms, he defended himself in the inaugural lecture he gave on 8 February 2010 when he was appointed to the chair of applied criminology at the *Conservatoire national des arts et métiers*.[190] My impression, however, is that with that lecture he garnered merely scorn from his opponents because, according to them, the lecture was devoid of scientific substance and, moreover, did not indicate in any way what he thought criminology in France should be like.[191] And indeed, if one reads the text of the lecture it is difficult to avoid agreeing that it is rich in flowery language but otherwise almost incomprehensible. Anyone who therefore wishes to view Bauer as the French counterpart to Wilson in the United States must immediately take note of the vast difference between them in terms of their academic standards.

---

[189]   Rigouste 2011.
[190]   Bauer (A.) 2010.
[191]   See Mucchielli's blog insécurité.blog.lemonde.fr, 11 March 2012.

Finally, it should be noted that the aforementioned manifesto deplored the fact that in recent decades there has been less and less cooperation between the key relevant disciplines and that that situation needed to be remedied. That conclusion is likely to have been prompted by Bauer's call for a *"criminologie plurielle"*. But this does not alter the fact that for outsiders it is also remarkable – for a country like France in any case – that in recent decades there has been little or no multidisciplinary or interdisciplinary research on important crime issues or on the functioning of the criminal justice system in which not only sociologists but also psychologists, psychiatrists, and lawyers have played an important role. That is especially strange in the case of psychologists and psychiatrists because, into the 1970s, France had leading scientists such as Hesnard and Heuer who also had a lot to contribute in terms of research. In the case of lawyers, it raises questions because many law faculties had institutes that also, at least in name, carried out criminological research as part of their remit.

These questions cannot be answered here because in France itself – quite differently from in Germany, as already pointed out – they have not become a topic of discussion.[192] Does this estrangement of disciplines have to do with a tradition in which the individuality of one's own scientific or scholarly discipline is too greatly emphasised? Is it because the universities lack funds to pursue more complicated research? It cannot in any case be due to the extent and development of crime problems in France. As any regular reader of *Le Monde* and other newspapers knows, such problems are certainly a challenge, especially in major cities like Marseilles. But whatever the reason, one of the practical consequences, for example, is that France does not have any integrated criminology textbooks or reference books like those published in the United Kingdom and Germany. Partly for that reason, it is almost impossible to gain a good understanding of recent developments in French criminology.

10.3.5. DEVELOPMENT OF CRIMINOLOGY IN BELGIUM

In Chapter 7 we saw how in Belgium criminology not only played an important role in the country's criminal policies until in the 1930s, but also became established at the universities via the setting up of schools of criminology whose operation, until long after the Second World War, was dominated by one or at most two professors, usually psychiatrists or lawyers. These main figures generally published a great deal but did not carry out any empirical research. There was little or no sociology, let alone sociological research, at those schools. Given their positions in the existing political system, it is not therefore surprising that their work testified to extensive involvement in what went on within the criminal

---

192   Mucchielli 2004, pp. 36–37.

justice system, but in many cases also to great loyalty to public authorities. In strictly criminological terms, there was one figure who was head and shoulders above the rest, including internationally, namely De Greeff.

Against this background, the development of criminology in Belgium since the 1970s – partly also under the influence of developments in the United States and the United Kingdom – can in general be termed innovative and dynamic.

In the context of the present work, it is not possible to examine how and to what extent that development took shape at each individual university. A brief summary will need to suffice, although with one exception, namely the pioneering work since the late 1960s at the Catholic University of Leuven which ushered in, as it were, the renewal of criminology in Belgium in the course of the following decades.

10.3.5.1. Pioneering Research at the Catholic University of Leuven

When one considers the few publications emerging from the Catholic University of Leuven's then School of Criminology in the 1960s, one encounters a contradictory situation. On the one hand, there was a chairman, René Dellaert, who was guided primarily by an interdisciplinary integrated concept of the criminal but who, on the other, was also clearly aware of the developments that took place in the United States in the 1960s.[193] On the other hand, of the members of staff, one, Lode Walgrave, followed German, American, and French examples in carrying out bio-anthropological measurements on young people, and another, Tony Peters, familiarised himself extensively with the American and British research on the functioning of prisons. And then – most striking of all – there was Steven De Batselier, who, in the spirit of De Greeff, had defended a remarkable psychological-phenomenological dissertation in 1966 on – as the subtitle reads – the origin, variety, and significance of behaviour that is labelled sexually perverted.[194] His lectures and presentations drew a full house everywhere. That was not only because of the unusual views that he propounded in all kinds of morally and politically sensitive areas, but also because of the engaging and at the same time rather mesmerising way he dealt with them. Those who attended his lectures will never forget them. Many of the contributions to the *liber amicorum* which was published in 1998 show something of the fascination he had for his listeners.[195]

De Batselier was not familiar with the American interactionist literature but the subtitle of his dissertation does in fact betray an interactionist approach to the behaviour that he had to deal with in his clinical practice. In his view,

---

[193]   De Batselier 1980; Dellaert 1969.
[194]   De Batselier 1966.
[195]   Debbaut, Kegel, Depuydt, Reyniers, Van Heer, Van Liempt, Van Pee and Van Vaerenberg 1998.

that behaviour was not intrinsically perverted – it became so by being termed so. And he had also established that a punitive approach to that behaviour in specific cases exacerbated the underlying problems rather than mitigated them. De Batselier therefore adopted positions that admittedly ran parallel to those

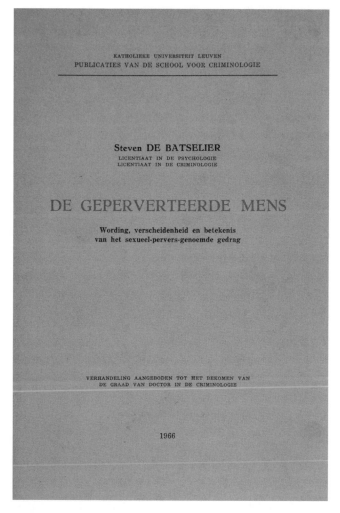

Steven DE BATSELIER, *De geperverteerde mens: wording, verscheidenheid en betekenis van het sexueel-pervers-genoemde gedrag*, Leuven, Publicaties van de School voor Criminologie, 1966.

of Becker and other interactionists in the United States but were not based on them – a strange combination of events.

In about 1970, he transformed his veiled criticism of the way society labelled behaviour as deviant into undisguised criticism of the functioning of society and, in particular, of everyone and everything that played a leading role in this. In the 1970s, he expressed that criticism – which fitted in to a certain extent with the anti-psychiatry movement that had made itself felt throughout the West in the 1960s – in the trilogy *Impasse* [*Dead End*] (1972), *De zachte moordenaars* [*The Gentle Murderers*] (1974), and *De extatische mens* [*Ecstatic Man*] (1977). These were republished as a collection in 1988 under the title *Mens, maatschappij en marginaliteit* [*Man, Society and Marginality*].[196]

De Batselier's criticism is not easy to summarise, but the basic premise is that normal people, i.e. people who have learned to behave in a conformist manner in all kinds of areas of life – in love just as much as in work – display psycho-pathological traits because that conformity has been accompanied by a loss of humanity. The psycho-pathological syndrome of the normal human being is therefore the result of a dehumanised and dehumanising society and thus forms, as it were, the counterpart to the socio-pathological syndrome of the dominant social structures. In order to escape from the clutches of this double pathology, one must first be aware of that situation. Someone who succeeds in doing so can become himself again and thus once more embody somewhat the ecstatic man who lies dormant within in all of us.

It would be a mistake to think that with this rather mystical solution to the world's problems De Batselier greatly distanced himself from the moral and political issues that were high on the political agenda specifically at that time. That was because he turned his criticism into a call for the decriminalisation of, inter alia, all kinds of sexual behaviour and drug use.[197] He expressed that call for the first time in 1971, at a symposium in Nijmegen on the victims of crime.[198] In a presentation that made a great impression, he then reversed the roles and asserted – invoking De Greeff – that it was actually the criminal justice system that created many victims and that criminology should first and foremost work towards the decriminalisation of behaviour, i.e. should remove behaviour from the purview of the current criminal law. It should advocate the breaching of bourgeois morality.

A few years later – in 1975 – Lode Van Outrive also spoke of the victims of the criminal justice system and – in the spirit of De Batselier – came to the conclusion that, as a system of social control, it not only created victims among offenders but also within the broad range of – as Peter Hoefnagels put it – "those other than the offenders", i.e. the direct victims of the crime, but also the relatives of the offenders and the victims, etc. He went on to assert that that system had become internally blocked and that the services and people who formed part of it were no longer capable of adapting themselves to the development of Western civilisation; that could only be achieved through collective political action. In

---

[196]   De Batselier 1988.
[197]   De Batselier 1982.
[198]   De Batselier 1971.

support of that argument, he invoked in particular – quite differently to De Batselier – the pioneers of American interactionism such as Lemert, the German sociologist Sack, and the authors of the Marxist *The New Criminology*, Taylor, Walton, and Young.[199]

In subsequent years, he elaborated on his views in various pamphlets and articles. These included his aggressive 1978 pamphlet – partly based on the

Tony PETERS, *Ongelijke levensvoorwaarden in de Centrale Gevangenis te Leuven*, Leuven, Acco, 1976.

research by Peters on the history of the Belgian prison system – about prisons as a system that had gone adrift, and the article in the journal *Déviance et société* in 1977 about interactionism and Marxism in criminology, in which he claimed to have demystified interactionism and given Marxism one last chance to

---

[199]   Van Outrive 1975.

prove itself.[200] Naturally enough, this did not make clear just what Van Outrive stood for himself. Because he never wrote his own introduction to criminology or anything similar, that remained forever unclear.

The differences of opinion did not prevent staff working in their own way to introduce the innovations in criminology that they considered necessary.[201] Peters' 1976 dissertation, for example – partly inspired by similar research in the United States and Britain – on the unequal living conditions in Louvain's central prison led in subsequent years to a number of studies which not only investigated – in particular that by Johan Goethals – the (negative) psychosocial implications of long-term imprisonment, but which also – for example those by Peters, Achiel Neys, Freddy Pieters, John Vanacker, and others – sought alternatives to imprisonment in the area of restorative justice.[202] Starting from the finding that the criminal justice system – certainly in terms of rehabilitation – not only often fails to rehabilitate the offender but that it also often fails to do justice to the interests and feelings of victims, they pursued victimological research in addition to penological research.[203] It was therefore hardly surprising that the *liber amicorum* for Peters dealt with the development of restorative justice and specifically its future. For Peters and his associates, that kind of justice offers a practicable route out of the dead end in which they believe the criminal justice system found itself.[204]

For his part, Lieven Dupont wrote a dissertation in 1979 on the principles of a proper criminal justice system that is still viewed as a crucial contribution to basic research in the area of criminal law. It is important to emphasise, however, that he definitely did not regard those principles as non-committal basic assumptions. Due to his major involvement in the work of the Peters penological research group, he increasingly began to consider those principles – certainly inspired by Constantijn Kelk's 1978 Utrecht dissertation on penitentiary law – more and more as a suitable starting point for properly regulating the legal status of prisoners in Belgium.[205] His application of those principles resulted in 1998 in his *Op weg naar een beginselenwet gevangeniswezen* [*Towards a Framework Act on the Prison System*].[206]

We should also note that in the 1970s Walgrave radically altered his point of view. In the late 1960s, as we have seen, he had begun with bio-anthropological research on juvenile delinquents, writing a dissertation on that subject. During the course of the 1970s, he became a critic of the existing juvenile protection system and an advocate of "emancipating juvenile criminology".[207] After years

---

200 Van Outrive 1977; Van Outrive 1978.
201 Casselman, Aertsen and Parmentier 2012a.
202 Goethals 1980; Neys, Peters, Pieters and Vanacker 1994; Robert and Peters 2003.
203 Peters and Goethals 1993.
204 Dupont and Hutsebaut 2001.
205 Kelk 2005.
206 Dupont 1998.
207 Walgrave 1980. This dissertation has not been published.

of research in a number of areas, he later linked up – in the 1990s – with the restorative justice movement and developed an international network of supporters of restorative justice for juveniles. Some time later, that network combined with the network formed by Peters and his colleagues on the basis of

Lieven DUPONT, *Beginselen van behoorlijke strafrechtsbedeling: bijdrage tot het grondslagenonderzoek van het strafrecht*, Antwerp, Kluwer, 1979.

their penological and victimological research to promote restorative justice. In this way, the European Forum for Victim-Offender Mediation and Restorative Justice was formed.[208]

---

[208] Walgrave 2012.

In the previous chapters, it became sufficiently apparent that whereas the prison system and – to a lesser extent – the protection of juveniles had long been able to count on the interest of all kinds of social reformers and scholars, that was less and less the case as regards the police. It was therefore extremely innovative – especially in the European context – that in the early 1970s Van Outrive, inspired by the sociological research on the police in the United States in the 1960s, joined with colleagues at the *Université catholique de Louvain* to arrange a basic study of the development, role, and effectiveness of the Belgian police. The author of the present work was engaged to carry out the Flemish component of the study. For all kinds of reasons, the project turned out quite differently from what had been expected. It resulted first of all in a dissertation on the political history of policing in Europe and only later in all kinds of studies of the police – the state of the municipal police, corruption among special investigative units[209] – that responded more directly to the initial intention.[210]

Finally, one must definitely not ignore the work of Jaak Van Kerckvoorde, who in the course of the 1970s became more and more a statistical methodologist. Besides his work in teaching and assisting with colleagues' research at the Catholic University of Leuven, he should be remembered especially as one of the main architects – perhaps the most important – of the current system of police and judicial statistics in Belgium. Van Kerckvoorde was too modest to compare himself with Quetelet but he nevertheless found it unacceptable that Quetelet's own country did not have a modern system of statistics for its criminal justice system. That was definitely one of the reasons why he made such efforts towards modernising it, but he was also naturally well aware of the importance of proper statistical data for scientific research and sound policy-making.[211]

10.3.5.2. General Innovation in Research

One of the previous chapters already briefly mentioned the 1988 dissertation by De Ruyver on the criminal policy of the socialist ministers of justice. That study was one of the signs in the 1980s that innovation had been gradually taking place at the other Belgian universities. That that included the University of Ghent was apparent from not only the dissertation by De Ruyver but also that by Eugène Verhellen from the same year, 1988, on juvenile protection and juvenile protection law.[212] At the *Vrije Universiteit Brussel*, Sonja Snacken's 1986 dissertation on short custodial sentences was a clear sign of innovation, followed in 1990 by a collection of essays by Christian Eliaerts, Els Enhus, and Rob Senden on developments within the police system.[213]

---

[209] Fijnaut 2012b; Fijnaut 1983c.
[210] Fijnaut 1979; Fijnaut 1985.
[211] Van Kerckvoorde 1995; Goethals 1998.
[212] Verhellen 1988.
[213] Snacken 1986; Eliaerts, Enhus and Senden 1990.

There were also similar signs at the Francophone universities, for example the 1985 book *Modèle éthologique et criminologie* by another renowned pupil of De Greeff (in addition to De Batselier), Christian Debuyst. In that work – very much influenced by American interactionism – the author suggests, inter alia, that it is very important not to first study someone's criminal behaviour and only

Brice De Ruyver, *De strafrechtelijke politiek gevoerd onder de socialistische Ministers van Justitie E. Vandervelde, P. Vermeylen en A. Vranckx,* Antwerp, Kluwer, 1988.

afterwards society's response to it. In his view, quite the opposite is necessary because that response forms, as it were, the lens through which we view that behaviour. In asserting this, Debuyst was distancing himself in his own way from De Greeff but not going anywhere near as far as De Batselier. In particular, he concluded that the famous *passage à l'acte* of someone who commits a crime could not be the *moment fondateur*, i.e. the starting point, for understanding that crime. Doing so, he wrote, would mean losing sight of the fact that the perception of that act is in itself already permeated by certain theories regarding such behaviour and such offenders.[214]

These publications appeared in a period during which there were a number of enormous scandals in Belgium regarding the enforcement of law and order: the murderous attacks by the "Nivelles Gang" on shops, restaurants and supermarkets; the attacks by the terrorist *Cellules communistes combattants* on, inter alia, banks; the Heysel Stadium disaster in which numerous football supporters lost their lives; and the murders of young girls by Marc Dutroux. These scandals were a major incentive for scientific research in these fields. It is not possible to examine that connection in greater detail here; we will therefore confine ourselves to summarizing the survey of criminological research drawn up at the end of the 1990s by Dan Kaminski, Sonja Snacken, and Veerle Van Gijsegem. As far as possible, use has also been made of Philippe Mary's analysis of criminal policy during that period.[215]

These surveys indicate that the research priorities, on the one hand, concerned to a great extent the problems of (local) feelings of safety and unsafety and, on the other, problems regarding the functioning of local police forces and cross-border police cooperation. They also paid a lot of attention to specific problems in the field of crime, disorder and nuisance, in particular those of football hooliganism and drug trafficking. By contrast, there was little research on the actual operation of the criminal justice system, in particular the judiciary. Such research was largely confined to pre-trial detention and – understandably – the many problems of the prison system, both the systematic overcrowding and the (imminent) privatisation of parts of the system. There was in fact also research on the position of victims in criminal proceedings and on the reform of the child protection system. Here and there, there was also investment in historical research, particularly on the history of the ideas behind the criminal policy and the history of the police.

Nevertheless, despite everything, there were still all kinds of remarkable gaps in the research carried out in the 1990s. The judicial system, for example – both the judiciary and the Public Prosecution Service – was not dealt with, even though these institutions played a truly crucial role in the problems that had revealed themselves in the various scandals. Nor was there any research into serious crime (whether or not organised) even though such crime – from the François corruption case on – had been involved in some of those scandals. Fortunately, these and other gaps were later filled in to some extent.[216]

---

[214]   Debuyst 1985; Digneffe and Adam 2004.
[215]   Kaminski, Snacken and Van Gijsegem 1999; Mary 1999, pp. 603–693.
[216]   Fijnaut, Van Daele and Verbruggen 1998; Fijnaut and Van Daele 1999.

It is also rather remarkable – compared to countries like the United Kingdom and Germany – that at the end of the twentieth century, no criminology introductions or textbooks had been published that covered, fully and deeply, the most important research that had been carried out in recent decades at the various universities. That is particularly remarkable given that so much research had been carried out and such a reference work would have been very useful in the increasingly crowded university courses in criminology.[217] Did the language problem make such an initiative difficult? Did the relations between the universities or between the various different research groups prevent such an undertaking? We do not know. All this makes the concise introduction by Georges Kellens, *Eléments de criminologie* (1998), even more notable.[218]

To what extent, finally, the theoretical, empirical, and policy-focused developments in criminology played a role – directly or indirectly, implicitly or explicitly – in the rising stream of research studies is a question that can scarcely be answered, precisely because of the lack of such reference works. That question will therefore be disregarded here. A proper answer would require painstaking consultation of the relevant publications.

10.3.6. DEVELOPMENT OF CRIMINOLOGY IN THE NETHERLANDS

The development of criminology in the Netherlands since the 1960s has in many ways been very different to that in Belgium. On the one hand, there were professors of criminology (and criminal law) at a number of Dutch universities – i.e. not just a single university as in Belgium – in the 1960s and 1970s who attempted to reform criminology in the most diverse ways. On the other hand, it is striking that the dynamic development of criminological research in Belgium since the 1980s took place for the most part at the universities, while the expansion of criminological research in the Netherlands has been channelled more and more via governmental (and semi-governmental) institutes and was therefore pursued largely outside academia.

In contrast, developments in criminology education in the two countries have in recent years taken a more parallel route. Nowadays, there are Bachelor's and Master's degree programmes at a number of Dutch universities that are similar to the undergraduate and graduate programmes that have existed at all major Belgian universities since the 1930s.

The first part of this section looks at the "changing of the guard" in university criminology that took place in the 1960s and 1970s. The evolution of Dutch

---

217   Vanderborght, Vanacker and Maes 2000; Vlaamse Interuniversitaire Raad 2008.
218   Kellens 1998.

criminology since that period is then considered, in the same way as in the section on the development of Belgian criminology.

10.3.6.1. Multifaceted but Turbulent Changing of the Guard

In the 1960s and 1970s, it was not only the leading figures at the criminology departments established in the 1930s and 1940s at the universities of Leiden, Utrecht, and Groningen who were replaced. During the same period, new institutes were also set up, or in any case new chairs of criminology were established, at a number of other universities, namely the University of Amsterdam, Free University Amsterdam, Erasmus University Rotterdam, Radboud University Nijmegen, and Tilburg University. The fact that a whole new generation of professors were appointed who pursued criminology – whether or not in combination with other disciplines, usually criminal law – meant that this complete changing of the guard could be expected to be accompanied not only by major innovation, but also by a certain level of turbulence. That expectation turned out to be justified.

This turbulence was not felt equally at all universities. The voices of professors such as Koos van Weringh (Amsterdam), Catharina Dessaur (Nijmegen), and Anton Geurts (Tilburg) were regularly raised in public debate, but generally did not cause much of a stir. There were various reasons for that: Van Weringh founded the Bonger Institute of Criminology but ultimately restricted his own research mainly to the history of criminology and the criminal justice system.[219] Dessaur was especially interested in the foundations of criminology and gained particular fame with the novels that she published under a pseudonym.[220] Geurts confined himself mainly to the topic of his dissertation, namely penitentiary law.[221]

A more controversial voice was that of Riekent Jongman, professor at the University of Groningen. That was because he and his co-workers not only carried out a great deal of research into the selective operation of the criminal justice system, but also asserted that class distinctions within Dutch society played a major role. For the supposedly egalitarian Netherlands, that was an uncomfortable message.[222] In conjunction with this research by Jongman, it has to be noted that important empirical research did in fact take place under the aegis of those other professors. One example is the ground-breaking research on the victims of crime by Jan Fiselier in Nijmegen in the 1970s. Together with the later dissertation by Marc Groenhuijsen at Leiden University, that

---

[219]   Van Weringh 1986.
[220]   Dessaur 1982.
[221]   Geurts 1962.
[222]   Van Swaaningen 1997, pp. 112–114.

research made a major contribution to the development of victimology in the Netherlands.[223]

What is striking when one reads the works of the professors just mentioned is that the new American or British criminological literature does play a role, but that that role is generally still limited. Literature from other European countries – in particular Germany – is just as important. The same applies to the works of professors who concerned themselves with criminology, the criminal law, and the criminal justice system from a socio-legal perspective. One example is the work of Antoon Peters, which breathed new life into the Utrecht School in the late 1960s, with American views on the ancient protective role of the criminal law and the exclusion of illegally obtained evidence.[224] One needs to note immediately, however, that within his university environment, a number of incisive works were produced on American and British interactionist criminology, in particular the labelling theory.[225] Another professor who drew on the American literature just as readily as that in German was Kees Schuyt. In 1971, he published an overview of the sociology of law that was based partly on the new American approach to that discipline – he had in fact studied sociology at Berkeley in the 1960s – but partly also on what German sociologists had long been saying about the law and legal systems.[226]

There were also professors, however, who were influenced far more strongly by the new American and British criminology. One who is worthy of particular note was Peter Hoefnagels, professor of criminology at the Erasmus University Rotterdam, who in 1969 produced what was by Dutch standards an extremely original introduction to criminology. That work, *Beginselen van criminologie*, was translated into English a few years later with the title *The Other Side of Criminology*.[227] In this introduction Hoefnagels discussed not only the traditional theories in criminology, the extent and types of crime, and the classic penalties but also insisted that what constitutes a crime from the legal perspective is in essence always the outcome of a struggle to define the behaviour in question. Further on he also devoted considerable attention to the ways in which the actual responses to crime influence the functioning of the criminal justice system and the position of the accused or person sentenced. He also drew attention to persons other than the perpetrators who suffer the negative impact of those responses: the victims, the immediate bystanders, etc. The latter point, in particular, was undoubtedly an important extension of the labelling theory, but it was not picked up on internationally.

---

[223] Fiselier 1978; Groenhuijsen 1985.
[224] Kelk, Moerings, Jörg and Moedikdo 1976, pp. 189–220; Kelk 1978.
[225] Moerings and Van de Bunt 1976.
[226] Schuyt 1971.
[227] Hoefnagels 1969; Hoefnagels 1973.

However, that was certainly not the case for the ideas of his colleague Louk Hulsman at Erasmus University Rotterdam, simply because the latter presented his views in person at numerous conferences and seminars in Europe and later throughout the world. In his inaugural lecture in 1965, Hulsman – strongly influenced by the views defended by Ancel in his *Défense sociale nouvelle* – questioned the conditions under which action should be taken against injustice in society by means of the criminal law rather than administrative or civil law. His answer to this fundamental criminal-political question was that that should not be determined in the first instance by moral convictions but by practical considerations: can the aggrieved party identify the party that caused the harm on his own, is it possible to bring a civil action, is the injustice so disadvantageous in social terms that enforcement under civil law is insufficient?[228] In line with that position, he subsequently developed not only criteria for criminalisation but at the same time also increasingly worked towards the decriminalisation of forms of behaviour which he believed did not need to be responded to by means of the criminal law.

Partly under the influence of interactionist criminology – i.e. its labelling variant – he eventually attempted not so much to restrict the domain of the criminal law but turned more and more – long before people like Nils Christie – against the criminal law as such, because he believed that that type of law, and certainly the manner in which it was systematically enforced, increased rather than reduced the problems, i.e. exacerbated them rather than resolved them.[229] It did so not only at the level of the persons who were socially excluded because of their criminal law label, but also at the level of the social problems that caused their conduct, i.e. misconduct.[230] Hulsman's increasing criticism of the criminal justice system finally culminated in a plea for the abolition of the criminal law.[231] That plea was not in fact purely negative in tone. Hulsman also had views on how "problematic situations" should actually be addressed, for example through mediation between offenders and victims regarding the harm involved.[232] In that sense, he was certainly one of the founders of what is today termed restorative justice. It is no coincidence, for the rest, that the topic of restorative justice came alive in Leuven at the same time: Hulsman had already been working closely in various ways since the 1980s with Peters, who had also gradually largely lost his faith in the criminal law, as noted above.[233]

Like Hulsman, Herman Bianchi also evolved over the years into an abolitionist. Unlike Hulsman, he had commenced his academic career at the Free University

---

[228] Hulsman 1965.
[229] Christie 1981.
[230] Hulsman 1986.
[231] Hulsman 1986.
[232] Van Hecke and Wemmers 1992.
[233] Van Swaaningen and Blad 2011, pp. 9–30; Blad 1996.

Amsterdam in 1956 not with an essentially rather functional conception of the criminal law but with an erudite dissertation in which he advocated the autonomy of criminology; this was in any case the wording of the first in the list of theses annexed to the dissertation.[234] In the 1960s, he began writing critically about

Louk HULSMAN, *Afscheid van het strafrecht: een pleidooi voor zelfregulering,* Houten, Het Wereldvenster, 1986 (Translated from the French edition with the cooperation of J. BERNAT DE CELIS and H. SMITS).

the principles of criminal law and asserted in his *Ethiek van het straffen* [*Ethics of Punishment*] (1964) that it would probably be better to replace punishment with reconciliation.[235] This scepticism towards the criminal justice system

---

234 Bianchi 1956.
235 Van Swaaningen 1997, pp. 118–121.

probably explains why he became extremely interested in the early 1970s in the discussions taking place in the United States and the United Kingdom regarding the interactionist or Marxist renewal of criminology. For Dutch readers, he not only relayed what was going on there, but also explained the consequences for developments in the Netherlands. In the spirit of his dissertation, this meant in the first place a plea for the preservation of non-governmental criminology that could constantly call into question the government's monopoly on combatting crime.[236] Later in the 1970s, American criminal policy strengthened his aversion to prisons and he began to believe in the abolition of the criminal law.[237]

This shift in his views led him to the idea that there should be *vrijplaatsen* (refuges) within society where people could themselves find satisfactory solutions to their problems. Such proposals found a response here and there within Dutch society, for example as regards accommodating refugees, but did not gain any broad support. In the academic world, Bianchi had already forfeited a great deal of credit with the publication in 1980 of his book *Basismodellen in de kriminologie* [*Basic Models in Criminology*],[238] which was so full of errors and scattershot remarks that many of those working in the field were unable to take it seriously. In particular, Van Weringh, his colleague at the other university in Amsterdam, ridiculed it mercilessly.

But this was still not the most bitter conflict that has ever arisen in the Netherlands in the field of criminology. Such a conflict broke out in 1978 when a journal announced that Wouter Buikhuisen – from 1966 to 1973 professor of criminology at the University of Groningen and in 1973 appointed general adviser on scientific research at the Ministry of Justice – had agreed to take over the chair of criminology at Leiden University from Willem Nagel because the university was willing to give him scope to carry out studies on the brains of offenders.[239] That news caused a great commotion not only in the media but also within the universities. It led to one of the most infamous smear campaigns against a scientist by a journalist ever in the Netherlands. The journalist Piet Grijs published a series of articles in the *Vrij Nederland* weekly that were then collected in a vitriolic and widely read diatribe entitled *Buikhuisen, dom en slecht* [*Buikhuisen, Stupid and Evil*]. Both Dessaur and Schuyt also wrote articles in prestigious journals in which they expressed their total opposition to the programme announced by Buikhuisen.[240]

The plans that Buikhuisen published the following year, 1979, for the research that he had in mind did not arrive out of the blue.[241] They were rooted not only

---

[236] Bianchi 1974a and Bianchi 1974b.
[237] Van Swaaningen, Snel, Faber and Blankenburg 1988, pp. 10–13.
[238] Bianchi 1980.
[239] KRI, 1978, no. 3, pp. 1, 3–4.
[240] Dessaur 1978; Schuyt 1978.
[241] Buikhuisen 1979.

to some extent in his 1966 inaugural lecture on the future of criminological research, but were also in line with subsequent articles and papers that he had published on crime and heredity, and – in the footsteps of Eysenck – on the conditioning of offenders.[242] His plans were clearly very much inspired by the discussions within an international criminological study group on the interplay

Wouter Buikhuisen, *Kriminologie in biosociaal perspektief*, Deventer, Kluwer, 1979.

between biological and social factors that can explain the origins of criminal behaviour.[243] The study group comprised a wide range of well-known and less well-known criminologists. Their research interests and research experience

---

[242]   Buikhuisen 1966; Buikhuisen 1968; Buikhuisen and Hemmel 1972; Buikhuisen 1978.
[243]   *Report of the Interdisciplinary Group on Criminology* n.d.

ranged from biological studies (of twins) to trace genetic factors that can explain delinquent behaviour, to studies in which not only biological factors but also psycho-physiological and/or social factors were examined to determine their explanatory value.[244] But regardless of the background to Buikhuisen's plans, the enormous controversy about their (alleged) content led Leiden University to no longer give him the scope to implement them. He later continued to defend them but without any practical result.[245]

When one considers this notorious "case" from the science sociology viewpoint of Kuhn, one can conclude that his view of paradigm shifts in science does have some gaps but also that Buikhuisen – if he had known why and how such changes could be successful – would have worked out his research plans better and presented them in a much more prudent manner. In my opinion, he was somehow entirely unaware of their highly controversial nature.[246] That was not, of course, something that some of his opponents could invoke as justification for their relentless assault on those plans.

10.3.6.2. Expansion of Criminological Research in the 1990s

In 1999, René van Swaaningen and John Blad published a detailed overview of the criminological research conducted in the Netherlands in the 1990s.[247] The overview shows that – as in Belgium – not only had more and more research taken place, but it had also covered an increasing number of fields, for example:

- public safety in the various neighbourhoods of large cities;
- the causes, extent, distribution, and nature of juvenile crime;
- crime by and against women;
- the role of ethnic minorities in crime problems, whether or not in conjunction with discrimination against them in Dutch society;
- the frequently occurring forms of violence in private and in public;
- the nature and development of organised crime, particularly in relation to drugs problems and drugs policy;
- support for victims of offences;
- prevention of crime and nuisance problems in the context of deficient public safety;
- the operation of the police at local level; and
- the implementation and results of criminal law measures and sanctions, including alternative sanctions.

---

[244]   Shah and Roth 1974.
[245]   Buikhuisen 1985; Buikhuisen and Mednick 1988.
[246]   Fijnaut 1980.
[247]   Van Swaaningen and Blad 1999.

Topics that were studied much less, or virtually not at all, included the creation of criminal legislation, the problem of socio-economic crime, and the actual operation of the Public Prosecution Service and the judiciary. But there are doubtless more.

More important in this context, however, is the issue of the American influence on the development of Dutch criminology in the final decades of the twentieth century. I will not venture a definitive answer to that question here because there has never been any specific investigation of the extent to which American criminology influenced research and, in particular, how that influence manifests itself nowadays. In their overview, Van Swaaningen and Blad observe only that in that period it was above all the opportunity, rational choice, control, and stress theories that were applied to a significant extent in the Netherlands. This finding alone, however, means that the corresponding research was strongly affected by American developments in criminology because those theories, at least in their more recent versions, quite simply happen to be of American origin. In that sense, one can state that at that time a powerful Americanisation of Dutch criminology took place. It should be noted however – as Van Swaaningen and Blad also mention – that the more radical variants of the interactionist perspective were not applied in research in a targeted manner, not to mention the variants of the Marxist perspective. Nor did any figure like Wilson emerge in the Netherlands to carry out high-quality research on the issues of crime and the response to it from a neo-classical perspective.[248]

But perhaps it is no longer appropriate to ask for that period about the impact of American or British criminology on criminology in Western Europe or at least in the Netherlands. That is quite simply because Dutch criminological research since the 1970s has become so transatlantic that that question cannot – in general – be answered any longer and has to some extent therefore become pointless. Where the Netherlands is concerned, such a shift in the question to be answered arises in any case when one considers the two general introductions to criminology that appeared around the year 2000, namely *Tegen de regels IV* [*Against the Rules IV*], compiled by Elisabeth Lissenberg, Sibo van Ruller and René van Swaaningen, and *Actuele criminologie* [*Current Criminology*] by Jan van Dijk, Irene Sagel-Grande, and Leo Toornvliet.[249] Both the bibliography and the content of these two introductions show that the major developments in American criminology since the 1920s have been to a great extent absorbed into Dutch criminology, theoretically, empirically, and thematically.

How far that absorption or internalisation of American criminology actually reaches can only be determined in detail, of course, at the level of individual

---

[248]   Van Swaaningen and Blad 1999, pp. 234–235.
[249]   Lissenberg, Van Ruller and Van Swaaningen 2001; Van Dijk, Sagel-Grande and Toornvliet 1995.

research projects and individual publications. If one takes my own work, for example, it can easily be demonstrated that that absorption in fact reaches quite far and can very well lead to out-and-out transatlantic interaction on specific topics.

In the mid-1980s – together with Liesbeth Nuijten-Edelbroek and Hans Spickenheuer – I closely examined the American and British research on the effectiveness of the police in combatting crime in order to evaluate experiments taking place in that regard in the Netherlands. In the same period, in the light of a debate in the Dutch Parliament on whether or not it was advisable to allow defence lawyers to attend police interrogations of suspects, I analysed all the American and British research on that matter.[250] In the late 1980s, with Hans Moerland and Jolande Uit Beijerse, I applied the findings of the research by the Chicago School on the influence of urban development on crime to the public safety problems in the south of Rotterdam.[251]

In the 1990s, my own research in the Netherlands and Belgium led me to increasingly seek cooperation with colleagues in the United States. That led, on the one hand, to a transatlantic initiative with James Jacobs on the nature of organised crime in highly developed urban areas such as New York and the Dutch "*Randstad*" (the large conurbation in the west of the country). On the other, it led to an international book project with Gary Marx on undercover policing.[252] The experience gained during those two projects then not only played an important role in my further research in these areas, but also in the establishment of the *European Journal of Crime, Criminal Law and Criminal Justice* in 1990.[253] The creation of that journal – in the light of the establishment of the European Union – was intended not only to provide a forum in Europe for scientific discussion of these topics, but also to create an academic bridge from Europe to the United States.[254]

10.4. CONCLUSION

The emergence of interactionist and Marxist criminology in the United States in the 1960s and 1970s not only led to deep divisions in the American criminological community, but also provoked a strong backlash in the form of a neo-classical and bio-social approach to criminology. The fact that that reaction also had strong ideological undertones naturally made the conflict considerably

---

[250] Fijnaut, Nuijten-Edelbroek and Spickenheuer 1985; Fijnaut 1987b.
[251] Fijnaut, Moerland and Uit Beijerse 1991.
[252] Fijnaut and Jacobs 1991; Fijnaut and Marx 1995.
[253] Fijnaut, Bovenkerk, Bruinsma and Van de Bunt 1998.
[254] Albrecht and Klip 2013.

more acrimonious. The highly ideological nature of the controversies meant that the benefits arising from the reception of European criminology after 1909, in particular in its criminal-sociological aspect, threatened to be ignored by both factions. As we saw in the previous chapter, the conflicts in the United States subsided to some extent during the 1980s and 1990s. The more peaceful discussion on the opposing views has on balance produced a richer criminology than existed before the 1960s.

Something similar also applies to criminology in Western Europe. After the Second World War, the research that had been carried out in the United States since the 1920s immediately became a rich source of inspiration and renewal for criminology in several Western European countries, especially in the United Kingdom, but also in the Netherlands and France. Subsequently, American interactionist and Marxist criminology represented a second wave of innovation on top of that research. The turmoil that the latter reform movement stirred up in the field of criminology was undoubtedly most intense in the United Kingdom, Germany, and the Netherlands. It also had an impact in France and Belgium but led to much less trouble there than in those three countries. Remarkably, it did not trigger a backlash – other than a few admittedly fierce but all in all still minor incidents – in any of these countries in the way it had in the United States in the form of a neo-classical and bio-social criminology.

There is no doubt that the clash of ideas brought about by the second reform movement in Western Europe led in a number of countries – especially, of course, in the United Kingdom, Germany, and the Netherlands – to similarly intense conflicts among criminologists as there had been in the United States. But in the same way as those conflicts in the United States have decreased substantially, they are also no longer fought with the same intensity in Western Europe. That does not necessarily mean that greater unanimity has arisen between the warring parties, on both sides of the Atlantic. My impression, rather, is that that conflict has in recent years not only entered far calmer academic waters, but has also led to a substantial theoretical, methodological, and thematic expansion and refinement of the criminological spectrum which all parties can identify with and which is therefore accepted by all of them.

It should also be noted that the increasingly vigorous links regarding criminological theory and policy that have grown up between the United States and Western Europe since the eighteenth century have in recent decades become still closer due to the increasing interaction between the two continents. As a result, an increasingly differentiated but also similar criminology has developed on either side of the Atlantic and – partly as a result – the criminal justice systems have also come to display increasing similarities on important points. It is for that reason that the title and subtitle of this chapter refer to the transatlantic integration of criminology. To a great extent, the time has passed when there was only occasional cooperation on such matters as the structure of the prison system and only one-sided reception of theories, research studies, and practices.

It is also appropriate to note that since the 1980s criminology has become a booming business. The main reason for this is undoubtedly that since that time the problems of crime and punishment have – for all kinds of reasons – become a major social priority and governments therefore feel compelled to fund criminological research (directly or indirectly) via their own institutions, the universities, and private research bodies. It goes almost without saying that this unprecedented quantitative reinforcement of criminology not only encourages its qualitative differentiation, but also increases its transatlantic integration. The enormous increase in the volume of research means that a growing number of issues have become the object of interest on both sides of the Atlantic. Moreover, one must not forget that modern information and communication technology makes it possible to satisfy that interest across the Atlantic without any delay and on an unprecedented scale.

CHAPTER 11

GENERAL CONCLUSION

To conclude this introduction to the transatlantic history of criminology and the criminal justice system, it is appropriate to look back at what we have seen during this survey. This will be done in the first section of this chapter. In conjunction with this retrospective, we will then also look to the future on the basis of the current status of criminology.

11.1. FROM THE PAST TO THE PRESENT

The foregoing chapters clearly demonstrate that criminology – in the form of a systematic discourse on crime and society's response to it – has a long history. That history reaches back into the Middle Ages but acquired greater shape and form in the course of the eighteenth and nineteenth centuries. However, its history as a scientific discipline is considerably shorter. It began at the end of the nineteenth century and gradually took on the usual institutional forms: books and journals, national and international associations, university chairs, and research institutes.

This so-called modern criminology clearly built, on the one hand, on the manifold ideas developed since the eighteenth century about the person of the offender, the nature, extent and development of crime problems, and preventive or repressive combatting of crime. On the other hand, it was also highly indebted to the institutions that, since the Middle Ages, have increasingly become the backbone of the criminal justice system, namely the police, the Public Prosecution Service and the judiciary, and the prison system. It should also be noted that this criminology not only radically transformed those ideas from a wide range of perspectives – biological, psychological, and sociological – but at the same time also called into question the principles, organisation, and functioning of the existing criminal justice system. The differentiation within the prison system, the development of the juvenile protection and probation systems, the psychiatrisation of sentencing, and the scientification of criminal investigation can be ascribed, both directly and indirectly, to the new science of criminology.

But this abstract summary is not sufficient for dealing with the development of modern criminology in relation to the criminal justice system. If we wish to do justice to the transatlantic history of that criminology during this period of more than a century, we need to view it from various different perspectives. Its history in the Western world is quite simply not a shining example of a discipline which, as it were, develops and progresses, continually and homogenously across the board, from a single fixed point. Quite the contrary.

11.1.1. THE VOLATILE HISTORY OF CRIMINOLOGY

One must first realise that in the past hundred years Western criminology has developed not only continuously but also discontinuously. Viewed in this way, its history can be roughly divided into three periods. The first runs from the end of the nineteenth century until the 1920s and can be categorised as the period during which – despite a great deal of sometimes passionate national and international debate regarding its principles, methods, and purposes – criminology in Western Europe developed biologically, psychologically, and sociologically and fanned out, especially in its bio-anthropological variant, to the United States.

The second period covers from the 1920s to the 1960s. During that period, however, the history of criminology on the European side of the Atlantic was entirely different to that on the American side. Whereas Western European criminology in that period was to a large extent devastated by Nazi or Marxist ideology, criminal sociology blossomed in the United States, with bio-anthropology becoming an undercurrent in its development.

The third period encompasses roughly the second half of the twentieth century and can be described as that during which criminology – again following fierce clashes regarding its principles, objects, methods, and relationships with government and society – became intertwined across the Atlantic, more closely than ever, into a scientific discipline with an unprecedented variety of theoretical perspectives, research methods, and themes.

Second, the foregoing history of criminology in the respective countries demonstrates very clearly that, since the invention of the discipline in Italy, its substantive evolution has been very different from one country to another in many respects. One must of course consider, first of all, the point at which and the extent to which the bio-anthropological ideas of the Italian School were initially adopted or contested, to a greater or lesser extent, in a number of European countries. If one positions those countries in a kind of spectrum, then Germany and the United States were the countries where those ideas gained most support and France was where they encountered the greatest opposition from a sociological perspective. Countries like the United Kingdom, Belgium, and the Netherlands fell somewhere between these two ends of the spectrum because the ideas of the Italian School ideas were generally received there with mixed feelings.

Moreover, it should be noted that the development of the ideas of the Italian School in the biological and psychological direction continued into the 1920s, especially in Germany. The development of the French School's ideas in a sociological direction took place from the 1920s on mainly in the United States. And whereas criminology in the Netherlands and Belgium during the interwar period did not undergo so pronounced a development in one direction or another, in the United Kingdom it hardly underwent any further development at all during that period. After the Second World War, however, it is difficult to make any sharp country-based differentiation in the development of criminology in one direction or another. That is not only because the transatlantic integration of criminology became stronger during that period, but also because this far-reaching internationalisation mainly involved sociological criminology. That form of criminology has in fact become the dominant form of criminology in the West.

Third, it is appropriate, following on from the above sketch of the history of criminology, to indicate the differences between countries that have arisen, and that still exist, when it comes to the institutionalisation of criminology. Whereas in Italy journals were founded, special professorial chairs were established, and institutions set up quite soon after the invention of this discipline, there were absolutely no such developments in the United Kingdom before the Second World War. In Germany, the institutionalisation of criminology until into the 1930s mainly involved specialised literature but not specific chairs or institutes. Its institutionalisation in the Netherlands and Belgium, on the other hand – especially after the First World War – acquired, as it were, Italian features through the establishment of separate schools and institutes of criminology at a significant number of universities, the corresponding allocation of specific criminological teaching assignments to internal and external lecturers, and the flourishing of a very varied literature. In the United States, institutionalisation during the relevant period took place mainly in Chicago at and around the

University of Chicago, in Boston at and around Harvard University and in Berkeley at and around the University of California.

After the Second World War, the institutional development of criminology underwent turbulent development not only in the United States but also in the United Kingdom: many universities established institutes pursuing criminology on a larger or smaller scale, in terms of both research and teaching. In the Netherlands and Belgium, there has since been a similar turbulent development based on the facilities that had already been created before the Second World War, although this has taken place in some respects at different speeds – for example the establishment of educational programmes – and in different forms, for example the setting up of separate research institutes. The institutional development of criminology in Germany and France in recent decades contrasts sharply with this, as can be inferred from the discussions currently taking place in both countries regarding its present state and its future. On the one hand, university education in criminology has only got off the ground marginally in those two countries. On the other, scientific research is not only on a limited scale but is also concentrated at just a few research institutes.

11.1.2. TIES BETWEEN CRIMINOLOGY, THE CRIMINAL JUSTICE SYSTEM, AND COMBATTING CRIME

Attention also needs to be paid to the interconnectedness of criminology and the criminal justice system and, more broadly, the preventive and repressive combatting of crime.[1] The above history of criminology shows very clearly that that discipline has from the outset developed in close conjunction with the criminal justice system and efforts to combat crime. In other words, "pure" criminology has never existed. The discipline has in fact always been inextricably linked with the practice of combatting crime and in particular with the institutions and services involved, in one way or another, with the application of the criminal law. It is therefore not the case that it was only with critical criminology, from the 1960s on, that the criminal justice system came within the purview of criminology. This system of sanctions has traditionally belonged to the core of its material concern. Beccaria's observations already concerned the organisation of the criminal justice system to a significant extent. Moreover, the publications of Lombroso, Ferri and Garofalo, and many of their successors – regardless of their disciplinary focus – to a large extent always related, and still relate, directly or indirectly, to the adaptation or redesigning of that system, whether or not as part of a certain policy on crime. This in fact immediately indicates that the intrinsic ties between criminology and the criminal justice

---

[1]   Ericson 2003.

system and combatting crime have essentially taken two main complementary forms.

On the one hand, criminology relies heavily on the results of the work of the institutions and services that play a major role in these areas, whether or not one is dealing with sociological research into the nature, extent, and development of crime problems or with psychological study of suspects or convicted persons. On the other hand, criminology has traditionally focused strongly on improving or reforming the actual operation of those institutions and services in order to more adequately address those problems. In that context, it can boast considerable successes, a number of which have been indicated above. It will in fact be clear that the two, as it were, go hand in hand: understanding their functioning presupposes understanding their effect, and, conversely, understanding their effect makes it possible to understand the way they work.

This invariably policy-oriented focus of criminology does not in itself need to pose problems for its scientific status but in certain circumstances it can nevertheless cause major problems in this respect. This was abundantly clear in the totalitarian police states that determined the fate of Europe throughout most of the twentieth century. As a result of its ideologisation in Nazi Germany and the Soviet Union, the traditional policy-oriented focus of criminology proved fatal. That extreme experience should keep criminologists alert to the fact that criminology cannot only – in the wake of Lombroso – be an empirical science but should also – in the wake of Beccaria – remain a normative one. My preference therefore has long been for integrated criminal science.

11.1.3. DECISIVE FACTORS IN THE DEVELOPMENT OF CRIMINOLOGY

Finally, we cannot ignore the question of the factors that have played a major role in the transatlantic history of criminology since the end of the eighteenth century. It will be clear that it is impossible to enumerate those factors here for the whole of that history. That history is simply too discontinuous and too heterogeneous. In other words, to a certain extent many developments in criminology have their own history and it is difficult to lump them together in order to interpret them. If one nevertheless attempts to define the factors that have, in general, played a more or less important role, in all kinds of combinations and degrees in the rich transatlantic history of this discipline, then one arrives in any case at the following four factors.

In the first place, general scientific changes have been a factor of great importance in this context, whether they concerned jurisprudence and psychology in the eighteenth century, biology, anthropology and physics in the nineteenth, or sociology, history, economics, and medicine in the twentieth.

New developments in these basic disciplines are often a strategic prerequisite for associated innovations in criminology.

Second, there must be people who are not only aware of the possibilities that scientific innovations can mean for the advancement of criminology, but who are also able to transform these opportunities into convincing theoretical observations and cogent practical proposals. Beccaria, Lombroso, Gross, and Sutherland – to name but a few who stand head and shoulders above many others – were able to do that, each in his own way. But putting such ideas into actual practice requires more than the presence of imaginative and energetic pioneers.

Third, the political circumstances must also be conducive to doing so. Political views and thus political power relationships have, in other words, played a major role in the development of criminology, certainly in relation to the criminal justice system. Without political support, it is not only difficult to organise criminology on any significant scale in terms of research and education, but also to allow it to flourish to the full in terms of policy and practical action.

Fourth, in order to achieve this, another factor is of great importance, namely the development of crime itself. Especially when the nature and/or extent and/or scale of crime problems mean that they have taken on worrying proportions – or are threatening to do so – in the eyes of influential bodies and/or political or economic interest groups and/or the general public, a need arises, as it were automatically, for targeted criminological research on those problems and how to tackle them. This happened, for example, around 1900 in relation to the so-called incorrigible criminal and at the end of the twentieth century, for example, with regard to the phenomenon of organised crime.

11.2. FROM THE PRESENT TO THE FUTURE

When, in the light of the distant and the recent past, one examines the introductions, textbooks, collections, and journals that have been published in America and Europe in the past few years in the broad field of criminology, one realises that this is a vibrant and wide-ranging discipline that has certainly not rejected its past.

That literature in fact discusses the theoretical movements that arose in the 1960s, 1970s, and 1980s – those in critical criminology and in bio-social and neo-classical criminology, and in the field of "green" or "cultural" criminology – together with the theoretical perspectives from the heyday of German and French criminology and from the time of the famous Chicago School.

Furthermore, the recent literature deals not only with all kinds of forms of crime and categories of offenders that were already on the criminological agenda at the end of the nineteenth century, but also with forms and categories that criminologists began to deal with mainly in the second half of the twentieth century, for example organised crime and its perpetrators, white-collar crime, war crimes and genocide, crimes against humanity, and, last but not least, terrorism.

Third, what is also striking is the way in which the organisation and functioning of the institutions in and around the criminal justice system are nowadays discussed in the literature. The way those institutions are treated today is based far more on empirical research than was the case in the past, and is usually more critical of the way they actually function.

It would not be going too far to say that in the West in the twentieth century, despite all kinds of discontinuity and battles of ideas, not only has a major criminological discipline arisen but also a discipline that is far more differentiated and thorough, theoretically, methodologically and thematically, than was the case 50, 60, 70, or 80 years ago.

This flourishing of criminology has not always only been welcomed. In particular, the fear is sometimes expressed that this expansion may turn, as it were, into the opposite, i.e. disintegration as a result of the far-reaching fragmentation of its subject, object, and methodology.[2] What should we think of this gloomy expectation or prediction? Is, in a manner of speaking, the end of criminology nigh? To answer that challenging question, it is important to reflect on how criminology might develop in the coming decades. A sketch of its possible future development in fact offers greater guidance in responding to the question of how to prevent the criminology of the future – to put it rather radically – destroying itself through fragmentation. Clearly, that question is only relevant if one already believes that criminology should in fact continue to exist. And so, a third question arises: are there in fact sound arguments for its preservation?

11.2.1. FUTURE DEVELOPMENT OF CRIMINOLOGY

As regards the future development of criminology, it is first of all important – in the wake of what has just been stated about its past and present – to establish that its expansion in recent decades had been the result not only of the almost unstoppable growth of its material object but also of the dynamics that have taken possession of criminology as such in that context.

In relation to the growth of its object, one can, on the one hand, point to the increase in – and recognition of – forms of very serious international crime (genocide, crimes against humanity, etc.), the further internationalisation of traditional forms of organised, socio-economic, fiscal, and professional crime,

---

[2]   Ericson and Carriere 1994.

and the inexorable growth of new forms of crime, such as scams, extortion, and exploitation with the aid of the Internet.[3] On the other hand, one should not lose sight of the fact that combatting crime, including the criminal justice system, has in recent years become a booming business in all sorts of ways – in terms of policy as well as in terms of institutions and services – both at national level and at the level of all kinds of major international institutions such as the European Union, the Council of Europe, and the United Nations.[4] And that booming business includes the growth of all sorts of private police services as well as the privatisation of the judicial system and the enforcement of penalties.

The dynamism that has made itself felt in criminology in recent decades includes, on the one hand, the theoretical differentiation that has manifested itself during that period. This has meant not only that the number of theoretical works has increased dramatically but also that the topics that have traditionally occupied criminologists are being examined in more and more different ways. On the other hand, one cannot ignore the fact that in some Western countries – for example the United Kingdom, the Netherlands, and Belgium – academic and political authorities have invested heavily in the institutionalisation of academic and governmental criminology. That investment has in fact been rewarded by a surge of publications on an ever-increasing number of elements and aspects of its material object.

The question that now naturally arises is whether this expansion of criminology will continue in the coming years and decades. I personally think that it will. But let me hasten to add that I do not really expect that expansion to be in the area of the (material) object and the (theoretical) subject, i.e. in the actual substance of criminology – though that is not to say that that substance is not amenable to expansion or refinement. In any case, if such developments occur, it will not be possible to stop them. But it will take some considerable time before the extensive and differentiated substance that now constitutes the subject and object are absorbed significantly into the body of criminological knowledge.

Rather, I see criminology expanding institutionally, in the sense that both an increasing number of Western countries – for example Germany and France – will invest more in criminological research and education, as well as more and more countries in other continents. These will include not only countries such as Japan, Korea, Turkey, Israel, and South Africa – which have long pursued criminology – but also countries such as China, India, Brazil, Argentina, and Indonesia, which, for various reasons, have a long way to go in this field.

---

[3]   Findlay 2000; Kyle and Koslowski 2001; Nordstroom 2007; Smeulers and Haveman 2008; Paoli, Greenfield and Reuter 2009.

[4]   Andreas and Nadelmann 2006; Pouligny, Chesterman and Schnabel 2007; Smeulers 2010; Redo 2012.

They can be expected to do so because crime and, much more broadly, safety and security will for various reasons be given a consistently higher place on their political agenda.[5]

Those reasons primarily concern the fact that the globalisation of safety and security issues is making it increasingly important for governments not only to anticipate cross-border crime problems but also to tackle them if they manifest themselves within their national borders to any significant extent. I believe, however, that another important reason is the ever-increasing urbanisation of the world as it expresses itself in the increasing number of megalopolises. That development will, after all, raise more and more fundamental questions about organising and enforcing the safety and security of people and property in the megalopolises of the future.

11.2.2. THE GLOBAL NEED FOR CRIMINOLOGY

These and other reasons will result, in my opinion, in an increasing number of institutes or schools of criminology being established around the world with a view to amassing and disseminating the knowledge needed to deal with these developments as effectively as possible. This means that there will be a kind of globalisation of criminology which will further reinforce its expansion not only geographically, but in the long run also as regards its substance. That globalisation will, for example, entail local and regional crime problems (and of course the responses to them) being raised within criminology that have hitherto not been very high on its agenda. It will also make it possible to perform comparative studies in greater depth on local forms of crime and how to combat them than is currently the case.[6] Similarly, it will provide greater scope for more integrated cross-border studies of the international dimensions of many forms of serious crime, whether it be arms dealing in the context of civil wars or the trafficking of women from one part of the world to red light districts in other continents or subcontinents.[7]

Besides these positive aspects, however, this development also has its downsides. One of these will be the need to prevent "the West" from attempting to exert its influence on criminology as it develops, or develops further, on other continents.[8] It is understandable that such intellectual colonisation will meet with a great deal of opposition, certainly in the former colonies of the Netherlands, the United Kingdom, France, etc. Partly for this reason, globalisation needs to

---

5   Ericson 2007, pp. 1–71, 204–219; Albrecht (H.-J.) 2007.
6   Barak 2000.
7   See, inter alia, Fijnaut, Bruggeman, Sievers, Spapens and Van Erve 2016.
8   Agozino 2004.

lead to "the West" diligently considering how crime used to be defined in those colonies and how the criminal law and other methods were once used to combat it. The growing academic interest in colonial policing in South America, Africa, and Asia is a good example of what is meant.

The latter consideration provides an answer to the third question that was raised above, namely whether a version of criminology is required that develops further internationally in a direction as indicated above. I believe that that question should be answered in the affirmative. There are various arguments to support this, two of which must in any case be emphasised.

The first positive argument is that global research in fields that are as socially sensitive as that of crime and insecurity (and how to combat them) must meet the highest standards in terms of expertise, impartiality, and independence. Contemporary criminology does to a large extent meet those standards, and it is therefore obvious that much is being done to promote the spread of such a version of the discipline. That may seem self-evident but it is certainly not, inter alia in the light of the increasing privatisation of criminology in those fields in the form of think tanks and consultants.

The second positive argument is that global research in those fields also demands an approach that assigns high priority to interdisciplinarity. In fact, criminology is unable to look back on an impressive past or present in that respect across the board, but even so, interdisciplinarity is in its genes. Not only has its development frequently been nourished by a wide variety of basic disciplines, but excellent examples can also be found in many subfields of interdisciplinary collaboration with historians, sociologists, lawyers, etc. An enticing view of the future will in fact encourage the practitioners of criminology to carry out interdisciplinary research more systematically and to teach on a more interdisciplinary basis.[9]

11.2.3. WILL FRAGMENTATION LEAD TO THE DEMISE OF CRIMINOLOGY?

The above positive response to the third question brings us, finally, to the question of how we can prevent criminology from becoming the victim of its own success due to fragmentation. In answering that question, one should first note that, in my view, criminology should not be kept alive simply for its own sake; sooner or later it will in fact disappear as such in some way or another. For the time being, it is of course important to ensure its continued existence. But how?

---

[9]   Fattah 1997, pp. 283–305.

In my opinion that cannot be achieved by seeking unification – as has sometimes been attempted in the past – of the theoretical perspectives that circulate within the discipline. Given the plural nature of its object, any attempt to do so is doomed to fail. Far more important is in any case to maintain the momentum of theoretical discussion within the discipline in relation to its material object, because such discussion ensures that the theoretical plurality of current and future criminology retains one and the same empirical point of reference.

The survival of criminology also cannot be promoted by reducing its material object or by returning it to its traditional proportions. If one were to attempt to do so, one would in fact risk criminology losing a great deal of its societal and scientific relevance and thus becoming marginalised. What is in any case more promising – in parallel with promoting theoretical discussion – is also to encourage discussion of the substance of its object. This will in fact prevent criminological research fragmenting into thousands of "single issues", with the link between them disappearing or being lost sight of. There is, for example, the impact of organised crime on safety in cities, the relationship between corruption and organised crime, and the links between organised crime and terrorism.

Finally, the conclusion must be that a criminology that can cope with the future predicted for it here does not exist – nor will it arise – of its own accord but must be deliberately organised. That will involve the following three things: the further development and distribution of multidisciplinary research institutes that also provide interdisciplinary teaching, the promotion of international journals that are theoretically and thematically open to the research and education taking place around the world, and the production of reference works that systematically reflect regional, continental, and intercontinental developments in specific subfields.

BIBLIOGRAPHY

Abbott, R., *Police Reform in Russia, 1858–1878*, Princeton University, Department of History, 1971 (dissertation).

About, I., "Naissance d'une science policière de l'identification en Italie, 1902–1922", *Les cahiers de la sécurité*, 2005, pp. 167–200.

—— "Classer le corps: l'anthropométrie judiciaire et ses alternatives, 1880–1930", in: A. Ceyhan and P. Piazza (eds.), *L'identification biométrique: champs, acteurs, enjeux et controverses*, Paris, Editions de la Maison des Sciences de l'Homme, 2011, pp. 39–62.

About, I. and V. Denis, *Histoire de l'identification des personnes*, Paris, La Découverte, 2010.

Académie Royale de Belgique (ed.), *Adolphe Quetelet, 1796–1874*, Brussels, Palais des Académies, 1977.

Achille, M., "Le service anthropométrique de M. Bertillon", *Archives d'anthropologie, de médécine légale et de psychologie normale et pathologique*, 1909, pp. 287–295.

Actes du deuxième congrès international d'anthropologie criminelle, biologie et sociologie (Paris, August 1889), Paris, G. Masson, 1890.

Actes du troisième congrès international d'anthropologie criminelle, biologie et sociologie, tenu à Bruxelles en août 1892 sous le haut patronage du gouvernement, Brussels, F. Hayez, 1893.

Actes du IIe congrès international de criminologie (Paris-Sorbonne, September 1950), Paris, Presses Universitaires de France, 1952–55, 6 vols.

Adams, B., *The Politics of Punishment: Prison Reform in Russia, 1863–1917*, Dekalb, Northern Illinois University Press, 1996.

Adler, J., "Rejoinder to Chambliss", *Criminology*, 1989, pp. 239–250.

Adler, F. and W. Laufer (eds.), *The Legacy of Anomie Theory*, New Brunswick, Transaction Publishers, 2000 (with an introduction by R. Merton).

Aertsen, I. and T. Peters, "Penologie en victimologie", in: J. Casselman, I. Aertsen and S. Parmentier (eds.), *Tachtig jaar criminologie aan de Leuvense universiteit: onderwijs, onderzoek en praktijk*, Antwerp, Maklu, 2012.

Agnew, R., "A general strain theory of community differences in crime rates", *Journal of Research in Crime and Delinquency*, 1999, pp. 123–155.

Agnew, R. and J. Kaufman (eds.), *Anomie, Strain and Subcultural Theories of Crime*, Farnham, Ashgate, 2010.

Agozino, B., "Imperialism, crime and criminology: towards the decolonisation of criminology", *Crime, Law and Social Change*, 2004, pp. 343–358.

Aichhorn, A., *Verwaarloosde jeugd*, Utrecht, Erven J. Bijleveld, 1967 (translated by J. Zuring).

Akers, R., "Theory and ideology in Marxist criminology: comments on Turk, Quinney, Toby and Klockars", *Criminology*, 1979, pp. 527–544.

—— *Criminological Theories: Introduction and Evaluation*, Los Angeles, Roxbury Publishing Company, 1994.

Alary, E., *L'histoire de la gendarmerie: de la Renaissance au troisième millénaire*, Paris, Calmann-Lévy, 2000.

Albats, Y., *KGB: State within a State*, London, I.B. Tauris, 1995 (translated by C. Fitzpatrick).

Albrecht, A., "Cesare Lombroso: a glance at his life work", *Journal of the American Institute of Criminal Law and Criminology*, 1910, pp. 71–83.

Albrecht, H.-J., "Kriminologische Forschung: Erwartungen an die Zukunft", in: A. Eser (ed.), *Kriminologische Forschung im Ubergang*, Freiburg im Breisgau, Max-Planck-Institut für ausländisches und internationales Strafrecht, 1997, pp. 49–78.

―― "Trafficking in human beings and human rights", in: S. Parmentier and E. Weitekamp (eds.), *Crime and Human Rights*, Amsterdam, Elsevier, 2007, pp. 302–332.

Albrecht, H.-J. and K. Boers, "Criminalité et justice criminelle en République Fédérale d'Allemagne: évolution dans les années 1990", in: L. van Outrive and P. Robert (eds.), *Crime et justice en Europe depuis 1990: état des recherches, évaluation et recommendations*, Paris, L'Harmattan, 1999, pp. 25–69.

Albrecht, H.-J. and A. Klip (eds.), *Crime, Criminal Law and Criminal Justice in Europe: A Collection in Honour of Prof. em. Dr. Dr. h.c. Cyrille Fijnaut*, Leiden, Martinus Nijhoff Publishers, 2013.

Albrecht, P.-A., *Kriminologie: eine Grundlegung zum Strafrecht*, Munich, Verlag C.H. Beck, 2005.

Aletrino, A., *Twee opstellen over crimineele anthropologie*, Amsterdam, Scheltema & Holkema's Boekhandel, 1898.

―― *Over ontoerekenbaarheid*, Amsterdam, Scheltema & Holkema's Boekhandel, 1899.

―― *Handleiding bij de studie der crimineele anthropologie*, Amsterdam, Tierie & Kruyt, 1902.

―― *Is celstraf nog langer geoorloofd en gewenscht?*, Amsterdam, Van Maas & Van Suchtelen, 1906.

―― *Zuster Bertha*, The Hague, Uitgeverij BZZTôH, 1982 (with an afterword by K. Joosse).

Alexander, F. and S. Selesnick, *The History of Psychiatry: An Evaluation of Psychiatric Thought and Practice from Prehistoric Times to the Present*, New York, The New American Library, 1968.

Alexander, F. and S. Staub, *The Criminal, the Judge and the Public: A Psychological Analysis*, New York, Collier Books, 1962.

Alff, W., "Voltaires Kommentar zu Beccarias Buch über Verbrechen und Strafen", in: G. Deimling (ed.), *Cesare Beccaria: die Anfänge moderner Strafrechtspflege in Europa*, Heidelberg, Kriminalistik Verlag, 1989, pp. 79–98.

Algemeen Commando van de Rijkswacht, *Geschiedenis van de rijkswacht*, Brussels, Ghesquière and Partners, 1979, 2 vols.

Allason, R., *The Branch: A History of the Metropolitan Police Special Branch, 1883–1983*, London, Secker & Warburg, 1983.

Allen, F., "Raffaele Garofalo, 1852–1934", in: H. Mannheim (ed.), *Pioneers in Criminology*, London, Stevens and Sons, 1960, pp. 318–340.

Alschuler, A., "The changing purposes of criminal punishment: a retrospective on the past century and some thoughts about the next", *University of Chicago Law Review*, 2003, pp. 1–22.

Alstorphius Grevelink, P., *Bedenkingen tegen het ontwerp van wet ter vernieuwde uitbreiding der celstraf*, The Hague, Martinus Nijhoff, 1874.

Ancel, M., *La défense sociale nouvelle (un mouvement de politique criminelle humaniste)*, Paris, Editions Cujas, 1966 (second revised and extended edition).

―― *La défense sociale*, Paris, Presses Universitaires de France, 1985.

Andreas, P. and E. Nadelmann, *Policing the Globe: Criminalization and Crime Control in International Relations*, New York, Oxford University Press, 2006.

Andrew, C. and O. Gordievsky, *KGB: The Inside Story of its Foreign Operations from Lenin to Gorbachov*, New York, Harper Collins, 1990.

Andrew, C. and V. Mitrokhin, *The Sword and the Shield: The Mitrokhin Archive and the Secret History of the KGB*, New York, Basic Books, 1999.

Anglade, E., *Etude sur la police*, Paris, C. Gérard, 1852.

Anoniem, "L'Ecole des Sciences Criminelles de l'Université de Louvain", *Revue de droit pénal et de criminologie*, 1930, pp. 149–160.

Applebaum, A., *Gulag: A History*, New York, Doubleday, 2003.

Arntzen, F. and E. Michaelis, *Psychologie der Zeugenaussage: Einführung in die forensische Aussagepsychologie*, Göttingen, Verlag für Psychologie, Dr. C.J. Hogrefe, 1970.

Arrigo, B. and D. Milovanovic (eds.), *Postmodernist and Poststructuralist Theories of Crime*, Surrey, Ashgate, 2010.

Artières, P. and G. Corneloup (eds.), *Le médecin et le criminel: Alexandre Lacassagne, 1843–1924*, Lyon, Bibliothèque Municipale de Lyon, 2004.

Asbury, H., *The Gangs of New York: An Informal History of the Underworld*, New York, Paragon House, 1990.

Aschaffenburg, G., 'Kriminalpsychologie und Strafrechtsreform', *Monatsschrift für Kriminalpsychologie und Strafrechtsreform*, 1904–05, pp. 1–7.

—— *Das Verbrechen und seine Bekämpfung: Einleitung in die Kriminalpsychologie für Mediziner, Juristen und Soziologen: ein Beitrag zur Reform der Strafgesetzgebung*, Heidelberg, Carl Winters Universitätsbuchhandlung, 1923 (third revised edition).

Asser, C., *Vluglige beschouwing van eenige voorname beginselen des strafregts, in verband met het ontwerp des lijfstraffelijken wetboeks*, The Hague, Gebroeders Van Cleef, 1827.

Aubert, J., M. Eude, C. Goyard et al., *L'état et sa police en France, 1789–1914*, Geneva, Librairie Droz, 1979.

Auboin, M., A. Teyssier and J. Tulard (eds.), *Histoire et dictionnaire de la police du moyen âge à nos jours*, Paris, Laffont, 2005.

Auerbach, L., *Denkwürdigkeiten des Geheimen Regierungsrathes Stieber*, Berlin, Julius Engelmann, 1884.

Autour de l'œuvre du dr. E. de Greeff, Leuven, Editions Nauwelaerts, 1956, 2 vols.

Avé-Lallemant, F., *Das deutsche Gaunertum in seiner sozialpolitischen, literarischen und linguistischen Ausbildung zu seinem heutigen Bestande*, Wiesbaden, Ralph Suchier, 1858.

Ayaz, W., R. Gilsenbach, U. Körber, K. Scherer, P. Wagner and M. Winther, *Feinderklärung und Prävention: Kriminalbiologie, Zigeunerforschung und Asozialenpolitik*, Berlin, Rotbuch Verlag, 1988.

Baayens-Van Geloven, Y., A. 't Hart et al., *Strafwetgeving in de negentiende eeuw*, Tilburg, Katholieke Hogeschool Tilburg, 1985, 5 vols.

Badinter, R., "Beccaria, l'abolition de la peine de mort et la Révolution française", *Revue de science criminelle et de droit pénal comparé*, 1989, pp. 235–251.

—— *La prison républicaine*, Paris, Fayard, 1992.

Bailleau, F. and A. Groenemeyer, "Introduction pour le 30e anniversaire de la revue", *Déviance et société*, 2007, pp. 371–374.

Baldaev, D., *Russian Criminal Tattoo*, London, FUEL, 2009.

—— *Drawings from the Gulag*, London, FUEL, 2010.

Balkema, J., G. Corstens, C. Fijnaut et al. (eds.), *Gedenkboek honderd jaar Wetboek van Strafrecht*, Arnhem, Gouda Quint, 1986.

Banton, M., *The Policeman in the Community*, London, Tavistock Publications, 1964.

—— *Police Community Relations*, London, Glasgow, 1973.

Barak, G., *Integrating Criminologies*, Boston, Allyn and Bacon, 1998.

Barak, G. (ed.), *Crime and Crime Control: A Global View*, Westport, Greenwood Press, 2000.

Baratta, A., "Strafrechtsdogmatik und Kriminologie: zur Vergangenheit und Zukunft des Modells einer gesamten Strafrechtswissenschaft", *Zeitschrift für die gesamte Strafrechtswissenschaft*, 1980, pp. 107–142.

Barnes, H., *The Repression of Crime: Studies in Historical Penology*, New York, George H. Doran Company, 1926.

—— *The Evolution of Penology in Pennsylvania: A Study in American Social History*, Indianapolis, Bobbs-Merrill, 1927.

Barnes, H. and N. Teeters, *New Horizons in Criminology*, Englewood Cliffs, Prentice-Hall, 1959.

Barry, J., "Alexander Maconochie, 1787–1860", in: H. Mannheim (ed.), *Pioneers in Criminology*, London, Stevens and Sons, 1960, pp. 68–90.

Bartier, J., "Quetelet politique", in: Académie Royale de Belgique (ed.), *Adolphe Quetelet, 1796–1874*, Brussels, Palais des Académies, 1977, pp. 20–45.

Bauer, A., *A la recherche de la criminologie: une enquête*, Paris, CNRS Editions, 2010.

Bauer, F., *Das Verbrechen und die Gesellschaft*, Munich, Ernst Reinhardt Verlag, 1957.

Bauer, G., *Moderne Verbrechensbekämpfung*, Lübeck, Verlag für Polizeiliches Fachschrifttum, 1970, 2 vols.

Baumann, I., *Dem Verbrechen auf der Spur: eine Geschichte der Kriminologie und Kriminalpolitik in Deutschland, 1880–1980*, Göttingen, Walstein Verlag, 2006.

—— "Im Schatten des Jugend-KZ: 'Vorbeugende Verbrechensbekämpfung' und die Debatte um 'Frühkriminalität' in den fünfziger Jahren der Bundesrepublik Deutschland", *Polizei & Geschichte*, 2009, pp. 32–41.

Baumer, E., "Untangling research puzzles in Merton's multilevel anomie theory", *Theoretical Criminology*, 2007, pp. 63–69.

Bauricius, L., *Over de gevangenissen in Nederland*, Leeuwarden, Schierbeek, 1838.

Baurmann, M., "Kriminalpolitik ohne Mass: zum Marburger Programm Franz von Liszts", *Kriminalsoziologische Bibliografie*, 1984, pp. 54–79.

Bayley, D. and H. Mendelsohn, *Minorities and the Police: Confrontation in America*, New York, Free Press, 1969.

Beavan, C., *Fingerprints: The Origins of Crime Detection and the Murder Case that Launched Forensic Science*, New York, Hyperion, 2001.

Beccaria, C., *Traité des délits et des peines*, Amsterdam, s.n., 1766 (translated from Italian by A. Morellet after the third revised, corrected and enlarged edition by the author).

—— *Des délits et des peines*, Paris, Guillaumin et Cie, Libraires, 1870 (with an introduction and commentary by M. Faustin Hélie).

—— *Over misdaden en straffen*, Antwerp, Kluwer Rechtswetenschappen, 1982 (translated from Italian and with an introduction and commentary by J. Michiels).

Bechtel, H., *State Police in the United States: A Socio-historical Analysis*, Westport, Greenwood Press, 1995.

Becker, H., *Outsiders: Studies in the Sociology of Deviance*, New York, Free Press, 1966.

—— (ed.), *The Other Side: Perspectives on Deviance*, New York, Free Press, 1967.

Becker, P., "Vom 'Haltlosen' zur 'Bestie': das polizeiliche Bild des Verbrechers im 19. Jahrhundert", in: A Lüdtke (ed.), *'Sicherheit' und 'Wohlfahrt': Polizei, Gesellschaft und Wissenschaft im 19. und 20. Jahrhundert*, Frankfurt, Suhrkamp, 1992, pp. 97–131.

—— "Der Verbrecher als 'monstruoser Typus': zur kriminologischen Semiotik der Jahrhundertwende", in: M. Hagner (ed.), *Der falsche Körper: Beiträge zu einer Geschichte der Monstrositäten*, Göttingen, Wallstein Verlag, 1995, pp. 147–173.

—— "Physiognomie des Bösen: Cesare Lombrosos Bemühungen um eine präventive Entzifferung des Kriminellen", in: C. Schmolders (ed.), *Der Exzentrische Blick: Gespräch über Physiognomik*, Berlin, Akademie Verlag, 1996, pp. 163–186.

—— "Von der Biographie zur Genealogie: zur Vorgeschichte der Kriminologie als Wissenschaft und diskursiver Praxis", in: H. Bödeker, P. Reill and J. Schlumbohm (eds.), *Wissenschaft als kulturelle Praxis, 1750-1900*, Göttingen, Vandenhoeck & Ruprecht, 1999, pp. 335–375.

—— *Verderbnis und Entartung: eine Geschichte der Kriminologie des 19. Jahrhunderts als Diskurs und Praxis*, Göttingen, Vandenhoeck & Ruprecht, 2002.

—— *Dem Täter auf der Spur: eine Geschichte der Kriminalistik*, Darmstadt, Primus Verlag, 2005 (2005a).

—— "Classifier, communiquer, confondre: l'histoire du 'regard pratique' dans les services de police en Allemagne au XIXe siècle", *Les cahiers de la sécurité*, 2005, pp. 225–250 (2005b).

Becker, P. and R. Wetzell (eds.), *Criminals and their Scientists: The History of Criminology in International Perspective*, Cambridge, Cambridge University Press, 2006.

Beeckman, M., *Arbeid van gevangenen en vrije arbeid*, Amsterdam, Roeloffzen & Hübner, 1892.

Beeley, A., *Social Planning for Crime Control: The Principles of Modern Criminology Applied to American Conditions*, Salt Lake City, University of Utah Press, 1935.

Beermann, R., "The Soviet law on commissions for cases of juveniles", *British Journal of Criminology*, 1961–62, pp. 386–391.

Beirne, P., "Adolphe Quetelet and the origins of positivist criminology", *American Journal of Criminology*, 1987, pp. 1140–1169 (1987a).

—— "Between classicism and positivism: crime and penality in the writings of Gabriel Tarde", *Criminology*, 1987, pp. 785–819 (1987b).

—— "Heredity versus environment: a reconsideration of Charles Goring's *The English Convict*", *British Journal of Criminology*, 1988, pp. 315–339.

—— *Inventing Criminology: Essays on the Rise of "homo criminalis"*, Albany, State University of New York Press, 1993.

Bell, J., "Reichskriminalpolizei", *Archiv für Kriminologie*, 1920, pp. 161–170.

Bellmann, F., *Die Internationale Kriminalistische Vereinigung, 1889-1933*, Frankfurt am Main, Peter Lang, 1994.

Bentham, J., *An Introduction to the Principles of Morals and Legislation*, London, University of London, 1970 (edited by J. Burns and H. Hart).

Béraud, G., *Précis de criminologie et de police scientifique*, Paris, Payot, 1938.

Berends, R., A. Huussen Jr, R. Mens and R. de Windt, *Arbeid ter disciplinering en bestraffing: Veenhuizen als onvrije kolonie van de Maatschappij van Weldadigheid, 1823-1859*, Zutphen, De Walburg Pers, 1984.

Berents, A., *Misdaad in de Middeleeuwen: een onderzoek naar de criminaliteit in het laat-middeleeuwse Utrecht*, Linschoten, Stichtse Historische Reeks, 1976.

Berlière, J.-M., *La police des moeurs sous la IIIe République*, Paris, Editions du Seuil, 1992.

—— *Le préfet Lépine: vers la naissance de la police moderne*, Paris, Editions Denoël, 1993.

—— "La police sous la IIIe République, la difficile construction", in: M. Auboin, A. Teyssier and J. Tulard (eds.), *Histoire et dictionnaire de la police du moyen âge à nos jours*, Paris, Laffont, 2005, pp. 351–402 (2005a).

—— "Anthropométrie", in: *Histoire et dictionnaire de la police du moyen âge à nos jours*, Paris, Laffont, 2005, pp. 550–553 (2005b).

—— "Bertillon, Alphonse (1853–1914)", in: M. Auboin, A. Teyssier and J. Tulard (eds.), *Histoire et dictionnaire de la police du moyen âge à nos jours*, Paris, Laffont, 2005, pp. 572–574 (2005c).

—— *Naissance de la police moderne*, Paris, Perrin, 2011.

Berlière, J.-M. and P. Fournié (eds.), *Fichés ? Photographie et identification, 1850–1960*, Paris, Perrin, 2011.

Berlière, J.-M. and R. Lévy, *Histoire des polices en France: de l'Ancien Régime à nos jours*, Paris, Nouveau Monde Editions, 2011.

Berman, N. and E. Burgess, "The development of criminological research in the Soviet Union", *American Sociological Review*, 1937, pp. 213–222.

Bernard, P., *From the Enlightenment to the Police State: The Public Life of Johann Anton Pergen*, Urbana, University of Illinois Press, 1991.

Bernburg. J., "Anomie, social change and crime: a theoretical examination of institutional anomie theory", *British Journal of Criminology*, 2002, pp. 729–742.

Bertillon, A., "De l'identification par les signalements anthropométriques", *Archives de l'anthropologie criminelle et des sciences pénales*, 1886, pp. 193–223.

—— "Sur le fonctionnement du service des signalements anthropométriques", *Archives de l'anthropologie criminelle et des sciences pénales*, 1888, pp. 138–157.

—— *Identification anthropométrique: instructions signalétiques*, Melun, Imprimerie Administrative, 1893.

—— "Les empreintes digitales", *Archives d'anthropologie, de médecine légale et de psychologie normale et pathologique*, 1912, pp. 36–52 (1912a).

—— "Note technique sur le nouveau portrait anthropométrique au 1/5", *Archives d'anthropologie criminelle, de médécine légale et de psychologie normale et pathologique*, 1912, pp. 629–631 (1912b).

Bertillon, S., *Vie d'Alphonse Bertillon: inventeur de l'anthropométrie*, Paris, Gallimard, 1941.

Bertrand, E., *Penitentiaire lessen*, Leuven, L'Ecrou, 1932–34, 3 vols.

Beschouwingen van de regterlijke collegien etc. over de eenzame opsluiting van gevangenen, vergeleken met de gemeenschappelijke gevangenisstraf, The Hague, Algemeene Lands-Drukkerij, 1857.

Beyens, K., S. Snacken and C. Eliaerts, *Privatisering van gevangenissen*, Brussels, VUBPress, 1992.

Beyers, L., "Rasdenken tussen geneeskunde en natuurwetenschap: Emile Houzé en de Société d'Anthropologie de Bruxelles, 1882–1921", in: J. Tollebeek, G. Vanpaemel and K. Wils (eds.), *Degeneratie in België*, Leuven, Universitaire Pers Leuven, 2003, pp. 43–78.

Bianchi, H., *Position and Subject-matter of Criminology: Inquiry Concerning Theoretical Criminology*, Amsterdam, North-Holland Publishing Company, 1956.

—— "York en Florence: op weg naar een nieuwe kriminologie", *Nederlands Tijdschift voor Kriminologie*, 1974, pp. 3–16 (1974a).

—— "Gouvernementele en non-gouvernementele kriminologie: een 'meta-probleem'", *Nederlands Tijdschrift voor Kriminologie*, 1974, pp. 201–216 (1974b).

—— "De radicale criminologen en Bonger", *Nederlands Tijdschrift voor Criminologie*, 1976, pp. 202–208.

—— *Basismodellen in de criminologie*, Deventer, Van Loghum Slaterus, 1980.

—— *Gerechtigheid als vrijplaats: de terugkeer van het slachtoffer in ons recht*, Baarn, Ten Have, 1985.

Bianchi, H., M. Simondi and I. Taylor (eds.), *Deviance and Control in Europe: Papers from the European Group for the Study of Deviance and Social Control*, London, John Wiley & Sons, 1975.

Bibl, V., *Die Wiener Polizei: eine kulturhistorische Studie*, Leipzig, Stein-Verlag, 1927.

Bientjes, J. and H. Offerhaus, *De rijkswerkinrichtingen Veenhuizen in hun oorsprong en wettelijke organisatie*, Assen, L. Hansma, 1904.

Biermé, M., *Jules Lejeune: 'un grand humain'*, Brussels, F. Larcier, 1928.

Binnenveld, H., *Filantropie, repressie en medische zorg: geschiedenis van de inrichtingspsychiatrie*, Deventer, Van Loghum Slaterus, 1985.

Birkmeyer, K., *Was lässt Von Liszt vom Strafrecht übrig? Eine Warnung vor der modernen Richtung im Strafrecht*, Munich, C.H. Beck'sche Verlagsbuchhandlung, 1907.

Birnbaum, K., *Kriminalpsychopathologie: systematische Darstellung*, Berlin, Verlag von Julius Springer, 1921.

Bischoff, M., *La police scientifique*, Paris, Payot, 1938.

Bittner, E., *Aspects of Police Work*, Boston, Northeastern University Press, 1990.

Black, D., *The Behavior of Law*, New York, American Press, 1976.

Blackstone, W., *Commentaries on the Laws of England: In Four Books: Book the Fourth: Of Public Wrongs*, London, A. Strahan and W. Woodfall, 1795.

—— "Commentaries", in: J. Heath (ed.), *Eighteenth Century Penal Theory*, Oxford, Oxford University Press, 1963, pp. 179–194.

Blad, J., *Abolitionisme als strafrechtstheorie: theoretische beschouwingen over het abolitionisme van L.H.C. Hulsman*, Arnhem, Gouda Quint, 1996.

Blamires, C., "Beccaria et l'Angleterre", in: M. Porret (ed.), *Beccaria et la culture juridique des lumières*, Geneva, Librairie Droz, 1997, pp. 69–82.

Blanckaert, C., "Des sauvages en pays civilisé: l'anthropologie des criminels, 1850–1900", in: L. Mucchielli (ed.), *Histoire de la criminologie française*, Paris, L'Harmattan, 1994, pp. 55–88.

Bleuler, E., *Der geborene Verbrecher: eine kritische Studie*, Munich, J. F. Lehmann, 1896.

Bloch, H. and G. Geis, *Man, Crime and Society*, New York, Random House, 1970.

Bloch, H. and A. Niederhoffer, *Les bandes d'adolescents*, Paris, Payot, 1969.

Blok, A., *De bokkerijders: roversbenden en geheime genootschappen in de landen van Overmaas, 1730–1774*, Amsterdam, Prometheus, 1991.

Blom-Cooper, L. (ed.), *Progress in Penal Reform*, Oxford, Clarendon Press, 1974.

Blondel, C., *La psycho-physiologie de Gall: ses idées directrices*, Paris, Felix Alcan, 1914.

Blumstein, A., "Prisons", in: J. Wilson and J. Petersilia (eds.), *Crime: Twenty-eight Leading Experts Look at the Most Pressing Problem of Our Time*, San Francisco, ICS Press, 1995, pp. 387–419.

Blumstein, A. and J. Wallman (eds.), *The Crime Drop in America*, Cambridge, Cambridge University Press, 2000.

Bödeker, H., P. Reill and J. Schlumbohm (eds.), *Wissenschaft als kulturelle Praxis, 1750–1900*, Göttingen, Vandenhoeck & Ruprecht, 1999.

Bodson, P., "Jean Nypels, 1803–1886", in: C. Fijnaut (ed.), *Gestalten uit het verleden: 32 voorgangers in de strafrechtswetenschap, de strafrechtspleging en de criminologie*, Leuven, Universitaire Pers Leuven, 1993, pp. 83–88.

Body-Gendrot, S., *Globalization, Fear and Insecurity: The Challenges for Cities North and South*, Houndmills, Palgrave Macmillan, 2012.

Body-Gendrot, S., K. Kerezsi, M. Hough, R. Lévy and S. Snacken (eds.), *Handbook of European Criminology*, Oxford, Routledge, 2013.

Böhme, A., "Allgemeine Wehrpflicht gegenüber dem Verbrechertum", *Archiv für Kriminologie*, 1933, pp. 1–3.

Boers, K., U. Ewald, H.-J. Kerner, E. Lautsch and K. Sessar (eds.), *Sozialer Umbruch und Kriminalität*, Bonn, Forum Verlag Godesberg, 1994, 2 vols.

Boies, H., *The Science of Penology: The Defence of Society against Crime*, New York, G.P. Putnam's Sons, 1901.

—— "Degeneration and regeneration, 1893", in: N. Rafter (ed.), *The Origins of Criminology: A Reader*, London, Routledge, 2009, pp. 255–259.

Bondio, M., *Die Rezeption der kriminalanthropologischen Theorien von Cesare Lombroso in Deutschland, 1880–1914*, Husum, Matthiesen Verlag, 1995.

—— "From the "atavistic" to the "inferior" criminal type: the impact of the Lombrosian theory of the born criminal on german psychiatry", in: P. Becker and R. Wetzell (eds.), *Criminals and their Scientists: The History of Criminology in International Perspective*, Cambridge, Cambridge University Press, 2006, pp. 183–205.

Bonenfant, P., *Le problème du pauperisme en Belgique à la fin de l'Ancien Régime*, Brussels, Académie Royale de Belgique, 1934.

Bonger, H., *Leven en werk van Dirck Volckertsz Coornhert*, Amsterdam, G.A. Van Oorschot, 1978.

Bonger, H. et al. (eds.), *Dirk Volckertszoon Coornhert: dwars maar recht*, Zutphen, De Walburg Pers, 1989.

Bonger, H., J. Valkhoff and B. van der Waerden (eds.), *Prof. mr. W.A. Bonger: verspreide geschriften*, Amsterdam, De Arbeiderspers, 1950, 2 vols. (with a short biography by H. Bonger and a study on the works by J. Valkhoff).

Bonger, W., *Criminalité et conditions économiques*, The Hague, Martinus Nijhoff, 1905.

—— *Criminality and Economic Conditions*, Boston, Little, Brown and Co., 1916.

—— *Geloof en misdaad: een criminologische studie*, Amsterdam, Boekhandel en Uitgevers-Maatschappij "De Ontwikkeling", 1917.

—— *Over de evolutie der moraliteit: rede, uitgesproken bij de aanvaarding van het hoogleraarsambt aan de Gemeentelijke Universiteit te Amsterdam, op 12 juni 1922*, Amsterdam, Boekhandel en Uitgevers-Maatschappij "De Ontwikkeling", 1922.

—— *Inleiding tot de criminologie*, Haarlem, De Erven F. Bohn, 1932.

—— "Development of the penal law in The Netherlands", *Journal of Criminal Law and Criminology*, 1933–34, pp. 260–270.

—— *Problemen der demokratie: een sociologische en psychologische studie*, Amsterdam, De Arbeiderspers, 1934.

—— "Het 'nieuwe' strafrecht", *Rechtsgeleerd Magazijn Themis*, 1935, pp. 236–266.

—— *Ras en misdaad*, Haarlem, H.D. Tjeenk Willink, 1939.

—— "Cesare Lombroso", in: H. Bonger, J. Valkhoff and B. van der Waerden (eds.), *Prof. mr. W.A. Bonger: verspreide geschriften*, Amsterdam, De Arbeiderspers, 1950, vol. 1, pp. 3–12 (1950a).

—— "Misdaad en socialisme: tegelijk een bijdrage tot de studie der criminaliteit in Nederland", in: H. Bonger, J. Valkhoff and B. van der Waerden (eds.), *Prof. mr. W.A. Bonger: verspreide geschriften*, Amsterdam, De Arbeiderspers, 1950, vol. 1, pp. 83–120 (1950b).

—— "De oorlog als sociologisch probleem", in: H. Bonger, J. Valkhoff and B. van der Waerden (eds.), *Prof. mr. W.A. Bonger: verspreide geschriften*, Amsterdam, De Arbeiderspers, 1950, vol. 2, pp. 97–109 (1950c).

—— *Inleiding tot de criminologie*, Haarlem, De Erven F. Bohn, 1954 (third printing, revised by G. Kempe).

—— *Criminality and Economic Conditions*, Bloomington, Indiana University Press, 1969 (abridged and with an introduction by A. Turk).

Bonhomme, G., *Meeningen of getuigenissen in het strafproces*, Maastricht, Leiter-Nypels, 1893.

Boomgaard, J., "Het Amsterdamse criminaliteitspatroon in de late Middeleeuwen", in: H. Diederiks and H. Roodenburg (eds.), *Misdaad, zoen en straf*, Hilversum, Verloren, 1991, pp. 102–118.

Bopp, W. and D. Schultz, *A Short History of American Law Enforcement*, Springfield, Charles C. Thomas, 1972.

Bordua, D., *The Police: Six Sociological Essays*, New York, John Wiley & Sons, 1967.

Bordua, D. and A. Reiss, Jr , "Law enforcement", in: P. Lazarsfeld, W. Sewell and H. Wilensky (eds.), *The Uses of Sociology*, New York, Basic Books, 1967, pp. 275–303.

Borgerhoff, T., "Le classement monodactylaire et la recherche des malfaiteurs par l'identification des traces digitales", *Revue de droit pénal et de criminologie*, 1914, pp. 251–279.

Bosch, J., "Beccaria et Voltaire chez Goswin de Fierlant et quelques autres juristes belges et néerlandais", *Tijdschrift voor Rechtsgeschiedenis*, 1961, pp. 1–21.

Bosly, H., "André Marchal, 1919–1983", in: C. Fijnaut (ed.), *Gestalten uit het verleden: 32 voorgangers in de strafrechtswetenschap, de strafrechtspleging en de criminologie*, Leuven, Universitaire Pers Leuven, 1993, pp. 313–318.

Bott-Bodenhausen, M., *Der Zugang zum Verbrecher: die Bedeutung der Tiefenpsychologie für Strafrechtswesen und Kriminologie*, Hamburg, Kriminalistik Verlag, 1965.

Bottomley, A., *Decisions in the Penal Process*, London, Martin Robertson, 1973.

Bovenkerk, F., "Robert Ezra Park, 1864–1944", in: K. Hayward, S. Maruna and J. Mooney (eds.), *Fifty Key Thinkers in Criminology*, London, Routledge, 2010, pp. 48–52.

Box, S., *Deviance, Reality & Society*, London, Holt, Rinehart and Winston, 1981.

Boyer, J., "Bertillon's new system of anthropology", *Scientific American*, 1907, pp. 534–535.

Braffort, L., *Essai de contribution à l'évolution du droit pénal: mémoire pour la fondation d'une Ecole des Sciences Criminelles à l'Université de Louvain*, Brussels, Larcier, 1929.

—— "De hervorming onzer strafrechtelijke instellingen", *Periodisch Bulletijn*, 1931, pp. 163–213.

Braithwaite, J., *Inequality, Crime and Public Policy*, London, Routledge & Kegan Paul, 1979.

—— *Crime, Shame and Reintegration*, Cambridge, Cambridge University Press, 1995.

Branham, V. and S. Kutash (eds.), *Encyclopedia of Criminology*, New York, Philosophical Library, 1949.

Brantingham, P. and P. Brantigham (eds.), *Environmental Criminology*, Prospect Heights, Waveland Press, 1991.

—— "Environmental criminology: from theory to urban planning practice", *Studies on Crime and Crime Prevention*, 1998, pp. 31–60.

Bratton, W. and P. Knobler, *Turnaround: How America's Top Cop Reversed the Crime Epidemic*, New York, Random House, 1998.

Brauneck, A.-E., "Was läszt die Kriminologie vom Strafrecht übrig?", *Monatsschrift für Kriminologie und Strafrechtsreform*, 1963, pp. 193–201.

Brookman, F., M. Maguire, H. Pierpoint and T. Bennett (eds.), *Handbook of Crime*, Cullompton, Willan Publishing, 2010.

Bruinsma, G., *Criminaliteit als sociaal leerproces: een toetsing van de differentiële-associatietheorie in de versie van K.D. Opp*, Arnhem, Gouda Quint, 1985.

Bruinsma, G., W. Huisman and R. van Swaaningen (eds.), *Basisteksten in de criminologie*, The Hague, Boom, 2005, 3 vols.

Bruinsma, G., E. Leuw, E. Lissenberg and A. van Vliet (eds.), *Vrouw en criminaliteit: vrouwen als plegers en slachtoffers van criminaliteit*, Meppel, Boom, 1987.

Bruno, Dr., *De physiognomiek van Lavater*, Amsterdam, Mulder, s.d.

Brunt, L., "De angst voor Babylon: etnografisch onderzoek in Londen, 1850–1914", *Sociologisch Tijdschrift*, 1987, pp. 437–468.

Brusten, M., J. Häuszling and P. Malinowski (eds.), *Kriminologie im Spannungsfeld von Kriminalpolitik und Kriminalpraxis*, Stuttgart, Ferdinand Enke Verlag, 1986.

Buchholz, E., R. Hartmann, J. Lekschas and G. Stiller, *Sozialistische Kriminologie: ihre theoretische und methodologische Grundlegung*, Berlin, Staatsverlag der Deutschen Demokratischen Republik, 1971.

Büchler, A., *De cellulaire gevangenisstraf voor jeugdige misdadigers in Nederland*, Groningen, J.B. Wolters, 1894.

Buikhuisen, W., *Criminologie en criminologisch onderzoek*, Assen, Van Gorcum & Comp., 1966 (1966a).

—— *Achtergronden van nozemgedrag*, Assen, Van Gorcum & Comp., 1966 (1966b).

—— "Erfelijkheid en criminaliteit", *Nederlands Tijdschrift voor Criminologie*, 1968, pp. 129–143.

—— *An Alternative Approach to the Aetiology of Crime*, The Hague, Wetenschappelijk Onderzoek- en Documentatiecentrum, 1978.

—— *Kriminologie in biosociaal perspectief*, Deventer, Kluwer, 1979.

—— *Kriminaliteit: uitgangspunten voor het verklaren van krimineel gedrag*, Deventer, Kluwer, 1985.

Buikhuisen, W., T. Drost and T. Schilt, *Het gezicht van de onverdraagzaamheid: analyse van factoren die aan onverdraagzaamheid ten grondslag liggen*, Assen, Van Gorcum, 1976.

Buikhuisen, W. and J. Hemmel, "Crime and conditioning", *British Journal of Criminology*, 1972, pp. 147–157.

Buikhuisen, W. and S. Mednick (eds.), *Explaining Criminal Behaviour*, Leiden, E.J. Brill, 1988.

Buker, H., "Formation of self-control: Gottfredson and Hirschi's general theory of crime and beyond", *Aggression and Violent Behavior*, 2011, pp. 265–276.

Bundeskriminalamt (ed.), *Bekämpfung der Jugendkriminalität*, Wiesbaden, Bundeskriminalamt, 1955.

—— (ed.) *Städtebau und Kriminalität: urban planning and crime*, Wiesbaden, Bundeskriminalamt, 1979.

—— (ed.) *Das Bundeskriminalamt stellt sich seiner Geschichte: Dokumentation einer Kolloquienreihe*, Deurne, Luchterhand, 2008.

Burack, B., "A critical analysis of the theory, method and limitations of the 'lie detector'", *Journal of Criminal Law and Criminology*, 1955, pp. 414–426.

Burnier, P., *Le crime et les criminels: études des théories lombrosiennes*, Lausanne, Imprimerie de la Société Suisse de Publicité, 1911.

Buro Studium Generale, *Clara Wichmann herdenkingsprogramma, september–oktober 1985*, Utrecht, Rijksuniversiteit Utrecht, 1985.

Burt, C., *The Young Delinquent*, London, University of London Press, 1925.

—— *The Young Delinquent*, London, University of London Press, 1945 (fourth and revised edition).

Busam, G., *Das Geständnis im Strafverfahren: kriminologische, kriminalistische und kriminalpsychologische Aspekte*, Lübeck, Schmidt-Römhild, 1983.

Bussmann, K.-D. and R. Kreissl (eds.), *Kritische Kriminologie in der Diskussion: Theorien, Analysen, Positionen*, Opladen, Westdeutscher Verlag, 1996.

Butler, B. and J. Petrulis, "Some further observations concerning Sir Cyril Burt", *British Journal of Psychology*, 1999, pp. 155–160.

Bijleveld, P., "Een paar opmerkingen over het vooronderzoek in strafzaken in het bijzonder bij ernstige misdrijven", *Tijdschrift voor Strafrecht*, 1899, pp. 243–250.

Cadogan, E., *The Roots of Evil: Being a Treatise on the Methods Dealing with Crime and the Criminal During the Eighteenth and Nineteenth Centuries in Relation to Those of a More Enlightened Age*, London, John Murray, 1937.

Cain, M., *Society and the Policeman's Role*, London, Routledge & Kegan Paul, 1973.

Caldwell, R., *Criminology*, New York, Ronald Press Company, 1956.

Calkoen, H., *Verhandeling over het voorkomen en straffen der misdaaden*, Amsterdam, s.n., 1778.

Callan, G. and R. Stephenson, *Police Methods for Today and Tomorrow*, Newark, Duncan Press, 1939.

Callier, A., *La défense sociale par la justice*, Ghent, Ad. Hoste, 1909.

Cameron, I., *Crime and Repression in the Auvergne and the Guyenne, 1720–1790*, Cambridge, Cambridge University Press, 1981.

Cameron, J., *Prisons and Punishment in Scotland from the Middle Ages to the Present*, Edinburgh, Canongate, 1983.

Cantor, N., *Crime, Criminals and Criminal Justice*, New York, Henry Holt and Company, 1932.

Caplan, J., "'One of the strangest relics of a former state': tattoos and the discourses of criminality in Europe, 1880–1920", in: P. Becker and R. Wetzell (eds.), *Criminals and their Scientists: The History of Criminology in International Perspective*, Cambridge, Cambridge University Press, 2006, pp. 337–361.

Carp, E., *Het misdadige kind in psychologisch opzicht*, Amsterdam, Scheltema & Holkema's Boekhandel en Uitgevers-Mij, 1932.

Carp, E., J. van Bemmelen and D. Wiersma, *Gerechtelijke psychiatrie*, Amsterdam, Scheltema & Holkema, 1956.

Carr, L., *Delinquency Control*, New York, Harper & Brothers, 1941.

Carrabine, E., P. Cox, M. Lee, K. Plummer and N. South, *Criminology: A Sociological Introduction*, London, Routledge 2009.

Carte, G. and E. Carte, *Police Reform in the United States: The Era of August Vollmer, 1905–1932*, Berkeley, University of California Press, 1975.

—— "O.W. Wilson: police theory in action", in: P. Stead (ed.), *Pioneers in Policing*, Maidenhead, McGraw-Hill Book Company, 1977, pp. 207–223.

Cartuyvels, Y., *D'où vient le code pénal?: une approche génealogique des premiers codes pénaux absolutistes au XVIIIe siècle*, Brussels, De Boeck Université, 1996.

Cartuyvels, Y., B. Champetier, A. Wyvekens and M. van de Kerchove, *Soigner ou punir?: un regard critique sur la défense sociale en Belgique*, Brussels, Publications des Facultés Universitaires Saint-Louis, 2010.

Casselman, J., *Etienne de Greeff, 1898–1961: psychiater, criminoloog en romanschrijver: leven, werk en huidige betekenis*, Antwerp, Maklu, 2010.

—— "De eerste vier voorzitters en hun onderwijsprogramma", in: J. Casselman, I. Aertsen and S. Parmentier (eds.), *Tachtig jaar criminologie aan de Leuvense universiteit: onderwijs, onderzoek en praktijk*, Antwerp, Maklu, 2012, pp. 17–40.

Casselman, J., I. Aertsen and S. Parmentier (eds.), *Tachtig jaar criminologie aan de Leuvense universiteit: onderwijs, onderzoek en praktijk*, Antwerp, Maklu, 2012 (2012a).

—— "Andere onderzoeksgebieden", in: J. Casselman, I. Aertsen and S. Parmentier (eds.), *Tachtig jaar criminologie aan de Leuvense universiteit: onderwijs, onderzoek en praktijk*, Antwerp, Maklu, 2012 , pp. 125–132 (2012b).

Center for Research on Criminal Justice, *The Iron Fist and the Velvet Glove: An Analysis of the U.S. Police*, Berkeley, Center for Research on Criminal Justice, 1977.

Ceyhan, A. and P. Piazza (eds.), *L'identification biométrique: champs, acteurs, enjeux et controverses*, Paris, Editions de la Maison des Sciences de l'Homme, 2011.

Challenge, The, of Crime in a Free Society: A Report by the President's Commission on Law Enforcement and Administration of Justice, New York, Avon Books, 1968 (with an introduction and afterword by I. Silver).

Chambliss, W., *On the Take: From Petty Crooks to Presidents*, Bloomington, Indiana University Press, 1988.

—— "On trashing Marxist criminology", *Criminology*, 1989, pp. 231–238.

Chapman, D., *Sociology and the Stereotype of the Criminal*, London, Tavistock Publications, 1968.

Chapoulie, J.-M., "Ernest W. Burgess et les débuts d'une approche sociologique de la délinquance aux Etats-Unis", *Déviance et société*, 2003, pp. 103–110.

Chauvaud, F., "Les jeunes délinquants de Seine-et-Oise et la colonie agricole et pénitentiaire de Mettray", in: P. Vigier et al., *Répression et prisons politiques*, Paris, Editions Creaphis, 1990, pp. 253–267.

Chauvenet, A. and F. Ocqueteau (eds.), *Dominique Monjardet: notes inédites sur les choses policières, 1999–2006, suivi de 'le sociologue, la politique et la police'*, Paris, Editions La Découverte, 2008 (with a preface by P. Joxe).

Chazal, J., *Etudes de criminologie juvénile*, Paris, Presses Universitaires de France, 1952.

Cheloukhine, S., "The roots of Russian organized crime: from old-fashioned professionals to the organized criminal groups of today", *Crime, Law and Social Change*, 2008, pp. 353–374.

Cherif Bassiouni, M., "AIDP: International Association of Penal Law: over a century of dedication to criminal justice and human rights", in: *Compendium of the International Association of Penal Law*, Ramonville St. Agne, Editions Erès, 1999, pp. 39–64.

Chesney, K., *The Victorian Underworld*, Harmondsworth, Penguin Books, 1979.

Chevigny, P., *Police Power: Police Abuses in New York City*, New York, Vintage Books, 1969.

—— *Cops and Rebels: A Study of Provocation*, New York, Pantheon Books, 1972.

Christiaens, J., *De geboorte van de jeugddelinquent*, Brussels, VUBPress, 1999.

Christiaensen, S., "Adolphe Prins, 1845–1919", in: C. Fijnaut (ed.), *Gestalten uit het verleden: 32 voorgangers in de strafrechtswetenschap, de strafrechtspleging en de criminologie*, Leuven, Universitaire Pers Leuven, 1993, pp. 109–123.

—— "Enoch C. Wines: transatlantisch bruggenlegger in het pentitentiaire debat van de negentiende eeuw", in: L. Dupont and F. Hutsebaut (eds.), *Herstelrecht tussen toekomst en verleden: liber amicorum Tony Peters*, Leuven, Universitaire Pers Leuven, 2001, pp. 115–142.

—— *Tussen klassieke en moderne criminele politiek: leven en beleid van Jules Lejeune*, Leuven, Universitaire Pers Leuven, 2004.

Christie, N., *Limits to Pain*, Oxford, Martin Robertson, 1981.

Ciacci, M. and M. Simondi, "Un courant novateur du savoir criminologique: l'expérience de l'European Group for the Study of Deviance and Social Control", *Déviance et société*, 1977, pp. 109–117.

Cicourel, A., *The Social Organization of Juvenile Justice*, New York, John Wiley & Sons, 1968.

Claringbould, J., *De voorwaardelijke invrijheidsstelling, geschetst in haren geschiedkundigen oorsprong en algemeenen aard*, Utrecht, P.J. Diehl, 1881.

Clark, R., *Crime in America: observations on its nature, causes, prevention and control*, New York, Simon and Schuster, 1970 (with an introduction by T. Wicker).

Clarke, R. and K. Heal, "Police effectiveness in dealing with crime: some current British research", *Police Journal*, 1979, pp. 24–41.

Clarke, R. and P. Mayhew, *Designing Out Crime*, London, Her Majesty's Stationary Office, 1980.

Clément, P., *La police sous Louis XIV*, Paris, Librairie Didier et Cie, 1866.

Clinard, M., "Sociologists and American criminology", in: *Actes du IIe congrès international de criminologie (Paris-Sorbonne, September 1950)*, Paris, Presses Universitaires de France, 1952–55, vol. 4, pp. 3–34.

—— *Sociology of Deviant Behavior*, New York, Rinehart & Company, 1957.

—— (ed.), *Anomie and Deviant Behavior: A Discussion and Critique*, New York, Free Press of Glencoe, 1964 (1964a).

—— "The theoretical implications of anomie and deviant behavior", in: M. Clinard (ed.), *Anomie and Deviant Behavior: A Discussion and Critique*, New York, Free Press of Glencoe 1964, pp. 1–56 (1964b).

Cloward, R. and L. Ohlin, *Delinquency and Opportunity: A Theory of Delinquent Gangs*, New York, Free Press, 1969.

Cohen, A., *Delinquent Boys: The Culture of the Gang*, New York, Free Press, 1967.

Cohen, S. (ed.), *Images of Deviance*, Harmondsworth, Penguin Books, 1971.

—— "Criminology and the sociology of deviance in Britain: a recent history and a current report", in: P. Rock and M. McIntosh (eds.), *Deviance and Social Control*, London, Tavistock Publications, 1974, pp. 1–40.

—— *Visions of Social Control*, Oxford, Polity Press, 1985.

—— *Against Criminology*, New Brunswick, Transaction Books, 1988.

Cole, S., *Suspect Identities: A History of Fingerprinting and Criminal Identification*, Cambridge, Harvard University Press, 2001.

Coleman, J., *The Criminal Elite: The Sociology of White Collar Crime*, New York, St. Martin's Press, 1985.

Colin, M. (ed.), *L'équipement en criminologie: actes du XIVe Cours International de Criminologie*, Paris, Masson et Cie, 1965.

Collin, F., *Enrico Ferri et l'avant-projet de code pénal italien de 1921*, Brussels, Ferdinand Larcier, 1925.

Colquhoun, P., *A Treatise on the Police of the Metropolis Explaining the Various Crimes and Misdemeanors which at Present are Felt as Pressure upon the Community and Suggesting Remedies to their Prevention*, London, H. Fry, 1796.

—— *A Treatise on the Police of the Metropolis*, London, H. Fry, 1800.

Congrès international pour l'étude des questions relatives au patronage des détenus et à la protection des enfants moralement abandonnés, Anvers 1890: compte rendu sténographique, Brussels, E. Guyot, 1891.

Constant, J., "La formation du juge pénal", *Revue de droit pénal et de criminologie*, 1947, pp. 553–586.

—— *Elements de criminologie: syllabus du cours professé à l'Ecole Provinciale d'Officiers de Police*, Liège, Imprimerie des Invalides, 1949.

—— "L'enseignement de la criminologie en Belgique", *Revue de droit pénal et de criminologie* (*Publication jubilaire*), 1957, pp. 197–210.

Constitutio Criminalis Theresiana, Heidelberg, Kriminalistik Verlag, 1986 (with an introduction by A. Forker).

Cool, S., *Het cellulair-stelsel verdedigd tegen de zienswijze van den minister van Justitie*, Amsterdam, Kirberger, 1856.

Cooley, E., *Probation and Delinquency: The Study and Treatment of the Individual Delinquent*, New York, Catholic Charities of the Archdiocese of New York, 1927.

Cools, M., T. Daems, A. de Boeck et al. (eds.), *75 jaar criminologie aan de Universiteit Gent*, Antwerp, Maklu, 2013.

Cools, M., T. Daems, "De oprichting van een criminologisch instituut te Gent op 10 mei 1938: een terugblik", in: M. Cools, T. Daems, A. de Boeck et al. (eds.), *75 jaar criminologie aan de Universiteit Gent*, Antwerp, Maklu, 2013, pp. 11–20.

Cools, M. and P. Ponsaers, "Nico Gunzburg: 'Ik heb een huis, wil u het hebben'", in: M. Cools, T. Daems, A. de Boeck et al. (eds.), *75 jaar criminologie aan de Universiteit Gent*, Antwerp, Maklu, 2013, pp. 21–32.

Coopman, E., *Handboekje van het gesproken portret*, Antwerp, Remes en Peppe, s.a.

Coornhert, D., *Boeventucht ofte middelen tot mindering der schadelyke ledighghanghers*, Muiderberg, Coutinho, 1985 (reissued and with commentary by A.-J. Gelderblom, M. Meijer Drees et al.).

Coppens, E., "De inquisitoire procedure in het canonieke recht", in: H. Diederiks and H. Roodenburg (eds.), *Misdaad, zoen en straf*, Hilversum, Verloren, 1991, pp. 37–47.

Corella, P. and L. Siegel (eds.), *Readings in Contemporary Criminological Theory*, Boston, Northeastern University Press, 1996.

Cornil, L., "Ouverture de l'Ecole des Sciences Criminologiques à l'Université de Bruxelles", *Revue de droit pénal et de criminologie*, 1936, pp. 1209–1217.

Cornil, P., "Contribution de la 'victimologie' aux sciences criminologiques", *Revue de droit pénal et de criminologie*, 1959, pp. 587–601.

—— "John Howard: European penal reformer", in: H. Klare (ed.), *Changing Concepts of Crime and its Treatment*, Oxford, Pergamon Press, 1966, pp. 171–183.

—— "Criminalité et déviance: essai de politique criminelle", *Revue de science criminelle*, 1970, pp. 239–308.

—— "Réflexions sur le cinquentenaire de l'Association Internationale de Droit Pénal", *Revue internationale de droit pénal*, 1975, pp. 387–401.

Cornish, D. and R. Clarke (eds.), *The Reasoning Criminal: Rational Choice Perspectives on Offending*, New York, Springer, 1986.

Corstens, G. and M. Groenhuijsen (eds.), *Rede en recht: opstellen ter gelegenheid van het afscheid van prof. mr. N. Keijzer van de Katholieke Universiteit Brabant*, Deventer, Gouda Quint, 2000.

Cortés, J. and F. Gatti, *Delinquency and Crime: A Biopsychosocial Approach: Empirical, Theoretical and Practical Aspects of Criminal Behavior*, New York, Seminar Press, 1972.

Cowell, D., T. Jones and J. Young (eds.), *Policing the Riots*, London, Junction Books, 1982.

Cremer-Schäfer, H. and H. Steinert, *Straflust und Repression: zur Kritik der populistischen Kriminologie*, Münster, Westfälisches Dampfboot, 1998.

Cressey, D., *Other People's Money: A Study in the Social Psychology of Embezzlement*, Glencoe, Free Press, 1953.

—— *Delinquency, Crime and Differential Association*, The Hague, Martinus Nijhoff, 1964.

—— *Theft of the Nation: The Structure and Operations of Organized Crime in America*, New York, Harper & Row, 1969.

—— *Criminal Organization: Its Elementary Forms*, London, Heinemann Educational Books, 1972.

—— "Criminological theory, social science and the repression of crime", *Criminology*, 1978, pp. 171–191.

Cressey, D. and D. Ward, *Delinquency, Crime and Social Process*, New York, Harper & Row, 1969.

Criminologie, La, au prétoire: colloque du 50ème anniversaire 1935–1985: Ecole des Sciences Criminologiques Léon Cornil, Brussels, E. Story-Scientia, 1987, 2 vols.

Critchley, D., *The Origin of Organized Crime in America: The New York City Mafia, 1891–1931*, New York, Routledge, 2009.

Cullen, F., "Were Cloward and Ohlin strain theorists?: delinquency and opportunity revisited", *Journal of Research in Crime and Delinquency*, 1988, pp. 214–241.

Cullen, F. and V. Burton (eds.), *Contemporary Criminological Theory*, New York, New York University Press, 1994.

Cullen, F. and S. Messner, "The making of criminology revisited: an oral history of Merton's anomie paradigm", *Theoretical Criminology*, 2007, pp. 5–37.

Cummings, S. and D. Monti (eds.), *Gangs: The Origins and Impact of Contemporary Youth Gangs in the United States*, Albany, State University of New York Press, 1993.

Currie, E., "The new criminology", *Crime and Social Justice*, 1974, pp. 109–113.

—— *Confronting Crime: An American Challenge*, New York, Pantheon Books, 1985.

—— *Crime and Punishment in America*, New York, An Owl Book, 1998.

Cusson, M., *Criminologie actuelle*, Paris, Presses Universitaires de France, 1998.

Dallemagne, J., "Etiologie fonctionnelle du crime", in: *Actes du troisième congrès international d'anthropologie criminelle, biologie et sociologie, tenu à Bruxelles en août 1892 sous le haut patronage du gouvernement*, Brussels, F. Hayez, 1893, pp. 140–152.

—— *Stigmates anatomiques de la criminalité*, Paris, G. Masson, 1896.

Daluege, K. and E. Liebermann v. Sonnenberg, *Nationalsozialistischer Kampf gegen das Verbrechertum*, Munich, Zentralverlag der NSDAP, 1936.

Daly, K. and L. Maher (eds.), *Criminology at the Cross-roads: Feminist Readings in Crime and Justice*, New York, Oxford University Press, 1998.

D'Arras d'Haudrecy, L., M.-S. Dupont-Bouchat and M. Dorban, *La criminalité en Wallonie sous l'Ancien Régime*, Leiden, E.J. Brill, 1976.

Darwin, C., *The Descent of Man, and Selection in Relation to Sex*, London, John Murray, 1871.

—— *The Descent of Man, and Selection in Relation to Sex*, New York, Appleton and Company, 1899.

—— *The Origin of Species by Means of Natural Selection or the Preservation of Favoured Races in the Struggle for Life*, Harmondsworth, Penguin Books, 1968 (edited with an introduction by J. Burrow).

Dastre, M., "Des empreintes digitales comme procédé d'identification", *Archives d'anthropologie criminelle, de criminologie et de psychologie normale et pathologique*, 1907, pp. 842–861.

Davie, N., *Les visages de la criminalité: à la recherche d'une théorie scientifique du criminel type en Angleterre, 1860–1914*, Paris, Editions Kimé, 2004.

—— *Tracing the Criminal: The Rise of Scientific Criminology in Britain, 186–1918*, Oxford, Bardwell Press, 2005.

—— "The impact of criminal anthropology in Britain, 1880–1918", http://criminocorpus. revues.org/319 (last accessed 9 April 2017).

De Batselier, S., *De geperverteerde mens: wording, verscheidenheid en betekenis van het sexueel-pervers-genoemde gedrag*, Leuven, Publikaties van de School voor Criminologie, 1966.

—— "De rol van het slachtoffer bij de totstandkoming van het delict", in: C. Hoorens, M. Schlösser, D. Duyvelaar, M. Gruyters and W. Wolters (eds.), *Slachtoffers van delicten: enkele beschouwingen over de maatschappelijke en juridische problemen van het slachtoffer*, Baarn, Anthos, 1971, pp. 19–29.

—— "Professor Dellaert emeritus", *Leuvens Bulletin LAPP*, 1976, pp. 197–202.

—— (ed.), *Prof. dr. René Dellaert: zijn leven en zijn werk*, Antwerp, Soethoudt, 1980.

—— *Algemene criminologie: decriminalisering*, Leuven, Onderzoekscentrum Marginaliteit, 1982.

—— *Mens, maatschappij, marginaliteit*, Leuven, Acco, 1988.

—— "René Dellaert, 1906–1979", in: C. Fijnaut (ed.), *Gestalten uit het verleden: 32 voorgangers in de strafrechtswetenschap, de strafrechtspleging en de criminologie*, Leuven, Universitaire Pers Leuven, 1993, pp. 237–248.

Debbaut, D., D. de Kegel, A. Depuydt, B. Reyniers, Y. van Heer, A. van Liempt, R. van Pee and J. van Vaerenberg (eds.), *Liber amicorum Steven de Batselier*, s.l., Druk in de Weer, 1998.

De Beaumont, G. and A. de Tocqueville, *Système pénitentiaire aux Etats-Unis et de son application en France: suivi d'un appendice sur les colonies pénales et de notes statistiques*, Paris, Charles Gosselin, 1833.

—— *On the Penitentiary System in the United States and its Application in France*, New York, Augustus M. Kelly, 1970 (translated by F. Lieber).

—— *On the Penitentiary System in the United States and its Application in France*, Carbondale, Southern Illinois University Press, 1977 (with an introduction by T. Sellin).

De Bont, R., "Meten en verzoenen: Louis Vervaeck en de Belgische criminele anthropologie, 1900–1940", *Bijdragen tot de Eigentijdse Geschiedenis*, 2001, pp. 63–136.

De Bonvoust Beeckman, M., *Arbeid van gevangenen en vrije arbeid*, Amsterdam, Roeloffzen & Hübner, 1892.

De Bosch Kemper, J., *Wetboek van strafvordering naar deszelfs beginselen ontwikkeld, en in verband gebragt met de algemeene regtsgeleerdheid*, Amsterdam, Johannes Müller, 1838.

Debuyst, C., *Modèle éthologique et criminologie*, Brussels, Pierre Mardaga, 1985.

—— "Etienne de Greeff, 1898–1961", in: C. Fijnaut (ed.), *Gestalten uit het verleden: 32 voorgangers in de strafrechtswetenschap, de strafrechtspleging en de criminologie*, Leuven, Universitaire Pers Leuven, 1993, pp. 221–235.

—— "Etienne de Greeff: une analyse complexe du comportement delinquant", in: L. Mucchielli (ed.), *Histoire de la criminologie française*, Paris, L'Harmattan, 1994, pp. 335–349.

—— "Les savoirs psychiatriques sur le crime: de Pinel (1801) à Morel (1857)", in: C. Debuyst, F. Digneffe, J.-M. Labadie and A. Pires (eds.), *Histoire des savoirs sur le crime et la peine: des savoirs diffus à la notion de criminel-né*, Brussels, De Boeck Université, 1995, pp. 213–292.

—— "L'école française dite 'du milieu social'", in: C. Debuyst, F. Digneffe and A. Pires (eds.), *Histoire des savoirs sur le crime et la peine: la rationalité pénale et la naissance de la criminologie*, Brussels, De Boeck Université, 1998, pp. 301–356.

Debuyst, C., F. Digneffe, J.-M. Labadie and A. Pires (eds.), *Histoire des savoirs sur le crime et la peine: des savoirs diffus à la notion de criminel-né*, Brussels, De Boeck Université, 1995.

Debuyst, C., F. Digneffe and A. Pires (eds.), *Histoire des savoirs sur le crime et la peine: la rationalité pénale et la naissance de la criminologie*, Brussels, De Boeck Université, 1998.

Dechêne, H., *Verwahrlosung und Delinquenz: Profil einer Kriminalpsychologie*, Munich, Wilhelm Fink Verlag, 1975.

De Clerck, K., *Veertig jaar School voor Criminologie aan de R.U.G.*, Ghent, Archief R.U.G., 1978.

Declercq, R., "Paul Trousse, 1910–1978", in: C. Fijnaut (ed.), *Gestalten uit het verleden: 32 voorgangers in de strafrechtswetenschap, de strafrechtspleging en de criminologie*, Leuven, Universitaire Pers Leuven, 1993, pp. 299–311.

De Damhouder, J., *Practycke ende handbouck in criminele zaeken, verchiert met zommeghe schoone figuren en beilde ter materie dienede*, Leuven, 1555 (reissued and explained by J. Dauwe and J. Monballyu with the support of the publishing company Den Wijngaert te Roeselaere in 1981).

Dedecker, R. and L. Slachmuylder, "De la critique de l'école classique à la théorie de défense sociale: la protection de l'enfance dans la pensée de Prins", in: P. Van der Vorst and P. Mary (eds.), *Cent ans de criminologie à l'ULB: Adolphe Prins, l'Union Internationale de Droit Pénal, le Cercle Universitaire pour les Etudes Criminologiques*, Brussels, Bruylant, 1990, pp. 125–140.

Deeman, P. and L. Gunther Moor (eds.), *Lokale en regionale inbedding van veiligheidshuizen*, Dordrecht, SMVP Producties, 2009.

De Feyter, S., *De bende van Jan de Lichte*, Leuven, K.U. Leuven, 1979 (licentiate's thesis at the Faculty of Arts and Philosophy).

De Fierlant, G., *Premières idées sur la réformation des lois criminelles*, s.l., s.n., 1774 (unpublished).

—— "Observations sur la torture et Observations sur l'insuffisance et les inconvéniens des peines afflictives et sur les avantages qu'il y auroit à les remplacer par des maisons de force", *Bulletin de la Commission Royale d'Histoire*, 1895, pp. 154–253 (edited by E. Hubert).

De Graaf, B., *Op weg naar Armageddon: de evolutie van fanatisme*, Amsterdam, Boom, 2012.

De Greef, G., *Précis de sociologie*, Brussels, Mayolez et Audiarte, 1909.

De Greeff, E., "La psychologie de l'assassinat", *Revue de droit pénal et de criminologie*, 1935, pp. 153–164, 213–235, 357–394.

—— *Amour et crimes d'amour*, Brussels, Joseph Vandenplas, 1942.

—— *Notre destinée et nos instincts*, Paris, Librairie Plon, 1945.

—— *Introduction à la criminologie*, Brussels, Vandenplas, 1946.

—— *Ames criminelles*, Tournai, Casterman, 1949 (1949a).

—— *La nuit est ma lumière: roman*, Paris, Editions du Seuil, 1949 (1949b).

—— *Criminologue et policier*, Brussels, Le Soutien, 1956 (1956a).

—— "Psychologie en psychopathologie van de angst", in: W. Grossouw, A. de Waelhens and E. de Greeff, *Studies over de angst*, Utrecht, Uitgeverij Het Spectrum, 1956, pp. 35–49 (1956b).

—— *L'homme et son juge*, s.l., Desclée de Brouwer, 1962.

Deimling, G. (ed.), *Cesare Beccaria: die Anfänge moderner Strafrechtspflege in Europa*, Heidelberg, Kriminalistik Verlag, 1989.

De Jong, D., J. van der Neut and J. Tulkens (eds.), *De vrijheidsstraf: bundel opstellen ter gelegenheid van de eeuwherdenking op 15 april 1986 te Groningen van de invoering van het Wetboek van Strafrecht en de eerste Beginselenwet van het gevangeniswezen*, Arnhem, Gouda Quint, 1986.

De Jong, M., P. Baan, J. van Bemmelen et al. (eds.), *Straffen en helpen: opstellen over berechting en reclassering aan geboden aan mr. Dr. N. Muller*, Amsterdam, Wereldbibliotheek, 1954.

De Jonge, G., *Strafwerk: over de arbeidsverhouding tussen gedetineerden en justitie*, Breda, Uitgeverij Papieren Tijger, 1994.

De Jongh, G., *Bedreigde levens: over reclassering, strafrecht en kinderrecht*, Arnhem, Van Loghum Slaterus' Uitgeversmaatschappij, 1941.

DeKeseredy, W., *Contemporary Critical Criminology*, London, Routledge, 2011.

DeKeseredy, W. and M. Schwartz, *Contemporary Criminology*, Belmont, Wadsworth Publishing Company, 1996.

Dekker, J., *Straffen, redden en opvoeden: het ontstaan en de ontwikkeling van de residentiële heropvoeding in West-Europa, 1814–1914, met bijzondere aandacht voor 'Nederlandsch Mettray'*, Assen, Van Gorcum, 1985.

De Koning, J., *De misdadiger en de misdaad: schetsen ten dienste der politie*, Heusden, L.J.Veerman, 1904.

De la Grasserie, R., *Des principes sociologiques de la criminologie*, Paris, V. Giard & E. Brière, 1901.

De Landecho, C., *Körperbau, Character und Kriminalität: kriminologische Anwendungsmöglichkeiten der Typologie Kretchmers*, Bonn, Ludwig Röhrscheid Verlag, 1964.

Del Bayle, J.-L., *Police et société*, Toulouse, Académie de Toulouse, 1988.

—— *Police et politique: une approche sociologique*, Paris, L'Harmattan, 2006.

DeLine, A. and A. Crosley, "A century of criminal law and criminology", *Journal of Criminal Law and Criminology*, 2010, pp. 1–6.

Dellaert, R. (ed.), *Verholen misdadigheid*, Leuven, Acco, 1969.

De Monté Verloren, J., *Geschiedenis van de wetenschap van het strafrecht en strafprocesrecht in de Noordelijke Nederlanden voor de codificatie*, Amsterdam, Noord-Hollandsche Uitgeversmaatschappij, 1942.

De Moor, J., *Paul Heger, 1846–1925*, Brussels, Imprimerie Scripta, 1935.

Denis, H., "Le socialisme et les causes économiques et sociales du crime", in: J. Wertheim Salomonson (ed.), *Congrès international d'anthropologie criminelle: compte rendu des travaux de la cinquième session tenue à Amsterdam du 9 à 14 septembre 1901*, Amsterdam, Imprimerie de J.H. de Bussy, 1901, pp. 256–269.

De Pinto, A., *Handleiding tot het wetboek van strafvordering*, The Hague, Gebroeders Belinfante, 1848.

Depreeuw, W., *Landloperij, bedelarij en thuisloosheid: een socio-historische analyse van repressie, bijstand en instellingen*, Antwerp, Kluwer Rechtswetenschappen, 1988.

—— "Louis Vervaeck, 1872–1943", in: C. Fijnaut (ed.), *Gestalten uit het verleden: 32 voorgangers in de strafrechtswetenschap, de strafrechtspleging en de criminologie*, Leuven, Universitaire Pers Leuven, 1993, pp. 149–162.

De Quiros, C., *Modern Theories of Criminality*, Boston, Little, Brown and Company, 1911 (translated from Spanish by A. de Salvio, with an introduction by W. Smithers).

Dercksen, A. and L. Verplanke, *Geschiedenis van de onmaatschappelijkheidsbestrijding in Nederland, 1914–1970*, Meppel, Boom, 1987.

De Rechter, G., "The School of Criminology and of Scientific Police of Belgium", in: T. Sellin (ed.), *The Police and the Crime Problem*, in: The Annals of the American Academy of Political and Social Science, Philadelphia, 1929, pp. 193–198.

Deroisy, A., *La répression du vagabondage, de la mendicité et de la prostitution dans les Pays-Bas Autrichiens durant la seconde moitié du XVIIIe siècle*, Brussels, 1966 (unpublished).

De Roos, J., *De strafmiddelen in de nieuwere strafrechtswetenschap*, Amsterdam, Scheltema & Holkema's Boekhandel, 1900.

—— *Inleiding tot de beoefening der criminele aetiologie met gebruikmaking van Nederlandsche gegevens*, Haarlem, De Erven F. Bohm, 1908.

—— "De ontwikkeling der crimineele aetiologie en hare beteekenis voor de theorie en de practijk van het strafrecht", *Tijdschrift voor Strafrecht*, 1911, pp. 277–301.

—— *Oorzaken der criminaliteit: methodiek en classificatie van misdadigers*, Baarn, Hollandia, 1914.

—— "Veranderende tijden", *Tijdschrift voor Strafrecht*, 1917, pp. 462–472.

De Ruyver, B., *De strafrechtelijke politiek gevoerd onder de socialistische ministers van Justitie E. Vandervelde, P. Vermeylen en A. Vranckx*, Antwerp, Kluwer, 1988.

De Ruyver, B. and J. Goethals, "Paul Heger, 1846–1925", in: C. Fijnaut (ed.), *Gestalten uit het verleden: 32 voorgangers in de strafrechtswetenschap, de strafrechtspleging en de criminologie*, Leuven, Universitaire Pers Leuven, 1993, pp. 125–131 (1993a).

—— "Auguste Ley, 1873–1956", in: C. Fijnaut (ed.), *Gestalten uit het verleden: 32 voorgangers in de strafrechtswetenschap, de strafrechtspleging en de criminologie*, Leuven, Universitaire Pers Leuven, 1993, pp. 185–193 (1993b).

De Ryckere, R., "Organisation de l'enseignement de la police judiciaire à Paris, Lausanne, Rome: rapport adressé, le 19 mai 1913, à M. Carton de Wiart, ministre de la Justice, à la suite de la mission dont il avait été chargé", *Archives d'anthropologie criminelle, de médecine légale et de psychologie normale et pathologique*, 1913, pp. 561–612.

De Secondat, C. (baron de la Brède et de Montesquieu), "*De l'esprit des lois ou du rapport que les lois doivent avoir avec la constitution de chaque gouvernement, les moeurs, le climat, la religion, le commerce, etc.*", in: D. Oster, *Montesquieu: oeuvres complètes*, Paris, Editions du Seuil, 1964, pp. 528–795.

Dessaur, C., "Het anti-humanisme in de criminologie: of: criminologie per injectiespuit", *Delikt en Delinkwent*, 1978, pp. 597–605.

—— *De droom der rede: het mensbeeld in de sociale wetenschappen: een poging tot criminosofie*, The Hague, Martinus Nijhoff, 1982.

Dessecker, A. and J.-M. Jehle, "Das Fach Kriminologie und die strafrechtsbezogenen Schwerpunktbereiche in der Juristenausbildung", *Monatsschrift für Kriminologie und Strafrechtsreform*, 2003, pp. 435–442.

De Vlugt, *De toepassing der progressiegedachte in het Nederlandsche gevangeniswezen*, Amsterdam, Drukkerij Holland, 1930.

De Vries, A. and F. van Tricht, *Geschiedenis der wetgeving op de misdadige jeugd*, Haarlem, H.D. Tjeenk Willink & Zoon, 1905, 2 vols.

De Vries, C., "De 'nieuwe richting' in de strafrechtswetenschap in Nederland, 1880–1910", in: E. Jonker, M. Ros and C. de Vries (eds.), *Kriminologen en reklasseerders in Nederland*, in: *Utrechtse Historische Cahiers*, 1986, no. 1, pp. 71–122.

De Vries, G., *Honderd jaar gemeenschapsregime in Esserheem-Veenhuizen, 1895–1995*, Arnhem, Gouda Quint, 1995.

De Vries, J., *Het vraagstuk der celstraf in zijn tegenwoordigen stand*, Amsterdam, Tierie & Kruyt, 1901.

De Vries, K., *Bijdrage tot de kennis van het strafprocesrecht in de Nederlandse steden benoorden Maas en Schelde*, Groningen, P. Noordhoff, 1955.

Devroe, E., L. Pauwels, A. Verhage, M. Easton and M. Cools (eds.), *Tegendraadse criminologie: liber amicorum P. Ponsaers*, Antwerp, Maklu, 2012.

Devroye, J., "The rise and fall of the American Institute of Criminal Law and Criminology", *Journal of Criminal Law and Criminology*, 2010, pp. 7–32.

De Wit, H., "De Beginselenwet 1886: onthullende beraadslagingen", in: D. de Jong, J. van der Neut and J. Tulkens (eds.), *De vrijheidsstraf: bundel opstellen ter gelegenheid van de eeuwherdenking op 15 april 1986 te Groningen van de invoering van het Wetboek van Strafrecht en de eerste Beginselenwet van het gevangeniswezen*, Arnhem, Gouda Quint, 1986, pp. 77–102.

D'Haenens, J., "Jacques Matthijs, 1907–1986", in: C. Fijnaut (ed.), *Gestalten uit het verleden: 32 voorgangers in de strafrechtswetenschap, de strafrechtspleging en de criminologie*, Leuven, Universitaire Pers Leuven, 1993, pp. 289–297.

Dicristina, B., "Durkheim's theory of homicide and the confusion of the empirical literature", *Theoretical Criminology*, 2004, pp. 57–91.

Diederiks, H., "Urban and rural criminal justice and criminality in the Netherlands since the Middle Ages: some observations", in: E. Johnson and E. Monkkonen (eds.), *The Civilization of Crime: Violence in Town and Country since the Middle Ages*, Chicago, University of Illinois Press, 1996, pp. 153–164.

Diederiks, H. and H. Roodenburg (eds.), *Misdaad, zoen en straf*, Hilversum, Verloren, 1991.

Dieu, F., *Politiques publiques de sécurité*, Paris, L'Harmattan, 1999.

—— *Sociologie de la gendarmerie*, Paris, L'Harmattan, 2008.

Dieu, F. and P. Mignon, *La force publique au travail: deux études sur les conditions de travail des policiers et des gendarmes*, Paris, L'Harmattan, 1999 (with a preface by P. Melchior).

Digneffe, F., "Conduites déviantes, identité et valeurs: la perspective de E. de Greeff", *Déviance et société*, 1989, pp. 181–198.

—— "Problèmes sociaux et représentations du crime et du criminel: de Howard (1777) à Engels (1845)", in: C. Debuyst, F. Digneffe, J.-M. Labadie and A. Pires (eds.), *Histoire des savoirs sur le crime et la peine: des savoirs diffus à la notion de criminel-né*, Brussels, De Boeck Université, 1995, pp. 137–212.

—— "Durkheim et les débats sur le crime et le peine", in: C. Debuyst, F. Digneffe and A. Pires (eds.), *Histoire des savoirs sur le crime et la peine: la rationalité pénale et la naissance de la criminologie*, Brussels, De Boeck Université, 1998, pp. 357–398.

Digneffe, F. and C. Adam, "Le développement de la criminologie clinique à l'Ecole de Louvain", *Criminologie*, 2004, pp. 43–70.

Digneffe, F. and M.-S. Dupont-Bouchat, "A propos de l'origine et des transformations des maisons pour jeunes délinquants en Belgique au XIXe siècle: l'histoire du pénitencier de Saint-Hubert (1840–1890)", *Déviance et société*, 1982, pp. 131–165.

Di Tullio, B., *Manuel d'anthropologie criminelle*, Paris, Payot, 1951.

—— "Naissance de la Société Internationale de Criminologie", in: *La criminologie: bilan et perspectives: mélanges offerts à Jean Pinatel*, Paris, Editions A. Pedone, 1980, pp. 1–12.

Dobler, J. and H. Reinke, "Sichere Reichshauptstadt? Kripo und Verbrechensbekämpfung, 1933–1945 – ein Werkstattbericht", in: W. Schulte (ed.), *Die Polizei im NS-Staat: Beiträge eines internationalen Symposiums an der Deutschen Hochschule der Polizei im Münster*, Frankfurt am Main, Verlag für Polizeiwissenschaft, 2009, pp. 655–685.

Doek, J., *Vijftig jaar ondertoezichtstelling: schets van ontstaan en ontwikkeling van een maatregel van kinderbescherming*, Zwolle, Tjeenk Willink, 1972.

Dölling, D., "Kriminologie im 'Dritten Reich'", in: R. Dreier and W. Sellert (eds.), *Recht und Justiz im Dritten Reich*, Frankfurt am Main, Suhrkamp, 1989, pp. 194–225.

Domela Nieuwenhuis, J., *De straf der afzonderlijke opsluiting, historisch en kritisch beschouwd, vooral in hare betrekking tot ons vaderland*, Amsterdam, J.H. Gebhard, 1859.

Domela Nieuwenhuis, J. and H. van der Hoeven, *Celstraf*, Baarn, Hollandia-Drukkerij, 1908.

Donnedieu de Vabres, H., *La justice pénale d'aujourdhui*, Paris, Armand Colin, 1929.

Dorgelo, J., *De koloniën van de Maatschappij van Weldadigheid*, Assen, Van Gorcum, 1964.

Dotremont, S. et al., *Le bâtonnier Louis Braffort: défenseur et martyr des libertés spirituelles*, Brussels, Larcier, 1944.

Downes, D., *The Delinquent Solution: A Study in Subcultural Theory*, London, Routledge & Kegan Paul, 1966.

Downes, D. and R. Morgan, "No turning back: the politics of law and order into the millennium", in: M. Maguire, R. Morgan and R. Reiner (eds.), *The Oxford Handbook of Criminology*, Oxford, Oxford University Press, 2007, pp. 201–240.

Downes, D. and P. Rock (eds.), *Deviant Interpretations: Problems in Criminological Theory*, Oxford, Martin Robertson, 1979.

—— *Understanding Deviance: A Guide to the Sociology of Crime and Rule Breaking*, Oxford, Clarendon Press, 1986.

Downes, D., P. Rock, C. Chinkin and C. Gearty (eds.), *Crime, Social Control and Human Rights: From Moral Panics to States of Denial: Essays in Honour of Stanley Cohen*, Cullompton, Willan Publishing, 2008.

Drähms, A., *The Criminal: His Personnel and Environment: A Scientific Study*, New York, The Macmillan Company, 1900 (with an introduction by C. Lombroso).

Dreier, R. and W. Sellert (eds.), *Recht und Justiz im Dritten Reich*, Frankfurt am Main, Suhrkamp, 1989.

Drenth, J., *Bijdrage tot de kennis der historische ontwikkeling van het accusatoire tot het inquisitoire strafproces*, Amsterdam, Noord-Hollandsche Uitgeversmaatschappij, 1939.

Dressler, O., *Die Internationale Kriminalpolizeiliche Kommission und ihr Werk*, Vienna, Wilhelm Santora, 1942.

Driver, E., "Charles Buckman Goring, 1870–1919", in: H. Mannheim (ed.), *Pioneers in Criminology*, London, Stevens and Sons, 1960, pp. 335–348.

Ducpétiaux, E., *De la mission de la justice humaine et de l'injustice de la peine de mort: de la justice de répression et particulièrement de l'inutilité et des effets pernicieux de la peine de mort*, Brussels, Cautaerts et Compagnie, 1827.

—— *Des progrès et de l'état actuel de la réforme pénitentiaire et des institutions préventives aux Etats-Unis, en France, en Suisse, en Angleterre et en Belgique*, Brussels, Société Belge de Librairie, 1837–38, 3 vols and an Atlas.

—— *Mémoire à l'appui du projet de loi sur les prisons, présenté à la Chambre des Représentants de Belgique, dans la séance du 3 decembre 1844, avec un appendice et trois plans de prisons cellulaires*, Brussels, Weissenbruch Père, 1845.

—— *Mémoire sur l'organisation des écoles de réforme soumis à m. le ministre de la Justice*, Brussels, T. Lesigne, 1848.

—— *Mémoire sur le paupérisme dans les Flandres*, Brussels, M. Hayez, 1850.

—— *Colonies agricoles, écoles rurales et écoles de réforme pour les indigents, les mendiants et les vagabonds, et spécialement pour les enfants de deux sexes, en Suisse, en Allemagne, en France, en Angleterre, dans les Pays-Bas et en Belgique, rapport adressé à m. Tesch, ministre de la Justice*, Brussels, T. Lesigne, 1851.

—— *Des conditions d'application du système de l'emprisonnement séparé ou cellulaire*, Brussels, Hayez, 1858.

Duesterberg, T., *Criminology and the Social Order in Nineteenth-Century France*, Indiana University, 1979 (doctoral thesis).

Dugdale, R., *"The Jukes": A Study in Crime, Pauperism, Disease and Heredity: Also Further Studies of Criminals*, New York, G.P. Putnam's Sons, 1884 (fourth edition, with an introduction by M. Round).

—— "The Jukes: a study in crime, pauperism and heredity", in: J. Jacoby (ed.), *Classics of Criminology*, Prospects Heights, Waveland Press, 1994, pp. 132–139.

Dunham, R. and G. Alpert (eds.), *Critical Issues in Policing: Contemporary Readings*, Prospect Heights, Waveland Press, 1989.

Dupont, L., *Beginselen van behoorlijke strafrechtsbedeling: bijdrage tot het grondslagenonderzoek van het strafrecht*, Antwerp, Kluwer Rechtswetenschappen, 1979.

—— "Jules Lejeune et la défense sociale", in: F. Tulkens (ed.), *Généalogie de la défense sociale en Belgique, 1880–1914: travaux du séminaire qui s'est tenu à l'Université Catholique de Louvain sous la direction de Michel Foucault*, Brussels, E. Story-Scientia, 1988, pp. 77–86.

—— "Edmond Picard, 1836–1924", in: C. Fijnaut (ed.), *Gestalten uit het verleden: 32 voorgangers in de strafrechtswetenschap, de strafrechtspleging en de criminologie*, Leuven, Universitaire Pers Leuven, 1993, pp. 97–107.

—— (ed.), *Op weg naar een beginselenwet gevangeniswezen*, Leuven, Universitaire Pers Leuven, 1998.

Dupont, L. and F. Hutsebaut (eds.), *Herstelrecht tussen toekomst en verleden: liber amicorum Tony Peters*, Leuven, Universitaire Pers Leuven, 2001.

Dupont-Bouchat, M.-S., "Le pénitencier de St. Hubert", *Saint-Hubert d'Ardenne-Cahiers d'histoire*, 1981, pp. 161–182.

—— "Le pénitencier de Saint-Hubert: la maison pénitentiaire des jeunes délinquants, 1840–1867", *Saint-Hubert d'Ardenne: cahiers d'histoire*, 1985, pp. 139–160.

—— "Stratégies du maintien de l'ordre en Belgique et en France au XIXe Siècle: la doctrine de la défense sociale", in: E. Heyen (ed.), *Historische Soziologie der Rechtswissenschaft*, Frankfurt am Main, Vittorio Klostermann, 1986, pp. 79–105.

—— "Ducpétiaux ou le rêve cellulaire", *Déviance et société*, 1988, pp. 1–28.

—— "Lambert de Hauregard, 1755–1855", in: C. Fijnaut (ed.), *Gestalten uit het verleden: 32 voorgangers in de strafrechtswetenschap, de strafrechtspleging en de criminologie*, Leuven, Universitaire Pers Leuven, 1993, pp. 23–32.

Duprat, C., "Punir et guérir: en 1819, la prison des philanthropes", in: M. Perrot (ed.), *L'impossible prison: recherches sur le système pénitentiaire au XIXe siècle*, Paris, Editions du Seuil, 1980, pp. 64–122.

Dupréel, E., *Ad. Quetelet: pages choisies et commentées*, Brussels, Office de Publicité, 1942.

Dupréel, J., "Quetelet et la criminologie", in: Académie Royale de Belgique (ed.), *Adolphe Quetelet, 1796–1874*, Brussels, Palais des Académies, 1977, pp. 65–73.

Durkheim, E., *Les règles de la méthode sociologique*, Paris, Presses Universitaires de France, 1968.

—— *Le suicide: étude de sociologie*, Paris, Presses Universitaires de France, 1969.

—— *De la division du travail social*, Paris, Presses Universitaires de France, 1973.

Dürkop, M., "Zur Funktion der Kriminologie im Nationalsozialismus", in: U. Reifner and B.-R. Sonnen (eds.), *Strafjustiz und Polizei im Dritten Reich*, Frankfurt am Main, Campus Verlag, 1984, pp. 97–120.

Durney, J., *The Mob: The History of the Irish Gangsters in America*, Naas, Leinster Leader, 2000.

Durviaux, S., "Le Cercle Universitaire pour les Etudes Criminologiques", in: P. Van der Vorst and P. Mary (eds.), *Cent ans de criminologie à l'ULB: Adolphe Prins, l'Union Internationale de Droit Pénal, le Cercle Universitaire pour les Etudes Criminologiques*, Brussels, Bruylant, 1990, pp. 21–44.

Editorial, "Berkeley's School of Criminology, 1950–1976", *Crime and Social Justice*, 1976, pp. 1–4.

Edwards, S., *The Vidocq Dossier: The Story of the World's First Detective*, Boston, Houghton Mifflin Company, 1977.

Eggink, J., *De geschiedenis van het Nederlandse gevangeniswezen*, Assen, Van Gorcum, 1958.

Egmond, F., *Banditisme in de Franse Tijd: profiel van de Grote Nederlandse Bende, 1790–1799*, Zutphen, De Bataafsche Leeuw, 1986.

—— "De boeven van Coornhert", in: C. Fijnaut and P. Spierenburg (eds.), *Scherp toezicht: van 'Boeventucht' tot 'Samenleving en criminaliteit'*, Arnhem, Gouda Quint, 1990, pp. 99–112.

—— *Op het verkeerde pad: georganiseerde misdaad in de Noordelijke Nederlanden*, Amsterdam, Bert Bakker, 1994.

—— "Between town and countryside: organised crime in the Dutch Republic", in: E. Johnson and E. Monkkonen (eds.), *The Civilization of Crime: Violence in Town and Country since the Middle Ages*, Chicago, University of Illinois Press, 1996, pp. 138–152.

Eibich, S., *Polizei, 'Gemeinwohl' und Reaktion: über Wohlfahrtspolizei als Sicherheitspolizei unter Carl Ludwig Friedrich von Hinckeldey, Berliner Polizeipräsident von 1848 bis 1856*, Berlin, Berliner Wissenschafts-Verlag, 2004.

Eichler, H. (ed.), *Römischer Congress für Kriminologie: Kameradschaftsarbeit von Teilnehmern und Mitarbeitern am Ersten Internationalen Kongress für Kriminologie im Rom – Oktober 1938*, Berlin, R.v. Decker's Verlag, 1939.

Eliaerts, C., "Paul Cornil, 1903–1985", in: C. Fijnaut (ed.), *Gestalten uit het verleden: 32 voorgangers in de strafrechtswetenschap, de strafrechtspleging en de criminologie*, Leuven, Universitaire Pers Leuven, 1993, pp. 277–288.

Eliaerts, C., E. Enhus and R. Senden (eds.), *Politie in beweging: bijdrage tot de discussie over de politie van morgen*, Antwerp, Kluwer, 1990.

Ellis, H., *The Criminal*, London, Walter Scott, 1890.

Elster, J., *Karl Marx: A Reader*, Cambridge, Cambridge University Press, 1999.

Emsley, C., *Policing and its Context, 1750–1870*, London, Macmillan Press, 1983.

—— *The English Police: A Political and Social History*, London, Longman, 1996.

—— *Gendarmes and the State in Nineteenth-Century Europe*, Oxford, Oxford University Press, 1999.

—— "The history of crime and crime control", in: M. Maguire, R. Morgan and R. Reiner (eds.), *The Oxford Handbook of Criminology*, Oxford, Oxford University Press, 2002, pp. 203–232.

—— "The changes in policing and penal policy in nineteenth-century Europe", in: B. Godfrey and G. Dunstall (eds.), *Crime and Empire, 1840–1940: Criminal Justice in Local and Global Context*, Cullompton, Willan Publishing, 2005, pp. 8–24.

Enforcement of the Prohibition Laws of the United States: message from the President of the United States transmitting a report of the National Commission on Law Observance and Enforcement relative to the facts as to the enforcement, the benefits, and the abuses under the prohibition laws, both before and since the adoption of the eighteenth amendment to the Constitution, Washington, Government Printing Office, 1931.

Engelen, D., "Het 'portrait parlé", *Tijdschrift voor Strafrecht*, 1910, pp. 378–389.

England, R., "Who wrote John Howard's text?: The state of prisons as a dissenting enterprise", *British Journal of Criminology*, 1993, pp. 203–215.

En hommage à Jean Constant, Liège, Université de Liège, Faculté de Droit, 1971.

Ericson, R., "The culture and power of criminological research", in: L. Zedner and A. Ashworth (eds.), *The Criminological Foundations of Penal Policy: Essays in Honour of Roger Hood*, Oxford, Oxford University Press, 2003, pp. 31–78.

—— *Crime in an Insecure World*, Cambridge, Polity Press, 2007.

Ericson, R. and K. Carriere, "The fragmentation of criminology", in: D. Nelken (ed.), *The Futures of Criminology*, London, Sage Publications, 1994, pp. 89–109.

Erikson, K., "Notes on the sociology of deviance", in: H. Becker (ed.), *The Other Side: Perspectives on Deviance*, New York, Free Press, 1967, pp. 9–21.

Erkens, J., "Kriminalbiologie und Kriminalpolizei", *Monatsschrift für Kriminalpsychologie und Strafrechtsreform*, 1931, pp. 491–498.

Eser, A. (ed.), *Kriminologische Forschung im Ubergang*, Freiburg im Breisgau, Max-Planck-Institut für ausländisches und internationales Strafrecht, 1997.

Esquirol, E., *Des maladies mentales considérées dans les rapports medical, hygiénique et medico-légal*, Paris, J.-B. Baillière, 1838.

Essential Works of Lenin, New York, Bantam Books, 1966 (edited and with an introduction by H. Christman).

Eugène, F., *Vidocq: der Mann mit hundert Namen*, Munich, Rogner & Bernhard, 1968 (with an afterword by L. Rubiner and a file by H. Zischler).

European Forum for Victim-Offender Mediation and Restorative Justice (ed.), *Victim-Offender Mediation in Europe: Making Restorative Justice Work*, Leuven, Universitaire Pers Leuven, 2000.

Evans, R., *Tales from the German Underworld: Crime and Punishment in the Nineteenth Century*, New Haven, Yale University Press, 1998.

Ewald, U. (ed.), *Social Transformation and Crime in Metropolises of Former Eastern Bloc Countries: Findings of a Multi-city Pilot Study 1993*, Bonn, Forum Verlag Godesberg, 1997.

Exner, F., *Kriminalistischer Bericht über eine Reise nach Amerika*, Berlin, Walter de Gruyter, 1935.

—— "Aufgaben der Kriminologie im neuen Reich", *Monatsschrift für Kriminalpsychologie und Strafrechtsreform*, 1936, pp. 3–16.

—— *Kriminalbiologie in ihren Grundzügen*, Hamburg, Hanseatische Verlagsanstalt, 1939.

—— *Kriminologie*, Berlin, Springer, 1949.

Eysenck, B. and H. Eysenck, "Crime and personality: item analysis of questionnaire responses", *British Journal of Criminology*, 1971, pp. 49–62.

Eysenck, H., *Crime and Personality*, London, Paladin, 1964.

Faber, S., *Strafrechtspleging en criminaliteit te Amsterdam, 1680–1811: de nieuwe menslievendheid*, Arnhem, Gouda Quint, 1983.

—— "Het rasphuis: wat is dat eigenlijk?", in: C. Fijnaut and P. Spierenburg (eds.), *Scherp toezicht: van 'Boeventucht' tot 'Samenleving en criminaliteit'*, Arnhem, Gouda Quint, 1990, pp. 127–144.

Faget, J. and A. Wyvekens, "Bilan de la recherche sur le crime et la justice en France de 1990–1998", in: L. van Outrive and P. Robert (eds.), *Crime et justice en Europe depuis 1990: état des recherches, évaluation et recommendations*, Paris, L'Harmattan, 1999, pp. 147–172.

Farrington, D., L. Ohlin and J. Wilson, *Understanding and Controlling Crime: Toward a New Research Strategy*, New York, Springer, 1986.

Fattah, E., *Criminology: Past, Present and Future: A Critical Overview*, Houndmills, Macmillan Press, 1997 (with a foreword by P. Rock).

Feber, G., *Beschouwingen over psychopathenstrafrecht*, Zwolle, Uitgevers-Maatschappij W.E.J. Tjeenk Willink, 1932 (with a foreword by B. Taverne).

—— *Beschouwingen over crimineele psychologie*, Zwolle, Uitgevers-Maatschappij W.E.J. Tjeenk Willink, 1934.

Féré, C., *Dégénérescence et criminalité: essai physiologique*, Paris, Félix Alcan, 1895.

Ferri, E., *La scuola criminale positiva*, Naples, Enrico Detken, 1885.

—— *La sociologie criminelle*, Paris, Artur Rousseau, 1893.

—— *Socialismus und moderne Wissenschaft*, Leipzig, Georg H. Wigand's Verlag, 1895 (translated with the permission of the author and extended by H. Kurella).

—— *Das Verbrechen als sociale Erscheinung: Grundzüge der Kriminal-Soziologie*, Leipzig, Georg H. Wigand's Verlag, 1896 (autorisierte Deutsche Ausgabe von H. Kurella).

—— *Socialisme et science positive (Darwin – Spencer – Marx)*, Paris, V. Giard & E. Brière, 1897.

—— *De misdadigers in de kunst*, Amsterdam, C.L.G. Veldt, 1905.

—— *Les criminels dans l'art et la littérature*, Paris, Félix Alcan, 1913.

Fetchenhauer, D. and J. Simon, "Eine experimentelle Uberprüfung der 'general theory of crime' von Gottfredson und Hirschi", *Monatsschrift für Kriminologie und Strafrechtsreform*, 1998, pp. 301–315.

Fetscher, I. (ed.), *Marx-Engels Studienausgabe*, Frankfurt am Main, Fischer Bücherei, 1966, 4 vols.

Finckenauer, J., "Crime as a national political issue, 1964–1976: from law and order to domestic tranquillity", *Crime & Delinquency*, 1978, pp. 13–27.

Finder, G., "Criminals and their analysts: psychoanalytic criminology in Weimar Germany and the First Austrian Republic", in: P. Becker and R. Wetzell (eds.), *Criminals and their Scientists: The History of Criminology in International Perspective*, Cambridge, Cambridge University Press, 2006, pp. 447–469.

Findlay, M., *The Globalization of Crime: Understanding Transitional Relationshps in Context*, Cambridge, Cambridge University Press, 2000.

Fine, B. and R. Millar (eds.), *Policing the Miners' Strike*, London, Lawrence & Wishart, 1985 (with a preface by M. McGahey).

Fink, A., *Causes of Crime: Biological Theories in the United States, 1800–1915*, Philadelphia, University of Pennsylvania Press, 1938.

Fiselier, J., "Bonger over vermogenscriminaliteit", *Nederlands Tijdschrift voor Criminologie*, 1976, pp. 160–173.

—— *Slachtoffers van delicten: een onderzoek naar verborgen criminaliteit*, Utrecht, Ars Aequi Libri, 1978.

Fitzgerald, M., *Prisoners in Revolt*, Harmondsworth, Penguin Books, 1977.

Fleerakers, F. (ed.), *Mens en recht: essays tussen rechtstheorie en rechtspraktijk: liber amicorum J. Broekman*, Leuven, Peeters, 1996.

Fletcher, J., "Summary of the moral statistics of England and Wales", in: P. Rock (ed.), *History of Criminology*, Aldershot, Dartmouth, 1994, pp. 175–186.

Fogelson, R., *Big-city Police*, Cambridge, Harvard University Press, 1977.

Forlivesi, L., G.-F. Pottier and S. Chassat (eds.), *Eduquer et punir: la colonie agricole et pénitentiaire de Mettray (1839–1937)*, Rennes, Presses Universitaires de Rennes, 2005.

Forsythe, B., "National Socialists and the English Prison Commission: the Berlin Penitentiary Congress of 1935", *International Journal of the Sociology of Law*, 1989, pp. 131–145.

Fosdick, R., "The passing of the Bertillon system of identification", *Journal of the American Institute of Criminal Law and Criminology*, 1915, pp. 363–369.

—— *European Police Systems*, New York, Century Co., 1916.

—— *American Police Systems*, New York, Century Co., 1920.

Foucault, M., *Surveiller et punir: naissance de la prison*, Paris, Gallimard, 1975.

Fouché: *Mémoires de Joseph Fouché, duc d'Otrante*, presented by M. Vovelle, Paris, Imprimerie nationale, 1992.

Fourth International Criminological Congress/Quatrième Congrès International de Criminologie, *Preparatory papers/Travaux préparatoires – General report/Rapport général*, The Hague/La Haye, Secretariat of the Congress/Secrétariat du Congrès, 1960, 2 vols.

Franke, H., *De dood in het leven: rouwadvertenties en openbare strafvoltrekkingen in Nederland*, The Hague, Nijgh & Van Ditmar, 1985.

—— *Twee eeuwen gevangen: misdaad en straf in Nederland*, Utrecht, Het Spectrum, 1990.

—— *De macht van het lijden: twee eeuwen gevangenisstraf in Nederland*, Amsterdam, Balans, 1996.

Frederiks, K., *Het oud-nederlandsch strafrecht*, Haarlem, De Erven F. Bohm, 1918.

Frégier, H., *Des classes dangéreuses de la population dans les grandes villes et des moyens de les rendre meilleures*, Brussels, s.n., 1840.

Frégier, H., *Histoire de l'administration de la police de Paris depuis Philippe-August jusqu'aux Etats-Généraux de 1789 ou tableau moral et politique de la ville de Paris durant cette période considéré dans ses rapports avec l'action de la police*, Paris, s.n., 1850.

Freud, S., *Abriss der Psychoanalyse: das Unbehagen in der Kultur*, Frankfurt am Main, Fischer Bücherei, 1971.

Fricke, D., *Bismarcks Prätorianer: die Berliner Polizei im Kampf gegen die deutsche Arbeiterbewegung, 1871–1898*, Berlin, Rütten & Loening, 1962.

Fried, A., *The Rise and Fall of the Jewish Gangster in America*, New York, Columbia University Press, 1993.

Friedlander, K., *De jeugdige delinquent: psychoanalytische beschouwingen over karaktervorming, criminaliteit en heropvoeding*, Haarlem, H.D. Tjeenk Willink & Zoon, 1952 (translated from English).

Friedrich, J., *Die Bedeutung der Psychologie für die Bekämpfung der Verbrechen: zugleich eine Kritik neuerer Straf-, Strafprozess- und Jugendgerichtsentwürfe und der herrschenden strafrechtlichen Schuldlehre*, Hannover, Helwingsche Verlagsbuchhandlung, 1915.

Fritz, G., *Räuberbanden und Polizeistreifen: der Kampf zwischen Kriminalität und Staatsgewalt im Südwesten des alten Reichs zwischen 1648 und 1806*, Remshalden, Verlag Manfred Hennecke, 2003.

Froment, M., *Histoire de Vidocq: écrite d'après lui-même*, Paris, Robert Laffont, 1967.

Funk, A., *Polizei und Rechtsstaat: die Entwicklung des staatlichen Gewaltmonopols in Preuszen, 1848–1914*, Frankfurt, Campus Verlag, 1986.

Fyvel, T., *The Insecure Offenders: Rebellious Youth in the Welfare State*, Harmondsworth, Penguin Books, 1966.

Fijnaut, C., *Opdat de macht een toevlucht zij? Een historische studie van het politieapparaat als een politieke instelling*, Antwerp, Kluwer Rechtswetenschappen, 1979, 2 vols.

—— "Een wetenschapsfilosofische beschouwing over de zaak-Buikhuisen", *Tijdschrift voor Criminologie*, 1980, pp. 65–81.

—— "Verklaren en bestrijden in de criminologie", *Panopticon*, 1981, pp. 549–574.

—— "Over de traditie van de politiewetenschap in West-Europa", in: P. van Lochem, C. Fijnaut and P. van Reenen, *Theoretische opstellen rondom de politie*, Apeldoorn, Nederlandse Politie Academie, 1983, pp. 21–42 (1983a).

—— "Criminologie en strafrecht(sbedeling): hun onderlinge verhouding rond de voorbije eeuwwisseling", in: A. 't Hart, W. Nieboer, G. Strijards and M. de Vries-Leemans (eds.), *Strafrecht in balans: opstellen over strafrecht aangeboden aan A.C. Geurts*, Arnhem, Gouda Quint, 1983, pp. 41–80 (1983b).

—— *De zaak-Francois: beschouwingen naar aanleiding van het vonnis*, Antwerp, Kluwer Rechtswetenschappen, 1983 (1983c).

—— "G.A. van Hamel: een behoudend strafrechtshervormer", *Delikt en Delinkwent*, 1984, pp. 8–24 (1984a).

—— "Die Fiktion einer integrierten Strafrechtswissenschaft gegen Ende des vergangenen Jahrhunderts", *Zeitschrift für die gesamte Strafrechtswissenschaft*, 1984, pp. 135–171 (1984b).

—— *De reguliere recherche in Nederland: enkele algemene beschouwingen over haar opbouw rond de voorbije eeuwwisseling*, Lochem, J.B. van den Brink, 1985.

—— *Verleden, heden en toekomst van de geïntegreerde strafrechtswetenschap*, Arnhem, Gouda Quint, 1986 (1986a).

—— "In de klem der verdeeldheid", in: J. Balkema, G. Corstens, C. Fijnaut et al. (eds.), *Gedenkboek honderd jaar Wetboek van Strafrecht*, Arnhem, Gouda Quint, 1986, pp. 125–156 (1986b).

—— "Het Leidse Strafrechtelijk en Criminologisch Instituut", in: P. ter Hoeven, R. Overeem, C. Hogenhuis and E. Rood-Pijpers (eds.), *Bezonnen hoop: opstellen aangeboden aan L.H.C. Hulsman*, Zwolle, W.E.J. Tjeenk Willink, 1986, pp. 75–88 (1986c).

—— "Gerardus Antonius van Hamel, 1842–1917", in: T. Veen and P. Kop (eds.), *Zestig juristen: bijdragen tot een beeld van de geschiedenis van de Nederlandse rechtswetenschap*, Zwolle, W.E.J. Tjeenk Willink, 1987, pp. 336–339 (1987a).

—— *De toelating van raadslieden tot het politiële verdachtenverhoor*, Antwerp, Kluwer, 1987 (1987b).

—— "Cesare Beccaria in de Noordelijke Nederlanden", *Delikt en Delinkwent*, 1990, pp. 144–157 (1990a).

—— "De Duitse criminele psychologie vóór Wereldoorlog II: een schoolvoorbeeld van psychologie voor juristen", *Panopticon*, 1990, pp. 298–316 (1990b).

—— "Organized crime: a comparison between the United States and Western Europe", *British Journal of Criminology*, 1990, pp. 321–340 (1990c).

—— "De actuele betekenis van de opvattingen van de I.K.V. over de strafrechtswetenschap", in: M. Groenhuijsen and D. van der Landen (eds.), *De Moderne Richting in het strafrecht: theorie, praktijk, latere ontwikkelingen en actuele betekenis*, Arnhem, Gouda Quint, 1990, pp. 181–194 (1990d).

—— "Coornhert: verlichter dan men denkt?" *Delikt en Delinkwent*, 1990, pp. 493–396 (1990e).

—— "De geboren misdadiger", *Tijdschrift voor Criminologie*, 1992, pp. 3–7.

—— (ed.), *Gestalten uit het verleden: 32 voorgangers in de strafrechtswetenschap, de strafrechtspleging en de criminologie*, Leuven, Universitaire Pers Leuven, 1993 (1993a).

—— "Florent Louwage", in: C. Fijnaut (ed.), *Gestalten uit het verleden: 32 voorgangers in de strafrechtswetenschap, de strafrechtspleging en de criminologie*, Leuven, Universitaire Pers Leuven, 1993, pp. 195–210 (1993b).

—— *Een kleine geschiedenis van de huidige organisatie van het Belgische politiewezen*, Antwerp, Kluwer Rechtswetenschappen, 1995.

—— "Beelden van de homo criminalis in de criminologie", in: F. Fleerackers (ed.), *Mens en recht: essays tussen rechtstheorie en rechtspraktijk: liber amicorum J. Broekman*, Leuven, Peeters, 1996, pp. 133–146.

—— "The International Criminal Police Commission and the fight against communism, 1923–1945", in: M. Mazower (ed.), *The Policing of Politics in the Twentieth Century: historical perspectives*, Oxford, Berghahn Books, 1997, pp. 107–128.

—— "Beccaria in de Nederlanden", in: *Liber amicorum Steven de Batselier*, s.l., Reyniers, 1998, pp. 187–202.

—— *Voorproeve van een geschiedenis van de Nederlandse politie, 1795–1957*, Tilburg-Leuven, 2000 (2000a).

—— "Over de individuele dader en zijn misdaad: het oeuvre van Etienne de Greeff, 1898–1961", in: T. Oei and M. Groenhuijsen (eds.), *Forensische psychiatrie anno 2000: actuele ontwikkelingen in breed perspectief*, Deventer, Gouda Quint, 2000, pp. 353–370 (2000b).

—— *De Europese Unie: een lusthof voor (strafrechtelijke) rechtsvergelijking*, Deventer, Gouda Quint, 2001.

—— "De la gendarmerie hollandaise à la márechaussee royale des Pays-Bas, 1805–1815", in: J.-N. Luc (ed.), *Gendarmerie, état et société au XIXe siècle*, Paris, Publications de la Sorbonne, 2002, pp. 423–436.

—— "De vroegste pleidooien voor de psychiatrisering van het gevangeniswezen", in: T. Oei and M. Groenhuijsen (eds.), *Actuele ontwikkelingen in de forensische psychiatrie*, Deventer, Kluwer, 2003, pp. 21–38 (2003a).

—— "Mr. G.A. van Hamel: afgevaardigde van het kiesdistrict Amsterdam IV in de Tweede Kamer", in: M. Groenhuijsen and J. Simmelink (eds.), *Glijdende schalen: liber amicorum J. De Hullu*, Nijmegen, Wolf Legal Publishers, 2003, pp. 149–184 (2003b).

—— "Cesare Lombroso: de revolutionaire grondlegger van de tegenwoordige criminologie", in: F. Verbruggen, R. Verstraeten, D. van Daele and B. Spriet (eds.), *Strafrecht als roeping: liber amicorum Lieven Dupont*, Leuven, Universitaire Pers Leuven, 2005, vol. 2, pp. 1093–1122 (2005a).

—— *Onwetendheid en wetenschap in de criminologie*, The Hague, Wetenschappelijk Onderzoek- en Documentatiecentrum, 2005 (2005b).

—— *De geschiedenis van de Nederlandse politie: een staatsinstelling in de maalstroom van de geschiedenis*, Amsterdam, Boom, 2007.

—— "De voorlopers van de moderne criminologie in België en Nederland", *Justitiële Verkenningen*, 2010, pp. 10–29 (2010a).

—— "Introduction of the New York double strategy to control organised crime in the Netherlands and the European Union", *European Journal of Crime, Criminal Law and Criminal Justice*, 2010, pp. 43–65 (2010b).

—— *Het nationale politiekorps: achtergronden, dilemma's, toekomstplannen*, Amsterdam, Uitgeverij Bert Bakker, 2012 (2012a).

—— "De wederwaardigheden van het onderzoek inzake politionele en gerechtelijke organisatie", in: J. Casselman, I. Aertsen and S. Parmentier (eds.), *Tachtig jaar criminologie aan de Leuvense universiteit: onderwijs, onderzoek en praktijk*, Antwerp, Maklu, 2012, pp. 107–124 (2012b).

—— "Searching for organised crime in history", in: L. Paoli (ed.), *Handbook on Organised Crime*, Oxford, Oxford University Press, 2013, pp. 53–95 (2013a).

—— "Introduction", in: H.-J. Albrecht and A. Klip (eds.), *Crime, Criminal Law and Criminal Justice in Europe: A Collection in Honour of Prof. em. Dr. Dr. h.c. Cyrille Fijnaut*, Leiden, Martinus Nijhoff Publishers, 2013, pp. xiii–xxii (2013b).

—— (ed.) *The Containment of Organized Crime and Terrorism: Thirty-five Years of Research on Police, Judicial and Administrative Cooperation*, Leiden, Brill, 2016.

Fijnaut, C., F. Bovenkerk, G. Bruinsma and H. van de Bunt, *Organized Crime in the Netherlands*, The Hague, Kluwer Law International, 1998.

Fijnaut, C., W. Bruggeman, L. Sievers, A. Spapens and W. van Erve, "The role of the police worldwide in the containment of the illegal production, the illegal trade and the illegal possession of small arms and light weapons", in: C. Fijnaut (ed.), *The Containment of Organized Crime and Terrorism; Thirty-five Years of Research on Police, Judicial and Administrative Cooperation*, Leiden, Brill, 2016, pp. 883–936.

Fijnaut, C. and B. de Ruyver, *Voor een gezamenlijke beheersing van de drugsgerelateerde criminaliteit in de Euregio Maas-Rijn*, Maastricht, Euregio Maas-Rijn, 2008.

Fijnaut, C., B. de Ruyver and F. Goossens (eds.), *De reorganisatie van het politiewezen*, Leuven, Universitaire Pers Leuven, 1999.

Fijnaut, C., J. Goethals, T. Peters and L. Walgrave (eds.), *Changes in Society, Crime and Criminal Justice in Europe*, The Hague, Kluwer Law International, 1955, 2 vols.

Fijnaut, C. and J. Jacobs (eds.), *Organized Crime and its Containment: A Transatlantic Initiative*, Deventer, Kluwer Law and Taxation, 1991.

Fijnaut, C. and G. Marx (eds.), *Undercover: Police Surveillance in Comparative Perspective*, The Hague, Kluwer Law International, 1995.

Fijnaut, C., H. Moerland and J. uit Beijerse, *Een winkelboulevard in problemen: samenleving en criminaliteit in twee Rotterdamse buurten*, Arnhem, Gouda Quint, 1991.

Fijnaut, C., E. Nuijten-Edelbroek and J. Spickenheuer, *Politiële misdaadbestrijding: een studie van het Amerikaanse, Engelse en Nederlandse onderzoek aangaande politiële misdaadbestrijding sedert de jaren zestig*, The Hague, Staatsuitgeverij, 1985.

Fijnaut, C. and L. Paoli (eds.), *Organised Crime in Europe and Beyond: Concepts, Patterns and Policies*, Dordrecht, Springer, 2004.

Fijnaut, C. and T. Spapens, *Criminaliteit en rechtshandhaving in de Euregio Maas-Rijn: de problemen van transnationale (georganiseerde) criminaliteit en de grensoverschrijdende politiële, justitiële en bestuurlijke samenwerking*, Antwerp, Intersentia, 2005.

Fijnaut, C., H. Spickenheuer and L. Nuijten-Edelbroek, *Politiële misdaadbestrijding: een studie van het Amerikaanse, Engelse en Nederlandse onderzoek aangaande politiële misdaadbestrijding sedert de jaren '60*, The Hague, Staatsuitgeverij, 1985.

Fijnaut, C. and P. Spierenburg (eds.), *Scherp toezicht: van 'Boeventucht' tot 'Samenleving en criminaliteit'*, Arnhem, Gouda Quint, 1990.

Fijnaut, C. and D. van Daele (eds.), *De hervorming van het openbaar ministerie*, Leuven, Universitaire Pers Leuven, 1999.

Fijnaut, C., D. van Daele, T. Kooijmans, B. vander Vorm and K. Verbist, *Criminaliteit en rechtshandhaving in de Euregio Maas-Rijn: de bestuurlijke aanpak van georganiseerde criminaliteit in Nederland en België*, Antwerp, Intersentia, 2010.

Fijnaut, C., D. van Daele and F. Verbruggen (eds.), *De uitdaging van de georganiseerde misdaad in België: het antwoord van de overheid*, Leuven, Universitaire Pers Leuven, 1998.

Gainot, B., "La gendarmerie dans la recomposition sociale post-révolutionnaire: la loi organique de 1798", in: J.-N. Luc (ed.), *Gendarmerie, état et société au XIXe siècle*, Paris, Publications de la Sorbonne, 2002, pp. 63–70.

Galassi, S., *Kriminologie im deutschen Kaiserreich: Geschichte einer gebrochenen Verwissenschaftlichung*, Stuttgart, Franz Steiner Verlag, 2004.

Galtung, J., *Gevangenis en maatschappij: een sociologisch-kriminologisch onderzoek naar strafbeleving*, The Hague, Bert Bakker, 1967 (with a preface by J. Galtung).

Ganshof van der Meersch, W., *Notice sur la vie et les travaux de Léon Cornil*, Brussels, Université Libre de Bruxelles, 1972.

Garland, D., "The criminal and his science: a critical account of the formation of criminology at the end of the nineteenth century", *British Journal of Criminology*, 1985, pp. 109–137.

—— *Punishment and Welfare: A History of Penal Strategies*, Aldershot, Gower, 1986.

—— "British criminology before 1935", in: P. Rock (ed.), *A History of British Criminology*, Oxford, Clarendon Press, 1988, pp. 133–147.

—— "Criminological knowledge and its relation to power: Foucault's genealogy and criminology today", *British Journal of Criminology*, 1992, pp. 403–422.

—— (ed.), *Mass Imprisonment: Social Causes and Consequences*, London, Sage Publications, 2001.

—— "Of crimes and criminals: the development of criminology in Britain", in: M. Maguire, R. Morgan and R. Reiner (eds.), *The Oxford Handbook of Criminology*, Oxford, Oxford University Press, 2002, pp. 7–50.

Garland, D. and R. Sparks (eds.), *Criminology and Social Theory*, Oxford, Oxford University Press, 2000.

Garner, J., "Editorial comment", *Journal of the American Institute on Criminal Law and Criminology*, 1910, pp. 2–7.

Garnot, B., *Crime et justice aux XVIIe et XVIIIe siècles*, Paris, Editions Imago, 2000.

Garofalo, R., *Criminologia: studio sul delitto, sulle sue cause et sui mezzi di repressione*, Turin, Fratelli Bocca, 1885.

—— *La superstition socialiste*, Paris, Félix Alcan, 1895.

—— *Criminology*, Boston, Little, Brown and Company, 1914 (translated by R. Millar, with an introduction by E. Stevens).

Gassin, R., *Criminologie*, Paris, Dalloz, 1988.

Gault, R., *Criminology*, New York, D.C. Heath and Company, 1932.

Gaylord, M. and J. Galliher, *The Criminology of Edwin Sutherland*, New Brunswick, Transaction Books, 1988.

Geis, G. and R. Meier (eds.), *White-collar Crime: Offences in Business, Politics and the Professions: Classic and Contemporary Views*, New York, Free Press, 1977.

Geisert, H., *The Criminal: A Study*, St Louis, B. Herder Book Co., 1930.

Geisert, M., *Le système criminaliste de Tarde*, Paris, Les Editions Domat-Montchrestien, 1935.

Gellately, R. and N. Stoltzfus (eds.), *Social Outsiders in Nazi Germany*, Princeton, Princeton University Press, 2001.

Gelsthorpe, L., "Clifford Shaw, 1895–1957", in: K. Hayward, S. Maruna and J. Mooney (eds.), *Fifty Key Thinkers in Criminology*, London, Routledge, 2010, pp. 71–75.

Genil-Perrin, G., *Psychoanalyse et criminologie*, Paris, Félix Alcan, 1934.

Gephart, W., *Strafe und Verbrechen: die Theorie Emile Durkheims*, Opladen, Leske und Budrich, 1990.

Gérard, P., *Ferdinand Rapédius de Berg: mémoires et documents pour servir à l'histoire de la Révolution Brabançonne*, Brussels, Demanet, 1842, 2 vols.

Gerard, P., F. Ost and M. van de Kerchove (eds.), *Actualité de la pensée de Jeremy Bentham*, Brussels, Publications des Facultés Universitaires Saint-Louis, 1987.

Geurts, A., *De rechtspositie van de gevangene*, Assen, Van Gorcum & Comp., 1962.

—— *Criminaliteit in wording?: Openbare les gegeven bij de aanvaarding van het ambt van lector in de criminologie en het penitentiaire recht aan de Katholieke Hogeschool te Tilburg op woensdag 13 december 1967*, Deventer, Kluwer, 1967.

Gewin, B., *Strafrecht en de z.g.n. 'nieuwe richting'*, Utrecht, G. Ruys, 1910.

Gibbons, D., *Talking about Crime and Criminals: Problems and Issues in Theory Development in Criminology*, Englewood Cliffs, Prentice-Hall, 1994.

Gibson, M., *Born to Crime: Cesare Lombroso and the Origins of Biological Criminology*, Westport, Praeger, 2002.

—— "Cesare Lombroso and Italian criminology: theory and politics", in: P. Becker and R. Wetzell (eds.), *Criminals and their Scientists: The History of Criminology in International Perspective*, Cambridge, Cambridge University Press, 2006, pp. 137–158.

Gillham, N., *Sir Francis Galton: From African Exploration to the Birth of Eugenics*, Oxford, Oxford University Press, 2001.

Gillin, J., *Criminology and Penology*, New York, Century Co., 1926.

—— *Taming the Criminal*, New York, Macmillan Company, 1931.

—— *Criminology and Penology*, New York, D. Appleton-Century Company, 1935 (revised edition).

Girling, E., I. Loader and R. Sparks, *Crime and Social Change in Middle England: Questions of Order in an English Town*, London, Routledge, 2000.

Giuliani, R., "Text of mayor Giuliani's farewell address", *The New York Times*, 27 December 2001.

Glaser, D., *The Effectiveness of a Prison and Parole System*, Indianapolis, Bobbs-Merrill Company, 1969 (abridged edition).

—— (ed.), *Handbook of Criminology*, Chicago, Rand McNally and Co., 1974.

—— "The counterproductivity of conservative thinking about crime", *Criminology*, 1978, pp. 209–223.

Glaser, L., *Counterfeiting in America: The History of an American Way to Wealth*, s.l., Clarkson N. Potter, Publisher, 1968.

Gleisal, J.-J., *Le désordre policier*, Paris, Presses Universitaire de France, 1985.

Glover, E., *The Roots of Crime*, London, Imago Publishing Company, 1960.

Glueck, S. and E. Glueck, *500 Criminal Careers*, New York, Alfred A. Knopf, 1930.

—— *One Thousand Juvenile Delinquents: Their Treatment by Court and Clinic*, Cambridge, Harvard University Press, 1934 (with an introduction by F. Frankfurter).

—— (eds.), *Preventing Crime: A Symposium*, New York, McGraw-Hill Book Company, 1936.

—— *Unraveling Juvenile Delinquency*, New York, The Commonwealth Fund, 1950.

—— *Delinquents in the Making: Paths to Prevention*, New York, Harper & Brothers Publishers, 1952.

—— *Of Delinquency and Crime: A Panorama of Years of Search and Research*, Springfield, Charles C. Thomas, 1974.

Goddefroy, E., "Les affaires criminelles et la police technique", *Archives d'anthropologie criminelle, de médecine légale et de psychologie normale et pathologique*, 1914, pp. 919–936.

Godfrey, B. and G. Dunstall (eds.), *Crime and Empire, 1840–1940: Criminal Justice in Local and Global Context*, Cullompton, Willan Publishing, 2005.

Goethals, J., *Psycho-sociale implicaties van de lange vrijheidsstraf*, Antwerp, Kluwer, 1980.

—— *Abnormaal en delinkwent: de geschiedenis en het actueel functioneren van de wet tot bescherming van de maatschappij*, Antwerp, Kluwer, 1991.

—— "Méthodologie de la statistique criminelle: l'oeuvre de Jaak van Kerckvoorde", *Déviance et société*, 1998, pp. 201–214.

—— "Laudatio", in: L. Dupont and F. Hutsebaut (eds.), *Herstelrecht tussen toekomst en verleden: liber amicorum Tony Peters*, Leuven, Universitaire Pers Leuven, 2001, pp. 9–31.

Goethals, J. and B. de Ruyver, "Fernand Heger, 1878–1957", in: C. Fijnaut (ed.), *Gestalten uit het verleden: 32 voorgangers in de strafrechtswetenschap, de strafrechtspleging en de criminologie*, Leuven, Universitaire Pers Leuven, 1993, pp. 179–183 (1993a).

—— "Jacques Ley, 1900–1983", in: C. Fijnaut (ed.), *Gestalten uit het verleden: 32 voorgangers in de strafrechtswetenschap, de strafrechtspleging en de criminologie*, Leuven, Universitaire Pers Leuven, 1993, pp. 319–327 (1993b).

Goffman, E., *Stigma: Notes on the Management of Spoiled Identity*, Englewood Cliffs, Prentice-Hall, 1963.

—— *Asylums: Essays on the Social Situation of Mental Patients and Other Inmates*, Harmondsworth, Penguin Books, 1970.

Goldsmith, A., "Fear, fumbling and frustration: reflections on doing criminological fieldwork in Colombia", *Criminal Justice*, 2003, pp. 103–125.

Goldstein, H., *Policing a Free Society*, Cambridge, Ballinger Publishing Company, 1977.

Göppinger, H., *Kriminologie: eine Einführung*, Munich, C.H. Beck'sche Verlagsbuchhandlung, 1971.

Göppinger, H. and G. Kaiser (eds.), *Kriminologie und Strafverfahren: Neuere Ergebnisse zur Dunkelfeldforschung in Deutschland: Bericht über die XVIII. Tagung der Gesellschaft für die gesamte Kriminologie vom 9. bis 12. Oktober 1975 in Freiburg*, Stuttgart, Ferdinand Enke Verlag, 1976.

Göppinger, H. and H. Leferenz (eds.), *Kriminologische Gegenwartsfragen: Vorträge bei der XIV. Tagung der Gesellschaft für die gesamte Kriminologie vom 13. bis 16. October 1967 in Köln*, Stuttgart, Ferdinand Enke Verlag, 1968.

Gordijn, H., *De sociologie van Emile Durkheim*, Amsterdam, J. de Bussy, 1969.

Goring, C., *The English Convict: A Statistical Study*, London, Her Majesty's Stationary Office, 1913.

Gottfredson, M. and T. Hirschi, *A General Theory of Crime*, Stanford, Stanford University Press, 1990.

Gramatica, F., *Principes de défense sociale*, Paris, Editions Cujas, 1964 (translated from Italian).

Grapin, P., *L'anthropologie criminelle*, Paris, Presses Universitaires de France, 1973.

Grassberger, R., *Gewerbs- und Berufsverbrechertum in den Vereinigten Staaten von Amerika*, Vienna, Verlag von Julius Springer, 1933.

—— "Hans Gross, 1847–1915", in: H. Mannheim (ed.), *Pioneers in Criminology*, London, Stevens and Sons, 1960, pp. 241–253.

Green, S., *Crime: Its Nature, Causes, Treatment and Prevention*, Philadelphia, J.B. Lippencott Company, 1889.

Greenberg, D. (ed.), *Crime and Capitalism: Readings in Marxist Criminology*, Philadelphia, Temple University Press, 1993.

Greenwood, P., J. Chaiken and J. Petersilia, *The Criminal Investigation Process*, Lexington, D.C. Heath and Company, 1977.

Greve, V., *Verbrechen und Krankheit: die Entdeckung der 'Criminalpsychologie' im 19. Jahrhundert*, Cologne, Böhlau Verlag, 2004.

Groenhuijsen, M., *Schadevergoeding voor slachtoffers van delicten in het strafgeding*, Nijmegen, Ars Aequi Libri, 1985.

Groenhuijsen, M. and J. Simmelink (eds.), *Glijdende schalen: liber amicorum J. De Hullu*, Nijmegen, Wolf Legal Publishers, 2003.

Groenhuijsen, M. and D. van der Landen (eds.), *De Moderne Richting in het strafrecht: theorie, praktijk, latere ontwikkelingen en actuele betekenis*, Arnhem, Gouda Quint, 1990.

Gross, H., *Handbuch für Untersuchungsrichter, Polizeibeamte, Gendarmen u.s.w.*, Graz, Leuschner & Lubensky's Universitätsbuchhandlung, 1893.

—— "Aufgabe und Ziele", in: *Archiv für Kriminal-Anthropologie und Kriminalistik*, 1898, pp. 1–4.

—— *Encyclopädie der Kriminalistik*, Leipzig, Verlag F.C.W. Vogel, 1901.

—— "Das Erkennungsamt der k.k. Polizeidirection in Wien", *Archiv für Kriminal-Anthropologie und Kriminalistik*, 1903, pp. 115–168 (1903a).

—— *De nasporing van het strafbaar feit: een leidraad voor ambtenaren en beambten van justitie en politie*, Heusden, L.J. Veerman, 1903 (adapted for the Netherlands by W. van der Does de Willebois) (1903b).

—— *Kriminalpsychologie*, Graz, Leuschner & Lubensky's Universitätsbuchhandlung, 1905.

—— "Ein kriminalistisches Reichsinstitut für Deutschland", *Archiv für Kriminal-Anthropologie und Kriminalistik*, 1913, pp. 193–199.

Gruder, L., "Die anthropometrische Messungen: ein Mittel zur Wiedererkennung rückfälliger Verbrecher", *Zeitschrift für die gesamte Strafrechtswissenschaft*, 1898, pp. 372–383.

Grünhut, M., *Penal Reform: A Comparative Study*, Oxford, Clarendon Press, 1948.

Grupp, S. (ed.), *The Positive School of Criminology: Three Lectures by Enrico Ferri*, Pittsburgh, University of Pittsburgh Press, 1968.

Grygier, T., "Soviet views on western crime and criminology", *British Journal of Delinquency*, 1950–51, pp. 283–293.

Gryphe: Revue de la Bibliothèque de Lyon, *Lacassagne: l'homme-livre*, 2004, no. 8.

Gudden, H., *Die Behandlung der jugendlichen Verbrecher in den Vereinigten Staaten von Nordamerika*, Nuremberg, Verlag der Friedrich Korn'schen Buchhandlung, 1910.

Guillaume, L., *Le congrès pénitentiaire international de Stockholm: mémoires et rapports sur l'état actuel des prisons et du régime pénitentiaire présentés au congrès et publiés sous la dierection de la Commission Pénitentiaire Internationale*, Stockholm, Bureau de la Commission Pénitentiaire Internationale, 1879.

Gürtner, F., "Das neue Reichsgesetz gegen gefährliche Gewohnheitsverbrecher", *Archiv für Kriminologie*, 1933, pp. 197–200.

Hacker, F., *Versagt der Mensch oder die Gesellschaft? Probleme der modernen Kriminalpsychologie*, Vienna, Europa Verlag, 1964.

Haff, K., *Rechtspsychologie: Forschungen zur Individual- und Massenpsychologie des Rechts und zur modernen Rechtsfindung*, Berlin/Vienna, Urban & Scharzenberg, 1924.

Haffmans, C., *Terbeschikking gesteld: geschiedenis, oplegging en executie van een strafrechtelijke maatregel*, Arnhem, Gouda Quint, 1984.

Hagan, J., *Modern Criminology: Crime, Criminal Behavior and its Control*, New York, McGraw-Hill Book Company, 1987.

Hagan, J. and W. Rymond-Richmond, *Darfur and the Crime of Genocide*, Cambridge, Cambridge University Press, 2009.

Hagner, M. (ed.), *Der falsche Körper: Beiträge zu einer Geschichte der Monstrositäten*, Göttingen, Wallstein Verlag, 1995.

Hall, A., *Crime in its Relations to Social Progress*, New York, Colombia University Press, 1902.

Hall, S., C. Critcher, T. Jefferson, J. Clarke and B. Roberts, *Policing the Crisis: Mugging, the State and Law and Order*, London, Macmillan Press, 1978.

Hallema, A., *In en om de gevangenis van vroeger dagen in Nederland en Nederlandsch-Indië: schetsen uit de geschiedenis der straffen en voornamelijk van de toepassing der vrijheidsstraffen binnen en buiten onze grenzen*, The Hague, Gebr. Belinfante, 1936.

Harmsen, G., "Bonger, Willem Adriaan", in: Biografisch woordenboek van het socialisme en de arbeidersbeweging in Nederland, https://socialhistory.org/bwsa/biografie/bonger (last accessed 9 April 2017).

Harring, S., *Policing a Class Society: The Experience of American Cities, 1865–1915*, New Brunswick, Rutgers University Press, 1983.

Harster, T., "Der Erkennungsdienst der Kgl. Polizeidirection München", *Archiv für Kriminal-Anthropologie und Kriminalistik*, 1910, pp. 116–137.

—— "Der Erkennungsdienst der Polizeidirektion München im neuen Heim", *Archiv für Kriminal-Anthropologie und Kriminalistik*, 1914, pp. 357–378.

Hart, H., *Essays on Bentham: Jurisprudence and Political Theory*, Oxford, Clarendon Press, 1982.

Hartsfield, L., *The American Response to Professional Crime, 1870–1917*, Westport, Greenwood Press, 1985.

Harvey, L., "The nature of 'schools' in the sociology of knowledge: the case of the 'Chicago School'", *Sociological Review*, 1987, pp. 245–278.

Haynes, F., *Criminology*, New York, McGraw-Hill Book Company, 1930.

Hayward, K., S. Maruna and J. Mooney (eds.), *Fifty Key Thinkers in Criminology*, London, Routledge, 2010.

Hayward, K. and M. Presdee (eds.), *Framing Crime: Cultural Criminology and the Image*, London, Routledge, 2010.

Healy, W., *The Individual Delinquent: A Textbook of Diagnosis and Prognosis for All Concerned in Understanding Offenders*, Boston, Little, Brown and Company, 1918.

Healy, W. and A. Bronner, *Delinquents and Criminals: Their Making and Unmaking: Studies in Two American Cities*, New York, Macmillan Company, 1926.

—— *New Light on Delinquency and its Treatment: Results of a Research Conducted for the Institute of Human Relations, Yale University*, New Haven, Yale University Press, 1936.

Heath, J. (ed.), *Eighteenth Century Penal Theory*, Oxford, Oxford University Press, 1963.

Heidensohn, F., *Crime and Society*, Houndmills, Macmillan, 1989.

—— *Women and Crime*, New York, New York University Press, 1995.

Heilbron, J., *Het ontstaan van de sociologie*, Amsterdam, Prometheus, 1990.

Heilmann, E., "Die Bertillonnage und 'die Stigmata der Entartung'", *Kriminologisches Journal*, 1994, pp. 36–46.

Heindl, R., "Bericht über den I.Internationalen Kriminalpolizeikongress in Monaco", *Archiv für Kriminal-Anthropologie und Kriminalistik*, 1914, pp. 333–353.

—— "Polizeiliche Bekämpfung des interlokalen Verbrechertums", *Archiv für Kriminologie*, 1920, pp. 191–224.

—— *System und Praxis der Daktyloskopie und der sonstigen technischen Methoden der Kriminalpolizei*, Berlin, Vereinigung der Wissenschaftlicher Verleger, 1922 (1922a).

—— *De dactyloscopie: eenige opmerkingen betreffende de techniek der justitiële politie*, Alphen aan den Rijn, N. Samson, 1922 (1922b).

—— *De organisatie der recherche*, Alphen aan den Rijn, N. Samson, 1924.

—— *Polizei und Verbrechen*, Berlin, Gersbach & Sohn Verlag, 1926.

—— *Der Berufsverbrecher: ein Beitrag zur Strafrechtsreform*, Berlin, Pan-Verlag Kurt Metzner, 1929 (1929a).

—— "The technique of criminal investigation in Germany", in: T. Sellin (ed.), *The Police and the Crime Problem*, in: The Annals of the American Academy of Political and Social Science, Philadelphia, 1929, pp. 223–236 (1926b).

Heinrich, J.-P., *Particuliere reclassering en overheid in Nederland*, Arnhem, Gouda Quint, 1995.

Hellwig, A., *Psychologie und Vernehmungstechnik bei Tatbestandsermittlungen: eine Einführung in die forensische Psychologie für Polizeibeamte, Richter, Staatsanwälte, Sachverständige und Laienrichter*, Berlin, P. Langenscheidt, 1927.

—— *Psychologie und Vernehmungstechnik bei Tatbestandsermittlungen: eine Einfürung in die forensische Psychologie für Polizeibeamte, Richter, Staatsanwälte, Sachverständige und Laienrichter*, Berlin, Verlag Arthur Sudau, 1943.

Henderson, C., *Introduction to the Study of the Dependent, Defective and Delinquent Classes and of their Social Treatment*, Boston, D.C. Heath & Co. Publishers, 1901.

Hennau, C. and J. Verhaegen, "Jacques-Joseph Hauss, 1796–1881", in: C. Fijnaut (ed.), *Gestalten uit het verleden: 32 voorgangers in de strafrechtswetenschap, de strafrechtspleging en de criminologie*, Leuven, Universitaire Pers Leuven, 1993, pp. 73–81.

Henry, G., *Cartouche*, Paris, Tallandier, 1984.

Henry, S. and S. Lukas (eds.), *Recent Developments in Criminological Theory*, Surrey, Ashgate, 2009.

Henry, S. and W. Einstadter (eds.), *The Criminology Theory Reader*, New York, New York University Press, 1998.

Henschel, A., "Der Geständniszwang und das falsche Geständnis", *Archiv für Kriminal-Anthropologie und Kriminalistik*, 1914, pp. 10–40.

Henze, M., "Netzwerk, Kongressbewegung, Stiftung: zur Wissenschaftsgeschichte der internationalen Gefängniskunde 1827 bis 1951", in: D. Schauz and S. Freitag (eds.), *Verbrecher im Visier der Experten: Kriminalpolitik zwischen Wissenschaft und Praxis im 19. und frühen 20. Jahrhundert*, Stuttgart, Franz Steiner Verlag, 2007, pp. 55–78.

Hering, K-H., *Der Weg der Kriminologie zur selbständigen Wissenschaft*, Hamburg, Kriminalistik Verlag, 1966.

Hermans, C., *De dwaaltocht van het sociaal-darwinisme: vroege sociale interpretaties van Charles Darwins theorie van natuurlijke selectie, 1859–1918*, Amsterdam, Uitgeverij Nieuwerzijds, 2003.

Hermans, H., *De Raad voor de Kinderbescherming*, Zwolle, W.E.J. Tjeenk Willink, 1984.

Herren, R., *Lehrbuch der Kriminologie: die Verbrechenswirklichkeit*, Freiburg, Verlag Rombach, 1982, 3 vols.

Hes, B., *Berechting van jeugdige delinquenten*, Groningen, P. Noordhoff, 1905.

Hesnard, A., *Psychologie du crime*, Paris, Payot, 1963.

Hess, H., "Fixing broken windows and bringing down crime: die New Yorker Polizeistrategie der neunziger Jahre", *Kritische Justiz*, 1998, pp. 32–57.

Hesselink, W., *Eerste optreden op de plaats eens misdrijfs: zeer beknopte handleiding voor eerstaanwezigen*, Arnhem, G.W. van der Wiel, 1909.

Hett, B., *Death in Tiergarten: Murder and Criminal Justice in the Kaiser's Berlin*, Cambridge, Harvard University Press, 2004.

Heuyer, G., *La délinquance juvenile: étude psychiatrique*, Paris, Presses Universitaires de France, 1969.

Heyen, E. (ed.), *Historische Soziologie der Rechtswissenschaft*, Frankfurt am Main, Vittorio Klostermann, 1986.

Hibbert, C., *The Roots of Evil: A Social History of Crime and Punishment*, Birmingham, Minerva Press, 1968.

Hill, F., *Crime: Its Amount, Causes and Remedies*, London, John Murray, 1853.

Hillesum, H., *Biographisch onderzoek naar de werking van het rijksopvoedingsgesticht voor meisjes en naar oorzaken der meisjesmisdadigheid*, Amsterdam, A.H. Kruyt, 1918.

Hingley, R., *Die Russische Geheimpolizei, 1565–1970*, Bayreuth, Hestia Verlag, 1970.

Hirsch, H., "Einführung in das Thema Strafrecht und Kriminologie unter einem Dach", in: U. Sieber and H.-J. Albrecht (eds.), *Strafrecht und Kriminologie unter einem Dach: Kolloquium zum 90. Geburtstag von prof. dr. dr. h.c. mult. Hans-Heinrich Jescheck*, Berlin, Duncker & Humblot, 2006, pp. 31–43.

Hirschi, T., "The family", in: J. Wilson and J. Petersilia (eds.), *Crime: Twenty-eight Leading Experts Look at the Most Pressing Problem of Our Time*, San Francisco, ICS Press, 1995, pp. 121–140.

Hobbs, D., *Doing the Business: Entrepreneurhip, the Working Class and Detectives in the East End of London*, Oxford, Clarendon Press, 1988.

—— (ed.), *Professional Criminals*, Aldershot, Dartmouth, 1995.

Hochstedler, E. (ed.), *Corporations as Criminals*, Beverly Hills, Sage Publications, 1984.

Höck, J., *Grundlinien der Polizeiwissenschaft mit besonderer Rücksicht auf das Königreich Baiern*, Nuremberg, in der Steinischen Buchhandlung, 1809.

Hoefnagels, G., *Beginselen van criminologie*, Deventer, Kluwer, 1969.

—— *The Other Side of Criminology*, Deventer, Kluwer, 1973.

Hohlfeld, N., *Moderne Kriminalbiologie: die Entwicklung der Kriminalbiologie vom Determinus des 19. zu den bio-sozialen Theorien des 20. Jahrhunderts: eine kritische Darstellung moderner kriminalbiologischer Forschung und ihrer kriminalpolitischen Forderungen*, Frankfurt am Main, Peter Lang, 2002.

Honnorat, G., "Etude sur les moyens de réprimer la criminalité internationale", *Mitteilungen der Internationalen Kriminalistischen Gesellschaft*, 1906, pp. 260–266.

Hood, R. (ed.), *Crime, Criminology and Public Policy: Essays in Honour of Sir Leon Radzinowicz*, London, Heinemann, 1974.

—— "Hermann Mannheim and Max Grünhut", *British Journal of Criminology*, 2004, pp. 469–495.

—— "Max Grünhut", in: *Oxford Dictionary of National Biography*, http://www.oxforddnb.com (last accessed 9 April 2017).

Hood, R. and R. Sparks, *Key Issues in Criminology*, London, Weidenfeld and Nicolson, 1978.

Hoorens, C., M. Schlösser, D. Duyvelaar, M. Gruyters and W. Wolters (eds.), *Slachtoffers van delicten: enkele beschouwingen over de maatschappelijke en juridische problemen van het slachtoffer*, Baarn, Anthos, 1971.

Hooton, E., *The American Criminal: An Anthropological Study*, Cambridge, Harvard University Press, 1939, 3 vols. (1939a).

—— *Crime and the Man*, Cambridge, Harvard University Press, 1939 (1939b).

—— "The American criminal", in: J. Jacoby (ed.), *Classics of Criminology*, Prospects Heights, Waveland Press, 1994, pp. 147–158.

Hoover, J., "Criminal identification", in: T. Sellin (ed.), *The Police and the Crime Problem*, in: The Annals of the American Academy of Political and Social Science, Philadelphia, 1929, pp. 205–213.

Hopff, G., "Das internationale Verbrechertum und seine Bekämpfung", *Mitteilungen der Internationalen Kriminalistischen Gesellschaft*, 1906, pp. 206–246.

Höpfel, F., "Der Einfluss des Nationalsozialismus auf das Strafrecht", *Zeitschrift für die gesamte Strafrechtswissenschaft*, 2003, pp. 906–920.

Horn, D., *The Criminal Body: Lombroso and the Anatomy of Deviance*, New York, Routledge, 2003.

Howard, J., *État des prisons, des hôpitaux et des maisons de force*, Paris, Lagrange, 1788 (translated from English).

Howson, G., *Thief-taker General: The Rise and Fall of Jonathan Wild*, London, Hutchinson, 1970.

Hudig, J., *De criminaliteit der vrouw*, Utrecht, Dekker & Van de Vegt, 1939.

Huff, C. (ed.), *Gangs in America*, Newbury Park, Sage Publications, 1990.

Hughes, R., *The Fatal Shore: A History of the Transportation of Convicts to Australia, 1787–1868*, London, Pan Books, 1988.

Hulsman, L., *Handhaving van recht*, Deventer, Kluwer, 1965.

—— *Afscheid van het strafrecht: een pleidooi voor zelfregulering*, Houten, Het Wereldvenster, 1986.

—— "Critical criminology and the concept of crime", *Contemporary Crises*, 1986, pp. 63–80.

Hutsebaut, F., "Louis Braffort, 1886–1944", in: C. Fijnaut (ed.), *Gestalten uit het verleden: 32 voorgangers in de strafrechtswetenschap, de strafrechtspleging en de criminologie*, Leuven, Universitaire Pers Leuven, 1993, pp. 211–219.

Huussen, Jr, A., "Coornherts Boeven-tucht", in: H. Bonger et al. (eds.), *Dirk Volckertszoon Coornhert: dwars maar recht*, Zutphen, De Walburg Pers, 1989, pp. 144–153.

Icard, S., "Code signalétique international", *Archives d'anthropologie criminelle, de médecine légale et de psychologie normale et pathologique*, 1912, pp. 561–615.

Ignatieff, M., *A Just Measure of Pain: The Penitentiary in the Industrial Revolution, 1750–1850*, London, Penguin Books, 1978.

Illinois Association for Criminal Justice (ed.), *The Illinois Crime Survey*, Montclair, Patterson Smith, 1968.

Imago: Zeitschrift für Anwendung der Psychoanalyse auf die Natur- und Geisteswissenschaften, 1931, no. 2.

Immink, P., *La liberté et la peine: étude sur la transformation de la liberté et sur le développement du droit pénal public en Occident avant le XIIe siècle*, Assen, Van Gorcum, 1973.

Inbau, F., "Scientific evidence in criminal cases: methods of detecting deception", *Journal of Criminal Law and Criminology*, 1934, pp. 1140–1158.

Inbau, F. and J. Reid, *Criminal Interrogation and Confessions*, Baltimore, Williams & Wilkins, 1962.

Irwin, J., *The Felon*, Berkeley, University of California Press, 1987.

Jablonka, I., "Un discours philantropique dans la France du XIXe siècle: la rééducation des jeunes délinquants dans les colonies agricoles pénitentiaires", *Revue d'histoire moderne et contemporaine*, 2000, pp. 131–147.

Jacoby, J. (ed.), *Classics of Criminology*, Prospects Heights, Waveland Press, 1994.

Jacobs, B., *Justitie en politie in 's-Hertogenbosch voor 1629*, Assen, Van Gorcum, 1986.

Jacobs, J., *Stateville: The Penitentiary in Mass Society*, Chicago, University of Chicago Press, 1977 (with a foreword by M. Janowitz).

—— *New Perspectives on Prisons and Imprisonment*, Ithaca, Cornell University Press, 1983.

—— "Facts, values and prison policies: a commentary on Zimring and Tonry, in: D. Garland (ed.), *Mass Imprisonment: Social Causes and Consequences*, London, Sage Publications, 2001, pp. 165–170.

—— *Mobsters, Unions and Feds: The Mafia and the American Labor Movement*, New York, New York University Press, 2006.

Jacobs, J., C. Friel and R. Radick, *Gotham Unbound: How New York City was Liberated from the Grip of Organized Crime*, New York, New York University Press, 1999.

Jacobs, J., C. Panarella and J. Worthington, *Busting the Mob: United States v. Cosa Nostra*, New York, New York University Press, 1994.

Jäger, H. (ed.), *Kriminologie im Strafprozesz: zur Bedeutung psychologischer, soziologischer und kriminologischer Erkentnisse für die Strafrechtspraxis*, Frankfurt am Main, Suhrkamp Verlag, 1980.

—— *Verbrechen unter totalitärer Herrschaft: Studien zur nationalsozialistischen Gewaltkriminalität*, Frankfurt am Main, Suhrkamp, 1982.

Jäger, J., *Verfolgung durch Verwaltung: internationales Verbrechen und internationale Polizeikooperation, 1880–1933*, Konstanz, UVK Verlagsgesellschaft, 2006.

—— "Internationales Verbrechen-Internationale Polizeikooperation, 1880–1930: Konzepte und Praxis", in: D. Schauz and S. Freitag (eds.), *Verbrecher im Visier der Experten: Kriminalpolitik zwischen Wissenschaft und Praxis im 19. und frühen 20. Jahrhundert*, Stuttgart, Franz Steiner Verlag, 2007, pp. 295–320.

Janse de Jonge, J., *Om de persoon van de dader: over straftheorieën en voorlichting door de reclassering*, Arnhem, Gouda Quint, 1991.

Jansen, M. en N. Petrov, *Stalin's Loyal Executioner: People's Commissar Nikolai Ezhov, 1895–1940*, Stanford, Hoover Institution Press, 2002.

Jasperse, C., K. van Leeuwen-Burow and L. Toornvliet (eds.), *Criminology between the Rule of Law and the Outlaws*, Deventer, Kluwer, 1976.

Jefferson, T. and R. Grimshaw, *Controlling the Constable: Police Accountability in England and Wales*, London, Frederick Muller/The Cobden Trust, 1984.

Jefferson, T. and J. Shapland, "Justice pénale, criminologie et production de l'ordre: les tendances de la recherche et la politique criminelle depuis 1980 en Grande-Bretagne", *Déviance et société*, 1991, pp. 187–221.

Jeffery, C., "The historical development of criminology", *Journal of Criminal Law, Criminology and Police Science*, 1959, pp. 3–19.

—— "The historical development of criminology", in: H. Mannheim (ed.), *Pioneers in Criminology*, London, Stevens and Sons, 1960, pp. 458–498.

—— *Criminology: An Interdisciplinary Approach*, Englewood Cliffs, NJ, Prentice-Hall, 1990.

Jehle, J.-M., *Kriminologie als Lehrgebiet*, Wiesbaden, Kriminologische Zentralstelle, 1992.

Jenkins, P., "The radicals and the rehabilitative ideal, 1890–1930", *Criminology*, 1982, pp. 347–372.

Jenkins, P., "Varieties of Enlightenment criminology", *British Journal of Criminology*, 1984, pp. 112–130 (1984a).

—— "Temperance and the origins of the new penology", *Journal of Criminal Justice*, 1984, pp. 551–565 (1984b).

Jens, L., *Criminaliteit te Utrecht in verband met familie en wijk*, Utrecht, Dekker & Van de Vegt, s.a.

Jescheck, H.-H. (ed.), *Franz von Liszt zum Gedächtnis: zum 50. Wiederkehr seines Todestages am 21. Juni 1919*, Berlin, Verlag Walter de Gruyter & Co., 1969.

Jescheck, H.-H. and T. Würtenberger (eds.), *Internationales Colloquium über Kriminologie und Strafrechtsreform*, Freiburg, Hans Ferdinand Schulz Verlag, 1958.

Johnson, B., "Taking care of labor: the police in American politics", *Theory and Society*, 1976, pp. 89–117.

Johnson, E. and E. Monkkonen (eds.), *The Civilization of Crime: Violence in Town and Country since the Middle Ages*, Chicago, University of Illinois Press, 1996.

Johnston, N., "John Haviland", in: H. Mannheim (ed.), *Pioneers in Criminology*, London, Stevens and Sons, 1960, pp. 91–112.

Johnstone, G. (ed.), *A Restorative Justice Reader: Texts, Sources, Context*, Cullompton, Willan Publishing, 2003.

Jones, D., *History of Criminology: A Philosophical Perspective*, New York, Greenwood Press, 1986.

Jones, H., *Crime in a Changing Society*, Harmondsworth, Penguin Books, 1965.

Jones, S., *Criminology*, London, Butterworths, 1998.

Jones, T., B. MacLean and J. Young, *The Islington Crime Survey: Crime, Victimization and Policing in Inner-city London*, Aldershot, Gower, 1986.

Jones, T. and T. Newburn, *Policy Transfer and Criminal Justice: Exploring US Influence over British Crime Control Policy*, Maidenhead, Open University Press, 2007.

Jonker, E., M. Ros and C. de Vries (eds.), *Kriminologen en reklasseerders in Nederland*, in: *Utrechtse Historische Cahiers*, 1986, no. 1.

Jonktys, D., *De pynbank wedersproken, en bematigt*, Amsterdam, Salomon Schouten, 1736.

Joosse, K., *Arnold Aletrino: pessimist met perspectief*, Amsterdam, Thomas Rap, 1986.

Kaiser, G., "Kriminologie im Verbund gesamter Strafrechtswissenschaft am Beispiel kriminologischer Forschung am Max-Planck-Institut in Freiburg", in: T. Vogler (ed.), *Festschrift für Hans-Heinrich Jescheck zum 70. Geburtstag*, Berlin, Duncker & Humblot, 1985, pp. 1035–1059.

—— *Kriminologie: ein Lehrbuch*, Heidelberg, C.F. Müller Juristischer Verlag, 1988 (1988a).

—— "Criminology in the Federal Republic of Germany in the 1980s", in: G. Kaiser, H. Kury and H.-J. Albrecht (eds.), *Criminological Research in the 80s and Beyond: Reports from the Republic of Germany, German Democratic Republic, Austria and Switzerland*, Freiburg, Max-Planck-Institut für ausländisches und internationales Strafrecht, 1988, pp. 1–11 (1988b).

—— *Kriminologie: ein Lehrbuch*, Heidelberg, C.F. Müller Verlag, 1996.

—— *Kriminologie*, Heidelberg, C.F. Müller Verlag, 1997 (1997a).

—— "Kriminologische Forschung: Programm und Wirklichkeit: Versuch einer Bilanz nach einem Vierteljahrhundert", in: A. Eser (ed.), *Kriminologische Forschung im Ubergang*, Freiburg im Breisgau, Max-Planck-Institut für ausländisches und internationales Strafrecht, 1997, pp. 19–78 (1997b).

—— "Strafrecht und Kriminologie ohne Berührungsfurcht", *Zeitschrift für die gesamte Strafrechtswissenschaft*, 2004, pp. 855–869.

—— "'Strafrecht und Kriminologie unter einem Dach' aus der Perspektive des Kriminologen", in: U. Sieber and H.-J. Albrecht (eds.), *Strafrecht und Kriminologie unter einem Dach: Kolloquium zum 90. Geburtstag von prof. dr. dr. h.c. mult. Hans-Heinrich Jescheck*, Berlin, Duncker & Humblot, 2006, pp. 66–77.

Kaiser, G. and H.-J. Albrecht (eds.), *Crime and Criminal Policy in Europe: Proceedings of the II. European Colloquium*, Freiburg, Max-Planck-Institut für ausländisches und internationales Strafrecht, 1990.

Kaiser, G. and I. Geissler (eds.), *Crime and Criminal Justice: Criminological Research in the Second Decade at the Max Planck Institute in Freiburg*, Freiburg im Breisgau, Max-Planck-Institut für auländisches und internationales Strafrecht, 1988.

Kaiser, G., H.-J. Kerner, F. Sack and H. Schelhoss (eds.), *Kleines kriminologisches Wörterbuch*, Heidelberg, C.F. Müller Juristischer Verlag, 1985 (second completely revised and extended edition).

Kaiser, G., H. Kury and H.-J. Albrecht (eds.), *Criminological Research in the 80s and Beyond: Reports from the Republic of Germany, German Democratic Republic, Austria and Switzerland*, Freiburg, Max-Planck-Institut für ausländisches und internationales Strafrecht, 1988.

Kaiser, G., H. Schöch, H.-H. Eidt and H.-J. Kerner, *Strafvollzug: eine Einführung in die Grundlagen*, Karlsruhe, C.F. Müller Juristischer Verlag, 1974.

Kalmann, H., "Die kriminalbiologische Untersuchung der Täterpersönlichkeit und ihr Wert für die polizeilichen Vorerhebungen", *Monatsschrift für Kriminalpsychologie und Strafrechtsreform*, 1931, pp. 175–183.

Kaluszynski, M., "Alphonse Bertillon et l'anthropométrie", in: P. Vigier et al., *Maintien de l'ordre et polices en France et en Europe au XIXe siècle*, Paris, Créaphis, 1987, pp. 269–285.

—— "Das Bild des Verbrechers in Frankreich am Ende des 19. Jahrhunderts: kriminologisches Wissen und seine politische Anwending", *Kriminologisches Journal*, 1994, pp. 13–35 (1994a).

—— "Identités professionelles, identités politiques: médecins et juristes face au crime au tournant du XIXème et dus XXème siècle", in: L. Mucchielli (ed.), *Histoire de la criminologie française*, Paris, L'Harmattan, 1994, pp. 215–233.

—— "Les artisans de la loi: espaces juridico-politiques en France sous la IIIe République", *Droit et société*, 1998, pp. 535–562.

—— "The international congresses of criminal anthropology", in: P. Becker and R. Wetzell (eds.), *Criminals and their Scientists: The History of Criminology in International Perspective*, Cambridge, Cambridge University Press, 2006, pp. 301–316.

—— "Alphonse Bertillon et l'anthropologie judiciaire: l'identification au cœur de l'ordre républicain", in: P. Piazza (ed.), *Aux origines de la police scientifique: Alphonse Bertillon, précurseur de la science du crime*, Paris, Karthala, 2011, pp. 31–47.

Kaminski, D., S. Snacken and V. van Gijsegem, "Crime et justice en Belgique: état de la recherche, 1990–1997", in: L. van Outrive and P. Robert (eds.), *Crime et justice en Europe depuis 1990: état des recherches, évaluation et recommandations*, Paris, L'Harmattan, 1999, pp. 83–117.

Kappeler, V., M. Blumberg and G. Potter, *The Mythology of Crime and Criminal Justice*, Prospect Heights, Waveland Press, 1996.

Karstedt, S. and W. Greve, "Die Vernunft des Verbrechens: rational, irrational oder banal? Der 'Rational-Choice'- Ansatz in der Kriminologie", in: K.-D. Bussmann and R. Kreissl (eds.), *Kritische Kriminologie in der Diskussion: Theorien, Analysen, Positionen*, Opladen, Westdeutscher Verlag, 1996, pp. 171–210.

Kaufmann, M., *Die Psychologie des Verbrechens: eine Kritik*, Berlin, Julius Springer, 1912.

Kavieff, P., *The Purple Gang: Organized Crime in Detroit, 1910–1945*, New York, Barricade Books, 2000.

Keckeisen, W., *Die gesellschaftliche Definition abweichenden Verhaltens: Perspektiven und Grenzen des labeling approach*, Munich, Juventa Verlag, 1974.

Kefauver, The, Committee Report on Organized Crime, New York, Didier, 1951.

Kefauver, E., *Crime in America*, London, Victor Gollancz, 1952 (edited and with an introduction by S. Shalett).

Kelk, C., *Recht voor gedetineerden: een onderzoek naar de beginselen van het detentierecht*, Alphen aan den Rijn, Samsom Uitgeverij, 1978.

—— "Lieven Dupont: pleitbezorger van beginselen van behoorlijk penitentiair recht", in: F. Verbruggen, R. Verstraeten, D. van Daele and B. Spriet (eds.), *Strafrecht als roeping: liber amicorum Lieven Dupont*, Leuven, Universitaire Pers Leuven, 2005, vol. 1, pp. 435–456.

Kelk, C., M. Moerings, N. Jörg and P. Moedikdo (eds.), *Recht, macht en manipulatie*, Utrecht, Uitgeverij Het Spectrum, 1976.

Kellens, G., "Jean Constant, 1901–1986", in: C. Fijnaut (ed.), *Gestalten uit het verleden: 32 voorgangers in de strafrechtswetenschap, de strafrechtspleging en de criminologie*, Leuven, Universitaire Pers Leuven, 1993, pp. 253–259.

—— *Eléments de criminologie*, Brussels, Bruylant, 1998.

Kellens, G., A. Lemaitre and J.-P. Koopmansch (eds.), *Criminologie et société: actes du colloque du 50ᵉ anniversaire de l'Ecole Liégeoise de Criminologie Jean Constant*, Brussels, Bruylant, 1998.

Kelling, G. and C. Coles, *Fixing Broken Windows: Restoring Order & Reducing Crime in our Communities*, New York, Martin Kessler Books, 1996 (with a foreword by J. Wilson).

Kellor, F., *Experimental Sociology: Descriptive and Analytical: Delinquents*, New York, Macmillan Company, 1901.

Kelly, R., *The Upperworld and the Underworld: Case Studies of Racketeering and Business Infiltrations in the United States*, New York, Kluwer Academic/Plenum Publishers, 1999.

Kempe, G., *Criminaliteit en kerkgenootschap*, Utrecht, Dekker & Van de Vegt, 1938 (with a preface by W. Pompe).

—— *Misdaad en wangedrag voor, tijdens en na den oorlog: opstellen over criminologie*, Amsterdam, Em. Querido's Uitgeversmij, 1947.

—— "Eenige opmerkingen over de ontwikkeling van de criminologische studie en het criminologisch onderricht in Nederland", in: *Opstellen over recht, wet en samenleving op 1 october 1948 door vrienden en leerlingen aangeboden aan prof. mr. W.P.J. Pompe*, Utrecht, Dekker & Van de Vegt, 1948, pp. 74–114.

—— "50 jaar criminologie in Nederland, 1907–1957", in: Psychiatrisch-Juridisch Gezelschap (ed.), *Gedenkboek 1907–1957*, Amsterdam, F. van Rossen, 1957, pp. 65–101.

—— *Reclassering in onze samenleving: voorlichten, recht doen, helpen*, Arnhem, Van Loghum Slaterus, 1958.

—— *Inleiding tot de criminologie*, Haarlem, De Erven F. Bohn, 1967.

Kempe, G. and J. Vermaat, *Criminaliteit in Drenthe*, Utrecht, Dekker & Van de Vegt, 1939 (with a foreword by R. Baron De Vos van Steenwijk).

Kemper, J., *Crimineel wetboek voor het Koninkrijk Holland: met eene inleiding en aanmerkingen*, Amsterdam, Allart, 1809.

Kennedy, R., *The Enemy Within: The McClennan Committee's Crusade againt Jimmy Hoffa and Corrupt Labor Unions*, New York, Da Capo Press, 1994 (with a new introduction by E. Guthman).

Kenney, D. and J. Finckenauer, *Organized Crime in America*, Belmont, Wadsworth Publishing Company, 1995.

Kerner, H.-J., H. Kury and K. Sessar (eds.), *Deutsche Forschungen zur Kriminalitätsentstehung und Kriminalitätskontrolle*, Cologne, Carl Heymanns Verlag, 1983, 3 vols.

Kidd, W., *Police Interrogation*, New York City, R.V. Basuino, 1940.

Kinberg, O., *Les problèmes fondamentaux de la criminologie*, Paris, Editions Cujas, 1957 (translated from Swedish).

Kinsey, R., J. Lea and J. Young, *Losing the Fight against Crime*, Oxford, Basil Blackwell, 1986.

Kizny, T., *La Grande Terreur en URSS, 1937–1938*, Paris, Noir sur Blanc, 2013.

Kist, B., "Pro Juventute", in: C. De Jong, P. Baan, J. van Bemmelen et al. (eds.), *Straffen en helpen: opstellen over berechting en reclassering aan geboden aan mr. Dr. N. Muller*, Amsterdam, Wereldbibliotheek, 1954, pp. 165–175.

Klaassen, K., *Misdaad en pers*, Utrecht, Dekker & Van de Vegt, 1939 (with a foreword by N. Muller).

Klare, H. (ed.), *Changing Concepts of Crime and its Treatment*, Oxford, Pergamon Press, 1966.

Klein, M., *The American Street Gang: Its Nature, Prevalence and Control*, New York, Oxford University Press, 1997.

Klockars, C., *The Professional Fence: Thirty Years of 'Wheelin' and Dealin'' in Stolen Goods*, New York, Free Press, 1974.

—— "The contemporary crises of Marxist criminology", *Criminology*, 1979, pp. 477–515.

Kloek, J., *Dialoog met de criminele psychopaat*, Utrecht, Aula-Boeken, 1968.

Knepper, P., *The Invention of International Crime: A Global Issue in the Making, 1881–1914*, New York, Palgrave Macmillan, 2010.

Knibbeler, J., "Verslag van een studiedag", *Algemeen Politieblad*, 1962, pp. 139–141.

Kocka, J. (ed.), *Interdisziplinarität: Praxis, Herausforderung, Ideologie*, Frankfurt am Main, Suhrkamp, 1987.

Koettig, P., "Fünf Jahre Daktyloskopie in Sachsen", *Archiv für Kriminal-Anthropologie und Kriminalistik*, 1908, pp. 155–162.

Kohl, A., "Adolphe Braas, 1889–1979", in: C. Fijnaut (ed.), *Gestalten uit het verleden: 32 voorgangers in de strafrechtswetenschap, de strafrechtspleging en de criminologie*, Leuven, Universitaire Pers Leuven, 1993, pp. 249–252.

Konty, M., "Microanomie: the cognitive foundations of the relationship between anomie and deviance", *Criminology*, 2005, pp. 107–131.

Kooijmans, T. and R. Letschert (eds.), *Vijfentwintig jaar strafrechtswetenschap en victimologie in Tilburg: vijf toppublicaties van Marc Groenhuijsen*, Deventer, Kluwer, 2012.

Kowalsky, S., "Who's responsible for female crime? Gender, deviance, and the development of soviet social norms in revolutionary Russia", *Russian Review*, 2003, pp. 366–386.

Kreissl, R., "Was ist kritisch an der kritischen Kriminologie", in: K.-D. Bussmann and R. Kreissl (eds.), *Kritische Kriminologie in der Diskussion: Theorien, Analysen, Positionen*, Opladen, Westdeutscher Verlag, 1996, pp. 19–44.

Kretschmer, E., *Körperbau und Character: Untersuchungen zum Konstitutionsproblem und zur Lehre von den Temperamenten*, Berlin, Springer, 1948.

Kreutziger, B., "Argumente für und wider die Todesstrafe(n): ein Beitrag zur Beccaria-Rezeption im deutschsprachigen Raum des 18. Jahrhunderts", in: G. Deimling (ed.), *Cesare Beccaria: die Anfänge moderner Strafrechtspflege in Europa*, Heidelberg, Kriminalistik Verlag, 1989, pp. 99–126.

Kuhn, T., *The Structure of Scientific Revolutions*, Chicago, University of Chicago Press, 1970.

Kunz, K.-L., *Kriminologie*, Bern, Haupt Verlag, 2004.

—— "Historische Grundlagen der Kriminologie in Deutschalnd und ihre Entwicklung zu einer selbstständigen wissenschaftlichen Disziplin", *Monatsschrift für Kriminologie und Strafrechtsreform*, 2013, pp. 81–114.

Kurella, H., *Naturgeschichte des Verbrechers: Grundzüge der criminellen Anthropologie und Criminalpsychologie*, Stuttgart, Ferdinand Enke, 1893.

—— *Cesare Lombroso als Mensch und Forscher*, Wiesbaden, J.F. Bergmann, 1910.

—— *Anthropologie und Strafrecht*, Würzburg, Curt Kabitzsch, 1912.

Küther, C., *Räuber und Gauner in Deutschland*, Göttingen, Vandenhoeck & Ruprecht, 1987.

Kyle, D. and R. Koslowski (eds.), *Global Human Smuggling: Comparative Perspectives*, Baltimore, John Hopkins University Press, 2001.

Labadie, J.-M., "Corps et crime: de Lavater (1775) à Lombroso", in: C. Debuyst, F. Digneffe, J.-M. Labadie and A. Pires (eds.), *Histoire des savoirs sur le crime et la peine: des savoirs diffus à la notion de criminel-né*, Brussels, De Boeck Université, 1995, pp. 295–345.

Lacassagne, A., "Marche de la criminalité en France de 1825 à 1880: du criminel devant la science contemporaine", *Revue scientifique*, 1881, pp. 674–684.

—— "Bibliografie", *Archives d'anthropologie criminelle, de criminologie et de psychologie normale et pathologique*, 1907, pp. 200–202.

—— "Cesare Lombroso, 1836–1909", *Archives d'anthropologie criminelle, de médicine légale et de psychologie normale et pathologique*, 1909, pp. 881–894.

—— "Des transformations du droit penal et les progrès de la medicine légale de 1810 à 1912", *Archives d'anthropologie criminelle, de criminologie et de psychologie normale et psychologque*, 1913, pp. 321–364.

—— "Alphonse Bertillon: l'homme, le savant, la pensée philosophique", Archives d'anthropologie criminelle, de médecine légale et de psychologie *normale et pathologique*, 1914, pp. 161–186.

Lacassagne, A and E. Martin, "Rapport", *Archives d'anthropologie criminelle, de criminologie et de psychologie normale et pathologique*, 1901, pp. 539–541.

Lacombe, D., "Les liaisons dangereuses: Foucault et la criminologie", *Criminologie*, 1993, pp. 51–72.

Lagrange, H., *La civilité à l'épreuve: crime et sentiment d'insécurité*, Paris, Presses Universitaires de France, 1995.

Lamers, E., *Het Nederlandse gevangeniswezen in de jaren 1945 tot en met 1953*, The Hague, Staatsdrukkerij- en Uitgeverijbedrijf, 1954 (1954a).

—— "Berechting: strafrechtspraak in de branding", in: C. De Jong, P. Baan, J. van Bemmelen et al. (eds.), *Straffen en helpen: opstellen over berechting en reclassering aan geboden aan mr. Dr. N. Muller*, Amsterdam, Wereldbibliotheek, 1954, pp. 145–164 (1954b).

Lamnek, S. and K. Köteles, "Profil und Entwicklung einer Fachzeitschrift: die Monatsschrift für Kriminologie und Strafrechtsreform", *Monatsschrift für Kriminologie und Strafrechtsreform*, 2004, pp. 192–221.

Landecker, W., "Criminology in Germany", *Journal of Criminal Law and Criminology*, 1941, pp. 551–575.

Landesco, J., "Organized crime in Chicago", in: Illinois Association for Criminal Justice (ed.), *The Illinois Crime Survey*, Montclair, Patterson Smith, 1968, pp. 815–1090.

Lane, R., *Policing the City: Boston, 1882–1885*, Boston, Harvard University Press, 1963.

—— "Urban police and crime in nineteenth-century America", in: M. Tonry and N. Morris (eds.), *Modern Policing*, Chicago, University of Chicago Press, 1992, pp. 1–50.

Lange, J., *Verbrechen als Schicksal: Studien an kriminellen Zwillingen*, Leipzig, Georg Tieme Verlag, 1929.

—— *Crime as Destiny: A Study of Criminal Twins*, London, Georg Allen & Unwin, 1931.

Lange, R., "Wandlungen in den kriminologischen Grundlagen der Strafrechtsreform", in: E. von Caemmerer, E. Friesenhahn and R. Lange (eds.), *Hundert Jahre Deutsches Rechtsleben: Festschrift zum hundertjährigen Bestehen des Deutschen Juristentages, 1860–1960*, Karlsruhe, Verlag C.F. Müller, 1960, pp. 345–381.

—— "Die Entwicklung der Kriminologie im Spiegel der Zeitschrift für die gesamte Strafrechtswissenschaft", *Zeitschrift für die gesamte Strafrechtswissenschaft*, 1981, pp. 151–197.

Lanteri-Laura, G., "Phrénologie et criminologie au début du XIXe siècle: les idées de F.J. Gall", in: L. Mucchielli (ed.), *Histoire de la criminologie française*, Paris, L'Harmattan, 1994, pp. 21–28.

Larguier, J., *Criminologie et science pénitentiaire*, Paris, Dalloz, 1985.

Larnaude, F. and J.-A. Roux (eds.), *Premier congrès de police judiciaire internationale, Monaco (avril 1914)*, Paris, H. Godde, 1926.

Larrieu, L., *Histoire de la maréchaussée et de la gendarmerie: des origines à la Quatrième République*, Villiers-sur-Marne, Phénix Editions, 2002.

Larson, J., "Present police and legal methods for the determination of the innocence or guilt of the suspect", *Journal of Criminal Law and Criminology*, 1925, pp. 219–271.

—— "Psychology in criminal investigation", in: T. Sellin (ed.), *The Police and the Crime Problem*, in: The Annals of the American Academy of Political and Social Science, Philadelphia, 1929, pp. 258–268.

Lasonder, L., *De beroepsmisdadigers en hunne strafrechtelijke behandeling*, Doetinchem, Nederl. Drukkers- en Uitgevers-Maatschappij "C. Misset", 1908.

Laub, J., "The life course of criminology in the United States: the American Society of Criminology 2003 presidential address, *Criminology*, 2004, pp. 1–26.

—— "Edwin H. Sutherland and the Michael-Adler report: searching for the soul of criminology seventy years later", *Criminology*, 2006, pp. 235–257.

Laub, J. and R. Sampson, "Unraveling families and delinquency: a reanalysis of the Gluecks' data", *Criminology*, 1988, pp. 355–380.

Laurent, E., *Les habitués des prisons de Paris: étude d'anthropologie et sociologie criminelles*, Paris, G. Masson, 1890.

—— *Le criminel aux points de vue anthropologique, psychologique et social*, Paris, Vigot Frères, 1908.

Lauzel, J.-P., *L'enfant voleur*, Paris, Presses Universitaires de France, 1974.

Lavater, J., *Physiognomische Fragmente*, Oldenburg, Heimeran, 1949 (selected and with a commentary by F. Märker).

Lawrence, P., "History, criminology and the 'uses' of the past", *Theoretical Criminology*, 2012, pp. 313–328.

Lazarsfeld, P., W. Sewell and H. Wilensky (eds.), *The Uses of Sociology*, New York, Basic Books, 1967.

Lea, J. and J. Young, *What is To Be Done about Law and Order? Crisis in the Eighties*, Harmondsworth, Penguin Books, 1984.

Léauté, J. (ed.), *Une nouvelle école de science criminelle: l'école d'Utrecht*, Paris, Editions Cujas, 1959.

—— *Les prisons*, Paris, Presses Universitaires de France, 1968.

Lebrun, J., "Cloîtrer et guérir: la colonie pénitentiaire de la Trappe, 1854–1880", in: M. Perrot (ed.), *L'impossible prison: recherches sur le système pénitentiaire au XIXe siècle*, Paris, Editions du Seuil, 1980, pp. 236–276.

Lechat, R., *De techniek van het crimineel onderzoek*, St-Lambrechts-Woluwe, Uitgeverij Moderna, 1950-1951, 3 vols.

Ledig, G., *Kriminologie*, Berlin, Walter de Gruyter, 1947.

Lefaucheur, N., "Psychiatrie infantile et délinquance juvénile", in: L. Mucchielli (ed.), *Histoire de la criminologie française*, Paris, L'Harmattan, 1994, pp. 313–332.

Leferenz, H., "Rückkehr zur gesamten Strafrechtswissenschaft?", *Zeitschrift für die gesamte Strafrechtswissenschaft*, 1981, pp. 200–221.

Leggett, G., *The Cheka: Lenin's Political Police*, Oxford, Clarendon Press, 1981.

Lehmann, P., "Die Kriminal-Polizei im Dienste der Strafrechtspflege", *Archiv für Kriminal-Anthropologie und Kriminalistik*, 1901, pp. 302–311.

Lehr, D. and G. O'Neill, *Black Mass: The Irish Mob, the FBI, and a Devil's Deal*, New York, Publicaffairs, 2000.

Leistner, G., "Erich Wulffen: ein Dresdner Jurist, Kriminologe und Schöngeist, 1862–1936", *Archiv für Polizeigeschichte*, 1999, pp. 2–13.

Lejins, P., "Thorsten Sellin: a life dedicated to criminology", *Criminology*, 1987, pp. 975–988.

Lekschas, J., H. Harrland, R. Hartmann and G. Lehmann, *Kriminologie: theoretische Grundlagen und Analysen*, Berlin, Staatsverlag der Deutschen Demokratischen Republik, 1983.

Le Maire, J., *La police de Paris en 1770*, in: Mémoires de la Société de l'histoire de Paris et de l'Ile-de-France, 1879.

Lemert, E., *Human Deviance, Social Problems & Social Control*, Englewood Cliffs, Prentice-Hall, 1967.

Le Nabour, E., *La Reynie: le policier de Louis XIV*, Paris, Perrin, 1991.

Lenders, P., *Vilain XIIII*, Leuven, Davidsfonds, 1995.

Lensen, L. and W. Heitling, *Tussen schandpaal en schavot: boeven, booswichten, martelaren en hun rechters*, Zutphen, Uitgeverij Terra, 1986.

Lenz, A., *Die Zwangserziehung in England (The Reformatory and Industrial Schools): eine kriminalpolitische Studie*, Stuttgart, Verlag von Ferdinand Enke, 1894.

—— *Die anglo-amerikanische Reformbewegung im Strafrecht: eine Darstellung ihres Einflusses auf die kontinentale Rechtsentwicklung*, Stuttgart, Verlag von Ferdinand Enke, 1908.

—— *Grundriss der Kriminalbiologie: Werden und Wesen der Persönlichkeit des Täters nach Untersuchungen an Sträflingen*, Vienna, Julius Springer, 1927.

Leonards, C., *De ontdekking van het onschuldige criminele kind: bestraffing en opvoeding van criminele kinderen in jeugdgevangenis en opvoedingsgesticht, 1833–1886*, Hilversum, Verloren, 1995.

Levi, M., *The Phantom Capitalists: The Organization and Control of Long-firm Fraud*, London, Heinemann, 1981.

Levin, Y. and A. Lindesmith, "English ecology and criminology of the past century", *Journal of Criminal Law, Criminology and Police Science*, 1937, pp. 801–816.

Levy, J., *Het indeterminisme (de psychische causaliteit)*, Leiden, Boekhandel en Drukkerij voorheen E.J. Brill, 1901.

Lévy, R., *Du suspect au coupable: le travail de police judiciaire*, Geneva, Meridiens Klincksieck, 1987.

Lévy-Bruhl, H., *Aspects sociologiques du droit*, Paris, Librairie Marcel Rivière et Cie, 1955.

Lewis, B., *The Offender and his Relations to Law and Society*, New York, Harper & Brothers Publishers, 1917.

Lewy, G., *The Nazi Persecution of the Gypsies*, New York, Oxford University Press, 2000.

Ley, J., *Les fondements medico-psychologiques et sociaux d'une réforme de la politique criminelle*, Montpellier, Masson et Cie, 1961.

Liang, O., "The biology of morality: criminal biology in Bavaria, 1924–1933", in: P. Becker and R. Wetzell (eds.), *Criminals and their Scientists: The History of Criminology in International Perspective*, Cambridge, Cambridge University Press, 2006, pp. 425–446.

Liebl, K. (ed.), *Kriminologie im 21. Jahrhundert*, Wiesbaden, Verlag für Sozialwissenschaften, 2007.

Lignian, F., "De anthropometrische signalementen volgens Alphonse Bertillon", *Nederlands Tijdschrift voor Geneeskunde*, 1894, pp. 987–996.

Lilly, J., F. Cullen and R. Ball, *Criminological Theory: Context and Consequences*, Thousand Oaks, Sage Publications, 1995.

Lindeboom, F., *De ontwikkeling van het strafstelsel in Sovjet-Rusland, 1917–1937*, Rotterdam, Libertas Drukkerijen, 1937.

Lindenau, H., "Kriminal-Polizei und Kriminologie", *Zeitschrift für die gesamte Strafrechtswissenschaft*, 1902, pp. 287–303.

—— "Das internationale Verbrechertum und seine Bekämpfung", *Mitteilungen der Internationalen Kriminalistischen Vereinigung*, 1906, pp. 192–205.

Lindenau, H. and G. Hopff, "Die Bekämpfung des internationalen Verbrechertums", *Mitteilungen der Internationalen Kriminalistischen Vereinigung*, 1906, pp. 370–423.

Lindesmith, A. and Y. Levin, "The Lombrosian myth in criminology", *American Journal of Sociology*, 1937, pp. 653–671.

Linebaugh, P., "Karl Marx, the theft of wood, and working-class composition", in: D. Greenberg (ed.), *Crime and Capitalism: Readings in Marxist Criminology*, Philadelphia, Temple University Press, 1993, pp. 100–121.

Lissenberg, E., S. van Ruller and R. van Swaaningen (eds.), *Tegen de regels IV: een inleiding in de criminologie*, Nijmegen, Ars Aequi Libri, 2001.

Litjens, H., *Onmaatschappelijke gezinnen: sociologisch onderzoek naar de onmaatschappelijkheid in Maastricht*, Assen, Van Gorcum & Comp., 1953.

—— *De criminaliteit in Limburg: een historisch overzicht*, Maastricht, Uitgevers-Mij. Drukkerij "Ernest van Aelst", 1973.

Livingston, E., *Introductory Report to the Code of Discipline: explanatory of the principles on which the code is founded, being part of the system of penal law prepared for the State of Louisiana*, Philadelphia, Lea and Carey, 1827.

Loader, I. and R. Sparks, "Contemporary landscapes of crime, order and control: governance, risk and globalization", in: M. Maguire, R. Morgan and R. Reiner (eds.), *The Oxford Handbook of Criminology*, Oxford, Oxford University Press, 2007, pp. 78–101.

—— (eds.), *Public Criminology*, London, Routledge, 2011.

Locard, E., "L'anthropométrie judiciaire à Paris en 1889", *Archives de l'anthropologie criminelle et des sciences pénales*, 1890, pp. 473–498.

—— "L'identification par les empreintes digitales", *Archives d'anthropologie criminelle, de criminologie et de psychologie normale et pathologique*, 1903, pp. 578–592.

—— "Les services actuels d'identification et la fiche internationale", in: *Archives d'anthropologie criminelle, de criminologie et de psychologie normale et pathologique*, 1906, pp. 145–206.

—— "La découverte des criminels par l'unique moyen des empreintes digitales", *Archives d'anthropologie criminelle, de médecine légale et de psychologie normale et pathologique*, 1912, pp. 834–839 (1912a).

—— "Polizeilaboratorien", *Archiv für Kriminalanthropologie und Kriminalistik*, 1912, pp. 204–217 (1912b).

—— "La preuve judiciaire par les empreintes digitales", *Archives d'anthropologie criminelle, de médecine légale et de psychologie normale et pathologique*, 1914, pp. 321–348.

—— *La police: ce qu'elle est: ce qu'elle devrait être*, Paris, Payot, 1919.

—— *Policiers de roman et de laboratoire*, Paris, Payot, 1924.

—— *L'enquête criminelle et les méthodes scientifiques*, Paris, Flammarion, 1933.

—— *La criminalistique à l'usage des gens du monde et des auteurs de romans policiers*, Lyon, Desvigne, 1937.

—— *Manuel de police technique*, Paris, Payot, 1948.

—— *Le portrait parlé*, Lyon, Desvigne, 1949.

Locke, J., *An Essay concerning Human Understanding*, London, Fontana/Collins, 1973 (abridged and edited with an introduction by A.D. Woozley).

Lofti, G., *KZ der Gestapo: Arbeitserziehungslager im Dritten Reich*, Frankfurt am Main, Fischer Taschenbuch Verlag, 2003 (with a preface by H. Mommsen).

Lombardi, G., *Sociologia criminale*, Naples, Casa Editrice Dott. Eugenio Jovene, 1944.

Lombardo, R., *The Black Hand: Terror by Letter in Chicago*, Urbana, University of Illinois Press, 2010.

Lombroso, C., *L'anthropologie criminelle et ses récents progrès*, Paris, Félix Alcan, 1891.

—— *Neue Fortschritte in den Verbrecherstudien*, Leipzig, W. Friedrich, 1894.

—— *L'homme criminel: étude anthropologique et psychiatrique*, Paris, Félix Alcan, 1895, 2 vols. (1895a).

—— *L'homme criminel: atlas*, Paris, Félix Alcan, 1895 (1895b).

—— *Kerker-Palimpseste: Wandinschriften und Selbstbekenntnisse gefangener Verbrecher: in den Zellen und Geheimschriften der Verbrecher gesammelt und erlautert*, Hamburg, Verlagsanstalt und Druckerei A.G., 1899 (edited in contact with H. Kurella).

—— *Die Ursachen und Bekämpfung des Verbrechens*, Berlin, Hugo Bermühler Verlag, 1902 (authorised translation by H. Kurella and E. Jentsch).

—— *Les palimpsestes des prisons*, Paris, A. Maloine, 1905.

—— *Neue Verbrecherstudien*, Halle, Carl Marhold, 1907 (authorised translation by E. Jentsch).

—— *L'homme de génie*, Paris, Félix Alcan, 1909.

—— *Criminal Man*, Durham, Duke University Press, 2006 (translated and with a new introduction by M. Gibson and N. Rafter).

—— *Boeven-litteratuur*, Amsterdam, C. Daniëls, s.a. (revised for the Netherlands by A. R. Steenstra and with a foreword by Cesare Lombroso).

—— *Genie und Irrsinn in ihren Beziehungen zum Gesetz, zur Kritik und zur Geschichte*, Leipzig, Verlag von Philipp Reclam jun., s.a. (translated by A. Lourth).

Lombroso, C. and G. Ferrero, *La femme criminelle et la prostituée*, Paris, Félix Alcan, 1896.

—— *Criminal Woman, the Prostitute and the Normal Woman*, Durham, Duke University Press, 2004 (translated and with a new introduction by N. Rafter and M. Gibson).

Lombroso, C. and R. Laschi, *Der politische Verbrecher und die Revolutionen anthropologischer, juristischer und staatswissenschaftlicher Beziehung*, Hamburg, Verlagsanstalt und Druckerei A.G., 1891.

—— *Le crime politique et les révolutions par rapport au droit, à l'anthropologie criminelle et à la science du gouvernement*, Paris, Félix Alcan, 1892, 2 vols.

Lombroso-Ferrero, G., *Cesare Lombroso: storia della vita e delle opere narrata dalla figlia*, Turin, Fratelli Bocca Editori, 1915.

Loosjes, G., *Bijdrage tot de studie van de criminaliteit der vrouw*, Haarlem, De Erven Loosjes, 1894.

Lorulot, A., *Crime et société: essai de criminologie sociale*, Paris, Stock, 1923.

Löschper, G., G. Manke and F. Sack (eds.), *Kriminologie als selbständiges, interdisziplinäres Hochschulstudium*, Pfaffenweiler, Centaurus-Verlagsgesellschaft, 1986.

Löschper, G. and T. von Trotha, "Statt einer Einleitung: ein Interview mit Fritz Sack", in: T. von Trotha (ed.), *Politischer Wandel, Gesellschaft und Kriminalitätsdiskurse: Beiträge zur interdisziplinären wissenschaftlichen Kriminologie: Festschrift für Fritz Sack zum 65. Geburtstag*, Baden-Baden, Nomos Verlagsgesellschaft, 1996, pp. 1–32.

Lösel, F., *Kriminalpsychologie: Grundlagen und Anwendungsbereiche*, Weinheim-Basel, Beltz Verlag, 1983.

Loubet del Bayle, J.-L. (ed.), *Police et société*, Toulouse, Académie de Toulouse, 1988.

Louwage, F., *Technique de quelques vols & escroqueries*, Ninove, Imprimerie Anneessens, 1932.

—— *Cours de police technique et de tactique de police criminelle*, Ninove, Imprimerie Anneessens, 1939.

—— *Psychologie et criminalité*, Ninove, Imprimerie Anneessens, 1945.

—— *Techniek en tactiek bij de crimineele politie*, Ninove, Drukkerij Anneessens, s.a.

Lowenthal, M., *The Federal Bureau of Investigation*, New York, William Sloane Associates, 1950.

Lowman, J. and B. MacLean (eds.), *Realist Criminology: Crime Control and Policing in the 1990s*, Toronto, University of Toronto Press, 1992.

Luc, J.-N. (ed.), *Gendarmerie, état et société au XIXe siècle*, Paris, Publications de la Sorbonne, 2002.

Lucchini, L., *I semplicisti (anthropologi, psicologi et sociologi) del diritto penale: saggio critico*, Turin, Unione Tipografico-Editrice, 1886.

—— *Le droit pénal et les nouvelles théories*, Paris, F. Pichon, 1892.

Luchterhandt, M., *Der Weg nach Birkenau: Entstehung und Verlauf der nationalsozialistischen Verfolgung der 'Zigeuner'*, Lübeck, Verlag Schmidt-Römhildt, 2000.

Lüderssen, K., *Kriminologie: Einführung in die Probleme*, Baden-Baden, Nomos Verlagsgesellschaft, 1984.

Lüderssen, K. and F. Sack (eds.), *Seminar abweichendes Verhalten*, Frankfurt am Main, Suhrkamp Verlag, 1975, 2 vols.

—— *Vom Nutzen und Nachteil der Sozialwissenschaften für das Strafrecht*, Frankfurt am Main, Suhrkamp Verlag, 1980, 2 vols.

Lüdtke, A., *Gemeinwohl, Polizei und Festungspraxis*, Göttingen, Vandenhoeck & Ruprecht, 1982.

—— (ed.), *'Sicherheit' und 'Wohlfahrt': Polizei, Gesellschaft und Wissenschaft im 19. und 20. Jahrhundert*, Frankfurt, Suhrkamp, 1992.

Lunden, W., *A Systematic Outline of Criminology with Selected Bibliography*, Pittsburgh, University of Pittsburgh, 1935.

—— "Emile Durkheim, 1858–1917", in: H. Mannheim (ed.), *Pioneers in Criminology*, London, Stevens and Sons, 1960, pp. 385–399.

Lynch, D., *Criminals and Politicians*, New York, Macmillan Company, 1932.

Lynch, M. (ed.), *Radical Criminology*, Aldershot, Dartmouth, 1997.

Lynch, M. and P. Stretesky (eds.), *Radical and Marxist Theories of Crime*, Surrey, Ashgate, 2011.

Maas, P., *The Valachi Papers*, New York, G.P. Putnam's Sons, 1968.

Macé, G., *Le service de la sûreté*, Paris, Bibliothèque-Charpentier, 1891.

MacDonald, A., *Criminology*, New York, Funk & Wagnalls Company, 1892 (with an introduction by C. Lombroso).

—— "Kriminalpolizei und Anthropologie", *Archiv für Kriminalanthropologie und Kriminalistik*, 1921, pp. 172–174.

MacDougall, E. (ed.), *Crime for Profit: A Symposium on Mercenary Crime*, Boston, Stratford Company, 1933.

Mackay, J., *Alan Pinkerton: the first private eye*, New York, John Wiley & Sons, 1997.

MacNamara, D., "August Vollmer: the vision of police professionalism", in: P. Stead (ed.), *Pioneers in Policing*, Maidenhead, McGraw-Hill Book Company, 1977, pp. 178–190.

Madelin, L., *Fouché, 1759–1820*, Paris, Librairie Plon, 1945, 2 vols.

—— *Fouché: Macht und Ehrgeiz*, Munich, Wilhelm Heyne Verlag, 1978.

Maguire, M., R. Morgan and R. Reiner (eds.), *The Oxford Handbook of Criminology*, Oxford, Clarendon Press, 1994.

—— *The Oxford Handbook of Criminology*, Oxford, Oxford University Press, 2002.

—— *The Oxford Handbook of Criminology*, Oxford, Oxford University Press, 2007.

—— *The Oxford Handbook of Criminology*, Oxford, Oxford University Press, 2012.

Maguire, M. and J. Pointing (eds.), *Victims of Crime: A New Deal*, Milton Keynes, Open University Press, 1988.

Maguire, M., J. Vagg and R. Morgan (eds.), *Accountability and Prisons: Opening up a Closed World*, London, Tavistock Publications, 1985.

Mannheim, H., *Criminal Justice and Social Reconstruction*, London, Kegan Paul, Trench, Trubner & Co., 1946.

—— *Group Problems in Crime and Punishment and Other Studies in Criminology and Criminal Law*, London, Routledge & Kegan Paul, 1955.

—— (ed.), *Pioneers in Criminology*, London, Stevens and Sons, 1960.

—— *Comparative criminology: a text book*, London, Routledge & Kegan Paul, 1966, 2 vols.

Manning, P., *Police Work: The Social Organization of Policing*, Cambridge, MIT Press, 1979.

Manouk, V., "Vers un retour aux fondements théoriques de la criminalité en col blanc", *Revue internationale de criminologie et de police technique et scientifique*, 2011, pp. 3–21.

Maple, J. and C. Mitchell, *The Crime Fighter: How You Can Make Your Community Crime-free*, New York, Broadway Books, 2000.

Marabuto, P., *La collaboration policière internationale en vue de la prévention et de la répression de la criminalité*, Nice, Ecole Professionnelle Don Bosco, 1935.

Maris, J. (ed.), *Tussen roeping en beroep: honderd jaar reclassering Leger des Heils in Nederland*, Arnhem, Gouda Quint, 1991.

Marquiset, J., *Le crime*, Paris, Presses Universitaires de France, 1964.

Martin, B. *Crime and Criminal Justice under the Third Republic: The Shame of Marianne*, Baton Rouge, Louisiana State University Press, 1990.

Martin, J., "The development of criminology in Britain", in: P. Rock (ed.), *A History of British Criminology*, Oxford, Clarendon Press, 1988, pp. 165–174.

Martin, R., R. Mutchnick and W. Austin, *Criminological Thought: Pioneers Past and Present*, New York, Macmillan Publishing Company, 1990.

Maruna, S. and A. Matravers, "N=1: criminology and the person", *Theoretical Criminology*, 2007, pp. 427–442.

Mary, P., "De la cellule à l'atelier: Prins et la naissance du traitement des détenus en Belgique", in: P. Van der Vorst and P. Mary (eds.), *Cent ans de criminologie à l'ULB: Adolphe Prins, l'Union Internationale de Droit Pénal, le Cercle Universitaire pour les Etudes Criminologiques*, Brussels, Bruylant, 1990, pp. 161–184.

—— *Délinquant, délinquance et insécurité: un demi-siècle de traitement en Belgique, 1944–1997*, Brussels, Bruylant, 1999.

Marx, G., *Undercover: Police Surveillance in America*, Berkeley, University of California Press, 1988.

Marx, K. and F. Engels, "Manifest der Kommunistischen Partei (1848)", in: I. Fetscher (ed.), *Marx-Engels Studienausgabe*, Frankfurt am Main, Fischer Bücherei, 1966, vol. 3, pp. 59–86.

Masten, V., *The Crime Problem: What to Do about It: How to Do It*, Elmira, Star-Gazette Co., 1909.

Matthews, R. and J. Young (eds.), *Issues in Realist Criminology*, London, Sage Publications, 1992.

Matthijs, J., *Openbaar ministerie*, Ghent, Story-Scientia, 1983.

Mathiesen, T., *The Defences of the Weak: A Sociological Study of a Norwegian Correctional Institution*, London, Tavistock Publications, 1972.

Mathyer, J., *Rodolphe A. Reiss: Pionnier de la Criminalistique*, Nadir, Editions Payot Lausanne, 2000.

Matsueda, R., "The current state of differential association theory", *Crime & Delinquency*, 1988, pp. 277–306.

—— "Differential social organization, collectieve action and crime", *Crime, Law and Social Change*, 2006, pp. 3–33.

Matza, D., *Delinquency and Drift*, New York, John Wiley and Sons, 1967.

—— *Becoming Deviant*, Englewood Cliffs, Prentice-Hall, 1969.

Maudsley, H., *Le crime et la folie*, Paris, Germer Baillière, 1874.

—— *The Pathology of Mind: A Study of its Distempers, Deformities and Disorders*, London, MacMillan and Co., 1895.

Mauer, M., "The causes and consequences of prison growth in the United States", in: D. Garland (ed.), *Mass Imprisonment: Social Causes and Consequences*, London, Sage Publications, 2001, pp. 4–14.

Mayet, L., *Notes sur les sciences anthropologiques et plus particulièrement l'anthropologie criminelle en Hollande et en Belgique: première partie: Hollande*, Lyon, A. Storck & Co., 1902.

—— *Notes sur les sciences anthropologiques et plus particulièrement l'anthropologie criminelle en Hollande et en Belgique: deuxième partie: Belgique*, Lyon, A. Storck & Co., 1903.

Mayo, K., *Justice to All: The Story of the Pennsylvania State Police*, Boston, Houghton Mifflin Campany, 1920 (with an introduction by T. Roosevelt, with a new introduction by W. Sproul).

Mays, J., *Crime and the Social Structure*, London, Faber and Faber, 1963.

Mazower, M. (ed.), *The Policing of Politics in the Twentieth Century: Historical Perspectives*, Oxford, Berghahn Books, 1997.

McArdle, A. and T. Erzen (eds.), *Zero Tolerance: Quality of Life and the New Police Brutality in New York City*, New York, New York University Press, 2001 (with a foreword by P. Chevigny).

McCarthy, B., "The attitudes and actions of others: tutelage and Sutherland's theory of differential association", *British Journal of Criminology*, 1996, pp. 135–147.

McGowen, R., "The body and punishment in eighteenth-century England", *Journal of Modern History*, 1987, pp. 651–679.

McIllwain, J., *Organizing Crime in Chinatown: Race and Racketeering in New York City, 1890-1910*, Jefferson, McFarland & Company, 2004.

McKim, W., "Selecting the fittest and eliminating the unfit, 1900", in: N. Rafter (ed.), *The Origins of Criminology: A Reader*, London, Routledge, 2009, pp. 260–265.

Mead, G., "The psychology of punitive justice", *American Journal of Sociology*, 1918, pp. 577–602.

Mechler, A., *Studien zur Geschichte der Kriminalsoziologie*, Göttingen, Otto Schwartz, 1970.

Mednick, S. and S. Shoham (eds.), *New Paths in Criminology: Interdisciplinary and Intercultural Explorations*, Lexington, Lexington Books, 1979.

Meershoek, G., *De geschiedenis van de Nederlandse politie: de gemeentepolitie in een veranderende samenleving*, Amsterdam, Boom, 2007.

Meier, B.-D., *Kriminologie*, Munich, Verlag C.H. Beck, 2007.

Meier, R., "The new criminology: continuity in criminological theory", *Journal of Criminal Law and Criminology*, 1977, pp. 461–469.

Melchers, A., *Kriminalstatistik im 19. Jahrhundert: ein Beitrag zur Geschichte der Kriminalsoziologie und ihrer Methodik*, Frankfurt am Main, Johann Wolfgang Goethe-Universität, 1992.

Melchior, J., *De bokkerijders: feiten en verhalen*, Maasbree, Uitgeverij de Lijster, 1981.

Melossi, D., "Thorsten Sellin, 1896-1994", in: K. Hayward, S. Maruna and J. Mooney (eds.), *Fifty Key Thinkers in Criminology*, London, Routledge, 2010, pp. 76–81.

Melossi, D. and M. Pavarini, *The Prison and the Factory: Origins of the Penitentiary System*, London, Macmillan Press, 1981.

Mercier, C., *Crime and Criminals: Being the Jurisprudence of Crime: Medical, Biological and Psychological*, London, University of London Press, 1918 (with an introduction by B. Donkin).

—— *Crime and Criminals Being the Jurisprudence of Crime: Medical, Biological and Psychological*, New York, Henry Holt and Company, 1919 (with an introduction by B. Donkin).

Mergen, A., *Die Wissenschaft vom Verbrechen: eine Einführung in die Kriminologie*, Hamburg, Verlag für kriminalistische Fachliteratur, 1961.

—— *Die Kriminologie: eine systematische Darstellung*, Berlin, Verlag Franz Vahlen, 1967.

Merle, R. (ed.), *Les mondes du crime: introduction à la compréhension du fait criminel*, Paris, Privat, 1968.

Merriam, C., "The police, crime and politics", in: T. Sellin (ed.), *The Police and the Crime Problem*, in: The Annals of the American Academy of Political and Social Science, Philadelphia, 1929, pp. 115–120.

Merton, R., "Social structure and anomie", *American Sociological Review*, 1938, pp. 672–682.

—— "Anomie, anomia and social interaction: contexts of deviant behavior", in: M. Clinard (ed.), *Anomie and Deviant Behavior: A Discussion and Critique*, New York, Free Press of Glencoe, 1964, pp. 213–242.

—— "Social structure and anomie", in: J. Jacoby (ed.), *Classics of Criminology*, Prospects Heights, Waveland Press, 1994, pp. 178–187.

—— "On the evolving synthesis of differential association and anomie theory: a perspective from the sociology of science", *Criminology*, 1997, pp. 517–525.

—— "Opportunity structure: the emergence, diffusion and differentiation of a sociological concept, 1930s–1950s", in: F. Adler and W. Laufer (eds.), *The Legacy of Anomie Theory*, New Brunswick, Transaction Publishers, 2000, pp. 3–80.

Messner, S. and R. Rosenfeld, *Crime and the American Dream*, Belmont, Wadsworth Publishing Company, 1997.

Meijer-Wichmann, C., *Misdaad, straf en maatschappij*, Utrecht, Erven J. Bijleveld, 1930.

—— *Vrouw en maatschappij*, Utrecht, Erven J. Bijleveld, 1936 (with an introduction by H. Roland-Holst-Van der Schalk).

Mezger, E., *Kriminalpolitik auf kriminologischer Grundlage*, Stuttgart, Ferdinand Enke Verlag, 1934.

—— *Kriminologie: ein Studienbuch*, Munich, C.H. Beck'sche Verlagsbuchhandlung, 1951.

Mezger, E., H.-H. Jescheck and R. Lange (eds.), *Deutsche Beiträge zum VII. Internationalen Strafrechtskongresz in Athen von 26. September bis 2. Oktober 1957*, Berlin, Walter de Gruyter, 1957.

Michael, J. and M. Adler, *Crime, Law and Social Science*, Montclair, Patterson Smith, 1971 (reprinted 1933, with a new introduction by G. Geis).

Middendorff, W., "Hans von Hentig: ein deutscher Kriminologe von Weltformat", *Kriminalistik*, 1976, pp. 129–132.

Miller, W., "Lower class culture as a generating milieu of gang delinquency", *Journal of Social Issues*, 1958, pp. 5–19.

Milspauch, A., *Crime Control by the Government*, Washington, The Brookings Institution, 1937.

Milton, S., "'Gypsies' as social outsiders in Nazi Germany", in: R. Gellately and N. Stoltzfus (eds.), *Social Outsiders in Nazi Germany*, Princeton, Princeton University Press, 2001, pp. 212–232.

Ministère de la Justice, *Réglement général des prisons*, Brussels, Imprimerie du Moniteur Belge, 1905.

—— *Notice sur l'organisation des établissements penitentiaires*, Leuven, Imprimerie Pierre Mafrans, 1929.

Mittermaier, W., *Gefängniskunde: ein Lehrbuch für Studium und Praxis*, Berlin, Verlag Franz Vahlen, 1954.

Modderman, A., *Straf-geen kwaad*, Amsterdam, Frederik Muller, 1864.

—— *De eenheid der wetenschap en het recht van het ideaal*, Leiden, E.J. Brill, 1879.

Moerings, M. and H. van de Bunt, "Etiketten plakken", in: C. Kelk, M. Moerings, N. Jörg and P. Moedikdo (eds.), *Recht, macht en manipulatie*, Utrecht, Uitgeverij Het Spectrum, 1976, pp. 155–188.

Moley, R., *State Crime Commissions: What They Are: How They Should Be Organized: What They Should Do*, New York, The National Crime Commission, 1926.

Monachesi, E., "Trends in criminological research in Italy", *American Sociological Review*, 1936, pp. 396–406.

Monballyu, J., "Het onderscheid tussen de civiele en de criminele en de ordinaire en de extraordinaire strafrechtspleging in het Vlaamse recht van de 16e eeuw", in: H. Diederiks and H. Roodenburg (eds.), *Misdaad, zoen en straf*, Hilversum, Verloren, 1991, pp. 120–132.

Monjardet, D., A. Chauvenet, D. Chave and F. Orlic, *La police quotidienne: éléments de sociologie du travail policier*, Paris, Université Paris VII, 1984.

Mönkemöller, O., *Psychologie und Psychopathologie der Aussage*, Heidelberg, Carl Winters Universitätsbuchhandlung, 1930.

Monkkonen, E., *Police in Urban America, 1860-1920*, Cambridge, Cambridge University Press, 1981.

—— "History of urban police", in: M. Tonry and N. Morris (eds.), *Modern Policing*, Chicago, University of Chicago Press, 1992, pp. 547–580.

Montefiore, S., *Stalin: The Court of the Red Tsar*, London, Phoenix, 2004.

Montesquieu, *Over de geest van de wetten*, Amsterdam, Boom, 2006 (translated and with an afterword by J. Holierhoek).

Moore, W., *The Kefauver Committee and the Politics of Crime, 1950-1952*, Columbia, University of Missouri Press, 1974.

Moran, R., "Biomedical research and the politics of crime control: a historical perspective", *Contemporary Crises*, 1978, pp. 335–357.

More, T., *Utopia*, Harmondsworth, Penguin Books, 1965.

Morel, B., *Traité des dégénérescenses physiques, intellectuelles et morales de l'espèce humaine et des causes qui produisent ces variétés maladives*, Paris, Masson, 1857.

Morellet, A., *Mémoires de l'abbé Morellet sur le dix-huitième siècle et sur la révolution*, Paris, Mercure de France, 1988.

Morris, A., *Criminology*, New York, Longmans, Green and Co., 1934.

—— *Women, Crime and Criminal Justice*, Oxford, Basil Blackwell, 1987.

Morris, N., *The Habitual Criminal*, London, Longmans, Green and Co., 1950.

—— *Maconochie's Gentlemen: The Story of Norfolk Island and the Roots of Modern Prison Reform*, Oxford, Oxford University Press, 2002.

Morris, N. and M. Tonry, *Between Prison and Probation: Intermediate Punishments in a Rational Sentencing System*, New York, Oxford University Press, 1991.

Morris, T., *The Criminal Area: A Study in Social Ecology*, London, Routledge & Kegan Paul, 1957 (with a foreword by H. Mannheim).

—— "British criminology, 1935-1948", in: P. Rock (ed.), *A History of British Criminology*, Oxford, Clarendon Press, 1988, pp. 150–164.

Morris, T. and P. Morris, *Pentonville: A Sociological Study of an English Prison*, London, Routledge & Kegan Paul, 1963.

Morrison, W., *Crime and its Causes*, London, Swan Sonnenschein & Co., 1891.

Morton, J., *The First Detective: The Life and Revolutionary Times of Eugène-François Vidocq, Criminal Spy and Private Eye*, London, Ebury Press, 2004.

Motifs […] du Code d'Instruction Criminelle et Exposé des Motifs du Code des Délits et des Peines présentés au corps législatif, s.l., s.n., s.d.

Mucchielli, L. (ed.), *Histoire de la criminologie française*, Paris, L'Harmattan, 1994 (1994a).

—— "Naissance de la criminologie", in: L. Mucchielli (ed.), *Histoire de la criminologie française*, Paris, L'Harmattan, 1994, pp. 7–18 (1994b).

—— "Naissance et déclin de la sociologie criminelle, 1880–1940", in: L. Mucchielli (ed.), *Histoire de la criminologie française*, Paris, L'Harmattan, 1994, pp. 287–312 (1994c).

—— "Le sens du crime: histoire des (r)apports de la psychoanalyse à la criminologie", in: L. Mucchielli (ed.), *Histoire de la criminologie française*, Paris, L'Harmattan, 1994, pp. 351–410 (1994d).

—— "L'impossible constitution d'une discipline criminologique en France: cadres institutionels, enjeux normatifs et développements de la recherche des années 1880 à nos jours", *Criminologie*, 2004, pp. 13–42.

—— "Criminology, hygienism and eugenics in France, 1870–1914: the medical debates on the elimination of 'incorrigible' criminals", in: P. Becker and R. Wetzell (eds.), *Criminals and their Scientists: The History of Criminology in International Perspective*, Cambridge, Cambridge University Press, 2006, pp. 207–229.

—— "Le CESDIP a 40 ans!", *Questions Pénales*, 2009, pp. 1–3.

Mueller, G., *Crime, Law and the Scholars*, Seattle, University of Washington Press, 1969.

Muir, W., *Police: Streetcorner Politicians*, Chicago, University of Chicago Press, 1977.

Mulder, G., "P.J.A. Feuerbach en het crimineel wetboek voor het Koninkrijk Holland", in: *Uit het recht: rechtsgeleerde opstellen aangeboden aan mr. P.J. Verdam*, Deventer, Kluwer, 1971, pp. 175–185.

Mulder, R., *Misdaad en macht: criminaliteit, strafrecht en criminologie in de DDR*, Amsterdam, Panholzer, 1980.

Müller, C., *Das Gewohnheitsverbrechergesetz vom 24. November 1933: Kriminalpolitik als Rassenpolitik*, Baden-Baden, Nomos Verlagsgesellschaft, 1997.

Muller, E., J. van der Leun, L. Moerings and P. van Calster (eds.), *Criminaliteit: criminaliteit en criminaliteitsbestrijding in Nederland*, Deventer, Kluwer, 2010.

Muller, N., "Nieuw strafrecht in nieuw Duitsland", *Maandblad voor Berechting en Reclassering*, 1933, pp. 253–272.

Müller-Hill, B., *Tödliche Wissenschaft: die Aussonderung von Juden, Zigeunern und Geisteskranken, 1933–1945*, Reinbek bei Hamburg, Rowohlt, 1984.

Mullins, C., *Crime and Psychology*, London, Methuen & Co., 1949 (fifth revised edition, with an introduction by E. Glover).

Muncie, J., E. McLaughlin and M. Langan (eds.), *Criminological Perspectives: A Reader*, London, Sage Publications, 1996.

Münsterberg, H., *On the Witness Stand*, New York, Clark Boardman Co., 1949.

Murchison, C., *Criminal Intelligence*, Worcester, Clark University, 1926.

Murphy, D. and M. Robinson, "The Maximizer: clarifying Merton's theories of anomie and strain", *Theoretical Criminology*, 2008, pp. 501–521.

Muyart de Vouglans P-F., *Réfutation des principes hasardés dans le traité des délits et peines*, Lousanne, Desaint, 1767 (translated from Italian).

Naffine, N., *Feminism and Criminology*, Philadelphia, Temple University Press, 1996.

Nagel, W., *De criminaliteit van Oss*, The Hague, D.A. Daamen's Uitgeversmaatschappij, 1949.

—— "De Utrechtse School", *Tijdschrift voor Strafrecht*, 1963, pp. 322–355.

—— *Het voorspellen van krimineel gedrag*, The Hague, Staatsuitgeverij, 1965.

—— "De Groningse School", *Nederlands Tijdschrift voor Criminologie*, 1966, pp. 81–93, 122–134.

—— "Beccaria en Calkoen", *Nederlands Tijdschrift voor Strafrecht*, 1968, pp. 67–84.

—— *Het werkschuwe tuig*, Alphen aan den Rijn, Uitgeverij Samsom, 1977 (1977a).

—— *Het betrekkelijke van kriminaliteit*, Alphen aan den Rijn, Uitgeverij Samsom, 1977 (1977b).

Napoli, P., *Naissance de la police moderne: pouvoir, normes, société*, Paris, Editions La Découverte, 2003.

Naucke, W., "Die Kriminalpolitik des Marburger Programms 1882", *Zeitschrift für die gesamte Strafrechtswissenschaft*, 1982, pp. 525–564.

—— "Die Modernisierung des Strafrechts durch Beccaria", in: G. Deimling (ed.), *Cesare Beccaria: die Anfänge moderner Strafrechtspflege in Europa*, Heidelberg, Kriminalistik Verlag, 1989, pp. 37–54.

Négrier-Dormont, L., *Criminologie*, Paris, Editions Litec, 1992.

Nehlsen, H. and G. Brun (eds.), *Münchener Rechtshistorische Studien zum Nationalsozialismus*, Frankfurt am Main, Peter Lang, 1996.

Nelken, D. (ed.), *The Futures of Criminology*, London, Sage Publications, 1994.

Nelli, H., *The Business of Crime: Italians and Syndicate Crime in the United States*, New York, Oxford University Press, 1976.

Népote, J., "Interpol: the development of international policing", in: P. Stead (ed.), *Pioneers in Policing*, Maidenhead, McGraw-Hill Book Company, 1977, pp. 280–296.

Newburn, T., *Criminology*, London, Routledge, 2013.

Newman, G. and Marongiu, P., "Penological reform and the myth of Beccaria", *Criminology*, 1990, pp. 325–346.

Newman, O., *Defensible Space: Crime Prevention through Urban Design*, New York, Macmillan Company, 1972.

Neys, A., "Ernest Bertrand, 1868–1949", in: C. Fijnaut (ed.), *Gestalten uit het verleden: 32 voorgangers in de strafrechtswetenschap, de strafrechtspleging en de criminologie*, Leuven, Universitaire Pers Leuven, 1993, pp. 163–177.

Neys, A. and T. Peters, "De geschiedenis van het gevangeniswezen", in: A. Neys, T. Peters, F. Pieters and J. Vanacker (eds.), *Tralies in de weg*, Leuven, Universitaire Pers Leuven, 1994, pp. 1–50.

Neys, A., T. Peters, F. Pieters and J. Vanacker (eds.), *Tralies in de weg*, Leuven, Universitaire Pers Leuven, 1994.

Niceforo, A., *La police et l'enquête judiciaire scientifique*, Paris, Librairie Universelle, 1907.

—— *Die Kriminalpolizei und ihre Hilfswissenschaften*, Grosz-Lichterfelde-Ost, P. Langenscheidt, s.a. (with an introduction and extended by H. Lindenau).

—— "L'enseignement de la police judiciaire scientifique dans les universités italiennes", *Mitteilungen der Internationalen Kriminalistischen Vereinigung*, 1914, pp. 559–574.

—— "Communication sur les instituts spéciaux de criminologie dans les universités italiennes et dans les facultés de Rome, de Turin et de Bologne", in: P. Larnaude and J.-A. Roux (eds.), *Premier congrès de police judiciaire internationale, Monaco (avril 1914)*, Paris, H. Godde, 1926, pp. 225–240.

Niederhoffer, A., *Behind the Shield: The Police in Urban Society*, Garden City, Anchor Books, 1969.

Nolte, W., *Psychologie für Polizeibeamte*, Berlin, Bali-Verlag Berger & Co., 1928.

Nonet, P. and P. Selznick, *Law and Society in Transition: Toward Responsive Law*, New York, Harper Colophon Books, 1978.

Nordstrom, C., *Global Outlaws: Crime, Money and Power in the Contemporary World*, Berkeley, University of California Press, 2007.

Norwood East, W., *Medical Aspects of Crime*, London, J. & A. Churchill, 1936 (with foreword by J. Simon).

Notice sur l'organisation des prisons en Belgique, Brussels, Imprimerie du Moniteur Belge, 1910.

Nijdam, A., *Goirle: een sociografische studie over de criminaliteit en de moraliteit van een grensgemeente rond de Tweede Wereldoorlog*, Wageningen, H. Veenman & Zonen, 1950.

Oberhummer, H., *Die Wiener Polizei: 200 Jahre Sicherheit in Österreich*, Vienna, Gerold, 1937–1938.

Oberman, G., *Verwaarloosde en misdadige jeugd: haar godsdienstig leven en geestelijke verzorging*, Groningen, J.B. Wolters' Uitgevers-Maatschappij, 1922.

Oei, T. and M. Groenhijsen (eds.), *Forensische psychiatrie anno 2000: actuele ontwikkelingen in breed perspectief*, Deventer, Gouda Quint, 2000.

—— (eds.), *Actuele ontwikkelingen in de forensische psychiatrie*, Deventer, Kluwer, 2003.

Office de la Protection de l'Enfance, *Les établissements affectés aux enfants de justice en Angleterre*, Brussels, M. Weissenbruch, 1920.

Olson, H., "Crime and heredity", in: *Research Studies of Crime as Related to Heredity*, Chicago, Municipal Court, 1925.

Ontwerp-lijfstraffelijk, Het, wetboek 1801 en 1804, Zutphen, De Walburg Pers, 1982, 2 vols. (edited by W. Frouws and H. van der Woude).

Opp, K.-D., *Abweichendes Verhalten und Gesellschaftsstruktur*, Darmstadt, Hermann Luchterhand, 1974.

Opstellen over recht, wet en samenleving op 1 october 1948 door vrienden en leerlingen aangeboden aan prof. mr. W.P.J. Pompe, Utrecht, Dekker & Van de Vegt, 1948.

Ordres de service de la prison centrale de Louvain, Leuven, Imprimerie, 1928.

Ortmann, R., *Abweichendes Verhalten und Anomie*, Freiburg im Breisgau, Max-Planck-Institut für ausländisches und internationales Strafrecht, 2000.

Ortner, H., A. Pilgram and H. Steinert (eds.), *New Yorker 'zero-tolerance'-Politik*, Baden-Baden, Nomos Verlagsgesellschaft, 1998.

Oster, D., *Montesquieu: oeuvres complètes*, Paris, Editions du Seuil, 1964.

Ottenhof, R. (ed.), *L'individualisation de la peine: de Saleilles à aujourd'hui*, Ramonville Saint-Agne, Editions Erès, 2001.

Ottolenghi, S., "Das wissenschaftliche Polizeiwesen in Italien", *Archiv für Kriminal-Anthropologie und Kriminalistik*, 1903, pp. 75–82.

—— "L'enseignement de la police scientifique et les fonctions du signalement et des investigations judiciaires dans l'administration de la Sûreté en Italie", in: P. Larnaude and J.-A. Roux (eds.), *Premier congrès de police judiciaire internationale, Monaco (avril 1914)*, Paris, H. Godde, 1926, pp. 240–243.

Overholser, W., "Isaac Ray", in: H. Mannheim (ed.), *Pioneers in Criminology*, London, Stevens and Sons, 1960, pp. 113–128.

Overwater, J., *De reclassering van strafrechtelijk meerderjarigen in Nederland*, Almelo, W. Hilarius Wzn, 1919.

Owen, R., *Book of the New Moral World Containing the Rational System of Society*, Glasgow, H. Robinson and Co., 1840.

Packer, H., *The Limits of the Criminal Sanction*, Stanford, Stanford University Press, 1968.

Pannenborg, W., *Bijdrage tot de psychologie van den misdadiger, in 't bijzonder van den brandstichter*, Groningen, M. de Waal, 1912.

Paoli, L., V. Greenfield and P. Reuter, *The World Heroin Market: Can Supply be Cut?*, New York, Oxford University Press, 2009.

Paoli, L. (ed.), *Handbook on Organised Crime*, Oxford, Oxford University Press, 2013.

Papke, D., *Framing the Criminal: Crime, Cultural Work and the Loss of Critical Perspective, 1830–1900*, Hamden, Archon Books, 1987.

Paramelle, F., *Histoire des idées en criminologie au XIXe et au XXe siècle: Gabriel Tarde*, Paris, L'Harmattan, 2005 (with a preface by J.-H. Robert).

Parent, C., *Féminismes et criminologie*, Brussels, De Boeck Université, 1998.

Parenti, C., *Lockdown America: Police and Prisons in the Age of Crisis*, London, Verso, 1999.

Parmelee, M., *The Principles of Anthropology and Sociology in their Relations to Criminal Procedure*, New York, Macmillan Company, 1908.

—— *Criminology*, New York, Macmillan Company, 1923.

Parmentier, S., L. Walgrave, I. Aertsen, J. Maesschalck and L. Paoli (eds.), *The Sparking Discipline of Criminology*, Leuven, Leuven University Press, 2011.

Parsons, P., *Crime and the Criminal: An Introduction to Criminology*, New York, Alfred A. Knopf, 1926.

Pasta, R., "Dei delitti e delle pene et sa fortune en Italie: les milieux juridiques et la lecture des 'philosophes'", in: M. Porret (ed.), *Beccaria et la culture juridique des lumières*, Geneva, Librairie Droz, 1997, pp. 119–149.

Patijn, J., *De voorwaardelijke invrijheidstelling*, The Hague, Martinus Nijhoff, 1938.

Paul, F., "Die Kollektivausstellung der Polizeibehörden auf der Städteausstellung in Dresden", *Archiv für Kriminal-Anthropologie und Kriminalistik*, 1903, pp. 316–348.

Pearce, F., *Crimes of the Powerful: Marxism, Crime and Deviance*, London, Pluto Press, 1976.

—— *The Radical Durkheim*, London, Unwin Hyman, 1989.

Pearce, F. and L. Snider (eds.), *Corporate Crime: Contemporary Debates*, Toronto, University of Toronto Press, 1995.

Perrot, M. (ed.), *L'impossible prison: recherches sur le système pénitentiaire au XIXe siècle*, Paris, Editions du Seuil, 1980 (1980a).

—— "Révolution et prisons", in: Perrot, M. (ed.), *L'impossible prison: recherches sur le système pénitentiaire au XIXe siècle*, Paris, Editions du Seuil, 1980, pp. 277–312 (1980b).

Persell, S., "Jean de Lanessan and the French positivist school of criminal reform, 1880–1914", *Criminal Justice Review*, 1987, pp. 1–6.

Peters, T., "Willem Adriaan Bonger, 1876–1940: bio-bliografische nota", *Politica*, 1966, pp. 265–279.

—— (ed.), *Criminografie: (ver)tekenen met cijfers?*, Leuven, Acco, 1974.

—— *Ongelijke levensvoorwaarden in de Centrale Gevangenis te Leuven*, Leuven, Acco, 1976 (1976a).

—— "De waardering van Bonger in zijn eigen tijd en nadien", *Nederlands Tijdschrift voor Criminologie*, 1976, pp. 209–216 (1976b).

—— "Edouard Ducpétiaux, 1804–1868", in: C. Fijnaut (ed.), *Gestalten uit het verleden: 32 voorgangers in de strafrechtswetenschap, de strafrechtspleging en de criminologie*, Leuven, Universitaire Pers Leuven, 1993, pp. 33–48.

Peters, T. and J. Goethals (eds.), *De achterkant van de criminaliteit*, Leuven, Universitaire Pers Leuven, 1993.

Petersen, M., *Gedetineerden onder dak: geschiedenis van het gevangeniswezen in Nederland van 1795 af, bezien vanuit zijn behuizing*, Alkmaar, Gevangenis Schutterswei, 1978.

Pfennig, I., "Kriminalbiologie im Nationalsozialismus – das Beispiel Franz Exner", in: H. Nehlsen and G. Brun (eds.), *Münchener Rechtshistorische Studien zum Nationalsozialismus*, Frankfurt am Main, Peter Lang, 1996, pp. 225–255.

Philips, D. and R. Storch, *Policing Provincial England, 1829–1856: The Politics of Reform*, London, Leicester University Press, 1999.

Piazza, P., "Alphonse Bertillon face à la dactyloscopie: nouvelle technologie policière d'identification et trajectoire bureaucratique", *Les cahiers de la sécurité*, 2005, pp. 251–270.

—— (ed.), *Aux origines de la police scientifique: Alphonse Bertillon, précurseur de la science du crime*, Paris, Karthala, 2011 (2011a).

—— "Alphonse Bertillon et les empreintes digitales", in: P. Piazza (ed.), *Aux origines de la police scientifique: Alphonse Bertillon, précurseur de la science du crime*, Paris, Karthala, 2011, pp. 120–143 (2011b).

Piepers, M., *Over samenwerking van juristen en psychiaters*, The Hague, s.n., 1907.

Pinatel, J., "Criminology and penal reform in France", *British Journal of Delinquency*, 1952, pp. 196–207.

—— *La criminologie*, Paris, Spes, 1960.

—— *Etienne de Greeff, 1898–1961*, Paris, Editions Cujas, 1967.

—— *Histoire des sciences de l'homme et de la criminologie*, Paris, L'Harmattan, 2001 (with a preface by R. Cario and J. Castaignède).

Pires, A., "La criminologie d'hier et d'aujourdhui", in: C. Debuyst, F. Digneffe, J.-M. Labadie and A. Pires (eds.), *Histoire des savoirs sur le crime et la peine: des savoirs diffus à la notion de criminel-né*, Brussels, De Boeck Université, 1995, pp. 13–68.

Pisciotta, A., "Scientific reform: the 'new penology' at Elmira, 1876–1900", *Crime & Delinquency*, 1983, pp. 613–630.

—— *Benevolent Repression: Social Control and the American Reformatory-prison Movement*, New York, New York University Press, 1994.

Pit, K., "Clara Wichmann: een kleine biografie", in: Buro Studium Generale, *Clara Wichmann herdenkingsprogramma, september–oktober 1985*, Utrecht, Rijksuniversiteit Utrecht, 1985, pp. 6–55.

Plack, A., *Plädoyer für die Abschaffung des Strafrechts*, Munich, List Verlag, 1974.

Platt, T., "Prospects for a radical criminology in the United States", *Crime and Social Justice*, 1974, pp. 2–10.

Platt, T. and P. Takagi, "Intellectuals for law and order: a critique of the new 'realists'", *Crime and Social Justice*, 1977, pp. 1–16.

—— "Biosocial criminology: a critique", *Crime and Social Justice*, 1979, pp. 5–13.

—— (eds.), *Punishment and Penal Discipline: Essays on the Prison and the Prisoners' Movement*, San Francisco, Crime and Social Justice Associates, 1982.

Pointing, J. (ed.), *Alternatives to Custody*, Oxford, Basil Blackwell, 1986.

Pollak, O., "Crime causation: selected bibliography of studies in the United States, 1939–1949", in: *Actes du IIe congrès international de criminologie (Paris-Sorbonne, September 1950)*, Paris, Presses Universitaires de France, 1952–55, vol. 4, pp. 131–168.

—— "Criminological research bulletin: survey of current research", in: *Actes du IIe congrès international de criminologie (Paris-Sorbonne, September 1950)*, Paris, Presses Universitaires de France, 1952–55, vol. 4, pp. 169–192.

Pollitz, P., *Die Psychologie des Verbrechers*, Leipzig, Verlag von B. Teubner, 1909.

Pols, M., *Strafrecht en strafrechtspraktijk voor de Fransche Revolutie*, The Hague, Martinus Nijhoff, 1889.

—— "De nieuwe richtingen in het strafrecht", in: *Jaarboek der Rijks-Universiteit te Utrecht, 1894–1895*, Utrecht, J. van Druten, 1894, pp. 1–38.

Polsky, N., *Hustlers, Beats and Others*, Harmondsworth, Penguin Books, 1971.

Pompe, W., *Beveiligingsmaatregelen naast straffen*, Utrecht, Dekker en Van de Vegt, 1921.

—— *De persoon des daders in het strafrecht: rede uitgesproken bij de aanvaarding van het hoogleraarsambt aan de Rijks-Universiteit te Utrecht op 28 oktober 1928*, Utrecht, Dekker & Van de Vegt, 1928.

—— "Het wetenschappelijk levenswerk van prof. dr. D. Simons", *Weekblad van het Recht*, 1931, nos. 12244–46.

—— "Voorwaardelijke invrijheidstelling", in: C. de Jong, P. Baan, J. van Bemmelen et al. (eds.), *Straffen en helpen: opstellen over berechting en reclassering aan geboden aan mr. Dr. N. Muller*, Amsterdam, Wereldbibliotheek, 1954, pp. 92–98.

—— *Geschiedenis der Nederlandsche strafrechtswetenschap sinds de codificatie-beweging*, Amsterdam, Noord-Hollandsche Uitgevers Mij, 1956.

Porret, M. (ed.), *Beccaria et la culture juridique des lumières*, Geneva, Librairie Droz, 1997.

Porter, B., *The Origins of the Vigilant State: The London Metropolitan Police Special Branch before the First World War*, London, Weidenfeld and Nicolson, 1987.

Pospielovsky, D., *Russian Police Trade Unionism: Experiment or Provocation?*, London, Weidenfield and Nicolson, 1971.

Pouligny, B., S. Chesterman and A. Schnabel (eds.), *After Mass Crime: Rebuilding States and Communities*, Tokyo, United Nations University Press, 2007.

Précis analytique et raisonné du système du docteur Gall sur les facultés de l'homme et les fonctions du cerveau, vulgairement cranoscopie, Paris, Rouen Frères, 1829.

Presdee, M., *Cultural Criminology and the Carnival of Crime*, London, Routledge, 2000.

Prichard, J., *Treatise on Moral Insanity and Other Disorders Affecting the Mind*, Philadelphia, E.L. Carey & A. Hart, 1837.

Prins, A., *La philosophie du droit et l'école historique*, Brussels, Librairie C. Muquardt, 1882.

—— *La démocratie et le régime populaire*, Brussels, Librairie C. Muquardt, 1884.

—— *Criminalité et répression: essai de science pénale*, Brussels, Librairie Européenne C. Muquardt, 1886.

—— *L'organisation de la liberté et le devoir social*, Brussels, Librairie Européenne C. Muquardt, 1895.

—— *Causerie sur les doctrines nouvelles du droit pénal*, Brussels, Bruylant-Christophe & Cie, 1896.

—— *Science pénale et droit positif*, Brussels, Bruylant-Christophe & Cie, 1899.

—— *De l'esprit du gouvernement démocratique: essai de science politique*, Brussels, Mish & Thron, 1905.

—— "Dégénérescense et criminalité", *Revue de droit pénal et de criminologie*, 1909, pp. 97–120.

—— *La démocratie après la guerre*, Brussels, Ferd. Larcier, 1918.

—— *La défense sociale et les transformations du droit pénal*, Geneva, Editions Médecine et Hygiène, 1986 (with an introduction by F. Tulkens).

Prins, A. and H. Pergameni, *Réforme de l'instruction préparatoire en Belgique*, Brussels, Claassens, 1871.

Proal, L., *Le crime et la peine*, Paris, Félix Alcan, 1892.

—— *Le crime et le suicide passionels*, Paris, Félix Alcan, 1900.

Proceedings of the First National Conference on Criminal Law and Criminology, Chicago, Illinois, June 7 and 8, 1909, Chicago, Northwestern University, 1910.

Proceedings of the Attorney General's Conference on Crime, held December 10–13, 1934, in Memorial Continental Hall, Washington, s.n., 1934.

Psychiatrisch-Juridisch Gezelschap (ed.), *Gedenkboek 1907–1957*, Amsterdam, F. van Rossen, 1957.

Quanten, D., *De School voor Criminologie en Criminalistiek als onderdeel van justitie- en politiebeleid in de jaren twintig*, Leuven, Katholieke Universiteit Leuven, School voor Criminologie, 1979.

Quennel, P. (ed.), *Mayhew's London*, London, Bracken Books, 1987.

Quensel, S., "Krise der Kriminologie: Chancen für eine interdisziplinäre Renaissance", *Kriminalsoziologische Bibliografie*, 1989, pp. 1–31.

Quetelet, A., *Recherches sur le penchant au crime aux differens âges*, Brussels, Hayez, 1831.

—— *Sur l'homme et le développement de ses facultés ou essai de physique sociale*, Paris, Bachelier, 1835.

—— *Du système social et des lois qui le régissent*, Paris, Guillaumin et Cie, 1848.

—— *Physique sociale ou essai sur le développement des facultés de l'homme*, Brussels, C. Muquardt, 1869.

—— *Anthropométrie ou mesure des différentes facultés de l'homme*, Brussels, C. Muquardt, 1871.

Quinche, N. (ed.), *Crime, science et identité: anthologie des textes fondateurs de la criminalistique européenne, 1860–1930*, Geneva, Editions Slatkine, 2006.

—— *Sur les traces du crime: de la naissance du regard indicial à l'institutionnalisation de la police scientifique et technique en Suisse et en France: l'essor de l'Institut de Police Scientifique de l'Université de Lausanne*, Geneva, Editions Slatkine, 2011.

Quinney, R. (ed.), *Crime and Justice in Society*, Boston, Little, Brown and company, 1969.

—— *The Social Reality of Crime*, Boston, Little, Brown and Company, 1970.

—— *Critique of the Legal Order: Crime Control in Capitalist Society*, Boston, Little, Brown and Company, 1973.

—— "The production of criminology", *Criminology*, 1979, pp. 445–457.

Quintus, J., *De cellulaire gevangenisstraf in Nederland, sinds hare invoering bij de wet van 28 juni 1851*, Groningen, Noordhoff, 1887.

Racine, A., *La délinquance des enfants dans les classes aisées*, Brussels, Librairie Falk, 1939.

Radzinowicz, L., *Ideology and Crime: A Study of Crime in its Social and Historical Context*, London, Heinemann, 1966.

—— *The Cambridge Institute of Criminology: Its Background and Scope*, London, Her Majesty's Stationary Office, 1988 (1988a).

—— "Herman Mannheim, 1889–1974", in: P. Rock (ed.), *A History of British Criminology*, Oxford, Clarendon Press, 1988, pp. 148–149 (1988b).

—— *The Roots of the International Association of Criminal Law and their Significance: A Tribute and a Re-assessment on the Centenary of the IKV*, Freiburg im Breisgau, Max-Planck-Institut für ausländisches und internationales Strafrecht, 1991.

Radzinowicz, L. and R. Hood, *A History of English Criminal Law and its Administration*, London, Stevens & Sons/Sweet & Maxwell, 1948–1986, 5 vols.

—— *The Emergence of Penal Policy in Victorian and Edwardian England*, Oxford, Clarendon Press, 1990.

Radzinowicz, L. and J. King, *The Growth of Crime: The International Experience*, New York, Basic Books, 1977.

Rafter, N., "Criminal anthropology in the United States", *Criminology*, 1992, pp. 525–545.

—— *Creating Born Criminals*, Urbana, University of Illinois Press, 1997.

—— "The unrepentant horse-slasher: moral insanity and the origins of criminological thought", *Criminology*, 2004, pp. 979–1008 (2004a).

—— "Ernest Hooton and the biological tradition in American criminology", *Criminology*, 2004, pp. 735–771 (2004b).

—— "The murderous Dutch fiddler: criminology, history and the problem of phrenology", *Theoretical Criminology*, 2005, pp. 65–96.

—— "Criminal anthropology: its reception in the United States and the nature of its appeal", in: P. Becker and R. Wetzell (eds.), *Criminals and their Scientists: The History of Criminology in International Perspective*, Cambridge, Cambridge University Press, 2006, pp. 159–181.

—— (ed.), *The Origins of Criminology: A Reader*, London, Routledge, 2009.

—— "Silence and memory in criminology – the American Society of Criminology 2009 Sutherland address", *Criminology*, 2010, pp. 339–355.

Rapport des commissaires du gouvernement près la prison de Pentonville pour l'année 1846, Brussels, Imprimerie du Moniteur Belge, 1848.

Rapport sur les établissements pénitentiaires de la Hollande, la Belgique et la Suisse, s.l., s.n., 1872.

Rapport onmaatschappelijke gezinnen, The Hague, Staatsdrukkerij- en Uitgeverijbedrijf, 1951.

Rapport van de staatscommissie, ingesteld bij Koninklijk Besluit van 31 juli 1902.

Rapport van de staatscommissie tot reorganisatie van het hoger onderwijs, ingesteld bij Koninklijk Besluit van 11 april 1946.

Rawlings, P., *Policing: A Short History*, Cullompton, Willan Publishing, 2002.

Rawlinson, P., "Capitalists, criminals and oligarchs: Sutherland and the new 'robber barons'", *Crime, Law and Social Change*, 2002, pp. 293–307.

Rebbein, K., "Zur Funktion von Strafrecht und Kriminologie im nationalsozialistischen Rechtssystem", *Monatsschrift für Kriminologie und Strafrechtsreform*, 1987, pp. 193–210.

Reckless, W., *The Crime Problem*, New York, Appleton-Century-Crofts, 1950.

Rédaction, La, "Avant-propos", *Archives de l'anthropologie criminelle et des sciences pénales*, 1886.

Redo, S., *Blue Criminology: The Power of United Nations Ideas to Counter Crime Globally: A Monographic Study*, Helsinki, European Institute for Crime Prevention and Control, 2012.

Reed, G. and P. Yeager, "Organizational offending and neoclassical criminology: challenging the reach of a general theory of crime", *Criminology*, 1996, pp. 357–382.

Regener, S., "Criminological museums and the visualisation of evil", *Crime, History and Societies*, 2003, pp. 43–56.

Reichskriminalpolizeiamt, *Organisation und Meldedienst der Reichskriminalpolizei*, Berlin, Kriminal-Wissenschaft und Praxis Verlag Elise Jaedicke, 1939.

Reifner, U. and B.-R. Sonnen (eds.), *Strafjustiz und Polizei im Dritten Reich*, Frankfurt am Main, Campus Verlag, 1984.

Reik, T., *Geständniszwang und Strafbedürfnis: Probleme der Psychoanalyse und der Kriminologie*, Leipzig, Internationaler Psychoanalytischer Verlag, 1925.

——— *Der unbekannte Mörder: psychoanalytischen Studien*, Hamburg, Hoffman und Campe Verlag, 1978.

Reiner, R., *The Politics of the Police*, Brighton, Harvester Press, 1985.

Reinke, H., "Une 'bonne' statistique pour la lutte contre la criminalité?: Observations sur les origines de la statistique criminelle en Allemagne au XIXe et au début du XXe siecle", *Déviance et société*, 1998, pp. 113–125.

Reiss, Jr, A., *The Police and the Public*, New Haven, Yale University Press, 1971.

——— "Crime control and the quality of life", *American Behavioral Scientist*, 1983, pp. 43–58.

——— "Why are communities important in understanding crime?", in: A. Reiss, Jr and M. Tonry (eds.), *Communities and Crime*, Chicago, University of Chicago Press, 1987, pp. 1–34.

Reiss Jr, A., and M. Tonry (eds.), *Communities and Crime*, Chicago, University of Chicago Press, 1987.

Reiss, R., "Un code télégrafique du portrait parlé", *Archives d'anthropologie criminelle, de criminologie et de psychologie normale et pathologique*, 1907, pp. 74–94.

——— "Die wissenschaftlichen Methoden bei der gerichtlichen und polizeilichen Untersuchungen", *Zeitschrift für die gesamte Strafrechtswissenschaft*, 1908, pp. 163–184.

——— *Manuel de police scientifique (technique)*, Paris, Payot, 1911 (1911a).

—— *Handleiding voor het signalement ('le portrait parlé') (Methode A. Bertillon) ten dienste van de politie met woordenlijst in de Fransche, Duitsche, Engelsche en Nederlandsche taal*, Haarlem, De Erven F. Bohn, 1911 (with permission of the author translated by R. van Steeden) (1911b).

—— *Manuel de portrait parlé*, Lausanne, T. Sack, 1914 (1914a).

—— *Contribution à la réorganisation de la police*, Paris, Payot, 1914 (1914b).

—— "Communication sur la fiche parisienne dite 'anthropométrique'", in: F. Larnaude and J.-A. Roux (eds.), *Premier congrès de police judiciaire internationale, Monaco (avril 1914)*, Paris, H. Godde, 1926, pp. 40–47.

Reiwald, P., *Die Gesellschaft und ihre Verbrecher*, Zürich, Pan-Verlag, 1948.

Remmelink, J., "Iets over Simon van der AA en 'zijn' internationale strafrechtelijke congressen", in: G. Corstens and M. Groenhuijsen (eds.), *Rede en recht: opstellen ter gelegenheid van het afscheid van prof. mr. N. Keijzer van de Katholieke Universiteit Brabant*, Deventer, Gouda Quint, 2000, pp. 27–40.

Renneville, M., "Entre nature et culture: le regard médical sur le crime dans la première moitié du XIXe siècle", in: M. Mucchielli (ed.), *Histoire de la criminologie française*, Paris, L'Harmattan, 1994, pp. 29–53 (1994a).

—— "La réception de Lombroso en France, 1880–1900", in: L. Mucchielli (ed.), *Histoire de la criminologie française*, Paris, L'Harmattan, 1994, pp. 107–135 (1994b).

—— "Le microbe et le bouillon de culture: Alexandre Lacassagne à la recherche d'une criminologie du milieu", *Gryphe: Revue de la Bibliothèque de Lyon*, 2004, pp. 14–19.

—— "Le Bertillonnage dans l'univers carcéral", in: P. Piazza (ed.), *Aux origines de la police scientifique: Alphonse Bertillon, précurseur de la science du crime*, Paris, Karthala, 2011, pp. 169–188.

Rennie, Y., *The Search for Criminal Man*, Lexington, Lexington Books, 1978.

Report of the Interdisciplinary Group on Criminology, The Hague, Ministerie van Justitie, s.d.

Report of the National Advisory Commission on Civil Disorders, New York, The New York Times Edition, 1968 (with an introduction by T. Wicker).

Reppetto, T., "Bruce Smith: police reform in the United States", in: P. Stead (ed.), *Pioneers in Policing*, Maidenhead, McGraw-Hill Book Company, 1977, pp. 191–206.

—— *American Mafia: A History of its Rise to Power*, New York, Holt Company, 2005.

Répression, La, de la traite des blanches: compte rendu du IVe congrès international tenu Madrid, les 24–28 octobre 1910 sous le haut patronage de S.M. le roi d'Espagne: actes et documents, Madrid, Imprenta de la Sucesora de M. Minuesa de Los Rios, 1912.

Reuss-Ianni, E., *Two Cultures of Policing: Street Cops and Management Cops*, New Brunswick, Transaction Books, 1984.

Reuter, L., "Die Ansichten des Marchese von Beccaria zu den Strafgesetzen, Verbrechen und Strafen: Strafgesetze, Strafjustiz und strafrechtliches Denken im 18. Jahrhundert", in: G. Deimling (ed.), *Cesare Beccaria: die Anfänge moderner Strafrechtspflege in Europa*, Heidelberg, Kriminalistik Verlag, 1989, pp. 55–78.

Rey, A. and L. Féron, *Histoire du corps des Gardiens de la Paix*, Paris, Firmin-Didot, 1896.

Reynolds, E., *Before the Bobbies: The Night Watch and Police Reform in Metropolitan London, 1720–1830*, Stanford, Stanford University Press, 1998.

Rhodes, H., *La science et les recherches criminelles: clues and crime*, Paris, Editions de la Revue Critique, 1934.

—— *Alphonse Bertillon: Father of Scientific Detection*, London, Georg G. Harrap, 1956.

Rials, S., *La déclaration des droits de l'homme et du citoyen*, Paris, Hachette, 1988.

Richardson, J., *The New York Police: Colonial Times to 1901*, New York, Oxford University Press, 1970.

—— *Urban Police in the United States*, Port Washington, Kennikat Press, 1974.

Richelson, J., *A Century of Spies: Intelligence in the Twentieth Century*, New York, Oxford University Press, 1997.

Rigouste, M., *Les marchands de peur: la bande à Bauer et l'idéologie sécuritaire*, Paris, Libertalia, 2011.

Robbers, G., *Sicherheit als Menschenrecht: Aspekte der Geschichte, Begründung und Wirkung einer Grundrechtsfunction*, Baden-Baden, Nomos Verlagsgesellschaft, 1987.

Robert, L. and T. Peters, "How restorative justice is able to transcend the prison walls: a discussion of the 'restorative detention' project", in: G. Weitekamp and H.-J. Kerner (eds.), *Restorative Justice in Context: International Practice and Directions*, Cullompton, Willan Publishing, 2003, pp. 95–122.

Robert, P., *Les bandes d'adolescents*, Paris, Editions Ouvrières, 1966.

—— "La sociologie du crime", in: R. Merle (ed.), *Les mondes du crime: introduction à la compréhension du fait criminel*, Paris, Privat, 1968, pp. 47–71 (1968a).

—— "La criminalité juvénile", in: R. Merle (ed.), *Les mondes du crime: introduction à la compréhension du fait criminel*, Paris, Privat, 1968, pp. 73–104 (1968b).

—— "Die 'Kriminologie' in Frankreich", in: G. Löschper, G. Manke and F. Sack (eds.), *Kriminologie als selbständiges, interdisziplinäres Hochschulstudium*, Pfaffenweiler, Centaurus-Verlagsgesellschaft, 1986, pp. 116–130.

—— "Le renouveau de la sociologie criminelle", in: L. Mucchielli (ed.), *Histoire de la criminologie française*, Paris, L'Harmattan, 1994, pp. 429–447.

—— *Le citoyen, le crime et l'état*, Geneva, Librairie Droz, 1999.

—— "Un regard critique sur trente années de *Déviance et société*", *Déviance et société*, 2007, pp. 375–386.

Robert, P. and C. Faugeron, *Les forces cachées de la justice: la crise de la justice pénale*, Paris, Le Centurion, 1980.

Robert, P. and F. Sack (eds.), *Normes et déviances en Europe: un débat Est-Ouest*, Paris, L'Harmattan, 1994.

Robinson, L., *History and Organization of Criminal Statistics in the United States*, Boston, Houghton Mifflin Company, 1911.

—— "History of criminal statistics, 1908–1933", *Journal of the American Institute of Criminal Law and Criminology*, 1934, pp. 125–139.

Roché, S., *Police de proximité: nos politiques de sécurité*, Paris, Editions du Seuil, 2005.

Rock, P., *Deviant Behaviour*, London, Hutchinson University Library, 1973.

—— "The sociology of crime, symbolic interactionism and some problematic qualities of radical criminology", in: D. Downes and P. Rock (eds.), *Deviant Interpretations: Problems in Criminological Theory*, Oxford, Martin Robertson, 1979, pp. 52–84.

—— (ed.), *A History of British Criminology*, Oxford, Clarendon Press, 1988.

—— (ed.), *History of Criminology*, Aldershot, Dartmouth, 1994.

—— "Cesare Lombroso as a signal criminologist", *Criminology and Criminal Justice*, 2007, pp. 117–133.

Rock, P. and M. McIntosh (eds.), *Deviance and Social Control*, London, Tavistock Publications, 1974.

Rode, C., *Kriminologie in der DDR: Kriminalitätsursachenforschung zwischen Empirie und Ideologie*, Freiburg im Breisgau, Max-Planck-Institut für ausländisches und internationales Strafrecht, 1996.

Rogier, L., *Evolutie der reclassering: gedenkschrift bij het vijftigjarig bestaan van de Katholieke Reclasseringsvereniging op 16 december 1966*, Nijmegen, Gebr. Janssen, 1966.

Rolin, A., "L'Union Internationale de Droit Pénal", *Revue de droit international et de législation comparée*, 1890, pp. 105–131, 279–302.

—— "La lutte contre le crime", *Revue de droit pénal et de criminologie*, 1907, pp. 209–228.

Röling, B., *De wetgeving tegen de zoogenaamde beroeps- en gewoontemisdadigers*, The Hague, Martinus Nijhoff, 1933.

—— "Het criminologisch werk van prof. dr. W.A. Bonger", *Tijdschrift voor Strafrecht*, 1942, pp. 89–114.

Roll, H., "Onderwijs in gerechtelijke geneeskunde en in politiewetenschap voor den aanstaanden jurist", *Tijdschrift voor Strafrecht*, 1914, pp. 310–336.

Ros, M., "Het Nederlandsch Genootschap tot Zedelijke Verbetering der Gevangenen, 1823–1915: een Foucaultiaanse visie op de macht van een reklasseringsvereniging", in: E. Jonker, M. Ros and C. de Vries (eds.), *Kriminologen en reklasseerders in Nederland*, in: *Utrechtse Historische Cahiers*, 1986, no. 1, pp. 5–70.

Roscher, G., "Bedürfnisse der modernen Kriminal-Polizei", *Archiv für Kriminal-Anthropologie und Kriminalistik*, 1899, pp. 244–255.

—— *Organisatie en hulpmiddelen der justitiële politie*, s.l., s.n., 1902 (translated from German by the Chairman of the Fraternity).

—— "Die daktyloskopische Registratur", *Archiv für Kriminal-Anthropologie und Kriminalistik*, 1904, pp. 129–141.

—— *Groszstadtpolizei: ein praktisches Handbuch der deutschen Polizei*, Hamburg, Otto Meiszners Verlag, 1912.

Roth, A., *Kriminalitätsbekämpfung in deutschen Groszstädten, 1850–1914*, Berlin, Erich Schmidt Verlag, 1997.

Roth, R., *Pratiques pénitentiaires et théorie sociale: l'exemple de la prison de Genève, 1825–1862*, Geneva, Librairie Droz, 1981.

Roth, T., "Verbrechensbekämpfung und Verfolgung sozialer Randgruppen – zur Beteiligung lokaler Kriminalpolizeien am NS-Terror", in: W. Schulte (ed.), *Die Polizei im NS-Staat: Beiträge eines internationalen Symposiums an der Deutschen Hochschule der Polizei im Münster*, Frankfurt am Main, Verlag für Polizeiwissenschaft, 2009, pp. 539–588.

Rothman, D., *The Discovery of the Asylum: Social Order and Disorder in the New Republic*, Boston, Little, Brown and Company, 1971.

Rousseau, J.-J., *Du contract social ou principes du droit politique*, Paris, Editions Garnier Frères, 1962.

Rousseaux, X., "Doctrines criminelles, pratiques pénales, projets politiques: le cas des possessions Habsbourgeoises, 1750–1790", in: M. Porret (ed.), *Beccaria et la culture juridique des lumières*, Geneva, Librairie Droz, 1997, pp. 223–252.

Rousseaux, X., F. Stevens and A. Tixhon, "Les origines de la statistique pénale en Belgique, 1795–1835", *Déviance et société*, 1998, pp. 127–153.

Rovers, B., *Resultaten van veiligheidshuizen: een inventarisatie en evaluatie van beschikbaar onderzoek*, 's-Hertogenbosch, BTVO, 2011.

Rubbens, E., *Edouard Ducpétiaux, 1804–1868*, Brussels, Albert Dewit, 1922–34, 2 vols.

Rubington, E. and M. Weinberg (eds.), *Deviance: The Interactionist Perspective*, London, Macmillan Company, 1969.

Ruff, J., *Crime, Justice and Public Order in Old Regime France: The Senéchaussées of Libourne and Bazas, 1696–1789*, London, Croom Helm, 1984.

Ruggiero, V., N. South and I. Taylor (eds.), *The New European Criminology: Crime and Social Order in Europe*, London, Routledge, 1998.

Rusche, G. and O. Kirchheimer, *Sozialstruktur und Strafvollzug*, Frankfurt, Europäische Verlagsanstalt, 1974 (translated from English).

—— *Peine et structure sociale: histoire et "Théorie critique" du régime pénal*, Paris, Les Editions du Cerf, 1994 (text presented by R. Lévy and H. Zander).

Rushton, J., "New evidence on Sir Cyril Burt: his 1964 speech to the Association of Educational Psychologists", *Intelligence*, 2002, pp. 555–567.

Rutherford, A., *Prisons and the Process of Justice*, Oxford, Oxford University Press, 1986.

Ruttiens, R., "La police judiciaire et sa réorganisation", *Revue de droit pénal et de criminologie*, 1910, pp. 280–289 (1910a).

—— "La police à l'exposition de Bruxelles", *Revue de droit pénal et de criminologie*, 1910, pp. 860–866 (1910b).

—— "L'Ecole de police de Rome", *Revue de droit pénal de de criminologie*, 1910, pp. 1126–1128 (1910c).

Rijksen, R., *Criminaliteit en bezetting*, Assen, Van Gorcum & Comp., 1957.

—— *Meningen van gedetineerden over de strafrechtspleging*, Assen, Van Gorcum & Comp., 1961.

Rijpperda Wierdsma, J., *Politie en justitie: een studie over Hollandschen staatsbouw tijdens de Republiek*, Zwolle, Drukkerij en Uitgeverij Erven J.J. Tijl, 1937.

Rylands, L., *Crime: Its Causes and Remedy*, London, T. Fisher Unwin, 1889.

Sack, F., "Neue Perspektiven in der Kriminologie", in: F. Sack and R. König (eds.), *Kriminalsoziologie*, Frankfurt am Main, Akademische Verlagsgesellschaft, 1968, pp. 431–476.

—— "Definition von Kriminalität als politisches Handeln: der 'labeling' approach", in: F. Stallberg (ed.), *Abweichung und Kriminalität: Konzeptionen, Kritik, Analysen*, Hamburg, Hoffmann und Campe Verlag, 1975, pp. 84–94.

—— "Kritische Kriminologie", in: G. Kaiser, H.-J. Kerner, F. Sack and H. Schellhoss (eds.), *Kleines kriminologisches Wörterbuch*, Heidelberg, C.F. Müller Juristischer Verlag, 1985, pp. 277–286.

—— "Kriminalität, Gesellschaft und Geschichte: Berührungsängste der deutschen Kriminologie", *Kriminologisches Journal*, 1987, pp. 241–268.

—— "Vom Wandel in der Kriminologie – und Anderes", *Kriminologisches Journal*, 1998, pp. 47–64.

—— "Das andere Lehrbuch – Prinzip Hoffnung", *Kriminologisches Journal*, 2006, pp. 49–61.

Sack, F. and R. König (eds.), *Kriminalsoziologie*, Frankfurt am Main, Akademische Verlagsgesellschaft, 1968.

Saint-Germain, J., *La Reynie et la police au Grand Siècle d'après de nombreux documents inédits*, Paris, Hachette, 1962.

Saleilles, R., *L'individualisation de la peine: étude de criminalité sociale*, Paris, Félix Alcan, 1898.

Sälter, G., *Polizei und soziale Ordnung in Paris*, Frankfurt am Main, Vittorio Klostermann, 2004.

Sampson, R. and W. Groves, "Community structure and crime: testing social-disorganization theory", *American Journal of Sociology*, 1989, pp. 774–802.

Sampson, R. and J. Laub, *Crime in the Making: Pathways and Turning Points through Life*, Cambridge, Harvard University Press, 1995.

Sassarath, S., "In memoriam Louis Braffort", *Revue de droit pénal et de criminologie*, 1940–46, pp. 363–365.

Satzungen der Internationalen Kriminalistischen Vereiniging (Union Internationale de Droit Pénal), Mitteilungen der Internationalen Kriminalistischen Gesellschaft, 1889, pp. 1–3.

Sauer, W., *Kriminalsoziologie*, Berlin, Verlag für Staatswissenschaften und Geschichte, 1933.

—— *Kriminologie*, Berlin, Walter de Gruyter, 1950.

Savant, J., *Le procès de Vidocq*, Paris, Le Club du Meilleur Livre, 1956 (original documents presented and with a commentary by J. Savant).

—— *Le vrai Vidocq*, Paris, Hachette, 1957.

Scarman, L., *The Scarman Report: The Brixton Disorders, 10–12 april 1981*, Harmondsworth, Penguin Books, 1982.

Schafer, S., *The Victim and his Criminal: A Study in Functional Reponsibility*, New York, Random House, 1968.

Schauz, D. and S. Freitag (eds.), *Verbrecher im Visier der Experten: Kriminalpolitik zwischen Wissenschaft und Praxis im 19. und frühen 20. Jahrhundert*, Stuttgart, Franz Steiner Verlag, 2007.

Schenk, D., *Auf dem rechten Auge blind: die braunen Wurzeln des BKA*, Cologne, Kiepenheuer & Witsch, 2001.

Schenk, W., *Wangedrag van kinderen: onderzoek naar aard en oorzaken ten aanzien van 600 Rotterdamsche kinderrechter-kinderen*, Baarn, Hollandia-Drukkerij, 1935.

Schlapp, M. and E. Smith, *The New Criminology: A Consideration of the Chemical Causation of Abnormal Behavior*, New York, Boni and Liveright, 1928.

Schlesinger, A., *Robert Kennedy and his Times*, New York, Ballantine Books, 1996.

Schlinzig, K., "100 Jahre Daktyloskopie in Deutschland: Polizeidirektion Dresden führte im März 1903 die Daktyloskopie ein", *Der Kriminalist*, 2003, pp. 112–113.

Schmeltz, G., *Sozialistische Kriminalistik und Kriminologie in der DDR*, Frankfurt, Verlag für Polizeiwissenschaft, 2010.

Schmid, N., "Der Einflusz von J.C. Lavaters Physiognomik auf die Anfänge der Kriminologie im 19. Jahrhundert", *Zeitschrift für Schweizerisches Recht*, 1984, pp. 465–488.

Schmolders, C. (ed.), *Der Exzentrische Blick: Gespräch über Physiognomik*, Berlin, Akademie Verlag, 1996.

Schneickert, H., "Neueinrichtungen der Berliner Polizei", *Archiv für Kriminal-Anthropologie und Kriminalistik*, 1911, pp. 1–26.

—— "Übersicht über die Tätigkeit und Erfolge einiger groszstädtischer Erkennungsämter", *Archiv für Kriminal-Anthropologie und Kriminalistik*, 1912, pp. 182–186.

—— *Einführung in die Kriminalsoziologie und Verbrechensverhütung*, Jena, Verlag von Gustav Fischer, 1935.

—— *Leitfaden der kriminalistischen Charakterkunde*, Jena, Verlag von Gustav Fischer, 1941.

Schneider, H., *Das Opfer und sein Täter: Partner im Verbrechen*, Munich, Kindler Verlag, 1979.

—— *Kriminologie*, Berlin, Walter de Gruyter, 1986.

—— "Kriminalpsychologie gestern und heute: Gustav Aschaffenburg als internationaler Kriminologe", in: *Monatsschrift für Kriminologie und Strafrechtsreform*, 2004, pp. 169–191 (2004a).

—— "Fortschritte der europäischen Kriminologie", *Monatsschrift für Kriminologie und Strafrechtsreform*, 2004, pp. 460–475 (2004b).

—— (ed.), *Internationales Handbuch der Kriminologie*, Berlin, Walter de Gruyter Verlag, 2007–09, 2 vols.

Schoemaker, D., *Theories of Delinquency: An Examination of Explanations of Delinquent Behavior*, New York, Oxford University Press, 1990.

Schreuder, W. (ed.), *Wetenschappelijk opsporingsonderzoek*, Leiden, A.W. Sijthoff's Uitgeversmaatschappij, 1952.

Schulte, W. (ed.), *Die Polizei im NS-Staat: Beiträge eines internationalen Symposiums an der Deutschen Hochschule der Polizei im Münster*, Frankfurt am Main, Verlag für Polizeiwissenschaft, 2009.

Schultz, H., "Abschied vom Strafrecht?", *Zeitschrift für die gesamte Strafrechtswissenschaft*, 1980, pp. 611–636.

Schulz, S., *Beyond Self-control: Analysis and Critique of Gottfredson & Hirschi's General Theory of Crime (1990)*, Berlin, Duncker & Humblot, 2006.

Schumann, K., "Approaching crime and deviance: a note on contributions by scientists, officials of social control and social activists during the last five years in West Germany", in: H. Bianchi, M. Simondi and I. Taylor (eds.), *Deviance and Control in Europe: Papers from the European Group for the Study of Deviance and Social Control*, London, John Wiley & Sons, 1975, pp. 59–76.

Schumann, K., H. Steinert and M. Vosz (eds.), *Vom Ende des Strafvollzugs*, Bielefeld, AJZ, 1988.

Schur, E., *Our Criminal Society: The Social and Legal Sources of Crime in America*, Englewood Cliffs, Prentice-Hall, 1969.

—— *Radical Non-intervention: Rethinking the Delinquency Problem*, Englewood Cliffs, Prentice-Hall, 1973.

Schuyt, C., *Rechtssociologie: een terreinverkenning*, Rotterdam, Universitaire Pers Rotterdam, 1971.

—— "Veroordeeld tot criminaliteit: een wetenschapsfilosofische en ethische reflectie op het voorgenomen onderzoek van prof. dr. W. Buikhuisen", *Nederlands Juristenblad*, 1978, pp. 389–399.

Schuyt, K., *Het spoor terug: J.B.Charles/W.H. Nagel, 1910–1983*, Amsterdam, Uitgeverij Balans, 2010.

Schwendinger, H. and J. Schwendinger, "When the study of delinquent groups stood still: in defence of a classical tradition", *Critical Criminology*, 1997, pp. 5–38.

Screvens, R., "Le promoteur de l'Ecole des Sciences Criminologiques", *Revue de droit pénal et de criminologie*, 1963, pp. 740–742.

Seelig, E., *Lehrbuch der Kriminologie*, Darmstadt, Verlag dr. N. Stoytscheff, 1963 (third edition, newly revised and extended by H. Bellavic).

Seelig, E. and K. Weindler, *Die Typen der Kriminellen*, Berlin, J. Schweitzer Verlag, 1949.

Sellin, J., *Pioneering in Penology: The Amsterdam Houses of Correction in the Sixteenth and Seventeenth Centuries*, Philadelphia, University of Pennsylvania Press, 1944.

—— *Slavery and the Penal System*, New York, Elsevier, 1976.

Sellin, T. (ed.), *The Police and the Crime Problem*, in: The Annals of the American Academy of Political and Social Science, Philadelphia, 1929.

—— *Research Memorandum on Crime in the Depression*, New York, Social Science Reseach Council, 1937.

—— *Culture Conflict and Crime*, New York, Social Science Research Council, 1938.

—— "L'étude sociologique de la criminalité", in: *Actes du IIe congrès international de criminologie (Paris-Sorbonne, September 1950)*, Paris, Presses Universitaires de France, 1952–55, vol. 4, pp. 109–130.

—— "Enrico Ferri: pioneer in criminology, 1856–1929", in: S. Grupp (ed.), *The Positive School of Criminology: Three Lectures by Enrico Ferri*, Pittsburgh, University of Pittsburgh Press, 1968, pp. 13–39.

—— "Enrico Ferri, 1856–1929", in: H. Mannheim (ed.), *Pioneers in Criminology*, London, Stevens and Sons, 1960, pp. 361–384.

—— "Culture conflict and crime", in: J. Jacoby (ed.), *Classics of Criminology*, Prospects Heights, Waveland Press, 1994, pp. 188–192.

Sellin, T. and J. Shalloo, *A Bibliographical Manual for the Student of Criminology*, Philadelphia, Rumford Press, 1935.

Semple, J., *Bentham's Prison: A Study of the Panopticon Penitentiary*, Oxford, Clarendon Press, 1993.

Sencie, F., "Prins et la loi belge de défense sociale", in: P. Van der Vorst and P. Mary (eds.), *Cent ans de criminologie à l'ULB: Adolphe Prins, l'Union Internationale de Droit Pénal, le Cercle Universitaire pour les Etudes Criminologiques*, Brussels, Bruylant, 1990, pp. 141–159.

Servais, J., *La police judiciaire des parquets*, Brussels, Cour d'Appel, 1921.

Shah, S. and L. Roth, "Biological and psychophysiological factors in criminology", in: D. Glaser (ed.), *Handbook of Criminology*, Chicago, Rand McNally and Co., 1974, pp. 101–173.

Shaw, C., *The Jack-roller: A Delinquent Boy's Own Story*, Chicago, University of Chicago Press, 1966 (with a new introduction by H. Becker).

Shaw, C. and H. McKay, "Differential systems of values", in: J. Jacoby (ed.), *Classics of Criminology*, Prospects Heights, Waveland Press, 1994, pp. 193–200.

Shaw, C., H. McKay and J. McDonald, *Brothers in Crime*, Chicago, University of Chicago Press, 1938.

Shaw, C. and E. Myers, "The juvenile delinquent", in: The Illinois Association for Criminal Justice (ed.), *The Illinois Crime Survey*, Montclair, Patterson Smith, 1968, pp. 645–732.

Shaw, C., F. Zorbaugh, H. McKay and L. Cottrel, *Delinquency Areas: A Study of the Geographic Distribution of School Truants, Juvenile Delinquents and Adult Offenders in Chicago*, Chicago, University of Chicago Press, 1929.

Shelley, L., "Soviet criminology after the Revolution", *Journal of Criminal Law and Criminology*, 1979, pp. 391–396 (1979a).

—— "Soviet criminology: its birth and demise, 1937–1936", *Slavic Review*, 1979, pp. 614–628 (1979b).

—— *Policing Soviet Society: The Evolution of State Control*, London, Routledge, 1996.

Shepstone, H., "The finger-print system of identification", *Scientific American*, 1910, pp. 256–257.

Sherman, L., "The sociology and the social reform of the American police, 1950–1973", *Journal of Police Science and Administration*, 1974, pp. 255–262.

Short, J., "Criminology, the Chicago School, and sociological theory", *Crime, Law and Social Change*, 2002, pp. 107–115.

Sieber, U. and H.-J. Albrecht (eds.), *Strafrecht und Kriminologie unter einem Dach: Kolloquium zum 90. Geburtstag von prof. dr. dr. h.c. mult. Hans-Heinrich Jescheck*, Berlin, Duncker & Humblot, 2006.

Sieverts, R., "Kriminalbiologisches Institut der Sicherheitspolizei", *Monatsschrift für Kriminalbiologie und Strafrechtsreform*, 1942, pp. 57–58.

Silverman, E., *NYPD Battles Crime: Innovative Strategies in Policing*, Boston, Northeastern University Press, 1999.

Simon, J., *Kriminalbiologie und Zwangssterilisation: eugenetischer Rassismus, 1920–1945*, Munich, Waxmann, 2001.

—— *Poor Discipline: Parole and Social Control of the Underclass, 1890–1990*, Chicago, University of Chicago Press, 1993.

Simon van der Aa, J., *De rijksopvoedingsgestichten in Nederland*, Amsterdam, Roeloffzen & Hübner, 1890.

Simons, D., "De strafrechtstheorie van Von Liszt", *Tijdschrift voor Strafrecht*, 1897, pp. 1–30.

—— *Het Wetboek van Strafrecht en de bestrijding van de misdadigheid*, The Hague, Gebroeders Belinfante, 1911.

—— *Problemen van strafrecht*, Amsterdam, Maatschappij voor Goede en Goedkope Lectuur, 1929.

Simons, R., "Le crime et la défense sociale", *Revue de droit pénal et de criminologie*, 1908, pp. 541–550, 658–671, 721–737.

Singer, R., *Just Deserts: Sentencing Based on Equality and Desert*, Cambridge, Ballinger Publishing Company, 1979.

Skolnick, J., "Scientific theory and scientific evidence: an analysis of lie-detection", *Yale Law Journal*, 1961, pp. 694–728.

—— *Justice without Trial: Law Enforcement in Democratic Society*, New York, John Wiley & Sons, 1967.

—— *The Politics of Protest*, New York, Ballantine Books, 1969.

—— *Justice without Trial: Law Enforcement in Democratic Society*, New York, MacMillan College Publishing Company, 1994.

Skolnick, J. and D. Bayley, *The New Blue Line: Police Innovation in Six American Cities*, New York, Free Press, 1986.

Smart, C., *Women, Crime and Criminology: A Feminist Critique*, London, Routledge & Kegan Paul, 1976.

Smaus, G., "Marx im Sack der kritische Kriminologie: über soziale Ungleichheit im Kriminalitätsdiskurs", in: T. von Trotha (ed.), *Politischer Wandel, Gesellschaft und Kriminalitätsdiskurse: Beiträge zur interdisziplinären wissenschaftlichen Kriminologie: Festschrift für Fritz Sack zum 65. Geburtstag*, Baden-Baden, Nomos Verlagsgesellschaft, 1996, pp. 151–165.

Smeets, J., *De affaire-Oss: van lokaal conflict tot nationale rel*, Amsterdam, Wereldbibliotheek, 2001.

Smeulers, A. (ed.), *Collective Violence and International Criminal Justice: An Interdisciplinary Approach*, Antwerp, Intersentia, 2010.

Smeulers, A. and R. Haveman (eds.), *Supranational Criminology: Towards a Criminology of International Crimes*, Antwerp, Intersentia, 2008.

Smith, B., *Police Systems in the United States*, New York, Harper & Brothers Publishers, 1940 (with a foreword by R. Fosdick).

—— *Police Systems in the United States*, New York, Harper & Row, 1960 (revised by B. Smith, Jr).

—— *The State Police: organization and administration*, Montclair, Patterson Smith, 1969 (reprinted 1925).

Smith, D., Jr, *The Mafia Mystique*, New York, Basic Books, 1975.

Smith, H. and R. Bohm, "Beyond anomie: alienation and crime", *Critical Criminology*, 2008, pp. 1–15.

Smith, S., *Crime, Space and Society*, Cambridge, Cambridge University Press, 1985.

Snacken, S., *De korte gevangenisstraf*, Antwerp, Kluwer, 1986.

—— "Leon Cornil, 1882–1962", in: C. Fijnaut (ed.), *Gestalten uit het verleden: 32 voorgangers in de strafrechtswetenschap, de strafrechtspleging en de criminologie*, Leuven, Universitaire Pers Leuven, 1993, pp. 261–276.

Snodgrass, J., "Clifford R. Shaw and Henry D. McKay: Chicago criminologists", *British Journal of Criminology*, 1976, pp. 1–17.

Söderman, H., "Science and criminal investigation", in: T. Sellin (ed.), *The Police and the Crime Problem*, in: The Annals of the American Academy of Political and Social Science, Philadelphia, 1929, pp. 237–248.

Soesman, F., *De crimineele sociologie: vrij naar de academische voordrachten van prof. Enrico Ferri, gehouden te Amsterdam van 17 sept. tot 11 oct. 1901*, Amsterdam, H. Campagne & Zoon, 1901.

Solomon, P., "A selected bibliography of soviet criminology", *Journal of Criminal Law, Criminology and Police Science*, 1970, pp. 393–432.

—— "Soviet criminology: its demise and rebirth, 1928–1963", in: R. Hood (ed.), *Crime, Criminology and Public Policy: Essays in Honour of Sir Leon Radzinowicz*, London, Heinemann, 1974, pp. 571–593.

—— *Soviet Criminologists and Criminal Policy: Specialists in Policy-making*, London, Macmillan Press, 1978.

Somerhausen, C. and L. Walgrave, "Aimée Racine, 1902–1980", in: C. Fijnaut (ed.), *Gestalten uit het verleden: 32 voorgangers in de strafrechtswetenschap, de strafrechtspleging en de criminologie*, Leuven, Universitaire Pers Leuven, 1993, pp. 335–347.

Sonnen, B.-R., *Kriminalität und Strafgewalt: Einführung in Strafrecht und Kriminologie*, Stuttgart, Verlag W. Kohlhammer, 1978.

Souchon, H., "Alexandre Lacassagne et l'Ecole de Lyon: réflexions sur les aphorismes et le concept du milieu social", *Revue de science criminelle et de droit pénal comparé*, 1974, pp. 534–559.

Sowle, C. (ed.), *Police Power and Individual Freedom: The Quest for Balance*, Chicago, Aldine Publishing Company, 1962.

Spapens, T., M. Groenhuijsen and T. Kooijmans (eds.), *Universalis: liber amicorum Cyrille Fijnaut*, Antwerp, Intersentia, 2011.

Spierenburg, P., *The Spectacle of Suffering: Executions and the Evolution of Repression: From a Preindustrial Metropolis to the European Experience*, Cambridge, Cambridge University Press, 1984.

—— "Boeventucht en vrijheidsstraffen: Coornherts betekenis voor het ontstaan en de ontwikkeling van het gevangeniswezen in Nederland", in: C. Fijnaut and P. Spierenburg (eds.), *Scherp toezicht: van 'Boeventucht' tot 'Samenleving en criminaliteit'*, Arnhem, Gouda Quint, 1990, pp. 11–30.

—— *The Prison Experience: Disciplinary Institutions and their Inmates in Early Modern Europe*, New Brunswick, Rutgers University Press, 1991.

—— "Long-term trends in homicide: theoretical reflections and Dutch evidence, fifteenth to twentieth centuries", in: E. Johnson and E. Monkkonen (eds.), *The Civilization of Crime: Violence in Town and Country since the Middle Ages*, Chicago, University of Illinois Press, 1996, pp. 63–105.

Stachhouwer, J., *Criminaliteit, prostitutie en zelfmoord bij immigranten in Amsterdam*, Utrecht, Dekker & Van de Vegt, 1950.

Stallberg, F. (ed.), *Abweichung und Kriminalität: Konzeptionen, Kritik, Analysen*, Hamburg, Hoffmann und Campe Verlag, 1975.

Stamhuis, E., *Protestantse bijdragen aan het Nederlandse strafrechtsdenken sinds 1880*, Amsterdam, VU Uitgeverij, 1988.

Stangl, W., "Kriminologie als Apologie der Macht: über Traditionen der Kriminologie am Beispiel Österreichs", Kriminologisches Journal, 1984, pp. 287–300.

—— *Wege in eine gefängnislose Gesellschaft: über Verstaatlichung und Entstaatlichung der Strafjustiz*, Vienna, Verlag der Österreichischen Staatsdruckerei, 1988.

Stanley, S. and M. Baginsky, *Alternatives to Prison: An Examination of Non-custodial Sentencing of Offenders*, London, Peter Owen, 1984.

Stead, P. (ed.), *Pioneers in Policing*, Maidenhead, McGraw-Hill Book Company, 1977.

Steffensmeier, D., *The Fence: In the Shadow of Two Worlds*, Totowa, Rowman and Littlefield Publishers, 1986.

Steinberg, R., "Die Beccaria-Rezeption in Ruszland während der Regierungszeit Katharinas II", in: G. Deimling (ed.), *Cesare Beccaria: die Anfänge moderner Strafrechtspflege in Europa*, Heidelberg, Kriminalistik Verlag, 1989, pp. 127–138.

Steinert, H., "The amazing new left law & order campaign: some thoughts on anti-utopianism and possible futures à propos Alan Hunt's 'The future of rights and justice'", *Contemporary Crises*, 1985, pp. 327–333.

Stern, V., *Bricks of Shame: Britain's Prisons*, Harmondsworth, Penguin Books, 1987.

Stevens, F., "Jean Vilain XIIII, 1712–1777", in: C. Fijnaut (ed.), *Gestalten uit het verleden: 32 voorgangers in de strafrechtswetenschap, de strafrechtspleging en de criminologie*, Leuven, Universitaire Pers Leuven, 1993, pp. 1–11.

Stevens, J., *Les prisons cellulaires en Belgique: leur hygiène physique et morale*, Brussels, Ferdinand Larcier, 1878.

Stieber, W., *Practisches Lehrbuch der Criminal-Polizei*, Berlin, U. Hayn, 1860.

—— *Praktisches Lehrbuch der Kriminalpolizei unter besonderer Berücksichtigung der Kriminologie und Kriminaltaktik*, Potsdam, A.W. Hayn's Erben, 1921 (second completely revised edition).

Stockis, E., *La dactyloscopie et l'identification judiciaire*, Charleroi, Imprimerie Maison Piette, 1908 (1908a).

—— *La fiche belge d'identité judiciaire: ce qu'elle doit être*, Charleroi, Imprimerie Maison Piette, 1908 (1908b).

—— "Quelques cas d'identification d'empreintes digitales", *Archives d'anthropologie criminelle, de médecine légale et de psychologie normale et pathologique*, 1908, pp. 257–266 (1908c).

—— "Les services d'identité judiciaire allemands", *Revue de droit pénal et de criminologie*, 1910, pp. 705–706.

Stöhr, A., *Psychologie der Aussage*, Berlin, Puttkammer & Mühlbrecht, 1911.

Strafella, F., "Ein Denkschrift über die Errichtung kriminalistischer Institute", *Archiv für Kriminal-Anthropologie und Kriminalistik*, 1916, pp. 313–323.

Strafella, F. and H. Zafita, "Hans Gross", *Archiv für Kriminal-Anthropologie und Kriminalistik*, 1916, pp. I–V.

Streng, F., "Der Beitrag der Kriminologie zu Entstehung und Rechtfertigung staatlichen Unrechts im 'Dritten Reich'", *Monatsschrift für Kriminologie und Strafrechtsreform*, 1993, pp. 141–168.

Stroobant, L., "Le rasphuys de Gand: recherches sur la répression du vagabondage et sur le système pénitentiaire établi en Flandre au XVIIe et au XVIIIe siècle", *Handelingen der Maatschappij van Geschied- en Oudheidkunde te Gent*, 1898, pp. 191–307.

Stuart, A., *De gemeenschappelijke of de afgezonderde opsluiting?*, Amsterdam, Van Kampen, 1857.

Sullivan, W., *Crime and Insanity*, London, Edward Arnold & Co., 1924.

Suringar, W., *Considérations sur la réclusion individuelle des détenus*, Paris-Amsterdam, Bouchard-Huzard/Van Heteren, 1843.

—— *Het vijfentwintigjarig bestaan van het Nederlands Genootschap tot Zedelijke Verbetering der Gevangenen plechtig herdacht*, Amsterdam, s.n., 1849.

—— *Openingsrede*, s.l., s.n., 1856.

—— *Le système cellulaire: considérations spéciales*, Leeuwarden, Suringar, 1860.

Susini, J., "L'influence d'Etienne de Greeff", in: *La criminologie: bilan et perspectives: mélanges offerts à Jean Pinatel*, Paris, Editions A. Pedone, 1980, pp. 233–245.

—— *La police: pour une approche nouvelle*, Toulouse, Presses de l'Institut d'Etudes Politiques de Toulouse, 1983 (with a preface by J.-L. del Bayle).

Sutherland, E., *Criminology*, Philadelphia, J.B. Lippincott, 1924.

—— *Principles of Criminology*, Chicago, J.B. Lippincott, 1934.

—— *Principles of Criminology*, Chicago, J.B. Lippincott, 1939.

—— *White Collar Crime*, New York, Holt, Rinehart and Winston, 1961 (with a foreword by D. Cressey).

—— *The Professional Thief: By a Professional Thief: An Astonishing Revelation of Criminal Life*, Chicago, University of Chicago Press, 1967.

—— *White Collar Crime: The Uncut Version*, New Haven, Yale University Press, 1983 (with an introduction by G. Geis and C. Goff).

Sutherland, E. and D. Cressey, *Principles of Criminology*, Chicago, J.B. Lippincott, 1955.

Sykes, G., *Crime and Society*, New York, Random House, 1963.

—— *The Society of Captives: A Study of a Maximum Security Prison*, Princeton, Princeton University Press, 1971.

—— "The rise of critical criminology", *The Journal of Criminal Law and Criminology*, 1974, pp. 206–213.

Sylvester, S., "Adolphe Quetelet: at the beginning", *Federal Probation*, 1982, pp. 14–19.

Szabo, D. and A. Normandeau (eds.), *Déviance et criminalité: textes*, Paris, Librairie Armand Colin, 1970.

Tamm, D., "Beccaria et le climat de réformes dans les pays du Nord", in: M. Porret (ed.), *Beccaria et la culture juridique des lumières*, Geneva, Librairie Droz, 1997, pp. 189–196.

Tange, C., *De Greeff et le problème du crime: l'attitude justicière chez l'homme criminel et son juge*, Brussels, Bruylant, 2001 (with an afterword by C. Debuyst).

Tannenbaum, F., *Wall Shadows: A Study in American Prisons*, New York, G.P. Putnam's Sons, 1922 (with an introduction by T. Osborne).

—— *Crime and the Community*, Boston, Ginn and Company, 1938.

Tarde, G., *La criminalité comparée*, Paris, Félix Alcan, 1886.

—— *La philosophie pénale*, Paris, A. Maloine, 1890 (1890a).

—— *Les lois de l'imitation: étude sociologique*, Paris, Félix Alcan, 1890 (1890b).

—— *Les lois sociales: esquisse d'une sociologie*, Paris, Félix Alcan, 1898.

—— *Penal Philosophy*, New Brunswick, Transaction Publishers, 2001(translated by R. Howell, with a new introduction by P. Beirne).

Taylor, D., *The New Police in Nineteenth-century England: Crime, Conflict and Control*, Manchester, Manchester University Press, 1997.

Taylor, I., *Law and Order: Arguments for Socialism*, London, Macmillan Press, 1982 (1982a).

—— "Against crime and for socialism", *Crime and Social Justice*, 1982, pp. 4–22 (1982b).

Taylor, I. and L. Taylor (eds.), *Politics and Deviance: Papers from the National Deviancy Conference*, Harmondsworth, Penguin Books, 1973.

Taylor, I., P. Walton and J. Young, *The New Criminology: For a Social Theory of Deviance*, London, Routledge & Kegan Paul, 1973.

—— "Advances towards a critical criminology", *Theory and Society*, 1974, pp. 441–476.

Teignmouth Shore, W. (ed.), *Crime and its Detection*, London, Gresham Publishing Company, 1931, 2 vols.

Ten Cate, C., *Tot glorie der gerechtigheid: de geschiedenis van het brandmerken als lijfstraf in Nederland*, Amsterdam, Wetenschappelijke Uitgeverij, 1975.

Ter Hoeven, P., R. Overeem, C. Hogenhuis and E. Rood-Pijpers (eds.), *Bezonnen hoop: opstellen aangeboden aan L.H.C. Hulsman*, Zwolle, W.E.J. Tjeenk Willink, 1986, pp. 75–88.

't Hart, A., W. Nieboer, G. Strijards and M. de Vries-Leemans (eds.), *Strafrecht in balans: opstellen over strafrecht aangeboden aan A.C. Geurts*, Arnhem, Gouda Quint, 1983.

Third International Congress on Criminology, Bedford College, London, 12th–18th September 1955: Summary of Proceedings with an Introduction by dr. H. Mannheim, London, The British Organising Committee, 1957.

Thomas, F., *De wetenschappelijke groei van de Belgische gerechtelijke geneeskunde*, Ghent, Rijkuniversiteit Gent, 1978.

Thomas, W., *The Unadjusted Girl: With Cases and Standpoint for Behavior Analysis*, London, George Routledge & Sons, 1924 (with a foreword by W. Dummer).

Thrasher, F., *The Gang: A Study of 1,313 Gangs in Chicago*, Chicago, University of Chicago Press, 1963 (abridged and with a new introduction by J. Short, Jr).

Thulfaut, G., *Kriminalpolitik und Strafrechtslehre bei Edmund Mezger, 1883–1962: eine wissenschaftsgeschichtliche und biografische Untersuchung*, Baden-Baden, Nomos Verlagsgesellschaft, 2000.

Tixhon, A., "Les statistiques criminelles belges du XIXe siècle: du crime au criminel: de la société a l'individu: le chiffre au service de l'état", *Déviance et société*, 1997, pp. 233–249.

Tjaden, M., "Voorwaardelijke veroordeling", in: M. de Jong, P. Baan, J. van Bemmelen et al. (eds.), *Straffen en helpen: opstellen over berechting en reclassering aan geboden aan mr. Dr. N. Muller*, Amsterdam, Wereldbibliotheek, 1954, pp. 41–57.

Tobias, J., *Crime and Industrial Society in the Nineteenth Century*, Harmondsworth, Penguin Books, 1972.

Tollebeek, J., G. Vanpaemel and K. Wils (eds.), *Degeneratie in België*, Leuven, Universitaire Pers Leuven, 2003.

Tonry, M. (ed.), *Confronting Crime: Crime Control Policy under New Labour*, Cullompton, Willan Publishing, 2003 (2003a).

—— "Evidence, elections and ideology in the making of criminal justice policy", in: M. Tonry (ed.), *Confronting Crime: Crime Control Policy under New Labour*, Cullompton, Willan Publishing, 2003, pp. 1–25 (2003b).

—— *Thinking about Crime: Sense and Sensibility in American Penal Culture*, New York, Oxford University Press, 2004.

Tonry, M. and N. Morris (eds.), *Modern Policing*, Chicago, University of Chicago Press, 1992.

Topinard, P., *L'Anthropologie*, Paris, C. Reinwald et Cie, 1879.

Trivelli, A., "De beteekenis der fotografie voor politie en justitie", *Tijdschrift voor Strafrecht*, 1908, pp. 362–373.

Trovillo, P., "A history of lie detection", *Journal of Criminal Law and Criminology*, 1939, pp. 848–881.

Tsitsoura, A., "La politique criminelle de la fin du XIXe siècle à la fin du XXe siècle", in: P. Van der Vorst and P. Mary (eds.), *Cent ans de criminologie à l'ULB: Adolphe Prins, l'Union Internationale de Droit Pénal, le Cercle Universitaire pour les Etudes Criminologiques*, Brussels, Bruylant, 1990, pp. 107–124.

Tudesq, A.-J., "Police et état sous la Monarchie de Juillet", in: J. Aubert, M. Eude, C. Goyard et al., *L'état et sa police en France, 1789–1914*, Geneva, Librairie Droz, 1979, pp. 59–81.

Tulkens, F., "Les principes du code pénal de Bentham", in: P. Gerard, F. Ost and M. van de Kerchove (eds.), *Actualité de la pensée de Jeremy Bentham*, Brussels, Publications des Facultés Universitaires Saint-Louis, 1987, pp. 615–662.

—— (ed.), *Généalogie de la défense sociale en Belgique, 1880–1914: travaux du séminaire qui s'est tenu à l'Université Catholique de Louvain sous la direction de Michel Foucault*, Brussels, E. Story-Scientia, 1988 (1988a).

—— "Un chapitre de l'histoire des réformateurs: Adolphe Prins et la défense sociale", in: F. Tulkens (ed.), *Généalogie de la défense sociale en Belgique, 1880–1914: travaux du séminaire qui s'est tenu à l'Université Catholique de Louvain sous la direction de Michel Foucault*, Brussels, E. Story-Scientia, 1988, pp. 17–46 (1988b).

—— "Jean Stevens, 1827–1898", in: C. Fijnaut (ed.), *Gestalten uit het verleden: 32 voorgangers in de strafrechtswetenschap, de strafrechtspleging en de criminologie*, Leuven, Universitaire Pers Leuven, 1993, pp. 49–55.

Tummers, F., *De 'nieuwere' richting in de strafrechtswetenschap critisch beoordeeld*, Nijmegen, L. Malmberg, 1911.

Turk, A., "Prospects and pitfalls for radical criminology: a critical response to Platt", *Crime and Social Justice*, 1975, pp. 41–45.

Türkel, S., "Criminalistic institutes and laboratories", in: T. Sellin (ed.), *The Police and the Crime Problem*, in: The Annals of the American Academy of Political and Social Science, Philadelphia, 1929, pp. 199–204.

Tyler, G., *Organized Crime in America: A Book of Readings*, Ann Arbor, University of Michigan Press, 1962 (with an introduction by E. Kefauver).

Ugeux, G.-A., "Jules Lejeune: ministre de la Justice, 1887–1894", *Revue de droit pénal et de criminologie*, 1955, pp. 3–46.

Uhl. K., *Das 'verbrecherische Weib': Geschlecht, Verbrechen und Strafen in kriminologischer Diskurs, 1800–1945*, Münster, LIT, 2003.

United States Senate, *Third Interim Report of the Special Committee to Investigate Organized Crime in Interstate Commerce*, New York, Arco Publishing Company, 1951.

Upson, L., "The International Association of Chiefs of Police and other American police organizations", in: T. Sellin (ed.), *The Police and the Crime Problem*, in: The Annals of the American Academy of Political and Social Science, Philadelphia, 1929, pp. 121–127.

Valier, C., "True crime stories: scientific methods of criminal investigation, criminology and historiography", *British Journal of Criminology*, 1998, pp. 88–105.

Valkhoff, J., "Willem Adriaan Bonger", *Nederlands Tijdschrift voor Criminologie*, 1976, pp. 146–151.

Van Bemmelen, J., *Van zedelijke verbetering tot reclassering: geschiedenis van het Nederlandsch Genootschap tot Zedelijke Verbetering der Gevangenen, 1823–1923*, The Hague, Martinus Nijhoff, 1923.

—— *De beteekenis van het strafrecht voor den normalen mensch*, The Hague, Martinus Nijhoff, 1931.

—— "Vijftig jaar strafrecht", in: Psychiatrisch-Juridisch Gezelschap (ed.), *Gedenkboek 1907–1957*, Amsterdam, F. van Rossen, 1957, pp. 7–22.

—— *Criminologie: leerboek der misdaadkunde*, Zwolle, Uitgeversmaatschappij W.E.J. Tjeenk Willink, 1958.

—— "Willem Adriaan Bonger, 1876–1940", in: H. Mannheim (ed.), *Pioneers in Criminology*, London, Stevens and Sons, 1960, pp. 443–457.

Van Bemmelen, J. and W. Pompe, "J. Simon van der Aa en B.M. Taverne", *Tijdschrift voor Strafrecht*, 1945, pp. 1–13.

Van Binsbergen, W., *Algemeen karakter van het crimineel wetboek voor het Koninkrijk Holland*, Utrecht, H. De Vroede, 1949.

Van Caenegem, R., *Geschiedenis van het strafrecht in Vlaanderen van de XIe tot de XIVe eeuw*, Brussels, Paleis der Academiën, 1954.

—— *Geschiedenis van het strafprocesrecht in Vlaanderen van de XIe tot de XIVe eeuw*, Brussels, Paleis der Academiën, 1956.

Van de Boogaart, H. and L. Seus, *Radikale Kriminologie: die Rekonstruktion zweier Jahrzehnte Wissenschaftsgeschichte Groszbritanniens*, Pfaffenweiler, Centaurus-Verlagsgesellschaft, 1991.

Van de Bunt, H., "Donald Ray Cressey, 1919–1987", in: K. Hayward, S. Maruna and J. Mooney (eds.), *Fifty Key Thinkers in Criminology*, London, Routledge, 2010, pp. 115–119.

Van Deinse, A., *De algemeene beginselen van strafregt, ontwikkeld en in verband beschouwd met de algemeene bepalingen der Nederlandsche strafwetgeving*, Middelburg, Altorffer, 1860.

Vandekerckhove, L., *Over het ontstaan van de gevangenisstraf: een kijk op het oude Rome*, Leuven, Acco, 1989.

—— "Hector Denis, 1842–1913", in: C. Fijnaut (ed.), *Gestalten uit het verleden: 32 voorgangers in de strafrechtswetenschap, de strafrechtspleging en de criminologie*, Leuven, Universitaire Pers Leuven, 1993, pp. 133–142.

Van de Kerckove, M., "L'organisation d'asiles spéciaux pour aliénés et aliénés dangereux: aux sources de la loi de défense sociale", in: F. Tulkens (ed.), *Généalogie de la défense sociale en Belgique, 1880–1914: travaux du séminaire qui s'est tenu à l'Université Catholique de Louvain sous la direction de Michel Foucault*, Brussels, E. Story-Scientia, 1988, pp. 113–140.

Van den Auwele, D. and O. Nefors, "Goswin de Fierlant, 1735–1804", in: C. Fijnaut (ed.), *Gestalten uit het verleden: 32 voorgangers in de strafrechtswetenschap, de strafrechtspleging en de criminologie*, Leuven, Universitaire Pers Leuven, 1993, pp. 11–22.

Van den Bergh, L., *De Belgiese kinderwet van 1912 met de Nederlandse kinderwetten vergeleken*, Amsterdam, Amsterdamsche Boek- en Steendrukkerij, 1915.

Van den Eerenbeemt, H., *In het spanningsveld der armoede: agressief pauperisme en reactie in Staats-Brabant*, Tilburg, Stichting Zuidelijk Historisch Contact, 1968.

—— *Van mensenjacht en overheidsmacht: criminogene groepsvorming en afweer in de Meierij 's-Hertogenbosch, 1795–1810*, Tilburg, Stichting Zuidelijk Historisch Contact, 1970.

—— *Armoede en arbeidsdwang: werkinrichtingen voor 'onnutte' Nederlanders in de Republiek, 1760–1795*, The Hague, Martinus Nijhoff, 1977.

Van den Haag, E., *Punishing Criminals: Concerning a Very Old and Painful Question*, New York, Basic Books, 1975.

Van den Honert, J., *Het wetboek van strafregt, toegelicht uit de beraadslagingen van de Tweede Kamer der Staten-Generaal*, Amsterdam, Gebroeders Diederichs, 1848.

Vanderborght, J., J. Vanacker and E. Maes (eds.), *Criminologie: de wetenschap, de mens*, Brussels, Politeia, 2000.

Van der Brugghen, I., *Etudes sur le système pénitentiaire irlandais*, Berlin/The Hague, Luederitz/Martinus Nijhoff, 1864 (revised by Fr. de Holtzendorff).

Van der Landen, D., *Straf en maatregel*, Arnhem, Gouda Quint, 1992.

Van der Meij, R., *Een studie over de grondslagen der zoogenaamde 'nieuwe richting' in de strafrechtswetenschap*, Leiden, S.C. van Doesburgh, 1904.

Van der Stegen, J., *Moyen de rendre les patrouilles utiles et moins onéreuses au plat-pays, surtout en Brabant*, s.l., s.n., 1778.

Van der Voo, H., *Cel of gemeenschap?*, The Hague, Drukkerij "Luctor et Emergo", 1929.

Van der Vorst, P. and P. Mary (eds.), *Cent ans de criminologie à l'ULB: Adolphe Prins, l'Union Internationale de Droit Pénal, le Cercle Universitaire pour les Etudes Criminologiques*, Brussels, Bruylant, 1990.

Van der Waerden, B., "Organisatievormen: met name: Reclasseringsraden", in: C. De Jong, P. Baan, J. van Bemmelen et al. (eds.), *Straffen en helpen: opstellen over berechting en reclassering aan geboden aan mr. Dr. N. Muller*, Amsterdam, Wereldbibliotheek, 1954, pp. 291–302.

Van de Voorde, H., "Frédéric Thomas, 1906–1986", in: C. Fijnaut (ed.), *Gestalten uit het verleden: 32 voorgangers in de strafrechtswetenschap, de strafrechtspleging en de criminologie*, Leuven, Universitaire Pers Leuven, 1993, pp. 329–334.

Van de Vrugt, M., *De Criminele Ordonnantiën van 1570: enkele beschouwingen over de eerste strafrechtcodificatie in de Nederlanden*, Zutphen, De Walburg Pers, 1978.

—— *Aangaende criminele saeken: drie hoofdstukken uit de geschiedenis van het strafrecht*, Deventer, Kluwer, 1982.

Van Duyl, D., *De voorwaardelijke invrijheidsstelling historisch en kritisch beschouwd, zoowel op zichzelf als in verband met de heerschende gevangenisstelsels*, Leiden, P. Somerwil, 1881.

Van Dijck, J., *Reconstructie van strafbare feiten: rede uitgesproken bij de aanvaarding van het hoogleraarsambt aan de Gemeenteuniversiteit van Amsterdam, op 26 juni 1922*, Alphen aan den Rijn, N. Samsom, 1922.

Van Dijk, J., H. Sagel-Grande and L. Toornvliet, *Actuele criminologie*, Lelystad, Koninklijke Vermande, 1995.

Van Embden, D., *Darwinisme en democratie: maatschappelijke vooruitgang en de hulp aan het zwakke*, The Hague, Martinus Nijhoff, 1901.

Van Eck, D., *Over de waarde der crimineele statistiek: openbare les gegeven bij de aanvaarding van het lectoraat in het strafprocesrecht en de criminologie aan de Roomsch-Katholieke Universiteit te Nijmegen op 19 september 1940*, Nijmegen, Dekker & Van de Vegt, 1940.

Van Geuns, C., *Proefondervindelijke bijdrage tot de psychologie der getuigenis*, Amsterdam, J.H. de Bussy, 1914.

Van Ginneken, J., "Gabriel Tarde en de ontdekking van de sociale psychologie", *Sociologisch Tijdschrift*, 1983, pp. 125–146.

Van Hamel, G., *De nietigheid van den verkoop van eens anders goed*, Leiden, S. C. van Doesburgh, 1865.

—— *Inleiding tot de studie van het Nederlandsche strafrecht*, Haarlem, De Erven F. Bohn, 1889.

—— (ed.), *Verspreide opstellen*, Leiden, Boekhandel en Drukkerij voorheen E.J. Brill, 1912, 2 vols.

—— "Zur Erinnerung und zum Abschied", *Mitteilungen der Internationalen Kriminalistischen Vereinigung*, 1914, pp. 440–445.

Van Hecke, T. and J. Wemmers, *Schadebemiddelingsproject Middelburg*, Arnhem, Gouda Quint, 1992.

Van Heerikhuizen, B., *W.A. Bonger: socioloog en socialist*, Groningen, Wolters-Noordhoff, 1987.

Vanhemelryck, F., *De criminaliteit in de ammanie van Brussel van de late Middeleeuwen tot het einde van het Ancien Régime, 1404–1789*, Brussels, Paleis der Academiën, 1981.

Van Heijnsbergen, P., *Geschiedenis der rechtswetenschap in Nederland: beknopt overzicht der geschiedenis onzer rechtswetenschap tot 1900*, Amsterdam, Meulenhoff, 1925.

Van Herwaarden, J., *Opgelegde bedevaarten: een studie over de praktijk van opleggen van bedevaarten (met name in de stedelijke rechtspraak) in de Nederlanden gedurende de late Middeleeuwen, ca 1300–ca 1550*, Amsterdam, Van Gorcum, 1978.

Van Hoorebeeke, E., *Etudes sur le système pénitentiaire en France et en Belgique*, Ghent, Librairie Générale de H. Hoste, 1843.

Vanhoudt, C., *Progressieve en regressieve evolutie in het strafrecht onder invloed der dictatuur*, Antwerp, De Sikkel, 1940.

Van Kan, J., *Les causes économiques de la criminalité: étude historique et critique d'etiologie criminelle*, Paris, A. Storck, 1903.

Van Kerckvoorde, J., "Adolphe Quetelet, 1796–1874", in: C. Fijnaut (ed.), *Gestalten uit het verleden: 32 voorgangers in de strafrechtswetenschap, de strafrechtspleging en de criminologie*, Leuven, Universitaire Pers Leuven, 1993, pp. 57–71.

—— "Statistique criminelle et statistique morale au XIXème siècle", in: L. Mucchielli (ed.), *Histoire de la criminologie française*, Paris, L'Harmattan, 1994, pp. 253–268.

—— *Een maat voor het kwaad*, Leuven, Universitaire Pers Leuven, 1995.

Van Maanen, H., *De ontwikkeling van het strafstelsel blijkens de ontworpen strafwetboeken van den laatsten tijd (Duitschland, Ooostenrijk, Zwitserland)*, Amersfoort, De Amersfoortsche Courant, 1912.

Van Mesdag, S., *De beteekenis van de studie der crimineele biologie en psychologie voor de toekomst van het strafrecht: openbare les gegeven bij de opening zijner colleges op 19 november 1935*, Groningen, J.B. Wolters' Uitgevers-Maatschappij, 1935.

Van Noije, L. and K. Wittebrood, *Sociale veiligheid ontsleuteld: veronderstelde en werkelijke effecten van veiligheidsbeleid*, The Hague, Sociaal en Cultureel Planbureau, 2008.

Van Outrive, L., "De strafrechtsbedeling en haar slachtoffers", *Tijdschrift voor Sociale Wetenschappen*, 1975, pp. 276–300.

—— "Interactionisme et neo-marxisme: une analyse critique", *Déviance et société*, 1977, pp. 253–289.

—— *De gevangenis: een systeem op drift*, Leuven, Davidsfonds, 1978.

Van Outrive, L. and P. Robert (eds.), *Crime et justice en Europe depuis 1990: état des recherches, évaluation et recommendations*, Paris, L'Harmattan, 1999.

Van Rappard, W., *Het ontwerp van een wetboek van strafvordering op zich zelve en in vergelijking met de bestaande Fransche wetgeving*, Zutphen, Thieme, 1828, 2 vols.

Van Rompaey, J., *Het grafelijk baljuwsambt in Vlaanderen tijdens de Bourgondische periode*, Brussels, Paleis der Academiën, 1967.

Van Rooy, H., *Criminologische contrasten tussen stad en land: Nijmegen en omstreken: openbare les gehouden op 3 juni 1947*, Wijchen, P.T. De Kleijn, 1947.

—— *Criminaliteit van stad en land: Nijmegen en omstreken*, Utrecht, Dekker & Van de Vegt, 1949.

—— "In memoriam prof. dr. E. de Greeff", *Nederlands Tijdschrift voor Criminologie*, 1961, p. 161.

Van Ruller, S., *Genade voor recht: gratieverlening aan ter dood veroordeelden in Nederland, 1806–1870*, Amsterdam, De Bataafsche Leeuw, 1987.

—— "Hoe de nationale deftigheid tweemaal triomfeerde: anderhalve eeuw parlementaire doodstrafdiscussie in Nederland", *Recht en Kritiek*, 1989, pp. 216–239.

Van Schreven, C., *Diefstal in groepsformatie gepleegd: een empirisch onderzoek met een criminologische beschouwing*, The Hague, Martinus Nijhoff, 1957.

Van Swaaningen, R., *Critical Criminology: Visions from Europe*, London, Sage Publications, 1997.

Van Swaaningen, R. and J. Blad, "La recherche criminologique aux Pays-Bas dans les années 1990", in: L. van Outrive and P. Robert (eds.), *Crime et justice en Europe depuis 1990: état des recherches, évaluation et recommendations*, Paris, L'Harmattan, 1999, pp. 193–246.

—— (eds.), *De ontmaskering van het strafrechtelijk discours: een bloemlezing uit het werk van Louk Hulsman*, The Hague, Boom Lemma Uitgevers, 2011.

Van Swaaningen, R., B. Snel, S. Faber and E. Blankenburg (eds.), *A tort et à travers: liber amicorum Herman Bianchi*, Amsterdam, VU Uitgeverij, 1988.

Vanstone, M., "The international origins and initial development of probation", *British Journal of Criminology*, 2008, pp. 735–755.

Van Warmelo, P., "Van der Keessel en Beccaria", *Tijdschrift voor Rechtsgeschiedenis*, 1967, pp. 573–583.

Van Weringh, J., "Aletrino als criminoloog", *BZZLLETIN*, 1982, pp. 93–96, 115.

—— *De afstand tot de horizon*, Amsterdam, Uitgeverij de Arbeiderspers, 1986.

Varendonck, J., *Experimenteele bijdrage tot de psychologie van het getuigenis*, Leuven, De Vlaamsche Boekenhalle, 1921.

Vargha, J., *Die Abschaffung der Strafknechtschaft: Studien zur Strafrechtsreform*, Graz, Leuschner & Lubensky, 1896–97, 2 vols.

Vaux, R., *Some Remarks on Crime-Cause*, Philadelphia, M'Laughlin Brothers' Book, 1879.

Veen, T. and P. Kop (eds.), *Zestig juristen: bijdragen tot een beeld van de geschiedenis van de Nederlandse rechtswetenschap*, Zwolle, W.E.J. Tjeenk Willink, 1987.

Verbruggen, F., R. Verstraeten, D. van Daele and B. Spriet (eds.), *Strafrecht als roeping: liber amicorum Lieven Dupont*, Leuven, Universitaire Pers Leuven, 2005, 2 vols.

Verger, H., *L'évolution des idées médicales sur la responsabilité des délinquants*, Paris, Ernest Flammarion, 1923.

Verhellen, E., *Jeugdbescherming en jeugdbeschermingsrecht*, Antwerp, Kluwer, 1988.

Ver Loren van Themaat, H., *Zorg voor den veroordeelde in het bijzonder na zijne invrijheidstelling*, Utrecht, P. Den Boer, 1910–11, 2 vols.

Verslag van de commissie van onderzoek inzake de afbreuk, door den arbeid in gevangenissen, rijkswerkinrichtingen en rijksopvoedingsgestichten aan den arbeid in de vrije maatschappij gedaan, The Hague, 1897.

Verslag van de werking van het stelsel van afzonderlijke opsluiting der gevangenen, The Hague, s.n., 1873.

Vervaeck, L., "Le professeur Lacassagne", *Revue de droit pénal et de criminologie*, 1924, pp. 913–930.

Vervaele, J., *Rechtsstaat en recht tot straffen*, Antwerp, Kluwer Rechtswetenschappen, 1990.

Veysey, B. and S. Messner, "Further testing of social disorganization theory: an elaboration of Sampson and Groves's 'community structure and crime'", *Journal of Research in Crime and Delinquency*, 1999, pp. 156–174.

Vidal, G., *Cours de droit criminel et de science pénitentiaire*, Paris, Arthur Rousseau, 1927–28, 2 vols.

Vidocq, E., *The Personal Memoirs of the First Great Detective*, Cambridge, Houghton Mifflin Company, 1935.

—— *Les voleurs*, Paris, Les Éditions de Paris, 1957 (texts repaired and presented by J. Savant).

Vigier, P. et al., *Maintien de l'ordre et polices en France et en Europe au XIXe siècle*, Paris, Créaphis, 1987.

—— et al., *Répression et prisons politiques*, Paris, Editions Creaphis, 1990.

Vilain XIIII, C., *Mémoire sur les moyens de corriger les malfaiteurs et les fainéants à leur propre avantage et de leur rendre utiles à l'état, précédé d'un premier mémoire inédit sur la même matière, présentés aux États de Flandre en 1771 et 1775, par le vicomte J.P. Vilain XIIII*, Brussels, Meline, 1841.

Visser, H., *Psychiatrisch toezicht in gevangenissen*, Amsterdam, Van Holkema & Warendorf, 1896.

Vlaamse Interuniversitaire Raad, *De onderwijsvisitatie Criminologische Wetenschappen [...] aan de Vlaamse universiteiten*, Brussels, 2008.

Vogel, J., "Einflüsse des Nationalsozialismus auf das Strafrecht", *Zeitschrift für die gesamte Strafrechtswissenschaft*, 2003, pp. 639–670.

Vogler, T. (ed.), *Festschrift für Hans-Heinrich Jescheck zum 70. Geburtstag*, Berlin, Duncker & Humblot, 1985.

Vold, G., T. Bernard and J. Snipes, *Theoretical Criminology*, New York, Oxford University Press, 2002.

Vollmer, A., *The Police and Modern Society*, Berkeley, University of California Press, 1936.

Vollmer, A. and A. Parker, *Crime and the State Police*, Berkeley, University of California Press, 1935.

Voltaire, *Commentaire sur le livre des délits et des peines (par un avocat de province)*, s.l., s.n., 1766.

Von Caemmerer, E., E. Friesenhahn and R. Lange (eds.), *Hundert Jahre Deutsches Rechtsleben: Festschrift zum hundertjährigen Bestehen des Deutschen Juristentages, 1860–1960*, Karlsruhe, Verlag C.F. Müller, 1960.

Von Hentig, H., "Alphonse Bertillon", *Archiv für Kriminal-Anthropologie und Kriminalistik*, 1914, pp. 358–359.

—— *The Criminal and his Victim*, New Haven, Yale University Press, 1948.

—— *Der Gangster: eine kriminalpsychologische Studie*, Berlin, Springer, 1959.

—— *Das Verbrechen*, Berlin, Springer, 1961.

—— "Gustav Aschaffenburg", in: H. Mannheim (ed.), *Pioneers in Criminology*, London, Stevens and Sons, 1960, pp. 421–428.

Von Hirsch, A., *Past and Future Crimes: Deservedness and Dangerousness in the Sentencing of Criminals*, Manchester, Manchester University Press, 1986.

Von Hirsch, A. and A. Ashworth (eds.), *Principled Sentencing*, Boston, Northeastern University Press, 1992.

Von Justi, J., *Grundsätze der Polizey-Wissenschaft*, Göttingen, Vandenhoeck, 1759.

Von Kraft-Ebing, R., *Lehrbuch der gerichtlichen Psychopathologie*, Stuttgart, Ferdinand Enke, 1900 (third revised edition).

Von Liszt, F., "Der Zweckgedanke im Strafrecht", *Zeitschrift für die gesamte Strafrechtswissenschaft*, 1883, pp. 1–47.

—— *Das Völkerrecht systematisch dargestellt*, Berlin, Verlag von O. Häring, 1898.

—— *Strafrechtliche Aufsätze und Vorträge*, Berlin, J. Guttentag, 1905, 2 vols. (1905a).

—— "Die Aufgaben und die Methode der Strafrechtswissenschaft", in: F. von Liszt, *Strafrechtliche Aufsätze und Vorträge*, Berlin, J. Guttentag, 1905, vol. 2, pp. 285–298 (1905b).

—— *Lehrbuch des deutschen Strafrechts*, Berlin, J. Guttentag, 1908.

—— *Das Völkerrecht systematisch dargestellt*, Berlin, Verlag von O. Häring, 1913.

—— "Die Entstehung der Internationalen Kriminalistischen Vereinigung", *Mitteilungen der Internationalen Kriminalistischen Vereinigung*, 1914, pp. 1–20.

—— "G.A. van Hamel (1. März 1917): ein Nachruf", *Zeitschrift für die gesamte Strafrechtswissenschaft*, 1917, pp. 553–569.

Von Meerscheidt-Hüllesem, E., "Die Erfolge der Bertillonnage in Deutschland", *Archiv für Kriminal-Anthropologie und Kriminalistik*, 1900, pp. 193–196.

Von Mohl, R., *Die Polizei-Wissenschaft nach den Grundsätzen des Rechtsstaates*, Tübingen, Laupp'schen Buchhandlung, 1834.

Von Pfeiffer, J., *Polizeiwissenschaft: natürliche, aus dem Endzweck der Gesellschaft entstehende allgemeine Polizeiwissenschaft*, Aalen, Scientia Verlag 1970, 2 vols. (new print of the edition Frankfurt am Main, 1779).

Von Trotha, T. (ed.), *Politischer Wandel, Gesellschaft und Kriminalitätsdiskurse: Beiträge zur interdisziplinären wissenschaftlichen Kriminologie: Festschrift für Fritz Sack zum 65. Geburtstag*, Baden-Baden, Nomos Verlagsgesellschaft, 1996.

Vovelle, M., *Fouché: mémoires*, Paris, Imprimerie Nationale, 1992.

Vrij, M., *Te recht!: rede uitgesproken bij de aanvaarding van het ambt van hoogleeraar aan de Rijksuniversiteit te Groningen op 10 maart 1928*, Groningen, J.B. Wolters' Uitgevers-Maatschappij, 1928.

—— *Ter effening: het subsociale als het derde element van het delict: afscheidscollege bij zijn aftreden als hoogleeraar aan de Rijksuniversiteit te Groningen op 25 october 1947 in de aula*, Groningen, J.B. Wolters' Uitgevers-Maatschappij, 1948.

—— "Pour commémorer le pionier G.A. van Hamel et pour combler une lacune", *Revue internationale de droit pénal*, 1951, pp. 361–392.

Wachsmann, N., "Habitual criminals' in the Third Reich: from indefinite confinement to extermination", in: R. Gellately and N. Stoltzfus (eds.), *Social Outsiders in Nazi Germany*, Princeton, Princeton University Press, 2001, pp. 165–191.

Wagniart, J.-F., *Le vagabond à la fin du XIXe siècle*, Paris, Berlin, 1999.

Wagner, J.-C., *Konzentrationslager Mittelbau-Dora 1943–1945*, Göttingen, Wallstein Verlag, 2009.

Wagner, P., *Volksgemeinschaft ohne Verbrecher: Konzeptionen und Praxis der Kriminalpolizei in der Zeit der Weimarer Republik und des Nationalsozialismus*, Hamburg, Christians, 1996.

Walby, K. and N. Carrier, "The rise of biocriminology: capturing observable bodily economies of 'criminal man'", *Criminology and Criminal Justice*, 2010, pp. 261–285.

Walder, H., *Triebstruktur und Kriminalität: kriminalbiologische Untersuchungen*, Bern, Verlag Hans Huber, 1952.

Walgrave, L., *De bescherming voorbij: ontwerp voor een emaniciperende jeugdcriminologie*, Antwerp, Kluwer, 1980.

—— "Onderzoek in de jeugdcriminologie", in: J. Casselman, I. Aertsen and S. Parmentier (eds.), *Tachtig jaar criminologie aan de Leuvense universiteit: onderwijs, onderzoek en praktijk*, Antwerp, Maklu, 2012, pp. 97–106.

Walker, N., *Crime and Insanity in England: The Historical Perspective*, Edinburgh, University Press, 1968.

—— *Sentencing in a Rational Society*, Harmondsworth, Penguin Books, 1972.

—— *Crime and Criminology: A Critical Introduction*, Oxford, Oxford University Press, 1987.

Walker, N. and S. McCabe, *Crime and Insanity: New Solutions to New Problems*, Edinburgh, Edinburgh University Press, 1973.

Walker, S., *The Police in America: An Introduction*, New York, McGraw-Hill, 1983.

—— "'Broken windows' and fractured history: the use and misuse of history in recent police patrol analysis", in R. Dunham and G. Alpert (eds.), *Critical Issues in Policing: Contemporary Readings*, Prospect Heights, Waveland Press, 1989, pp. 382–394.

Walsh, A. and K. Beaver (eds.), *Biosocial Criminology: New Directions in Theory and Research*, New York, Routledge, 2009.

Walton, P. and J. Young (eds.), *The New Criminology Revisited*, London, Macmillan Press, 1998.

Wasserman, D. and R. Wachbroit, *Genetics and Criminal Behavior*, Cambridge, Cambridge University Press, 2001.

Wassermann, R., *Begriff und Grenzen der Kriminalstatistik: eine logische Untersuchung*, Leipzig, Verlag von Wilhelm Engelmann, 1909.

Weber, D., *Homo criminalis: Belgische parlementsleden over misdaad en strafrecht, 1830–1940*, Brussels, VUBPress, 1996.

Weingart, P., J. Kroll and K. Bayertz, *Rasse, Blut und Gene: Geschichte der Eugenik und Rassenhygiene in Deutschland*, Frankfurt am Main, Suhrkamp Verlag, 1992.

Weisburd, D. and T. McEwen (eds.), *Crime Mapping & Crime Prevention*, Monsey, Criminal Justice Press, 1998.

Weiss, C., "Zum Problem der Einführung eines einheitlichen Erkennungssystem", *Archiv für Kriminal-Anthropologie und Kriminalistik*, 1911, pp. 142–146.

—— "Zur Reform unserer Kriminalpolizei", *Archiv für Kriminologie*, 1920, pp. 225–234.

Weitekamp, G. and H.-J. Kerner (eds.), *Restorative Justice in Context: International Practice and Directions*, Cullompton, Willan Publishing, 2003.

Werkentin, F., M. Hofferbert and M. Baurmann, "Criminology as police science or: how old is the new criminology?", *Crime and Social Justice*, 1974, pp. 24–41.

Werle, G., *Justiz-Strafrecht und polizeiliche Verbrechensbekämpfung im Dritten Reich*, Berlin, Walter de Gruyter, 1989.

Wertheim Salomonson, J. (ed.), *Congrès international d'anthropologie criminelle: compte rendu des travaux de la cinquième session tenue à Amsterdam du 9 à 14 septembre 1901*, Amsterdam, Imprimerie de J.H. de Bussy, 1901.

West, D., *The Young Offender*, Harmondsworth, Penguin Books, 1968.

Westhoff Jr, J., *Lokbeambten (agents provocateurs)*, Amsterdam, Roeloffzen en Hubner, 1893.

Westley, W., *Violence and the Police: A Sociological Study of Law, Custom and Morality*, Cambridge, MIT Press, 1970.

Wetzell, R., *Inventing the Criminal: A History of German Criminology, 1880–1945*, Chapel Hill, University of North Carolina Press, 2000.

White, W., *Crimes and Criminals*, New York, Farrar & Rinehart, 1933.

Whyte, W., *Street Corner Society: The Social Structure of an Italian Slum*, Chicago, University of Chicago Press, 1955.

—— *Street Corner Society: The Social Structure of an Italian Slum*, Chicago, University of Chicago Press, 1993.

Wichmann, C., *Beschouwingen over de historische grondslagen der tegenwoordige omvorming van het strafbegrip*, Leiden, Boekhandel en Drukkerij voorheen E.J. Brill, 1912.

Wiersma, D., *Praedispositie tot misdaad: openbare les gehouden bij de aanvang zijner lessen als privaat-docent in de criminele psychologie aan de Rijks-Universiteit te Leiden*, Leiden, S.C. van Doesburgh, 1929.

Wilbrink, J., *Bedelarij, landlooperij en de rijkswerkinrichtingen*, Arnhem, G.W. van der Wiel, 1902.

Wildt, M., *Generation des Unbedingten: das Führungskorps des Reichssicherheitshauptamtes*, Hamburg, Hamburger Edition, 2002.

Wilkins, L., *Social Policy, Action and Research: Studies in Social Deviance*, London, Tavistock Publications, 1964.

Willekes MacDonald, F., *De psychiater in het strafproces*, Haarlem, De Erven F. Bohn, 1885.

Willems, W., *Op zoek naar de ware zigeuner: zigeuners als studieobject tijdens de Verlichting, de Romantiek en het Nazisme*, Utrecht, Uitgeverij Jan van Arkel, 1995.

Williams, A., *Les mémoires de Beria*, Paris, JClattès, 1974.

—— *The Police of Paris, 1718–1789*, Baton Rouge, Louisiana State University Press, 1979.

Williams III, F. and M. McShane, *Criminological Theory*, Englewood Cliffs, Prentice Hall, 1988.

Williams, K., *Textbook on Criminology*, London, Blackstone Press Limited, 1991.

Wilson, J., "A reader's guide to the Crime Commission reports", *The Public Interest*, 1967, pp. 64–82.

—— *Varieties of Police Behavior: The Management of Law and Order in Eight Communities*, Cambridge, Harvard University Press, 1970.

—— *Thinking about Crime*, New York, Vintage Books, 1985 (revised edition).

—— "Crime and public policy", in: J. Wilson and J. Petersilia (eds.), *Crime: Twenty-eight Leading Experts Look at the Most Pressing Problem of Our Time*, San Francisco, ICS Press, 1995, pp. 489–507.

Wilson, J. and R. Herrnstein, *Crime & Human Nature: The Definitive Study of the Causes of Crime*, New York, Simon & Schuster, 1986.

Wilson, J. and J. Petersilia (eds.), *Crime: Twenty-eight Leading Experts Look at the Most Pressing Problem of Our Time*, San Francisco, ICS Press, 1995.

Wilson, O., *Police Planning*, Springfield, Charles C. Thomas, 1973.

Wilson, T., *Criminal Anthropology*, Washington, Government Printing Office, 1891.

Wilson-Vine, M., "Gabriel Tarde, 1843–1904", in: H. Mannheim (ed.), *Pioneers in Criminology*, London, Stevens and Sons, 1960, pp. 228–240.

Wines, E., *International Congress on the Prevention and Repression of Crime, Including Penal and Reformatory Treatment: Preliminary Report of the Commissioner Appointed by the President to Represent the United States in the Congress, in Compliance with a Joint Resolution of March 7, 1871*, Washington, Governement Printing Office, 1872.

Wines, F., "Criminal anthropology, 1895", in: N. Rafter (ed.), *The Origins of Criminology: A Reader*, London, Routledge, 2009, pp. 199–203 (2009a).

—— "Crime in the 1880 U.S. Census", in: N. Rafter (ed.), *The Origins of Criminology: A Reader*, London, Routledge, 2009, pp. 289–294 (2009b).

Winfree, Jr, L. and H. Abadinsky, *Understanding Crime: Theory and Practice*, Belmont, Wadsworth, 2003.

Winkelhorst, A., "Spuren der Beccaria-Rezeption in John Howards 'The state of the prisons in England and Wales', 1777 und 1784", in: G. Deimling (ed.), *Cesare Beccaria: die Anfänge moderner Strafrechtspflege in Europa*, Heidelberg, Kriminalistik Verlag, 1989, pp. 139–147.

Wittebrood, K., *Slachtoffers van criminaliteit: feiten en achtergronden*, The Hague, Sociaal en Cultureel Planbureau, 2006.

Wittlin, T., *Beria: vie et mort du chef de la police secrète sovietique*, Paris, Elsevier, 1976 (translated from the American by A. Bernard).

Wodon, L. and J. Servais (eds.), *L'oeuvre d'Adolphe Prins*, Brussels, Université Libre de Bruxelles, 1934.

Wolfgang, M., "Cesare Lombroso, 1835–1909", in: H. Mannheim (ed.), *Pioneers in Criminology*, London, Stevens and Sons, 1960, pp. 232–291.

Woodiwiss, M., *Organized Crime and American Power*, Toronto, University of Toronto Press, 2001.

Wright, G., *Between the Guillotine and Liberty: Two Centuries of the Crime Problem in France*, New York, Oxford University Press, 1983.

Wulffen, E., *Psychologie des Verbrechers: ein Handbuch für Juristen, Ärzte, Pädagogen und Gebildete aller Stände*, Berlin, P. Langenscheidt, 1913, 2 vols. (second edition).

—— *Kriminalpsychologie: Psychologie des Täters*, Berlin, P. Langenscheidt, 1926.

Würtenberger, T., "Criminology and penology in Western Germany", *British Journal of Delinquency*, 1953–54, pp. 26–38.

—— "Die Kriminalbiologische Gesellschaft in Vergangenheit und Gegenwart", in: H. Göppinger and H. Leferenz (eds.), *Kriminologische Gegenwartsfragen: Vorträge bei der XIV. Tagung der Gesellschaft für die gesamte Kriminologie vom 13. bis 16. October 1967 in Köln*, Stuttgart, Ferdinand Enke Verlag, 1968, pp. 1–9.

Wyndham, H., *Criminology*, London, Ernest Benn, 1928.

Yablonsky, L., *The Violent Gang*, Harmondsworth, Pelican Books, 1967.

Young, J., "Radikale Kriminologie in Groszbritannien: die Entfaltung eines konkurrierenden Paradigmas", *Kriminologisches Journal*, 1988, pp. 247–264.

—— "Robert Merton, 1910–2003", in: K. Hayward, S. Maruna and J. Mooney (eds.), *Fifty Key Thinkers in Criminology*, London, Routledge, 2010, pp. 105–114.

Young, J. and R. Matthews (eds.), *Rethinking Criminology: The Realist Debate*, London, Sage Publications, 1992.

Young, P., *Social Treatment in Probation and Delinquency: Treatise and Casebook for Court Workers, Probation Officers and Other Child Welfare Workers*, New York, McGraw-Hill Book Company, 1937.

Zafita, H., "Zur Theorie des polizeilichen Erkennungswesens", *Archiv für Kriminal-Anthropologie und Kriminalistik*, 1915, pp. 351–370.

Zaki, M., *Le rôle des laboratoires de police technique au point de vue de la police judiciaire et de l'instruction préparatoire*, Lyon, Desvigne, 1929.

Zedner, L., "Useful knowledge? Debating the role of criminology in post-war Britain", in: L. Zedner and A. Ashworth (eds.), *The Criminological Foundations of Penal Policy: Essays in Honour of Roger Hood*, Oxford, Oxford University Press, 2003, pp. 197–236.

Zedner, L. and A. Ashworth (eds.), *The Criminological Foundations of Penal Policy: Essays in Honour of Roger Hood*, Oxford, Oxford University Press, 2003.

Zimring, F., "Imprisonment rates and the new politics of criminal punishment", in: D. Garland (ed.), *Mass Imprisonment: Social Causes and Consequences*, London, Sage Publications, 2001, pp. 145–149.

Zuckerman, F., *The Russian Political Police at Home and Abroad, 1880-1917: Its Structure, Functions, Methods and its Struggle with Organized Opposition*, New York University, History Department, 1973 (dissertation).

Zvekic, U. (ed.), *Essays on Crime and Development*, Rome, UNICRI, 1990.

Zijderveld, A., *De theorie van het symbolisch interactionisme*, Meppel, Boom, 1973.

Zysberg, A., "Politiques du bagne, 1820-1850", in: M. Perrot (ed.), *L'impossible prison: recherches sur le système pénitentiaire au XIXe siècle*, Paris, Editions du Seuil, 1980, pp. 165–205.

REGISTER OF NAMES